# In Defense of Self and Others...

# In Defense of Self and Others...

*Issues, Facts & Fallacies —*
*The Realities of Law Enforcement's*
*Use of Deadly Force*

**THIRD EDITION**

Urey W. Patrick, FBI—Retired

John C. Hall, JD, FBI—Retired

CAROLINA ACADEMIC PRESS
Durham, North Carolina

Library of Congress Cataloging-in-Publication Data

Names: Patrick, Urey W. (Urey Woodworth), author. | Hall, John C. (John
  Creighton), author.
Title: In defense of self and others ... : issues, facts & fallacies--the
  realities of law enforcement's use of deadly force / Urey W. Patrick, John
  C. Hall.
Description: Third edition. | Durham, North Carolina : Carolina Academic
  Press, [2016] | Includes bibliographical references and index.
Identifiers: LCCN 2016024790 | ISBN 9781611636826 (alk. paper)
Subjects: LCSH: Police shootings--United States. | Police--United States.
Classification: LCC HV8139 .P37 2016 | DDC 363.2/32--dc23
LC record available at https://lccn.loc.gov/2016024790

e-ISBN 978-1-53100-356-2

Carolina Academic Press, LLC
700 Kent Street
Durham, North Carolina 27701
Telephone (919) 489-7486
Fax (919) 493-5668
www.cap-press.com

# Contents

# Foreword

I first met Pat on September 30, 1986. Through a remarkably complex series of unlikely events, I found myself driving to Quantico, Virginia, where the FBI Academy is co-located with the United States Marine Corps—this is not a coincidence—with instructions to park at the pistol range for instruction in submachine guns, where Pat would check me out on several light automatic weapons. You see, I'd just published *Red Storm Rising*, and was at work on *Patriot Games*, in which Jack Ryan would have to defend himself with such weapons against an attack from Irish terrorists of the fictional Ulster Liberation Army. The FBI has many such weapons in its possession, mostly for training purposes, and Pat, I was told, was (and remains) an expert with such arms. So, I drove there, parked, and walked in the range shack. To my right was a conference room in which I saw some heavier weapons lying on a table. I remember one was an AK-47 of Soviet manufacture, sitting there with the bolt closed. My Boy Scout training came back to me: weapons are supposed to be left in a condition that makes them obviously safe, which usually means an open bolt, which exposes an empty chamber. Curious at this oversight, I lifted the weapon and pulled back on the bolt handle and set the weapon back down. It turned out that I was wrong. Fully automatic weapons, since they fire from an open bolt, are actually safer when the bolts are closed on an empty chamber. You live and learn. On a later trip I met John Hall, a member of the bar and a pretty good guitar player and Country & Western singer, in addition to being a skilled investigator and weapons expert. John had been made Unit Chief of the Firearms Unit and was Pat's immediate boss. His keen legal mind (John would make a pretty good judge) did most of the policy and legal research in this book. John is recognized throughout the law enforcement world as *the* authority on deadly force law and was the impetus for the complete revision of federal deadly force policies.

Pat's a big boy, an inch or so taller than I am, with a Zapata mustache and a manner that seems to say Texas rather loudly. In fact, he's a Princeton grad, and a former naval officer, but he looks like the sort of fellow you see driving a Kenworth diesel tractor on an interstate highway, complete to the ostrich-skin cowboy boots, however he speaks quietly and politely, and his vocabulary indicates a man with a brain. In due course we were out on the range. Pat demonstrated the two weapons in which I had expressed interest, the American-made Ingram SMG, in 9mm caliber, and the well-known Israeli Uzi. Pat showed me (unnecessarily) how they worked, and soon I was shooting the Ingram, which, I immediately learned, looks good in the movies, but is difficult to shoot accurately, even with the enormous screw-on suppressor (*not* a silencer) on the muzzle. The Ingram rapidly climbs upward and to the right, and after three or four rounds, you are a danger to birds rather than people. Its rate of fire, however, is very rapid indeed, and you can empty a magazine in two seconds flat. It probably won't kill anybody, but the noise (absent the suppressor) is certain to get everyone's attention. Even with the short strap that attached near the muzzle, to hold the weapon down in the target area, the Ingram is very difficult to control. Not what Jack Ryan needed to stay alive, Pat made clear to me.

The somewhat bulkier Uzi, on the other hand, is far easier to control, with a slower rate of fire, and it will actually hit a target, if you use the sights (yes, I know: in the movies such weapons are fired from the hip, but you can't really hit anything that way, and the purpose of firing a weapon is to put steel on target). Afterwards Pat and I sat in his office and I explained the tactical environment into which I was going to drop Jack Ryan. Pat approved of my scenario, offering a few bits of advice along the way, all of them relevant. Then he told me that the next time I came to the FBI Academy, to bring my pistol with me, and he'd teach me how to shoot properly.

*Teach me how to shoot properly?* I thought. *I learned how to do that when I was twelve years old!*

But I'd just seen Pat with the Uzi, and I remembered that the chief firearms instructor at the FBI Academy just might know some things I did not, and I agreed. And a few weeks later I had to give a speech at the Academy, and I brought my Browning Hi-Power with me. For this lesson we went to the indoor range. Choosing a target lane, and attaching a Q-target to the clip, Pat showed me how to hold a pistol in a steady Weaver grip and stance, and after donning our ear-protectors, I let fly. I immediately learned that shooting a pistol and hitting a target is rather more difficult than it appears on TV and in the movies. It's easier than hitting a straight drive on a golf course, but harder than eating a Big Mac. Well, it turned out that I did have much to learn, but Pat turned out to be a superb teacher, and a closet intellectual.

I yelled at him for some years to write a book. Why? He knows this subject and others. First of all, Pat's a cop, and an unusually smart one at that. Next, he knows firearms better than anyone I have ever met, both how to use them and the scientific principles that make them work. When two FBI agents, Ben

Grogan and Jerry Dove, were killed in Miami, Florida, in 1986, Pat was part of the team that analyzed the event, in which both bad guys were also killed. Pat's work resulted in specifications for a new FBI pistol (written by Pat) and the implementation of the revolutionary FBI Ammunition Test Series (one of John's ideas). Their efforts led to the design and adoption of a sub-sonic 10mm cartridge by the FBI that largely replicated the effectiveness of the older .45 ACP in a smaller diameter (as a result of which an automatic pistol can carry at least one more round), and with lesser recoil to distract the shooter. Pat and John initiated and managed the complete conversion of the FBI from revolvers to semi-automatic pistols. Pat created the training program for the conversion program and the FBI basic training curriculum, as well as the new "practical" firearms training that are included in all Bureau training.

The 10mm in turn led to the development of the .40 S&W (a shorter 10mm) that has since become the standard law enforcement caliber, killing off less effective, smaller rounds like the 9mm and the .38/357 class. As a part of this ongoing process, Pat completed a scientific study on the issue of how bullets kill, the results of which were the basis of the FBI ammunition test protocols and used to define bullet performance parameters for law enforcement ammunition analysis and procurement. This study rewrote the accepted knowledge on the subject. Pat essentially proved that Sam Colt was right back in the mid-1800s when he invented and manufactured handguns that fired large, heavy, but relatively slow bullets. That old .45 Colt cartridge remains a premier man-stopper in the world, though the weapons chambered for it tend to be overly large and heavy for proper concealment. Pat also wrote the FBI Sniper Manual, reading which I learned more about rifles than I had ever known.

Under Pat's tutelage I also turned into a fairly decent pistol shot. As good as Pat? Not quite.

I was sufficiently impressed that in 1989, I made Pat into a continuing character in my novels, Major Case Inspector Pat O'Day, where I try to emphasize his intellectual gifts in addition to his skill with firearms, because the majority of the effort in police work will always be intellectual—intelligence gathering and analysis. Pat continues this trait to this date, consulting in deadly force incidents, in which he mostly explains reality to investigators, litigators and juries, as opposed to the mistaken prejudices which come to us from Hollywood, and are remarkably difficult to overcome, egregiously false though they may be.

This book is a textbook, mostly aimed at police officers, the attorneys who defend them in court, students of law enforcement and its many badly informed critics. For that purpose it is admirably clear and easy to understand. It combines John's unique depth of knowledge of the law with Pat's comprehensive and extensive practical expertise in weapons and deadly force factors. Reading it will make for better cops, and for cops who will be more likely to return home alive at end of watch after having done good work while on duty. That is a harder task than most of us realize. It's important to remember that the term "public defender" is less likely to mean an attorney paid by the government to ensure due process for indigent (accused) criminals than it is to mean a well-trained police officer who enforces the law on the street in a fair and *professional* manner. Those cops are also the principal protectors of our federal Constitution, and, along with that, our civil liberties. Any free society depends absolutely on fair and honest cops. If this book helps to teach them to be real professionals, then it will have served a worthy purpose.

Tom Clancy
Huntingtown, MD

# Preface to the Third Edition

*"These are the times that try men's souls."*
—Thomas Paine, *The American Crisis* (1776)

Thomas Paine penned these words while serving with George Washington's army in the brutally cold first winter of our war for independence. They were a clarion call to all who valued freedom and independence to stand up and be counted. That call has been repeated in critical times throughout our country's history. It is relevant today. Historically, we Americans have taken comfort in the knowledge that we are a nation of laws and not of men, secure in the faith that we choose to be guided and governed by fixed principles derived from human experience and embodied in our Constitution rather than by the volatile whims of the mob and the moment. Those principles are being challenged today and those who cherish them must again stand up and be counted.

As we present this third edition of the book that was first published over a decade ago, it is gratifying to report that the fundamental principles governing the authority of law enforcement officers to defend themselves and others against imminent threats of serious physical injury continue unchanged. Indeed, since this book was first published the U.S. Supreme Court has held that the ancient common law right of self-defense is a fundamental right and guaranteed by the Constitution to all Americans.

Notwithstanding these positive trends in the courts, there are some dark clouds on the horizon. While there is no reason to believe that these constitutional rights will be erased by court decisions or amendments to the Constitution, there is a very real risk that they may be subverted by individuals and groups who view them as archaic obstacles to their social and political goals. For those who hold this view, neither the facts nor the law are relevant.

There is no better illustration of this problem than the "Ferguson" incident that is discussed in detail in Chapter 1 of this book. In August 2014, a white officer of the Ferguson (Missouri) Police Department shot and killed an unarmed black man. Within minutes of the incident, and before the facts could be known, some in the media were reporting nationwide that the man had his hands raised in surrender at the time he was shot. Some accounts reported that the man was shot in the back as he attempted to run away. Riots and looting broke out in Ferguson and other cities across the country. The officer's actions were publicly condemned by activists, by unquestioning members of the media, and by pandering political leaders from every level of government. Subsequently, a thorough investigation by the U.S. Department of Justice determined that the initial reports from the media were based on a deliberate lie and that there was no evidence to support federal charges against the officer. Despite the facts, "Ferguson" continues to be promoted as the embodiment of the unlawful use of deadly force by a racially motivated police officer and, more perniciously, that this is characteristic of all police everywhere. This "Ferguson" model is being used to increase social and political pressures on law enforcement agencies to modify their policies and training to prevent any such incidents in the future. If successful, the delicate balance struck by the Constitution between the rights of the individual and the rights of society will be subjectively skewed in favor of the criminal suspect to the detriment of society and its law enforcement officers.

The Ferguson incident has spawned what is now being described as "the Ferguson effect"—the apparent reluctance of law enforcement officers to enforce the law aggressively and to protect themselves in the process. There are knowledgeable experts who attribute the recent rise in violent crimes to this phenomenon. Although many in high places deny its existence, many law enforcement leaders, including FBI Director James Comey, have cited "the Ferguson effect" as contributing to this unfortunate and unmistakable trend.

Incidents such as that which occurred in Ferguson must remind us that it is not sufficient that law enforcement officers be well trained in the lawful constraints on their authority to use force, or that their departments implement sound policies and guidance that reflect the law and the realities of police work. It is equally important in a free society that the people have some understanding of their own responsibilities to ensure that their officers are judged fairly. It is the hope of the authors that this book will continue to serve in some way to counter confusion and ignorance and thereby contribute to the maintenance of public safety and justice.

In closing, we must recognize Brian MacMaster whose help and suggestions on this third edition have been instrumental to its completion. Brian is a consummate professional with over 40 years experience in law enforcement and still counting. In Maine the Attorney General's Office of Investigations that Brian has headed for decades investigates all police deadly force incidents. He has investigated more police shootings than anybody in the country and his experience, expertise and perceptions have been invaluable to us. He is an even better friend. Thank you Brian—we could not have done this without you.

The same appreciation must be extended to Ms. Sophia Kil whose invaluable assistance with the legal research served to make this book much better and more complete than it otherwise could have been, and eased the authors' burdens immeasurably. Thank you Sophia.

Finally, the authors would be remiss if we did not express our deep appreciation to the readers who have made the first two editions of this book a success, and to the staff at Carolina Academic Press for making our book writing endeavors so pleasant and rewarding.

# Preface to the Second Edition (2010)

*"People sleep peaceably in their beds at night only because rough men stand ready to do violence on their behalf."*

—George Orwell

The authors must express their deep appreciation to all those readers who have made the first edition of this book so successful. We have been particularly gratified by its reception within the legal, law enforcement, and military communities. We must also express our thanks to Carolina Academic Press. They made the first edition possible, and they prodded us into producing this second edition.

Any book that purports to address the myriad legal and practical issues that govern the use of deadly force by law enforcement officers can never be truly complete. Although the fundamental constitutional principles that govern this subject matter have remained fairly constant over the past twenty-five years, the countless factual patterns to which those principles must be applied require constant study and evaluation. The first edition of this book was published five years ago, and to state a tautological platitude, things change! The now ubiquitous use of electronic control devices such as the eponymous TASER is but one example of that. The validation of this second edition is further exemplified by the fact that it is approximately 40% larger in volume alone, and that figure does not reflect the expansion of the book's substantive content.

Every chapter has been revised to some degree. New information has been incorporated. New issues have been addressed and more recent court decisions have been incorporated to recognize and explain developments in constitutional law. Additional case studies have been added to illustrate the manner in which the legal principles and the practical realities affect the legal outcomes. And an entirely new chapter has been added to address some of the legal and practical issues relating to the use of non-deadly force.

The perspective of this second edition is unchanged from that of the first edition—a "reasonable officer at the scene." The U.S. Supreme Court mandated that perspective in 1989[1] and it has not changed either. It is a perspective with which we are intimately familiar due to our decades of experience in law enforcement. We believe that the interests of society are synonymous with, and inseparable from, the interests of its law enforcement officers. We have been strengthened in that belief by the continuing trends in the courts that clearly and consistently reflect that harmony of interests. The law is the source that defines the duties of law enforcement officers. And it is the law that clothes them with the authority to protect themselves while they perform those duties.

The authors have been motivated from the beginning to disseminate and substantiate this positive message throughout the law enforcement community. Since the decisions of law enforcement officers will always be reviewed in the courts of public opinion as surely as in the courts of law, it is also our hope and intention that this book will be a resource for those outside the law enforcement community that can foster greater understanding of the realities that define and influence the perspective and decision making of that reasonable officer at the scene. To the extent that such an educational effect may result in less agenda-driven outrage over police uses of force and more informed examination of police risks and realities by the public, it would be an even more successful achievement—one for which we have hopes.

---

1. *Graham v. Connor*, 490 U.S. 386, 396 (1989).

# Preface to the First Edition (2005)

*"I decline utterly to be impartial as between the fire brigade and the fire."*
— Sir Winston Churchill (1926)

There are some topics about which decent folk cannot afford to be impartial. Sir Winston's statement provides a good example. There is an obvious parallel between the fireman and the policeman. Just as the fireman's helmet represents our determination as a community to protect ourselves from the dangers posed by fire, the law enforcement officer's badge and gun represent our determination as a community to protect ourselves from the dangers posed by those individuals whose actions threaten our safety. The folly of taking a neutral stance between that which is dangerous and that which we create to protect us from that danger should be self-evident.

This book is about the use of deadly force by law enforcement officers. It makes no pretense of being impartial "as between the fire and the fire brigade." Its perspective is clearly and unabashedly that of law enforcement. That is not due to the subjective reason that the authors share almost 60 years of law enforcement experience between them, but for the objective reasons that the law enforcement perspective is compelling for both the interests of society and the dictates of the Constitution.

The interests of any society that purports to be committed to the rule of law are inherently synonymous with the interests of those who enforce that law. It would be an anomaly to suggest otherwise. That does not mean that we are to ignore the gravity of the authority granted to law enforcement officers, or the need to closely scrutinize the exercise of that authority. It simply means that to further society's interests in effective law enforcement it is essential to ensure that those who serve that interest are guided and judged by standards that are objective and fair and that they fully comprehend the range of factors that affect an officer's decision to use deadly force.

The law enforcement perspective is also mandated by the U.S. Supreme Court as the means of assessing whether an officer's decision to use force is "objectively reasonable" under the Fourth Amendment to the Constitution. Observing *"the fact that officers are often forced to make split-second judgments— in circumstances that are tense, uncertain, and rapidly evolving—about the amount of force that is necessary in a particular situation"* the Court concluded that the issue must be viewed *"from the perspective of a reasonable officer at the scene, rather than with the 20/20 vision of hindsight...."* [2]

Judicial recognition of the uniqueness of the law enforcement perspective in applying constitutional standards is well established. The Supreme Court once noted that:

> ... *when used by trained law enforcement officers, objective facts, meaningless to the untrained, [may permit] inferences and deductions that might well elude an untrained person.*[3]

A federal appellate court explained the practical implications of this principle *for the courts*:

> ... *we must avoid substituting our personal notions of proper police procedures for the instantaneous decision of the officer on the scene. We must never allow the theoretical, sanitized world or our imagination to replace the dangerous and complex world that policemen face every day.*[4]

A second federal appellate court described its implications *for juries*:

> *When a jury measures the objective reasonableness of an officer's action, it must stand in his shoes and judge his action based upon the information he possessed....*[5]

The practical effect of these judicial developments is to emphasize that it is not possible to accurately determine whether a particular law enforcement action is objectively reasonable under the Constitution without viewing the relevant facts from the law enforcement perspective.

The significance of that perspective is readily seen when contrasted with the pervasive misperceptions that prevail outside the law enforcement community with respect to the legal and practical realities that affect an officer's decision to use deadly force. For example, it is apparently a commonly held belief that

---

2. *Graham v. Connor*, 490 U.S. 386 (1989).
3. *United States v. Cortez*, 449 U.S. 411, at 418 (1980).
4. *Smith v. Freland*, 954 F.2d 343, at 347 (6th Cir. 1992).
5. *Sherrod v. Berry*, 856 F.2d 802, at 804–5 (7th Cir. 1988).

officers are required to know for a *certainty* that a non-compliant suspect is armed with a gun and *actually* intends to shoot the officer before the officer is justified in believing that deadly force is justified to counter an immediate danger. Those who are accustomed to seeing the silver screen hero wait until the villain's gun is clearly visible and pointed in his direction before shooting the villain are unlikely to understand why a police officer shot a suspect who was *believed to be reaching* for a gun. The reality that "action beats reaction" and that the law "*does not require police officers to wait until a suspect shoots to confirm that a serious harm exists*"[6] is lost in the *misperception* depicted so dramatically on the screen.

Another commonly held view is that a gunshot wound always results in visible, dramatic, and instantaneous reactions from those who have been shot. Those who have thrilled to see the Hollywood hero fire a shot (it matters not from what type or caliber of weapon) that strikes the villain (it matters not where), lifting him bodily from his feet and propelling him through a conveniently located plate-glass window, will probably not comprehend why it was necessary for a police officer to shoot an assailant multiple times in order to stop his attack. The reality of wound ballistics, which teaches that bullets don't knock people down and that officers have no reliable means of instantaneously halting a threat, is lost in the *misperception* of instant and dramatic response portrayed on the screen.

And, of course, those who have cheered the hero as he, or she, successfully and with bare hands took on an aggressive assailant who was armed "only" with a knife, or club, or nothing at all, will find it incredible that a law enforcement officer judged it necessary to use deadly force to counter such threats. The reality that law enforcement officers are frequently killed or seriously injured during such encounters because the outcome is largely subject to the vagaries of chance is not as entertaining or comforting as the *misperception* that the hero or heroine always wins.

Few things highlight the disconnect between reality and misperception more graphically than the way cases are usually evaluated in the public forum as opposed to the way those same cases are evaluated in the courts of law. The obvious reason for this disconnect is that in the courts the final judgment is based on the facts and the law while in the public forum the vocal judgments are generally made before the facts are known and without reference to the law by those whose views are unaffected by either. Equally important, the courts are bound to view the facts and circumstances of a given case through the per-

---

6. *Elliott v. Leavitt*, 99 F.3d 640, at 643 (4th Cir. 1996).

spective of a reasonable officer at the scene while in the public forum the perspective is too often the product of the misperceptions described above or the deliberate manipulation of opinion to serve other agendas.

Unfortunately, the clamor of ignorance can sometimes drown out the voice of reason. If we are to remain a society committed to the objective rules of law, the evaluation of an officer's actions cannot be relegated to the subjective whims of the ill-informed. There are established processes for assessing the legality of an officer's decision to use deadly force. The obvious challenge is to ensure the safety of law enforcement officers and the community while deterring the abuse of authority. Unchecked power leads to tyranny as surely as unenforced law leads to anarchy. To avoid either extreme, the legal rules and the physical realities that govern the use of deadly force must be clearly understood both by the officers who make the decisions and those who subsequently judge them, whether in the court of public opinion or a court of law.

The *rules of law* can readily be found in statutes or judicial interpretations of constitutional provisions. The *physical realities* that give meaning to the legal rules are found in the collective knowledge and practical experience of law enforcement. Those physical realities include the objective factors that define a threat; the limited time available to see, recognize, react, initiate, and implement a response to that threat; the sensory distortion that occurs in any high-stress incident; and the limited means available to compel a timely halt to the threatening activity.

Objective and realistic legal standards have been developed in the last several years as the lower courts have followed the mandate of the Supreme Court and interpreted and applied the law through the prism of that practical knowledge and experience. These remarkable achievements are amply documented in this book.

The challenge remains to achieve in the court of public opinion what has been achieved in the courts of law. To do so, law enforcement agencies must assume the burden of proactively educating the community and addressing the disconnection commonly present between the realities and the misperceptions. There is no other realistic way for the community to comprehend the law enforcement perspective, and no better way to ensure that the public can "stand in the shoes" of its officers and evaluate their decisions objectively.

# In Defense of Self and Others...

# Chapter 1

# The Tragedy, the Travesty and the Truth

## Ferguson, Missouri, August 9, 2014

There are a number of good reasons to begin the third edition of this book with a discussion of the shooting incident that occurred in Ferguson, Missouri, on August 9, 2014. Although the facts of this incident are not unique, the aftermath has been truly remarkable, and highlights the general lack of knowledge and understanding—at many levels—of the lawful authority of law enforcement officers to use force, including deadly force, when necessary to defend themselves and others from threats of serious physical injury. This ignorance is all the more remarkable since this lawful authority has been clearly established for decades, and was further defined and clarified by the United States Supreme Court 30 years ago.

This chapter will provide a factual account of events based on the most reliable data available, describe how a false narrative was deliberately spread (and by whom), and present the conclusions of the United States Department of Justice (DOJ) with respect to the legality of the officer's decision to use deadly force in light of the constitutional standards.

# Part One: The Tragedy

Tragedy: An event causing great suffering, destruction, and distress.

*"Tragedy is like strong acid—it dissolves away all but the very gold of truth."*

—*D. H. Lawrence*

This summary of events is based on investigations conducted by the FBI, St. Louis County police detectives, federal prosecutors, and a St. Louis County grand jury. These investigative results are reported in the March 4, 2015, memorandum of the U.S. Department of Justice.

On August 9, 2014:

Officer Darren Wilson, Ferguson (Missouri) Police Department was in uniform and on duty in his official SUV. Around noon he received a dispatch reporting a "stealing in progress" at a nearby market. The dispatch provided descriptions of two men involved and their clothing.

Shortly thereafter Officer Wilson saw two men (later identified as Michael Brown and Dorian Johnson) matching the descriptions walking in the middle of the street. Officer Wilson called for backup and ordered the two men to move out of the street onto the sidewalk. When they did not comply he moved his vehicle at an angle to block their path. When he attempted to open the driver's side door he was unable to do so because of the close proximity of Michael Brown. [Dorian Johnson later stated that Brown pushed the door shut.]

A struggle ensued between Michael Brown and Officer Wilson through the open window of the SUV. Officer Wilson sustained injuries to his neck consistent with being struck. Officer Wilson later stated that he believed that Brown was attempting to grab his (Wilson's) service pistol.

During the struggle for control of Officer Wilson's service pistol, Wilson managed to fire two shots. One shot struck Michael Brown in his right hand and the other missed.

After the shots were fired, Michael Brown and Dorian Johnson ran away. Officer Wilson exited his vehicle and pursued the pair on foot. [At some point during this pursuit, Dorian Johnson disappeared from the scene.] Michael Brown ran several yards then stopped, turned, and advanced toward Officer Wilson, who ordered him to stop. When Brown did not stop, Officer Wilson fired several rounds from his pistol, striking Michael Brown several times. Brown went down and died at the scene.

The shooting occurred at approximately 12:02 p.m. Within minutes, local residents poured onto the street as word spread that Michael Brown had been shot "execution-style" while trying to surrender to a white police officer.

By 12:14 p.m. other Ferguson police officers began to arrive on the scene. The growing and increasingly hostile crowd began calling for the killing of police officers. Riots, looting, and arson began and continued for several days, resulting in frequent confrontations between citizens and police, and extensive destruction of private property.

On August 11, 2014, United States Attorney General Eric Holder announced a federal inquiry into the Michael Brown shooting to determine if federal civil rights laws had been violated.

Independent of that inquiry, after reviewing the available evidence—including statements from numerous witnesses—on November 24, 2014, a St. Louis County grand jury declined to return an indictment against Officer Wilson. This was followed by another round of disorder, arsons, and looting.

On November 28, 2014, Officer Wilson resigned from the Ferguson Police Department, citing "credible threats" against him and other police officers.

The tragedy of Ferguson is multifaceted. An 18-year-old black man was shot and killed by a 28-year-old white police officer. The conflicting allegations that the white officer shot the black man in the back, or shot him while he was facing the officer with his hands raised in surrender were zealously promoted and spread, although there was no credible evidence to substantiate these accusations.

The riots, arsons, and looting added another destructive dimension to the tragedy. Countless businesses were destroyed or severely damaged by the riots. Huge quantities of private property—e.g., television sets, computers, cell phones, alcoholic beverages, groceries, and even diapers—were stolen, indiscriminately destroyed, or carried away by the unruly mob.

The most disturbing aspect of the tragedy is the degree to which a false narrative was so readily believed, the rapidity with which it was spread, and its continuing, widespread, and destructive impact. The falsehood was "spawned" and spread by Dorian Johnson—Michael Brown's companion—whose credibility was subsequently destroyed by credible witnesses, the physical evidence, and his own self-contradictory statements to the media, investigators, and a grand jury. The depth and breadth of his fabrications are further described in Part Two.

# Part Two: The Travesty

Travesty: An absurd or grotesque misrepresentation.

*"A lie can travel half way around the world while the truth is putting on its shoes."*

—Mark Twain

The grotesque misrepresentation of events began almost immediately after the shooting incident that Saturday afternoon in Ferguson. The fatal shooting of Michael Brown by Officer Wilson occurred at about 12:02 p.m. Within minutes, and well before the facts could have been ascertained, crowds began to gather in the street. By 12:14 p.m. there were obscene chants to kill the police officers present at the scene. The anger was undoubtedly fueled by the rumor that a white police officer shot and killed Michael Brown execution-style while Brown's hands were raised in surrender and he was pleading "Don't shoot."

The source of this story was Dorian Johnson, Michael Brown's companion throughout the morning who claimed to have witnessed the events. Almost immediately after the shooting incident Johnson made several statements to the gathering crowd and to the media. He later made several statements to FBI agents and St. Louis County police detectives, to federal prosecutors, and to a St. Louis County grand jury. It is interesting to read his several descriptions of the events. Here is a summary:

About 7:00 a.m. on the morning of August 9, 2014 Johnson and Michael Brown got together.

About 11:00 a.m. they decided to go to the Ferguson Market to get cigarillos. Brown, who was 6'5" and weighed close to 300 lbs., stole cigarillos from behind the counter "as though he was entitled to them," and then walked out, shoving aside the substantially smaller store clerk who tried to stop him. According to Johnson, Brown was "surprisingly aggressive" and "bold." After leaving the store, they were walking single-file on the yellow line in the center of the street when they encountered Officer Wilson driving in the opposite direction in his marked Ferguson Police Department (FPD) vehicle.

Officer Wilson ordered the two men to move to the sidewalk. When they did not, he backed his vehicle up at an angle to block their progress. Officer Wilson attempted to open the driver's side door, but the door bounced off Michael Brown and slammed shut. Johnson said that he could understand why Officer Wilson might have thought that Michael Brown slammed the door shut. Johnson asserts that Officer Wilson then reached through the window with his left hand and grabbed Brown by the throat. Johnson said that a struggle ensued but "at no point did Brown ever strike, punch, or grab any part of Wilson." Officer Wilson used his right hand to draw his gun, and aiming it out the window said "I'm going to shoot."

Johnson said that Officer Wilson fired, " … hitting Brown in the torso." In another statement, he said that Officer Wilson " … neither fired a shot inside the SUV, nor did Brown have his hand(s) near the gun" when the shot was fired. Johnson said, "The bullet traveled outside the car and struck [Brown] in the chest."

Shortly after the shooting, Johnson told a local TV station that the officer got out of the SUV and pursued Michael Brown, and then " … fired another shot. And it struck my friend in the back."

Johnson described this event somewhat differently on MSNBC's *Al Sharpton Show*: "By this time, the officer is out of the car … And the officer is walking with his gun drawn … As he got closer, he fired one more shot. That shot struck my friend in the back."

*Note: According to Johnson, Michael Brown has now been shot twice, once in the chest and once in the back.*

One month later, Johnson presented a third version of this same event under oath before the grand jury: "I'm watching the officer … It was the second shot fired, pow, the officer shot. *I don't know if it hit, I wasn't that close.*" (Emphasis added.)

In a fourth version of the same event before the same grand jury Johnson testified: "Once the second shot fired off, I see his body do a little jerking movement, not to where it looked like he got hit in his back … it maybe could have grazed him."

By all accounts, after the encounter at Wilson's SUV, both Johnson and Brown ran. Johnson apparently got a head start, because he says that Brown ran past him, telling him, "Keep running, bro" and that Officer Wilson passed him in pursuit of Brown. Officer Wilson then fired a second shot that, in one version *"appeared"* to strike Brown in the back, or, in a second version *"definitely struck [Brown] in the back."* After hearing a news account of an autopsy report indicating that Brown was not shot in back, Johnson told a St. Louis grand jury that " … *the bullet likely grazed*" Brown's arm.

Johnson told the grand jury that Brown stopped running, and with his hands above his head, turned and faced Officer Wilson and said either "I don't have a gun" or "I'm unarmed." It isn't clear how Johnson knew what Brown was thinking, but he testified that *"Brown started to say it again,"* but Officer Wilson—while walking toward Brown—fired one volley of at least four shots and Brown fell down and died. Johnson testified that Brown either fell dead right where he stood, or he may have taken a half step forward but he insisted that Brown never moved toward Officer Wilson. Johnson also told the grand jury that he *"stood and watched face-to-face as every shot was fired as Brown's body fell to the ground."*

At some point Johnson ran from the scene, went home, and changed his shirt to avoid being recognized as one of the perpetrators of the strong-arm robbery at the market earlier that day. He then returned to the scene where a large crowd was gathering. He made multiple statements to those present and to the media to the effect that Officer Wilson shot Michael Brown execution-style as he held up his hands in surrender. From these statements emerged the slogan, "Hands up. Don't shoot."

In Part Three of this chapter, the "grotesque misrepresentation" of the truth is contradicted by all credible witnesses as well as physical and forensic evidence. The travesty becomes even more deplorable and pernicious when one considers the strong possibility that its author, Dorian Johnson, was not present to witness the fatal shooting of Michael Brown. By all accounts, including his own, after the shots were fired near Officer Wilson's SUV he ran away and ducked behind a car as Brown and Officer Wilson ran past him.

Several credible witnesses to these events either never saw Johnson at all, or saw him run away after the first shots near the SUV and never saw him return. One witness, after seeing Johnson in media interviews asserted that he " ... could not have seen what he is claiming to have seen ... After the initial shot ... [Johnson] took off running as well, and did not reappear until much later, once Brown's body was covered." A second witness stated that she first saw Johnson take off when the first shots were fired near the SUV, and she never saw him again. A third witness said that Brown's companion (Johnson) "disappeared" after the first shots near the SUV. A fourth said that Johnson took off running somewhere into the apartment complexes. And yet another said that Johnson ducked behind a white car, ran around it, and went in another direction. *There is **no credible witness** who placed Johnson at the scene when Officer Wilson fired the fatal shots.*

But, the travesty does not end with Dorian Johnson. As documented in the DOJ report, several other people claimed in media interviews to have seen Michael Brown put his hands up in surrender before he was shot and killed by Officer Wilson. When interviewed by FBI agents and St. Louis County detectives every single one of these individuals admitted that they did not witness the shooting but just repeated what they had heard from others. The willingness of so many to accept the lie without a shred of proof, and then adopt it as their own and spread it, is truly a travesty beyond comprehension or measure.

After eliminating those "witnesses" who admitted that they did not actually witness the events, 41 individuals remained who insisted that they were eyewitnesses to the shooting. Of these 41, only eight were deemed credible—i.e., their statements to investigators or to the grand jury were consistent with their prior statements, and with the physical and forensic evidence. *None of these witnesses claimed to have seen an execution-style shooting of a surrendering Michael Brown.*

Another nine witnesses gave statements that for a variety of reasons did not support a prosecution of Officer Wilson. *None of these witnesses claimed to have seen an execution-style shooting of a surrendering Michael Brown.*

The remaining 24 individuals who claimed to have witnessed the death of Michael Brown were discredited for a variety of reasons—inconsistent prior statements, recanting their prior statements, or inconsistencies between their statements and the physical and forensic evidence. It is noteworthy that *all of these discredited "witnesses" claimed to have seen Michael Brown raise his hands in surrender before being fatally shot.*

In the words of the DOJ report: "*There is no witness who has stated that Brown had his hands up in surrender whose statement is otherwise consistent with the physical evidence.*"

C. S. Lewis once wrote: "*No clever arrangement of bad eggs can produce a good omelet.*" Those words seem appropriate as we assess the malodorous consequences of *the lie*—authored by Dorian Johnson, adopted and exploited by hundreds of others, and mindlessly believed by countless thousands. That, indeed, is a travesty.

# Part Three: The Truth

Truth: The quality or state of being true as opposed to being false.

*"This truth is incontrovertible. Panic may resent it, ignorance may deride it, malice may distort it, but there it is."*

—Winston Churchill

Having established what *did not* happen, we can determine what did. The DOJ report of March 4, 2015, objectively delineates and documents the credible information. It refutes the allegations of excessive force leveled against Officer Wilson by the *discredited witnesses* cited above, and concludes that he acted in self-defense. A closer examination of the DOJ report on the events as they occurred follows:

(1) At Officer Wilson's SUV—"*The evidence establishes that the shots fired by [Officer] Wilson while he was seated in the SUV were in self-defense and thus were objectively reasonable under the Fourth Amendment.*"

Officer Wilson stated that when he tried to exit his vehicle to speak with the two men, Brown blocked him from opening the door. Brown reached through the open window and began punching Officer Wilson in the face. " … *Wilson had injuries to his jaw consistent with being struck.*" The two men struggled for control of Wilson's pistol and Wilson managed to fire a shot that struck Brown's hand. "*The physical evidence corroborates Wilson's account in that the bullet was recovered from the door panel just over Wilson's lap, the base of Brown's hand displayed injuries consistent with it being within inches of the muzzle of the gun….*" Three other credible witnesses stated that they saw Brown's upper body and/ or arms inside the vehicle.

The report concludes: "*Under well-established Fourth Amendment precedent, it is not objectively unreasonable for a law enforcement officer to use deadly force in response to being physically assaulted by a subject who attempts to take his firearm.*"

(2) As Brown was running away with Officer Wilson in pursuit: "*The evidence does not support concluding that [Officer] Wilson shot Brown while Brown's back was toward Wilson.*"

Although there were several witnesses who claimed to have seen Officer Wilson shoot Brown in the back as he ran away, "*These statements are contradicted by all three autopsies, which concluded that Brown had no entry wounds to his back.*"

While these conclusions refute the assertions that Michael Brown was shot in the back as he was running away, they do not suggest that it would have been unlawful for him to do so. In fact, the report notes: "*An officer may use deadly force under certain circumstances even if the suspect is fleeing.*" (See Chapter 3 for further discussion of an officer's lawful authority to use deadly force to prevent the escape of a dangerous person.)

(3) When Brown stopped running and turned to face Officer Wilson: "*The evidence establishes that the shots fired by [Officer] Wilson after Brown turned around were in self-defense and thus were not objectively unreasonable under the Fourth Amendment.*"

The physical evidence reveals that Brown ran about 180 feet (60 yards) from the SUV, turned to face Wilson, then moved toward him. Wilson stated that Brown "balled or clenched" his fists and "charged" forward, ignoring commands to stop. "*Knowing that Brown was much larger than him and that he had previously attempted to overpower him and take his gun, Wilson stated that he feared for his safety and fired at Brown…. Brown then reached toward his waistband, causing Wilson to fear that Brown was reaching for a weapon. Wilson stated that he continued to fear for his safety at this point and fired at Brown again. Wilson finally shot Brown in the head as he was falling or lunging forward, after which Brown immediately fell to the ground.*"

The report specifically notes that Wilson's description of events is supported by the physical evidence and by several credible witnesses, all of whom support Officer Wilson's assertion that Brown had turned to face him and "ran or charged" toward him when Wilson fired the fatal shots. "*Although some of the witnesses stated that Brown briefly had his hands up or out at about waist-level, none of these witnesses perceived Brown to be attempting to surrender at any point when Wilson fired upon him.*" (Emphasis added.)

Two individuals are identified in the report as the principal sources of the claim that Brown was shot with his hands up in surrender, Witness 101 (Dorian Johnson) and Witness 127. Both claimed that Brown turned around with his hands up in surrender, that he never moved toward Wilson after turning to face him with his hands up, and that he fell to the ground with his hands raised. Their statements are contradicted by the statements of other, demonstrably more credible witnesses and by the physical evidence.

Photographs taken at the scene depict Brown on the ground with his left hand at his waistband and his right hand at his side. Furthermore, Brown's blood on the street indicates that he moved forward *at least 21.6 feet (more than 7 yards)* from the point where he turned to face Wilson to the point where he fell. Most importantly, the report states: " … *there are no witnesses who could testify credibly that Wilson shot Brown while Brown was clearly attempting to surrender.*"

The DOJ reports notes: "*The media has widely reported that there is witness testimony that Brown said 'don't shoot' as he held his hands above his head. In fact, our investigation did not reveal any eyewitness who stated that Brown said 'don't shoot.'*" (Emphasis added.)

# Conclusion

Based on the most reliable evidence—i.e., credible witnesses and physical and forensic evidence, including three autopsies—it is possible to reconstruct a coherent and credible narrative of what happened.

At about noon on August 9, 2014, Officer Darren Wilson of the Ferguson Police Department saw two men walking in the middle of the street as he was patrolling in his department issued SUV. Officer Wilson had received a radio transmission moments before that a nearby convenience store had been robbed, that two men were implicated, and descriptions of the men and their clothing were included in the transmission. Officer Wilson observed that the general descriptions of the two men and their clothing matched those of the men implicated in the robbery. Officer Wilson stopped his SUV and ordered the two men to move to the sidewalk. When they failed to do so, he backed his vehicle up in a position to block their path. The two men were subsequently identified as Michael Brown and Dorian Johnson.

Officer Wilson attempted to get out of his vehicle, but he was unable to open the door because Michael Brown slammed the door shut. Michael Brown reached through the open driver's side window, punched Officer Wilson in the face, and tried to gain control of the officer's pistol. The former is confirmed by the injuries to the left side of Officer Wilson's neck and face; the latter is confirmed by the existence of Brown's DNA on Officer Wilson's pistol.

As they struggled for control for the pistol, Officer Wilson fired one shot at contact range that struck Brown in his right hand. The close proximity of the two men is confirmed by the existence of stippling and burnt gunpowder in the vicinity of the wound on Brown's hand. Officer Wilson fired a second shot that missed Brown.

Immediately after Brown sustained the gunshot wound to his hand, he and his companion—Dorian Johnson—began running away. Officer Wilson did not fire any shots at Brown as he ran away. Brown ran about 180 feet, or 60 yards, from the SUV before stopping and turning around to face Officer Wilson. Brown advanced at least 21.6 feet in the direction of Officer Wilson, ignoring repeated commands to stop. Officer Wilson fired a total of 10 rounds in three strings within a span of about eight seconds. Either 6 or 8 of these rounds struck Brown, all in the front of his body, the last and fatal shot being to his head. Brown fell face-forward to the ground. Investigative photos taken at the scene immediately after the shooting depict Brown with his left hand at his waistband and his right hand down by his side.

The investigation of this incident conducted by the Federal Bureau of Investigation (FBI), the St. Louis County Police Department, a St. Louis County grand jury, and federal prosecutors, consumed more than six months. The U.S. Department of Justice concluded that Officer Wilson acted in self-defense, and that his decision to use deadly force was not objectively unreasonable under the Fourth Amendment to the Constitution, or relevant federal civil rights statutes. The governing legal principles highlighted in this case, and the practical realities that give them substance, are the topics of the following chapters.

# Chapter 2

# The Law—A Brief Survey of History and Procedures

*"An official sued under [Section] 1983 is entitled to qualified immunity unless it is shown that the official violated a statutory or constitutional right that was 'clearly established' at the time of the challenged conduct."*

—*Plumhoff v. Rickard*, 572 U.S.(2014)

*"If the law at that time did not clearly establish that the officer's conduct would violate the Constitution the officer should not be subject to liability, or, indeed, even the burden of litigation."*

—*Brosseau v. Haugen*, 543 U.S. 194 (2004)

## Historical Perspectives

Until the twentieth century, state law was the only significant legal authority relating to the use of deadly force by law enforcement in the United States. Apart from the U.S. Marshals Service, which was founded in 1789, law enforcement was the responsibility of state and local government. There was no clearly defined federal law on the subject of the use of deadly force; had there been, it would have had no application to state and local officers because the relevant provisions of the U.S. Constitution did not apply to the states in the early years of the Republic. There were essentially two parallel universes: state and local law enforcement agencies, governed by their respective constitutions and statutes, which were not relevant to the federal government, and federal law enforcement agencies—to the extent they existed—governed by the federal Constitution and federal statutes, which were not binding on the states. That changed dramatically in the mid-twentieth century, as the U.S. Supreme Court began the process of selectively incorporating provisions of the federal Bill of

Rights into the Fourteenth Amendment Due Process Clause, making them binding on the states.

As a consequence of this "selective incorporation" process, most of the provisions of the Bill of Rights are equally binding on state and federal activities. Most importantly for our discussion is the incorporation of the Fourth Amendment into the Due Process Clause in 1949.[1] As a consequence, all searches and seizures, whether conducted by federal, state, or local authorities, must meet a uniform standard of "reasonableness." That includes not only the factual standard necessary to justify a particular seizure, but the kind and level of force permitted to achieve it. Although state laws may be more restrictive than the federal standards, they cannot be less so. Before discussing the current constitutional standards regarding the use of force by law enforcement officers, it will be helpful to take a brief look at the historical developments that brought us to this point.

# The Common Law

The influence of the English Common Law on American laws and institutions was both natural and profound. When the early settlers came to the New World, they brought with them the language, religion, customs, and laws of the mother country; since most of the early colonists came from the British Isles, that meant English customs and laws. From that day until now, the principles of the English Common Law have permeated our own legal system, including principles that govern the use of force by law enforcement officers. With respect to the authority of police officers to use deadly force, the eighteenth century English jurist William Blackstone explained that such authority would exist in the following circumstances:

> [1] Where an officer in the execution of his office ... kills a person that assaults or resists him.
>
> [2] If an officer ... attempts to take a man charged with felony, and is resisted; and in the endeavor to take him, kills him.
>
> [3] In all these cases, there must be an apparent necessity ... otherwise, without such absolute necessity, it is not justifiable.[2]

The first statement may be characterized as a *self-defense* provision; the second, as the *fleeing felon* rule; and the third, as a requirement of *necessity* be-

---

1. *Wolf v. Colorado*, 338 U.S. 25 (1949).

2. Blackstone, *Commentaries on the Laws of England*, v. 4, p. 179–80 203–4, University of Chicago Press (1979).

fore deadly force may be used in either circumstance. It is notable that under the Common Law this rule is an affirmative defense against criminal prosecution rather than an affirmative grant of authority.

Following the establishment of American independence, most states continued to operate under the Common Law rules, including the "fleeing felon" rule. After all, felonies were by definition serious offenses, frequently punishable by death. And in the days when communications were only as fast as the legs of a man or a horse—and organized police forces were essentially nonexistent— the likelihood of capturing a fleeing felon after he escaped the scene of his crime was remote at best.

For most of our 200-plus year history, the states exercised their police powers unaffected by the federal Constitution or the federal courts. This was due to the unique nature of our constitutional system. Today, it is easy to forget that the Constitution was written primarily for the purpose of creating a new central government and defining its limited powers. Concerns about the potential expansion of these powers led to the adoption of a Bill of Rights two years after the Constitution was ratified. Thus, the restrictions on governmental authority found in the Bill of Rights were not aimed at the states, but at the federal government. This original intent of the framers of the Constitution was affirmed by the Supreme Court decision of *Barron v. Baltimore*[3] in 1833. That interpretation would remain essentially unaltered for more than a century.

## The Fourteenth Amendment & Due Process

The seeds for change came in 1868 after the Civil War with the adoption of the Fourteenth Amendment, which, unlike the Bill of Rights, was aimed directly at the states. Specifically, it prohibits the states from depriving any person of "life, liberty or property" without "due process." This language already existed in the Fifth Amendment to the Constitution, but applied only to the federal government. Now the states were similarly constrained. The second step came in 1871 with the passage of two federal statutes, Title 42 U.S. Code, Section 1983, and Title 18 U.S. Code, Sections 241 and 242, designed to enforce the provisions of the Fourteenth Amendment through civil and criminal remedies in federal courts.

Notwithstanding the obvious importance of these developments, they remained largely symbolic, with little practical impact on state and local police

---

3. 32 U.S. 243 (1833).

powers until the twentieth century. "Due process" was historically viewed as guaranteeing a process or procedure, rather than providing substantive rights. Such rights as found in the Bill of Rights were simply not relevant. In the 1930s the Supreme Court began to accept appeals from individuals challenging the practices in the states that were viewed as denying a defendant some of the rights found in the Bill of Rights. One such case was *Powell v. Alabama*[4] in 1932. Viewing "due process" as requiring the states to comply with a general standard of "fundamental fairness," the court held that a defendant in a criminal case had the right to be represented by counsel, and that the state had an obligation to provide counsel if the defendant could not provide one himself. In reaching this decision, the court made no reference to the Bill of Rights or to the right to counsel found in the Sixth Amendment, referring only to the requirement of due process in the Fourteenth Amendment.

Similar cases followed as the Supreme Court selectively applied principles from the Bill of Rights and applied them to the states without making reference to the Bill of Rights. This process of "selective incorporation" eventually included most, but not all, of the major rights found in the Bill of Rights. Included in this "incorporation" process as noted above was the Fourth Amendment, with its prohibition of *"unreasonable searches and seizures."* As a consequence, every seizure of a person by law enforcement officers, whether an arrest or an investigative stop, must be reasonable with respect to both the facts needed to justify it, and the force used to accomplish it. Moreover, these standards were now enforceable through lawsuits or criminal prosecutions brought in state or federal courts. The "criminal procedure revolution" had begun.

This revolution was greatly facilitated by two Supreme Court decisions in 1961 that fashioned remedies for alleged violations of federal constitutional rights by state and local law enforcement officers. The first, *Mapp v. Ohio*,[5] by requiring the suppression of unconstitutionally seized evidence in state criminal trials; the second, *Monroe v. Pape*,[6] by opening the door for lawsuits in federal court against state and local officials for alleged violations of federal constitutional rights.

Inasmuch as the Eleventh Amendment to the Constitution prohibits lawsuits against the individual states without their consent, the Supreme Court's decision in *Monroe v. Pape* interpreted Section 1983 to allow *lawsuits only against*

---

4. 287 U.S. 45 (1932).
5. 367 U.S. 643 (1961).
6. 365 U.S. 157 (1961).

*natural persons, not government entities.* In 1967 the Court added a new wrinkle by holding in *Pierson v. Ray*[7] that a police officer sued under Section 1983 enjoyed a defense of qualified immunity, often referred to as the "good faith" defense.[8]

In combination, these factors meant that neither the state that enacted a law, nor the municipality that passed an ordinance, could be sued under Section 1983, and an officer acting under the authority of either was generally held to be entitled to a good faith belief in its lawfulness. That is not to say that there were no effective constitutional challenges to the police use of force during this period. It simply meant that the focus of such challenges was necessarily on the officer's actions, rather than on the policy or law that may have prompted them. Consequently, efforts to reach beyond the officer to source of the problem and the "deep pockets" of the state or municipality were consistently thwarted.

An illustrative case is *Ashcroft v. Mattis*,[9] in which a Missouri police officer shot and killed a fleeing burglary suspect pursuant to a Missouri statute that codified the Common Law "fleeing felon" law. In the resulting Section 1983 lawsuit against the officer, it was determined by the trial court that the officer was entitled to the defenses of probable cause and good faith. A federal appellate court concurred on the issue of the officer's good faith, but concluded that the state's statute under which he acted violated the "fundamental right to life" as guaranteed by the Fourteenth Amendment Due Process clause. The U.S. Supreme Court set aside the lower decision on the procedural ground that since the only viable defendant, the officer, was shielded by the good faith defense, there remained no "case or controversy" to justify federal jurisdiction. The law had truly become a tangled web, and it would require two additional Supreme Court cases to untangle it. They were not long in coming.

In the 1978 decision of *Monell v. Department of Social Services*[10] the Supreme Court reversed a portion of its decision in *Monroe v. Pape* and held that <u>municipalities and counties could be sued under Section 1983 if the challenged actions were *caused by a policy or custom of that entity*</u>. This is sometimes confused with the doctrine of "vicarious liability," in which an employer is automatically liable for the actions of the employee. Under the *Monell* decision the municipal or county agency is only liable for the wrongful actions of an employee

---

7. 386 U.S. 547 (1967).

8. A fuller discussion on the qualified immunity defense is found later in this chapter.

9. 431 U.S. 171 (1977).

10. 436 U.S. 658 (1978).

if its policies, practices, or customs caused those actions. Two years later, in *Owen v. City of Independence*,[11] the Court held that local government entities sued under Section 1983 could not assert the qualified immunity defense.

The way was now paved for direct constitutional challenges to state laws and departmental policies relating to police use of deadly force. From that time until the present, it has been federal court, rather than state court, that has provided the forum for most legal challenges to the use of deadly force by law enforcement; likewise, it has been federal constitutional law, rather than state law, that has been the standard used to resolve the issues.

The legal standards governing police use of deadly force by law enforcement officers are remarkably similar throughout the country. Generally, state laws permit officers to use deadly force whenever necessary *to defend themselves or others* from perceived danger of serious physical injury. Moreover, state laws generally permit officers to use deadly force *to prevent escape* of those who may be termed "dangerous suspects." To say that the statutory language is similar among the states does not necessarily mean that the interpretations of those statutes are uniform. There is no question that the same words may have different meanings to different people. One need only survey the diversity of opinions among U.S. Supreme Court justices on any given question of constitutional law to discern the truth of this point. Nevertheless, the consensus of view on major principles is greater than some may suspect.

# The Process of Legal Challenges

The federal constitutional standards governing the use of deadly force by law enforcement officers have been largely defined and refined through litigation; that is, through lawsuits filed against law enforcement officers and/or their agencies. There are different mechanisms depending upon whether the defendant is a government employee or a government agency, and there is a further distinction to be made between state and local defendants and those who are part of the federal government. It also should be noted that in both state and federal systems it is possible for criminal charges to be brought against law enforcement officers who have used deadly force in a manner that rises to the level of a crime. However, those cases are relatively rare and do not tend to produce court opinions from which instruction can be derived. Accord-

---

11. 445 U.S. 622 (1980).

ingly, we will focus our attention on the civil lawsuits, which are both frequent and instructive.

# Suits against Individual Law Enforcement Officers

## State & Local Law Enforcement Officers

The law and constitution of their respective states determines the personal legal liability of state and local officers under state law. Federal constitutional standards determine legal liability when federal constitutional issues are raised. All of the states permit civil lawsuits to be brought against individual state and local officers. These are usually in the form of "tort" suits, alleging assault and battery, false arrest, false imprisonment, etc. To provide some level of protection for officers named in such suits, the states generally require some showing of intentional action, or at the least, gross negligence, on the part of the officers. Simple negligence is generally not enough. Needless to say, this avenue is not a particularly attractive one for most erstwhile plaintiffs, or their attorneys. They will find the federal courts a much more attractive and profitable arena.

As previously noted, the primary avenue for lawsuits against state and local law enforcement officers is Title 42, U.S. Code, Section 1983, which permits state and local officers to be sued in federal court for alleged violations of the U.S. Constitution. It has also been noted that officers sued under this statute may assert the defense of "qualified immunity." Described generally as a "good faith" defense, the U.S. Supreme Court has held that it shields an officer from liability as long as the challenged conduct did not violate any "clearly established" law of which a reasonable person should have known.[12] This is particularly important since officers are often called upon to make life-and-death decisions in tense and rapidly evolving circumstances. The Court has held that just as officers are entitled to rely upon the validity of *the law*, they are equally entitled to rely upon *the facts* available to them at the time they act, as long as they were reasonable in believing them to be accurate.[13]

---

12. See *Pierson v. Ray*, 386 U.S. 547 (1967), and *Harlow v. Fitzgerald*, 457 U.S. 800 (1982).

13. See *Anderson v. Creighton*, 107 S. Ct. 3034 (1987).

## Federal Law Enforcement Officers

Because the language of Section 1983 explicitly refers to those acting under color of state law, it has no application to federal law enforcement officers. Although there is no comparable statute imposing liability on those acting under color of federal law, the Supreme Court has filled in the gap. In *Bivens v. Six Unknown Named Agents of the Federal Bureau of Narcotics* the Court held that federal employees may be sued for alleged violations of federal constitutional rights.[14] Consequently, though the mechanisms differ, law enforcement officers at every level of government may be sued for actions that allegedly violate the federal Constitution. When sued under *Bivens*, federal agents have the same defense of qualified immunity available to their state and local counterparts.

# Suits against Local Government Agencies

State governmental agencies can be sued in state court for violations of state law to the extent that sovereign immunity has been waived by the state. While the Eleventh Amendment to the U.S. Constitution precludes suits in federal court against a state, that preclusion does not shield local governmental agencies (municipalities and counties) from such suits.[15]

As noted above, the *Monell* decision in 1978 held that a local governmental entity (municipality or county) may be sued under Section 1983 when a policy or practice of the entity causes the constitutional violation.[16] The Court declined to adopt the principle of "vicarious liability," which would have made local agencies automatically liable for the constitutional violations of their employees. Instead, the employer is only liable if its own policies or practices caused the unconstitutional behavior. When such suits are filed against local governmental entities they, unlike their employees, are not entitled to the qualified immunity defense.[17]

---

14. 403 U.S. 388 (1971).

15. See *Lake Country Estates v. Tahoe Regional Planning Agency*, 440 U.S. 391 (1979), and *Edelman v. Jordan*, 415 U.S. 651 (1974).

16. See *Monroe v. Pape*, 365 U.S. 167 (1961), and *Monell v. Department of Social Services*, 436 U.S. 658 (1978).

17. *Owen v. City of Independence*, 445 U.S. 622 (1980).

# Suits against Federal Agencies

Just as with state governments, the federal government cannot be sued without a waiver of sovereign immunity. The Federal Tort Claims Act (FTCA) constitutes the federal government's limited waiver and permits lawsuits against the federal government for negligent or other wrongful acts of its employees.

The FTCA is a good illustration of "vicarious liability" in that it makes the federal government liable for a wide range of unlawful acts by its employees. Unlike Section 1983 suits, the plaintiff is not required to establish that a constitutional violation occurred, nor does the plaintiff have to establish a causal connection between the act of the employee and some policy or practice of the employer. By the express terms of the FTCA, the federal government is entitled to all defenses that would be available to the employee.

# Summary Judgment and the Qualified Immunity Defense

Summary judgment is a legal tool used by the courts to minimize unnecessary litigation. Once a lawsuit is filed, and the discovery process is completed, the defense may file a motion for summary judgment, contending that no material facts are in dispute, and that the case should be resolved in the defendant's favor without the necessity of a jury trial. The trial court's decision on that motion is appealable. If the defendant does not prevail on the summary judgment motion, then the disputed facts are resolved by a jury.

As previously noted, neither the federal nor the state governments may be sued unless they waive their sovereign immunity. Sovereign immunity arose in the early days of the evolution of the Common Law when it was it concluded that the sovereign—king or queen—was not subject to the same laws as everyone else. You could not sue the sovereign because he or she was ... well, sovereign. When the Common Law was brought to the New World the doctrine of sovereign immunity came with it. And even though we no longer have a king or queen, the notion that the highest officials or components of government are above the common herd is still with us. Hence, the need for waivers of sovereign immunity before the federal or state governments can be sued. Such immunity does not exist for municipalities, state and local officers, or federal law enforcement officers.

When law enforcement officers are sued for alleged violations of the Constitution they are entitled to the whole range of defenses available to any defendant in a lawsuit. But they are entitled to more. It is not enough for plaintiffs to assert and prove that an officer violated their constitutional rights; they must prove that the officer knew or should have known of those constitutional rights and violated them anyway. Unlike "absolute immunity," which precludes any lawsuit, "qualified immunity" permits the suit but shields the officer from liability as long as the challenged conduct did not violate any clearly established right of which a reasonable officer should have known. While this defense is available to government officials at all levels of government, it is particularly important for law enforcement officers who, in the words of the Supreme Court, must often make decisions "*in circumstances that are tense, uncertain, and rapidly evolving.*"[18] Importantly, it applies to reasonable mistakes of *fact* and *law*.

The Supreme Court describes qualified immunity as "*a two-pronged inquiry*":

> "*[1] ... whether the facts, '[t]aken in the light most favorable to the party asserting the injury ... show the officer's conduct violated a [federal] right.*"[19]
> "*[2] ... whether the right in question was 'clearly established' at the time of the violation.*"[20]

The Court explained that lower courts have discretion to decide the order in which to engage these two prongs,[21] but courts may not resolve genuine disputes of fact in favor of the party seeking summary judgment. Issues of fact are to be resolved by a jury.

A good illustration of how the qualified immunity defense benefits law enforcement officers is found in ***Brosseau v. Haugen.***[22] Officer Rochelle Brosseau shot Kenneth Haugen in the back as he was attempting to flee in his vehicle from the scene of an altercation. He survived his wound and filed a lawsuit against Officer Brosseau in U.S. District Court alleging excessive force in violation of the Fourth Amendment. Officer Brosseau filed a motion for summary judgment, asserting that she did not violate Haugen's constitutional rights, and, even if she did, that she was entitled to "qualified immunity" be-

---

18. *Graham v. Connor*, 490 U.S. 386, 396 (1989).
19. *Tolan v. Cotton*, 572 U.S. _____(2014), citing *Saucier v. Katz*, 533 U.S. 194, 201 (2001).
20. *Id.*, citing *Hope v. Pelzer*, 536 U.S. 730, 739 (2002).
21. *Pearson v. Callahan*, 555 U.S. 223, 236 (2009), see also, *Carroll v. Carman*, 574 U.S. _____ (2014).
22. 543 U.S. 194 (2004).

cause at the time of the shooting her actions were not precluded by any clearly established law.

In resolving summary judgment motions, courts are required to adopt the version of events espoused by the non-moving party, in this case Haugen. According to that version, Officer Brosseau responded to a report of a fight between Haugen and two other men in the driveway of his mother's home. One of these two men (one of Haugen's former partners in crime) had reported to Officer Brosseau the previous day that Haugen was in possession of stolen tools. Officer Brosseau also learned of an outstanding no-bail warrant against Haugen for drug and other charges. When Haugen saw Officer Brosseau arrive at his mother's residence, he ran away and disappeared in the neighborhood. Meanwhile, his erstwhile opponents seated themselves in their pickup truck at the street end of the driveway. Shortly thereafter, two other officers arrived and joined the search for Haugen.

Haugen was seen 30 to 40 minutes later running back towards his mother's house with Officer Brosseau in pursuit. Haugen jumped into his Jeep, which was parked in the driveway facing the street, locked the doors, and attempted to start the engine. Officer Brosseau drew her gun and ordered him to get out of the Jeep. When Haugen ignored her orders, she broke the driver's side window with her gun, and attempted to get the keys from Haugen. Despite her efforts to prevent it, Haugen managed to start the engine of the Jeep and accelerated forward. At this point, in addition to the pickup truck and its two occupants at the end of the driveway, a small car occupied by Haugen's girlfriend and her three-year-old daughter was parked facing the Jeep about four feet away. As the Jeep moved forward, Officer Brosseau jumped back from the driver's side door, and fired one shot through the rear driver's side window striking Haugen in the back. Despite his wound, Haugen, in his own words "stood on the gas," navigated "the small tight space," drove across the neighbor's yard, and continued down the street. When he realized he was wounded, he stopped the Jeep and surrendered. He subsequently pleaded guilty to a felony, admitting that he drove his vehicle in a manner indicating "a wanton or willful disregard for the lives … of others."

In light of this version of the facts, the district court granted Officer Brosseau's motion for summary judgment. The Ninth Circuit Court of Appeals reversed that decision, ruling that Officer Brosseau violated Haugen's clearly established constitutional rights. The Supreme Court took the case on appeal and reversed the Ninth Circuit. Because of its longstanding practice of resolving only the issues necessary to dispose of a case, the Court side-stepped the constitutional question—i.e., did the officer violate the plaintiff's constitutional rights—and focused on the issue of qualified immunity:

*"We express no view as to the correctness of the Court of Appeals' decision on the constitutional question itself. We believe that, however that question is decided, the Court of Appeals was wrong on the issue of qualified immunity."*[23]

Citing several federal appellate cases that found no Fourth Amendment violation when officers shot fleeing suspects in vehicles who presented risks to others, the Supreme Court reversed the Ninth Circuit, concluding that at the time of her action, it was not clearly established that Officer Brosseau's shooting of Haugen violated the Fourth Amendment. The Court noted that Officer Brosseau's explanation for shooting Haugen was her "fear for the other officers on foot [she] believed were in the immediate area, for the occupied vehicles in [Haugen's] path and for any other citizens who might be in the area."[24]

The significance of qualified immunity for law enforcement officers can hardly be exaggerated. Officer Brosseau would not have been found liable even if it had been determined that she violated Haugen's constitutional rights because of the unsettled nature of the law. The Supreme Court emphasized that the purpose of the qualified immunity defense is not limited to protecting officers from liability:

*"If the law at the time did not clearly establish that the officer's conduct would violate the Constitution, the officer should not be subject to liability, or indeed, <u>even the burden of litigation.</u>"*[25]

***J.L.D. v. City of Los Angeles, et al.***[26] provides an interesting illustration of how summary judgment can work with an unusual set of facts. Two police officers attempted to arrest Reginald Doucet for petty theft and indecent exposure. Doucet resisted, forcing both officers to their knees and pummeling them with his fists. One of the officers shot and killed Doucet. Both officers recalled only one shot being fired, striking Doucet in the torso, and causing him to fall backwards. A lawsuit was filed in federal district court against the City of Los Angeles and the officer who fired the fatal shot. The district court granted summary judgment to the defendants. On appeal, the federal appellate court reversed. A medical examiner's report disclosed that Doucet had actually been shot twice, once in the torso and once in the base of his neck. The shot to the neck traveled in a downward direction through Doucet's chest, and produced

---

23. *Id.*, at 197.
24. *Id.*
25. *Id.*
26. 555 Fed. Appx. 670; 2014 U.S. App. LEXIS 3136 (9th Cir. 2014).

his death. An expert witness opined that the officer, from his stated and demonstrated position, could not have positioned his pistol to produce the neck wound. As a consequence of this dispute of material facts, the appellate court upheld summary judgment for the first shot (to the torso), but denied it for the second shot (to the neck). The appellate court explained:

> "We must assume the correctness of the district court's conclusion that [the officer] was entitled to use deadly force to repel an attacker who had forced him to the ground and continued an attack. But assuming, as we must, that [the officer] fired two shots, the first to Doucet's torso from a kneeling position and the second after Doucet fell backwards, from an angle downward into Doucet's neck, we are unable to conclude as a matter of law that the use of force in its totality was reasonable ... Although it is not clear how much time transpired between the two shots, [plaintiff's expert] opined that there 'would also be a corresponding delay between the two shots. The two shots would not have discharged in rapid succession as would typically be described as a two shot burst.' That opinion creates a fact issue on whether the second shot was reasonable."

As noted above, summary judgment can only be granted when there are no material facts in dispute. Clearly, in this case, there were material facts in dispute regarding the justification for the second shot, and the location of the wounds to Doucet's body. There are a number of plausible explanations that could resolve the dispute in the officer's favor, but the dispute must be resolved before summary judgment can be granted. Otherwise, there is likely to be a trial.

The recent Supreme Court decision in *City and County of San Francisco, California, et al. v. Sheehan*,[27] raises a multitude of issues that will be discussed in later chapters, but the dispositive issue was qualified immunity, so we will begin the discussion here.

Teresa Sheehan, a woman who suffers from a schizoaffective disorder, lived in a group home for individuals with mental illness. When she began acting erratically and threatened to kill her social worker with a knife, police officers Reynolds and Holder were dispatched to help escort Sheehan to a facility for temporary evaluation and treatment. The officers went to Sheehan's apartment, knocked on the door, announced their identity to Sheehan and that they were there to help her. When she did not respond, the officers used a key to enter the room. Sheehan grabbed a kitchen knife with an approximately five-inch blade and advanced on the officers, yelling threats and ordering them to

---

27. 575 U.S. ____ (May 18, 2015) (slip opinion).

leave. The officers retreated from the room and Sheehan remained inside with the door closed. The officers called for backup, but concerned that Sheehan was still armed with a knife, decided to reenter the apartment before backup arrived. In making that decision they did not consider whether her disability should be accommodated. They knew she was unwell, and that she had recently threatened to kill her social worker and two uniformed police officers.

The officers reentered the room with weapons drawn. Sheehan, still armed with a knife yelled at them to leave. One of the officers began spraying Sheehan with pepper spray but she would not drop the knife. She continued to advance on the officers with knife in hand. When she was only a few feet away Officer Holder shot her twice without result, and Officer Reynolds then fired multiple shots and Sheehan fell. Sheehan survived to file a lawsuit against the City and County of San Francisco for arresting her without accommodating her disability, and against the two police officers for violating her Fourth Amendment rights. The U.S. District granted summary judgment to the defendants, holding that officers making an arrest are not required to determine whether their actions would comply with the Americans with Disabilities Act (ADA), and, moreover, the officers did not violate Sheehan's Fourth Amendment rights by entering her apartment or by their use of force.

On appeal the Ninth Circuit Court of Appeals vacated the judgment of the District Court, holding that it was for a jury to determine whether San Francisco should have accommodated Sheehan's disability by "respecting her comfort zone," and essentially allowing the passage of time to deescalate the situation. As to the officers, the court held that their initial entry into Sheehan's apartment was lawful, and that the officers acted lawfully by reentering and using their firearms when pepper spray was not effective in stopping her advance. However, the court opined, a jury could determine that the officers "provoked" Sheehan by "needlessly forcing that second confrontation." The court then found that "it was clearly established" that an officer cannot "forcibly enter the home of an armed, mentally ill subject who had been acting irrationally and had threatened anyone who entered when there was no objective need for immediate entry."

The defendants, San Francisco and the two officers, appealed to the Supreme Court, raising two questions: First, whether the ADA's requirement to accommodate mentally ill persons applies to arrests; and, second, whether the officers can be held personally liable for the injuries Sheehan suffered. For reasons not altogether clear, San Francisco changed course after the Supreme Court granted certiorari, and assumed the position that "the ADA governs the manner in which a *qualified* individual with a disability is arrested." (Emphasis added.) Thus, the position turned from whether the ADA applies to arrests, to an assumption that it does. Because that issue was not properly briefed the Supreme Court declined to decide it. As to the second question of the officers' liability, the Court held that " ... *they are entitled to qualified immunity.*"

A minority of the justices would have declined to resolve both questions, but the majority was sensitive to the fact that while the first question related to the liability of the city, the second related to the liability of the individual officers. In a footnote to the opinion, the majority wrote:

> *"At a minimum, these officers have a personal interest in the correctness in the judgment below, which holds that they may have violated the Constitution ... Because of the importance of qualified immunity ... the Court often corrects lower courts when they wrongly subject individual officers to liability."[28]*

Having decided the qualified immunity question to the officers' benefit, the Court gratuitously addressed some of the issues relating to the officers' actions. Their conclusions are worth citing in some detail.

> " ... *the officers did not violate any federal right when they opened Sheehan's door the first time ... [They] knocked and announced that they were police officers and ... they wanted to help her. When Sheehan did not come to the door, they entered her room. This was not unconstitutional."[29]*

> " ... had Sheehan not been disabled, the officers could have opened her door the second time without violating any constitutional rights."

> "In addition, [the officers] knew that Sheehan had a weapon and had threatened to use it to kill three people. They also knew that delay could make the situation more dangerous."

> " ... after the officers opened Sheehan's door the second time, their use of force was reasonable. [Officer] Reynolds tried to subdue Sheehan with pepper spray, but Sheehan kept coming at the officers until she was 'only a few feet from a cornered Officer Holder.'"

> "At this point, the use of potentially deadly force was justified."

> "Nothing in the Fourth Amendment barred [the officers] from protecting themselves, even though it meant firing multiple rounds."

---

28. See, e.g., *Carrol v. Carman*, 574 U.S.____(2014); *Wood v. Moss*, 572 U.S. ____(2014); *Plumhoff v. Ricard*, 572 U.S.____(2014); *Stanton v. Sims*, 571 U.S. ____(2013); and *Reichle v. Howard*, 566 U.S.____(2012).

29. The Court observed that "*[L]aw enforcement officers may enter a home without a warrant to render emergency assistance to an injured occupant or to protect an occupant from imminent injury.*" Citing *Brigham City v. Stuart*, 547 U.S. 398 (2006), and *Kentucky v. King*, 563 U.S. _____(2011).

"Under Ninth Circuit law, an entry that otherwise complies with the Fourth Amendment is not rendered unreasonable because it provokes a violent reaction."

"Indeed, even if [the officers] misjudged the situation, Sheehan cannot 'establish a Fourth Amendment violation based merely on bad tactics that result in a deadly confrontation that could have been avoided.'"

It is remarkable how frequently issues are raised in litigation that have no bearing on the legal issues. For example, plaintiffs often call upon experts in police training or policy to testify that an officer violated one or the other. That occurred in this case when an expert testified that the officers did not follow their training. The Court responded:

> *"Even if an officer acts contrary to her training, however, (and here, given the generality of that training, it is not at all clear that [the officers] did so), that does not itself negate qualified immunity where it would otherwise be warranted. Rather, so long as 'a reasonable officer could have believed that his conduct was justified,' a plaintiff cannot 'avoid summary judgment by simply producing an expert's report that an officer's conduct leading up to a deadly confrontation was imprudent, inappropriate, or even reckless.'"*

In conclusion, the Court held:

> *" ... we hold that qualified immunity applies because these officers had 'no fair and clear warning of what the Constitution requires.' Because the qualified immunity analysis is straightforward, we need not decide whether the Constitution was violated by the officers' failure to accommodate Sheehan's illness."*

This last quote from the **Sheehan** decision highlights both the positive and the negative consequences of summary judgment and the qualified immunity defense. On the positive side, qualified immunity shields officers from liability unless they have violated a *"clearly established law"* of which a reasonable officer should have known. And a right is clearly established *"only if its contours are sufficiently clear that a reasonable official would understand that what he is doing violates that right."* On the negative side, qualified immunity often results in important constitutional questions remaining unanswered. On balance, it must be viewed as a positive factor, *"giving [officers] breathing room to make reasonable but mistaken judgments,"* and protecting *"all but the plainly incompetent or those who knowingly violate the law."*[30]

---

30. *Malley v. Briggs*, 475 U.S. 335, 341 (1986).

# Chapter 3

# Federal Constitutional Standards

*" … courts should be cautious about second-guessing a police officer's assessment, made on the scene, of the danger presented by a particular situation."*
—*Ryburn v. Huff*, 132 S.Ct. 987, 191–92 (2012)

*"It stands to reason that, if police officers are justified in firing at a suspect in order to end a severe threat to pubic safety, the officers need not stop shooting until the threat is over."*
—*Plumhoff et al. v. Rickard*, 572 U.S. ____(2014)
(slip opinion p. 11)

There are three provisions of the federal Constitution that affect the use of force by law enforcement officers and each has specific applications briefly described as follows:

**The Fourth Amendment** prohibits *"unreasonable searches and seizures,"* and applies to *seized persons*—i.e., those arrested or otherwise detained by law enforcement officers.[1]

**The Due Process Clause** found in the Fifth and Fourteenth Amendments restricts the authority of the federal and state governments, respectively, and governs the use of force against *persons not seized* within the meaning of the Fourth Amendment, as well as *pre-trial detainees*.[2]

**The Eighth Amendment** protects *convicted prisoners* from *"cruel and unusual punishments."*[3]

While all three provisions are important in their respective contexts, the focus of this book is on the use of deadly force by law enforcement officers engaged in traditional police functions "on the street." Accordingly, neither the

---

1. See *Graham v. Connor*, 490 U.S. 386 (1989).
2. See *Bell v. Wolfish*, 441 U.S. 520 (1979).
3. *Ingraham v. Wright*, 430 U.S. 651, at 671 (1977).

Eighth Amendment, nor that portion of the Due Process Clause that relates to pre-trial detainees, is within the parameters of our discussion.

# The Fourth Amendment Standard

The Fourth Amendment states:

> *"The right of the people to be secure in their persons, houses, papers, and effects against unreasonable searches and seizures shall not be violated, and no warrants shall issue but upon probable cause, supported by oath or affirmation, and particularly describing the place to be searched and the persons or things to be seized."*

# The Seizure Requirement

Because the Fourth Amendment specifically prohibits *"unreasonable searches and seizures,"* it is the **only** constitutional provision at issue when law enforcement officers seize a person.[4] The Supreme Court has defined a seizure of a person as a " ... *governmental termination of freedom of movement through means intentionally applied."*[5] Fourth Amendment seizures of individuals fall into one of three categories—arrest, investigative detention, and *de minimus* seizures—and each *"carries with it the right to use some degree of force to effect it."* Thus, all Fourth Amendment seizures are, by definition, *forcible* government actions. The appropriateness of the type and level of force necessary to achieve a *seizure* is more often dictated by the actions of the person being seized than by the officers doing the seizing. Deadly force can never be justified solely for the purpose of seizing a non-dangerous person. As the cases discussed below illustrate, it can only be justified by the necessity to protect officers or others from serious physical injury.

The threshold question in deciding whether the Fourth Amendment has any application to a law enforcement officer's use of force is whether a seizure has occurred. There are four components to the Supreme Court's definition:

a. Government action;
b. Intentional termination of freedom of movement;
c. Intended person;
d. Intended means.

---

4. See *Graham, supra.*
5. *Brower v. County of Inyo*, 486 U.S. 593 (1989).

## Government Action

The requirement of "government action" is grounded in the constitutional principle that the provisions of the Bill of Rights only constrain the power of the government. Initially, the Bill of Rights applied only to the federal government, and had no application to the states. As a consequence of the process of "selective incorporation" described in Chapter 2, the strictures of the Fourth Amendment constrain the actions of officers at every level.

## Intentional Termination of Freedom of Movement

A Fourth Amendment seizure is an intentional act; it cannot be accidental or inadvertent. In *Tennessee v. Garner*[6] the Supreme Court held that when a police officer shot a burglary suspect dead as he was attempting to flee the scene, a *seizure* had occurred. The Court explained, "*Whenever an officer restrains the freedom of a person to walk away, he has seized that person.*"[7] One federal appellate court apparently missed this point in *Carr v. Tatangelo*,[8] concluding that a seizure had occurred when a police officer shot and wounded a drug suspect who then ran across the street to his house, where he remained for several minutes before surrendering. The court reasoned:

> "*The seizure occurred when Carr was struck by a bullet from [the officer's] gun ... Although Carr was not immediately stopped by the bullet ... he nevertheless was seized within the meaning of the Fourth Amendment when the bullet struck or contacted him.*"[9]
>
> *It isn't quite clear how the suspect who ran away after being shot was deprived of his freedom to walk away. He was clearly not restrained from regaining the cover of his house, and would have not have been restrained from firing at the officer from that position of advantage. The facts do not support the conclusion that Carr was deprived of his freedom of movement when the bullet struck him. By his own admission, he did not realize he had been shot until sometime after he entered the house, and it was several minutes later that he surrendered and was taken into custody.*

The *Garner* decision clearly established that when there is no termination of freedom of movement there is no Fourth Amendment *seizure*. See also, *Scott*

---

6. 471 U.S. 1, 7 (1985).
7. *Id.*, at 7.
8. 338 F.3d 1259 (11th Cir. 2003).
9. *Id.*, at 1267.

*v. Harris*, where the Supreme Court reiterated, "*A Fourth Amendment seizure occurs ... when there is a governmental termination of freedom of movement through means intentionally applied.*"[10] In *Adams v. City of Auburn Hills*,[11] Kevin Adams sped from the scene of a domestic altercation. A police officer fired several shots at his speeding car, apparently hoping to bring the vehicle to a halt by puncturing one of the tires. Adams was not struck by any of the bullets, but there were bullet holes in the left rear wheel and mud flaps. Adams escaped the scene and later surrendered. He sued the officers and the city, alleging excessive force in violation of the Fourth Amendment. The appellate court ruled that no *seizure* occurred since Adams was not deprived of his ability to leave the scene: "*The use of deadly force alone does not constitute a seizure ... absent an actual physical restraint.*"[12]

A recent case highlights the precise nature of this definition. The officer who hit the target achieved the seizure, the officer who missed did not. In *McGrath v. Taveres*,[13] Officer Edwin Almeida of the Plymouth (Massachusetts) Police Department responded to an activated burglar alarm at a liquor store at 3:15 a.m. En route to the location of the liquor store with his cruiser's blue lights activated, Officer Almeida observed a vehicle heading in the opposite direction commit several traffic violations. He notified dispatch that he had spotted a car leaving the liquor store's vicinity and was going to pull it over. Although he activated his lights and siren the car did not pull over. It eventually slowed down at an intersection roughly four blocks later, allowing Officer Almeida to get a quick look at the driver, but then sped off again with Officer Almeida in pursuit. Responding to the initial dispatch of the burglary alarm, Officer Richard Taveres joined in the chase. Eventually, the suspect vehicle failed to make the turn at an intersection and crashed into a stone wall. The two officers pulled up behind the vehicle, Officer Taveres to the rear of the passenger's side and Officer Almeida to the rear of the driver's side. Officer Almeida ordered the driver to exit the vehicle, but the suspect revved the engine and maneuvered his car between two police vehicles. In doing so he struck Officer Almeida's cruiser and crashed into a telephone pole. The driver did not comply with commands to turn off his engine and get out of the car, but instead revved the engine and drove in the direction of Officer Taveres. By this time both officers had their weapons drawn, and Officer Taveres fired two

---

10. 550 U.S. 372, 381 (2007), quoting *Brower v. County of Inyo*, 489 U.S. 593, 596–597 (1989).
11. 336 F.3d 515 (6th Cir. 2003).
12. *Id.*, at 519–520.
13. 2014 U.S. App. LEXIS 14776 (2014).

shots striking the car's windshield. One bullet struck the driver in the upper right arm. As the vehicle passed Officer Taveres and continued in Officer Almeida's direction, Officer Taveres fired two more shots, one of which entered the front passenger window and struck the driver in the back. Officer Almeida then fired seven shots, but none struck the driver. After hitting the curb and becoming airborne, the vehicle came to a complete stop. The driver, 16-year-old Anthony McGrath, was removed from the vehicle and given first aid until paramedics arrived. He was then taken to a nearby hospital where he died shortly thereafter.

McGrath's mother filed a lawsuit against Officers Almeida and Taveres, the chief of police, and the town of Plymouth, alleging the use of excessive force in violation of the Fourth and Fourteenth Amendments. The officers moved for summary judgment. The federal district court granted summary judgment to the defendants, holding that Officer Taveres's use of deadly force was objectively reasonable as a matter of law, and no constitutional violation occurred. As to Officer Almeida, he did not seize McGrath since all of his shots missed the target.

The federal appellate court affirmed the district court's judgment, including its determination that Officer Almeida had not seized McGrath. The court noted:

> "We agree that there was no seizure, not solely because none of Almeida's shots hit Anthony, but also because Almeida's missed shots did not restrain Anthony's freedom of movement."[14]

Even if an officer succeeds in shooting and wounding a subject, there is no seizure if that person's freedom of movement is not terminated. In *Brooks v. Gaenzle*,[15] officers responded to the report of a burglary in progress at a residence. As the officers tried to enter the house from the garage, someone inside fired a shot that went through the door, barely missing the officers' heads. The officers then saw a suspect run from the house and begin to climb a fence. One officer fired a shot that struck but did not stop the fleeing suspect, who fled the scene and was arrested three days later. In a lawsuit against the officers, Brooks asserted that they used excessive force in violation of his Fourth Amendment rights. The federal appellate court dismissed that claim, holding that no *seizure* occurred:

---

14. *Id.*, footnote 7.

15. 614 F.3d 1213 (10th Cir. 2010), *cert. denied*, 2011 U.S. LEXIS 1027 (U.S., Jan. 24, 2011).

*"For a seizure to occur ... the government must do something that gives it
the opportunity to control the suspect's ability to evade capture or control."*[16]

The court went further and observed that even if a seizure had occurred,
the officers used an objectively reasonable level of force under the circumstances presented.

## Intended Person

In *Medeiros v. O'Connell*, an officer fired shots at an armed and dangerous
man who had commandeered a school van to effect his escape.[17] One of the shots
went astray inside the van, striking and fatally injuring a student. The family
of the victim sued the officer in federal court under Title 42, U.S. Code, Section 1983, alleging that the officer's use of deadly force that resulted in the
death of their son violated the Fourth Amendment.[18] The federal district court
held, and the federal appellate court affirmed, that the Fourth Amendment
did not apply to the case. The officer had intentionally fired the fatal shot, but
had clearly not intended to strike the student. That was a tragic accident, not
a Fourth Amendment seizure. Absent the seizure, no Fourth Amendment violation occurred.[19]

A more recent illustration of this principle is found in *Melvin v. Karman,
et al.*,[20] where an officer intervened to protect a man named Whitehead, who
was lying on the ground being assaulted by three individuals. When the officer announced his presence, two of the men fled, but the third, Jesse Ramon,
advanced on the officer with a gun in his hand. When Ramon failed to drop
the gun as ordered by the officer, the officer fired five shots. Four of the rounds
struck Ramon, but one struck Whitehead, killing him. In the ensuing action
against the officer, the federal appellate court upheld the officer's motion for
summary judgment, and observed:

---

16. *Id.*

17. 150 F.3d 164 (2nd Cir. 1998).

18. This statute permits civil actions against state and local officials as well as municipal and county agencies based on alleged violations of federal constitutional rights.

19. See also, *Landol-Rivera v. Cruz Cosma*, 906 F.2d 791 (1st Cir. 1990) (No "seizure" occurred when hostage unintentionally wounded by police gunfire); *Troublefield v. City of
Harrisburg*, 789 F. Supp. 160 (MD PA 1992) (Officer's "accidental" discharge of firearm that
injured handcuffed suspect did not constitute a "seizure"); and *Glasco v. Ballard*, 768 F.
Supp. 176 (ED VA 1991) (Officer's accidental shooting of shoplifting suspect did not constitute a "seizure.").

20. 550 Fed. Appx. 218 (5th Cir. 2013).

*"Absolutely nothing in the record suggests that [the officer], facing an armed assailant and reasonably concerned for his own safety, took the time deliberately to direct one of his bullets for the purpose of killing Whitehead, who was on the ground and an innocent victim of the assault the officer was attempting to end."*

An unintended killing of a person by an officer does not constitute a seizure. For example, in ***Baskin v. City of Houston et al.***,[21] an officer accidentally shot and killed a bank robbery suspect during a physical struggle. Summary judgment was granted to the defendants because there was " ... *no evidence that the shooting was anything but accidental.*" In attempting to determine the intent of an officer in these cases, some courts have shown a willingness to apply what might be termed a "straight-face" test. In ***Kellen v. Frink***, for example, a federal district court concluded that a seizure had occurred when a game warden fired a shotgun loaded with rifled slug into a fleeing vehicle, despite the officer's explanation that he only fired to "mark" the van for later identification.[22] In the court's view, the consequences of firing a shotgun into an occupied van were so foreseeable as to clearly demonstrate intent.

## Intended Means

Finally, to constitute a *seizure*, the termination of freedom must be caused by the very means intended for the purpose. Even when law enforcement officers clearly intend to seize a person, if the termination of freedom of movement is caused by an unintended event, there is no *seizure*. In ***Cameron v. City of Pontiac***, police officers engaged in a foot chase of a burglary suspect.[23] When the fleeing suspect failed to heed the officers' commands to stop, the officers fired shots at him without effect. The suspect climbed a fence and ran onto a highway where he was struck and killed by a passing automobile. A subsequent lawsuit against the police officers alleged that by firing shots at an unarmed, nondangerous suspect, they had unconstitutionally used deadly force in violation of the Fourth Amendment. That argument would have had some merit if the officers had succeeded in their purpose. However, the case was dismissed in favor of the police on the grounds that there was no "*seizure.*" The court explained:

*"The officers' show of authority by firing their weapons, while designed to apprehend Cameron, did not stop or in any way restrain him ... [His]*

---

21. 378 Fed. Appx. 417; 2010 U.S. App. LEXIS 9808 (5th Cir. 2010).
22. 745 F. Supp. 1428 (SD Ill., 1990).
23. 813 F. Supp. 782 (6th Cir. 1987).

*freedom of movement was restrained only because he killed himself by electing to run onto a heavily traveled, high speed freeway … [T]he manner in which [Cameron] met his death was completely independent of the application of deadly force by [the officers]; the moving vehicle by which Cameron was struck was a distinct, unrelated, unexpected, superseding, but effective medium … It would be unfair, and possibly absurd to permit a fleeing felon, uninjured by a pursuing police officer, to benefit from his unwise choice of an escape route."*[24]

Another federal appellate court reached the same conclusion in a case where a passenger on a motorcycle fleeing from the police was run over by a pursuing police car when he fell off of his bike and onto the highway. The ensuing lawsuit against the police alleged various violations of the Constitution, including a Fourth Amendment claim that the officers used deadly force to seize a non-dangerous, fleeing person. The court held that no Fourth Amendment seizure occurred because while the officers clearly intended to seize the motorcycle and its two passengers, there was no evidence that they intended to do so by running them over with the police car. The Supreme Court concurred in the lower court's judgment.[25]

The Supreme Court has cautioned against an overly strict interpretation of the phrase *"through means intentionally applied."*[26] It is enough *"that a person be stopped by the very instrumentality set in motion or put in place to achieve that result."*[27] A case in point is ***Vaughan v. Cox***,[28] where a police officer pursuing a speeding pickup truck fired a shot into the truck in an effort to stop its progress by disabling the truck or its driver, but instead striking a passenger. A federal appellate court held that although the officer did not intend to shoot the passenger, he intended to seize both the driver and the passenger, and he fired the shot into the truck for that purpose. Since Vaughan (the passenger) *"was hit by a bullet that was meant to stop him, he was subjected to a Fourth Amendment seizure."*[29] Put simply: (1) the officer intended to *seize* Vaughan; (2) he fired a shot to further that purpose; (3) the shot succeeded — although in a different manner than anticipated. Having determined that a

---

24. *Id.*

25. See *County of Sacramento v. Lewis*, 118 S. Ct. 1708 (1998). The Supreme Court affirmed the appellate court's analysis, and decided the case in favor of the police on other constitutional grounds.

26. *Brower v. County of Inyo*, 498 U.S. 593, 598 (1989).

27. *Id.*, at 599.

28. 343 F.3d 1323 (11th Cir. 2003).

29. *Id.*, at 1329.

*seizure* had occurred, the court denied summary judgment, concluding that a jury could well decide that the officer was not justified in using deadly force to seize the non-dangerous occupants of the pickup truck.

# Fourth Amendment Authority to Use Deadly Force

Before describing the permissible uses of deadly force under the Fourth Amendment, it will be helpful to define our terms. "Deadly force" has never been definitively defined by the Supreme Court, but is often loosely described in lower court decisions and in law enforcement policies and training as force that creates a reasonable likelihood, or a substantial risk, of death or serious injury. The defect in this definition is the ambiguity created by the use of the two terms, *death* and *serious injury*. The terms are not synonymous, and a risk of one is hardly comparable to a risk of the other. This ambiguity often raises unnecessary questions, and invites unnecessary litigation. For example, in *Miller v. Clark County*,[30] plaintiff argued that the use of a police dog to "bite and hold" him was comparable to the use of deadly force in violation of the Fourth Amendment. Miller was being pursued by police officers for a traffic infraction when he ran into a wooded area. An officer yelled that if he didn't come out, a police dog would be sent to find him. When he did not respond, the dog was released and shortly thereafter found and seized Miller by biting him on the upper arm. The dog maintained his hold for about 60 seconds until an officer arrived and placed Miller under arrest. Miller was taken to the hospital where he was treated for severe injuries to his arm. Conceding that the use of a police dog for that purpose constituted a *seizure*, and a significant use of force, the federal appellate court rejected the argument that it was deadly force. The court defined deadly force as "*force that creates a significant risk of death*" and further explained:

> "*To be characterized as deadly, force must present 'more than a remote possibility' of death in the circumstances under which it is used … Mere 'possibilities' and 'capabilities' do not add up to 'reasonable probability.'*"[31]

It is likely that the "*death or serious injury*" formula originated from the justification for using deadly force in defense of self or others which typically uses

---

30. 340 F. 3d 959 (9th Cir. 2003).
31. *Id.*, at 963.

the same terms. It is clear that both can be simplified without doing violence to the substance of either. The *Miller* decision has already provided a workable *definition* of "*deadly force*" as *force that creates a significant risk of death*; while the Supreme Court has already provided the *justification* for using deadly force as *probable cause to believe there is an imminent threat of serious physical harm*.[32] Thus, a *threat of serious physical harm* justifies the use of force that *creates a significant risk of death*. These terms will be discussed further in Chapter 4.

The Fourth Amendment permits law enforcement officers to use deadly force to achieve seizures in two general contexts:

1) To *protect themselves or others* from immediate threats of serious physical injury; and/or
2) To *prevent the escape* of a fleeing "dangerous" person.

## To Protect Themselves and Others from Immediate Threats

A closer look at the concept of "self-defense" will highlight its fundamental role in the lawful use of deadly force. If there is such a thing as a universal rule relating to the authority of law enforcement officers to use deadly force, this is it. Indeed, the right of self-defense is deeply grounded in the history of Anglo-American jurisprudence. William Blackstone, the eighteenth century English jurist, wrote in his *Commentaries*:

> "*Self-defense ... is justly called the primary law of nature, so it is not, neither can it be ... taken away by the law of society.*"[33]

The U.S. Supreme Court echoed this principle in an 1891 case:

> "*[T]he Rules which determine what is self-defense are of universal application ...*"[34]

In the same case, the Court further illustrated the nature and content of this "universal" rule:

> "*The Rules which determine what is self-defense are of **universal application** ... and it would be a sufficient defense that he honestly **believed***

---

32. *Tennessee v. Garner*, 471 U.S. 1, at 19 (1985).
33. Blackstone, *Commentaries on the Laws of England*, Volume 3, p. 4, University of Chicago Press (1979).
34. *New Orleans & N.E.R. Co. v. Jopes*, 142 U.S. 18 (1891).

*he was in **imminent danger**, and had reasonable ground for such belief. In other words, the law of self-defense justifies an act done in honest and reasonable belief of immediate danger."*[35] (Emphasis added.)

Three points are noteworthy in the Court's statement. First, the factual standard for justifying self-defense is a reasonable belief in imminent danger. Second, reasonable belief is synonymous with "probable cause." And, third, the terms "imminent" and "immediate" are used interchangeably.

The basic nature of the right of self-defense was further buttressed by the Supreme Court in the 1896 decision of ***Rowe v. United***,[36] which focused on whether a threatened person must first attempt to evade an attack, or attempt a lesser level of response before using deadly force. The facts of the case are highly instructive. Rowe and a man named Bozeman were in a bar when Bozeman "subjected Rowe to offensive language." In response, Rowe kicked at Bozeman, "but not in a way to indicate an intent to cause serious injury." When Rowe walked away, Bozeman attacked him with a knife and Rowe shot him to death. In Rowe's trial for manslaughter, the trial judge instructed the jury that " *... although [Bozeman] sprang at [Rowe] with knife in hand, for the purpose of cutting him to pieces, yet if [Rowe] could have stepped aside or paralyzed the arm of his assailant, his killing was not in the exercise of self-defense."* Not surprisingly in light of that instruction, Rowe was convicted. On appeal, the Supreme Court reversed and held:

> *"[Rowe] was entitled ... to remain where he was, and to do whatever was necessary, or what he had reasonable grounds to believe at the time was necessary, to save his life or to protect himself from great bodily harm ... Under the circumstances, it was error to make the case depend in whole or in part upon the enquiry whether [Rowe] could, by stepping aside have avoided the attack, or could have carefully aimed his pistol as to paralyze the arm of his assailant without more seriously wounding him."*[37]

An interesting twist in this case was the trial judge's instruction to the jury that since Rowe had started the physical fight by kicking at Bozeman, " *... under no possible circumstances ... could he be justified in killing the deceased."* The Supreme Court rejected that view, focusing instead on the moment when Rowe faced the threat of great bodily harm.

---

35. *Id.*
36. 164 U.S. 545 (1896).
37. *Id.*, at 559.

In the 1921 case of **Brown v. United States**,[38] the Supreme Court again reviewed a case in which it was contended that a person confronted with an immediate threat should retreat, or simply attempt to disable his assailant, before using deadly force in self-defense. The Court wrote:

> "*Many respectable writers agree that if a man reasonably believes that he is in immediate danger of death or grievous bodily harm from his assailant, he may stand his ground, and if he kills him (his assailant), he has not exceeded the bounds of lawful self-defense. That has been the decision of this court ... Detached reflection cannot be demanded in the presence of an uplifted knife. Therefore ... it is not a condition of immunity that one in that situation must pause to consider whether a reasonable man might not think it possible to fly with safety or to disable his assailant rather than to kill him.*"[39]

Reviewing these historic cases that interpret an individual's right of self-defense under the Common Law, it is remarkable to observe how the principles they enunciate are reflected in the modern constitutional principles that govern the authority of law enforcement officers to use deadly force in defense of self and others: (1) a reasonable belief in the existence of an imminent threat of serious physical injury; (2) the focus on the moment that threat emerges; (3) the absence of an obligation to retreat; and (4) the absence of a need to first consider other or lesser alternatives. As the following cases will amply illustrate, the law accepts the principle that an *immediate danger* justifies an *immediate response.*

Bringing the issue forward to the twenty-first century, the Supreme Court, in its 2008 decision of **District of Columbia v. Heller**,[40] cited the "*inherent right of self-defense*" as central to the right to keep and bear arms embodied in the Second Amendment to the Constitution. The Court cited that right no fewer than nine times, and indicated that the right extends beyond self-defense to include the defense of others. Since the case arose in the District of Columbia, a federal preserve, its constraints apply only to the federal government. But that would change two years later, when the Supreme Court decided the case of **McDonald v. City of Chicago**,[41] thereby extending the protections of the Second Amendment to the states through the Fourteenth Amendment Due Process Clause. As in the *Heller* decision, the Court based its decision squarely on the

---

38. 256 U.S. 961 (1921).
39. *Id.*, at 963.
40. 554 U.S. 570 (2008).
41. 564 U.S. 742 (2010).

individual and inherent right of self-defense. Summarizing the underlying purposes of the Second Amendment right to keep and bear arms, the Court noted its historical relevance to the establishment and maintenance of state militias, but emphatically rejected the idea that it was the only—or even the most important—reason for that right. The Court wrote:

> "*[In **Heller**] ... we rejected the suggestion that the right was valued only as a means of preserving the militias ... On the contrary, we stressed that the right was also valued because the possession of firearms was thought to be essential for self-defense. As we put it, self defense was the central component of the right itself.*"

Obviously, the inherent right to defend oneself and others from threats of death or serious bodily harm does not diminish or end when one becomes a law enforcement officer. If anything, it assumes the character of a responsibility. The duties of law enforcement officers routinely expose them to dangers that the citizen may never experience, or can often avoid. As the cases discussed throughout this book amply illustrate, there is no area of constitutional law that reflects greater deference to the interests of law enforcement officers and the communities they serve than that which governs their authority to act in defense of self and others. Officers are not required to assume risks beyond those inherent in the duties of the law enforcement profession. As the cases clearly illustrate, *an immediate threat of serious injury to officers or others justifies an immediate and effective response.*

# Immediate Threats

Since the law clearly justifies the use of deadly force to counter immediate threats of serious physical injury, it is imperative to understand what constitutes an immediate threat. Given the infinite number of variables that can arise, it is not possible to construct a definition, or even a formula, to relieve officers of the need to make their own reasonable judgments based on the facts and circumstances confronting them *at the moment*. However, a survey of relevant cases will provide examples of "facts and circumstances" acknowledged by the courts to constitute immediate threats. From these examples, coupled with the collective experience of law enforcement, it is possible to identify general indicators of threatening behaviors which, when applied to specific facts, can guide and support an officer's reasonable belief in the existence of an immediate threat of serious injury. It is worth observing that the practical experiences of law enforcement officers in real-world threat assessments serve to inform and educate the courts, and not the other way around. Stated succinctly, the law can establish the standard, but law enforcement experience defines and illustrates it.

**Suspect Armed with a Firearm.** It might be thought axiomatic that a person threatening officers with a firearm fits the description of "immediate threat." That is generally true. And yet the fact that there are court decisions on the issue illustrates the point that even apparently obvious cases can raise questions that must be resolved in the courts. A particularly illustrative case is *Elliott v. Leavitt.*[42] Two officers arrested a DUI[43] suspect, handcuffed him, and placed him in the front passenger seat of the police car. As the officers were standing outside the vehicle talking, the suspect, *still handcuffed*, produced a handgun and pointed it in the direction of the officers. Before he fired a shot, the two officers quickly drew their own handguns and fired 22 rounds, fatally wounding the suspect. Although the facts seem relatively straightforward (a suspect threatened officers with a firearm), a lawsuit was filed against the officers in federal district court alleging violations of the Constitution. The issues raised by the plaintiff, and the manner in which the court addressed them, are worthy of attention.

The federal district court denied summary judgment for the officers, not because there was no threat but because in the court's view a jury could conclude that they could have responded differently to that threat—for example, by taking evasive action to avoid the danger. The officers appealed.

The federal appellate court reversed the judgment of the district court, and focused on the core issue—the existence of the immediate threat:

> *"The Constitution simply does not require police to gamble with their lives in the face of a serious threat of harm."*[44]

Regarding the immediacy of the threat:

> *"The Fourth Amendment does not require police officers to wait until a suspect shoots to confirm that a serious threat of harm exists ... No citizen can fairly expect to draw a gun on police without risking tragic consequences. And no court can expect any human being to remain passive in the face of an active threat on his or her life."*[45]

---

42. 99 F.3d 640 (4th Cir. 1996).
43. DUI—Driving Under the Influence.
44. *Id.*, at 641.
45. *Id.*, at 643, 644.

Regarding the plaintiffs' suggestion that the officers could have averted the danger by moving away from the car, the court characterized such assertions as " … *more reflective of the 'peace of a judge's chambers' than of a dangerous and threatening situation on the street.*"[46]

Regarding the assertion of excessive force based on the number of shots (22) fired by the officers, the court responded:

> "*The district court's concern that the number of shots fired was excessive is likewise misplaced. The number of shots by itself cannot be determinative as to whether the force used was reasonable. Both officers fired almost simultaneously … and the evidence indicates that the shooting took place within a matter of seconds. That multiple shots were fired does not suggest the officers shot mindlessly as much as it indicates that they sought to ensure the elimination of a deadly threat.*"[47]

This contention, which emerges frequently, is based on the assumption that human beings respond instantly to gunshot wounds, and that officers can instantly perceive that the threat is over. While it is clear that the justification for using deadly force ends when a reasonable officer would perceive that the threat has ended, it is a dangerously false assumption that there are instantaneous, visible, and desired responses to gunshot wounds. (See Chapter 5—Wound Ballistics for an extensive discussion.)

The relevant issue is not how many shots were fired, but when they were fired. When disputed by the parties, this issue can thwart a summary judgment motion by the defense. This is amply illustrated in ***Margeson v. White County, Tennessee, et al.*,**[48] where three officers attempted to arrest a mentally disturbed man known to possess firearms. When confronted by the officers the man "*jumped up and grabbed his guns.*" Several of the officers ordered him to drop a shotgun he was holding. Instead, he pointed the gun at one of the officers. That officer fired the first shot, and other officers joined in. At one point, the subject was seen to fall to the floor and get up with a handgun. The shooting continued. It was later determined that the man suffered 21 separate gunshot wounds, and another 24 bullet holes were lodged in the home. It was noted that several of the rounds were 00 buckshot pellets from the shotguns that several of the officers were using. Notwithstanding the number of wounds sustained, the man survived long enough to be transported to a hospital, where he later died.

---

46. *Id.*
47. *Id.*, at 643.
48. 2014 U.S. App. LEXIS 17464. (6th Cir. 2014).

The defendants' motion for summary judgment was denied, not because they had used deadly force, but because of a factual dispute regarding the necessity to fire so many rounds. The court explained it this way:

*" ... a jury could certainly conclude that shooting at a man 43 times, including at least 12 shots after he had fallen to the ground, amounts to an unreasonable and excessive use of force ... A jury could also conclude, on the other hand, that the officers' actions were reasonable, based on [the man's] alleged failure to surrender, even after having been shot down. Either way, there are disputed facts at issue that only a jury can properly decide."*

In these two cases, there was no question that the suspects possessed firearms. But it is important to note that officers need not actually <u>see</u> a firearm in order to have a reasonable belief that one is possessed by, or readily accessible to, a suspect. One example is when officers reasonably perceive that a person is threatening them with a firearm, but it turns out to be something else. This occurred in *Aipperspach v. McInerney, et al.,*[49] when a young man named Al-Hakim appeared to be threatening suicide with a handgun in a wooded area. Over a period of about three-and-a-half minutes officers repeatedly ordered Al-Hakim to drop the gun, but he continued to point the gun at his body or head. At one point he aimed the gun in the direction of the officers, and was warned that if he did it again they would shoot. Shortly thereafter, Al-Hakim apparently attempted to shift his position, but he slipped and fell backwards. As he moved to regain his balance he pulled the gun away from his chin and swung it around in the direction of the officers, who, over a period of about four seconds, fired multiple rounds at Al-Hakim. A news helicopter circling overhead captured these actions on film, and confirmed the officers' account of the events. As it turned out, the black handgun held by Al-Hakim was actually a Daisy 008 BB gun. Al-Hakim died from his injuries and a lawsuit was filed against the police, asserting that they used excessive force in violation of the Fourth Amendment.

The federal district court granted the defendants' motion for summary judgment, and the plaintiffs appealed. Finding that the officers' use of deadly force was a seizure of Al-Hakim under the Fourth Amendment, the appellate court concluded that " ... *the officers were confronted by a suspect who held what <u>appeared to be a handgun</u>* [emphasis added], *refused repeated commands to drop the gun, pointed it at [one officer], and then waved it in the direction of officers*

---

49. 2014 U.S. App. LEXIS 17201. (8th Cir. 2014).

*deployed along the ridge line … In these circumstances, objectively reasonable officers had probable cause to believe that Al-Hakim posed a threat of serious physical harm to the officers."*

An interesting side note to this case was the plaintiff's contention that the district court ignored the video taken from the news helicopter, which could have permitted a jury to find that Al-Hakim was actually trying to surrender rather than threatening the officers. The appellate court adopted the district court's view that the video provided only the aerial perspective of the person who recorded it, *"and therefore could not answer the issue of objective reasonableness from the perspective of an officer on the ground."*

The officers in this instance reasonably believed that the pellet gun was a firearm. In *Penley v. Eslinger, et al.*,[50] a 15-year-old boy modified a plastic air pistol to look like a firearm and took it to school. When it was learned that he was armed and students fled from the classroom, he briefly held one classmate hostage. By the time law enforcement officers arrived at the scene, the boy had left the classroom and was walking through the campus. When one of the officers confronted him and commanded that he drop the gun, the boy put the gun to his chin, said that he was going to die one way or another, and "slithered" into a nearby bathroom. The bathroom had one entrance, an overhead roll-up style door that remained open throughout the standoff that followed. Deputy Maiorano took up a position about 65 feet from the bathroom entrance and began efforts to communicate with the boy. The boy made no response to these efforts apart from giving his name. He walked back and forth from one side of the bathroom to the other, pointing his gun alternately in Deputy Maiorano's direction and at his own chin. Believing that the weapon was real, Deputy Maiorano advised the other officers at the scene that the boy was "wielding a large semiautomatic pistol." As negotiations continued, a SWAT team sniper was called to the scene. In the meantime, the boy continued pointing the weapon in the direction of the officers. Believing that the boy posed a danger to himself, the other officers, and the children that were exposed to the open area, the sniper fired one shot that struck the boy in the head. After the shooting it was discovered that the gun was not real.

A suit was filed in federal district court against the sheriff and the officer who fired the fatal shot. The district court granted the defendants' motions for summary judgment and the plaintiffs appealed. The federal appellate court affirmed the lower court's decision, finding, *inter alia*, that *"[The boy] demonstrated his dangerous proclivities by bringing to school what reasonable officers*

---

50. 605 F.3d 843 (11th Cir. 2010).

*would believe was a real gun. He refused to drop the weapon when repeatedly commanded to do so. Most importantly, he pointed his weapon several times at [two of the officers]. We have held that a suspect posed a grave danger under less perilous circumstances than those confronted by [these officers].*"

A person who threatens officers with a gun, or *what appears to be a gun*, does so at his peril, and supports a reasonable belief that he poses an immediate threat of serious physical injury that justifies the use of deadly force.[51] They also illustrate the point that seemingly simple, straightforward, and even undisputed facts can still lead to creative legal challenges.

*Fleeing Suspect Armed with a Firearm.* The authority to use deadly force to prevent the escape of an <u>unarmed</u>, fleeing suspect is discussed later in this chapter. Here we focus on the fleeing suspect <u>armed with a firearm</u>. It should be self-evident that the possession of a firearm makes the fleeing suspect an immediate threat to pursuing officers as well as anyone he encounters in the course of his flight. In *Montoute v. Carr*, a police officer responded to a disturbance call involving a man with gun.[52] The officer arrived on the scene and saw a man armed with a shotgun. Ignoring the officer's command to stop and drop the gun, the man ran from the officer with the shotgun still in his hands. After repeated warnings to stop and drop the shotgun were ignored, the officer fired a shot that struck and wounded the suspect. In a subsequent lawsuit against the officer, the plaintiff contended that the officer's use of deadly force to prevent escape of a fleeing suspect was inconsistent with constitutional law. The court declined to decide the case on that basis, deciding instead that the suspect armed with the shotgun posed an "immediate threat" to the officer. The court reasoned that even though the suspect was apparently fleeing and not pointing the shotgun at the officer, he could have done so "in a split second" before the officer could have effectively responded.

The significance of the *Montoute* decision lies in the recognition of the reality that suspects armed with firearms, even those apparently fleeing, continue to pose "immediate" threats to officers and others as long as they retain possession of their firearms and remain within gunshot range. The ability of the fleeing, armed suspect to fire at a pursuing officer exceeds the ability of

---

51. See, e.g., *Rice v. Reliastar Life Insurance Co., et al.*, 2014 U.S. App. LEXIS 20581 (5th Cir. 2014) (Officer shot man who threatened him with shotgun); *Smith v. City of Brooklyn Park, et al.*, 757 F.3d 765 (8th Cir. 2014) (Officer shot man who threatened him with shotgun); *Tellez v. City of Belen, et al.*, 2014 U.S. App. LEXIS 9303 (10th Cir. 2014) (Officer shot man armed with pellet gun and spear); *Lenning v. Brantley County, Georgia, et al.*, 2014 U.S. App. LEXIS 16627 (11th Cir. 2014) (Officer shot man who threatened him with shotgun).

52. 114 F.3d 181 (11th Cir. 1997).

the officer to respond by taking cover or effectively returning fire. (See Chapter 6—Physiological Imperatives and the discussion on "action versus reaction.") That being the case, fleeing suspects armed with firearms more logically fall within the rules that govern "immediate threats" rather than those that govern the prevention of escape of fleeing suspects.

A more recent case further illustrates this point. In *Brooks v. Gaenzle*,[53] deputies responded to a burglary in progress. Their information was that burglars had broken into a garage in an attempt to burglarize the attached house. When the deputies arrived at the scene and attempted to enter the house through the garage door, someone inside the house fired a shot that went through the garage door, barely missed the deputies, and sprayed them with "shrapnel." The deputies saw one burglar flee the house and climb a fence. When the fleeing burglar ignored a deputy's command to stop, the deputy fired a shot that struck, but did not stop, the burglar, who was apprehended three days later. He filed a lawsuit alleging use of excessive force in violation of the Fourth Amendment, and the defendants responded with a motion for summary judgment.

The federal district court granted the defendants' summary judgment motion, finding that the Fourth Amendment did not apply since no "*seizure*" had occurred. But the court went further and opined that even if a "*seizure*" had occurred, the deputies had used an objectively reasonable degree of force because they had probable cause to believe that the fleeing burglary suspect had committed a crime involving the infliction or threatened infliction of serious physical harm. Moreover, at the time the deputy shot him, the suspect "*was involved in the commission of an inherently violent crime where, during the course of a burglary, someone shot at the deputies at close range before fleeing.*" Accordingly, the deputy acted reasonably because "*a reasonable officer in his position would have, under the circumstances presented, feared for his safety and the safety of others.*" (Emphasis added.) The federal appellate court affirmed the district court's decision.

The courts' focus on the shot that was fired at the deputies, distinguishes this case from the pure "fleeing suspect" category, which focuses on the *prospective* danger posed by an escaping suspect rather than the *present* dangers posed to officers attempting to apprehend an armed and dangerous fleeing suspect. It is also important to note that the deputy did not have to actually see a gun in order to reasonably believe that the subject was armed and dangerous.

---

53. 614 F.3d 1213 (10th Cir. 2010) *cert. denied*, 2011 U.S. LEXIS 1027.

That point is further illustrated in *Quiles v. City of Tampa, et al.*,[54] which began with a traffic stop. When asked for identification, the driver gave the officer a driver's license in the name of another person whose license had been suspended. The officer, now assisted by another officer, ordered the driver to step out of the car. As he began to get out of the vehicle he attempted to run away. A struggle ensued as the officers sought to restrain the man. During that struggle one of the officers and the man fell to the ground, and the second officer said "watch your gun, watch your gun." The man broke free from the first officer and began to run away, at which point the second officer fired two shots striking and killing him. As recorded on one of the officer's dash cameras, the entire episode lasted 17 seconds.

Suit was brought against the City of Tampa Police Department and the officer who fired the fatal shots, alleging excessive force in violation of the Fourth Amendment. The federal district court determined that the officer reasonably believed that the man had taken the other officer's gun, but denied the officer's motion for summary judgment on the grounds that he did not give a verbal warning before using deadly force. The federal appellate court reversed, concluding that the officer's use of deadly force was objectively reasonable, and violated no constitutional right. In the court's view, the officer " ... *believed reasonably (although mistakenly) that [the man] had stolen and was still in possession of [the other officer's] gun."*

A reasonable belief is sufficient to support an officer's judgment that he faces an immediate threat of serious physical harm. It is not essential that the officer be certain in that judgment.[55] Note that the man was shot as he was *fleeing* the scene of the encounter. The appellate court had no difficulty with this fact, observing: "*An objectively reasonable officer possessing the same knowledge ... could have believed that the use of deadly force against Quiles was justified, to prevent serious injury to the officers and to bystanders."*

Although most of the cases discussed in this chapter were resolved by summary judgment because there were no material facts in dispute, the factual issues in *Lee v. Andersen, et al.*,[56] were resolved by a jury. Officer Andersen and a state trooper were following a group of young men who were riding bicycles. Two of the cyclists, including Lee, jumped a curb and rode away. Officer Andersen ac-

---

54. 2015 U.S, App. LEXIS 56 (11th Cir. 2015).

55. See, e.g., *Aipperspach v. McInerney*, 2014 U.S. App. LEXIS 17201 (8th Cir. 2014) (Subject brandishing pellet gun); *Pollard v. City of Columbus, et al.*, 2015 U.S. App. LEXIS 3538 (6th Cir. 2015) (Subject quickly reaching into car and raising clasped hand in shooting posture.).

56. 616 F.3d 803 (8th Cir. 2010).

tivated his squad car's lights and followed the two onto a school's grounds where he saw the other cyclist pass a gun to Lee. Lee dropped his bicycle and began running. Officer Andersen and his partner got out of their vehicle with their service pistols in hand and began chasing Lee on foot while yelling "Police. Drop the gun." As they rounded a corner, Lee turned back towards Officer Andersen, who fired one shot that missed, and Lee continued to run away with Officer Andersen in pursuit. When Lee turned a second time with the gun in his hand, Officer Andersen fired three more shots that struck Lee. After being struck by the bullets, Lee fell to the ground. Officer Andersen continued to yell, "Drop your gun," but Lee appeared to be getting up to a sitting position, and the officer fired five more shots. Lee had been struck by eight bullets, and died at the scene. Other officers arrived shortly thereafter, and a .380 caliber pistol was found at the scene.

The case presented to the jury by the plaintiffs was that Lee did not have a gun, that he ran from the officers out of fear after they had knocked him off his bicycle, that Officer Andersen had no reason to use force against Lee, that the gun found near the body was planted by one of the officers, and that a "young, aggressive cop committed a horrible wrongful killing."

The jury returned a verdict finding that Officer Andersen did not use excessive force against Lee, and the federal district court denied the plaintiffs' motion for a new trial. The federal appellate court affirmed the district court's judgment, finding that the evidence supported the jury's verdict that Officer Andersen did not use excessive force against Lee, and the U.S. Supreme Court declined to take the case on appeal.[57]

It should be self-evident that suspects armed with firearms, even those apparently fleeing, continue to pose "immediate" threats to officers and others as long as they retain possession of their firearms and remain within gunshot range. The ability of the fleeing, armed suspect to fire at pursuing officers exceeds the ability of the officers to respond in a timely way—either by taking cover or effectively returning fire. That being the case, fleeing suspects armed with firearms logically fall within the rules that govern "immediate threats." Whether they may also fall within the rules relating to "prevention of escape" will be discussed below.

*Suspect Armed with a Knife.* If the threats posed by suspects armed with firearms give rise to debate in the courts, it should be no surprise that the debate gains more impetus, and is more intense, when the weapon is a knife or similar instrument. While it is true that a knife does not pose the distant threat inherent with a firearm, the courts have consistently recognized the threats

---

57. *Lee v. Andersen*, 178 L.Ed. 2d 557 (2010).

posed by resisting suspects armed with knives, particularly when the suspect is in relatively close proximity to the officers. A case in point is *Roy v. Inhabitants of Lewiston, Maine*.[58] A police officer shot and wounded Roy, an intoxicated man armed with two knives, who was wanted for an assault committed earlier that day, and who was advancing on him and two other officers despite repeated warnings to stop and drop the knives. The man sued the police officers and the city, alleging constitutional violations. The contention was that the threat posed by knife-wielding, intoxicated Roy should have been resolved without the use of deadly force. For example, the officers could have retreated or used lesser levels of force to subdue Roy. The federal district court granted summary judgment to the police, and the appellate court affirmed, with this explanation:

> " ... *one might think a hard look was warranted where three officers had to shoot and badly injure an intoxicated man who, although armed with two small knives, was flailing and stumbling about rather ineffectually ... [However]*, <u>Roy was armed</u> *[emphasis added]; he apparently tried to kick and strike at the officers; he disobeyed repeated instructions to put down the weapons; and the officers had other reasons, already described, for thinking him capable of assault.*"[59]

An equally emphatic recognition that a knife is a dangerous weapon is found in *Newcomb v. City of Troy*,[60] in which an officer shot and wounded a suspect at the scene of a robbery attempt where the suspect held a store clerk at knife-point. In a subsequent lawsuit, the plaintiff contended that he had put the knife in his pocket at the time he was shot and was therefore unarmed. The district court judge responded to this argument:

> *The suspect was armed with a knife, and had convincingly demonstrated his willingness to wield that knife against the store clerks. Plaintiff ... contends that ... he was 'unarmed.' This contention is premised on a novel definition of that term. Plaintiff did not become 'unarmed' merely because he placed the weapon in his pants pocket.*[61]

The reluctance of officers to use deadly force against an individual armed "only with a knife" is further illustrated in *Mace v. Palentine*.[62] Officers responded to complaints of a disturbance at a mobile home park where they

---

58.  42 F.3d 691 (1st Cir. 1994).
59.  *Id.*
60.  719 F. Supp. 1408 (ED Mich. 1989).
61.  *Id.*, at 1416.
62.  333 F.3d 621 (5th Cir. 2003).

found a heavily intoxicated man armed with an 18- to 20-inch sword. As the officers attempted to reason with him, he continued to brandish and make punching motions with the sword. When he raised the sword toward the officers, one of the officers shot him in the right arm, causing him to drop the sword. He died later in the hospital and a suit was filed against the officer who fired the shot, alleging excessive force. The court held:

> "[The] officer was faced with an intoxicated, violent and uncooperative individual who was wielding a sword within eight to ten feet of several officers in a relatively confined space. It is not objectively unreasonable for an officer in that situation to believe that there was a serious danger to himself and the other officers present."[63]

It is not clear whether the officer deliberately aimed at the suspect's arm, but two points are worth mentioning: (1) the officer was not required to attempt a lesser level of force in the face of the immediate threat, and (2) shooting someone with a firearm is an application of deadly force regardless of the location of the wound or the eventual outcome. It is worthwhile recalling that the U.S. Supreme Court, in three cases discussed earlier in this chapter, explicitly acknowledged the dangers posed by knife-wielding assailants.[64]

An issue that arises frequently in cases alleging excessive force by law enforcement officers is that the officers caused or contributed to the need to use deadly force by using bad tactics in trying to address the threat. This occurred in *Han v. City of Folsom, et al.*[65] Three officers responded to an incident at a residence where a family member, 23-year-old Joseph Han, had been acting in a "mentally unstable" manner. Upon arriving at the residence the officers were asked to enter the home and speak to Han. They found Han in his room, holding a three-to-four-inch camping knife. He ordered the officers to leave his room, and approached them while holding the knife. Two different officers fired their Tasers at Han, but they were ineffective. One of the officers then shot Han with his gun before backing out of the room. Soon after, one of the officers fired his Taser at Han, and another then shot Han with his gun before he was finally subdued. Han later died from the gunshots, and a suit was filed against the officers and their department alleging excessive force under the Fourth Amendment. The federal district court granted summary judgment

---

63. *Id.*, at 624.

64. See, *New Orleans & N.E.R Co. v. Jopes*, 142 U.S. 18 (1891); *Rowe v. United States*, 164 U.S. 545 (1896); and *Brown v. United States*, 256 U.S. 961 (1921).

65. 551 Fed. Appx. 923; 2014 U.S. App. LEXIS 342. (9th Cir. 2014).

for the officers because their actions were not objectively unreasonable in light of the facts and circumstances confronting them. The federal appellate court affirmed that judgment, noting that undisputed evidence established that Han moved toward the officers with his knife in the confines of his room and did not comply with the officers' commands to drop it.

A second issue raised in this case was that the officers acted unreasonably by creating the need to use force "*by confronting Joseph inside his room when they could have chosen to retreat and monitor [him] from outside the room.*" To this assertion, the appellate court responded:

> "*But our cases do not 'permit a plaintiff to establish a Fourth Amendment violation based merely on bad tactics that result in a deadly confrontation that could have been avoided.'*" *(Citing **Billington v. Smith**, 292 F.3d 1177, 1190 (9th Cir. 2002))*

The court emphasized that even if an officer's pre-shooting conduct negligently provokes a suspect to violence, "*that negligent [conduct] will not transform an otherwise reasonable subsequent use of force into a Fourth Amendment violation.*"

It is worth reiterating the Supreme Court's recent decision in **City and County of San Francisco, California v. Sheehan** discussed at length in Chapter 2. In that case Sheehan was armed with a knife, and had threatened officers who attempted to enter her apartment. When she advanced on the officers with knife in hand, she was pepper sprayed without result. She was then shot twice, still without result, and then shot several times before she fell. After concluding that the officers were entitled to qualified immunity with respect to their use of deadly force, the Supreme Court addressed the issue of the officers' pre-shooting conduct:

> "*Indeed, even if [the officers] misjudged the situation, Sheehan cannot establish a Fourth Amendment violation based merely on bad tactics that result in a deadly confrontation that could have been avoided. Courts must not judge officers with the '20/20 vision of hindsight.'*"

These cases are highly significant, particularly in light of the frequent media reaction to a police shooting of an assailant who "only had a knife." It is never quite clear whether those who have that perspective think that the knife is not a dangerous weapon—in which case they are ill-informed—or whether they object to an officer having the advantage of a superior weapon to counter it— in which case the problem goes beyond ignorance. The courts consistently recognize that knives and other bladed weapons can pose immediate threats of serious physical injury to law enforcement officers and others, and when they do, deadly force is justified to counter them.[66]

**Suspect Armed with an Impact Weapon.** Obviously, impact weapons can be used to inflict serious physical injury, and law enforcement officers are legally justified in using deadly force to protect themselves from assault with them. A good example is found in **Pena v. Leombruni** in which a police officer confronted a man at a shopping mall who was urging his dog to attack passing shoppers.[67] When the suspect turned his dog loose on the officer, the officer used "pepper spray" on both the dog and the suspect. The dog wisely retreated, but the suspect attacked the officer with a slab of concrete. The officer shot and seriously wounded the suspect. In the inevitable lawsuit that followed, the courts had no difficulty concluding that the suspect, armed with the concrete slab, posed an immediate threat to the officer's safety.

Similarly, in **Plakas v. Drinski** a police officer shot and killed a suspect who, although handcuffed in the front, managed to get a fireplace poker and was advancing on the officer.[68] The federal appellate court stated:

> "As a matter of law there can be no other conclusion but that Plakas threatened [the officers] with a weapon intending to inflict serious physical harm...."[69]

In **McCormick v. City of Fort Lauderdale**,[70] an officer attempted to arrest McCormick, who had assaulted a woman with an ornate walking stick just minutes before. Upon approaching him, the officer saw that McCormick still had the stick in his hands. When other efforts to disarm the suspect failed, including pepper spray, the officer attempted to knock the weapon out of his hands with his baton and continued ordering him to drop it. When McCormick raised the stick above his head and advanced on the officer, the officer backed up, tripped and fell to the ground, at which point McCormick ran towards the officer with the stick raised above his head. The officer fired one shot, striking McCormick in the chest. Undeterred, McCormick renewed his advance on the officer until other officers pepper-sprayed McCormick again (without

---

66. See also, *Sigman v. Town of Chapel Hill*, 161 F.3d 782 (4th Cir. 1998); *Reynolds v. County of San Diego*, 84 F.3d 1162 (9th Cir. 1996); *Harris v. Serpas, et al.*, 745 F.3d 767 (5th Cir 2014); *Wilson v. City of Chicago, et al.*, 758 F.3d 875 (7th Cir. 2014); *Morgan v. Cook, et al.*, 686 F. 3d 494 (8th Cir. 2012); *James v. Chavez, et al.*, 511 Fe. Appx. 742 (10th Cir. 2013).

67. 200 F.3d 1031 (7th Cir. 1999).

68. 19 F.3d 1143 (7th Cir. 1994).

69. *Id.*, 1362. See also, *Schulz v. Long*, 44 F.3d 643 (8th Cir. 1995) (Officer justifiably shot and killed mental patient who was threatening officers with an axe.).

70. 333 F.3d 1234 (11th Cir. 2003).

effect), and finally used a stun gun to subdue and handcuff him. McCormick filed a lawsuit alleging excessive force. The federal appellate court upheld a grant of summary judgment for the officer, noting that a stick can be a deadly weapon, and concluding:

> "[The officer] had probable cause to believe that McCormick had earlier committed a violent felony, could reasonably perceive that McCormick posed an imminent threat of violence to the officers and other bystanders, and noted that McCormick continued to ignore commands to drop his weapon."[71]

More recently, in **Buchanan v. Gulfport Police Department, et al.,**[72] officers observed a man swinging a baseball bat at passing vehicles. When confronted by the officers, the suspect dropped the bat but refused commands to step away from it. When he leaned toward the bat as if to pick it up, officers "tased" him twice. Neither was effective. The suspect picked up the bat, raised it above his head, and charged at an officer. Two officers shot him. Cameras incorporated into the Tasers recorded most of these events. The suspect, Buchanan, was charged with disorderly conduct for swinging the bat at passing traffic and fined $336.00. He was also indicted for aggravated assault on a peace officer, but was found guilty of misdemeanor simple assault for which he received a six-month suspended sentence.

Buchanan filed suit against the officers in federal district court alleging, among other things, excessive force for tasing and shooting him. The court granted summary judgment to the officers regarding the excessive force claim inasmuch as he had been found guilty of assault, and the jury had determined implicitly that he had threatened the officers with serious harm by charging them with the upraised bat prior to being shot. The court noted that "*deadly force is permitted if an officer reasonably perceives a threat of serious harm to himself or others.*"

Obviously, impact weapons can inflict serious injury and death. But apart from that direct threat, they have the potential of incapacitating an officer and, even if only momentarily, the assailant has access to the officer's firearm. It is axiomatic that in any encounter between a law enforcement officer and a suspect, "there is always at least one gun at the scene." For this reason, any risks of injury caused by personal weapons must be considered secondary to the risk of losing possession of one's firearm to an assailant. It may be argued that not every suspect who succeeds in momentarily incapacitating an officer with

---

71. *Id.*, at 1246.
72. 530 Fed. Appx. 307 (5th Cir. 2013).

personal weapons will take the officer's firearm and use it against him, but no reasonable officer would choose to trust his survival to the intentions of his assailant, and the law doesn't require an officer to take that chance.

*Unarmed Suspect Attempting to Gain Access to a Weapon.* If the suspect armed with a firearm constitutes the most obvious example of an "immediate threat," the unarmed suspect occupies the other end of the spectrum. That is not because an unarmed person cannot pose an immediate threat. It is because the potential danger is often not recognized when a "traditional weapon" is not present. And yet, in reality, an aggressively resisting, albeit unarmed, suspect can be extremely dangerous. First, there is the potential injury that may be inflicted by an unarmed person even without a traditional weapon. And, second, there is the potential danger posed by the suspect gaining control of a weapon, including an officer's firearm, as discussed above.

In *Colston v. Barnhart*, the suspect Colston violently resisted two officers who were attempting to control him following a traffic stop, knocking both officers to the ground.[73] One of the officers drew his service weapon and fired one shot that missed, and then fired two more that struck Colston as he moved toward the police car. In the ensuing lawsuit, the federal district court judge denied a motion for summary judgment filed in behalf of the officer. The federal appellate court reversed the lower court's decision and explained:

> "At the time [Officer] Barnhart drew his weapon and fired the first shot, Colston was standing between [the officers] in a position to inflict serious harm on the <u>officers with or without a weapon</u> [emphasis added]. When [Officer] Barnhart fired the two shots that hit Colston, Colston had moved only two steps from Barnhart, toward Barnhart's patrol car, where his shotgun was located … Barnhart had no way to know whether Colston intended to flee or inflict further injury or death on the officers. We cannot say that a reasonable officer in Barnhart's place would not have believed that Colston posed an immediate danger of serious bodily harm or death....."[74]

In *Colston*, the officers knew for a certainty that there was a firearm present in their vehicle and that the suspect was moving in its direction, even though they could not know for a certainty that he intended to get the gun. But

---

73. 130 F.3d 96 (5th Cir. 1997).

74. *Id.*, at 100. See, also, *Salim v. Proulx*, 93 F.3d 86 (2nd Cir. 1996) (Officer justifiably shot juvenile suspect during physical struggle when officer believed suspect was about to gain control of officer's gun); and see 162 F.3d 986 (8th Cir. 1998) (Officer justifiably shot unarmed suspect who resisted arrest, knocked officer down, kicked officer in chest, and reached for officer's gun.).

the knowledge that a gun was in the vehicle was sufficient in the court's view to support a reasonable belief that the suspect posed an immediate threat to them. They were not required to stake their survival on the hope that his intention was more benevolent. A similar result has been reached by the courts where officers have clearly seen suspects reaching toward areas where the officers reasonably believed a weapon to be located, even though they lacked certain knowledge. The issue is not whether the suspect is actually attempting to gain access to a weapon; it is whether the facts and circumstances known to the officers at the time support a reasonable belief that he is doing so.

Similarly, the risks posed to officers by apparently unarmed but aggressive suspects can be enormous. A good case to illustrate this point is *Smith et al. v. Hennessey.*[75] The facts are critical to understanding the officer's experience and the court's decision. Detective David Smith was off duty and driving home late at night with family members in a police vehicle. He was passed by a car with tires squealing, and traveling at 70 mph in a 30 or 35 mph residential zone. The driver, later identified a Ryan Hennessey, swerved in and out of traffic, almost colliding with an oncoming vehicle. Instead of pulling over when Detective Smith turned on his blue lights and gave chase, Hennessey turned off his headlights and accelerated. Shortly thereafter, Hennessey lost control of his car, crashed into a curb, and came to a stop.

Detective Smith, knowing that backup officers were on the way but not knowing the extent of Hennessey's injuries, got out of his police car and walked over to Hennessey's car, intending to render first aid and arrest Hennessey for felony reckless driving. Not being in uniform, and unaware of what awaited him, Detective Smith approached Hennessey's car with his gun in one hand and a flashlight in the other. Hennessey was slumped in the driver's seat with his eyes closed and the driver's side window down. Detective Smith identified himself as a police officer and told Hennessey to place his hands on the steering wheel. When there was no response, Detective Smith repeated his commands. Hennessey looked up at Officer Smith's badge and asked, "If I don't, are you going to shoot me?" Detective Smith answered, "If I have to." Instead of putting his hands on the wheel as ordered, Hennessey started his car, put it in gear and tried to drive away, but the car was too damaged to move. Hennessey began grabbing at Detective Smith's flashlight. From this point forward, the court provides a graphic description of what followed:

> "*Detective Smith decided to handcuff Hennessey, and told him to put his hands outside the window, while shouting to his daughter (who was in*

---

75. 292 F.3d 1177 (9th Cir. 2002).

*the police car) to bring his handcuffs … Just as his daughter handed him the handcuffs, Hennessey started hitting him … [He] then grabbed Detective Smith by the throat with one hand and grabbed him by his tie with the other hand. Detective Smith tried to back away, leaving Hennessey behind the closed car door, but Hennessey clambered out of his car window, hanging on to Detective Smith. Then he yelled 'Shoot me, motherfucker!' and came at Detective Smith swinging. Detective Smith hit Hennessey repeatedly with his flashlight, hitting one blow squarely on the forehead, but to no effect. Then Hennessey started kicking Detective Smith in the stomach and groin. Detective Smith tried to back away from Hennessey and fend off his blows and kicks, but Hennessey charged him, and held him in a bear hug, and grabbed his gun by the barrel. Hennessey landed a solid blow to Detective Smith's head, cutting him, knocking his glasses off, and forcing him back … As he warded off Hennessey's blows to his head and groin, Detective Smith fought for control of his gun. He could feel Hennessey trying to pry his thumb off the gun. Then he felt the gun's slide move backward toward the locked position, where it would prevent the gun from shooting. Detective Smith feared for his life and didn't want to disarm his own weapon, so he moved the slide forward, fighting Hennessey's pressure on the gun. At this point … when the men were still struggling for control of the gun, Detective Smith fired, hitting and killing Hennessey."*

Some witnesses gave versions of the events that differed somewhat from what Detective Smith described. But there was sufficient agreement on the *material facts* for the federal appellate court to conclude:

*"Detective Smith was locked in hand-to-hand combat and losing … Hennessey actively, violently, and successfully resisted arrest and physically attacked Detective Smith and tried to turn Smith's gun on him. No one who saw the fight disputes that Hennessey was the aggressor … Hennessey was trying to get the detective's gun, and was getting the upper hand. <u>Hennessey posed an imminent threat of injury or death; indeed the threat of injury had already been realized by Hennessey's blows and kicks.</u>"* (Emphasis added.)

Accordingly:

*"Under the circumstances, a reasonable officer would perceive a substantial risk that Hennessey would seriously injure or kill him, either by beating and kicking him, or by taking his gun and shooting him with it. Indeed, once Hennessey grabbed the barrel of Detective Smith's gun and*

*tried to pry it from his hand, a reasonable officer would infer a substantial possibility that he was fighting for his life. Maybe he could have hoped that Hennessey simply wanted to disarm him, not shoot him, but that would have been a gamble."*[76]

In both cases discussed above, there was no question about the presence of a weapon, or of the potential danger of a suspect gaining control of it. But an officer does not have to know for a certainty that a weapon is present in order to have a reasonable belief that a suspect is attempting to gain access to one.

In *Small v. City of Alexandria, et al.*,[77] a police officer responded with EMTs to a motel where a woman had reported that her boyfriend, Richard Goss, was intoxicated and she needed assistance. For reasons not clear, the dispatcher categorized the boyfriend as suicidal. When the EMTs entered the motel room, Goss was sitting in the middle of the bed and "rambling." Uncertain what to do, the EMTs left the motel room and waited for the arrival of their supervisor. The officer remained in the doorway of the motel room and conversed with Goss. Goss made several statements to the officer, such as "stay alert," "stay alive," "you got your weapon, I got mine too." The officer then asked Goss's girlfriend, who was standing outside, if Goss had any weapons inside, or if Goss had a weapon. The officer did not hear the girlfriend's reply, but he heard Goss say "I got mine too." As Goss said this, he moved toward the side of the bed, and reached downward toward the bottom of the top mattress. The officer yelled, "Don't do it!" but Goss did not stop moving. The officer fired two shots in rapid succession, moved for cover to the doorway, and then fired a third, "seconds after the first," and Goss died at the scene. No weapon was found underneath the mattress.

Goss's girlfriend filed a lawsuit against the officer raising both Fourteenth Amendment due process claims and excessive force under the Fourth Amendment. The federal district court granted the officer's motion for summary judgment, and the Fourth Amendment excessive force claim was appealed to the federal appellate court. The appellate court affirmed the district court's grant of summary judgment, noting that the only evidence on the record described Goss's behavior immediately prior to the shooting, including his references to having a weapon and his persistent movement to reach under the bed. Accordingly, the court held:

*"The summary judgment evidence does not show that [the officer's] use of force was clearly excessive."*

---

76. *Id.*, at 1185–1186.
77. 2015 U.S. App. LEXIS 14332 (5th Cir. 2015).

Another example of a suspect appearing to be reaching for a weapon is *Thomas v. Baldwin*,[78] in which police officers went to the residence of Brian Mc-Griff to execute a search warrant for stolen weapons. Upon arrival the officers breached the door, identified themselves, shouted that they had a warrant, and entered the apartment with guns drawn. As the officers entered the bedroom they discovered a man named Thomas, and another individual named Miller. Officer Baldwin ordered the two men to get on the ground and show their hands. Miller complied by lying on a mattress, but Thomas slowly got to his knees without lying down. Officer Baldwin repeated his command for Thomas to get to the ground, and turned slightly away to call for assistance from fellow officers. When he turned back, Thomas was "quickly rising from the mattress on the floor. [His] left hand was clenched and he moved his right hand toward the left hand." At this point, Officer Baldwin shot Thomas one time. Thomas jumped out of a window, and was found outside about 20 yards from the apartment. Police later found a knife in the room near the bedroom where Officer Baldwin was standing. Thomas died from the gunshot wound, and a suit was filed against Officer Baldwin alleging excessive force.

The federal district court granted summary judgment to Officer Baldwin, and the case was appealed to the federal appellate court. The court upheld the summary judgment ruling and explained:

> *"Here, the evidence shows that Baldwin's use of deadly force was objectively reasonable as a matter of law ... This court has found a police officer's use of deadly force to be objectively reasonable in similar factual situations—when the subject does not comply with an officer's orders and reaches for something out of the officer's sight."*

*The court then listed some of the specific factors that support summary judgment:*

> *"Baldwin and his team were executing a search warrant to locate stolen firearms. Owing to the dangerous nature of the situation, they entered the property with guns drawn ... As he entered the bedroom ... Baldwin identified himself as a police officer and yelled multiple times for Thomas and Miller to get on the ground. Only Miller complied ... Thomas did not ... instead, he fell to his knees and looked around as if he was searching for something. Baldwin turned away for a moment, then saw Thomas moving quickly back up with one hand clenched as if he were holding a gun or a knife. Thomas then brought his hands together in a threatening manner, at which point Baldwin shot him."*

---

78. 2014 U.S. App. LEXIS 24060 (5th Cir. 2014).

One interesting element in this case is the court's response to the plaintiff's contention that no knife was found near where Thomas was standing:

> "… [T]he fact that no weapon was found in Thomas's vicinity does not contradict Baldwin's account that Thomas was on his knees and had his hand clenched. This court has been clear that whether the decedent actually possessed a weapon is irrelevant so long as the police officer reasonably believed he possessed a weapon."

These cases demonstrate how an unarmed suspect can be reasonably perceived as posing an immediate danger to officers or others by virtue of gaining access to a firearm, either the officers' or their own. Nevertheless, for a variety of reasons, perhaps not always understood by the officers themselves, they routinely subject themselves to great risk of death and serious physical injury at the hands of aggressive but apparently unarmed suspects. It is something of a paradox that officers readily see the danger in a suspect attempting to gain access to an area where a weapon *may* be located, while failing to discern the danger in that same suspect attempting to gain access to an area where a weapon is *definitely* located—i.e., the officer. It can hardly be doubted that any person who aggressively attacks a law enforcement officer poses an immediate danger of serious injury to that officer. That danger is dramatically elevated by the presence of the officer's firearm. Nonetheless, that scenario is not commonly acknowledged in law enforcement policies and training programs as warranting the use of deadly force.

Perhaps it is a failure to accurately assess the peril posed by an unarmed suspect's actions, or a failure to recognize the risks involved in engaging in a physical struggle with such assailants. Possibly it is the consequence of training or policy that officers feel compelled to assume such risks. Undoubtedly, it is often based on the mistaken belief that even in the face of an immediate threat they are required by law to consider other options, and to view deadly force only as a last resort. Maybe it is due to all of the above. What can be stated without reservation is that the Constitution does not require law enforcement officers to sacrifice their lives for their country.

When law enforcement officers elect to defend themselves against an aggressive, physical attack by an unarmed suspect through means other than deadly force, they are gratuitously assuming greater risks to themselves than that which is required by law. That does not mean that the officers' decision was necessarily wrong; after all, the use of deadly force is discretionary. But such decisions should be informed ones, based on a clear understanding of the dangers posed and the latitude afforded by the law to officers to protect themselves in the face of such dangers. It should not be the product of misunderstanding with respect to either the facts or the law.

With respect to the facts, confusion can exist regarding the nature of the threat posed by an unarmed, but aggressive, assailant. It may be thought that a trained officer has the advantage in such encounters, all else being equal. But that view is based on a false premise because things are not equal and the inequity often works to the disadvantage of the officer. The challenges facing the officer and the suspect are not the same. The officer must subdue the assailant while protecting his firearm and remaining within the boundaries of conduct prescribed by law and policy. The assailant has no such constraints. It is not his job to subdue the officer, and he has no need to protect a firearm. He need only achieve a "lucky" punch, or otherwise gain a momentary advantage, in order to gain access to the officer's firearm.

*Unarmed Suspect Using Personal Weapons.* It is notable that the court in *Hennesey* discussed above acknowledged the risks posed to officers by aggressively non-compliant suspects who use personal weapons—i.e., hands, feet, etc.—in a manner to injure or kill. Apart from the risk of a suspect gaining access to an officer's firearm, there is a legitimate risk of an officer being killed or seriously injured by personal weapons. A relevant case is ***Davenport v. Causey.***[79] Officer Sam Causey of the Crossville, Tennessee, police department made a traffic stop of a vehicle being driven by Austin Davenport. Most of the events that followed were captured on the police car's dash camera. Davenport got out of his vehicle and walked toward the rear. Officer Causey got out of his vehicle and approached Davenport, instructing him to return to his vehicle. Davenport returned to the side of his vehicle but leaned against it, folding his arms. Because Davenport was non-compliant, Officer Causey called for backup and decided to place Davenport in custody. When Officer Causey reached for Davenport, Davenport brushed his hand away. Davenport was 44 years old, five feet, nine inches tall, and weighed 277 pounds. Officer Causey was 34 years old, five feet, eight-and-a-half inches tall, and weighed 200 pounds. Officer Causey decided to use his Taser, but when he used it on Davenport there was no discernible reaction, except Davenport's grabbing the wires and taking up the slack as he walked toward Officer Causey. At about this time, Officer Pugh arrived. Davenport began walking backward, continuing to pull the Taser wires and wrapping them around his hand. Officer Causey walked toward Davenport in order to use the Taser in the "stun drive format," at which point Davenport began punching Officer Causey, first on the shoulder, then in the abdomen, and finally on the head, knocking Officer Causey to the ground. Davenport then turned his attention to Officer Pugh, who was 60 years old

---

79. 521 F.3d 544 (6th Cir. 2008).

and about the same size as Officer Causey. Davenport struck Officer Pugh three quick blows, causing him to stagger backwards. As he prepared to hit Officer Pugh a fourth time, Officer Causey shot Davenport, severely wounding him. The lapsed time, *from the initiation of the traffic stop to the point when Officer Causey shot Davenport was 68 seconds.* Davenport filed a lawsuit against Officer Causey, alleging excessive force. The federal appellate court ruled that Officer Causey was entitled to summary judgment, noting that Davenport was non-compliant, he actively resisted arrest and attacked two officers, he used enough force to knock Officer Causey down, and he struck the officers with <u>close-fisted blows</u>. The significance of this to the court was its view that "*closed-fisted blows … may constitute deadly force blows.*"[80] (Emphasis added.) That can also be true when law enforcement officers strike individuals with closed fists.[81]

Another illustration of an "unarmed" individual attacking a police officer is *Johnson v. Rankin,*[82] in which an officer responded to a "Priority One" emergency call reporting a "burglary in progress" at an apartment building. It is important to note that Priority One calls are reserved for situations in which someone is in physical danger. In this instance, someone was trying to break down a door. When the officer arrived he saw a man violently banging on a glass door, apparently trying to gain entry into the building. From a distance of about 35 feet away, the officer drew his weapon, identified himself as a police officer, and repeatedly ordered the suspect—a man named Denyakin—to stop, show his hands, and get down on the ground. Denyakin stopped banging on the door, lowered his hands to his side, and shoved his right hand in his pants as if "digging for an object." Denyakin then charged at the officer and did not stop when ordered to do so. The officer later testified that although he did not see a weapon, Denyakin's behavior led him to believe that he was in serious physical danger. The officer fired his weapon eleven times in a span of about three seconds. All of the rounds struck Denyakin, killing him.

The case was tried by a jury, which ruled in favor of the officer on all counts. On appeal, the plaintiff challenged the relevance of certain "bad act" evidence regarding Denyakin's alcoholism and his behavior during an earlier encounter with police. In particular, plaintiff contended that Denyakin could not have charged the officer because of the high blood alcohol content (BAC) (0.28%) at the time of the incident. The court was not impressed, observing that dur-

---

80. *Id.*, at 550.

81. See, *Sallenger v. Oakes*, 473 F.3d 731 (7th Cir. 2007) (Court held that officers striking person with closed-fisted punches to the head would constitute the use of deadly force, and would be unreasonable unless justified under the Fourth Amendment.).

82. 547 Fed. Appx. 263 (4th Cir. 2013).

ing the prior incident, when his BAC was 0.22%, Denyakin "walked without stumbling … threatened to beat his girlfriend, punched her apartment window, drew a bloody symbol on her door," and responded to the officer's statement that he could shoot him if he didn't show his hands.

The appellate court rejected all of the plaintiff's claims on appeal, and noted that the incident which preceded this one demonstrated " … *that Denyakin could walk, respond lucidly to a police officer, and behave violently while drunk. The testimony regarding Denyakin's alcoholism further illustrates his heightened ability to act while intoxicated. Specifically, the testimony shows that Denyakin had developed a tolerance to alcohol that allowed him to function with a high BAC. We therefore find that the evidence speaks to Denyakin's ability to function while intoxicated, which bears on whether Denyakin could have charged at [the officer] while drunk."*

These cases emphasize the extreme risks facing law enforcement officers when they choose, or are compelled by circumstances, to engage in physical struggles with violently resisting individuals who are armed only with their personal weapons. It is a dangerous fallacy to think that the well-trained and equipped officer has the advantage. It has been observed through the ages that all human encounters, whether in the sporting arena, on the battlefield, or on the street, are subject to the vagaries of *chance*. It can be readily discerned from history, as well as from personal experience and observation, that the "best man" does not always win. In the words of the ancient proverb:

> *"The race is not to the swift, nor the battle to the strong … nor yet favor to the man of skill; but time and chance happeneth to them all."*[83]

If God and the ancients have known this all along, perhaps it is time that we take note of it as well. The role of *chance* in an encounter can be lessened to varying degrees through training, good tactical judgment, and skill. It can never be eliminated. Whatever the reasons may be for officers to gratuitously assume risks of death or injury to themselves—and sometimes they have no choice—they should understand that they are staking the outcome of the encounter to some degree on mere *chance*.

Not only is the assumption of greater risk foolhardy, it is "gratuitous" because it isn't necessary. Law enforcement officers are not legally required to assume unreasonable risks to themselves. That means, among other things, that they are not required to use, or even consider, less intrusive options before

---

83. Ecclesiastes 9:11.

using deadly force to counter immediate threats to their lives.[84] It also means that they are not required to allow an assailant to disable them — even temporarily — and gamble their survival on the intentions of their assailants. It is worth repeating the statement of the federal court of appeals quoted above:

> *"The Constitution simply does not require police to gamble with their lives in the face of a serious threat of harm."*[85]

If the Constitution does not require officers to gamble with their lives, it stands to reason that neither should law enforcement policies and training. (Those topics are covered in later chapters of this book.) Law enforcement is a dangerous job. That is a given. And those who choose that profession are choosing to assume those risks that are inherent in the job. But the risks an officer must assume are generally those that cannot be perceived in advance, and therefore cannot be fully guarded against. Law enforcement officers often knowingly choose to sacrifice themselves on behalf of *the endangered*. But they should not be expected to sacrifice themselves on behalf of *the dangerous*. Given the choice between the safety of law enforcement officers — whom we hire to protect us — and the safety of criminal suspects who choose to assail them, the law clearly strikes the balance in favor of the officers.

The cases discussed thus far should make it clear that law enforcement officers are not required to assume unreasonable risks while performing their duties. This means that they are not required to allow themselves to be shot, stabbed, or struck with a club, or punched, or otherwise rendered incapable of defending themselves — even temporarily. It also means that they are not required to allow themselves to be rendered incapable of defending themselves through any other means, including electronic or chemical weapons. In areas such as these, where there is no significant body of law yet available to provide specific guidance, the general principles of law already discussed should encourage the development of policies and training to fill any remaining gaps. In the FBI's deadly force training curriculum there are several examples of typical factors that may be viewed by FBI agents as posing an imminent danger justifying the use of deadly force. Among those factors is the following, which is relevant to this section:

---

84. For further explanation of the constitutional rule that officers are not required to select the least intrusive force option, only a reasonable one, see the discussion beginning on page 80.

85. *Elliott v. Leavitt*, 99 F.3d 640 (4th Cir. 1996). See also *Monroe v. City of Phoenix*, 248 F.3d 851 (9th Cir. 2001) (Officer shot unarmed man who physically attacked him.).

*"The suspect has the capability of inflicting death or serious injury, or otherwise incapacitating Agents without a deadly weapon, and is indicating an intention to do so."*

The absence of any significant body of case law on an issue does not preclude law enforcement agencies from developing policies and training to fill the gap and address serious threats that confront officers. As noted earlier, law enforcement experience, reflected in well-reasoned policies and training, not only serves to protect the officers, by addressing actual events that emerge in the real world involving the behaviors of real human beings, they also serve to inform and educate the courts.

**Vehicles as Weapons.** Motor vehicles present unique challenges for law enforcement officers. Their mass and mobility create significant dangers to officers, other motorists, and pedestrians, whether used intentionally for that purpose, or just to evade arrest. Law enforcement officers cannot know the purpose or intent of a driver who is operating a vehicle in a manner that endangers others; they can only perceive the threat and attempt to address it. How to do that is the challenge.

It is not always easy to distinguish between the threats posed by suspects who use their vehicles to purposefully strike officers or other persons, and those where the threats are created by the reckless manner in which a vehicle is used to evade police. Fortunately for society, the courts have recognized both as justifications to use deadly force to end the threat. An example of the first scenario is found in **Levesque v. City of Mesa, et al.**,[86] where a person caused a disturbance in a local bar by allegedly pointing a firearm at another person and then left in his truck. When confronted by two officers who were on foot, he accelerated in the general direction of the officers who shot and killed him. An eyewitness to the event asserted that she did not believe the officers were actually in danger. In a subsequent lawsuit, the federal district court granted summary judgment to the officers, finding that " ... *the [officers'] actions were objectively reasonable under the circumstances* ..." The federal appellate court upheld the lower court's decision. With respect to the eyewitness's opinion the court stated:

*"The fact that an eyewitness proffered the opinion that she did not believe that the officers were actually in danger is immaterial because the test of objective reasonableness is based on the 'perspective of the officer on the scene.'"*

---

86. 444 Fed. Appx. 978 (9th Cir. 2011). See, also, *Wilkinson v. Torres, et al.*, 610 F.3d 546 (9th Cir. 2010) (*cert. denied, Scott v. Torres*, 2011 U.S. LEXIS 1418, 2011).

Most cases involving vehicles arise from the threats posed to officers and the public as the result of reckless driving. The Supreme Court has addressed this issue in several recent cases, beginning with *Scott v. Harris*.[87] Victor Harris was clocked driving his vehicle at 73 mph on a two-lane road with a 55 mph speed limit. A deputy sheriff tried to pull the speeding vehicle over but Harris sped away, reaching speeds exceeding 85 mph. Other officers, including Deputy Timothy Scott, joined the pursuit. At one point, Harris drove into a shopping center where pursuing officers attempted to box him in. He evaded the trap by turning sharply, colliding with Deputy Scott's car, exiting the parking lot and speeding down a two-lane highway with Deputy Scott in close pursuit. Six minutes and nearly 10 miles after the chase began, Deputy Scott received permission from a supervisor to use a PIT (Precision Intervention Technique) maneuver, intended to cause the fleeing vehicle to spin out of control. Believing the vehicles were moving too fast to safely use the PIT maneuver, Deputy Scott applied his push bumper to the rear of Harris's vehicle, causing it to leave the roadway, run down an embankment and overturn. Harris was seriously injured and rendered a quadriplegic. He filed suit in federal court alleging Deputy Scott used excessive force in violation of his constitutional rights.

Deputy Scott filed a motion for summary judgment on an assertion of qualified immunity. That motion was denied by the lower federal courts. As discussed in the previous chapter, where there are disputes regarding material facts, courts are required to accept the version most favorable to the party opposing the summary judgment motion. Accordingly, the lower courts adopted the version espoused by Harris and denied summary judgment. The Supreme Court reversed the lower courts in an 8–1 decision written by Justice Scalia. Since it is virtually impossible to improve upon his gift of expression, the reader is invited to read his comments at length in the italics below.

According to Harris's version, there was little actual threat to pedestrians or other motorists, the roads were mostly empty, he remained in control of his vehicle, he slowed for turns and intersections, and he typically used his indicators for turns. This description prompted Justice Scalia's comment that reading this description " ... *one gets the impression that [Harris], rather than fleeing from police, was attempting to pass his driving test.*"

Fortunately, the Supreme Court detected an "*added wrinkle*"—a video tape! The Court wrote:

> "*The videotape tells quite a different story. There we see [Harris's] vehicle racing down narrow, two-lane roads in the dead of night at speeds*

---

87. 550 U.S. 372 (2008).

*that are shockingly fast. We see it swerve around more than a dozen other cars, cross the yellow line, and force cars traveling in both directions to their respective shoulders to avoid being hit ... run multiple red lights and travel for considerable periods of time in the occasional center left-turn-only lane, chased by numerous police cars forced to engage in the same hazardous maneuvers just to keep up. Far from being the cautious and controlled driver the lower court depicts, what we see on the video more closely resembles a Hollywood-style car chase of the most frightening sort, placing police officers and innocent bystanders alike at great risk of serious injury."*

Viewing the facts through that prism, the Court concluded that Deputy Scott did not violate the Fourth Amendment. Acknowledging that Deputy Scott's actions posed a "*high likelihood of serious injury to Harris,*" the Court wrote that those risks had to be considered "*in light of the threat to the public that Scott was trying to eliminate.*" The Court balanced the risks posed by Deputy Scott to Harris against the risks posed by Harris to "*the lives of any pedestrians who might have been present, to other civilian motorists, and to the officers involved in the chase.*" The Court added:

*"We think it appropriate ... to take into account not only the number of lives at risk, but also their relative culpability. It was [Harris], after all, who intentionally placed himself and the public in danger ... By contrast, those who might have been harmed had Scott not taken the action he did were entirely innocent. We have little difficulty in concluding it was reasonable for Scott to take the action he did."*

To the argument that the innocent public could have been protected and the accident avoided if the police had simply ceased their pursuit, the Court responded:

*"We think the police need not have taken that chance and hoped for the best. Whereas Scott's action—ramming [Harris] off the road—was certain to eliminate the risk that [Harris] posed to the public, ceasing pursuit was not ... [Harris] might have been just as likely to respond by continuing to drive recklessly as by slowing down and wiping his brow ... we are loath to lay down a rule requiring the police to allow fleeing suspects to get away whenever they drive so recklessly that they put other people's lives in danger."*

The Court concluded:

*"The Constitution assuredly does not impose this invitation to impunity-earned-by-recklessness. Instead, we lay down a more sensible rule: a po-*

*lice officer's attempt to terminate a dangerous high-speed car chase that threatens the lives of innocent by-standers does not violate the Fourth Amendment, even when it places the fleeing motorist at risk of serious injury or death."*

The Court did not explicitly describe Deputy Scott's action in ramming Harris's car off the road as "deadly force," but acknowledged that this action placed Harris at significant risk of death or serious injury. The Court reasoned that whether or not it was deadly force, it was reasonable.

More recently, in ***Plumhoff, et al. v. Rickard***,[88] the Supreme Court addressed the issue of police officers using deadly force by shooting and killing the driver of a car that engaged the officers in a high-speed chase, and then continued efforts to escape the police after his vehicle had been brought to a halt. Near midnight on July 18, 2004, Lieutenant Joseph Forthman of the West Memphis (Arkansas) Police Department stopped a car that had only one operating headlight. There were two occupants, Donald Rickard, the driver, and Kelly Allen, his passenger. While interacting with Rickard, Lieutenant Forthman noticed an indentation in the windshield "roughly the size of a head or a basketball," and glass shavings on the dashboard, raising concerns that a pedestrian might have been struck by that vehicle. Rickard failed to produce a driver's license, and appeared to be nervous. When he was asked to step out of the car, he sped away. Lieutenant Forthman gave chase and was soon joined by five other police cruisers. The high-speed chase proceeded eastbound on I-40, reaching speeds in excess of 100 mph and passing more than two dozen vehicles. The officers attempted to stop Rickard using a "rolling roadblock," but were unsuccessful. Eventually, Rickard exited I-40, making a quick right turn that caused contact with a pursuing police car, and caused Rickard's vehicle to spin out into a parking lot where it collided with Officer Plumhoff's cruiser. Rickard put his car in reverse, making contact with one of the police cruisers. With his bumper flush against the bumper of the cruiser, his tires spinning, and his car rocking back and forth, he continued his efforts to escape, and struck another police cruiser.

In the meantime, two officers—including Evans and Plumhoff—approached Rickard's car with guns in hand. Evans pounded on the passenger side window, but Rickard continued his efforts to escape. Officer Plumhoff fired three shots into Rickard's car. Rickard reversed in a 180-degree arc and maneuvered onto another street, forcing Officer Evans to take evasive action to avoid being struck. As Rickard continued fleeing down that street, two

---

88. 572 U.S. _____ (2014).

other officers fired a total of 12 shots. Rickard then lost control of the car and crashed into a building. A total of 15 rounds had been fired by the officers. As the Supreme Court noted: *"Rickard and Allen both died from some combination of gunshot wounds and injuries suffered in the crash that ended the chase."*

A lawsuit was filed in federal court by Rickard's minor daughter, alleging that the officers used excessive force in violation of the Fourth and Fourteenth Amendments. The federal district court denied the officers' motion for summary judgment, holding that their conduct violated the Fourth Amendment and was contrary to established law. In the court's view, the danger presented by a high-speed chase <u>cannot</u> justify the use of deadly force because the danger was caused by the officers' decision to continue the chase! The federal appellate court affirmed the district court's decision, likewise holding that the officers' actions violated the Fourth Amendment. A unanimous Supreme Court reversed, holding that *"The officers' conduct did not violate the Fourth Amendment. Even if the officers' conduct had violated the Fourth Amendment [they] would still be entitled to summary judgment based on qualified immunity."*

It may be of interest to highlight the salient points addressed by the Supreme Court in reaching its opinion. Citing its earlier decision in ***Scott v. Harris***, discussed above, the Court explained:

> *"We see no basis for reaching a different conclusion here."*
> [1] *"... the chase in this case exceeded 100 miles per hour and lasted over five minutes ..."*
> [2] *"Rickard passed more than two dozen other vehicles, several of which were forced to alter course."*
> [3] *"Rickard's outrageously reckless driving posed a grave public safety risk."*
> [4] *"And while it is true that Rickard's car eventually collided with a police car and came temporarily to a near standstill, that did not end the chase. Less than three seconds later [he] resumed maneuvering his car."*
> [5] *"Just before the shots were fired, when the front bumper of his car was flush with that of one of the police cruisers, Rickard was obviously pushing down on the accelerator because the car's wheels were spinning ..."*
> [6] *"... then Rickard threw the car into reverse 'in an attempt to escape.'"*
> [7] *"... at the moment when the shots were fired, all that a reasonable officer could have concluded was that Rickard was intent on resuming his flight and that, if he was allowed to do so, he would once again pose a deadly threat for others on the road."*

*[8] "Rickard's conduct even after the shots were fired—as noted he managed to drive away despite the efforts of the police to block his path—underscores the point."*

*[9] "... it is beyond serious dispute that Rickard's flight posed a grave public safety risk, and ... the police acted reasonably in using deadly force to end that risk."*

Another issue that rears its head with some frequency is the number of rounds fired by the officers—in this case 15. To the plaintiffs assertion that the number of rounds fired was excessive, the Supreme Court responded succinctly:

*"We reject that argument. It stands to reason that, if police officers are justified in firing at a suspect in order to end a severe threat to public safety, the officer need not stop shooting until the threat has ended."*

The 15 shots were fired within a span of about 10 seconds, and as the Court observed, even after the shots had been fired, *"Rickard never abandoned his attempt to flee ... he managed to drive away and to continue driving until he crashed."* To bolster the argument that too many shots were fired, plaintiff pointed to the presence of Rickard's passenger, Allen, who was also struck and killed. The Court responded:

*"If a suit were brought on behalf of Allen ... the risk to Allen would be of central concern. But Allen's presence in the car cannot enhance Rickard's Fourth Amendment right. After all, it was Rickard who put Allen in danger by fleeing and refusing to end the chase, and it would be perverse if his disregard for Allen's safety worked to his benefit."*

The significance of the *Scott* and *Plumhoff* cases is not so much in the Court's conclusions that officers may use deadly force to stop someone who poses imminent threats to the safety of law enforcement officers and others. That has been an accepted rule of constitutional law for a long time. The significance of these cases lies in their recognition that the risks posed by motor vehicles can be just as real when the operator is demonstrating a reckless disregard for the safety of others, as when the vehicle is being intentionally used to cause death or serious injury. While that may seem obvious to many of us, that has not been reflected in the case law or law enforcement policies for many years. Even in these two cases, where the dangers posed to the public by individuals "armed with vehicles" seemed so self-evident to the Supreme Court, two federal district courts and two federal appellate courts ruled against the officers who brought those threats to an end.

It is illuminating to briefly look at the lower court proceedings in the *Plumhoff* case, both to appreciate the significance of the Supreme Court's ruling and to highlight the perverse reasoning in the lower courts that would place the safety of the "dangerous" over that of the "endangered." The plaintiff alleged that it was a violation of the Fourth Amendment to use deadly force to terminate the high-speed chase, and that even if the officers were permitted to fire their weapons they fired too many rounds. The district court agreed that the officers violated *clearly established law*, and declared that the danger presented by a high-speed chase <u>cannot</u> justify the use of deadly force because the danger was caused by the officers' decision to continue the chase. As if that were not bad enough, the 6th Circuit Court of Appeals agreed and affirmed the ruling!

*The Number of Shots Fired.* Before moving to the next section that focuses on the use of deadly force to prevent escape, we will address the issue raised in the *Plumhoff* case regarding the number of shots fired by police officers in the defense of life. It is worth repeating the Supreme Court's response to the assertion that the officers "*acted unreasonably in firing a total of 15 shots*":

> "*It stands to reason that, if police officers are justified in firing at a suspect in order to end a severe threat to public safety, the officers need not stop shooting until the threat is over.*"

Several of the cases cited and discussed in this chapter involved multiple shots fired by the police in defense of themselves or others. In *Steele v. City of Cleveland*,[89] six officers initiated a traffic stop for an expired license plate. When the subject began wrestling with one of the officers for control of the officer's gun, three of the officers fired at him, striking him "*in excess of 12 times*" in his back and shoulder area by multiple guns. Nevertheless, the federal district court granted the officers' motions for summary judgment, and the appellate affirmed, concluding:

> " ... *the plaintiff has failed to show the violation of a constitutional right ... Here, the sole evidence of record shows that Steele, in violation of the officers' repeated orders, dove suddenly into his car and reached for a gun. At the time the officers shot him, he was physically wrestling one of those officers for control of the weapon, and was winning.*"

In *Wilkinson v. Torres*,[90] an officer in pursuit of a minivan executed a pursuit immobilization technique (PIT) maneuver, causing the minivan to enter a yard. As the minivan struck a telephone pole and then reversed, Officer Torres

---

89. 2010 U.S. App. LEXIS 8791 (6th Cir. 2010).
90. 610 F.3d 546 (9th Cir. 2010) (*cert. denied*, 2011 U.S. LEXIS 1418).

saw a fellow officer on the ground and yelled at the driver of the minivan to stop. When the driver failed to stop, the officer fired eleven rounds into the vehicle, killing the driver. The plaintiffs in the following lawsuit claimed that the officer fired two volleys, and should have halted after the first volley to assess the need for further action. The federal district court denied the officer's motion for summary judgment, but the federal appellate court reversed, holding:

> "[The] officer was entitled to qualified immunity as to the excessive force claim because a reasonable officer in his position had probable cause to believe that the driver posed an immediate threat...."

As to the number of shots fired, the court wrote:

> "Because we conclude as a matter of law that deadly force was authorized to protect a fellow officer from harm, it makes no difference in this case whether [Officer Torres] fired seven rounds or eleven rounds."[91]

In *Smith v. City of Brooklyn Park*,[92] the federal district court granted summary judgment to officers who shot a man multiple times when he pointed a shotgun at the officers. The federal appellate court upheld that judgment and added:

> "While 16 or 17 wounds seems a large number for two officers facing one suspect, it still does not negate the objective evidence that [the subject] was armed during the encounter."

In *Cooper v. Rutherford*,[93] a mother and son were injured when officers fired at an armed bank robber who was attempting to steal the car in which they were riding. The officer (defendant) fired 24 shots, some of which struck and wounded the mother and son. A lawsuit was filed in federal district court against the officer by the innocent victims alleging excessive force under the Fourth Amendment and a violation of the Fourteenth Amendment Due Process Clause. The district court denied the officer's motion for summary judgment, but the appellate court reversed that decision stating: " ... *the officer was entitled to qualified immunity as to the Fourth Amendment claims for unreasonable seizure because preexisting law did not provide the officer with fair notice that firing 24 shots was constitutionally unreasonable under the circumstances.*"

---

91. The apparent discrepancy in the number of shots fired arises from plaintiff's assertion that the officer fired two volleys, the first of seven rounds, and the second of four more. The obvious point of this assertion would be that the last four were unnecessary, and therefore excessive. As noted, the court was not impressed.

92. 757 F.3d 765 (8th Cir. 2014).

93. 2012 U.S. App. LEXIS 17427 (11th Cir. 2012).

A different conclusion was reached in *Margeson v. White County, et al.*,[94] an apparent "suicide by cop" case, where officers fired multiple shots, inflicting 21 separate gunshot wounds. It was later asserted that the officers fired between 36 and 43 shots total, but the officers countered that at least some of the shots were from shotguns loaded with 00 buckshot. Summary judgment for the officers was denied, because " … *a jury could certainly conclude that shooting at a man 43 times, including at least 12 shots after he had fallen to the ground, amounts to an unreasonable and excessive use of force …*"

This sampling of cases reflects a fairly broad understanding in the courts of the limitations imposed by time and the realities of wound ballistics on the ability of law enforcement officers to counter an immediate threat of serious physical injury.[95] These topics are discussed in depth in Chapters 5 and 7.

# Deadly Force to Prevent Escape

Thus far we have considered cases where the authority to use deadly force was justified by the need to address *immediate* threats posed by criminal suspects, whether resisting arrest or attempting to evade arrest by flight. In all of those cases, the issue was the immediacy of the threat, regardless of the underlying offense. We will now focus on cases where the justification to use deadly force is based on *the gravity of the offense* rather than the immediacy of a threat of serious physical to officers or others. Prior to 1985, there were no federal constitutional standards governing the use of deadly force to prevent the escape of a person when there was probable cause to believe that person had committed a crime, either a felony or a misdemeanor. The individual states had their own rules to govern this issue, and many of them retained the Common Law rule described in Chapter 2, and permitted the use of deadly force to prevent the escape of fleeing felons, regardless of the nature of the felony. It was sufficient that the crime was categorized as a felony as opposed to a misdemeanor. The following quote provides a fair rationalization for the rule:

> "*If effective law enforcement is to be maintained, the race must not be to the swift. The fleeing criminal, regardless of his offense, must be considered the author of his own misfortune.*"[96]

---

94. 2014 U.S. App. LEXIS 17464 (6th Cir. 2014).
95. See, *Lee v. Andersen*, 616 F.3d 803 (8th Cir. 2010) (*cert. denied*, 178 L. Ed. 2d 557).
96. 14 McGil LJ, at page 311 (1955).

In the 1985 decision of *Tennessee v. Garner*,[97] the U.S. Supreme Court declared the so-called "fleeing felon" rule unconstitutional. The issue before the Court was a state statute in Tennessee that tracked the Common Law rule and permitted the use of deadly force to prevent the escape of *any* felony suspect.

A Memphis police officer shot and killed a 15-year-old unarmed burglary suspect as he attempted to flee the scene of his crime. The use of deadly force under these circumstances was consistent with the Common Law rule, as well as the state statute in existence at that time. A lawsuit was filed in federal court alleging violations of the Constitution, and the case eventually reached the Supreme Court. Applying a balancing test between the interests of the fleeing suspect in his own life and the community's interests in apprehending criminal suspects, the Court concluded that it is not necessarily better that all felony suspects be shot than that they escape. On the contrary, if the suspect "*poses no immediate threat to the officer and no threat to others the harm resulting from failing to apprehend him does not justify the use of deadly force to do so.*"[98] The Court held that <u>deadly force can be used</u> when "*necessary to prevent escape and when the officer has probable cause to believe that the suspect poses a significant threat of death or serious physical injury to the officer or others.*"[99]

The Court offered the following illustrations of a suspect who poses a "significant threat":

> "*... if the suspect threatens the officer with a weapon or there is probable cause to believe that he has committed a crime involving the infliction or threatened infliction of serious physical harm, deadly force may be used if necessary to prevent escape, and if, where feasible, some warning has been given.*"[100]

The *Garner* decision marked the demise of the "fleeing felon" rule; no longer would it be constitutionally reasonable to use deadly force to prevent the escape of a fleeing suspect simply because the suspected crime was classified as a felony. The Court noted that the legal terms traditionally used to classify crimes—i.e., "felony" and "misdemeanor"—do not provide an adequate basis for deciding when deadly force is justified to prevent the escape of an offender. However, the Court did not hold that using deadly force to prevent escape is *always* unconstitutional. In fact, the decision explicitly recognizes constitutional authority to do so. The Court simply shifted the focus **from** *the classification* **to** *the nature* of the suspect's crime. The resulting two-pronged test

97. 471 U.S. 1.
98. *Id.*, at 9–10.
99. *Id.*, at 4.
100. *Id.*, at 10.

requires (1) probable cause to believe that the fleeing suspect is "*dangerous*" by virtue of his prior actions; and (2) the use of deadly force is *necessary* to effect the seizure. Each of these prongs is discussed below.

# "Dangerous" Fleeing Suspects

What makes a fleeing suspect "dangerous?" The first factor suggested by the Court is "*if the suspect threatens the officer with a weapon.*" Clearly, such an action would justify deadly force in "immediate self-defense," but given the context in which it is used by the Court, it should be read to mean that deadly force would be reasonable <u>to prevent the suspect's escape</u> at any time *after* committing that offense. This explanation becomes even more clear when it is recalled that the Court described the issue in *Garner* as "*the constitutionality of the use of deadly force <u>to prevent the escape</u>*" of a suspect. That reading is consistent with the second factor, which is, "*there is probable cause to believe that <u>he has committed a crime involving the infliction or threatened infliction of serious physical harm</u>....*"

Both factors require, at a minimum, that the suspect "threatened" infliction of serious physical harm. These factors are written in the disjunctive, so that either factor would define the suspect as "dangerous." The primary difference between the two factors is *when* the threatened action occurred. The first refers to a suspect who "*threatens* [present tense] *the officer with a weapon,*" while the second refers to a suspect who "*has committed* [past tense]" a harm-threatening offense.

Accordingly, the first constitutional requirement for justifying the use of deadly force to prevent escape of a criminal suspect is a probable cause belief that the suspect has committed an offense involving threatened infliction of serious physical harm. For a suspect to qualify as "dangerous," within the meaning of *Garner*, there is nothing to suggest that the danger posed must be "immediate." If that were the case the "fleeing dangerous suspect" rule would add nothing to the "immediate self-defense" rule, and whether the criminal suspect was advancing on the officer or attempting to flee would make no difference. The *Garner* decision establishes a presumption that one who has committed a crime involving infliction or threatened infliction of serious physical harm poses a continuing danger to society. This view is supported to some degree by language of the Supreme Court in *Scott v. Harris*,[101] where the Court explained this aspect of the *Garner* rule in this manner:

---

101. 550 U.S. 372 (2007).

*"By way of example only, **Garner** hypothesized that deadly force may be used 'if necessary to prevent escape' when the suspect is known to have 'committed a crime involving the infliction or threatened infliction of serious physical harm' so that <u>his mere being at large poses an inherent danger to society.</u>"*[102]

A case that illustrates the application of the rule is *Forrett v. Richardson*, where an unarmed, fleeing suspect was shot and wounded by a police officer.[103] The police were searching for a man who a short time before had broken into a home, tied up the three occupants, shot and wounded one of them, and then fled the scene. The officers located a pickup truck matching one observed at the crime scene, but failed to immediately locate either the suspect or any weapon in the vehicle. Shortly thereafter, however, the officers saw a man who matched the description of the suspect. The man fled at the sight of the officers, and refused to comply with repeated commands to stop. When the suspect climbed a fence and appeared on the verge of escaping, one of the officers gave a final warning and then fired one shot that struck and wounded the suspect. No weapon was found in possession of the suspect or in the area.

In the subsequent lawsuit, the plaintiff alleged that the officer had violated the Fourth Amendment rule as articulated by the Supreme Court in *Garner* by using deadly force against a fleeing suspect who was unarmed and posed no immediate threat to the officers or others. The federal appellate court rejected the plaintiff's claim and explained:

*"... the suspect need not be armed or pose an immediate threat to the officers or others at the time of the shooting."*[104]

The *Forrett* case is one of the few cases to date that has addressed the *pure* fleeing suspect issue. There are probably several reasons for that, but at least three are suggested. First, as noted throughout this book, law enforcement officers are frequently hesitant to use deadly force even when confronted by immediate threats to their safety. It should not be surprising that they are even more reluctant to do so in the absence of an immediate threat.[105] Second, more

---

102. *Id.*, footnote 9.

103. 112 F.3d 416 (9th Cir. 1997).

104. *Id.*, at 420.

105. In the opinion of the authors, this is the most prevalent and powerful factor at play. Police officers' restraint goes largely unnoticed and unrecognized for the simple reason it most often results in no incidents and no headlines, and no misinformed or manipulated community outrage. When it is noticed, it is most often praised as a commendable exercise of discretion. However, there is a hidden consequence of such restraint. Criminal

often than not, when deadly force is used against a fleeing suspect the suspect is armed with a firearm, using a vehicle in a manner that creates a danger to the officers and the public, or otherwise posing an "immediate threat." Accordingly, the courts are seldom called upon to reach the core issue of the fleeing "dangerous" suspect who poses no immediate threat. (The *Montoute* case, discussed above, is a good example.)[106] Third, despite what the Constitution permits, many law enforcement agencies have deadly force policies that impose stricter rules than the law. This is particularly true as they relate to fleeing suspects.

A typical example can be found in the deadly force policy adopted by the U.S. Department of Justice in 1995. Following a somewhat standard paragraph permitting the use of deadly force to counter an "imminent danger" of death or serious physical injury, the policy addressed the "prevention of escape" issue:

> *Deadly force may be used <u>to prevent the escape</u> of a fleeing subject if there is probable cause to believe: (1) the subject has committed a felony involving the infliction or threatened infliction of serious physical injury or death, and (2) the escape of the subject would pose an imminent danger of death or serious physical injury to the officer or to another person.*

The first requirement essentially restates the Supreme Court's language in *Garner*, while the second requirement nullifies the first by imposing the "imminent danger" standard. In so doing, the constitutional standard created in the *Garner* decision was rejected and substituted with a rule that was not only stricter, but also incomprehensible.

Responding to pressure from its law enforcement components, including the FBI, in 2004 the DOJ amended its deadly force policy by removing all references to "prevention of escape." The positive aspect of this development is the elimination of inconsistency and ambiguity from an important policy statement. The negative aspect is yet another law enforcement policy that ignores the dangers posed to society by dangerous criminal suspects who remain at large as long as they are able to outrun pursuing law enforcement officers.

In *Garner*, the Supreme Court was required to strike a balance between *"The suspect's fundamental interest in his own life ..."* and society's *"interest in*

---

suspects who fall within the Supreme Court's definition of "dangerous" are permitted to remain at large to perpetrate further crimes upon the community, and to pose further danger to the officers who must next encounter them.

106. Also see Chapter 15 Case Histories—*David Lopez, et al. v. LVMPD* for another example of a "pure" prevention of escape use of deadly force.

*effective law enforcement*."[107] The Court struck that balance in favor of the fleeing suspect when he is not dangerous, but in favor of society when there is
probable cause to believe that he is. It is difficult to escape the conclusion that
gratuitously restrictive policies reverse the effect of that decision by shifting
the balance of risk from the fleeing dangerous suspect to society and its law
enforcement officers.

# Necessity

Under the *Garner* decision, in addition to having probable cause to believe that a fleeing suspect poses a significant threat to officers or others, the
use of deadly force to prevent the escape must be *necessary*. The clear intention of this rule is to limit the use of deadly force to prevent escape to those
instances where the fleeing suspect is both dangerous and unwilling to submit to arrest. While court cases are lacking to illustrate the circumstances, it
seems logical that if officers can effect the arrest without subjecting themselves and others to significant risks, deadly force would not be necessary.
That could happen because officers manage to chase down and subdue the
suspect through means other than deadly force, and it could be as simple as
the suspect choosing to surrender.

An issue relevant to the "necessity" requirement is the Court's instruction
that "*some warning*" be given "*where feasible*." The Court gave no detailed guidance, but the term "warning" suggests that it means more than just a command to "halt." This requirement is obviously based on the possibility that a
fleeing suspect, no matter how dangerous, may choose to surrender if informed
that failure to do so could have dire consequences. The first point to emphasize is that the rule applies only to fleeing suspect cases, and not to those involving immediate threats to life. The second point, which the Court emphasized,
is that if it is not feasible to give such a warning—for example, if to do so
would place the officers or others in danger—then it is clearly not required.

# Applying the Fourth Amendment Standard

In *Graham v. Connor*, the Supreme Court provided one of the most significant and comprehensive decisions to date on the manner in which the

---

107. 471 U.S. 1, at 8 (1985).

Fourth Amendment is to be applied in reviewing a law enforcement officer's decision to use *any* level of force to effect a seizure.[108] The Court framed the issue as follows:

> " ... *[w]hether the officers' actions are <u>objectively reasonable</u> in light of <u>the facts and circumstances confronting them</u> ... judged from <u>the perspective of a reasonable officer on the scene</u>, rather than with the 20/20 vision of hindsight.*"[109] (Emphasis added.)

The underlined portions of this statement provide a useful framework for discussing the propriety of an officer's decision to use deadly force in a given case.

## "Objectively Reasonable"

It is noteworthy that the Constitution does not require that law enforcement officers be "right." It requires only that they be "reasonable." The constitutional standard of "objective reasonableness" provides a logical means of fairly assessing an officer's actions in any context.

To properly apply the "reasonableness" standard, it is critical to understand that it is " ... *not capable of precise definition or mechanical application.*"[110] This is a particularly important point to counter the tendency within the law enforcement community to develop policies and training programs that attempt to do that very thing. The impulse to establish precise rules that can be learned by rote, by which officers can thoughtlessly and mechanically order their actions, and by which those actions can then be mechanically assessed administratively is understandable. Unfortunately, that impulse is neither desirable nor practicable. Events that emerge during encounters between law enforcement officers and criminal suspects defy such neat solutions. A good faith error on the part of law enforcement officers may be "wrong," and yet be "reasonable." The Supreme Court acknowledges the need for flexibility, and has pointed out that the Fourth Amendment " ... *is not violated by an arrest based on probable cause, even though the wrong person is arrested ... nor by the mistaken execution of a valid search warrant on the wrong premises.... <u>With respect to a claim of excessive force, the same standard of reasonableness at the moment applies.</u>...*"[111] (Emphasis added.)

---

108. 490 U.S. 386 (1989).
109. *Graham v. Connor, supra*, at 396–97.
110. *Id.*, at 396, citing *Bell v. Wolfish*, 441 U.S. 520, at 559 (1979).
111. *Id.*, at 396.

Law enforcement policy makers and instructors must resist the temptation to reduce these critical issues to overly simple rigid rules of application. Apparent gains in clarity will be offset by a corresponding loss of flexibility in responding to rapidly changing situations. The root word for the term "reasonable" connotes a thought process. The goal should not be to train officers to act thoughtlessly and mechanically according to some predetermined formula. Rather, the goal must be to train officers to "think" quickly in light of the facts and circumstances confronting them, and then to respond effectively and rationally. Our best intended efforts cannot relieve officers of the responsibility to "reason," and the goal of rational policies and training will be to inform their ability to do so.

A second and extremely important aspect of "reasonableness" is that it does not require officers to select the least intrusive level of force, just a reasonable one. This point was first addressed by the Supreme Court in a 1983 case that had nothing to do with a use of force issue.[112] Police officers had inventoried the contents of an arrestee's shoulder bag and discovered illegal drugs. The defense challenged the inventory on the grounds that the police could have accomplished the purported purpose of protecting the arrestee's property by the less intrusive means of inventorying the shoulder bag as a unit, without looking inside. The defense argued that the availability of this less intrusive option made the more intrusive action "unreasonable." Conceding the availability of the less intrusive option, the Supreme Court nevertheless held that the Fourth Amendment does not require police officers to choose "the least intrusive alternative, only a reasonable one."[113]

Although the Court was explaining "reasonableness" in the context of a "search," the same standard applies to a seizure. Accordingly, this defining standard has been consistently applied by the courts to the use of force by law enforcement officers who are engaged in making Fourth Amendment seizures.[114]

There are no cases to better illustrate the application of this principle than *Plakas v. Drinski*.[115] A police officer shot and killed a handcuffed subject who attacked the officer with a fireplace poker. In a lawsuit against the officer and

---

112. *Illinois v. Lafayette*, 462 U.S. 640 (1983).

113. *Id.*, at 647. See also *U.S. v. Martinez-Fuerte*, 428 U.S. 543 (1983).

114. See, e.g., *Roy v. Lewiston*, 42 F.3d 691 (1st Cir. 1994); *Salim v. Proulx*, 93 F.3d 86 (2nd Cir. 1996); *Elliott v. Leavitt*, 99 F.3d 640 (4th Cir. 1996); *Collins v. Nagle*, 992 F.2d 489 (6th Cir. 1989); *Plakas v. Drinski*, 19 F.3d 1143 (7th Cir. 1994) *cert. denied*, 115 S. Ct. 81 (1994); *Tauke v. Stine*, 120 F.3d 1363 (8th Cir. 1997); *Warren v. Las Vegas*, 111 F.3d 139 (9th Cir. 1997); *Medina v. Cram*, 252 F.3d 1124 (10th Cir. 2001); and *Menuel v. Atlanta*, 25 F.3d 990 (11th Cir. 1994).

115. *Supra.*

his department, the plaintiff did not dispute that the suspect was armed with the poker, that he attacked the officer, and that, prior to the attack, had said to the officer, "Either you're going to die here or I'm going to die here." Rather, the plaintiff's contention was that the officer could and should have used less intrusive means to resolve the threat. Specifically, it was pointed out that one of the officers on the scene had a canister of CS gas on his belt and that there was a K-9 unit in the vicinity that could have been called to the scene to subdue the subject.

Rejecting the plaintiff's contention, the federal district court granted summary judgment for the police, which the appellate court affirmed with the following explanation:

> "There is no precedent in this Circuit (or any other) which says that the Constitution requires law enforcement officers to use all feasible alternatives to avoid a situation where deadly force can justifiably be used. There are, however, cases which support the assertion that where deadly force is justified under the Constitution, there is no constitutional duty to use non-deadly alternatives first."[116]

The significance of these decisions for the safety of law enforcement officers cannot be overstated. Notwithstanding that significance, there is a persistent tendency within the law enforcement community itself to require officers to go through a process of considering lesser alternatives before using deadly force. In *Plakas*, the court queried:

> "As [the suspect] moved toward [the officer], was he (the officer) supposed to think of an attack dog, of ... CS gas, of how fast he could run backwards? Our answer is, and has been, no, because there is too little time for the officer to do so and too much opportunity to second-guess that officer."[117]

The court's opinion is fully consistent with the Supreme Court's caution in *Graham v. Connor* that allowance must be made for the fact that officers " ... are often forced to make split-second judgments—in circumstances that are tense,

---

116. *Id.*, at 1148.

117. *Id.*, at 1149. Regarding the plaintiff's argument that the police could have used a dog to subdue the suspect, the court observed: "It is unusual to hear a lawyer argue that the police ought to have caused a dog to attack his client, but he is right that such an attack *might* have led to a better result for his client (and would, in our view, have led to a different sort of lawsuit)."

*uncertain, and rapidly evolving—about the amount of force that is necessary in a particular situation.*"[118]

Requiring officers who are facing immediate threats to their safety to consider lesser alternatives before using deadly force, or to use deadly force only as a "last resort,"—i.e., after all other options have been tried—is at best contrary to established constitutional principles, and at worst unnecessarily dangerous for the officers. They are contrary to the law because of the long-standing legal principle, discussed earlier, that the natural right of self-defense cannot be taken away or superseded, or even diminished, by any law of society. They are dangerous because they impose a time-consuming mental process on officers under circumstances that are often "tense, uncertain, and rapidly evolving," and where they are already confronting immediate threats to their safety.

Under the Common Law, to deny the right to act promptly and decisively was viewed as a denial of the inherent right of self-defense. Likewise, the Supreme Court long ago rejected the idea that a person confronted with an immediate threat is required to "pause" and consider alternatives.[119] Totally apart from the practical and moral considerations, these strong and long-standing legal precedents should prompt careful review of law enforcement policies and training that gratuitously restrict the right of law enforcement officers to effectively defend themselves. In the face of immediate threats of death or serious physical injury, deadly force should not be viewed as *a last resort* ... it should be viewed as *a first response*. That is consistent with the constitutional standard.

# Relevant Factors

It is typical in lawsuits for plaintiffs' attorneys to attempt to raise every possible issue and factor that might prove helpful in winning the client's case.[120] That is understandable. However, rules of evidence have evolved over the years to ensure that only relevant matters are brought into play. The Supreme Court has provided some general guidance as to what should be viewed as "relevant" when law enforcement officers are alleged to have used excessive force when making an arrest or other Fourth Amendment seizure: *the facts and circumstances*

---

118. *Supra*, at 396.

119. See *Brown v. U.S.*, 256 U.S. 335 (1921). The most pervasive example of this is the incorporation of the *force continuum* concept in law enforcement policy, training, and after-the-fact analysis of police officer use-of-force decisions. See Chapter 6—Training vs. Qualification.

120. See Chapter 13—Plaintiff's Dilemma.

*confronting the officers at the moment.* More specifically, the Court has suggested the following as examples of relevant factors: (1) The *severity of the crime* suspected; (2) Whether the suspect poses an *immediate threat* to the safety of the officers or others; (3) Whether the suspect actively is *resisting* arrest or *attempting to evade arrest by flight.* Clearly, the enumeration of these factors does not preclude the existence of others. To suggest otherwise would contradict the Court's admonition that the Fourth Amendment standard of reasonableness " ... *is not capable of precise definition or mechanical application.*"[121] To ensure that the focus remains on *the facts and circumstances confronting the officers at the moment,* the Court explicitly identified some factors that are not relevant.

# Irrelevant Factors

*Officers' Subjective Intent.* In *Graham,* the Court explicitly held that subjective factors, such as the officer's intent or motivation, are irrelevant. The Court emphasized that the standard is one of "objective reasonableness." Accordingly, the Court explained that the best of intentions cannot convert an unreasonable use of force into a reasonable one, and, conversely, the worst of intentions cannot convert a reasonable use of force into an unreasonable one.

*Suspects' Subjective Intent.* Several lower federal courts have held that a suspect's state of mind cannot be relevant. Even assuming that an officer could have some knowledge of a suspect's state of mind, the officer's objectively reasonable belief that a suspect poses an immediate threat of serious physical injury to the officer or others is not diminished by the fact that the suspect's mental capacity has been diminished by drugs, alcohol, or mental illness. As one court said, "*It requires very little mentation to be dangerous. Even a rattlesnake is dangerous, but does not possess the requisite mental capacity to be prosecuted for homicide.*"[122]

Particularly relevant to this discussion is the apparent increase in cases that suggest the suspects were intent on forcing the police to kill them. Often referred to in professional circles as "suicide by cop," the cases reviewed for this book suggest that the phenomenon is on the increase. The cases fall into three categories: (1) Those in which individuals with mental issues pose imminent threats to police officers or others compelling the use of deadly force to ad-

---

121. *Graham v. Connor, supra,* at 396.
122. See, e.g., *Pena v. Leombruni,* 200 F.3d 1031 (7th Cir. 1999).

dress the threat; (2) those in which the individuals are known to have mental issues, and clearly demonstrate the intent to make the police kill them; and (3) those in which the circumstances support a strong inference that the individuals intended to achieve that result.

A case to illustrate the first category is *De Boise v. Taser International, et al.*,[123] in which the subject, who suffered from schizophrenia, became delusional one evening and left his home naked. The following morning, he was seen by neighbors roaming through the neighborhood, beating houses with a stick, and claiming to be God. He returned home that night, still naked and delusional, demanded his mother worship him, and held her head to the floor. She eventually managed to leave the house and call 911. Officers from the St. Louis Police Department were dispatched to the house with knowledge that the man was emotionally disturbed, violent, and used physical force against people or property. Upon arriving at the residence the officers were told by De Boise's mother that there was a gun in the house. The officers could hear loud noises coming from the home, including screaming, glass breaking, and heavy furniture being thrown. De Boise then came out of the house, still naked, and was confronted by officers who ordered him to lie face down on the grass. He complied, but when an officer approached him he jumped to his feet with clenched fists. When he ignored repeated commands to lie on the ground one of the officers fired his Taser, which caused De Boise to drop to the ground. But he continued to struggle and ignore the officers' commands. Over the next few minutes De Boise was subjected to 10 Taser discharges. He was then subdued by officers, but went into cardiac arrest and died. A suit in federal court was resolved in favor of the police, and summary judgment was affirmed by the federal appellate court.

The second category of cases is illustrated in *Rice v. Reliast Life Insurance Company*[124] in which a family member called police reporting that his uncle, Gerald Rice, was sitting in his truck with a loaded shotgun to his head and threatening to commit suicide. When officers arrived at the residence they were told that Rice had taken a lot of medication, and that he had a problem with law enforcement. From the kitchen, the officers could see Rice sitting in the truck with a gun to his head, and repeatedly asked him to put the gun down. Rice refused, saying he wanted to come into the kitchen to get a beer. Moments later the officers heard a single gunshot, but quickly determined that Rice had not injured himself. Instead of getting rid of the gun as ordered by the officers,

---

123. 2014 U.S. App. LEXIS 14276 (8th Cir. 2014).
124. 2014 U.S. App. LEXIS 20581 (5th Cir. 2014).

Rice got out of the truck and began walking toward the kitchen saying, "I want to commit suicide." One of the officers fired four shots, striking Rice three times in the chest. Rice died of these wounds. While several issues were raised in the ensuing lawsuit, the federal district court granted summary judgment on the excessive force claim, and the federal appellate court affirmed, stating:

> " ... we hold that [the officer] did not violate Rice's right to be free of excessive force."

In response to the plaintiffs' assertion that Rice did not have the gun in his hand when he entered the kitchen, the court noted that there was an audio recording of the officer shouting for Rice to drop the gun seconds before the fatal shots were fired.

The third category of cases is illustrated in **Penley v. Eslinger, et al.,**[125] (discussed earlier in this chapter) where a 15-year-old boy modified a plastic air pistol to look like a real gun and took it to school. When the boy was confronted by police, he pointed the weapon at officers and was shot. The decision to use deadly force was upheld by the courts. Although there is no clear evidence that the teen was intending to compel the officers to shoot him, it is difficult to escape that conclusion.

**_Facts Discovered after the Event_**. As noted previously, the Supreme Court has held that officers are not required to be *right* in order to be *reasonable*. Obviously, that principle presumes that any error—e.g., the wrong person arrested, the wrong house searched, etc.—was discovered after the action was taken. In other words, after additional or new information was received. There have been several cases—including several discussed above—where law enforcement officers acted on the belief that a suspect was reaching for a firearm, only to discover later that no firearm was present. Two early cases, **Sherrod v. Berry**[126] and **Reese v. Anderson,**[127] are instructive. In the first case, a police officer shot and killed a suspect following a vehicle stop related to a robbery report. The officer fired the fatal shot when he believed the suspect was reaching for a weapon inside the car. No weapon was found. During the ensuing lawsuit against the officer, the jury was permitted to hear the evidence regarding the absence of a weapon. The jury returned a verdict against the officer. On appeal, the appellate court set aside the jury verdict on the ground that it was error to allow evidence that the suspect was unarmed. The court stated:

---

125. 605 F.3d 843 (11th Cir. 2010).
126. 856 F.2d 802 (7th Cir. 1988).
127. 926 F.2d 494 (5th Cir. 1991).

*"When a jury measures the objective reasonableness of an officer's action, it must stand in his shoes and judge the reasonableness of his action based upon the information he possessed ... Knowledge of facts and circumstances gained after the fact (that the suspect was unarmed) has no place in the trial court's or jury's post-hoc analysis...."*[128]

In the second case, the facts were similar. An officer shot a suspect following an armed robbery report and vehicle pursuit when the suspect failed to comply with the officer's commands to keep his hands raised and reached down toward the car seat. Again, it was determined that the suspect was not armed. And similarly the federal appellate court ruled that such information was irrelevant to the determination of reasonableness. The court concluded:

*" ... [the officer's] shooting of [the suspect] was reasonable and not excessive.... also irrelevant is the fact that [the suspect] was actually unarmed."*[129]

Attempts to hold officers accountable for facts they could not have known at the moment they acted, apart from being unfair on its face, ignores the Supreme Court's admonition in *Graham v. Connor* against relying on *"20/20 hindsight."* Several more recent cases discussed earlier in this chapter illustrate the same point: Officers must deal with the facts and circumstances confronting them *"at the moment."*[130]

***Policy Violations.*** In virtually every case where an officer's decision to use deadly force is challenged, plaintiffs attempt to use any evidence that the officer made mistakes or did something wrong as evidence that he violated the Constitution. Most often, the claim is that the officer violated departmental policy. Courts have consistently rejected such claims as not being relevant to the question of whether the officer's actions violated the Constitution. As one federal appellate court explained the point:

*"The issue is whether [the officer] violated the Constitution, not whether he should be disciplined by the local police force."*[131]

---

128. *Sherrod v. Berry, supra,* at 804–5.

129. *Reese v. Anderson, supra,* at 500 & 501.

130. See, e.g., *Luna v. Mullenix,* 2014 U.S. App. LEXIS 24067 (5th Cir. 2014); and *Pollard v. City of Columbus,* 2015 U.S. App. LEXIS 3538 (6th Cir. 2015).

131. *Smith v. Freland,* 954 F.2d 343 (6th Cir. 1992). See also, *Salim v. Proulx,* 93 F.3d 86 (2nd Cir. 1996); *Greenidge v. Ruffin,* 927 F.2d 789 (4th Cir. 1991); *Carter v. Buscher,* 973 F.2d 1328 (7th Cir. 1992); *Mettler v. Whitledge,* 165 F.3d 1197 (8th Cir. 1999); *Scott v. Henrich,* 39 F.3d 912 (9th Cir. 1994); and *Medina v. Cram,* 252 F.3d 1124 (10th Cir. 2001).

The Supreme Court provided some support for this position in *Whren v. United States*,[132] where plainclothes officers in a high-drug area of the District of Columbia observed suspicious behavior from the occupants of a vehicle. Suspecting drug activity, the officers stopped the vehicle ostensibly for a traffic violation, and found illegal drugs in the vehicle. The defendants raised a number of arguments in court in an effort to have the drugs suppressed. The one that is relevant to our purposes was the argument that the stop was a violation of the District of Columbia police regulations. Rejecting the argument that violations of departmental regulations require the suppression of evidence, the Supreme Court countered: "*They cite no holding to that effect....*"

It may be recalled that this issue was raised in *City and County of San Francisco, California, et al. v. Sheehan*,[133] (discussed in Chapter 2) where it was alleged that the officers violated their training. The Supreme Court said:

> "*Indeed, even if an officer acts contrary to her training ... (and here, given the generality of that training, it is not at all clear that [the officers] did so), that does not itself negate qualified immunity where it would otherwise be warranted. Rather, so long as 'a reasonable officer' could have believed that his conduct was justified, a plaintiff cannot avoid summary judgment by simply producing an expert's report that an officer's conduct leading up to a deadly confrontation was imprudent, inappropriate, or even reckless.*"

In *Scott v. Edinburg*,[134] one of the allegations by the plaintiff was that an officer violated his department's policy when he fired a shot into a moving vehicle killing the driver. The policy prohibited "shooting into a moving vehicle" and "the use of deadly force against a non-dangerous fleeing felon." The federal appellate court ruled:

> "*Title 42 U.S.C. 1983 protects plaintiffs from constitutional violations, not violations of state laws, or, in this case, departmental regulations and police practices.*"[135]

No federal court has held otherwise, and the fact that this issue continues to emerge is a tribute to the persistence of some plaintiffs' attorneys.

*Officers' Pre-seizure Conduct*. Another issue often raised is whether an officer's pre-seizure conduct is relevant to a subsequent decision to use deadly force.

---

132. 517 U.S. 806 (1996).
133. 575 U.S. _____ (May 18, 2015) (Slip opinion).
134. 346 F.3d 752 (7th Cir. 2003).
135. *Id.*, at 758.

The argument typically takes one of three strategies: First, officers' pre-seizure conduct <u>allowed</u> the suspect to pose a threat; or second, the officers' pre-seizure conduct <u>provoked</u> the threat; or third, the officers' pre-seizure conduct <u>created</u> the threat.

The strategy of the first example is to shift the focus from the actions of the suspect to the actions of the law enforcement officer, and, in effect, to make the officers responsible for the suspect's actions as well as their own. The strategy of the second example is to suggest that the suspect would never have been inclined to pose a threat but for the provocation of the officers' actions; and the third asserts that the officers' pre-seizure conduct created a threat that was never intended by the suspect.

All three strategies have to overcome the basic premise that the Fourth Amendment applies to "*seizures*," and that what occurs outside the context of a seizure is simply not relevant. We refer again to the **Sheehan** case discussed above, where the Supreme Court stated:

> *Indeed, even if [the officers] misjudged the situation, [the plaintiff] cannot establish a Fourth Amendment violation based merely on bad tactics that result in a deadly confrontation that would have been avoided.*

As the Supreme Court clearly stated in **Graham v. Connor**, the focus is on the facts and circumstances confronting officers "*at the moment*" they made a decision to use a particular level of force. The following cases illustrate how lower courts have applied this principle.

In **Plakas v. Drinski** the federal appellate court declined to review the officer's actions preceding the deadly confrontation to determine if the actions were proper.[136] The court expressed the view that such a review would "*nearly always reveal that something different could have been done if the officer knew the future before it occurred.*"[137] The court then addressed the suggestion that the officer's actions preceding the seizure "caused" the problem:

> "*Other than random attacks, all such cases begin with the decision of a police officer to do something, to help, to arrest, to inquire. If the officer had decided to do nothing, then no force would have been used. In this sense, the police always causes the trouble. But it is trouble which the police officer is sworn to cause, which society pays him to cause, and which, if kept within constitutional limits, society praises the officer for causing.*"[138]

---

136. *Supra.*
137. *Id.*, at 1150.
138. *Id.*

A second case provides further insight. In **Carter v. Buscher** police officers devised a plan to arrest a man who had contracted to have his wife killed.[139] The arrest plan went awry, and the suspect opened fire on the police, killing one officer and wounding another before being killed himself. The deceased suspect's wife (the intended victim of the murder plot!) sued the police alleging that " ... *by reason of their ill conceived plan ... the [officers] ... provoked a situation whereby unreasonable deadly force was used in an attempt to seize [the suspect]*."[140] Observing that "*pre-seizure conduct is not subject to Fourth Amendment scrutiny*," and that no seizure occurred until the suspect was shot, the court concluded:

> "*Even if [the officers] concocted a dubious scheme to bring about [the suspect's] arrest, it is the arrest itself and not the scheme that must be scrutinized under the Fourth Amendment.*"[141]

The point of these decisions is that the Fourth Amendment prohibits "unreasonable seizures," and police actions that precede the "seizure" are beyond the bounds of the Fourth Amendment.[142]

A case that addresses the second strategy that officers' pre-seizure conduct provoked a threat is **Davis v. Romer**,[143] in which Officer J. Romer attempted to execute an arrest warrant on Charal Thomas, who was sitting in the driver's seat of his vehicle. Thomas refused to get out of his vehicle, and when Officer Romer reached inside the driver's window, Thomas suddenly began driving away. Officer Romer jumped on the vehicle's running board and ordered Thomas to stop, but Thomas ignored the order and continued to drive toward the entrance to the freeway. Officer Romer, who was still standing on the running board of the vehicle, drew his weapon and fatally shot Thomas. A lawsuit followed, and Officer Romer moved for summary judgment that was granted. On appeal, it was argued that Officer Romer *caused* the dangerous encounter by grabbing the vehicle and jumping on the running board of the vehicle. The appellate court explicitly rejected that argument and observed:

> "*Here, the [evidence] demonstrates that Romer was standing by the driver's door when Thomas suddenly drove to the left with Romer's arm in-*

---

139. 973 F.2d 1328 (7th Cir. 1993).

140. *Id.*, at 1330.

141. *Id.*, at 1333.

142. For additional cases on this point, see, *Napier v. Town of Windham*, 187 F.3d 177 (1st Cir. 1999); *Salim v. Proulx*, 93 F.3d 86 (2nd Cir. 1996); *Greenidge v. Ruffin*, 927 F.2d 789 (4th Cir. 1991); *Fraire v. Arlington*, 957 F.2d 1268 (5th Cir. 1992); *Mettler v. Whitledge*, 165 F.3d 1197 (8th Cir. 1999); *Menuel v. City of Atlanta*, 25 F.3d 990 (11th Cir. 1994).

143. 2015 U.S. App. LEXIS 1714 (5th Cir. 2015).

*side the vehicle. Moreover, it is undisputed that Romer was standing on the running board of the vehicle as it was being driven on the service road and headed toward the freeway. Clearly, Thomas's actions put the officer in harm's way, and there was a very real danger that Romer would sustain serious injury or death."*

The third strategy described above, that an officer's pre-seizure conduct actually *created the threat*, typically arises in cases involving vehicles where the argument is that an officer stepped into the path of a moving vehicle, creating a threat that was not intended by the driver. A typical case is **McGrath v. Tavares, et al.**,[144] where two officers responding to a burglary alarm at a liquor store attempted to stop a suspicious vehicle. During a high-speed chase the suspect failed to make a turn and crashed into a stone. When the two officers got out of their vehicles and attempted to arrest the suspect, he revved his engine and maneuvered his vehicle in reverse between the two police cars. When ordered repeatedly to stop and get out of the vehicle, he eventually revved his car's engine and accelerated forward towards one of the officers, who fired two shots, striking the suspect in the arm but not stopping him. As the suspect drove in the direction of the second officer, two more shots were fired and the suspect, a 16-year-old boy, was fatally wounded.

In the ensuing lawsuit against the officers, the federal district granted summary judgment to the officers, and the appellate court affirmed, observing:

*"At the moment when the shot were fired, all that a reasonable officer could have concluded was that [the driver] was intent on resuming his flight and that ... he would once again pose a deadly threat for [the officers, as well as for] others on the road."*

These cases clearly illustrate the principle that an officer's pre-seizure conduct is irrelevant in assessing the constitutionality of the seizure itself. As one federal appellate court explained it:

*"The fact that an officer negligently gets himself into a dangerous situation will not make it unreasonable for him to use force to defend himself ... Thus, even if an officer provokes a violent response, that negligent act will not transform an otherwise reasonable subsequent use of force into a Fourth Amendment violation."*[145]

---

144. 2014 U.S. App. LEXIS 14776 (1st Cir. 2014).
145. *Hennessey v. Smith*, 292 F.3d 1177 (9th Cir. 2002).

# The Perspective of a Reasonable Officer on the Scene

Perhaps the most important language in the *Graham* decision is the emphasis on the need to review the constitutionality of an officer's decision to use a particular level of force *"from the perspective of a reasonable officer on the scene."*[146] The Supreme Court noted in earlier decisions that a law enforcement officer's perspective is unique, observing in one case:

> *" ... when used by trained law enforcement officers, objective facts, meaningless to the untrained ... [may permit] inferences and deductions that might well elude an untrained person."*[147]

The uniqueness of that perspective is the product of an officer's knowledge, training, and experience regarding numerous practical factors that are fully discussed in subsequent chapters of this book. Those practical factors are not only critical to an officer's ability to make an appropriate decision regarding the use of force, they are equally critical to any fair and realistic assessment of an officer's decision in an administrative review, in a court of law, or in the court of public opinion.

# The Due Process Standard

Both the Fifth and Fourteenth Amendments prohibit deprivation of " ... *of life, liberty, or property, without due process of law...."*

The duplication of this "due process" guarantee stems from the fact that the Fifth Amendment, as adopted in 1791, applied solely to the federal government, while the Fourteenth Amendment was adopted in 1868 for the specific purpose of imposing constraints on the powers of the states. It is the same standard but with different applications.

At the time it was included in the Constitution "due process" would have been a familiar expression to anyone conversant with English and American history. Although it did not enumerate specific rights, it came to be synonymous with the "law of the land" mentioned in Magna Carta in 1215, and embodied the principle that a person could not be subjected to governmental actions affect-

---

146. *Supra*, at 396.
147. *United States v. Cortez*, 449 U.S. 411, at 418 (1980).

ing his life, liberty, and property without some *legal process*. It was highly valued by those who espoused the need for bulwarks against the arbitrary power of government, but it was viewed as a general expression of principle rather than a guarantee of anything specific. By the early twentieth century, the clause had come to encompass *substantive* rights as well as procedural rights, as the Court began incorporating specific guarantees found in the Bill of Rights (and some that were not), making them applicable to the states through the Fourteenth Amendment. No longer was due process viewed as a guarantee of a legal process before one could be deprived of life, liberty, or property. It now meant that one was protected from unreasonable searches and seizures (the Fourth Amendment), which included the protections against excessive force. Without these developments, the scope of this book would be almost entirely limited to federal law enforcement officers.

But due process meant more than just the incorporation of other provisions of the Bill of Rights. The concept of due process had a meaning of its own, independent of those specific provisions enshrined in the Bill of Rights. We've already noted that the Fourth Amendment protects the rights of the people against *unreasonable seizures*—e.g., arrests and investigative detentions—while the Eighth Amendment protects convicted prisoners against *cruel and unusual punishments*. Put simply, the Due Process Clause applies to whatever is left.

The U.S. Supreme Court has frequently noted the generalized nature of the due process guarantee. Recently, the Court acknowledged that the "*guideposts for responsible decision making in this unchartered area are scarce and open-ended*."[148] Throughout the twentieth century, the Court struggled to come up with some semblance of a workable definition. Those efforts produced some remarkable formulations such as " *... those principles that are so rooted in traditions and conscience of our people as to be ranked as fundamental*";[149] and those principles that are "*implicit in the concept of ordered liberty*."[150] Other formulations followed, but none advanced the cause of clarity. One of the most memorable, but equally ambiguous efforts came in the 1952 Supreme Court case of ***Rochin v. California*** where Justice Frankfurter wrote that any governmental action that "shocked the conscience" would constitute a violation of due process.[151] The good Justice did not specify whose conscience was supposed to be shocked. This lack of precision has prompted the Court to limit its ap-

---

148. *Albright v. Oliver*, 510 U.S. 271, 272 (1994).
149. *Snyder v. Massachusetts*, 291 U.S. 97 (1934).
150. *Palko v. Connecticut*, 302 U.S. 319, at 325 (1937).
151. 342 U.S. 165 (1952).

plication to those circumstances where there is no other "*explicit textual source of constitutional protection against a particular sort of intrusive governmental conduct.*"[152]

The critical nature of law enforcement decisions regarding the use of deadly force imposes the need for the clearest possible constitutional guidance. A lack of clarity can lead to excesses of caution or zeal—to the detriment of officers' legitimate concerns for their safety and of the rights of citizens. Fortunately, recent court decisions shed more light on the kinds of conduct likely to violate due process. A significant refinement of this standard came in the 1998 Supreme Court decision in *County of Sacramento v. Lewis*.[153] Although this is not a use-of-force case *per se*, the Court's refinement of the due process standard is relevant.

Lewis was the passenger on a motorcycle being pursued by officers for speeding. In the course of the pursuit, the motorcycle tipped over, dumping Lewis onto the highway and into the pathway of the pursuing police car. A lawsuit brought by his estate against the officers and the department under Title 42, U.S. Code, Section 1983, alleged violation of Lewis's Fourth Amendment right to be free from unreasonable seizure and his Fourteenth Amendment due process right to life.

The federal district court granted summary judgment to the officers and the department on the grounds that no Fourth Amendment seizure occurred since the officers did not intend to seize Lewis by running over him, and the plaintiff failed to cite any case to support the view that high-speed police pursuits were governed by the due process standard.

The federal appellate court reversed the trial court's decision with respect to the due process issue, ruling that high-speed pursuits were encompassed in the constitutional provision. The court then concluded that due process would be violated if the police conduct displayed a "deliberate indifference or reckless disregard" for a person's right to life or personal safety.

The Supreme Court agreed that due process is the appropriate constitutional provision to govern high-speed pursuits, but rejected the appellate court's view that "*deliberate indifference*" is the correct standard. Conceding that "deliberate indifference" would be the appropriate standard in some circumstances, the Court observed that such could only be true when *actual deliberation* is practicable. For example, the Court explained that claims of inadequate medical care for pre-trial detainees must be viewed differently from claims that of-

---

152. *Graham v. Connor*, 490 U.S. 386, 395 (1989).
153. 118 S.Ct. 1708 (1998).

ficers used excessive force in response to a violent disturbance. In the former case, there is time and opportunity for "deliberation," whereas, in the latter instance, police *"are supposed to act decisively and to show restraint at the same moment, and their decisions have to be made in haste, under pressure, and frequently without the luxury of a second chance."* [154] In such circumstances, " ... *only a purpose to cause harm* [emphasis added] *unrelated to the legitimate object of arrest will satisfy the element of arbitrary conduct shocking to the conscience, necessary for a due process violation."* [155] Applying this standard to the facts, the Court concluded that even if the officers' decision to engage in and continue the high-speed pursuit *"offended the reasonableness held up by tort law or the balance struck in law enforcement's own codes of sound practice ..."* [156] it did not violate due process.

To the extent that this decision appears to establish a "subjective" standard for due process violations, as opposed to the "objective" standard that governs Fourth Amendment violations, that notion was dispelled in the recent Supreme Court decision in ***Kingsley v. Hendrickson, et al.*** [157] The issue in that case was "whether, to prove an excessive force claim, a pretrial detainee must show that the officers were *subjectively* aware that their use of force was unreasonable, or only that the officers' use of that force was *objectively* unreasonable."

The facts involve a pretrial detainee, Kingsley, awaiting trial in county jail. One evening during a cell check an officer noticed a piece of paper covering the light fixture above Kingsley's bed, and ordered him to remove it. He refused to do so despite several commands. He was told that officers would remove the paper and that he would be moved to a receiving cell in the interim. When four officers came to carry out the task, Kingsley refused their commands to stand, put his hands behind his back, and back up to the door. Despite his wishes, he was cuffed, removed from the cell, and placed face down on a bunk in a receiving cell with his hands cuffed behind his back. What happened next is disputed. The officers claim that he resisted their efforts to remove the handcuffs. Kingsley denies that, and claims that one officer put his knee in Kingsley's back, then slammed his head into the concrete bunk. There is no dispute that an officer applied a Taser to Kingsley's back for about five seconds, and left him cuffed in his cell for 15 minutes. He filed suit against several officers for using excessive force in violation of the Due Process Clause of the Fourteenth Amendment.

---

154. *Id.*, at 1720.
155. *Id.*, at 1711–12.
156. *Id.*, at 1721.
157. 576 U.S. _____(2015).

The question presented to the Supreme Court was whether the requirements of an excessive force claim brought by a pretrial detainee "must satisfy a subjective standard or only the objective one." Notwithstanding the Court's decision in *County of Sacramento v. Lewis*, which seemed to apply a subjective standard by holding that " *... only a purpose to cause harm ...*" would violate the Due Process Clause, the Court in *Kingsley* held that courts must use an objective standard: " *... a pretrial detainee must show that the force purposely or knowingly used against him <u>was objectively unreasonable</u>.*" In addressing "*a legally requisite state of mind*" the Court identified two questions:

> "*The first concerns the defendant's state of mind with respect to his physical acts ... The second question concerns the defendant's state of mind with respect to whether his use of force was 'excessive'... Thus, the defendant's state of mind is not a matter that a plaintiff is required to prove... [A] pretrial detainee must show only that the force purposely or knowingly used against him was objectively unreasonable.*"

If this reads like the Fourth Amendment standard enunciated in *Graham v. Connor*, the Court's explanation reinforces that idea. For example, the Court cites *Graham* in explaining that a court cannot apply this standard mechanically. "*Rather, objective reasonableness turns on the 'facts and circumstances of each particular case.'*" And, "*A court must make this determination from the perspective of a reasonable officer on the scene, including what the officer knew at the time, not with the 20/20 vision of hindsight.*"

The Court offered the following factors that could bear on the issue of reasonableness regarding the degree of force used against a pretrial detainee:

(1) The relationship between the need for force and the amount of force used;
(2) The extent of the detainee's injuries;
(3) Any effort made by the officer to temper or to limit the amount of force;
(4) The severity of the security problem;
(5) The threat reasonably perceived by the officer; and
(6) Whether the detainee was actively resisting.

The Court split 5–4 in the *Kingsley* decision, and it remains to be seen what the impact will be. It should be noted that the Court did not reverse the decision in *County of Sacramento v. Lewis*, instead going to some lengths to reconcile the apparent differences. This decision continues a theme established in other Supreme Court decisions where the issue was the constitutionality of an officer's decision taken under circumstances that are "*tense, uncertain, and rapidly evolving—about the amount of force that is necessary in a particular sit-*

*uation*." Just as with the Fourth Amendment standard, the due process standard gives considerable deference to an officer's judgment in high-stress and fast-moving situations. Accordingly, the Court distinguishes between those instances when there are "*extended opportunities to do better*" and those when "*unforeseen circumstances demand an officer's instant judgment....*" In the latter instance, "*even precipitate recklessness fails to inch close enough to harmful purpose*" to shock the conscience.

<u>*The Duty to Intervene*</u>. This issue typically arises in cases where an individual has been arrested and secured, an officer uses excessive force against the arrestee, and other officers on the scene do not intervene to protect the arrestee. A relevant case is ***Simcoe v. Gray, et al.***,[158] where the plaintiff alleged that after he had been arrested and handcuffed, and while lying on the ground, Officer Gray repeatedly smashed his face into the ground and stood on his hands after he was handcuffed, and that other officers failed to intervene. The federal district court granted summary judgment to the officers on all of the issues, including the failure to intervene claim, and the federal appellate court reversed based on disputed facts regarding the use of excessive force and the failure to intervene. Regarding the latter the court wrote:

> *It is widely recognized that all law enforcement officials have an affirmative duty to intervene to protect the constitutional rights of citizens from infringement by other law enforcement officers in their presence ... and a police officer is liable for failing to intercede when excessive force is being used when there was 'a realistic opportunity to intervene to prevent the harm from occurring.'* (Citing *Anderson v. Branen*, 17 F.3d 552, 557 (2d Cir. 1994).[159]

The duty to intervene has emerged in both Fourth Amendment and due process cases, depending on the context of the actions. The same is true of the duty to provide medical care.

<u>*The Duty to Provide Medical Care*</u>. As long ago as 1983, the U.S. Supreme Court held that the Fourteenth Amendment Due Process Clause requires government officials to provide medical care to those who have been injured during arrest by police.[160] A recent application of this rule is found in ***Valderrama v. Rousseau, et al.***[161] The case involved a vehicle stop in the early morning hours.

---

158. 2014 U.S. App. LEXIS 16588 (2nd Cir. 2014).

159. See, *Robinson v. Payton, et al.*, 2015 U.S. App. LEXIS 11049 (8th Cir. 2015); and *Goodwin v. City of Painesville, et al.*, 2015 U.S. App. LEXIS 4417 (6th Cir. 2015).

160. *City of Revere v. Mass. Gen. Hosp.*, 463 U.S. 239, (1983).

161. 2015 U.S. App. LEXIS (11th Cir. 2015).

For reasons not altogether clear, Detective Rousseau shot the passenger in the genitals. A lawsuit was filed against Detective Rousseau and two other officers alleging, among other things, deliberate indifference to his medical needs. This claim was based on the fact that there was a delay of approximately three and a half minutes between the shooting and the call for an ambulance. Furthermore, the call for an ambulance did not report a gunshot but a laceration. A gunshot wound would have been given higher priority, and the ambulance would have arrived at least seven minutes sooner. A lawsuit was filed against the officers, alleging, among other claims, deliberate indifference to his serious medical needs. The officers were granted summary judgment on all of the claims except that of deliberate indifference to his medical needs. On this issue, the appellate court held: "*We conclude there is evidence from which a reasonable jury could find that [the officers] disregarded the risk of serious harm the gunshot wound presented.*"[162]

When a law enforcement officer makes the decision to use deadly force, it is to be expected, and must be accepted, that the decision will be closely scrutinized at various levels. At the same time, the officers who bear the burden of making such grave decisions have the right to expect that their actions will be judged fairly and objectively. As the foregoing legal discussion illustrates, that expectation is generally met in the courts where long-established constitutional principles, interpreted in the light of practical realities confronting law enforcement officers, balance the interests of society and the individual.

The protection of the lives and safety of those who enforce the law is the responsibility of the society that gives them that mission and reaps the benefit of that service. The nature of law enforcement dictates that officers will continue to be exposed to risks of death and injury while performing their duties. It is important to recognize that the Constitution and law of the land do not require officers to assume risks beyond those inherent in the job.

---

162. See also, *Scozzari v. Miedzianowski, et al.*, 2012 U.S. App. LEXIS (6th Cir. 2012); and *Cornejo v. City of Los Angeles, et al.*, 2015 U.S. App. LEXIS 12743 (9th Cir. 2015).

# Chapter 4

# The Use of Deadly Force

A definition: Deadly force is " … *force that creates a significant risk of death.*"[1]

Law enforcement officers are not trained to take no action to protect themselves and others. To the contrary, they are trained that they have a duty to protect themselves and others. In balancing the concept of "no action" against the concept of a "duty to perform," we must remember that law enforcement officers are trained and practiced to protect themselves and the public. They are expected to be proactive in the pursuit of their duty.

The training provided to law enforcement officers stresses that they must recognize risks of imminent death or serious injury and react to protect themselves and others. Law and good policy are uniform.[2] "Law enforcement and correctional officers … may use deadly force only when necessary, that is, when the officer has a reasonable belief that the subject of such force poses an imminent danger of death or serious physical injury to the officer or to another person."[3]

Therefore, to justify a use of deadly force, it must (1) be necessary to prevent or end (2) an imminent danger of death or serious injury[4] that the offi-

---

1. *Miller v. Clark County*, 340 F.3d 959, 963 (9th Cir. 2003).

2. Unremarkable in that law enforcement policy is subsidiary to, reflective of, and governed by the law to a degree unparalleled in other professions. Good policy closely mirrors the law—bad policy does not. See Chapter 11 for a wider discussion.

3. U.S. Department of Justice Policy Statement: Use of Deadly Force.

4. The Supreme Court has provided the justification for using deadly force as probable cause to believe there is an imminent threat of serious physical harm. Simply stated, a threat of serious physical harm justifies the use of force that creates a significant risk of death. To say, as most deadly force policies do (DOJ a case in point) that deadly force may be used to prevent an imminent risk of *death or serious injury* is an unnecessary formulation. Serious injury alone is the harmful consequence that deadly force may be used to prevent—death is but *the most serious* end product of serious injury. The phrase "death or serious injury" has assumed a totemic status, repeated mechanically and without discernment or distinction. It is a talisman that incorporates all the injurious consequences that justify a use of deadly force. But death is a symptom of serious injury—admittedly the most dire of all. Other examples of symptoms of serious injury would be loss of an eye, broken leg, ruptured spleen, bleeding, etc. and symptoms do not need to be enumerated to justify the use of

cer has reason to believe exists and that (3) imperils self or others. Hence, deadly force is "necessary" under the DOJ policy when there is a reasonable belief that there exists an "imminent danger" of death or serious injury. Notice that there is no reference to the means available to counter that "imminent danger." The policy is consistent with the constitutional standard that does not require officers to consider alternative levels of force once the "imminent danger" element is satisfied. It is the reasonable belief in the "imminent danger" that creates the "necessity" for deadly force because only deadly force promises to be effective enough within the crucial time constraints needed to protect against imminent danger.

"Imminent" means simply that the danger could happen at any moment—it need not have happened, or be happening yet, but *could* happen at any moment. "Reasonable belief," like "probable cause," is a level of belief that is the constitutional standard of a "reason to believe" that in turn must arise from the perceptions, knowledge, experience, and reasonable inferences of the officer at the moment the decision is made to use deadly force.

The best use of justified deadly force is preemptive. That means that it is timely enough, and effective enough, to prevent an *imminent* risk of serious injury (about to happen) from becoming a *definite* attempt to cause serious injury (in fact happening). Often, the decision to use deadly force is not timely enough to be preemptive (for any number of reasons such as hesitation, the action/reaction cycle, surprise attack, etc.). Then the justified use of deadly force can only be preventive in nature—intended to stop the actual attempt to cause injury, or the real infliction of injury, from continuing.

An analysis of a decision to use deadly force by a law enforcement officer must look at what the officer knew or reasonably believed at the moment the decision was made. The issue is whether the officer's belief that there was an imminent danger of serious injury to self or others was a reasonable one based on what was known and what was reasonably inferred by the officer. The first issue to address is whether the perception of imminent danger at the moment that the decision was made to shoot was reasonable.[5]

---

deadly force. The authors do recognize the traditional eminence of the phrase "death or serious injury" and we understand that it is not incorrect. Nevertheless, in the interests of clarity and simplicity of concept, we will resist the allure of the incantation and limit ourselves as much as possible to the Supreme Court's phrasing of the standard: *deadly force may be used to prevent the imminent risk of serious injury.*

5. The necessity for an officer to make nearly instantaneous decisions in order to best protect his life or the life of others under urgent, dire, and extremely stressful conditions is accepted and well recognized throughout law enforcement practice, training, and policy. For example: "Determining whether deadly force is necessary may involve instantaneous

Law enforcement officers are trained to recognize a variety of danger signals that are indicative of an imminent attack, such as non-compliance with orders, presence of a weapon, or unseen hands, to name a few. Situational context is an important factor. Proximity is another. The law enforcement officer invariably and necessarily must approach in order to interact and do his job. The likelihood of being actually shot, struck, or successfully hit by an assailant increases exponentially as distance decreases.[6] The actions of the person being confronted are a factor that can be especially acute when a basic understanding of the nature of the individual is present. (See Chapter 8 for an extended discussion of tactical factors.)

There is no mandate in the law to run through a laundry list of various force options. There is no mandate in the law that preordains a sequence of actions prior to the use of deadly force. The question is, and must be: Was the officer objectively reasonable in his perception that the individual posed a reasonable risk of imminent injury or death? Nevertheless, there are two lesser force options that are regarded as preconditions to using deadly force in the popular conception of self-defense as embodied in the Hollywood stereotype: verbal warnings and warning shots.

Law enforcement officers are trained to issue a verbal warning when feasible, i.e., when taking the time to issue such a warning will not delay the use of deadly force to such an extent that it increases the risk of death or serious injury. There are important caveats regarding verbal warnings. The first is that

---

decisions that encompass many factors, such as the likelihood that the subject will use deadly force on the officer or others if such force is not used by the officer; the officer's knowledge that the subject will likely acquiesce in arrest or recapture if the officer uses lesser force or no force at all; the capabilities of the subject; the subject's access to cover and weapons; the presence of other persons who may be at risk if force is or is not used; and the nature and the severity of the subject's criminal conduct or the danger posed."
U.S. Department of Justice Commentary Regarding the Use of Deadly Force in Non-Custodial Situations; Section III, Principles on Use of Deadly Force.

6. For a clear example of this, consider the law enforcement officers killed by firearms in the 14-year period of 1999–2014. A total of 746 officers were killed with firearms in that period. 495 of them were killed at a distance of 10 feet or less (64.7%)—354 of those inside five feet (46.3%). 162 were killed between 11 and 50 feet (21.2%) and 48 (6.3%) were killed at distances greater than 50 feet.

Source: A compendium of the FBI Uniform Crime Reports "Law Enforcement Officers Killed & Assaulted" for the years 1999–2014.

This statistical example does not include officers killed with vehicles, knives, personal weapons, etc., all of which require close proximity to be used successfully. The point to be stressed is that the likelihood of injury and death in the event of an attack significantly increases as distance decreases. That is an unavoidable risk for all law enforcement officers, and a risk factor they are regularly trained to recognize.

there should be a high probability that deadly force may be warranted in the first place or else there would be no cause to even consider a warning. Otherwise, the verbal warning is nothing more than a bluff. Law enforcement officers are trained that if the situation does not merit the use of deadly force, they are no more justified warning of it than they would be actually using it. In fact, issuing a verbal warning is nothing more than an attempt to utilize a lesser force option in a deadly force situation.

A second caveat is that the issuance of a warning must be left to the discretion of the officer. The officer may or may not attempt a verbal warning prior to using deadly force, or even while engaged in using deadly force. But the absence of a warning is not a measure of the reasonableness or the justification for the use of deadly force, especially in incidents where the onset of the threat is immediate and unmistakable in the perception of the officer involved. The only mention of verbal warnings in the law is in the specific context of using deadly force to prevent the escape of a dangerous person (see Chapter 3). There is no other legal basis for it.

Whereas verbal warnings have some limited foundation in the law, warning shots have no basis in the law whatsoever. If a warning shot causes an injury, it does not implicate the Fourth Amendment unless it was clearly foreseeable and intentional. That would seem to put a warning shot in the same constitutional category as an unintentional discharge—no violation of a constitutional right. And there would be no due process implication unless it represented a reckless disregard for harmful consequences.

In practical terms, there are serious tactical and situational issues that argue against firing warning shots. First, it is inconceivable to consider a warning shot unless the need to use deadly force is reasonably imminent in the first place—same as with verbal warnings. So a warning shot is similar to a verbal warning in that it represents a lesser level of force used in hopes of preempting the necessity to use deadly force in a situation that already justifies deadly force—a manifestation of hope that the additional delay and the waste of ammunition will be enough to prevent serious injury. In addition, a warning shot is an uncontrolled, unaimed shot in violation of the firearms training principle to *know* where a shot is going. It can result in unintended, unanticipated consequences. (Chapter 6 expands on warning shots.)

It is unreasonable to expect any law enforcement officer to allow an attacker a fair chance to prevail either through greater skill, strength, or mere chance. The officer is not expected to gamble his life or physical safety on the whimsy of chance. Issuance of verbal warnings or waiting to see what happens next are options, but options that delay the use of deadly force. If the delay is to the extent that it substantially increases the possibility of significant harm to self or others, then it is neither feasible nor reasonable.

In reality, the decision to delay the otherwise justifiable use of deadly force in hopes that lesser means will fortuitously prevail is a common occurrence throughout law enforcement. Frequently, police officers will delay using deadly force preemptively, although it is clearly justified. They hold off until the risk of death or injury evolves beyond imminent to actual, with consequences detrimental to their own safety. Law enforcement officers commonly take on far greater risk to their personal safety than is necessary under the dictates of law, policy, or training. The officer almost always recognizes that there is an imminent risk, i.e., the person "could be reaching for a gun," but delays the use of deadly force until a weapon is sighted or an attack is actually initiated and the risk suddenly transforms from "imminent" to "present." Those decisions are within the individual officer's discretion, although arguably unreasonable in view of the potential consequences.[7]

As the legal discussion in Chapter 3 clearly illustrates, the Supreme Court has established the outer limits for the lawful use of deadly force, and described two distinct circumstances where such force may be used: First, *defense of self and others* from an imminent threat of serious injury; and second, arrest or *prevention of escape* of a "dangerous" individual. Law enforcement agencies must then establish their respective deadly force policies within the boundaries of those limits

As a rule, many, if not most, choose to limit *by policy* the permissible use of deadly force to a point defined within the outer bounds delineated by the U.S. Supreme Court rather than reach to the very outer limits constitutionally allowed. For example, in 1995 the U.S. Department of Justice (DOJ) adopted a deadly force policy that included a fully undiluted "defense of self and others" concept. The DOJ policy restricted the use of deadly force to prevent es-

---

7. Of interest is the fact that most police officers who have been assaulted and injured or nearly killed are far more likely to act sooner to dispel an imminent risk. That is how good training and personal experience reinforce each other to better promote reasonable perception of imminent danger in time to consider a use of force at a more propitious stage of the incident. Most police officers have not directly experienced an injury or near death in a violent incident, and many do not recognize an imminent risk of death or injury when it is in fact reasonable to do so. The tendency is to deny and delay until the risk is manifest and no longer merely imminent. One aspect of deadly force training involves educating police officers that "imminent risk" is reasonable and real much sooner in a confrontation than they may realize. The training is intended to inculcate an understanding that they can incur risk unnecessarily, certainly sooner than they think—and although doing so is within their discretion, they should do so out of informed choice, not ignorance.

cape to incidents in which the suspect's escape would pose an imminent danger of death or serious injury. This limitation by policy is far more restrictive than the constitutional authorization for use of deadly force to prevent escape of a dangerous person. There is no requirement in the standard prescribed by the Supreme Court for an imminent danger of death or serious injury posed by the escape. The effect of this limitation is that there can be no "prevention of escape" justification that would not already be justified "in defense of self or others."[8] It is not at all clear when a dangerous person's *escape* could be realistically deemed to pose an imminent danger; and, assuming that such a peculiar circumstance could be determined, it adds nothing to the authority to use deadly force that is not already encompassed by the defense-of-self-or-others clause.[9]

By extension, the DOJ policy became the deadly force policy for all DOJ subordinate agencies, including the Federal Bureau of Investigation (FBI). The FBI recognized the potential for confusion in attempting to interpret and apply the prevention-of-escape provision and insisted on an interpretation of the defense-of-self-or-others clause that would permit its agents to use deadly force when necessary to prevent escape of individuals *from the scene of violent confrontations during which those subjects inflicted or attempted infliction of death or serious physical injury* (language of the policy). It was the FBI's contention that such an interpretation was consistent with the imminent danger concept and should not be governed by the prevention-of-escape provision. This variant was approved by the DOJ for inclusion in the FBI's version of the deadly force policy.

The threat of serious injury must be a reasonable perception on the part of the officer at the time the decision to employ deadly force is made *in defense of self or others*. The use of deadly force to prevent the escape of a dangerous subject is different, as discussed below. It is not necessary that death or serious injury occur prior to the use of deadly force. It is not necessary that attempts to inflict a death or serious injury have occurred. Nor is it pertinent if post-incident analysis reveals that no actual attempts to inflict serious injury were made. An assessment of the justification for the use of deadly force must be made solely based upon the perceptions of the officer (or officers) involved at the

---

8. This paradox caused considerable pressure to be brought to bear by federal law enforcement components, including the FBI. DOJ responded to the controversy in 2004 by simply eliminating references to "prevention of escape" in the policy.

9. There are other problems with the formulation of this aspect of the policy. See Chapter 3 for an examination of the DOJ policy and the nonsensical, if not paradoxical, implications of the policy regarding prevention of escape.

time the decision was made to use deadly force, and viewed through a prism of objective factors which define a threat and appropriate responses.

The essential elements to be considered are the inherent danger reasonably perceived at the time and the physical realities that apply at the time. These physical realities include the factors of action versus reaction times, the abilities of the involved parties, the limited time available to recognize, react, initiate, and implement a response, the sensory distortions that will occur in any high-stress, life-threatening incident, and the limited means available to compel a timely halt to the threatening activity. These elements must be judged from the perspective of a reasonable officer under the particular circumstances and not with the application of 20/20 hindsight.

In examining the use of force in a specific incident, it is helpful to break down the assessment into the interrelated factors. First, was the officer's perception of danger reasonable? This analysis will assess the situation and circumstances of the incident in question from the point of view of the officer, including what was reasonably known about the individual, the time and location of the incident, and the individual's behavior. Compliance with verbal orders and visual cues is a critical indicator of potential danger during an incident. Noncompliance with commands or instructions is a common precursor to resistance or violence. Recognition of and reaction to visual cues are equally important factors, although frequently overlooked. Visual cues include obvious manifestations such as a marked police car with its emergency lights activated, or a uniformed police officer with weapon in hand making hand gestures. They may also include more subtle signals such as a law enforcement officer walking towards an individual and reaching for his arm. Police training universally recognizes noncompliance as a danger signal.

The intent or the mental state of the adversary being confronted is a frequent, and mistaken, element offered as a mitigating factor in examining the justification of the use of deadly force. However, there is no way the officer involved can have knowledge of intent beyond what the adversary's actions lead him to reasonably believe. Thus an examination of the causative factors for an officer's judgment, decision-making, and resultant actions must rest on the officer's reasonable perceptions based on what the individual actually did. Intent, mental state, or "competence" is irrelevant, except to the extent that observable mental state in the form of anger, rage, or determination will support the reasonable perception of danger. However, it is absolutely unnecessary for an individual to be mentally competent in order to pose a reasonable threat. Actual mental state is irrelevant to any determination of reasonableness in the use of deadly force.

*"Very little mentation* [sic] *is required for deadly action. A rattlesnake is deadly but could not form the mental state required for conviction of murder."*[10]

(See Chapter 3 for legal issues regarding mental capacity and Chapter 9 for a discussion of suicide by cop—perhaps the most frequent situation in which mental capacity becomes the basis for allegations of unreasonableness.)

Second, was it reasonable for the officer to believe that the threat of death or serious injury was imminent? It must be emphasized that this discussion is focused on the use of force in defense of self and others. Imminence of threat is not relevant to the use of deadly force to prevent escape of a dangerous subject. Prevention of escape is justifiable as a last resort measure to protect pursuing officers and unknown citizens from the danger of a "dangerous person" at large.

Assessing the factor of imminent threat in self-defense situations requires an examination of a number of issues from the perspective of the officer. Among these are the likelihood of a weapon being present, the capability of that weapon, the proximity of the parties at risk relative to the weapon's capability, the exposure of the officer or others, the adversary's actions independently of any weaponry and the likelihood of injury if those actions continue unabated, the realities of action versus reaction, and the limited effectiveness of the means at hand.

"Imminent threat" is a critical concept underlying the justified use of deadly force. It is a concept that is not simple in its definition (that the danger could happen at any moment—it does not have to have happened, or be happening yet, but *could* happen at any moment) and yet dependent upon an inter-related accumulation of physical realities and characteristics that complicate the application of the concept to the assessment of a use of deadly force. Although not reflected in case law, in the separate public sphere of community support, media understanding and policy influences, "imminent threat" is perhaps the single most misunderstood, misconstrued and abused factor underlying the assessment of a use of deadly force. And ultimately, the public sphere will exert influence on the legal sphere.

Disputes over the meaning and application of "imminent threat" are the basis for most, if not all, public disagreements regarding the justification of a police use of deadly force. The allegations invariably center on the assertion that

---

10. *Pena v. Leombruni*, 200 F.3d 1031 (7th Cir. 1999). This particular quote from Chapter 3 is repeated here because it is a favorite of the authors, and it nicely encapsulates the relevance of mental state in assessing dangerousness.

there was no threat that justified deadly force despite case law, training, policies, and the realities of deadly force confrontations (as explained throughout this book).

The imminence of a threat is necessarily relative to factors of time, distance, reaction constraints, and the "lethal reach" of the weapon or instrument constituting the source of the threat. The time factor in this context is the time needed to create an actual unpreventable attempt to inflict injury. It is how long it takes for an adversary to get within a zone of lethal reach of the victim. Lethal reach is defined as that point (distance and time) within which the attack can reach and harm the victim regardless of the victim's reactions and responses. It varies with the weapon or instrument used to generate the danger of harm. It also varies with the individuals involved in the confrontation and the physical surroundings in which the event is occurring.

The time factor for an adversary armed with a gun is tenths of a second—the time it takes to point and shoot the weapon. It is also independent of the direction the adversary is facing or the distance of the victim from the adversary. Absent cover, the lethal reach of a firearm is hundreds of yards. Guns are omni-directional—they can be fired in any direction without any perceptible difference in the time required to do so and without any necessity of precise or specific aiming. A randomly fired bullet is every bit as injurious as an aimed one if it hits a person. The bullet is lethal hundreds of yards away regardless of aiming, intent or the direction the shooter may be facing. A gun can cause grave injury without any decrease in distance between the attacker and the victim. That is why the mere presence of a firearm constitutes an objective imminent threat and the lethal reach of a firearm is essentially line of sight independent of range.

The time factor for an adversary armed with a knife may be several seconds or even longer—the time it takes to close the distance to a point close enough to get to the victim regardless of what the victim does in response. Intervening obstacles and the direction the adversary is facing can have some effect upon the time it will take to bring the victim within lethal reach. Lethal reach of a knife is some distance beyond the arm's reach of the knife-wielder because the detrimental effects of surprise, reaction times, and tactical issues (backing up in haste, tripping over nearby obstacles, etc.) mean that the attacker's initiative can cover additional distance beyond arm's reach and get within the arm's reach needed to cut or stab with the knife.

The distance factor is a function of the actual physical reach of the weapon coupled with the aggravating effects of reaction times and stress. As mentioned, in order to cut or stab with a knife, the attacker must be within arm's reach. But because of the time it takes the victim to recognize and then respond to the attack and the aggravating effects of stress and surprise that always increase the reactions times of the victim, the actual lethal reach of a knife is extended considerably beyond arm's reach to as much as 30 feet or so. That is why training regarding the risk intrinsic to a knife-wielding person uses the 21-foot rule. It is not a directive to shoot a knife-wielding person at 21 feet. It is a flag to alert the officer that within such distances, the officer is within lethal reach of the knife because of the time it takes to recognize, respond and avert a sudden attack.

Thus, circumstances of time and distance relative to the weapon or instrument of harm are unavoidably linked to an assessment of the reasonableness of the perception of imminent threat. They are objectively determinable factors that the objectively reasonable observer must assess, and that the members of the public and critics of use of force by law enforcement seldom, if ever, assess with any objective accuracy. The circumstances of time and distance relative to the weapon or instrument of harm are subject to the physical realities of reaction times, the effects of stress and surprise and tactical issues of unplanned acts, unexpected obstacles and mistakes of movement. That is why the perception of "imminent threat" must be objectively assessed from the personal viewpoint of the individual officer deciding to use deadly force. Others will always have different perceptions, different angles, different points of focus, different comprehension—something critics and the public have difficulty understanding and applying to the essential concept of "imminent threat."

It should go without saying that a perception of imminent threat is not a mandatory "shoot" point. Officers can and do take on increased risk despite a reasonable perception of imminent threat of serious injury. Often this can be due to hesitation, policy-induced uncertainty, training deficiencies or other factors. It can also be a conscious choice compelled by the circumstances. This is a decision within the discretion of the individual officer, subject to that officer's training, experience, observations and understanding of his or her own capabilities, and the officer's assessment of the circumstances. The practice of law enforcement is not, and cannot be, risk free.

For example, assume that a bank robbery has occurred in which the bank robber shot people inside the bank (a felony). A description of the bank robber is broadcast. Unknown to all is the fact that the bank robber ditched his gun in a dumpster soon after leaving the bank. Thirty minutes later, an officer sees a man fitting the description of the bank robber walking down the street with empty hands. He walks up behind the man and orders him to stop and to show his hands. The man then abruptly turns around as he reaches inside his jacket with one hand. The perception that this was the bank robber and that he was reaching for a gun would be reasonable, and the officer's decision to shoot instead of waiting to see what happened next would also be reasonable. The officer is certainly within lethal reach and the circumstances support an immediate perception of harm.

Now change only the underlying incident. Assume that the lookout was for the arrest of a man for income tax evasion (also a felony) and the officer sees a man fitting that description and approaches him the same way, giving the same commands to stop and show your hands with the same result—the man turns and reaches under his coat.

Although this second situation does in fact signal "threat," an immediate perception of imminent risk of serious injury is not reasonable despite the exact same circumstances of non-compliance and sudden unsolicited movements. The officer must accept the increased risk of waiting longer to see. Officers are trained, practiced and expected to distinguish risk within the threat circumstances in which it occurs. It is true that the income tax evader may in fact be drawing a gun while the potential bank robbery suspect may have been reaching for his cell phone. Non-threatening suspects in more benign circumstances than this have killed police officers, but it is rare and an objective assessment cannot support a reasonable perception of an imminent threat of harm justifying a decision to use deadly force. This illustrates the unavoidable uncertainty inherent to law enforcement work and the equally unavoidable responsibility to distinguish threat and accept or resolve risk based on the totality of circumstances in which it occurs.

The objective factors of this aspect of deadly force assessment most misunderstood are action versus reaction, and the limited effectiveness of the weapons used in law enforcement. In any confrontation, the initiator of an action will always beat the reaction of the respondent. Law enforcement officers are always in the position of having to *react* to the actions of those with whom they are dealing. They are further put at risk by the fact that they cannot know what a particular individual is going to do or intends to do. They can only react to what the individual does, and what they reasonably infer to be the individual's intent in the context of the situation, the individual, and the preceding actions. This illustrates the unavoidable necessity for law enforcement officers to act despite a level of uncertainty that will always exist.

In practical application, this means that a police officer is not required to wait until a shot is fired or even until a weapon is visible before being justified in using deadly force. If the circumstances support the reasonable belief that a weapon is present and about to be used, deadly force may be justified whether the weapon is in fact present or used. This is the stricture of action versus reaction. A well-trained police officer understands that he cannot wait to see what happens. Nor is the officer required to be certain that injury is imminent. The perception of its imminent likelihood must only be reasonable. The law enforcement officer is *always* in the position of having to react to the actions of other people, trying to interpret those actions and then trying to move quickly enough to overcome the lag time that inevitably arises between an individual's action and the officer's reaction. (See Chapter 7 for a full discussion.)

The term *weapon* is not exclusively limited to obviously recognizable items such as guns or knives. Any mechanism, tool, or implement meets the definition of weapon if *employed* in a manner reasonably perceived to threaten serious injury. For example, a motor vehicle is an exceedingly effective and dangerous weapon when driven at an individual. The act of driving a car away from an officer while dragging the officer alongside occurs surprisingly often and is just as dangerous an act. Even though the weapon (the car) is not directed "at" the officer in such a case, the driver's actions, despite verbal and visual cues, are a direct and imminent threat to the officer involved that can be stopped only by stopping the actions of the driver. A piece of pipe, a baseball bat, or a dog are weapons when employed against another, as are the hands and feet of one physically resisting. Even if the adversary does not bring a weapon to the encounter, the officer always does. The risk of losing control of that weapon to a stronger or more physically skilled or simply luckier adversary is a real one. A determined aggressor can overcome a hesitant officer, or can simply prevail by the omnipresent fortune of chance that is a factor in every physical confrontation. Whether the use of such lesser weapons justifies deadly force in response can only be assessed on a case-by-case basis.

Clearly not everyone who resists arrest merits being shot. The issue is whether the officer in the specific incident was reasonable in believing that the use of deadly force was the best means available to prevent serious injury or death. There are numerous cases of unarmed individuals physically overpowering an officer by surprise, skill, or a simply a "lucky punch" and then injuring or killing the officer. And there are far more cases of unarmed individuals physically resisting with no significant consequences resulting. Law enforcement is not a risk-free endeavor, and never can be. Officers are trained to recognize and resolve risks within the parameters of their own experience, training, and judgment. Thus every use of deadly force must be separately and independently analyzed based on the totality of the event itself and the perceptions and judgments of the officers involved. As an aside, when deadly force is used it must be directed at the individual employing the weapon and not the weapon itself to have any reasonable chance of successfully dispelling or terminating the threat posed.

Possibly the most misunderstood reality of deadly force incidents is the wounding effectiveness of firearms, and particularly the effectiveness of a handgun projectile—the primary law enforcement weapon for protection of self and others. Deadly force (most commonly represented by use of a firearm although any implement may be employed) may be used to stop or dispel an imminent threat of serious injury. The unavoidable realities of wound ballistics dictate that even if the officer succeeds in shooting an attacker, it is no guarantee that the attack will be stopped before it can cause harm. This means, for example, that an attacker armed with a firearm can still pull the trigger despite receiving a mortal wound in the process of the attack; an attacker using knife, club, fists, metal pipe, or motor vehicle may persist and cause injury before incapacitation can occur. The realities of wound ballistics are such that there is no reliable and opportune way to ensure timely incapacitation of a determined attacker.

When the threat is perceived to have stopped or dissipated, then the application of deadly force should cease. The ideal application of force will result in the immediate incapacitation of the subject posing the threat. "Immediate incapacitation" is defined as the imposition of a sudden physical inability to pose any further risk of injury to others. Unfortunately, immediate incapacitation is rare due to the realities and vagaries of wounding factors and wound effectiveness, which comprise the field of wound ballistics. The harsh truth is that incapacitation takes time. (See Chapter 5 for a full discussion.)

Where one individual may surrender and comply at the sight of a gun, the next may not give up despite mortal wounds and will die fighting, and the officer can never know beforehand which will happen. Those who do not choose to stop can pose a significant threat for quite some time. There are numerous cases in which individuals have continued to resist, and kill and injure, even though mortally wounded, until the gross effects of their wounds finally sapped their physical ability to continue to fight. And there are all manner of responses in between these two extremes. Thus, the only certain way to insure protection of self or others against imminent serious injury is to force physiological incapacitation upon the individual posing the threat, and that takes time.

This is the truth of wound ballistics. It decrees that even though the officer has fired effectively, it may not be enough to stop or dispel the threat of serious injury in time. The most common observable reaction to being shot is no immediate reaction, barring injury to the central nervous system. The actual impact or initial effects of most bullet wounds are relatively minor and commonly unrecognized under the stress of the encounter. This is virtually certain in situations where fear, anger, adrenaline, or the presence of substances like narcotics or alcohol may further mask or inhibit pain and awareness. Law enforcement officers are trained to apply deadly force for as long as they perceive the threat of injury to persist, and cease when they perceive it has ended, or dissipated.

The critical imperative of action/reaction times in the law enforcement setting is that the officer's time lapse (perception of event, decision plus response time, resulting in a shot fired) _begins_ in response to an action initiated by the person confronted. A law enforcement officer cannot see the future or read minds. The officer can only react to what the person being confronted does. And even if the officer's use of deadly force is ultimately lethal, the incapacitating effects of the wounds may not take effect quickly enough. This is the unbending reality of reaction times and wound ballistics.

A third factor that arises in all deadly force confrontations is the human physiological response mechanism to sudden, life-threatening danger, characterized by the popularized label "fight-or-flight syndrome." Simply speaking, "fight or flight" describes the collective set of subconscious, involuntary survival responses to sudden danger that are normally dormant. The physiological effects enhance major muscle group performance to "fight or flee" to the detriment of fine motor control. Senses are altered in unpredictable ways to unpredictable degrees.

These perfectly natural, and inescapable, physiological responses will affect different individuals in different ways—but they will *always* be present in every individual at least in part, in some form, and at some level of intensity. They are triggered by adrenaline and by involuntary, subconscious responses that evolved to enhance survival in the face of life-threatening physical danger. The effects can complicate understanding and analysis of deadly force incidents because they can appear to create a conflict between the individual's account of events and the forensic record.

The human mind does not operate like an overhead video recorder. The "tape" of events recalled by the participant in the aftermath of a "fight-or-flight" incident will be incomplete and it will narrow in scope. It will be limited to specific stimuli that were focused upon, and that may prove variably inaccurate in the cold light of investigation. Each of the people involved acts independently, simultaneously, and, most importantly, unpredictably. Each one sees and experiences different events from different perspectives. None of the participants will have an exact recall of precisely what transpired and when. None will have seen things from the same perspective, at the same time, focused on the same objects or affected by the same stress-induced distortions of senses and recall. This is not evidence of a cover-up or subterfuge. It is indicative of the imperfect ability of the human entity to flawlessly observe, identify, and record all the details of a high-stress, life-endangering incident in a comprehensive, unemotional, non-subjective, and mechanical manner while simultaneously coping with the fear of imminent death or serious injury and the urgent necessity to react and survive.[11] (See Chapter 7 for a full discussion.)

A fourth factor that frequently arises in analyses of deadly force incidents is the question as to whether reasonable alternatives were available. This is commonly misunderstood to imply that there is some mandate for the officer involved to consider lesser alternatives. The consequence of this misunderstanding is the promotion of lesser alternatives as the basis for criticism and condemnation of the officer's actions. This is incorrect. The use of deadly force is justified if it is an objectively reasonable response. That is the constitutional standard! And it does not have to have been the only reasonable response, nor the last resort response. If it is a reasonable response for the circumstances it is a justified response. The standard of reasonableness has been clearly enunciated by the Court, and consistently applied in numerous subsequent actions.

> *"The 'reasonableness' of a particular use of force must be judged from the perspective of a reasonable officer on the scene, rather than with the 20/20 vision of hindsight. The Fourth Amendment is not violated by an arrest based on probable cause, even though the wrong person is arrested, nor is it violated by the mistaken execution of a valid search warrant on the wrong premises. With respect to a claim of excessive force, the same standard of reasonableness at the moment applies: Not every push or shove, even if it may later seem unnecessary in the peace of a judge's chambers, violates the Fourth Amendment. The calculus of reasonableness must embody allowance for the fact that police officers are often forced to make split-second judgments—in circumstances that are tense, uncertain, and rapidly evolving—about the amount of force that is necessary in a particular situation."*[12]

If deadly force is justified and an attempt to utilize a lesser alternative significantly increases the risk of serious injury or leads to those results, then it is an exercise in poor judgment. If it is ultimately successful, it can only be attributed to luck. Reliance on fate and good fortune is not an acceptable means for resolving an imminent threat of serious injury, although many officers do exactly that, albeit largely unwittingly, as they go to great lengths and assume ever increasing personal risks to delay or avoid the use of deadly force.

---

11. Although the legal justification for using deadly force is to prevent an imminent risk of serious injury, "death or serious injury" is a proper formulation for describing the stimuli that triggers "fight or flight." Fear of imminent serious injury may be enough to trigger the response, to be sure—but the sudden perception that *death* is imminent is virtually certain to do so.

12. *Graham v. Connor*, 490 U.S. 386, 396–97 (1989).

An officer cannot control the actions of the suspect. Further, it is unreasonable and unrealistic to expect an officer to let a situation develop until he is certain that he or others will be hurt, or not hurt. On the other hand, deadly force is never a mandated response. That decision is correctly left to the officer at the scene. The necessity for individual judgment can never be ignored.

A final factor to examine is the issue of the duration of application of deadly force. Did the use of deadly force begin when it was reasonably perceived that a threat of injury to self or others was imminent, and did it cease when it was reasonably recognizable that the threat of injury had in fact ended? The action-versus-reaction effect can easily lead to invalid assessments of matters such as the number of shots fired, the location of entry wounds, and the point at which the threat ceased. These questions will arise when the subjects of a police use of deadly force are found to have received wounds in the side or the back, or numerous shots are fired, or shots are fired beyond the point at which cool and clear hindsight tells us the threat ended.

Viewed in isolation, such matters are frequently assumed to be indicative of excessive force, unreasonable use of force, or deficient training or policy. In reality, they are symptomatic of the dynamics of any deadly force confrontation and the irreducible effects of action versus reaction. They must be analyzed as interrelated segments of a seamless and rapidly evolving continuum of actions and reactions taking place in seconds and fractions of seconds, subject to the physical realities of action/reaction, sensory distortion, wound ballistics, and tactical limitations.

It takes time for perceptions to arise and be acted upon. An officer will begin firing, during which time the individual turns or falls or otherwise reacts to being shot at and/or wounded. During that time, shots fired by the officer are striking the individual who has turned. By the time the officer perceives the change, and stops shooting, the wounds have been inflicted in areas at which the officer was not aiming and the officer is most likely unaware of it. The tunnel vision that focuses the mind on the threat to life in a survival situation does not readily pick up nuances of body angle and motion that occur in mere fractions of a second. Trained to fire until the threat ends, the well trained officer will be firing when the threat does end, but react to that perception mere moments (and probably some shots) after the fact. These are not indicative of intent or over reaction. These are indications of the physical limits imposed by the realities of action, reaction, and the times required to engender physiological responses

The critical issue is whether the decision to shoot was reasonable under the circumstances. The number of shots fired and the sequence of those shots are seldom relevant. Deadly force events tend to be continuous in nature—a seamless encounter with little or no break or respite in the perception of the officer(s) involved—and rarely match Hollywood's extended gunfight replete with frequent pauses, alternate plans, and numerous antagonists. The continued application of deadly force as assaults unfold against an officer and others similarly endangered is reasonable and consistent with training. Police officers are trained to keep shooting until they perceive that the risk of injury has ended. That is a reasonable and justified application of deadly force.[13]

Secondly, the same factors of action/reaction and lag times unavoidably apply to the end of a shooting incident as apply to its beginning. During a deadly force encounter, the officer is engaged in making immediate split-second decisions, running-dodging-shooting-reacting all under the stress of possible injury and death; all being experienced in sudden, unexpected, and unpracticed ways with the unavoidable uncertainty of results. It takes time to perceive a change of stimuli and stop that series of responses. It is common for shots to overlap the actual end of a particular threat because cognizance of the end of the confrontation must overcome the active imperative of defense. Analytical observers can easily pinpoint the exact moment in time that a threat ended, after the fact, in a stress-free environment, utilizing 20/20 hindsight. It is unreasonable to the extreme to expect an officer caught up in the harsh, split-second environment of a life-or-death encounter to be able to make that same clinical judgment.

Justified use of force in defense of self and others does not require affirmative answers in all analytical topic areas. It does require that the totality of issues covered under these questions lead to a reasonable conclusion that, at that moment, the perception that there was an imminent risk of injury was reasonable. And additionally, the means used were timely and safe in the sense of not increasing the risk of injury to self or others by delaying effective action. The totality of facts and circumstances should support the conclusion that the officer reasonably perceived an imminent threat, applied deadly force to stop or dispel that threat, and ceased at such a point that it was reasonably

---

13. It is not at all exceptional for an officer armed with a semi-automatic weapon to be able to fire numerous shots in the space of one or two seconds. Second, it is not at all exceptional for someone being shot—even multiple times—to take several seconds or even minutes to exhibit the effects of the wounds. Thus officers are properly trained to keep shooting until they perceive that the threat has ended. They can and do end up shooting dangerous people multiple times because it takes time for wounds to take effect—seconds, sometimes minutes. During that interval between beginning to shoot and wounds taking effect, it is not at all exceptional for a trained officer to fire numerous shots.

apparent *to a participating officer* that the threat had in fact stopped or been dispelled.

Deadly force is never mandatory. It is an option that may be employed at the discretion of the officer involved. A rational deadly force policy, and the laws from which such policy ensues, state clearly that deadly force *may* be used when the officer reasonably believes that the threat of death or serious physical harm to self or others is imminent. In the case of a fleeing person, deadly force *may* be used when necessary to prevent the escape of a "dangerous person" as defined by the U.S. Supreme Court in *Tennessee v. Garner.*[14]

*Prevention of escape* has no prerequisite perception of imminent risk of death or injury. There is a requirement to issue a verbal warning, if feasible, which is logical where there is no imminent threat, affording the fleeing subject a reasonable opportunity to surrender. It is not logical where the fleeing subject poses an imminent threat to self or others, as can easily be the case. In that eventuality, the use of deadly force is more accurately seen *in defense of self and others*, not to prevent escape.

Deadly force policy does not state that deadly force *must* be employed. The analytical focus in every deadly force case must be the articulated perceptions, judgments, and consequent actions of the officer or officers involved, juxtaposed with the available forensic evidence and with a thorough understanding of the ineluctable physical realities that apply. The standard of reasonableness is an objective one. Could an objectively reasonable officer in the same situation make the decisions and take the actions at issue? Put another way, "an unreasonable use of force is one that no objectively reasonable law enforcement officer would have used."[15]

> *"[W]e must avoid substituting our personal notions of proper police procedure for the instantaneous decision of the officer at the scene. We must never allow the theoretical, sanitized world of our imagination to replace the dangerous and complex world that policemen face every day. What constitutes 'reasonable' action may seem quite different to someone facing a possible assailant than to someone analyzing the question at leisure."*[16]

---

14. The Court defined a "dangerous person" as one who has "inflicted, or threatened to inflict" physical harm. 471 U.S. 1 (1985).

15. Petrowski, TD, JD, "Use-Of-Force Policies and Training—A Reasoned Approach" FBI Law Enforcement Bulletin, U.S. Department of Justice, Washington, D.C., October 2002, page 26.

16. *Smith v. Freland*, 854 F.2nd 343, 347 (6th Circuit 1992).

# Chapter 5

# Wound Ballistics

The handgun is the primary weapon in law enforcement. It is the one weapon any officer or agent can be expected to have available whenever needed. Its purpose is to apply deadly force to not only protect the life of the officer and the lives of others, but to prevent serious physical harm to them as well.[1] When an officer shoots someone, it is done with the explicit intention of immediately incapacitating that person in order to stop whatever threat to life or physical safety the person has created. "Immediate incapacitation" is defined as the sudden physical inability to pose any further risk of death or injury to others.[2] The reality is that immediate incapacitation is very difficult to achieve in the human target. The more common result is an eventual incapacitation that requires some passage of time to occur, time that a law enforcement officer involved in a deadly force confrontation can ill afford but cannot avoid.[3]

The concept of immediate incapacitation is the only legitimate goal of any law enforcement use of deadly force and is the underlying rationale for decisions regarding weapons, ammunition, calibers, and training. While this concept is subject to conflicting theories, widely held misconceptions, and varied opinions generally distorted by personal experiences,[4] it is critical to any analysis of a deadly force incident, as well as essential in the selection of weapons, ammunition, and calibers for use by law enforcement officers.[5]

---

1. FBI Deadly Force Policy, paraphrased.

2. Ideally, immediate incapacitation occurs instantaneously.

3. Patrick, UW, "Handgun Wounding Factors and Effectiveness," FBI Academy Firearms Training Unit, U.S. Department of Justice, Federal Bureau of Investigation, 1989.

4. Fackler, ML, MD, "What's Wrong with the Wound Ballistics Literature, and Why," Letterman Army Institute of Research, Presidio of San Francisco, CA, Report No. 239, July, 1987.

5. Fackler, ML, MD, Director, Wound Ballistics Laboratory, Letterman Army Institute of Research, Presidio of San Francisco, CA, letter, "Bullet Performance Misconceptions," International Defense Review 3; 369–70, 1987.

# Mechanics of Projectile Wounding

In order to assess the likelihood of incapacitation with any handgun round, an understanding of the mechanics of wounding is necessary.[6] There are four components of projectile wounding.[7] Not all of these components relate to incapacitation, but each of them must be considered. They are:

1. *Penetration.* The tissue through which the projectile passes and disrupts or destroys in passing.
2. *Permanent Cavity.* This is the volume of space once occupied by tissue that has been destroyed by the passage of the projectile. It is a function of penetration and the frontal area of the projectile. Quite simply, it is the hole left by the passage of the bullet.
3. *Temporary Cavity.* This is the expansion of the permanent cavity by stretching due to the transfer of kinetic energy during the projectile's passage.
4. *Fragmentation.* Projectile pieces or secondary fragments of bone that are impelled outward from the permanent cavity and may sever muscle tissues, blood vessels, etc., apart from the permanent cavity.[8, 9] Fragmentation is not necessarily present in every projectile wound. It may or may not occur and should be considered a secondary effect.[10]

Projectiles incapacitate only by damaging or destroying the central nervous system or by causing significant blood loss. To the extent the wound components cause or increase the effects of these two mechanisms, the likelihood of incapacitation increases. Because of the impracticality of shooting solely to hit the central nervous system (i.e., brain or spinal cord), this examination of

---

6. Discussion here is limited to handgun bullet effects as handguns are the primary weapons for law enforcement use. The dictates of wound ballistics are the same for other projectile wounds, such as shotguns and rifles. The greater destructive potential of shoulder-fired munitions can increase the likelihood of incapacitation; however, the mechanics of incapacitation remain the same. Incapacitation is compelled by central nervous system damage and/or blood loss sufficient to induce brain dysfunction. More damaging projectiles may be more effective, but only because of increased tissue destruction and thus more rapid blood loss.

7. Josselson, A, MD, Armed Forces Institute of Pathology, Walter Reed Army Medical Center, Washington, DC, lecture series to FBI National Academy students, 1982–83.

8. DiMaio, VJM, MD, *Gunshot Wounds*, Elsevier Science Publishing Company, New York, NY, 1987: Chapter 3, Wound Ballistics: 41–49.

9. Fackler, ML, MD, Malinowski, JA, "The Wound Profile: A Visual Method for Quantifying Gunshot Wound Components," *Journal of Trauma* 25: 522–29, 1985.

10. Fackler, ML, MD, "Missile Caused Wounds," Letterman Army Institute of Research, Presidio of San Francisco, CA, Report No. 231, April, 1987.

wound ballistics relative to law enforcement use is focused upon torso wounds and the probable results.[11]

# Mechanics of Handgun Wounding

All handgun wounds will combine the components of penetration, permanent cavity, and temporary cavity to a greater or lesser degree. Fragmentation, on the other hand, does not reliably occur in handgun wounds due to the relatively low velocities of handgun bullets. Fragmentation reliably occurs in high-velocity projectile wounds (impact velocity in excess of 2,000 feet per second) inflicted by soft point or hollow point bullets.[12] In such a case, the permanent cavity is stretched so far, and so fast, that tearing and rupturing can occur in tissues surrounding the wound channel that may have also been weakened by fragmentation damage.[13, 14] Temporary cavity can significantly increase tissue damage in rifle bullet wounds.[15]

Since the highest handgun velocities generally do not exceed 1,400–1,500 feet per second (fps) at the muzzle, reliable fragmentation could only be achieved by constructing a bullet so frangible as to eliminate any reasonable penetration. Such a bullet will break up too fast to penetrate to vital organs.[16]

In cases where some fragmentation has occurred in handgun wounds, the bullet fragments are generally found within one centimeter of the permanent

---

11. Patrick, UW, "Handgun Wounding Factors and Effectiveness," FBI Academy Firearms Training Unit, U.S. Department of Justice, Federal Bureau of Investigation, 1989.

12. Josselson, A, MD, Armed Forces Institute of Pathology, Walter Reed Army Medical Center, Washington, DC, lecture series to FBI National Academy students, 1982–83.

13. Fackler, ML, MD, "Ballistic Injury," *Annals of Emergency Medicine* 15: 12 December 1986.

14. Fackler, ML, MD, Surinchak, JS, Malinowski, JA, *et al.* "Bullet Fragmentation: A Major Cause of Tissue Disruption," *Journal of Trauma* 24: 35–39, 1984.

15. Fragmenting rifle bullets in some of Fackler's experiments have caused damage 9 centimeters from the permanent cavity. Such remote damage is *not* found in handgun wounds. Fackler stated at the workshop that when a handgun bullet does fragment, the pieces typically are found within one centimeter of the wound track.

16. An excellent example was the Glaser Safety Slug, a projectile designed to break up on impact and generate a large but shallow temporary cavity. Fackler, when asked to estimate the survival time of someone shot in the abdomen with a Glaser slug, responded, "About three days, and the cause of death would be peritonitis." Fackler, ML, MD, Director, Wound Ballistics Laboratory, Letterman Army Institute of Research, Presidio of San Francisco, CA, letter, "Bullet Performance Misconceptions," *International Defense Review* 3; 369–70, 1987.

cavity. "The velocity of pistol bullets, even of the new high-velocity loadings, is insufficient to cause the shedding of lead fragments seen with rifle bullets."[17] It is obvious that any additional wounding effect caused by such fragmentation in a handgun wound is inconsequential.

Of the remaining factors, the temporary cavity is frequently and grossly overrated as a factor when analyzing wounds.[18] Nevertheless, historically it has been used in some cases as the primary means of assessing the wounding effectiveness of bullets. The most notable example was the Relative Incapacitation Index (RII) that resulted from a study of handgun effectiveness sponsored by the Law Enforcement Assistance Administration (LEAA). In this study, the assumption was made that the greater the temporary cavity, the greater the wounding effect of the round. This assumption was based in turn upon the necessary assumption that the tissue bounded by the temporary cavity was damaged or destroyed.[19] Long since discredited, the RII concept has continued to exert a pernicious influence in the field.

In the LEAA study, virtually every handgun round available to law enforcement was tested. The temporary cavity was measured, and the ammunition was ranked based on the results. The depth of penetration and the permanent cavity were ignored. The result according to the RII is that a bullet that causes a large but shallow temporary cavity is a better incapacitating agent than a bullet that causes a smaller temporary cavity with deep penetration.[20] Such conclusions ignored the factors of penetration and permanent cavity. Since vital organs are located deep within the body, it should be obvious that to ignore penetration and permanent cavity is to ignore the only proven means of damaging or disrupting vital organs.

Further, the temporary cavity is caused by contiguous tissue being stretched away from the permanent cavity. That tissue is not being destroyed. By definition, a cavity is a space in which nothing exists.[21] A temporary cavity is only

---

17. DiMaio, VJM, MD, *Gunshot Wounds*, Elsevier Science Publishing Company, New York, NY, 1987, page 47.

18. Lindsey, Douglas, MD, "The Idolatry of Velocity, or Lies, Damn Lies, and Ballistics," *Journal of Trauma* 20: 1068–69, 1980.

19. Bruchey, WJ, Frank, DE, "Police Handgun Ammunition Incapacitation Effects," National Institute of Justice Report 100–83. Washington, DC, U.S. Government Printing Office, 1984, Vol I: *Evaluation*.

20. Patrick, UW, "Handgun Wounding Factors and Effectiveness," FBI Academy Firearms Training Unit, U.S. Department of Justice, Federal Bureau of Investigation, 1989.

21. *Webster's Ninth New Collegiate Dictionary*, Merriam-Webster Inc., Springfield, MA, 1986, "An unfilled space within a mass."

a temporary space caused by tissue being pushed aside. That same space then disappears when the tissue returns to its original configuration.

Frequently, forensic pathologists cannot distinguish the wound track caused by a hollow point bullet (large temporary cavity) from that caused by a solid bullet (very small temporary cavity). There may be no physical difference in the wounds. If there is no fragmentation, "remote damage due to temporary cavitation can be minor *even with high-velocity rifle projectiles*" (emphasis added).[22] Even those who have espoused the significance of temporary cavity agree that it is not a factor in handgun wounds:

> *"In the case of low-velocity missiles, e.g., pistol bullets, the bullet produces a direct path of destruction with very little lateral extension within the surrounding tissues. Only a small temporary cavity is produced. To cause significant injuries to a structure, a pistol bullet must strike that structure directly. The amount of kinetic energy lost in the tissue by a pistol bullet is insufficient to cause the remote injuries produced by a high-velocity rifle bullet."*[23]

The reason is that most tissue in the human target is elastic in nature. Muscle, blood vessels, lung, bowels—all are capable of substantial stretching with minimal damage. Studies have shown that the outward velocity of the tissues in which the temporary cavity forms is no more than one tenth of the velocity of the projectile.[24] This is well within the elasticity limits of tissue such as muscle, blood vessels, and lungs. Only inelastic tissue like liver, or the extremely fragile tissue of the brain, would show significant damage due to temporary cavitation.[25]

The tissue disruption caused by a handgun bullet is limited to two mechanisms. The first or crush mechanism is the hole that the bullet makes passing through the tissue. The second or stretch mechanism is the temporary cavity formed by the tissues being driven outward in a radial direction away from the path of the bullet. Of the two, the crush mechanism, the result of penetration and permanent cavity, is the *only* handgun wounding mechanism that damages tissue.[26]

---

22. Fackler, ML, MD, Surinchak, JS, Malinowski, JA, *et al.*, "Bullet Fragmentation: A Major Cause of Tissue Disruption," *Journal of Trauma* 24: 35–39, 1984.

23. DiMaio, VJM, MD, *Gunshot Wounds*, Elsevier Science Publishing Company, New York, NY, 1987, page 42.

24. Fackler, ML, MD, Surinchak, JS, Malinowski, JA, *et al.*, "Bullet Fragmentation: A Major Cause of Tissue Disruption," *Journal of Trauma* 24: 35–39, 1984.

25. Fackler, ML, MD, "Ballistic Injury," *Annals of Emergency Medicine* 15: 12 December 1986.

26. Wound Ballistic Workshop: "9mm vs. .45 Auto," FBI Academy, Quantico, VA, September, 1987. Conclusion of the Workshop.

To cause significant injuries to a structure within the body using a handgun, the bullet must penetrate the structure.

The temporary cavity has no reliable wounding effect in elastic body tissues. Temporary cavitation is nothing more than a stretch of the tissues, generally no larger than ten times the bullet diameter (in handgun calibers), and elastic tissues sustain little, if any, residual damage.[27, 28, 29]

# The Human Target

With the exceptions of hits to the brain or upper spinal cord, the concept of reliable and reproducible immediate incapacitation of the human target by gunshot wounds to the torso is a myth.[30] The human target is a complex and durable one. A wide variety of psychological, physical, and physiological factors exist, all of them pertinent to the onset of incapacitation. However, except for the location of the wound and the amount of tissue destroyed, none of these factors are within the control of the law enforcement officer.

A human being is a notoriously difficult target upon which to force immediate physiological incapacitation. Physiologically, a determined adversary can be stopped reliably and immediately only by a shot that disrupts the brain or upper spinal cord. Failing a hit to the central nervous system, the *only* other means by which incapacitation can be forced is via a loss of blood sufficient to lower blood pressure and induce unconsciousness for lack of oxygen in the brain.[31]

In a healthy standing adult, adequate blood pressure can be maintained until at least a 20% loss of blood volume occurs at which point the effects of decreased blood pressure begin to be felt. Healthy young people can tolerate a sudden loss of approximately 25% of their blood volume without significant effect or permanent injury, if laying flat on their back.[32] Further complicating

---

27. Fackler, ML, MD, "Ballistic Injury," *Annals of Emergency Medicine* 15: 12 December 1986.

28. Fackler, ML, MD, Malinowski, JA, "The Wound Profile: A Visual Method for Quantifying Gunshot Wound Components," *Journal of Trauma* 25: 522–29, 1985.

29. Lindsey, D, MD: "The Idolatry of Velocity, or Lies, Damn Lies, and Ballistics," *Journal of Trauma* 20: 1068–69, 1980.

30. Wound Ballistic Workshop: "9mm vs. .45 Auto," FBI Academy, Quantico, VA, September, 1987. Conclusion of the Workshop.

31. Patrick, UW, "Handgun Wounding Factors and Effectiveness," FBI Academy Firearms Training Unit, U.S. Department of Justice, Federal Bureau of Investigation, 1989.

32. Newgard, K, MD, "The Physiological Effects of Handgun Bullets," *Wound Ballistics Review*, Journal of the International Wound Ballistics Association, Vol. 1, No. 3, Fall 1992.

the problem is the fact the body has compensatory mechanisms that are triggered by physical trauma and which work to reduce blood loss.

These compensatory mechanisms are triggered by blood pressure sensors in the heart and major vessels that results in a hormonal increase in the bloodstream. These hormones cause a faster heartbeat and an increase in the heart's contractive force, which increases heart output. The nervous system reacts by constricting the venous system, which contains 60% of the circulating blood volume, and this further compensates for drop in blood pressure. As blood pressure falls, body fluids enter the capillaries to further replenish vascular volume. This is proportionate to the loss of blood volume and is significant in its effect. However, the body's compensatory mechanisms will be inadequate for blood loss in excess of 25%.[33] From the perspective of compelling incapacitation, blood loss in such quantity takes time, and absolutely cannot happen immediately.

Assuming that the thoracic artery is severed (the largest artery), it will take almost five seconds at a minimum for a 20% blood loss to occur in an average sized male. But:

> "*Most wounds will not bleed at this rate because:*
> *1) bullets usually do not transect (completely sever) blood vessels;*
> *2) as blood pressure falls, the bleeding slows;*
> *3) surrounding tissue acts as a barrier to blood loss;*
> *4) the bullet may only penetrate smaller blood vessels;*
> *5) bullets can disrupt tissue without hitting any major blood vessel resulting*
> *in a slow ooze rather than rapid bleeding; and*
> *6) physiological compensatory mechanisms.*"[34]

This analysis does not account for oxygen contained in the blood already within the brain.[35] Even in cases where the heart stops beating and blood flow to the brain ceases, there is enough residual oxygen in the brain to support willful, voluntary action for 10 to 15 seconds.[36] It is impossible to predict how long an individual can function before incapacitation sets in. However, because residual oxygen is present within the brain's blood supply regardless of the severity of wounding and rate of blood loss elsewhere, it is clear that 10–15

---

33. *Ibid.*

34. *Ibid.* Body fluids replenish vascular volume proportionately to the loss of blood volume. This can be significant until blood loss exceeds 25%.

35. *Ibid.*

36. Wound Ballistic Workshop: "9mm vs. .45 Auto," FBI Academy, Quantico, VA, September, 1987. Conclusion of the Workshop.

seconds is the minimum time necessary for incapacitation to occur due to blood loss. It is equally clear that except for wounds to the central nervous system, significant amounts of time in excess of that minimum can elapse between the infliction of a gunshot wound and the consequent incapacitation compelled by the effects of the wound.

One additional study lends compelling credence to this reality. Levy examined the activity of gunshot and knife victims in Dade County, Florida, who died from their wounds.[37] Specifically, the percentage of gunshot victims who survived *five minutes or more* (emphasis added) with chest and abdominal wounds was 64%, and 36% for those with head and neck injuries. A number of individual cases are presented in which the victim, including those shot through the heart, engaged in strenuous physical activity before dying. The breakdown for stabbing victims surviving *five minutes or more* (emphasis added) prior to dying was 50% with chest and abdominal wounds, and 50% with head and neck injuries. The implications for the law enforcement officer who uses deadly force to compel a quick and effective end to a threat of death or serious injury are clear. The implications for the investigator, jury, or citizen sitting in judgment of the officer's decisions and actions are equally compelling, but the realities are not widely known.

In fact, physiological factors probably play a relatively minor role in achieving rapid incapacitation in most shooting incidents. Barring central nervous system hits, there is no physiological reason for an individual to be incapacitated by even a fatal wound until the blood loss is sufficient to drop blood pressure and/or the brain is deprived of oxygen. The effects of pain, which might contribute to incapacitation, are commonly delayed in the aftermath of serious injury such as a gunshot wound. The body engages in survival patterns. The well-known "fight or flight" syndrome is a composite of assorted patterns that can be experienced (discussed in Chapter 7). Pain is irrelevant to survival and is commonly suppressed until some time later. In order to be a factor, pain must be perceived and must cause an emotional response. In many individuals, pain is ignored even when perceived, or the response is anger and increased resistance, not surrender.[38]

Psychological factors are probably the most prevalent relative to achieving rapid incapacitation from a gunshot wound to the torso. Awareness of the in-

---

37. Levy, V, *et al.*, "Survival Time in Gunshot and Stab Wound Victims," *The American Journal of Forensic Medicine and Pathology* 1988; 9(3).

38. Patrick, UW, "Handgun Wounding Factors and Effectiveness," FBI Academy Firearms Training Unit, U.S. Department of Justice, Federal Bureau of Investigation, 1989.

jury (often delayed by the suppression of pain); fear of injury, death, blood, or pain; intimidation by the weapon or the act of being shot; preconceived notions of what people do when they are shot; or the simple desire to quit can all lead to rapid incapacitation even from minor wounds.

A good example occurred during a bank robbery in a Midwestern state in the 1980s that was captured on bank surveillance cameras. An armed guard was standing in the lobby of the bank and attempted to stop the robbery. The bank robber fired one shot at the guard, who immediately collapsed to the floor. His inert body was visible face down on the floor in the camera's subsequent frames and his revolver was on the floor beside him, until the last few frames. First his revolver disappears from the camera view and then he does.

What actually happened was that the guard fainted when the robber shot at him. He was not hit. He was not injured in any way. He simply passed out. That was immediate incapacitation. However, it occurred for purely psychological reasons that are neither reliable nor reproducible, and they are transient in their effect, none of which are desirable. The subconscious psychological reaction that can create transient incapacitation by "altering the physiology without damaging it is called neurogenic shock."[39] Also termed "emotional fainting," the effect is induced by sudden strong emotions (such as fear) and may be more prevalent than recognized.[40]

As it happened, when the guard regained consciousness, he saw his revolver lying on the floor. He surreptitiously reached out and pulled it back under his torso. The camera, taking serial still shots every few seconds, did not catch that. It also did not catch the moment he leapt to his feet and ran for cover as the robber was being shot by a second officer off camera. So the surveillance photos show him and his gun on the floor, then the gun gone, then the guard gone. It makes a great classroom exercise.

Psychological factors are also the primary cause of incapacitation failures. The will to fight on can be a powerful activator, as a review of battlefield commendations for heroism will make clear. People, whether good or bad, fight and function effectively despite horrific and even fatal wounds, and there is no way to foresee which individual will do so. A singularly notorious law enforcement example is the famous FBI shoot-out in Miami, Florida, in 1986.

---

39. Fackler, ML, MD, "Questions and Comments," *Wound Ballistics Review*, Journal of the International Wound Ballistics Association, vol. 4 (1) 1999, page 5.

40. *Ibid.* page 5.

Briefly, two armed robbers were intercepted by eight FBI agents and a lengthy gunfight occurred during which both robbers (Michael Platt and William Matix) were killed, but not before two FBI agents were killed and five wounded. The ability of a person to function through sheer willpower despite severe and even fatal physical trauma was demonstrated on both sides in this shoot-out.

One of the robbers, Michael Platt, inflicted all the damage on the agents despite multiple severe gunshot wounds he received himself throughout the action. In fact, one minute into the fight Platt received a wound later described as "non-survivable," yet continued to move and fight.[41, 42] Approximately three to four minutes after receiving that fatal wound, Platt killed Special Agents Ben Grogan and Jerry Dove at the rear of their car. Platt was shot 12 times and Matix six by the time the gunfight was ended by SA Ed Mireles.[43] "Platt's effectiveness was not because he was uninjured, but because he persevered even with devastating injuries any one of which might have stopped an ordinary assailant."[44]

All five FBI agents who were wounded continued to function and fight back despite their wounds.[45] The best example for this discussion is FBI Special Agent Ed Mireles. SA Mireles lost the use of his left arm due to a gunshot wound suffered in the opening stages of the fight that destroyed flesh and bone in his arm. He was on the ground and fading in and out of consciousness due to the cumulative effects of shock and blood loss, but continued to fight back for the duration of the shoot-out. SA Mireles fired five shotgun rounds from a 12-gauge pump-action shotgun that he could only operate with one hand, inflicting buckshot wounds on both assailants. Then he got up and approached Platt and Matix as they sat in Grogan and Dove's car and ended the gunfight by shooting them both in the head with his handgun. By his own account, SA Mireles was not aware of his injury until he tried to use his arm to push him-

---

41. Barnhart, JS, MD, Associate Medical Examiner, Dade County Medical Examiner Department, Miami, FL, Case No: 86-0968, April 25, 1986.

42. Anderson, WF, MD, *Forensic Analysis of the April 11, 1986, FBI Firefight*, University of Southern California School of Medicine, Los Angeles, CA 1996, page 40.

43. *Ibid.* page 16.

44. *Ibid.* page 86.

45. The Special Agents in this incident were Ben Grogan (killed), Jerry Dove (killed), Gordon McNeill (wounded), Ed Mireles (wounded), John Hanlon (wounded), Dick Manauzzi (wounded), Gil Orrantia (wounded), and Ron Risner (uninjured). Every one of them scored hits on Platt and Matix except for SA Manauzzi, who lost his weapon early in the incident and was unable to locate another weapon before it ended. Their courage, strength, and perseverance epitomize the very best of the FBI in particular and law enforcement in general.

self up off the ground and could not, which caused him to look at his arm and see the wound and exposed bones. By the end of the gunfight, he was functioning on sheer will and rage.[46]

A person may be unaware of the wound and thus experience no stimuli to force a reaction. Strong will, survival instinct, or sheer emotion such as rage or hate can keep a grievously injured individual fighting, as is common on the battlefield and on the street. The effects of chemicals can be powerful stimuli preventing incapacitation. Adrenaline alone can be sufficient to keep a mortally wounded adversary functioning and fighting. Stimulants, anesthetics, painkillers, or tranquilizers can all prevent incapacitation by suppressing pain, awareness of injury, or eliminating normal inhibitions arising from a concern over the injury. Drugs such as cocaine, PCP, and heroin are dissociative in nature. One of the experiential effects of dissociative stimulants is that the individual "exists" outside of his body. He sees and experiences what happens to his body, but from the perspective of an outside observer. This viewpoint leaves the individual in control of the body as a tool for fighting or resisting yet unaffected by pain or injuries inflicted on the body, if not unaware of them.

Sheer will alone, unaffected by any substance-induced behavioral or physiological modifications, can significantly enhance an individual's survival potential even in the aftermath of grievous injury. The will to survive appears to be " ... one of several characteristics which separates an officer who survives a felonious assault from one who is killed in the line of duty."[47]

Personal determination to survive is a significant factor affecting the ultimate survival chances of the individual. It is a factor that must be instructed, and one that each individual law enforcement officer must recognize, accept, and believe. The simple truth to be driven home is that just because you are injured, you don't have to die.

Measurable physical factors such as energy deposit, momentum transfer, size of the temporary cavity, or calculations such as the RII are insignificant or erroneous. The impact of the bullet upon the body is no more than the recoil of the weapon in the hand of the shooter. The ratio of bullet mass to target mass is too extreme.

The popularly cited, but vastly misleading, term "knock-down power" of a given bullet clearly implies the ability of a bullet to physically move its target.

---

46. Author's interview of SA Ed Mireles during the FBI post-shooting incident analysis team investigation, 1986.

47. Pinizzotto, AJ, PhD, Davis, EF, MS, Miller, CE, "In the Line of Fire: Violence against Law Enforcement," U.S. Department of Justice, Uniform Crime Reports Section, FBI Academy, Quantico, VA, October 1997, page 13.

This is nothing more than the momentum of the bullet. It is the transfer of momentum that will cause a target to move in response to the blow received. "Isaac Newton proved this to be the case mathematically in the 17th Century, and Benjamin Robins verified it experimentally through the invention and use of the ballistic pendulum to determine muzzle velocity by measurement of the pendulum motion."[48]

The fallacy of "knock-down power" is amply illustrated by calculating the heights (and resultant velocities) from which a one-pound weight and a ten-pound weight must be dropped to equal the momentum of 9mm and .45ACP projectiles at muzzle velocities, respectively. The results are revealing. In order to equal the impact of a 9mm bullet at its muzzle velocity, a one-pound weight must be dropped from a height of 5.96 feet, achieving a velocity of 19.6 fps. To equal the impact of a .45ACP bullet, the one-pound weight needs a velocity of 27.1 fps and must be dropped from a height of 11.4 feet. A ten-pound weight equals the impact of a 9mm bullet when dropped from a height of 0.72 *inches* (velocity attained is 1.96 fps), and equals the impact of a .45 when dropped from 1.37 *inches* (achieving a velocity of 2.71 fps).[49]

The popular wisdom tells us that a bullet with "knock-down power" will knock a standing man off his feet. That is also the Hollywood special effects version of getting hit with a bullet. The victim is lifted off his feet and propelled backwards. It is an easily tested concept. Hang a target weighing 150 pounds (to use a *small* adult size) from a rope and shoot it with the caliber and bullet being touted as having such devastating "knock-down power"—and notice how much it actually moves when hit. As an alternative, stand a 50-pound log chunk on the ground and shoot it dead center. In both cases, little or no movement will be induced in the target by the strike of the bullet. "Knock-down power" is not a valid concept in small arms projectiles and calibers.

The "shock" of a bullet's impact is another common, and erroneous, concept applied to evaluations of gunshot wounds. However, the measurable impact as described above is insufficient in magnitude and duration to contribute to any "shock" effect. There simply is no "shock wave" effect in tissue due to the differences in properties of air and tissue—air is compressible, tissue is not. In air, the shock wave created by a bullet's passage is physiologically inconsequential. In tissue, the shock wave just isn't present. Use of the term "shock" when discussing a bullet's wounding effect is common, but mistaken.

---

48. Goddard, S, "Some Issues for Consideration in Choosing Between 9mm and .45ACP Handguns," Battelle Labs, Ballistic Sciences, Ordnance Systems and Technology Section, Columbus, OH, presented to the FBI Academy, February 16, 1988, pages 3–4.

49. *Ibid.* pages 3–4.

*The shock from being hit by a bullet is actually much like the shock from being called an idiot; it is an expression of surprise and has nothing to do with physical effects or physiological trauma.*[50]

A bullet simply cannot knock a man down. If it had the energy to do so, then equal energy would be applied against the shooter (albeit mitigated by the weight and design of the firearm) and he too might be knocked down or would certainly have trouble retaining control of the weapon. That is simple physics, and has been established for hundreds of years.[51] The amount of energy deposited in the body by a bullet is approximately equivalent to being hit with a Major League fastball.[52] Tissue damage is the only physical link to incapacitation, but excluding the central nervous system, it cannot be a causative factor compelling incapacitation within the desired time frame, i.e., instantaneously.

The human target can be incapacitated reliably and immediately only by the disruption or destruction of the brain or upper spinal cord. Otherwise, incapacitation is subject to a random host of variables, the most important of which are beyond the control of the shooter. Incapacitation becomes an eventual event, not necessarily an immediate one. If the proper psychological factors that contribute to incapacitation are present, even a minor wound can be immediately incapacitating. If they are not present, incapacitation can be significantly delayed even with grievous and non-survivable wounds.

# Fallacies of Popular Shooting Incident Analyses

Field results are a collection of individualistic reactions on the part of each person shot that can be analyzed and reported as percentages. However, no individual responds as a percentage, but as an all-or-nothing phenomenon

---

50. Fackler, ML, MD, "Questions and Comments," pages 9–10.

51. Newton, Sir Isaac, *Principia Mathematica*, 1687, in which are stated Newton's Laws of Motion. The Second Law of Motion states that a body will accelerate or change its speed at a rate that is proportional to the force acting upon it. In simpler terms, for every action there is an equal but opposite reaction. The acceleration will, of course, be in inverse proportion to the mass of the body. For example, the same force acting upon a body of twice the mass will produce exactly half the acceleration.

52. Lindsey, Douglas, MD, presentation to the Wound Ballistics Workshop, Quantico, VA, 1987.

that the law enforcement officer cannot possibly predict and which may provide misleading data upon which to calculate wounding effectiveness.

There is no valid, scientific analysis of actual shooting results in existence, or being pursued, to date. It is an unfortunate vacuum because a wealth of data exists, and (sadly) new data is being generated every day. There are some well publicized so-called analyses of shooting incidents being promoted; however, they are greatly flawed. Conclusions are reached based on samples so small that they are meaningless. The author of one, for example, extols the virtues of his favorite cartridge because he has collected ten cases of one-shot stops with it.[53] Preconceived notions are the basis on which the shootings are categorized. Shooting incidents are selectively added to the "data base" with no indication of how many may have been passed over or why. There is no correlation between hits, results, and the location of the hits upon vital organs.

It would be interesting to trace a life-sized anatomical drawing on the back of a target, fire 20 rounds at the "center of mass" of the front, then count how many of these optimal, center-of-mass hits actually struck the heart, aorta, vena cava, or liver.[54] It is rapid hemorrhage from these organs that will best enhance the likelihood of timely incapacitation. Yet nowhere in the popular press extolling these studies of real shootings are we told what the bullets hit.

These so-called studies are further promoted as being somehow better and more valid than the work being done by trained researchers, surgeons, and forensic labs. They disparage controlled laboratory work, claiming that the "street" is the real laboratory and their collection of results from the street is the real measure of caliber effectiveness, as interpreted by them of course. Yet their data from the street is collected haphazardly, lacking scientific method and controls, with no noticeable attempt to verify the less-than-reliable accounts of the participants with actual investigative and forensic reports. Cases are subjectively selected with no indication how many are not included because they do not fit the assumptions of the authors. The numbers of cases cited are statistically meaningless, and the underlying assumptions upon which the collection of information and its interpretation are based are themselves based

---

53. He defines a one-shot stop as one in which the subject dropped, gave up, or did not run more than 10 feet. That is problematic on its face.

54. This exercise was suggested by Dr. Martin L. Fackler, U.S. Army Wound Ballistics Laboratory, Letterman Army Institute of Research, San Francisco, CA, as a way to demonstrate the problematical results of even the best results sought in training, i.e., shots to the center of mass of a target. It illustrates the very small actually critical areas within the relatively vast mass of the human target.

on myths such as knock-down power, energy transfer, hydrostatic shock, or the temporary cavity methodology of discredited work such as RII.[55]

Further, it appears that a lot of people are predisposed to fall down when shot. This phenomenon is independent of caliber, bullet, or hit location, and is beyond the control of the shooter. It can only be proven in the act, not predicted beforehand. It requires only two factors to be triggered in the individual: a shot and cognition of being shot by the target. Lacking either factor, people are not at all predisposed to fall down and don't. When this predisposition is prevalent, the choice of caliber and bullet is essentially irrelevant. People largely fall down when shot, and the apparent predisposition to do so appears to exist with equal force among the good guys as among the bad. The causative factors are obviously psychological in origin. Thousands of books, movies and television shows have educated the general population that when shot, one is supposed to fall down—and many do exactly that.

The serious problem, and the critical reason it is necessary to understand the realities of incapacitation, is that individual who is *not* predisposed to fall down. Or that individual who is unaware of having been shot by virtue of alcohol, adrenaline, narcotics, or the physiological fact that in most cases of grievous injury the body suppresses pain for a period of time. Lacking pain, there may be no physiological effects from being shot that can make the individual aware of the wound. Thus the vital issue regarding the use of deadly force: if such an individual threatens one's life, how best to compel him to stop by shooting him?

The factors governing incapacitation of the human target are many, and variable. The actual destruction caused by any small arms projectile is too small in magnitude relative to the mass and complexity of the target. An effective bullet will destroy about 2 ounces of tissue in its passage through the body. That represents 0.07 of one percent of the mass of a 180-pound man. Unless the tissue destroyed is located within critical areas of the central nervous system, it is physiologically insufficient to force incapacitation upon the unwilling or unaware target. It may certainly prove to be lethal, but a body count is not evidence of timely incapacitation. Probably more people in this country have been killed by the lowly .22-rimfire than all other calibers combined. Based on body count, that would dictate the use of .22-rimfire weapons for self-defense. Nobody makes that argument. The more important question that sadly is seldom asked is: what did the individual do when hit?

---

55. Patrick, UW, "Handgun Wounding Factors and Effectiveness," FBI Academy Firearms Training Unit, U.S. Department of Justice, Federal Bureau of Investigation, 1989.

There is a problem in trying to assess calibers by small numbers of shoot-ings. For example, as has been done, if a number of shootings were collected in which only one hit was attained and the percentage of one-shot stops was then calculated, it would appear at first glance to be a valid system. However, if a large number of people are predisposed to fall down, the actual caliber and bullet are irrelevant. What percentage of those stops was thus pre-ordained by the psychological make-up of the target? How many of those targets were not at all disposed to fall down? How many multiple shot failures to stop occurred? What is the definition of a stop? What did the successful bullets hit and what did the unsuccessful bullets hit? How many failures were in the vital organs, and how many were not? How many of the successes? What is the number of the sample? How were the cases collected? What verifications were made to vali-date the information? How can the verifications be checked by independent investigation?

Because of the extreme number of variables within the human target, and within shooting situations in general, even a hundred shootings is statistically insignificant. If anything can happen, then anything will happen, and it is just as likely to occur in the first ten shootings as in ten shootings spread over a thousand incidents.

Although no cartridge is certain to work all the time, surely some will work more often than others, and any edge is desirable in one's self-defense. This logic is as compelling as it is simple. The incidence of failure to incapacitate will vary with the severity of the wound inflicted.[56] It is safe to assume that if a tar-get is always 100% destroyed, then incapacitation will also occur 100% of the time. If 50% of a target is destroyed, incapacitation will occur less reliably, de-pending on the specific 50% that is destroyed. It must be stressed here that the desired incapacitation of a threatening target is a matter of *timeliness*—a function of forcing the physical inability to pose a threat inextricably coupled with the *time necessary* for that inability to become real.

Failure to incapacitate may be rare in such a case but it can happen, and in fact has happened on the battlefield. Men in combat have lost the lower half of their bodies (50% destruction) yet continued to return fire for a period af-terwards. Incapacitation is still less rare if 25% of the target is destroyed.

The magnitude of small arms bullet destruction is far less than these ex-treme examples (less than 1% of a human target), but the relationship remains the same. The round that destroys 0.07% of the target will incapacitate more often than the one that destroys 0.04%. However, only very large numbers of

---

56. Severity is a function of location, depth, and volume of tissue destroyed.

shooting incidents will quantify it. The difference may be only 10 out of a thousand, but that difference is an edge and that edge should be on the officer's side. One of those ten may be the person trying to kill him.

# The Simple Truth

Physiologically, no caliber or bullet is certain to incapacitate any individual unless specific areas of the central nervous system are hit. Psychologically, some individuals are incapacitated by the infliction of minor wounds. Some are incapacitated even though no wound has been inflicted at all. Individuals who are stimulated by fear, anger, adrenaline, drugs, alcohol, and/or sheer will and determination to survive may not be incapacitated *in time* even if mortally wounded.

The will to survive and to fight despite horrific damage to the body is commonplace on the battlefield and on the street. Barring a hit to the brain, the *only* way to force incapacitation is to cause sufficient blood loss as to cause the subject to no longer function, and that takes time. Even if the heart is instantly destroyed, there will be sufficient residual oxygen in the brain to support full and complete voluntary action for 10–15 seconds. This also explains why a police officer "had to shoot him so many times," a criticism that often forms the basis for an allegation of unreasonable or excessive force in legal actions sought against the officer following a shooting incident. It is also the reason that law enforcement training teaches officers to keep shooting until they perceive that the threat they are facing has ended.

Kinetic energy does not wound. Temporary cavity does not wound. The much-discussed "shock" of bullet impact is a fable, and "knock-down" power is a Hollywood special effect. The critical element in wounding effectiveness is penetration. The bullet *must* pass through the large blood-bearing organs and be of sufficient diameter to promote rapid bleeding. Penetration less than 12 inches is too little, and, in the words of two of the participants in the 1987 FBI Wound Ballistics Workshop, "too little penetration will get you killed."[57, 58] Given desirable and reliable penetration, the only way to increase bullet effectiveness is to increase the severity of the wound by increasing the size of the hole made by the bullet. Any bullet that will not penetrate *through* vital organs from

---

57. Fackler, ML, MD, presentation to the Wound Ballistics Workshop, Quantico, VA, 1987.

58. Smith, O'BC, MD, presentation to the Wound Ballistics Workshop, Quantico, VA, 1987.

less than optimal angles is not acceptable. Of those that will penetrate, the edge will always be with the bigger bullet.[59]

Penetration is a function of velocity and mass. If you use a non-deforming projectile, increasing either factor will increase penetration. Full metal jacket (FMJ) bullets are excellent penetrators in flesh—but they only create caliber-sized holes. To enhance hemorrhage, you must make a bigger hole. The .45 makes bigger holes than the .40 and both make bigger holes than the 9mm.

Once you go to a deforming projectile (jacketed hollow point—JHP) to increase the size of the hole over and above caliber, mass versus velocity must be balanced. Higher velocity increases the rate of deformation and as deformation increases, the drag on the bullet passing through flesh increases exponentially. Increased drag decreases penetration. That's why a JHP will not penetrate as far as a FMJ, given same mass/caliber/velocity.

If there is insufficient mass, then the rate of deformation coupled with the loss of mass inevitable with deformation limits penetration even more. Lose too high a proportion of mass and the bullet not only fails to penetrate but it also tends to come apart. That is the problem with low-weight/high-velocity projectiles ... 115gr 9mm, 140–150gr .40 and 185gr .45. The mass is reduced in order to increase the velocity without exceeding pressure specifications. Velocity sells ... it doesn't necessarily wound adequately, though. It sounds counter-intuitive, but especially with deforming bullets, "more mass-less velocity" translates into deeper more reliable wound tracks.

For example, elephant hunters shoot 500gr FMJ bullets at low-end rifle velocities for a reason. Lighter, faster bullets don't penetrate enough. Deforming bullets don't penetrate. When Weatherby Arms first came out with the .460 Weatherby to compete with the .458 Winchester Magnum, the velocities were spectacular in comparison (Weatherby's trademark), but the FMJ bullet would break up and deform—dangerous stuff with an angry elephant. As another example, in most states, the .22 calibers (.223, .22/250, etc.) are illegal for deer hunting—for the same reasons. Fast, light bullets don't work as well against larger denser targets.

The real benefit of increased velocity is to extend effective range, by which we mean the range at which you can accurately hit your target without significant compensatory correction in sights and trajectory. The slower the projectile, the shorter your effective ranges. That is not much of a consideration with self-defense handguns.

---

59. Fackler, ML, MD, presentation to the Wound Ballistics Workshop, Quantico, VA, 1987.

Within a given caliber, heavier bullets will wound better than lighter ones. To enhance wounding, you can go to deforming bullets within the caliber, or go to a bigger caliber and add deformation to increase the hole even more. Deforming bullets abound that balance deformation against penetration and provide good wounding, but bear in mind that deformation is also problematic— it does not occur reliably. It is dependent upon a wide assortment of variables, intervening obstacles, clothing, distance … when it occurs, it is a bonus. Mass helps penetrate those obstacles and still inflict good wounds, but mass is severely limited by caliber considerations. In 9mm, the 147gr is the heaviest feasible bullet. In .40, the limit is 180gr (and that is pushing the pressure limitations—165gr is the optimal weight). In .45 the heaviest feasible bullet is 230gr. The more mass a bullet has, the more it can lose and still work.

Simply put, wounding effectiveness (and thus the odds of attaining rapid incapacitation) can only be increased by inflicting more, deeper, and bigger bullet holes. There are three common criticisms used in contradiction of this simple truth.

The first criticism is general—it alleges that excessive penetration will create an unacceptable hazard to the safety of others. Specifically, the fear is that the bullet will penetrate the subject and injure innocent people behind him. This is greatly over-hyped for several reasons. It ignores officer training and the ingrained sense of responsibility that training imbues in officers that commonly results in law enforcement officers holding their fire because they see people in the line of fire. Law enforcement officers are trained to look for and avoid cross-fire and line-of-fire risks to others. That training is constantly reinforced in regular firearms training as well as arrest and tactical training. It also ignores another salient point. Statistically, roughly 70% of the shots fired in the universe of law enforcement deadly force confrontations miss the subject, yet the critics of adequate handgun bullet penetration argue that the 30% of bullets that hit the subject and might penetrate beyond him are somehow more dangerous than the 70% that never hit him in the first place.

Bullet penetration that will not reliably pass through vital organs deep within the body, from less than optimal angles, through intervening limbs, heavy clothing, or other unforeseen obstacles, will not lead to rapid incapacitation. Inadequate penetration increases the chances that the officer in the fight will be injured or killed because it delays (at best) or does not (at worst) initiate the hemorrhage necessary to compel incapacitation.

The other two common criticisms of the formulation of necessary wounding factors (more, deeper, and bigger bullet holes) generally arise from those advocates of smaller calibers who perceive in the formula the implicit premise that the .45 is better than the 9mm. These two criticisms are both intended to illustrate how the smaller caliber is as good as the larger one. It is the age-old argument between advocates of smaller calibers (invariably 9mm) and advocates of larger calibers (the .45).

First, they state that a good 9mm round will expand to .45 caliber, tacitly implying that the two are therefore identical. This ignores several actual facts. First, and most important, is the reality that bullet expansion (regardless of caliber) is problematic in real use. It does not happen repetitively or with certainty. It does not even happen reliably within the body of the same subject shot a number of times with the same caliber and round. Expansion depends upon a host of variables, including intervening material, angle of impact, impact velocity, and impacted tissue (flesh, bone, etc.), to name a few. So the only size of hole that is in fact certain and reliable is the unexpanded diameter of the bullet. By that measure, a 9mm is always 0.355" in diameter and a .45 always 0.452". They are not the same.

This argument, assuming for discussion that bullet expansion is reliable, eschews comparing the expanded 9mm bullet (a nominal 0.45" diameter) to the *expanded* .45 bullet (a nominal 0.60–0.70" diameter). It compares the expanded 9mm to the unexpanded .45 and asserts equivalence. This is not to say that smaller calibers are inadequate wounding agents. It is to say that the insistence of the smaller caliber advocate to argue that smaller calibers can be equivalent to larger calibers by using expanding bullets is nonsensical.

The second argument advanced by smaller caliber advocates is that shot placement is the ultimate factor, and smaller, lighter recoiling calibers are easier to train with and facilitate proper shot placement. Basically, the argument is that caliber doesn't matter—shot placement does. However, the underlying incentive is convenience. Interestingly, these advocates do have a minimum caliber level at which they draw the line (almost invariably 9mm), but few shootings ever embody optimal shot placement. It is even more irrational to presume optimal placement is possible or likely because of the dynamic and unpredictable nature of deadly force confrontations. The circumstances always dictate against ideal shot placement. The reality is that shot placement will be essentially random. In most shootings, that will work because most adversaries quit—they choose to stop and it becomes unnecessary to compel incapacitation upon the adversary. Smaller guns, lighter recoil, and larger capacity do not increase wounding effectiveness but do make the instructor's job easier.

Shot placement in a deadly force confrontation will always be more serendipitous than designed. As discussed elsewhere in this book, the stress and physiological responses to stress, the dynamics of life-or-death confrontations, the surprise, the lack of rehearsal and practice, independent action/reaction, and the sheer speed of onset all make cool, calm, proper shot placement virtually impossible—certainly unlikely. Shot placement in actual shooting situations is random, by virtue of the inescapable nature of shooting situations.

And if shot placement does happen to be ideal, more, deeper, and bigger bullet holes will be better. If shot placement is marginal, or not ideal, then more, deeper, and bigger bullet holes will be better still. The formulation is not a statement of superiority of one caliber over another—it is simply a statement of what is necessary to improve wounding effectiveness and thus improve the chances of attaining immediate incapacitation. If one has a choice of calibers, it argues for the larger caliber and guides bullet selection within that caliber. If one is restricted to a specific caliber, it gives guidance on bullet selection within that caliber in order to improve wounding effectiveness.

There is one qualitative difference between larger and smaller calibers, academically speaking. That difference is that a larger caliber will tangentially damage or sever an artery that a smaller caliber, hitting in the exact same spot, will not. That is a function of the wider diameter of the larger caliber—it "reaches" tissue that the smaller caliber slips past. For example, where a smaller bullet can pass close beside an artery without severing it, a larger (wider) bullet in the exact same spot would damage or sever that artery. And in that case, the difference between the effectiveness of the two is 100%.

To put it another way, a 9mm through the heart is a vastly more effective wound than a .45 through the shoulder. That leads to an important corollary: the perfectly placed shot that does not penetrate vital organs is every bit as bad; it is inadequate for self-defense. That further exemplifies the reason why even small calibers such as the .22, .25 and .32 are seldom touted as acceptable self-defense calibers even though their smaller sized weapons and significantly diminished recoil are easier to handle and shoot accurately than the bigger calibers.

One of the glaring revelations that arose in the aftermath of the 1986 FBI shoot-out in Miami was the failure of the ammunition issued to the Special Agents to meet the wounding standards discussed above. The specific round used was a lightweight, high-velocity round widely popular throughout law enforcement at the time. It was designed to expand rapidly and limit penetration, "dumping" its energy totally within the target and thereby eliminating any danger of "over penetration." The round did exactly as it was designed to do. Early in the shootout Michael Platt crawled out of the right side passenger window. As he did so Special Agent Jerry Dove hit him with a shot that penetrated Platt's right upper arm and entered the right side of his chest between the fifth and sixth ribs. The expanded bullet entered the lower lobe of his right lung and was recovered near the hilum of the right lung. The path of the bullet would have penetrated the upper heart/aorta if the bullet had continued to penetrate.[60] This was the above cited "non-survivable" wound inflicted on Platt.

Over the course of the next several minutes, Platt continued to move and fight, killing Special Agents Grogan and Dove over three minutes later. By the end of the shoot-out, Platt had lost essentially half his blood volume from this and other wounds. The bullet performed exactly as it was designed to do—expand violently and penetrate no more than 6–7 inches. It was a failure. It was based on performance parameters that do not promote rapid incapacitation.

The Miami shoot-out provided additional impetus for a re-evaluation of FBI weapons and ammunition. One far-reaching development was the design and initiation of the FBI Ammunition Test Protocol to extensively test bullets relative to defined standards of penetration, permanent cavity, and reliability.[61] The FBI defined performance standards were designed to identify bullets that did what the realities of wound ballistics told us had to be done to incapacitate the human target.[62,63] The standards were translated into reproducible testing procedures.

The consequences within the firearms industry were drastic—for the first time ever law enforcement defined exactly what it wanted in terms of bullet terminal performance, based on tactical realities and wound ballistic imperatives. The industry responded and the qualitative and quantitative improvements in ammunition design for use by law enforcement was stunning. It continues. The FBI performance standards and the industry-wide response among ammunition manufacturers have provided law enforcement with more signifi-

---

60. Anderson, WF, MD, *Forensic Analysis of the April 11, 1986, FBI Firefight*, University of Southern California School of Medicine, Los Angeles, CA 1996, pages 37–40.

61. The FBI Ammunition Test protocol was designed by the authors and implemented in December 1988. Annual reports of the results were published on a calendar year basis. FBI shooting incidents were constantly studied to ensure test results were validated in comparison to actual bullet performance. Anomalous comparative results were resolved by amending test protocol to replicate observed data.

62. Patrick, UW, "Handgun Wounding Factors and Effectiveness," FBI Academy Firearms Training Unit, U.S. Department of Justice, Federal Bureau of Investigation, 1989.

63. "In 1989, the FBI's Firearms Training Unit released a report that provided law enforcement with the first meaningful operational definition of cartridge effectiveness. This report represented the first major attempt to apply the scientific method to evaluate handgun cartridges. Other research predated this report; however … lacked the rigor contained in the 1989 report and could be better described as preliminary research or informed opinion than as quality empirical research."

Stone, WE, PhD, "Improvements in Handgun Ammunition," FBI Law Enforcement Bulletin, U.S. Department of Justice, Washington, DC, January 1995, page 1.

cantly improved ammunition than ever existed before.[64] Countless more lives have been protected and saved because the myths and suppositions of wound ballistics and bullet effectiveness have been replaced with scientific method and objective analysis.

64. *Ibid.* pages 1–5.

# Chapter 6

# Training vs. Qualification

## Legal Issues Related to Training

"Failure to train" lawsuits emerged in the latter part of the twentieth century as a means for plaintiffs to reach beyond the modest resources of an individual police officer and into the more lucrative "deep pockets" of the police department. The contours of this modern-day lawsuit are the product of the unique scheme established under Title 42 U.S. Code, Section 1983, for seeking redress for constitutional violations by local law enforcement officers. Section 1983 provides the legal mechanism for lawsuits against individual officers acting under color of state law who are alleged to violate federal constitutional rights. By Supreme Court interpretation, a municipality or county also may be legally liable if it can be established that the local government agency *caused* the officer's unconstitutional behavior through a policy, custom, or practice.

In a major 1989 decision, *City of Canton v. Harris*,[1] the Court considered whether municipalities or counties could ever be liable for constitutional violations resulting from a "failure to train" their employees. The Court concluded "*there are limited circumstances in which an allegation of a 'failure to train' can be the basis of liability under [Section] 1983.*" However, those "limited circumstances" are present only when "*...the failure to train amounts to deliberate indifference to the rights of persons with whom the police come into contact...*" and, when the identified deficiency is "*closely related to the ultimate injury.*" Thus, a "failure to train" lawsuit under Section 1983 must contain three essential elements:

a.  A federal constitutional violation,
b.  A policy of inadequate training, *and*
c.  A causal connection between the two.

---

1. 489 U.S. 378 (1989).

Alleged deficiencies in training have no legal significance in federal court apart from the assertion that they caused a constitutional violation. Any such claim relating to the use of deadly force would be based on either the Fourth or Eighth Amendments, or the Due Process Clause, and it must allege more than simple negligence. (Chapter 3 discusses this at greater length.)

Because *respondeat superior* (vicarious liability) does not apply in Section 1983 lawsuits, establishing that an officer violated the Constitution is not sufficient to attach liability to the agency. It is necessary to establish that the agency had a policy of providing deficient training and that the policy caused the officer's unconstitutional behavior. While it is not necessary to establish that the policy itself is unconstitutional, it is necessary to show that it is deficient to the point that it reflects a "deliberate indifference" to the potential risks on the part of the policy makers. This presents a formidable challenge to potential plaintiffs who seek to challenge law enforcement training programs.

The Court's recognition of this can be seen in its discussion. The Court noted that it is not sufficient to show that a particular officer was inadequately trained, because "...*the officer's shortcomings may have resulted from factors other than a faulty training program*."[2] Moreover, the predictable claim that the injury could have been avoided had an officer received more or better training "...could be made about almost any encounter resulting in injury, yet not condemn the adequacy of the program to enable officers to respond properly to the *usual and recurring* situations with which they must deal [emphasis added]."[3]

The point is that proof of an officer's unconstitutional behavior, coupled with proof that the violation might not have occurred if the officer's training had been different in some respect, does not necessarily satisfy the plaintiff's burden. The Court emphasized:

> "*Only where a municipality's failure to train its employees in a relevant respect evidences a 'deliberate indifference' to the rights of its inhabitants can such a shortcoming be properly thought of as a city 'policy or custom' that is actionable under [Section] 1983.*"[4]

One may wonder why this discussion is limited to state and local government agencies. That is because of the peculiar nature of Section 1983 litigation that requires a "bridge" between an officer's alleged wrongdoing and some wrongdoing on the part of the officer's department before departmental liability at-

---

2. 489 U.S. at 390–91.
3. *Ibid.* at page 391.
4. *Ibid.* at page 389.

taches. Since the Federal Tort Claims Act (FTCA) essentially makes a federal agency liable for the wrongful acts of its employees committed within the scope of their employment, no such bridge is necessary to reach the "deep pockets" of the federal agency. Thus, if a federal agent is sued for violating a person's constitutional rights, the agent's employing agency is generally sued simultaneously under the FTCA because the alleged wrongful act was committed within the scope of the agent's employment. The agent's act is the basis for the agency's liability. There is no necessity to allege and prove that the agency did anything such as providing deficient training. Consequently, "failure to train" lawsuits are limited to Section 1983 actions against local governmental agencies.

Once it is established that an officer violated the plaintiff's constitutional rights, and that it is the policy of the department to provide training that is so deficient as to demonstrate a "deliberate indifference" to the rights of its inhabitants, it is still necessary to prove a causal connection between the two. As the Court noted in *Canton*:

> "...for liability to attach...the identified deficiency in a city's training program must be closely related to the ultimate injury."[5]

Clearly, these relatively high standards of fault and causation reflect the Court's reluctance to open further the floodgates to "unprecedented liability" claims against local government entities. They also undoubtedly reflect the Court's concern about the degree to which the federal judiciary might get involved in "...an endless exercise of second-guessing municipal employee training programs...an exercise we believe the Federal courts are ill-suited to undertake."[6]

# Types of Training

In the context of deadly force, the two most obvious forms of relevant training are firearms and judgment. Because firearms are viewed as inherently dangerous instrumentalities, the need to train officers in their safe and proficient use falls into the category of "self-evident" truths. There can be differences of view as to the precise type and quantity of training, its frequency, the standards of performance, etc., but it is irrational to argue that such training is not essential. Officers who are not skilled in the safe and proficient use of their firearms present inordinate levels of risk to unintended targets. The consequences may not rise to the level of constitutional violations, but they will gen-

---

5. *Ibid.* at page 391.
6. *Ibid.* at page 392.

erally fall within the realm of "negligence," thus making the agencies liable under relevant state "tort claims" statutes.

Training is a subject that is intimately intertwined with the issues that arise regarding the use of deadly force. It comes up in three general areas of controversy. Frequently, in the civil suits that are an inevitable part of the aftermath of most incidents involving the use of deadly force by law enforcement, training is alleged to be inadequate, ineffective, or poorly implemented. The implication is that more or better or more refined training will reduce or eliminate law enforcement use of deadly force. This is a position adopted with regularity by activist groups, many of which are outraged by any use of deadly force by law enforcement regardless of the facts and circumstances of the incident.

A second controversy is one that arises within the law enforcement community. Training is commonly viewed as a shield against civil suits and the content and implementation are focused on allaying administrative fears of civil liability. This viewpoint is understandable given the frequency that allegations of inadequate training are raised against law enforcement, but it is a mistake because it tends to obscure if not negate real training issues of officer judgment, risk assessment, survival skills, and tactical and policy approaches to mitigate risks to officers and citizens. Ultimately, we arrive at the final controversy: that of training versus firearms qualification.

Training versus qualification is a critical distinction that must be made and implemented within any law enforcement firearms program. In simple terms, qualification is a periodic affirmation that the individual retains or has regained the minimum skills required by the department to be allowed to carry a firearm. Training is the means by which the individual learns to use those skills and acquire new ones in realistic, unforeseen, and unpracticed ways that are specifically related to conditions relevant to the individual's job and duty.

Qualification is an absolute necessity. A police officer is authorized to carry a weapon in the performance of duty and is expected to do so without posing a risk to the public at large. To state the obvious, skill with a firearm is a learned skill. The law enforcement agency will define a set of skills and a means of measuring those skills that will enable it to make the institutional judgment that a particular individual is or is not proficient enough to be allowed to carry a firearm. This is a duty the agency owes to itself, its officers/agents, and more importantly to the community at large that the agency is meant to protect.

The qualification course is thus the agency's measure of the individual's proficiency. If the defined result is obtained in the qualification course, the individual can be judged to be sufficiently proficient to be allowed to carry a firearm. Of course, the process by which the individual learns the skills necessary to pass qualification is training. That process is giving the individual the skills and the ability to use them to meet the qualification requirements. In turn, those requirements must be legitimately related to the responsibilities and functions of the officer/agent and to the firearm to be utilized by the individual.

Thus, law enforcement basic training programs invariably utilize the specific firearm that will be issued to the qualified officer. To state another self-evident truism, it would be meaningless to train a recruit in the basic marksmanship skills necessary to qualify with a weapon system different than the one to be issued. An agency that issues semi-automatic pistols must train its people to qualify with semi-automatic pistols, not revolvers. Although many basic marksmanship skills are the same in effect, the manner in which those skills are utilized will vary with the weapons system that is issued and used.

For example, the ability to align the sights of the firearm relative to the intended target is a basic marksmanship skill. The sights of the weapon are the means by which the shooter can see where the shot will strike. That is a basic skill common to firearms training. However, there is a variety of sighting systems in existence and each one requires a different technique to accurately and effectively align the sights.

Conventional open iron sights require the alignment of three points in space—the rear sight, the front sight, and the target. An aperture sight system has the same three parts (rear sight, front sight, and target) but enables the shooter to utilize them differently and thus align only two points in space. An optical sight introduces still different factors that the shooter must learn to use. A telescopic sight has still different considerations and techniques that must be learned. Yet all sighting systems perform the same basic marksmanship function—to show the shooter where the shot will strike. The point is that the training program must be tailored to the equipment and the weapons systems to be used.

Qualification then becomes the measurement of minimum required performance necessary to be a law enforcement officer/agent in that particular agency using those particular weapons systems. The agency can attest to the community, and by implication the courts, that the officer was sufficiently proficient to be employed and to carry the weapon. Qualification is an essential condition of employment. If the officer cannot demonstrate the necessary proficiency, that officer cannot be allowed to carry the firearm. Further, qualification must be periodically reaffirmed. Every agency has qualification requirements that must be met on a regular basis by its officers because the agency has a duty to regularly assess the skill level of its officers to ensure they continue to meet the defined proficiency level. In the same vein, drivers must renew driver's licenses, pilots must successfully pass regular FAA mandated check rides, and bankers must undergo audits of their procedures and accounting practices by federal bank examiners.

The skills measured by qualification are entry-level skills, and they are perishable. They will diminish with lack of use over time.

> "*In the US, many departments train their officers only to the level of minimum state standards, which are inadequate for achieving high-level proficiency. The bulk of their training often is presented in concentrated blocks, after which learned psychomotor skills rapidly deteriorate, rather than through continual reinforcement at intervals, which tends to build and maintain skills over time. And, deplorably, many officers are never exposed to firearms training of any kind that allows them to practice perception, decision-making, and responses at the speed of an actual gunfight. All this leaves them dangerously deficient in many aspects of quality performance in a crisis…*"[7]

Therefore, a qualification program must be designed to both refresh those critical skills and measure the individual's proficiency with them. But,

> "*…while there is obvious benefit to range shooting, standing at the fifteen-yard line at a barricade shooting three shots strong-handed and three shots weak-handed just does not equate to the elements the officer will experience if he or she is involved in a tactical encounter containing moving multiple suspects and lethal threat.*"[8]

The FBI, for example, requires its trainees to meet basic qualification requirements approximately halfway through the basic training cycle. Immediately prior to graduating and being sworn in as Special Agents, the trainees must once again qualify. If a trainee cannot qualify, that trainee cannot be a Special Agent of the FBI. Qualification with the handgun is a condition of employment as imperative for the trainee as achieving the minimum specified academic grades in the classroom. Subsequently, the FBI requires Special Agents to qualify four times a year for the duration of their career. Experience has shown that qualifying four times a year meets the dual requisites of maintaining skill levels and affirming the necessary proficiency with those skills.

As time passes, skill levels decline. One of the realities of law enforcement is that most of the officers/agents who carry firearms do not practice with those firearms, except as scheduled and required by their agency. Thus, in the FBI,

7. Lewinski, W, Ph.D., Force Science Institute, Mankato, MN, Force News #276.

8. Blum, LN, PhD, *Force Under Pressure—How Cops Live and Why They Die*, New York, Lantern Books, Booklight Inc., 2000, page 25.

the average agent will not practice firearms skills except when scheduled to do so at one of the mandated firearms training sessions.

As a generalized illustration, an agent who qualifies with a 90% score will not practice those skills again until the next firearms session, perhaps two months later. When that agent shoots two months later, the ability to align sights, control the trigger, meet time limitations, reloading requirements, etc., will have diminished to the point that if a qualification course were fired first thing, the agent might score 85%. The firearms session is spent on remedial training and practice to refresh and enhance the agent's skills. When the qualification course is fired later in the session, the agent will score again in the 90% range.

Any diminution of skill will of course vary with the individual. A motivated individual who practices independently of the mandated sessions will probably see little or no diminution. An individual with marginally acceptable skills will lose proficiency to the point that qualification can be problematic. Frequently, those individuals require extra remedial training simply to raise their skill levels back to the point they can once again marginally qualify. Some individuals have an aptitude for handling and using firearms just as some people have a greater talent for golf, cooking, or carpentry. Such an individual will naturally retain a higher proficiency level than the one with less talent or aptitude for shooting. And although an individual with exceptional skill will always experience significantly less diminution of skill, diminution of skill will always occur in all shooters where regular practice is absent. All that varies is the rate of decline and the innate skill level at which each individual will "bottom out."

For example, the agent who qualifies with a score of 100% may shoot 98% the next session, and 100% at the end of it. The diminution of skill is always present over time. The magnitude will vary with the ability of the individual. This is not an endless process that inexorably erases skill over time, however—each individual will ultimately reach a level of innately retained skill. That is the base level at which the individual's proficiency, absent regular practice and refresher use, will essentially "bottom out." At that point, further degradation of skill virtually ceases. A shooter does not forget how to shoot, but proficiency and efficiency of the skill is noticeably diminished. That innate base skill level cannot be predetermined, but it will be substantially below the individual's potential. This is simply another example of the age-old admonition—"use it or lose it!"

Diminution of skill is complicated by the fact that the duration and intensity of basic training will raise the proficiency levels of a trainee to an artificially high level that cannot be maintained within the field firearms program that follows. For example, an FBI trainee will shoot three to four times a week over the 16-week training program. The trainee will fire over 4,000 rounds during those 16 weeks. This is an intense and focused program. When that trainee graduates and goes to the field as a Special Agent, firearms training will occur four times a year. The agent will fire approximately 300 rounds per session (1,200 rounds per year). The average agent's proficiency will drop to the agent's innate ability, which is invariably less than the proficiency level that the agent attained in basic training. Regular firearms training will maintain skill levels at that more realistic level. The magnitude of the diminution of proficiency will certainly vary with the individual, but it is always a factor and always in effect. That is also why marginal shooters in basic training will experience even greater difficulty qualifying in the field when they receive less instruction, less time shooting, and fewer opportunities to practice.

Qualifying four times a year is the minimum frequency determined to be necessary by the FBI to maintain the skill levels of its Special Agents within bureau defined parameters. It is not sufficient to substantially improve those skill levels, but merely to maintain them at the individual's historically established and innate level. This is a function, too, of the qualification requirements of the FBI. Other agencies may define less stringent proficiency requirements that can be maintained and reaffirmed with fewer range sessions. Some may require more stringent standards. For example, most special weapons and tactics teams will require monthly firearms training and more frequent qualifications. Determination and definition of qualification requirements is a function that legitimately falls within the institutional authority and discretion of the individual law enforcement agency.

There is no minimum national standard, no legal mandate, no model program to offer guidance, although most states have established minimum training requirements that will govern law enforcement agencies within the state. Absent state mandated minimums, each agency must establish its own qualification requirements, be able to justify those requirements relative to the duty it owes the community to ensure its officers are safe and proficient, and then objectively test those skills at defined intervals to certify the maintenance of minimum requirements.

The goal of a qualification program is to certify that the qualified individual possesses the necessary marksmanship skills at a sufficient level of proficiency to be safe carrying a firearm in the performance of duty—safe to himself and others, and safe within the community at large. The individual agency must define the skills necessary and relevant to the job, establish a training program to instill those skills, and implement a qualification program to regularly measure and certify those skills.

*"Under the high-arousal states dictated by the natural fear response, you will usually give little or no conscious thought to your actions. Your body has been programmed by Mother Nature to go into autopilot mode, and you respond automatically based on your training and past experiences."*[9] [see Chapter 7 regarding the "fight-or-flight" syndrome]

To cite an example, by the time an FBI trainee graduates, the trainee will have fired the FBI qualification course at least 20 or 30 times. In the field, that agent will fire the FBI qualification course three times or more per firearms session, and thus another 12 times a year, on average. After 10 years on the job, that agent will have fired the FBI qualification course at least 150 times. When that agent fires the FBI qualification course the 50th time or the 150th time, that agent is not learning anything. That agent did not learn any new skills, or new applications for established skills, in any of those qualification courses beyond basic training. It is a rote procedural exercise that must be employed on a regular basis to certify the retention of critical job related skills. It is not training. The tendency to consider qualification shooting as training is a mistake.

*"A danger inherent in limiting training methods to procedure training is that the habits developed by experienced officers are used as a mental model from which the officer generates his or her expectations regarding the encounter. Mental models that apply past habits are likely to impede the officer's ability to correctly integrate the currently relevant information necessary to maintain officer safety within unusual tactical encounters."*[10]

Training is the improvement of established skills, the learning of new skills, and the application of established skills in new, unforeseen, but job relevant ways. The reason a law enforcement officer carries a firearm is to protect himself and others from death or serious injury. Training must enhance the ability to use the firearm for that purpose and to successfully protect life and prevent injury. That is a simple statement that encompasses a multifaceted subject area including tactical issues, judgment issues, survival issues, and the realities of high-stress confrontations—none of which come into play in a qualification course. *"The brain will not do what an officer hopes or expects it to*

9. Artwohl, Alexis, PhD, Christensen, Loren, *Deadly Force Encounters*, Paladin Press, Boulder, CO, 1997, page 15.
    10. Blum, LN, PhD, page 41.

*do. It will do as it has practiced... [The] brain will follow previously conditioned mental and behavioral patterns."*[11]

The FBI Pistol Qualification Course (PQC), as adopted in the late 1980s, consisted of firing a total of 50 rounds at a stationary and unobscured target at fixed and known distances from precisely defined positions within specific unchanging time limits. The agent would first fire a total of 18 rounds from four mandated positions utilizing a conventional barricade at 25 yards within 1 minute and 15 seconds. Then on a signal, the agent would run straight forward to the 15-yard line, draw and fire 12 rounds at the target from a standing position directly in front of the target in 25 seconds. The next stage required the agent to move forward to the seven-yard line, draw and fire 10 rounds at the target in 20 seconds. The final stage required the agent to step to the five-yard line and fire the remaining 10 rounds into the target, five rounds strong hand only, five rounds weak hand only, in 15 seconds with a magazine change. Forty hits within the torso-sized target out of the 50 shots fired were the minimum necessary to qualify.

The PQC was an excellent test of the basic marksmanship skills necessary to demonstrate and certify the necessary proficiency to be allowed to carry a firearm on a daily basis in the community. It tested grip, sight alignment, trigger control, positions, movements between positions with safe handling and manipulation of the weapon and its controls, loading and reloading, and proficient, accurate firing of the weapon within carefully prescribed and controlled parameters (of time, range, and position). In fact, it was an ideal qualification course. The agent who successfully fired the PQC was demonstrably safe and competent with the weapon. But it was not a preparation for a deadly force confrontation—a shooting incident. The PQC was a rote exercise. It could never be anything more than that. It did not change every time it was fired. It tested the same skills in the same way, time after time, year after year.

To pick one stage of the PQC for illustrative purposes, no shooting incident will ever present an agent or officer with the scheduled and practiced opportunity to draw and fire 12 rounds while standing erect in front of a stationary adversary exactly 15 yards away who does not move or resist. Fewer still will provide the agent or officer with clear start and stop signals, 25 seconds in which to act, largely benign environmental conditions, and no uncertainty as to the identity, location, or actions of the adversary.

Rather, actual shootings are characterized by their sudden, unexpected occurrence; by rapid and unpredictable movements of both officer and adversary; by partial and obscured target opportunities; by poor light and unforeseen

---

11. Blum, LN, PhD, page 55.

obstacles; and by the life-or-death stress of sudden, close, personal violence. They require the ability to identify and discriminate between valid hostile targets and innocent bystanders or non-threatening participants. Judgments and decisions critical to protection of self and others from death or serious injury must be rendered in split seconds. They are further complicated by the physical realities of violent confrontations that are absent in a rote exercise such as a qualification course, including action versus reaction, the realities of wound ballistics, and the inevitable sensory distortions that occur in manners and degrees that vary with the individual.[12]

A qualification course is a rote exercise that does not require any exercise of judgment as to the appropriate use of deadly force. The shooter starts shooting when signaled, and stops when signaled without any consideration of the necessity or appropriateness of the act of shooting. There is no uncertainty as to the target, its location, or its actions and intentions. The shooter always shoots at the same target in the same place in the same manner under the same

---

12. This epiphany occurred to one of the authors early in his assignment at the Firearms Training Unit at the FBI Academy. This was prior to any recognition of wound ballistic studies, practical shooting courses, judgment training, or the confluence of these disparate disciplines into a cohesive whole. The training goal was essentially draw, fire a shot to center mass, and go home—you have done your job and it's over. This was endemic to law enforcement, not a failing confined to the FBI. The author had a trainee who had been a Pennsylvania State Trooper. He was dedicated, motivated, and an excellent student with substantial life experiences in law enforcement. He qualified and graduated easily. While serving in his first office in 1982, his wife became pregnant. She had difficulty sleeping as the pregnancy advanced, so they used separate bedrooms at that time. One night he was wakened by the sound of his wife praying in a loud and persistent manner. He investigated and found that a would-be rapist was in her bedroom trying to assault her. The praying was her tactic to attract his attention. He accosted the rapist, who turned with a gun in his hand. The agent shot him one time in the chest from no more than five feet away. In his own words, "I knew I hit him. I saw my sights, squeezed the trigger, all just like in training. I saw the bullet strike...but nothing happened." The agent stood there stupefied, staring at his gun, unable to comprehend what had occurred or why his training had not worked. In his mind he had done exactly as he had been trained, which was true—and it did not work as he had been led to believe it would. The rapist fled. The agent did not recover his equanimity in time to pursue. The rapist was later located several blocks away with a gunshot wound to the chest. He could have just as easily used the temporary vulnerability of the agent to assault or kill him. The agent was not prepared for the reality that he experienced and more importantly it was clear that training had to do more—there had to be more conscious application to actual usage, actual events, and the realities of deadly force confrontations. Anything less was a disservice—and remains so to this day. The Miami shootout occurred several years later, and the entire FBI went through the same epiphany about ammunition, weapons, and the realities of deadly force confrontations.

time constraints. There is no need to be concerned for the safety of others. There is nothing unpracticed, unanticipated, or unknown in the resolution of the course. Yet these are the factors that real training must address.

> *"Adaptive expertise requires that officers participate in long-term, guided, and extensive practice experience. Their training must address norma-tive, ongoing situations that will be frequently encountered in interac-tions with resistive or dangerous subjects. Thereafter, variability, ambiguity, and inconsistencies need to be inserted into the task to force the trainee to stretch his or her learning to a level of competence that permits them to rapidly respond to difficult or unanticipated events."*[13]

All too often a law enforcement agency will then confuse the necessary and periodic qualification program with training. The two are not the same, and the lack of a relevant training program may in fact lead to civil liability. Train-ing is significantly enhancing and improving established skills, imparting new skills, and teaching the use of established skills in new and unanticipated ways. Qualification does not accomplish any of this.

A more ubiquitous failing is "teaching the qualification course." This occurs when a rigorous evaluation of the purpose and content of a training curricu-lum is not regularly given credence or attempted. If the instructional staff is lim-ited in ability or understanding of the greater purpose, and performance is measured by the percentage of students who successfully qualify, the instruc-tional staff will soon concentrate on teaching the qualification course rather than teaching the skills necessary to shoot effectively regardless of circumstance. This is characteristic of instructional staffs that are neither original, imagina-tive, nor service oriented to the officer in the field. The student will be drilled on the specific positions, ranges, and courses of fire that comprise the quali-fication course.

The instructional staff members will be proud of their high rate of qualifi-cation, even brag that they can "teach a stump to shoot," overlooking that in the process they have not adequately prepared the trainee to survive a deadly force confrontation. They do not understand that the importance of firearms training does not arise from the frequency that a firearm will be used in the law enforcement function, but solely due to the absolutely critical nature of the event when it must be used.

When a training curriculum is geared to its qualification course, the in-structors will like it because they look good due to the resulting perfect (or

---

13. Blum, LN, PhD, page 41.

near-perfect) qualification rates. The staff will not have to confront any need to justify, critique, or enhance instructional doctrines, and complacency and staff self-satisfaction will inhibit objectivity and open-mindedness. It is a huge disservice to the trainees once they leave the predictable routines of the range and the specific, limited performance goals expected of them. It is demeaning as well because in reality law enforcement trainees are limited only by the expectations of the instructional staff responsible for them. Unfortunately, training is not evaluated by its effectiveness relative to officer judgment, decision-making, and instinctive application of skills. It tends to be rated by the facile and easily compiled qualification rate. That is not sufficient.

Two additional examples from the FBI will serve to illustrate the inadequacies of a qualification program relative to substantive training considerations. Prior to 1983, post-qualification training in the FBI was essentially nonexistent. The assumption was that an agent who successfully qualified possessed all the skills necessary to resolve a shooting incident.

In 1983, the Firearms Training Unit (FTU) of the FBI Academy researched other shooting applications, especially those practiced and advocated by adherents of the sport of "practical pistol shooting" under the aegis of the International Practical Shooting Confederation (IPSC). The courses of fire sanctioned by IPSC utilized reactive steel targets, partial targets, unknown ranges, unrehearsed courses, unusual obstacles, and a scoring system that emphasized rapid hits.

In 1984, the FTU implemented its own practical shooting program, reorganizing the New Agent Firearms Training Program into a two-semester curriculum. The first semester trained basic marksmanship and culminated in the mandatory qualification process. The second semester exposed the trainees to a series of progressively more complex practical shooting problems that the trainees were required to resolve using their established firearms skills, judgment, and initiative, without prior rehearsal or instruction. The instructors would take advantage of the trainees' initial performance as a basis for advanced instruction, to be incorporated in subsequent runs through the course.

One of the first and most basic practical courses that the trainees would face was a simple multiple target course. The trainee would stand in the open to one side of a relatively unfamiliar item of cover such as a mailbox. The item of cover was not on the firing line, but off in the grass and not centered in front of the target array. At unknown and varied distances down range was an array of three cardboard targets and one steel head plate spread horizontally for approximately 25 yards across the range. One target would be at about 20 yards, another at six yards and partially obscured so only the head was exposed, and the third at 16 yards perhaps half obscured, for example. The head plate would be downrange at roughly 15 yards. When told to start, the trainee was required to place at least two hits on each of the three cardboard targets and then knock over the head plate. The trainee was timed from the start signal until the instant the head plate fell over. If any target had less than two hits on it, a penalty was incurred. Scoring more than two hits was fine—the training goal was to oblige the trainee to be sure of at least two good hits. The other goal was to recognize the availability of protective cover, and to fire on the entire array of targets from behind cover.

It was not uncommon to see a trainee attempt to resolve this course by moving horizontally along the paved firing line, stopping directly in front of each target to fire at it from a picture perfect standing position, then moving to a position directly in front of the next one to fire at it, and so on. The qualification training had conditioned the trainee to stand directly in front of the target, assume a textbook firing position, draw and fire as expected at the target, holster, move in front of the next one, and repeat. Some of the trainees even adjusted their position forward or backwards to more closely create a range from the target with which they were familiar.

> "...human beings are creatures of habit. Habituated patterns of behavior become automatic responses. [T]he brain will do as it has practiced. It will not do what the officer hopes will happen, it will do as it has been conditioned to do."[14]

However, with a little training the students quickly learned to move to a position of cover first. Then, from behind cover they could draw and fire at all of the targets without moving, except to adjust position behind the cover as necessary. It sounds simplistic, but they learned that the bullet fired from the weapon would reach the target regardless of the angle or distance, provided they utilized their basic skills, although the situation was unfamiliar and unconventional relative to their experience. And they learned that, with no time constraints other than to score hits as quickly as possible, they did not need to race a clock, but needed to shoot within their individual skill level to ensure fast but certain hits and not faster but likely misses. In this short, simple practical course the trainees learned they could utilize their ingrained skills effectively in ways they had not practiced, and had not anticipated. That is training.

From such simple initial courses, the curriculum advanced into other, more involved courses of fire. All courses were characterized by unusual target positions, unusual obstacles, intermingled "shoot/don't-shoot targets," and unrehearsed movements and goals.

---

14. Blum, LN, PhD, page 75.

Another telling example involved shooting in and around a motor vehicle. When the practical training curriculum was first developed, analysis of FBI shooting incidents revealed that more than half of them involved cars. This breakdown was true year in and year out. Yet, no FBI trainee was given any exposure to shooting in and around a car. The first attempts to do so were always revealing.

One of the first car courses required the trainee to sit in the driver's seat, holstered, and with the seat belt properly worn, parked on the range with both hands on the steering wheel. Two targets were set up outside the car, a cardboard target directly in line with the driver's side window and about two yards from the car. The second target was a steel reactive target set up 10–15 yards downrange from the car, and offset slightly to the front of the car so the trainee did not have a clear shot from within the car. The course simulated a walk-up ambush of an agent sitting in a car.[15] At the start signal, the trainee was required to draw and hit the close target at least twice, then knock down the steel target to stop the clock. Several things became apparent.

First, it is not easy to quickly draw a weapon when sitting in a car with the seat belt on. The first time trainees (and instructors, for that matter) tried to draw a weapon, they tried to do so in the conventional manner to which they were accustomed. However, trying to draw the weapon that way invariably causes the elbow to hit the seat back that obstructs grasping the weapon. The seat belt also hinders access to the weapon. Thus we learned that in a car the draw needs to be a different series of movements: the left hand releases the seat belt buckle as the body turns to the left and the right hand grasps the weapon, which facilitates a fast and expeditious draw from the holster. However, neither instructors developing the course nor trainees engaging in it did it right the first time.

This drives home the value of training. The goal is to prepare the agent/officer to better react to the sudden and unrehearsed imperatives of a deadly force confrontation. In this example, the car training ensures that the agent/officer who is someday the victim of an attack while seated in a car has previously experienced the awkward and different movements necessary to efficiently

---

15. The relevance of this simple simulation is regularly reaffirmed. In May 1995, Ralph McLean was being sought for several police shootings and killings in Washington, DC, and Prince George's County, MD. A task force was surveilling an area in which McLean was expected to appear. FBI Agent William Christian was sitting in his car in a parking lot when McLean saw him and approached on foot from behind, shooting him at close range through the car window. SA Christian was killed. McLean was pursued to a parking garage. He killed himself with a gunshot to the head.

draw a weapon. It minimizes the risk that the first time the agent/officer attempts to draw the side arm under such constraints is not the one time that his life depends on doing it quickly and proficiently. *"This type of training rests on the premise that officers never should face a situation in the field completely unlike anything previously faced in training."*[16]

Other lessons were driven home in this simple car course. Everybody shooting the course for the first time would lean out of driver's side window to shoot at the close target, extending the gun hand and arms in an approximation of the correct shooting posture as utilized hundreds of times previously on the firing line. Yet doing so exposed the shooter's head and upper chest to the assailant at point blank range—indeed, thrust those vital areas even closer towards the assailant. It not only increased exposure, it invited the assailant to grapple over the weapon.

The trainees were shown how to fall back along the seat inside the car as they drew the weapon, firing through the window and from inside the car. This way the trainee used the car door as cover that masked much of the trainee's head and torso from the assailant and allowed even faster accurate hits on the target. Another benefit was that it hid the trainee from the viewpoint of the second target/assailant. Now the trainee could open the offside door and exit the car, using the car as cover, and move to an even more protected position behind the front tire/engine block to fire at the second target.

None of the tactics/lessons cited were apparent to any of the shooters who attempted to resolve the course with no training other than that received during qualification trials. All of them were slow, inefficient, and unnecessarily vulnerable to being shot. And all of them quickly saw and learned the difference. They were using the same basic firearms skills, but doing so in ways that they had never practiced or imagined—and that is quite simply a definition of a gunfight, thus illustrating the critical distinction between training and qualification.

A law enforcement agency has to require regular qualifications to certify that the specified firearms skills are retained at the specified minimum level. Any agent/officer who cannot meet the qualification requirement cannot be allowed to carry a weapon in the scope of employment. But qualification is not training. That same agency must also train its armed employees in how to use those skills to better enhance their abilities to survive and prevail in a deadly force confrontation. Training does not, however, require the immersion and repetition that goes into imparting and maintaining the proficiency

---

16. Arnspiger, BR, Bowers, GA, MA, "Integrated Use-of-Force Training Program," FBI Law Enforcement Bulletin, U.S. Department of Justice, Washington, DC, November 1996, page 2.

necessary to qualify. Training can be far simpler in form and duration, use less time and resources, and still be effective, as can be seen from the description of the basic car course above. A trainee will complete that course in less than 30 seconds, and fire no more than five or six rounds. Two or three runs through the course will suffice, leaving time and resources for other and diversified training.

Training does not have to be measured by the number of rounds fired or time expended per training session. Effective training of the law enforcement officer is better served by more frequent sessions of limited but targeted duration. Instead of requiring an officer to spend one day a quarter on the firing range shooting 250 rounds (to cite a common and justifiable qualification frequency), good training can be realized by spending one hour a week shooting a specific course such as the car course described above. Spending a day at the range firing 250 rounds in practice and qualification is excellent to maintain, certify, and perhaps improve basic firearms skills. It is not training for a gunfight. Firing ten rounds a week in novel but simple and unrehearsed courses that simulate scenarios and factors that are relevant to actual gunfights is excellent training.

> *"The adaptive growth process occurs when the learning material presented is just beyond the trainee's level of competence. Solving the problems presented in the training then requires the trainee to 'stretch' his or her ability and adapt his or her knowledge to new information and skills."*[17]

The same growth in ability, confidence, and knowledge occurs when the officer being trained is put in a situation that requires the use of established skills and techniques in new and innovative ways. It is all training.

Secondly, law enforcement personnel must be trained in circumstances pertinent to their reasonably anticipated employment circumstances. An officer working night shifts should be exposed to shooting in various nighttime scenarios. A state trooper who works predominantly in and around motor vehicles should be exposed more to shooting problems in and around vehicles than a foot patrolman in an urban neighborhood.

Training is limited only by the imagination and initiative of the instructors and the historical experience of the agency as comprised within its own personnel and its own record of officer-involved shootings. *"Exposing officers to situations that closely replicate what they might face in the field allows them to learn and practice effective responses. In addition to mastering specific techniques, they*

---

17. Blum, LN, PhD, page 41.

*gain the critical thinking and decision-making skills that shave life-saving seconds from response times."* [18]

One approach that has been successfully utilized in some departments is to establish shift-based training. For example, officers working a night shift are called to report to the range during their shift. Consequently, they arrive in their assigned vehicle, wearing their regular duty weapons and equipment. The instructor directs them into the specific course set-up, evaluates and instructs them in the course, and sends them back on duty. Typically, such a training session would require the expenditure of no more than five to ten rounds and 20 to 30 minutes. Shift-based training also ensures that the officer is being trained with regularly available equipment and readily within parameters pertinent to actual working conditions. That is a good and effective approach to training.

Although shift-based training may not be feasible for some departments, good training is still readily attainable. The keys are frequency (not necessarily duration) and relevance to the working environments of the officers.

There are other training avenues that should be considered in addition to live-firing programs. One factor that is often overlooked in deadly force training programs is the element of judgment. Ultimately, it is the decisive factor that governs not only survival in a deadly force confrontation, but also justification in the inevitable legal and institutional assessments that follow every use of force by a law enforcement officer. The decision to use deadly force is discretionary with the individual officer. Deadly force *may* be used to prevent an imminent risk of death or serious injury and, therefore, it is the reasonableness of the officer's perception of that risk that will be assessed and that will lead to vindication of the officer's judgment that deadly force was necessary.

Judgment cannot be taught as a rote skill to be learned like trigger control or sight picture. However, it can be tested, practiced, and improved across a wide variety of scenarios and utilizing a variety of instructional means designed for the purpose of requiring the application of individual judgment. Certainly judgment is in play in any practical firearms course—the shooter must constantly assess and judge range, target priority, personal exposure, and the risk to non-hostile targets versus the need to hit hostile targets quickly and effectively. However, there are numerous other training avenues that engage individual judgment more critically.

Computer-based training systems represent one alternative. These systems present the trainee with a live action scenario projected on a screen. The trainee in-

---

18. Arnspiger, BR, Bowers, GA, MA, page 6.

teracts with the people in the scenario. The best systems utilize "branching" in their scenarios so that the events on the screen will "branch" to different situations depending on what the trainee does. The instructor monitoring the training session can direct what "branch" the scenario follows. Some branching can be automatic as well. The trainee is typically armed with a laser weapon identical in model and working features to the issued weapon. The laser weapon fires blanks, and the sound impulse of the blank firing is what triggers the laser. The computer senses where on the screen the laser hits and the scenario will "branch," depending on whether the trainee hit a vital area, hit a non-vital area, or missed. The system can be programmed to require multiple vital hits, for example, before the subject goes down. Trainees can interact with the same scenario more than once, but branching can create different experiences each time.

Computer-based firearms simulators are excellent for judgment training, and for interacting with people and situations that will react unpredictably and independently. It can immerse a trainee in an intense situation with much of the stress, dynamic uncertainty, and necessity to quickly exercise sound judgment based on training, experience, and perceptions—exactly as is required in an actual deadly force confrontation. The system is susceptible to being "gamed" over time, however. It will only be as effective as the library of scenarios it contains, and when all the permutations have been experienced over time, it quickly becomes no more effective a training tool than the firearms qualification course.

Computer-based systems must have their scenarios modified, if not replaced, on a regular basis (every few years or so, depending on how extensive the scenarios and their various permutations are). That is expensive and, sadly, expense is an all too determinative factor in any training program. It is also best if the scenarios are created with the agency's assistance to better insure they are consistent with the law and with the agency's particular policies and training needs. That, too, is expensive. One way to resolve the need for new and varied scenarios is to share libraries with other agencies using compatible systems. That will increase the useful life span of the scenarios on hand and delay the need and expense to replace them—but it is only a delay. Of course, in a new-recruit training environment the library of scenarios on hand will be fresh and "new" for each new class of students. Obviously, the scenarios will last far longer, in terms of training effectiveness, in recruit training. Computer-based systems are expensive to acquire, but relatively inexpensive to utilize and maintain for as long as the scenarios are useful.

Another effective and extremely popular training system is known by its trademarked name "Simunitions®." Simunitions® rounds are fired in service weapons converted for the purpose to ensure that normal service rounds cannot be fired during training and to simulate recoil with reduced-pressure/ reduced-velocity rounds for more realistic training. Conversion kits for specific weapons are used. The weapons function no differently than they would with service ammunition. Alternatively, dedicated weapons can be utilized for Simunitions® training—a more expensive proposition. The ammunition is non-lethal by design. It fires a frangible projectile that will be felt by the person getting shot, and that "marks" the point of impact with paint.

The use of Simunitions® has obvious training merits. It puts the trainee into a situation as realistic as an actual deadly force confrontation, lacking only the risk of death or serious injury. It does in fact incur a risk of getting hit, and getting hit hurts.[19] Simunitions® tests and trains all aspects of deadly force interactions—judgment, tactics, physical and emotional stress, shooting ability, and effectiveness. It is superb and it is expensive—the conversion kits for all weapons to be utilized in the training and protective apparel for everybody engaged in the training must be acquired. Secondly, the Simunitions® ammunition must be regularly replaced as it is shot up. For those reasons, Simunitions®-based training may be less appropriate at the recruit training level and better suited for follow-up training of field personnel on the job. It has become very popular in law enforcement training and its use is becoming ever more prevalent, to the very great benefit of law enforcement.

An effective training program constantly must be tested against an agency's experiential history of deadly force incidents. That experience will evolve over time and the training and related policy authorities must regularly and *objectively* scrutinize deadly force incidents as they accumulate to identify emerging trends, developments, or unexpected deficiencies. This cannot be a faultfinding process. Training, equipment, tactics, and policy must correlate with the demonstrated requirements and practices of the officers involved in deadly force encounters. The scrutiny must identify what works and why, what doesn't work and why, and what must be better, from the perspective of aspiring to improve the chances for officer survival. The training content will thereby progressively change and improve over time, validated by the institution's unique historical experience.

> "We [see] too many officers paying a price for inadequate training that
> [is] too dear. The challenges are sobering indeed. For example, it would

---

19. The proponents of Simunitions® refer to this as "impact awareness." Personal experience will fully substantiate the contention that "impact awareness" is an effective training tool. Protective clothing is required for all persons engaged in Simunitions® training, and there are minimum safe stand-off ranges specified by the manufacturer—no closer than one foot for the .38 Special and 9mm Simunitions® ® rounds, for example.

*take an officer who receives a typical amount of academy and in-service training in psychomotor skills, including firearms, more than 30 years to amass the amount of training and experience the average teenage athlete receives in a given sport during his or her high school career."*[20]

The alarming performance consequences of this deficiency have been revealed in a variety of research experiments. For instance, "decision errors" will arise when an officer is suddenly confronted by an assailant who unexpectedly points a gun at him at close range. The result is that most officers' only response is to try to draw their own weapon, putting themselves "hopelessly behind the reactionary curve." Many of them "drew awkwardly and had difficulty putting the gun on target." Unfortunately, decision-making and firearms skills are too often *"taught at the speed of qualification, not at the speed of a gunfight, and we develop and use psychomotor skills at the speed we practice them."*[21]

*"We need to train officers to the point that none of their cognitive resources need to be placed on the mechanics of operating their weapon. For effective performance, all of an officer's focus needs to be on decision-making, [with mechanical operations occurring automatically and subconsciously]."*[22]

Legally, the courts have recognized that law enforcement departments are duty bound to train their officers. The required standard is one of reason. The courts have declined to specify what training is necessary. There is no legally mandated minimum any more than there is a legally mandated curriculum or content. But there is a mandate that training be provided, and that it be relevant to the needs of the officers and the responsibilities owed to the community. Although not a legal duty, the authors believe that there is a moral duty owed to the officer to maximize their chances for survival in a deadly force confrontation, and we believe that a moral duty is owed to society to enable the officer to survive and prevail in a deadly force confrontation without imposing unreasonable or negligent risks on members of the community.

It follows that common sense and good faith attempts to define and provide targeted training relevant to the work environment of the officers being trained will suffice. But to rely upon the qualification program to meet the legal man-

---

20. *Ibid.*

21. *Ibid.* "We have to train in real-world circumstances." In another experiment, Force Science examined the common belief by officers that they can safely avoid an edged weapon assault by moving aside from the line of attack. But in reality, when they're weighted down with duty boots and 20 lbs. of gear, a knife-wielding suspect can be slashing them before they can dodge him.

22. *Ibid.*

dates for training is a mistake. Although the skills required to qualify are the same skills required to prevail in a deadly force incident, the stresses, obstacles, timing, and imperatives of a deadly force incident are so different from the comfortable and rehearsed stage of a qualification course that the relevance and the critical likelihood of success are not reasonably transposed. Qualification is not training.

Another essential feature of effective and relevant training that is not present in rote procedural training (and never can be) is threat assessment. Law enforcement officers must be trained to respond to the threat of violence and not wait to respond to the actual violence when it may occur. The use of deadly force is reasonable, and justified, to *prevent* an imminent risk of death or serious injury. It is preemptive by definition as well as design. Frequently, officers hesitate or fail to recognize the risk they face (i.e., threat assessment), and a decision to use deadly force is reactive, i.e., it is an attempt to stop an actual attack from continuing. That is a reality, but it is not a requirement. Ideally, a decision to use deadly force will be preemptive and thereby prevent an imminent risk of harm from becoming an actual attempt to do harm. That is the reason that deadly force training must incorporate the concept of threat assessment. A use-of-force training curriculum that is based on threat assessment will result in an escalating approach when escalation is appropriate and a timely response when it is not.[23] It enhances the officer's ability to recognize when the use of force is no longer necessary.

For example, the FBI incorporates threat assessment in its deadly force curriculum. Four categories of impending deadly threat are taught in the judgment training that is incorporated in the FBI's deadly force program.[24] If a Special Agent has probable cause to believe that any of the four conditions exists, then the use of deadly force may be a reasonable decision. Examples of the four conditions are:

1. The subject possesses a weapon, or is attempting to gain access to a weapon, under circumstances indicating an intention to use it against the agent or others.
2. The subject is armed and moving to gain the tactical advantage of cover.

---

23. Petrowski, TD, JD, "Use-Of-Force Policies and Training—A Reasoned Approach (Part Two)," FBI Law Enforcement Bulletin, U.S. Department of Justice, Washington, DC, November 2002, page 30.

24. Hall, JC, JD "FBI Training on the New Federal Deadly Force Policy," FBI Law Enforcement Bulletin, U.S. Department of Justice, Washington, DC, April 1996, pages 25–32.

3. The subject has the capability of inflicting death or serious injury, *or can otherwise incapacitate* agents *without* a deadly weapon and is indicating an intention to do so. [Emphasis added.]
4. The subject is attempting to escape the vicinity of a violent confrontation in which the subject inflicted or attempted the infliction of death or serious injury.

A corollary point is that it is not possible to design and implement a training program that will prevent a lawsuit being filed by constraining or prescribing in specificity the use of force by an officer. It cannot be done—yet many departments are intent upon establishing training programs that do exactly that. The primary goal, never acknowledged openly, being to pre-empt legal action.

The truth is that the "victim" of any police use of force is free to file legal action and will do so alleging any number of improper, illegal, excessive, reckless, or unreasonable actions. The format and content of the training program will not prevent it. The only proper and justifiable goal of a training program is to provide the law enforcement employees with the skills, practiced judgments, and experiences that will best enable them to survive a deadly force confrontation and to protect others in the process. A relevant and well-planned training program that gives its officers the skills and experiences prerequisite to the proper and timely decisions necessary to prevail will not prevent lawsuits, but it can ensure that the lawsuits do not succeed.

A contemporary example of training and policy implemented to forestall legal actions is the widely popular "Force Continuum" concept. The first continua appeared in law enforcement training in the late 1960s. They were intended to provide officers with guidelines for the use of force, filling a notable void in law enforcement at that time.[25] They were designed to be training aids, not use-of-force policies. However, the concept evolved over the years from a "training aid" intended to graphically illustrate and help foster understanding of the progressive nature of uses of force. It is now the embodiment of a concept of progressive use of force defined in the form of stairs, pyramids, tables, or ladders, and incorporated into use-of-force policies as a model for making judgments and decisions about using force.

Force continuum theory requires a law enforcement officer to begin at the lowest level of defined force necessary to effect the purpose sought, and then comply with an escalating scale of force as necessary in response to the results

---

25. Williams, GT, "Force Continuums—A Liability to Law Enforcement?" FBI Law Enforcement Bulletin, U.S. Department of Justice, Washington, DC, June 2002, page 14.

observed from the lower level used. Simply, a force continuum requires an officer to progressively escalate from one force level to the next until the officer is successful in controlling the subject. It also requires, by implication if not actual mandate, that the officer de-escalate from one level to the next lowest in response to reduced resistance. The terms "escalation" and "de-escalation" are irrevocably linked with the concept of force continuum, which contributes to the practical and legal problems inherent to the theory. It is results based in its effect rather than needs based — implicitly, one force level must be attempted unsuccessfully before the next level can be tried.

The concept and theory of force continua is seductively attractive to law enforcement administrators and training managers. It is seemingly logical, easily defined, and easily instructed, with clearly established steps in the progression and cues or levels of resistance that are defined for each step. And it is easily laid out, defined, and defended in the face of inquiry — legal or otherwise. Many defend it as a way to prevent lawsuits. Yet, in actuality, it represents an unrealistic, almost wishful ideal.

It appears to have been developed on the premise that controlling a resistant subject, or confronting a physically violent one, entails an orderly, sterile, and inevitably sequential progress, "climbing the ladder or stair steps of force to the reasonable and proper level of force before instantly de-escalating."[26] But a deadly force confrontation is anything but a clear progression of enforcement tools and tactics. In reality, it is better described as "a series of mistakes corrected as they are made."[27]

The practical effects of force continuum theory are two-fold. First, it builds inevitable hesitation in the minds of the officers compelled to act within its strictures. Force continua are by definition complex systems.[28] Proponents maintain that a continuum easily allows an officer to instantly respond with higher levels of force, but they also, by definition, require officers to instantly de-escalate whenever possible. Both require highly subjective judgments and assessments on which to act, and on which to analyze the acts after the fact. The officer must continuously assess the actions of the subject and the effects of the force being used to decide whether the next step on the ladder can be taken. The officer must also continuously consider lesser alternatives of force to know when to de-escalate. The process is one of constantly trying to mesh observed reality with the idealized constructions of the continuum, based on a man-

---

26. *Ibid.* page 15.
27. *Ibid.* page 15.
28. *Ibid.* page 16.

dated assumption that the continuum is correct, comprehensive, and controlling.

In the reality of deadly force confrontations, law enforcement officers who hesitate are often injured or killed. Yet the courts do not require officers to ponder the level of force used, nor to consider whether the force used is somewhat higher than that which the continuum suggests, or which someone may second guess later. "An officer trained to progress through a force option menu inevitably will hesitate too long to eliminate all less intrusive options."[29] Policies and training must focus on overcoming hesitation, not encouraging it.[30, 31]

The second failing of force continuum theory is that it opens the door for unlimited second-guessing and parsing levels of force and subjective decision-making in the inevitable legal actions that will follow every deadly force confrontation. The result is an ambiguous and subjective inquiry into the best level of force, applying the clarity of hindsight, rather than the reasonableness and necessity of the decision to use force. This is an even more significant problem where the force continuum theory has been advanced to include "less-lethal" options. This unfortunate development requires that once a decision is made to use deadly force, then the officer must review and select from options within that level of force. "*This creates a continuum within a continuum, making an unacceptably long decision process even longer.*"[32]

If the need for firearms training may be viewed as self-evident within the law enforcement community, the same cannot be said with respect to judgment training as to *when* the officer is justified in using deadly force. It is not an

---

29. Petrowski, TD, JD, "Use-Of-Force Policies and Training—A Reasoned Approach," FBI Law Enforcement Bulletin, U.S. Department of Justice, Washington, DC, October 2002, page 29.

30. Petrowski, TD, JD, "Use-Of-Force Policies and Training—A Reasoned Approach (Part Two)," FBI Law Enforcement Bulletin, U.S. Department of Justice, Washington, DC, November 2002, page 29.

31. When asked the difference between a good naval officer and a great one, Admiral Arleigh A. Burke famously declared, "About six seconds." The quintessential destroyerman known for his aggressive, high-speed battle tactics, Burke believed that hesitation caused by a lack of confidence or preparation gives adversaries a dangerous advantage: they can order the disposition of their forces, fire their weapons, and gain the upper hand. Six seconds can be the critical margin between life and death, and victory or defeat. Law enforcement confrontations are exponentially shorter in duration and drastically closer in spacing than naval engagements, so hesitation of a magnitude much less than six seconds can be equally as fatal.

32. Petrowski, TD, JD, "Use-Of-Force Policies and Training—A Reasoned Approach," FBI Law Enforcement Bulletin, U.S. Department of Justice, Washington, DC, October 2002, page 29.

overstatement to say that until the 1980s, relatively little attention was paid to this issue. Undoubtedly, most agencies devoted some time to instructing their officers on their deadly force policy or appropriate legal standards. However, there is little evidence that such training constituted more than a fraction of the overall training programs, and considerably less than that devoted to firearms training itself. Moreover, such training was more likely to be classroom lecture and discussion rather than any practical application.

That picture has changed remarkably in the past two decades, probably due to the increase in lawsuits arising from instances where police officers have used deadly force. That is not to suggest that there was an increase of such incidents, only an increase in legal challenges due to the legal developments described in Chapter 3. When a lawsuit arises from police use of deadly force, it is difficult to conceive a case where the focus would be on firearms training itself. Deficiencies in firearms training are more likely to lead to unintentional injuries than to unconstitutional use of deadly force. Accordingly, the focus is on an officer's decision to use deadly force in a given circumstance and the training that may have influenced that decision.

In *Canton*, the Court explained that an agency's failure to train could be construed as a policy when "...the need for more or different training is so obvious and the inadequacy so likely to result in the violation of constitutional rights, that the policymakers of the city can reasonably be said to have been deliberately indifferent to the need."[33]

To illustrate when a policy of inadequate training could be characterized as likely to result in constitutional violations, the Court explained:

> "...*city policy makers know to a moral certainty that their police officers will be required to arrest fleeing felons. The city has armed its officers with firearms, in part to allow them to accomplish that task. Thus, the need to train officers in the constitutional limitations on the use of deadly force...can be said to be 'so obvious' that a failure to do so could properly be characterized as 'deliberate indifference' to constitutional rights.*"[34]

To recognize the need for judgment training is one thing. To establish a realistic program to satisfy that need is another thing altogether. Common sense would seem to suggest that a comprehensive program should encompass at least two components: academic and practical applications.

The academic portion should comprise classroom instruction on the deadly force policy and any supporting commentaries designed to explain it. A solid

---

33. 489 U.S. at 390.
34. *Ibid.* footnote 10.

foundational understanding of the policy is the first step in making it second nature to the trainee. This is also the opportunity for management to communicate the philosophy and objectives of the policy to the trainee, thereby instilling confidence. For example, the instructional outline used by the FBI since 1995 for training agents in the deadly force policy includes the following introductory paragraph:

> *"The policy is not to be construed to require Agents to assume unreasonable risks. In assessing the need to use deadly force, the paramount consideration should always be the safety of the Agents and the public."*

Such language is intended not only to provide a positive statement of the intent of the policy but is also intended to serve as a constant reminder and guide to those who must conduct administrative reviews of an agent's decision to use deadly force.

The academic portion of the training should be sufficient to provide a fundamental understanding of the policy to the trainee. The use of written scenarios can be invaluable to illustrate proper application. However, it must be recognized that while the academic portion is essential, it is not sufficient in itself to adequately train a law enforcement officer in the proper application of deadly force. There must be a practical application component.

Practical application training can take different forms. It can be done with written scenarios that require the trainee to provide the appropriate response and justification. It can be in the form of an interactive computer program that requires the trainee to actually react to scenarios by punching the appropriate computer key. It can be in the form of interactive video programs that incorporate the use of a firearm and require the trainee to make judgments *and* to display tactical and firearms skills. It can be in the form of "live actor" scenarios that pit the trainee against role-playing human adversaries. The more realistic it is, the more effective the training.

Even though all of the examples listed above can be helpful in providing practical judgment training, those that most closely replicate the actual experience will be the most valuable. For example, both interactive videos and role player scenarios have the potential of causing many of the same physiological and psychological reactions in the trainee that can be caused by actual fast-moving, life-threatening events. Whatever the method of training, and whatever the frequency of repetition, judgment training is essential to prepare officers to defend themselves and others from threats of serious physical injury. It is an equally essential ingredient for the successful defense of the officers and their agencies from the legal challenges that are certain to follow.

# Use-of-Force Instruction

Any discussion of training issues would be remiss without considering the "Use of Force" as an instructional topic and how it is taught. Concurrently with the rise in popularity of the force continuum concept as both a teaching aid and a standard for the use of force has become apparent the equally facile treatment of deadly force and non-deadly force as one uniform subject. This treatment of the subject matter is misleading and conducive to a less comprehensive understanding among law enforcement officers of the standards and limitations of using force. This in turn results in ill-informed allegations of improper training, improper understanding of use-of-force standards, and flawed analyses of use-of-force incidents. It is a conceptual issue more than a usage issue.

First, it must be clearly understood that *all* uses of force by law enforcement are "seizures" as defined by the courts and will be judged under the Fourth Amendment standard of objective reasonableness as discussed in Chapter 3. However, all uses of force are not the same in terms of the standards for their use and the circumstances under which they are justified and thus the manner in which they should be instructed.

Non-deadly force is that force used by law enforcement officers on a daily basis. It is inherent to the law enforcement function and implicit in any interaction between a law enforcement officer and a citizen. For example, law enforcement officers are empowered to make arrests; to detain people for investigative purposes; to subdue and control people for purposes of arrest, detention, and safety; to compel compliance of resistant or uncooperative individuals; and to command compliance with laws, ordinances, and societal dictates. The wide array of law enforcement activities that involve use of force vary from the benign (directing traffic around an accident scene) to the proactively dangerous (arresting an armed and dangerous subject). The uniformed presence of an officer directing traffic requires compliance with the officer's commands, and is in fact a use of force, albeit arguably the lowest level of force possible—official presence. At the other end, there is the armored and well-armed SWAT team that uses injurious physical force to subdue a dangerous individual who is resisting arrest. That represents a significantly greater level of force. All law enforcement functions involve use of force.

Clearly, law enforcement functions restrict the physical freedom of the affected individuals in a variety of ways. For example, being arrested, or resisting police directions (passively or actively), or attempting to escape, or intruding upon and obstructing police actions, or concealing or destroying evidence, or endangering themselves or others, or simply posing an obstruction by their presence at a police scene—all require some level of force by law enforcement officers either in response to the action or in order to pre-empt the action for the greater safety of all involved and the benefit of society. All these examples require some level of force exerted by law enforcement to achieve the legitimate law enforcement purpose at hand. Further, in every instance in which law enforcement uses force, that force can be escalated if the initial levels of force prove unsuccessful.

There is no policy, process, or procedure for choosing a specific level of force to apply—no mandated entry level of use. The standard for using non-deadly force has been defined by the Supreme Court in its application of the Fourth Amendment. Law enforcement officers may use *the degree of force reasonably necessary* to achieve the specific law enforcement purpose—but no more than that. The latter is a critical distinction to understand, and it applies to both the nature of the force used and the duration of its application. It is a limitation on the amount of non-deadly force that may be legally used—that which is reasonably necessary to attain a legitimate purpose and no more. Force that exceeds that is patently unreasonable and unjustified. There is also the strong implication that the initial level of force chosen—the "entry level" as it were—must be reasonably proportionate to the circumstances. This does *not* mean that the law enforcement officer must use equal force, or attempt barely adequate force. "Reasonably necessary force" inherently embraces factors of efficiency, rapidity and effectiveness in the interests of timely resolution and safety. The duration of an application of force is dependent upon and justified by the duration of resistance. When the need that prompted the use of force ends or is resolved, the justification for any continuation of force also ceases.

For example, the police officer directing traffic cannot reasonably resort to a chemical agent to get the attention of a motorist. If the officer's official presence is insufficient, then there is the recourse to loud commands, whistles, gestures, perhaps slapping a fender. It is hard to conceive of a reasonable necessity to use any greater level of force to direct traffic. On the other hand, officers arresting an armed and dangerous person may initiate the interaction by physically tackling and throwing the person to the ground at gunpoint. The circumstances and the goal (efficiently arrest a dangerous individual without getting hurt) make reasonable the choice of a higher entry-level force. In all cases, if the entry-level force attempted is unsuccessful then the officer(s) can escalate. If circumstances warrant, the officer(s) can escalate far beyond the next logical force level. That is counter-intuitive to the advocates of a force continuum, and an example of the ill-conceived nature of continuums. The standard is *that level of force reasonably necessary ... and no more.*[35]

---

35. Of course, implicit in the standard is that officers can also de-escalate. Using that degree of force reasonably necessary implies a responsibility to recognize when a lesser degree

Contrast that limitation with the standard for the use of deadly force. "Law enforcement and correctional officers ... may use deadly force only when necessary, that is, when the officer has a reasonable belief that the subject of such force poses an imminent danger of death or serious physical injury to the officer or to another person."[36]

Deadly force may be used when necessary to prevent death or serious injury. There is no limitation on its form or nature. Deadly force is strictly limited in the circumstances in which it may be used, but is totally unlimited in the form it may take. This means that if deadly force is necessary under the circumstances, then it is legal and justified to use any means at hand and it is legal and justified to cause the death of the person creating the necessity. Simply put, the courts do not care if the subject is shot, stabbed, beaten, blown up, or run over with a car *if* the subject poses a reasonable imminent risk of death or serious injury. The dire consequences to be prevented—death or serious injury—justify the means.

Non-deadly force is unlimited in the circumstances in which it can be used, but strictly limited in form, method, and nature to that which is reasonably necessary to attain a legitimate purpose. Deadly force is unlimited in form, method, and nature but strictly limited to two specific circumstances in which it may be used. This distinction is important, even though the use of either type of force will be judged under the Fourth Amendment.

The duration of any and all uses of force is contingent upon, and directly related to, the duration and nature of the resistance or behavior that required using force. For example, the minimal levels of force needed to maintain a seizure are seldom more than official presence and perhaps verbal commands. This very low level of force can be applied for hours if not days. Nevertheless, this arguably unlimited duration is in fact limited to the duration of the seizure and must end when the need to maintain that seizure ends.

For these reasons, the best use-of-force instruction will separate the two subjects of non-deadly and deadly force. Non-deadly force should be taught separately and distinctly from deadly force and treated as a topic inherent to tactics, arrest procedures, and law enforcement functions. Deadly force is so serious in purpose, and so consequential in application—the limited circumstances in which it is justified are so critical—that it merits treatment as a stand-alone topic. This should also foster greater and more comprehensive understanding of deadly force and its unique status and application and thereby better prepare

---

of force is sufficient and thus all that is necessary and de-escalate to that lower level. De-escalation occurs when resistance subsides, or reasonably anticipated resistance or need does not materialize as the event develops, or for similar reasons.

36. U.S. Department of Justice Policy Statement: Use of Deadly Force.

officers to articulate not only their perceptions and decision making processes, but also their understanding of the law and departmental policies.

# Warnings & Warning Shots

There are two other issues that need to be incorporated within law enforcement firearms training curricula as well as the training content regarding deadly force and its use. The first is the concept and use of verbal warnings and the second is the issue of warning shots. Each of them exemplifies a lesser degree of force than deadly force. Each is inextricably interrelated to the use of deadly force because neither one has any valid application except in a situation in which deadly force is necessary or very likely to become necessary. For that reason, both topics need to be addressed as integral parts of deadly force training and follow-up firearms training. A second reason to include both topics is the extensive but incorrect popular belief that one (a verbal warning) is a necessary precondition to using deadly force, and the other (a warning shot) is a viable last-ditch good faith measure to give a person one last chance to avoid deadly force. However, there is no legal standard that preordains a sequence of lesser force actions prior to the use of deadly force.

Law enforcement training commonly encourages the use of a verbal warning when *feasible*. "Feasible" means that there is time and opportunity to do so without incurring excessive (unreasonable) added risk. Officers must not be placed in the position of thinking they must delay the necessary use of deadly force until they have issued a verbal warning. Even more unrealistically, some advocates outside of law enforcement impute a necessity to be sure the warning is understood before using deadly force. Neither is necessary nor reasonable.

There are important caveats regarding verbal warnings. The first is that there has to be a high probability that deadly force may be warranted in the first place or else there is no cause to even consider a warning. Otherwise, the verbal warning is nothing more than a bluff. Law enforcement officers should be trained that if the situation does not merit the use of deadly force, they are no more justified warning of it than they would be actually using it. A verbal warning is nothing more than a less-than-deadly force option used in a deadly force situation in an attempt to forestall the actual use of deadly force.

A second caveat is that the issuance of a warning must be left to the discretion of the officer involved. The officer may or may not decide to issue a verbal warning prior to using deadly force, or the officer may issue the warning while actively engaged in using deadly force, or both may occur. But the absence of a warning is not a measure of the justification for the use of deadly force, even more so in those incidents where the onset of the threat is sudden, immediate, and unmistakable.

A third very significant factor is often overlooked. Quite simply, the only mention of verbal warnings in the law is within the specific context of using deadly force to prevent the escape of a dangerous person (see Chapters 3 & 4). There is no other legal foundation for it, no mention of it except in that single specifically defined and limited circumstance. The use of deadly force to prevent an imminent risk of serious injury does not incorporate any intimation of a need to even consider a verbal warning.

Whereas verbal warnings have some limited foundation in the law, i.e., they are necessary *when feasible* solely within the narrow and specific circumstance of preventing the escape of a dangerous individual, warning shots have no basis in the law whatsoever. If a warning shot causes an injury, it does not implicate the Fourth Amendment unless it was clearly foreseeable and intentional. That would seem to put a warning shot in the same constitutional category as an unintentional discharge—no violation of a constitutional right. And there would be no due process implication unless it represented a reckless disregard for harmful consequences.

In practical terms, there are serious tactical and situational issues that argue against firing warning shots. First, it is inconceivable to consider a warning shot unless the need to use deadly force is reasonably imminent in the first place—same as with verbal warnings. So a warning shot is similar to a verbal warning in that it represents a lesser level of force used in hopes of preempting the necessity to use deadly force in a situation that already justifies deadly force. Essentially, it is an attempt to delay the use of deadly force in circumstances that would justify the use of deadly force—a manifestation of hope that the additional delay and the waste of ammunition will be enough to prevent serious injury.

Second, a warning shot is haphazard. Its intended effect is a show of force and a loud noise. Its ultimate effect in actuality is indiscriminate and randomized—if fired up, it must come down and if fired down, it may ricochet. If fired horizontally, it will travel a long way. The final destination of the *bullet* is unknown, unpredictable, and unsafe. It can injure or kill unknown victims in unknown locations remote from the dangerous incident—victims unaware of the event and uninvolved with it. Innocent bystanders can and do get injured in proximity to deadly force confrontations because the imminent threat is so urgent that the necessity to impose that risk of injury on them is reasonable—under the circumstances. Simply put, the wrong person can get shot for all the right reasons and that is not unreasonable, nor is it indicative of an unjustified use of force.

However, a warning shot can injure innocent bystanders who are far removed from the incident and have no reasonable proximate risk. It would be difficult in a moral sense to justify unintentionally shooting an unknown victim remote from the scene with a warning shot that was fired in hopes of avoiding having to shoot a dangerous individual threatening imminent serious injury. Imposing a haphazard risk of remote injury on distant, uninvolved citizens to avoid inflicting injury on the specific person who is creating the threat of injury does not make a lot of sense.

Third, law enforcement firearms training constantly stresses the necessity to know where the shot is going; to be aware of unintended targets such as innocent bystanders, fellow officers, and unanticipated passersby. Officers involved in shooting situations regularly hold their fire or shift positions to avoid endangering unintended targets. A warning shot is inconsistent with that training and practice.

Fourth, warning shots can trigger unanticipated consequences. There is nothing more certain than a gunshot to galvanize everybody involved into action. Where those engaged in the incident believe that an imminent risk of serious injury is present, a gunshot will immediately convince them that the imminent risk has suddenly become an actual attack. The impetus of sudden gunfire may lead to undesirable, unintended, and unanticipated results. For example, an officer fires a warning shot in response to a fleeing suspect and other officers hear the shot and shoot the suspect as he emerges into their view, assuming it is necessary and justified.

Although gunshots are distinctive and readily identifiable as such, determining the origin of the shots is problematic at best unless one has witnessed it. In the various environs in which shootings occur, the sound of a gunshot reverberates and reflects in unpredictable ways. It introduces an unexpected stimulus into an already tense and uncertain situation with unforeseeable consequences.

On balance, warning shots should be discouraged in practice and through training for all the reasons mentioned above. However, many, if not most, departmental firearms policies contain blanket prohibitions of warning shots. That can create an equally undesirable quandary regarding them. There actually are conceivable circumstances in which a warning shot *is* reasonable.

Consider the use of deadly force to prevent the escape of a dangerous individual. Under those very limited circumstances in which deadly force is justified, a warning shot might suffice to stop the escape. Inarguably, there is a reluctance to shoot plainly dangerous individuals solely to prevent escape, even though the circumstances allow it. If a warning shot successfully induces the individual to submit, it might not be unreasonable especially if precautions were taken to prevent the bullet itself from endangering unknown others remote from the scene. However, the use of a warning shot in this specific situation cannot be the only use of force—if it does not induce surrender, the officer should be prepared to quickly fire an aimed shot to stop the escape.

A second circumstance justifying a warning shot is best explained anecdotally. Early in the authors' experience, an FBI agent working undercover in a motorcycle gang had his cover blown. At the time, he was alone and confronting a dozen armed and angry outlaw bikers who were going to attack him, perhaps kill him. They were in an isolated rural area and the agent was armed with a six-shot revolver—the issued weapon in the FBI at the time. The imminent risk of serious injury, perhaps death, was unmistakable and deadly force was clearly justified. As the agent later stated, he recognized that at best he could shoot six of them as he was going down. He elected to fire a warning shot in addition to verbal warnings that he would shoot them. That shot dispersed the biker gang. The agent was unharmed.

Now, the firearms policy of the FBI contains an unequivocal prohibition on firing warning shots. Nevertheless, the agent was not disciplined or even admonished for firing a warning shot because of the circumstances. His judgment was validated, and rightly so. But even though the administrative result was proper, it was also clearly situational and result oriented and established that the policy is not what it says. What counts is what those sitting in review think of the results. That is not characteristic of good policy. (See Chapter 14 for a discussion of policy considerations.)

It is prudent to strongly discourage warning shots for all the reasons discussed above, and to instill that discouragement through training—but not necessarily by a blanket policy prohibition. That is certainly the most prevalent approach for dealing with warning shots, but it is one that sooner or later will lead to a result-based situational exception to the policy. Inconsistencies in the application of a policy can contribute to the reluctance of officers to act based on their judgment and their assessment of the needs of the situation they are in. The situations in which a warning shot can be a reasonable choice are so rare in occurrence and unique in circumstance that it is better to treat the concept as a training issue, strongly discouraged and severely limited in permissible use. Then policy can prohibit the routine use of warning shots if some exception is made for the case-by-case consideration of any actual use of a warning shot.

# Chapter 7

# Physiological Imperatives

The physiological realities of deadly force confrontations include the factors of action-versus-reaction times, the sensory distortions that occur in any high-stress, life-threatening event, the cognitive and behavioral changes that can occur, and the realities of wound ballistics and the human target (the latter were discussed at length in Chapter 5). These physiological realities are present to varying degrees in *every* deadly force confrontation. The magnitude of the effects may fluctuate, but the occurrence and presence of the effects are unavoidable. They cannot be wished away or ignored in any meaningful analysis of a deadly force incident. As with all other aspects of a deadly force confrontation, these elements must be recognized, assessed, and judged from the perspective of a reasonable officer under the particular circumstances and not with the application of 20/20 hindsight.

## Action vs. Reaction

One of the least recognized physiological factors inherent in all deadly force incidents is that of "action versus reaction." This is apparent despite the fact that reaction times are widely quantified and understood scientifically in numerous professional and recreational pursuits and in the popular understanding of human interactions. However, in analyzing deadly force confrontations, the effects of action/reaction times are frequently ignored or belittled, usually to support allegations that the officer involved should have, or could have, reflected on the unfolding events and acted in a manner to ensure no harm came to the plaintiff.

Unfortunately, the realities are unavoidable and they cannot be ignored or explained away. Most deadly force confrontations begin and end within three seconds. Time is a critical factor—time to think, to act, to react, and to do it all within the imperatives of the law, departmental policy, and training strictures. In the space of three seconds or less, it will all be done.

The reality of action versus reaction as it appertains to a deadly force incident is as much ignored or fantasized as the realities of wound ballistics. Yet, action versus reaction is every bit as critical a factor that must be recognized in any use-of-force incident analysis. Reaction time is very simple to define: it is that time necessary for a person to recognize a stimulus, decide upon an action in response, then initiate and complete the response. To end or alter the response thus occurring would then require a separate reaction time sequence. The second sequence incurs additional time because it first requires recognition of the effects of the initial response, a decision as to what to do, and the time necessary to initiate and complete the new response. The cycle becomes a cascading series, incurring ever more time as it progresses.

Action and reaction sequences take quantifiable amounts of time to complete. This is an unavoidable reality. Although it is a truism that events can occur simultaneously, it is a physical fact that none of them can happen instantaneously. It takes time for a person to perceive an event or stimulus, identify it, formulate a reaction plan (decision time), and then send the requisite nerve impulses to the requisite muscle groups to activate the plan (response time). There then follows the "mechanical time" necessary to physically perform the actions decided upon.

Decision time is that time necessary to perceive a signal or stimulus, identify it, and reach a decision about what to do in response to it. Decision time occurs once in a reaction time sequence, assuming nothing changes. Response time is that time required for the brain to send the necessary nerve impulses to the necessary muscle groups to activate the response. Response time also happens once in a reaction time sequence, assuming nothing changes. And mechanical time is the time necessary for the response to occur, or continue to occur. Mechanical time can accumulate with repetitive responses. All three taken together constitute "reaction time."

A simple example of the interplay of these time components is the act of shooting a gun. First, the shooter must decide to shoot, which takes time (decision time). Then the shooter's brain must direct the shooter's hands and fingers to move as necessary to fire the gun—grip, aim, and pull the trigger (response time). Finally, the gun must be fired and the time taken for each shot to be fired, which does not require any further decision or response time, just the continuation of the action (mechanical time).

This mechanical time does not include the reaction time sequence that leads to the decision to shoot nor the time necessary to implement the decision to shoot. It is simply the time necessary to perform the bodily movements to fire a shot. This time is required to physically move the trigger through the length of its travel. The trigger movement then releases the hammer or firing pin that must now move and strike the primer of the cartridge. The cartridge must then fire and the projectile must then travel the length of the barrel and exit the muzzle of the firearm. Typically this requires roughly 0.3 to 0.4 seconds *per shot fired.*

If something changes, a new decision/response/mechanical sequence must follow. Staying with the example of shooting a gun, if we assume that the target no longer merits being shot, then the shooter must first recognize and identify that fact and decide to stop shooting (decision time). The nerve impulses must travel from the brain to the gun hand and direct the gun hand to stop pulling the trigger. The gun hand must stop pulling the trigger. Typically a decision/response sequence can take 0.5 to 1.0 second to complete in ideal circumstances. Thus the shooting previously decided upon can be *continuing* during the decision/response time and the actual cessation of shooting will lag the recognition that cessation is necessary. This explains why law enforcement officers firing multiple shots in deadly force confrontations can shoot their adversary as or after the individual falls, or in other seemingly inappropriate ways, and not be aware of it. This particular phenomenon is commonly exacerbated by the fact that the person being shot is moving independently and unpredictably while the officer is shooting. The result can be bullet entry wounds in unusual locations, yet that is perfectly consistent with the dynamics of deadly force confrontations and the action/reaction realities.

Recognizing that reaction time is a substantive factor, and that real time must elapse and it is immutable and unavoidable, it is apparent that action (an initial event) will always beat reaction (response to the event). Simply expressed, an action will always occur before an appropriate reaction can be initiated and implemented. Action always beats reaction. This is a reality that is a focus of training throughout law enforcement because law enforcement officers are always in the position of having to react to what somebody does. Second, as stress intensifies and as decision points multiply, reaction time only increases—it never reflects reaction times attained in training; it never decreases. Just as marksmanship skills deteriorate under duress, so do reaction times—always.

The practical effect in the field of deadly force usage is that no law enforcement officer is required to wait or can be expected to wait until he or she is absolutely certain what it is that an individual is going to do, or has in his or her hand. If the circumstances support a perception of imminent danger. The officer does not have to wait to see if the person is actually going to shoot or stab or act to inarguably hurt someone. To wait for certainty is to ensure that no response can possibly prevent or avert the subsequent death or injury.

Acceptance of the fact that actions/reactions impose significant time lapses in high-intensity, short-duration human events and thus affect responses and outcomes is widespread. It is established science widely recognized and accepted without question. In aviation, the Federal Aviation Administration presupposes a minimum reaction time of 0.6 to 1.0 seconds in its operational analyses. Yet in collision avoidance maneuvers, it is not uncommon to see up to five seconds elapse before an aircraft *begins* evasive action [emphasis added].[1]

It is fundamental to vehicle operation and accident analysis. The Los Angeles Police Department defines reaction time as: "The time that elapses between the driver's perception/decision and the time the brakes are applied or the steering wheel turned. The average human reaction time, under these circumstances, is 0.75 of a second."[2] This also has been termed "Mental Processing Time" in other research and determined to average 1.5 seconds. In the context of driving a vehicle, this combines detection of stimuli or sensory input ( ... something is in the road ... ), recognition of the meaning of the input ( ... the something is a person ... ), and response selection and programming ( ... steer left instead of braking ... ).[3]

The above-cited sequences do not represent the total reaction time. Once the response has been selected and programmed, it will take additional time for it to be implemented. There remains in the reaction time sequence sum that time necessary for movement and the time necessary for the device to respond. Movement is the time required to perform the programmed muscle movements. Device response time is the time required for the device being implemented to work.[4] In the context of the example above regarding braking a car, the driver's foot has to move from the accelerator to the brake pedal and press down (movement). Then the vehicle itself will require an unavoidable and absolute minimum time to slow, depending on speed and road conditions. Mechanical devices take time to activate, even after the responder has acted.

For example, a driver stepping on the brake pedal *cannot* stop a car immediately. Instead, the stopping is a function of physical forces, gravity, and friction. For illustration, assume the car is traveling at 55 mph (80.67 feet/sec) on a dry, level road. With a reaction time of 1.5 seconds, the car will travel 1.5 x 80.67 or 121 feet *before* the brakes are even applied. When the brakes engage, external physical forces will determine the stopping distance. In this example, that is 134.4 feet. Therefore total stopping distance = 120.9 ft (reaction time) + 134.4 ft (device response time) = 255.3 ft.[5]

---

1. U.S. Dept. of Transportation, Federal Aviation Administration, Civil Aeromedical Institute. Physiological Operations, "Physiological Training—High Speed Flight," January 1972, page 24.

2. Los Angeles Police Department Training Division, Driver Training Unit, Instructor Lesson Plan "Vehicle Operation Factors," The Human Factor—Reaction Time (1975).

3. "How Long Does It Take to Stop? Methodological Analysis of Driver Perception-Brake Times," *Transportation Human Factors*, 2, pages 195–216, 2000.

4. *Ibid.*, pages 195–216.

5. *Ibid.*, pages 195–216.

Researchers writing in the *Wound Ballistics Review* of the International Wound Ballistics Association (IWBA) have explored reaction times as related to the act of shooting. They defined and measured two components. The first component tested was response time, defined as the time required for the brain to send the impulse to the gun hand and fire the weapon. Forty-six officers were positioned with their weapons out, aimed at the target, primed to fire on the signal. Using electronic timers, they fired one shot when the start signal sounded, and the timer stopped at the sound of the muzzle blast. This protocol eliminated any recognition or decision time. The officers were prepared to fire at the signal and no decision-making time was required. They knew they would shoot on the signal. Each fired three shots with finger on the trigger, and three starting with finger off the trigger, for data purposes.

The mean time lapse for a shot with finger on the trigger was 0.365 seconds. This means that on average an officer (having *already* made the decision to shoot) will perceive a stimulus, initiate the necessary nerve impulse, and 0.365 seconds later the muzzle blast sounds. The mean time lapse for finger off the trigger was 0.677 seconds.[6]

These times are consistent with simple, no-choice-required reaction times as reported in other fields and literature. Interestingly, visual signals incur more time to process than do audio signals.[7] This time interval can be considered the mechanical time necessary to fire a shot, since in this experiment the judgment and decision to shoot have been made.[8]

These times are substantiated by actual shooting results. Several multiple-shot shooting incidents reviewed by the author have been captured on video-

---

6. Tobin EJ, Fackler, ML, MD, "Officer Reaction—Response Times in Firing a Handgun," IWBA *Wound Ballistics Review*, Vol. 3 (1), 1997, pages 6–9.

7. A representative sample in addition to sources previously cited:

Underwood, BJ. *Experimental Psychology, 2nd Ed*, NY, Appleton, Century Crofts, 1949, pages 9, 33, 256.

Wordsworth, RS, Schlosberg H, *Experimental Psychology*, NY, Holt, 1954, page 42.

Kelso, JAS. (Ed.) *Human Behavior, An Introduction*, Hillsdale, NJ, Lawrence Erlbaum Assoc., 1982, pages 70–73, 144–46.

8. As an aside, the researchers also examined the issue of how fast someone can turn his torso. Using videotape, visual markers and electronic timing, the researchers had test subjects turn their torsos 90° and 180° from facing the camera. It took 0.23 seconds for a 90° turn, and 0.53 seconds for a 180° turn. This bit of research was done to provide a forensic explanation of the all-too-common phenomenon in police shootings where an officer swears the suspect was looking at him when he fired, but entry wounds are subsequently found in the suspect's flank or back.

Tobin EJ, Fackler ML, MD, "Officer Reaction—Response Times in Firing a Handgun," page 9.

tape. By timing the muzzle blasts recorded on the tape, it is possible to time the shots themselves. These shootings were situations in which the shooter fired multiple shots without interruption or reason to stop shooting or change focus. In other words, the decision and response times were incurred and the shots followed continuously for a brief period. Consistently, 0.3 to 0.4 seconds elapsed between each shot in the series.[9, 10, 11]

The second component tested was decision time, defined as that time necessary to perceive a signal, identify it, and make the decision to fire a shot. This test protocol used a computer-controlled firearms simulator and three scenarios screened at random.

One scenario was an obvious "no-shoot" scenario to force the test officers to first perceive and identify whether the situation was a "shoot" event, rather than know ahead of time they would shoot in all scenarios. Of the two "shoot" scenarios, one was a simple case of a man stepping out of a doorway with a shotgun and pointing it at the officer. The other was a more complex assassination scenario in a busy courtyard with other people present, and a far less obvious weapon. The researchers used a common visual start point for the electronic timer, and stopped the timer on the sound of the muzzle blast. The officers started with their weapons drawn and pointed at the target area, finger on the trigger. This measured total reaction time—decision time plus the response time discussed above (and including mechanical time).

The mean time lapse from start to shot for the simple scenario was 0.576 seconds. Subtracting the mean response time of 0.365 results in a mean decision time of 0.211 seconds. However, the complex scenario predictably resulted in a mean time lapse of 1.260 seconds, and a resultant mean decision time of 0.895 seconds.[12] Clearly, complex scenarios increase reaction time. Two or more choices substantially increase reaction time exponentially, and "stress generally increases reaction time by a factor of 50 to 100%."[13]

9. Patrick, UW, "Analysis & Report," October 20, 2002, *Juan-Jose Guerra Morales v. U.S.*, U.S. District Court, Eastern District of Michigan, Southern Division, Civil Action No: 01-74269.

10. Patrick, UW, "Supplementary Report," April 30, 2003, *Juan-Jose Guerra Morales v. U.S.*, U.S. District Court, Eastern District of Michigan, Southern Division, Civil Action No: 01-74269.

11. Patrick, UW, "Analysis & Report," July 10, 2000, *Patricia Pace, et al., v. Nicholas Capobianco, et al.*, U.S. District Court, Southern District of Georgia, Case No: CV100-032.

12. Tobin EJ, Fackler ML, MD, "Officer Decision Time in Firing a Handgun," IWBA *Wound Ballistics Review*, Vol. 5 (2), Fall 2001, pages 8–10.

13. Tobin EJ, Fackler ML, MD, "Officer Reaction—Response Times in Firing a Handgun," page 7.

*"The impact upon an officer of unexpected, rapidly changing, or chaotic circumstances will often be a disruption, disturbance, or lag in time in decision-making and tactical responses until he or she accurately identifies what has to be done. This disruption occurs because the brain experiences a temporary perceptual shock when something serious happens that it wasn't ready for."*[14]

Reaction times are greatly affected by the degree to which the individual expects to have to respond. A situation where the need to activate a response is expected will result in the absolute best reaction time possible. A best estimate is 0.7 seconds. Of this, 0.5 seconds is decision time and 0.2 is response/mechanical time. When the situation is unexpected, the reaction time is somewhat slower, about 1.25 seconds. This is due to the increase in decision time to over a second with response time still about 0.2 seconds. In a surprise situation, there is extra time needed to interpret the event and to decide upon response and the increased reaction time is essentially beyond valid estimation. Reaction time depends entirely upon the extent and urgency of the surprise. As noted by the FAA in studying collision avoidance maneuvers, it is not uncommon to see up to five seconds elapse before an aircraft *begins* evasive action [emphasis added].[15]

The increased reaction time is due to a number of factors, including the need to interpret the novel situation and to decide among alternative possible responses. Moreover, people in surprise situations tend to hesitate, expecting the other to take some compensatory action, which increases reaction time. In law enforcement, this manifests itself in the form of a "disbelief" factor—disbelief that this person being confronted is suddenly, really going to try to inflict harm. Effective training can minimize or dispel this factor—as does experience.

The critical imperative of action/reaction times in the law enforcement setting is that the officer's reaction time sequence (decision plus response plus mechanical time resulting in a shot fired) *begins* in response to an action initiated by the person confronted. A law enforcement officer cannot see the future or read minds. The officer can only react to what the subject of investigation does.

The generally accepted rule of thumb is that it takes 0.7 to 1.0 seconds for an individual to first recognize another's action, identify the nature of the action, and then formulate and initiate a response (the reaction). This is an im-

---

14. Blum, LN, PhD, *Force Under Pressure—How Cops Live and Why They Die*, NY, Lantern Books, Booklight Inc., 2000, page 39.

15. U.S. Dept. of Transportation, Federal Aviation Administration, Civil Aeromedical Institute. Physiological Operations, "Physiological Training—High Speed Flight," January 1972, page 24.

mutable physiological reality. The response itself will then entail additional time, depending on its nature, before any effect can be expected. For example, to react by drawing a holstered weapon could then add another 0.5 to 1.25 seconds to the interval preceding firing a shot in self-defense.

Reaction times are increased by a substantial magnitude when the individual is under stress, emotional duress (such as fear), or operating in new and uncertain circumstances. The increase can amount to 50–100% more time than normal, i.e., calm and unstressed reaction times. Yet in the space of the first 0.7 to 1.0 seconds of the event, an unseen weapon can be raised and fired several times. A well-trained police officer understands that he cannot wait to see what happens. Nor is the officer required to be certain that death or injury is imminent. The perception of its imminent likelihood must only be reasonable.

Action versus reaction coupled with the mandates of wound ballistics dictates a reality that can seem to counter common sense or conventional wisdom. Perhaps no more telling example can be found than that of an armed officer confronting a person with a knife. In experiments performed at the Firearms Training Unit (FTU), FBI Academy, Quantico, Virginia, the goal was to quantify in terms of distance the dangerousness of a person with a knife. Obviously, at patently long ranges a man with a knife poses no imminent threat to a man with a gun. However, law enforcement officers cannot stay at a safe distance and pick off knife wielders from long range. They must attempt to resolve the situation peacefully, and that requires closing with the individual. On the other hand, officers must be aware that a knife is an implement of deadly force and at some point, close is too close to protect against a sudden attack.

In the experiments done at the FTU, an instructor stood with a rubber knife at a measured distance from another instructor with a blank-firing handgun. The one with the knife initiated an attack against the one with the gun at his discretion and without warning, charging at him with the intent of stabbing/slashing him with the rubber knife.

Beyond a distance of 21 feet, the agent with the handgun had time to evade the initial attack and shoot, if the gun were already in hand. Inside 21 feet, most of the agents could still fire a shot by the time the attacker reached them with the knife, as the attacker concurrently was able to stab or slash the agent. The harsh reality in such a circumstance is that unless the shot happens to hit the attacker in the central nervous system, the attack will succeed (see Chapter 5—Wound Ballistics). At closer ranges, the attack was successful before the agent could raise his weapon and fire a shot. When the agent started from a holstered position, he was stabbed/slashed every time when the attack commenced inside 21 feet. Some instructors managed to draw and fire an unaimed shot from the hip; most did not. Again the reality of wound ballistics intrudes.

The effects of a bullet wound (other than to the central nervous system) simply take too long to compel incapacitation. For a variety of reasons, those risks may be accepted by the individual officer who decides to approach within the danger zone of a person armed with a knife. That is properly left to the officer's discretion, as guided by experience, training, and the situation at hand. The importance of the so-called 21-foot rule is to flag the risk and its exponential increase as distance decreases and thereby enhance the officer's awareness and preparation.[16] The law enforcement function always requires balancing the responsibility to act against issues of personal safety (see Chapter 11—Risks and Responsibilities).

Yet when a law enforcement officer shoots a person armed with a knife, invariably the assumption arises in allegations and interest group criticisms that it was an unjustified shooting since the person "only" had a knife and the officer had a gun, or the person was 20 feet away when he made a threatening move, or the person could not have hurt anyone, or the officers should not have approached. Frequently, too, police officers let potentially violent individuals armed with a knife get too close to them. Usually they surrender. On the occasions they don't, police officers get killed or injured as a result.[17]

Failure to recognize and account for the reality of action versus reaction can obscure the real issue. It simply is not humanly possible to eliminate the time delays imposed by reaction sequences. The critical question remains, as always, not where or when shots were fired or even the number of shots fired, but was the decision to shoot reasonable and justified under the circumstances.

---

16. A cautionary note is necessary—the agents engaged in the original experiment were well-practiced, expert firearms instructors. Their skills in gun handling, including drawing and firing, are significantly better than the residual skills possessed by the average agent or police officer. Importantly, there was no element of surprise. They knew what was going to happen, lacking only the knowledge of when the test subject would start the attack. This indicates that the average agent or officer will be at risk at distances in excess of 21 feet. More recent experimentation indicates that the dangerous distance is actually 30–35 feet, especially because most officers react unsystematically and erratically—tripping, fumbling for their weapon, failing to defend against the blade, frantically backing up with the only goal being to get out of reach and failing to do so. The spontaneous, indeed panicked, avoidance response only serves to increase the officer's exposure and vulnerability in both time and opportunity.

17. In fact, at some point it will always be necessary to approach within reach of the individual, whether to effect the arrest, disarm, or otherwise resolve the matter. The approach might be delayed, but it cannot be eliminated. Therefore, the "21-foot rule" is a training device that will assist the officer(s) involved in making an informed decision to incur increased personal risk. When it does become necessary to advance increasingly within reach, the officer is cognizant of the severe risk and prepared accordingly.

Secondly, each individual involved in the incident will have his or her own unique perceptions and reaction times. One person's perception cannot be the controlling factor for assessing the reasonableness of another person's perception of an event. Each must be assessed and analyzed from the unique perspective of each individual independently.

The onset of a deadly force incident is an event that is most likely to be sudden and unexpected. Most officers (64%) who have been the victims of a violent physical or potentially lethal assault were not aware that the assault was coming. Of the 36% who were aware that assault was pending, half of them stated later that there was no time to prepare in any way for the attack.[18] The law enforcement officer is *always* in the position of reacting to what the adversary does.

Analysis of a deadly force incident must recognize and assess each individual as an independent entity—one officer may react slower than another and thus not fire a shot. That is not an indication that the first officer was wrong or reckless. One may simply be unaware of the emerging imminent risk, another may be looking somewhere else and another may be a fool. One may simply be slower to react than another. The totality of the circumstances must be determined and evaluated and the effects on each participant assessed from the unique perspective of each participant.

# Fight or Flight

A second physiological reality that is also *always* present in deadly force confrontations is the well named fight-or-flight syndrome. This involuntary reaction to a perceived threat to survival is automatic and reflexive in its effectuation. The physical changes brought on are controlled by a part of the nervous system called the "autonomic nervous system."[19] The autonomous and subconscious level of the central nervous system takes command of the metabolism. Adrenaline is pumped into the system. Blood vessels in the extremities are squeezed down or closed off, increasing blood flow to the large muscle groups and the brain itself. Blood pressure and pulse are both greatly elevated. Heart rate increases to promote blood flow to the brain in order to enhance vision, brain function, and physical reactions. Blood pressure increases. Small blood vessels constrict and fine motor skills and dexterity are diminished in

---

18. Pinizzotto, AJ, PhD, Davis, EF, MS, Miller, CE, "In the Line of Fire: Violence against Law Enforcement," U.S. Department of Justice, Uniform Crime Reports Section, FBI Academy, Quantico, VA, October 1997, page 17.

19. Artwohl, Alexis, PhD, Christensen, Loren, *Deadly Force Encounters*, Paladin Press, Boulder, CO, 1997, pages 33–34.

favor of major muscle groups—the basic means of fighting or fleeing. This results in a loss of dexterity and a loss of fine motor control. (To draw an analogy, imagine peeling a hard-boiled egg—an easy task with normal dexterity and fine motor control. Now imagine doing it with leather work gloves on.) Fight-or-flight processes of the brain are not under the conscious control of the individual. Neurological activity occurring in the fight-or-flight area of the brain is instinctive. It is fueled by the type and quantity of hormones dumped into the system to mobilize the body for emergency reaction.[20]

The large muscle groups are primed for physical violence, or flight. Tunnel vision dominates, focused on the threat source to the exclusion of peripheral factors. So-called "tunnel hearing" is also evident. Participants may or may not hear sounds, noises, or voices as the event unfolds. Many officers in shooting incidents have no recollection of the sound of their gun, or never heard a partner's gun discharge, or the gun being fired at them, or did not recognize the "pop" they heard as a gunshot. For example, officers engaged in shootings consistently have no idea how many shots they fired. It is not unusual that they cannot recall hearing any shots at all. Some report an audio-sensory focus on the sounds of shots to the exclusion of all other sounds. The mental processes are isolated. Time perception is frequently distorted so the individual perceives the unfolding events in extreme slow motion, or sometimes unnaturally speeded up. These effects are commonly referred to as "sensory distortions."[21] However, sensory distortion can be very misleading in its connotations. It might be more accurate to call these perceptual changes "sensory alteration" or "sensory specialization" rather than "sensory distortion."

The senses are not distorted, but are focused with ruthless and augmented capacities upon the perceived threat in order to maximize the likelihood of survival. Seen in that sense, the senses are not distorted at all—they are narrowly concentrated and enhanced more or less to the exclusion of stimuli that are not perceived as bearing on the issue of survival. However, the significant fact to understand is regardless of what it is called, it is extremely prevalent in all deadly force confrontations in one form or another, in varying degrees of intensity, and among all participants to the confrontation.[22]

The consequence is that an observer analyzing the incident after the fact, with no life-threatening stress altering the observer's perceptions and senses,

20. Blum, LN, PhD, *Force Under Pressure—How Cops Live and Why They Die*, Lantern Books, Booklight Inc., New York, NY, 2000, page 7.

21. *Ibid.* pages 51–53.

22. A survey of 157 officers from multiple agencies involved in shootings over the period 1994–1997 produced the following data: 62% experienced the incident in slow motion

may not understand how the officer involved did not hear his gun fire, or did not see the bystander next to the gunman, or could not recount his movements in fine detail during the event. Sensory distortions also explain the common occurrence of multiple commands, a factor that is frequently cited as evidence of poor training and incompetence in the lawsuits that inevitably follow such incidents. An officer may not hear other officers issuing commands and may thus feel compelled to issue his own series of commands. The officer feels an urgency to be heard and to be obeyed by the individual in order to establish and maintain the control that is vital for survival. All of the officers present and aware of the imminent danger feel that urgency and many will respond to it. These are all incidental factors that the subconscious survival reflex does not waste any attention or resources upon. It dominates the response and sensory perceptions of the officer to focus all senses on the primacy of individual survival.

The perceptual changes brought on by fight-or-flight syndrome can take various forms. It is not possible to predict which sensory changes an individual will experience or to what degree. It is fair to say that sensory alteration will be present. It will affect every party to a deadly force confrontation (good guys and bad). And it will manifest itself in each individual in different ways and totally unpredictable degrees. It is probable that the intensity of sensory alteration will vary in direct reaction to the level and urgency of unanticipated elements contained within the incident.[23]

Examples of the various forms that sensory alteration can manifest are as follows:

a.  **Tunnel Vision**—Peripheral vision is diminished. Field of vision narrows to the threat, and depth perception deteriorates or is lost. Thus people in

---

while 17% perceived time to speed up; 84% noted diminished sound and 16% experienced intensified sound; 79% had tunnel vision and 71% experienced heightened visual acuity; 74% responded on "automatic pilot" with little or no conscious thought; 52% reported memory loss for part of the event, and 46% had memory loss for some of their own behavior; 39% experienced dissociation (detachment, out-of-body observance of the event); 26% had intrusive, unrelated, and distracting conscious thoughts during the event; 21% experienced memory distortion (saw, heard, or experienced something that did not happen or actually happened differently than their memory of it); and 7% reported temporary paralysis. This latter is more likely a facet of speeded-up time imposed on the action-reaction time interval making it seem as if they are frozen in place waiting for the reaction to take effect. See: Artwohl, Alexis, PhD, "Perceptual and Memory Distortion During Officer-Involved Shootings," *FBI Law Enforcement Bulletin*, U.S. Department of Justice, Washington, DC, October 2002, pages 19–23.

23. Blum, pages 51–53.

deadly force incidents often do not see bystanders, or people or actions external to the threat.

b.  **Increased Visual Acuity**—Details within the tunnel vision focus are recognized and vividly retained, such as seeing the bullet in the air, a ring on the gun hand of the subject clearly recalled but not the face of the shooter, or the shape of the knife blade being thrust.[24]

c.  **Altered Hearing**—Diminished sound is the most common, ranging from total loss of sound to sounds that seem muffled and distant. Frequently officers in shooting incidents do not hear, and cannot recall, shots being fired. Voices and commands may not be heard, nor sirens or other loud sounds. This effect can also take the form of louder than normal sounds, especially relative to shots being fired at the officer. Both diminished or muted sound and augmented sound can occur in the same individual in the same incident. An officer may hear the adversary whisper something to him (tunnel hearing, for want of a better term), but be unaware of a fellow officer nearby yelling commands. The focus is on the adversary, not the partner.

d.  **Time Distortion**—Events seem to speed up or slow down. An action that actually takes milliseconds to unfold may clearly appear to the people involved to last for minutes, or the reverse. The time may seem to speed up so rapidly that events and actions can barely be perceived. As with altered hearing, both phenomena can occur during the same event.

e.  **Dissociation**—A sense of detachment, of independent outside observation. The individual feels almost nothing, emotionally or physically, but

---

24. An interesting example of sensory alteration occurred in a shooting case investigated by the author. The assailant attacked uniformed Border Patrol agents wielding the broken neck of a glass bottle as a weapon. After being shot twice by one officer in the first room, he advanced on a second officer standing in the doorway to a larger second room. This officer shot him once as he came through the doorway while backing up a couple of steps. The first officer also shot one more time, after which the assailant fell to the floor. A third officer within ten feet of the second officer later advised that he never heard a single shot fired, but he knew the officer near him fired a shot because he saw the flame erupt from the gun muzzle and he smelled the smoke. He has no memory of the assailant falling— he recalls the subject moving forward and he helped handcuff the man on the floor, but he hasn't a clue of the man's intervening actions. It must be noted that muzzle flash is not at all apparent in good lighting, such as was present in this case, even to an individual who expects a shot and is looking for the flash. The enhanced sense of smell is also interesting. It is doubtful at best that anyone would see a muzzle flash or smell the gun smoke from a shot in this huge room with high ceilings, numerous bystanders, and bright lighting if asked to do so under controlled conditions. And this particular officer was only a witness, not a participant. He never drew his own weapon, never made a move nor issued a command— he never had time to do so.

focuses on staying alive, and remembers events as if he had been watching a movie play out before his eyes.

f.  **Temporary Paralysis**—A temporary, but potentially fatal, effect caused when the autonomic nervous system is desperately trying to catch up to the sudden realization that survival is at stake and something must be done immediately.[25] This is a less likely effect than the other examples listed above, especially among trained professionals. After all, preventing this type of involuntary response is one cogent priority of training.

g.  **Memory Distortion**—Memory is not a flawless videotape that can play back exactly the same way each time a person tries to remember a past event. It is normal for memories to change over time. The changed memory may or may not represent reality more accurately.[26] Under fight-or-flight stress, the normal deliberative rational thinking process is replaced by experiential thinking that is faster, more effortless, and automatic in processing information. The slow, deliberative, cognitive process of logic and reflection by which the rational thinking process builds memory is a luxury that cannot be risked in the urgencies of fight or flight. The result is a fragmented memory based on the highlights that flash across the experiential process rather than an integrated narrative.[27]

> *"When the threat directed at an officer requires that he or she engage in an extremely rapid response for survival, the officer does not take the time to think consciously about the situation she or he is in. The 'conscious' part of the officer's brain shuts down during survival mode. The nervous signals and brain activity that enable the officer to react for self-preservation travel and follow a much quicker reflex arc via the spinal cord (e.g., muscle reflexes)."*[28]

Interestingly, "tunnel vision" is frequently manifested forensically in the form of hits inflicted to the weapon or the weapon hand/arm of the adversary. For example, in one case a man who was holding a knife in his right hand suddenly assaulted an officer from about 20 feet away. The officer fired four rounds

---

25. Artwohl, Alexis, PhD, Christensen, Loren, *Deadly Force Encounters*, Paladin Press, Boulder, CO, 1997, page 42.

26. Artwohl, Alexis, PhD, "Perceptual and Memory Distortion During Officer-Involved Shootings," *FBI Law Enforcement Bulletin*, U.S. Department of Justice, Washington, DC, October 2002, pages 19–22.

27. *Ibid.* page 19.

28. Blum, LN, PhD, page 38.

as the man ran at him. The subsequent forensic examination determined that all four rounds hit the man in the right arm. The officer was totally unaware of this until advised of the results of the forensic ballistic examinations. When asked if he intended to hit the man in the arm, he answered that he did not know—it all happened so quickly. He was focused on the man and when the man charged he just raised his gun and fired.

Subconsciously, when the attack abruptly occurred his fight-or-flight focus narrowed or tunneled on the specific threat to his life—the knife in the man's hand rapidly getting closer to him. That focus led him to subconsciously (and unaware) aim his weapon at the point on which he was focused—and all of his shots were fired at that threat point.[29]

This happened despite his training and the knowledge that incapacitation is best achieved by damage to centrally located vital organs, and that peripheral wounds cannot compel incapacitation on a determined person nor dissipate the threat.

This fact was proven yet again in this case—the man paused briefly when struck in the arm by the first shot. He did not drop the knife. He continued his attack, at which point a second officer standing off to the side fired three shots striking him in the torso. The man finally stopped his advance within two feet of the first officer and sank to the floor. Despite the four severe gunshot wounds to his right arm and fatal wounds to his torso, he still held the knife. It had to be wrested from his grip. The second officer was not the target of the attack so his concentration was on the attacker, and not the attacker's weapon.

The normal consciousness will continue to function under the influence of fight-or-flight, but may have little effect. Survival incident participants frequently report their conscious state is more like that of an outside observer, watching what happens and even entertaining non-relevant thoughts about

---

29. Practical firearms training constantly stresses keeping the eyes on the target and raising the weapon up to the line of sight so that vision and firearm are synchronously aimed at the target. Tactically, officers should be trained to keep their firearm and their eyes functioning as a coordinated unit so that when searching or moving through a dangerous area, the weapon is always pointed along the line of sight to where the eyes are looking. Thus if a sudden threat unexpectedly appears, the officer's visual perception and weapon orientation are in immediate, synchronized, and maximal position to respond efficiently. In practical training, the officer learns to shoot where he looks, as he looks. It is not surprising that when this innate "shoot where you look" response is activated under the influence of fight or flight, hits to the weapon and/or weapon hand/arm are later discovered. It happens frequently.

family or fears or how this event was going to change their routine later on. One officer related that as his gunfight progressed, he was thinking about the grocery list his wife had given him that morning and whether he would have time to shop. The conscious mind is a hindrance to the organism in a fight-or-flight survival situation. It is too slow, too easily distracted, and the subconscious mind isolates it and ignores it. The subconscious mind controls the individual, who then falls back on habits and reactions that are either ingrained by thorough and effective training, or are the responses of the ever present evolutionary imperative, i.e., fight tooth and nail or run.

Fight or flight is a survival syndrome that has been orchestrated over time by evolution. It originated in the days of fang and tooth, predator and prey, to maximize the individual's chances of survival when confronted with an attack or threatened with loss of life. It is with us today. It is a short-term phenomenon, and can leave the individual in a state of near physical collapse, with symptoms including nausea, dizziness, elevated pulse rate, and/or a physical sensation of weakness due to the flood of hormones and magnified physical exertions that comprise the syndrome.

"Neurological activity occurring in the 'fight or flight' area of the brain is instinctive—fueled by the hormones that mobilize the body for emergency reaction."[30] The resultant biological alarm response arouses the person in preparation for decisive physical action. Among the effects observed in the body's preparatory activation are the following:

a.  Increased arterial blood pressure, blood supply to the brain, heart rate, and cardiac output.
b.  Increased stimulation of major muscle groups.
c.  Increased plasma, free fatty acids, triglycerides, and cholesterol.
d.  *Decreased* blood flow to the kidneys, gastrointestinal system, and skin.[31]

These effects prepare the body to fight or flee. Increased blood flow to the brain enhances the neurological functions driving the flight-or-flight response. Increased blood flow to the central organs and away from the extremities prepares the body against injury and works to diminish the effects of blood loss. Increased blood flow to the major muscle groups (arms and legs) maximizes the ability to fight or run—to strike blows, to defend, and/or attack. Decreased blood flow to skin and extremities will decrease fine motor control, unnecessary for the programmed decisive physical exertion to come. The physical changes are designed to galvanize the individual into action and pro-

30. Blum, page 7.
31. *Ibid.* pages 135–36.

vide the extra energy and focus to fight as hard and run as fast as possible to survive.[32]

A critical effect, also discussed in Chapter 5, is insensitivity to pain. During the period the fight-or-flight syndrome holds sway, the individual affected will feel little pain, and commonly is totally insensitive to it.[33] Pain is a factor that could detract from the individual's focus on survival and the ability to fight or flee. It is a distraction that inhibits decisive physical action, and thus the autonomic nervous system suppresses it. It is not biologically relevant to immediate survival. Pain becomes a factor after the event is over. This phenomenon is common throughout the literature on combat. It is commonly reported in the post-shooting incident analyses routinely conducted in the aftermath of law enforcement deadly force incidents.[34]

A number of cognitive and behavioral changes also commonly occur among participants during and in the aftermath of deadly force incidents. It is important to recognize and understand these changes because they frequently appear to support allegations of lying or cover-up in the legal actions that invariably follow any law enforcement use of deadly force. The truth is that the chemical changes in the brain engendered by the autonomic nervous system's invocation of fight or flight cause these changes to occur. It is an involuntary and unconscious effect that the individual cannot understand or explain in the aftermath of the incident, but it is no less real in its manifestation.

The several cognitive/behavioral changes that can arise are:

a.  **Automatic Behavior**—Most participants in high-stress, high-risk events give little or no conscious thought to their behavior. They instinctively do what their experience has programmed them to do.

b.  **Memory Gaps**—It is normal that people involved in a deadly force encounter do not remember parts of what happened, or all that they did. Memory is selective.

c.  **Intrusive Thoughts**—It is common that the conscious mind engages in thoughts that may not be relevant to the incident at hand while the subconscious is furiously engaged in controlling and formulating responses. Thoughts of one's family, future events or plans, or even past experiences similar to the current one are all common. For example, referring again to SA Ed Mireles' experience in Miami in 1986, as he ran across the street

---

32. Artwohl, pages 38–39.

33. *Ibid.* page 39.

34. See the brief account of FBI Special Agent Ed Mireles' actions in the infamous FBI Miami shoot-out of April 1986, recounted in Chapter 5.

to join SSA Gordon McNeill he was hit in the right arm and abruptly fell down hard. His thought at the time was that he had run into the back of McNeill's car and he recalled thinking, "God I hope nobody saw that!" He was unaware of his wound until he tried to use his arm to push himself up and had to look to see why it wasn't working.

d.   **Memory Distortions**—The individual may think he or she saw, heard, or experienced something during the event, but investigation or forensic evidence reveals that it happened differently or could not have happened at all.[35] The goal of any training program should be to instill the necessary habits and reactions to such an extent that when the fight-or-flight syndrome does kick in and the officer is operating instinctively under the control of the autonomic nervous system, these are the responses that are programmed and utilized. Training instills conditioned experiential responses that the subconscious will utilize.

The fact that physiological realities always are present also explains the seemingly anomalous things that become apparent in the aftermath of all deadly force incidents. The officer involved in the shooting does not remember how many shots were fired. The officer vividly remembers the adversary looking him in the eyes when he shot, but the autopsy reveals bullet entry wounds in the adversary's flank or back. The officer never heard the commands being shouted by his partner beside him. The officer swears he only fired two shots, but the adversary has four bullet wounds. The adversary has a bullet entry wound that indicates it was inflicted as he lay on the ground, but the officer swears he stopped shooting when he saw him fall. The adversary was hit multiple times, but any one of the shots would have been fatal. The officer says he shot the subject in the front of the store, but the subject is found in the back of the store and the officer cannot remember seeing him move there.[36]

The phenomenon of shots being fired that subsequent forensic examination reveals hit the subject after he was down, or turned away, or falling is a relatively common one. The allegation that invariably follows is that the officer used excessive force, or was shooting with negligent abandon, or was not justified in firing those shots. In some cases, criminal charges are filed on no other basis than

---

35. Artwohl, pages 42–47.

36. An FBI agent was involved in a shooting incident in the Midwest in which several agents fired a number of rounds, as did the adversary who was killed. The agent was armed with a pistol that has a capacity of 15 rounds. When asked if he knew how many shots he fired, the agent said "Absolutely—15!" When asked how he knew that, the agent smiled and said, "My gun was empty." That same agent was unaware he had been wounded in his calf until another agent noticed blood pooling on the floor back in the office.

the location of gunshot wounds relative to the subject's position. It should be clear that, given the reality of action/reaction time sequences and the physiological sensory alterations of fight or flight, these incidents are fully explainable.

In the time it takes for an officer to perceive that the threat has ended and activate the necessary physical response to stop shooting, one or more additional shots likely will have been fired as the previous decision/response/mechanical sequence plays out. The continued act of shooting does not require decision/response time except to alter it or end it. It continues as the senses take in stimuli and the brain assesses and decides what to do next.

For example, in a controlled experiment using electronic timers, 20 police officers were instructed to fire as many shots as possible between two audible signals. The officers started with their handguns drawn and aimed at the target, finger on the trigger. The time interval used was two seconds. Seventeen of the 20 shooters (85%) fired one or two shots after the stop signal.[37] There can be no doubt that reaction/response times will delay the end of a series of shots. The inevitable presence of sensory alterations to whatever degree manifested in the individual involved will only exacerbate this delay.

The most pernicious factor that affects objectively and correctly analyzing a law enforcement use of deadly force is memory—pernicious in the sense that failure to understand the realities and limitations of human memory will lead to unfounded suspicions and allegations of lying or covering up. Memory is problematic in the most benign of circumstances. It becomes even more troublesome as the circumstances become more stressful, more unexpected, and more dynamic—startling in onset, brief in duration, and sudden in termination. That is a fair, generic description of a deadly force incident. It is not conducive to a detailed, comprehensive, and infallible recall of the events.

> "*To be mistaken about details is not the result of a bad memory but of the normal functioning of human memory. When we want to remember something, we don't simply pluck a whole memory intact from a "memory store." The memory is actually constructed from stored and available bits of information; we unconsciously fill in any gaps in the information with inferences. When all the fragments are integrated into a whole that makes sense, they form what we call a memory. Still other factors affect the accurate perception, and therefore recollection, of an event. Was there*

---

37. Tobin EJ, Fackler ML, MD, "Officer Reaction-Response Time Delay at the End of a Shot Series," IWBA *Wound Ballistics Review*, Vol. 5 (2), Fall 2001, pages 11–12.

*violence? How much? Was it light or dark? Did the eyewitness have any
prior expectations or interests?"*[38]

Routinely, law enforcement officers are asked to provide an outline account,
perhaps a walk-through narrative, of the event in the immediate aftermath.
This is a necessary and invaluable investigative tool. The investigators must
have some idea of what happened, where, to whom, and in what sequence in
order to conduct an objective and thorough investigation. However, no participant's account of the event can be complete. Common sense tells us that the
narrative will be a "macro-version" missing numerous details, probably conflicting with other witness accounts (civilian and police), and inconsistent to
some degree with the forensic record embodied in the crime scene at which
the investigators are looking. However, this is normal. Memory does not work
like a video camera. It is better thought of as a collection of still photos like a
surveillance camera taking pictures at repetitive intervals such as 2–3 seconds
apart. That also illustrates how details can be unobserved and thus not remembered—they happened between shots. Assorted physiological effects (i.e.,
tunnel vision, et al.) further limit the parameters of what is actually seen. Then
the mind automatically fills in the gaps to create a seamless whole that makes
sense ... but that can also omit actual details apparent to the objective observer
after-the-fact. Under the exigent circumstances of a "fight-or-flight" event,
memory will be even more restricted and limited.

One obvious reason is that memory is ineluctably related to vision—much
of the data recorded in memory is taken in through the eyes. If memory is
likened to a recording, the senses are the camera. But the senses discern very
little that is not directly and immediately relevant to the issue of survival. Consider just one simple example—vision and how it "tunnels" in such circumstances. The severely restricted field of view critically limits the "visual data"
available to form a memory. The officer cannot remember that which he or
she did not see.

Another term for this phenomenon is "*selective attention.*" While the brain,
via the eyes, is intensely focused on a particular stimulus (the life-threatening
action or event), it can easily fail to recognize another, perhaps equally important piece of information peripheral to that stimulus. The mind is intently
focused upon one element in the environment and the sensory system not only
ignores other, distracting elements, it actively suppresses recognition to pre-

---

38. Loftus, Elizabeth, PhD, Ketcham, Katherine, *Witness for the Defense—The Accused,
the Eyewitness and the Expert,* St. Martin's Press, 175 Fifth Avenue, New York, NY (1991),
page 23.

vent distraction from the immediately urgent point of attention. It affects recall after the fact. Information subconsciously deemed unrelated or irrelevant will have a very low rate of recall. Officers, because of their severely focused observations (*selective attention*) in deadly force circumstances will fixate on specific elements of the incident, resulting in very specific and vivid, though not necessarily accurate, memory for aspects of the incident while concurrently limiting their recollection of other facts.

Human memory after the fact is incomplete, inconsistent with the physical record, and suffers inexplicable gaps. Not all information that is observed is retained. Just as it has limited capacity to receive or recognize information, the brain also has limited capacity to retain or store information. That natural and unavoidable fact nevertheless lends the appearance of dissimilation and alibi to the officer's narrative. Subsequently, the mind will attempt to rectify the gaps and inconsistencies of the memory record. "*All memory involves reconstruction. We put together pieces of episodes that are not well connected, and we continually make judgments about whether a particular piece belongs in the memory or not. One expects to see shuffling of pieces with a process that works like this.*"[39] The individual is not aware of it happening—it is seamless and natural, and not evidence of duplicity.[40]

> "*Truth and reality, when seen through the filter of our memories, are not objective facts but subjective, interpretative realities. We interpret the past, correcting ourselves, adding bits and pieces, deleting uncomplementary or disturbing recollections, sweeping, dusting, tidying things up. Thus our representation of the past takes on a living, shifting reality; it is not fixed and immutable, not a place way back there that is preserved in stone, but a living thing that changes shape, expands, shrinks, and expands again, an amoeba-like creature with powers to make us laugh, and cry, and clench our fists. Enormous powers—powers even to make us believe in something that never happened.*"
>
> "*The 'drawers' holding our memories are obviously extremely crowded and densely packed. They are also constantly being emptied out, scat-*

---

39. Reprinted with permission from *Issues in Science and Technology*, Loftus. "Memory Faults and Fixes," Summer 2002, p. 41–50, by the University of Texas at Dallas, Richardson, TX.

40. "Are we aware of our mind's distortions of our past experience? In most cases, the answer is no. As time goes by and the memories gradually change, we become convinced that we saw or said or did what we remember. We perceive the blending of fact and fiction that constitutes a memory as completely and utterly truthful. We are innocent victims of our mind's manipulations." Loftus and Ketcham, page 20.

*tered about, and then stuffed back into place. Like curious, playful chil-
dren searching through drawers for a blouse or pair of pants, our brains
seem to enjoy ransacking the memory drawers, tossing the facts about,
and then stuffing everything back in, oblivious to order or importance.
As new bits and pieces of information are added into long-term memory,
the old memories are removed, replaced, crumpled up, or shoved into
corners. Little details are added, confusing or extraneous elements are
deleted, and a coherent construction of the facts is gradually created that
may bear little resemblance to the original event."*

*"Memories don't just fade, as the old saying would have us believe;
they also grow. What fades is the initial perception, the actual experience of the events. But every time we recall an event, we must reconstruct
the memory, and with each recollection the memory may be changed—
colored by succeeding events, other people's recollections or suggestions,
increased understanding, or a new context."*[41]

A law enforcement officer involved in a deadly force incident will be interviewed more than once over time. There will be the initial narrative and/or
walk-through to assist the investigation. There will be a formal interview at
some later date as a part of the investigation. There may additional interviews.
Sooner or later there will be a deposition in response to the inevitable civil suit
being filed.

With each successive account, the officer's version will develop. New details
may be remembered. Previous details may be forgotten or denied. The passage of time, subsequent events, revelation of additional information, and
even suggestive comments by interviewers will all intrude and can affect the memory of the event.

*"Our memories are vulnerable to 'post-event information': to details,
ideas, and suggestions that come along after an event has happened. People integrate new materials into their memory, modifying what they believe they personally experienced. When people combine information
gathered at the time of an actual experience with new information acquired later, they form a smooth and seamless memory and thereafter
have great difficulty telling which facts came from which time."*[42]

None of it is evidence of falsehood or cover-up. And it does not say that
the eyewitness account of the officer is not valid. The officer's account is valu-

---

41. *Ibid.* page 20.
42. Loftus, page 43.

able. It may be the best descriptive evidence of what happened. And the more it can be corroborated with other evidence, the better. The critical lesson to be applied when assessing an officer's account of what happened is that memory is not seamless. It is not comprehensive. It is not necessarily consistent and repeatable. It provides the outline that investigation must fill in. All of this is totally consistent with the physiological reality of human memory, and is indicative of a truthful account—to the best ability of the officer involved. The reverse is also true—comprehensive, consistent, and unchanging recollection of what happened is symptomatic of collaboration and collusion.[43]

Physiological realities are inescapable. Reaction time is an immutable and irreducible factor that must be considered in any analysis of the imminence of danger or the potential for risk. Time and distance relative to human reactions are important considerations. There is no such thing as an instantaneous event or reaction—it cannot happen and it cannot be assumed in any deadly force analysis. The sensory alterations that arise and the cognitive/behavioral changes that can occur are always present, but unpredictable in terms of when and how and to what degree they will influence any given individual. And the individual officer's recall of what happened will never be comprehensively detailed nor will it be immutable over time.

The purpose of this discussion is not to suggest that these physiological factors are endemic or quantifiable. They are not. Some individuals will experience few such factors; some will experience many. Some will experience a variety of them off and on during the incident. Some will experience only one, and that one may vary in effect over the duration of the incident. However, these effects cannot be ignored in an analysis of the use of deadly force and the interaction of the people involved. Often overlooked is the fact that these physiological realities apply to all human beings in general. Those on the side of law enforcement will experience them, and so will the assailants and adversaries on the other side of the event.

---

43. The U.S. Department of Justice assembled a committee in 1996 that came up with a set of guidelines for law enforcement. *Eyewitness Evidence: A Guide for Law Enforcement* offers a set of national guidelines for the collection and preservation of eyewitness evidence that includes recommendations such as asking open-ended questions, not interrupting eyewitness's responses, and avoiding leading questions, among many other concerns related to eyewitness testimony.

The publication is not a legal mandate but rather a document that hopes to promote sound professional practice. Investigators and attorneys would be as well advised to apply the same precautions and concerns to the eyewitness accounts of law enforcement officers involved in a deadly force incident. The officers deserve no less.

# Chapter 8

# Tactical Factors and Misconceptions

Tactical factors include the dynamics and environmental circumstances of shooting incidents, the abilities of the involved parties, and the limited means available to compel a timely halt to the threatening activity. Any consideration of tactical factors also must look at weapon limitations and utilization, peripheral gear such as body armor, chemical agents, or impact weapons, and the obstacles and features of the environment within which the deadly force incident occurred. These elements must be assessed objectively in any analysis of a deadly force confrontation.

Each incident will be composed of a unique set of factors, circumstances, and obstacles within which the law enforcement officer will have to function, as always subject to the ever present realities of wound ballistics and physiological responses. All deadly force incidents are dynamic, fluid, and unpredictable as they evolve from start to finish and involve necessarily unanticipated, if not random, developments that must be recognized, adapted to, and resolved.

## Deadly Force Incident Dynamics

Few, if any, deadly force confrontations will present the officer with an opportunity to take a careful, precisely aimed shot at a stationary person, selecting a specific aiming point intended to compel incapacitation with minimal delay. Rather, deadly force confrontations are characterized by their sudden, surprising onset; by rapid and unpredictable movements of both officer and adversary; by limited and partial target opportunities; by poor light and unforeseen obstacles; by unexpected and unrehearsed events; and by the life-or-death stress of sudden, close, personal violence happening at unpracticed speeds within critically brief time constraints.

Frequently, deadly force confrontations will involve more than one adversary. Proper training is designed to imbue the law enforcement officer with the ability to first recognize and prioritize multiple threats then react against those threats quickly and efficiently in order of descending risk to self and others. For example, confronted with two targets at 10 yards, one with a knife and one with a gun, the well-trained officer would shoot at the one with the gun first then deal with the knife wielder. Within arm's reach, the problem becomes more complex. The officer must now assess which is most likely to inflict injury soonest, or which might inflict the most grievous injury when either can inflict dire, if not mortal, harm.

Several factors must be recognized and processed relative to how they enhance or diminish the risk from that particular threat: the location of the gun and the knife; the attitude or dangerous qualities attributable to the wielder of each weapon, known or perceived; the "readiness" of each weapon—is the gun holstered, held down, and the knife raised overhead, or is the gun aimed and the knife down? These are but a few examples of the types and complexities of data an officer encountering multiple adversaries must assess and process. Based on the officer's assessment of relative risk, a prioritized response will ensue. The response the officer must decide upon is which requires first attention, and which must wait a second or fraction of a second before being acted against. And the decision must be made immediately.

The law enforcement officer confronted with multiple threats cannot afford to wait and see if the first threat has been successfully resolved before addressing the next one. In fact, it is extremely unlikely that an officer could know whether or not the shots fired were successful in the time available in such a scenario.[1]

In simple terms, assuming the use of deadly force is justified, law enforcement officers should be trained to shoot at least two shots at the first threat and then immediately respond to the next threat—fire at that one—and then move to the next one or return to the first one. If neither threat is stopped, at least one or all may be disrupted or deflected sufficiently to serve the ultimate goal—protection of self and others. Additionally, disruption of the threat(s) can benefit the officer by enabling a better opportunity to apply deadly force more effectively. It is a tenet of law enforcement training, based on experience and science, to keep shooting as long as the threat presents itself and stop when the officer recognizes that the threat has ended. This is the lesson learned from the realities of wound ballistics (see Chapter 5). However, the physiological responses to a deadly force confrontation, such as tunnel vision, can make that level of tactical awareness problematic. One goal of training is that the officer

---

1. Patrick, UW, "Handgun Wounding Factors and Effectiveness," FBI Academy Firearms Training Unit, U.S. Department of Justice, Federal Bureau of Investigation, 1989.

can recognize the onset of sensory alterations such as tunnel vision and adapt to it. To use but one sensory alteration as an example, the officer cannot prevent tunnel vision, but he or she can recognize it and adapt to it by looking left, right, up, and down when feasible rather than focusing exclusively on the most compelling threat.

It merits emphasizing that these situations are life-or-death situations. Law enforcement use of deadly force is not an arrest technique. It is not a means for achieving a statutory law enforcement responsibility. Officers do not shoot to subdue, to arrest, or to compel compliance. The use of deadly force is limited to protection of self and others from the risk of death or serious injury or, much more rarely, the prevention of escape of a dangerous individual. It has no other justifiable purpose.

Therefore, training is quite properly oriented towards "center of mass" shooting, to use the popular verbal shorthand ubiquitous throughout law enforcement. The term is habitually and reasonably construed to mean that the law enforcement target is the center chest area of the human target. This is somewhat misleading and will contribute to confusion when shooting incidents are examined after the fact and the person was hit elsewhere. Although true in a range environment and certainly the optimum target point mandated by the realities of wound ballistics, "center of mass" is true in actuality only in the simplistic sense that if the adversary presents a full frontal view without any intervening obstruction or impediment, then the center chest is in fact the center of mass target to be hit. In truth, this is seldom the case.

As an aside, this is another compelling reason for effective training as opposed to a continuation of qualification courses and practices. A stationary, full frontal and unobstructed target is the norm in qualification courses and practices. It is not the norm in deadly force confrontations. In fact, the sudden realization that there is nothing presented as a target that resembles the stationary, full frontal, and unobstructed target of the qualification course can result in uncertainty, hesitation, and ultimately failure to react promptly and effectively.

It is more correct to say the law enforcement officer is trained to shoot at the center of *whatever is presented for a target*. Shooting at the center of whatever is visible as a target is the only accurate definition of target aiming point and must be ingrained through practical training. Good shot placement is multiple hits in the center of that part of the adversary that is presented, regardless of anatomy or angle. Shoot what you see—you may not have time or opportunity for a better target.

A review of law enforcement shootings clearly reveals that regardless of the number of rounds fired in deadly force confrontations, most of the time only one or two solid torso hits will be attained. This is because of the nature of deadly force confrontations and the extreme difficulty of shooting a handgun with precision under such dire and stressful conditions. The probability of multiple hits with a handgun is minimized in high-stress, high-risk confrontations where adversaries are moving, unforeseen obstacles come into play, and the physiological/cognitive/behavioral changes inherent to the onset of the fight-or-flight syndrome are in effect. Experienced law enforcement officers implicitly recognize that fact. When a potential deadly force confrontation can be reasonably anticipated and they have the time to prepare in advance, those preparations are characterized by employing shoulder weapons instead of handguns as the primary weapon. Because most deadly force confrontations are not anticipated and cannot be planned in advance, the officer(s) involved cannot be prepared in advance with heavier armament.

The handgun, with all its limitations, is the primary weapon in law enforcement. It is the primary weapon for defense against an unexpected attack. It will almost certainly be the *only* weapon available to meet an unexpected attack. As a corollary tactical principle, no law enforcement officer should ever plan to meet an *expected* attack armed only with a handgun. Nevertheless, the majority of shootings occur in manners and circumstances in which the officer either does not have any other weapon available, or cannot get to it. One of the tactical realities of deadly force confrontations is that the handgun is the only weapon a law enforcement can reasonably be expected to have at hand whenever needed and it must be relied upon, and must prevail.

It is pertinent to note that during the sixteen-year period of 1999–2014, of the 765 officers killed with firearms, 597 (78.0%) of them were killed within distances of 20 feet or less.[2] The nature of the law enforcement function requires that law enforcement officers must close the distance between themselves and the subject(s) of their attentions. Perhaps the most significant tactical reality of deadly force confrontations is that law enforcement officers are trained, practiced, and expected to intervene and resolve potentially hazardous situations. This requires the officer to intrude and to seek to close with the adversary in order to subdue, control, and ultimately arrest as necessary. In simple terms, this is the law enforcement duty and managing that duty forms the law enforcement response.

Responsible law enforcement does not recognize an option to decline involvement where the safety of an individual, a group of individuals, or a community at large is at risk. An assortment of allegations is commonly raised in

---

2. A compendium of FBI Uniform Crime Reports, "Law Enforcement Officers Killed and Assaulted," 1999–2014.

civil suits instituted following a law enforcement shooting incident. Such allegations include claims that the officer(s) involved: should not have intervened, or should have gone away, or should have avoided closing with the individual and thereby forcing the incident. None are valid. Law enforcement officers are sworn to protect the community and its citizens, and to do so they must resolve such incidents in favor of the safety of the community and its citizens. In order to do that, those same law enforcement officers must close with the individual(s) who pose the threat. And in doing that, they must protect themselves in order to protect the community and its citizens. The 78% killed within 20 feet of their adversary bear stark witness to this tactical reality.

## Weapon Retention Issues

Several considerations relate to the use of the handgun as the primary weapon in law enforcement. One is weapon retention. During the sixteen-year period of 1999–2014, 765 officers were killed with firearms—58 of them with their own weapon.[3] On average, four law enforcement officers are killed every year with their own weapon.

One countermeasure attempted by some departments is to mandate the use of security holsters that severely restrict the ability of someone to remove the weapon from the holster. This is an attractive but risky option. Unfortunately, these same security holsters make it awkward and difficult at best for the officer to remove the weapon from the holster. The result is that an additional delay is built into the officer's response to the sudden onset of a deadly force confrontation. Weapon retention is better resolved by enhanced officer awareness of potential risk, control techniques, and relevant policy stipulations, such as mandating no weapons in booking rooms, etc.[4]

---

3. *Ibid.* The annual totals range from a low of one each in 2000, 2006, 2012, and 2013 to a high of 11 victim officers killed with their own weapon in 2003. Among those 11 killings is one victim officer who was beaten to death with his own baton. And in 2011 and 2012, two officers each year were beaten to death (and one in 2014)—no weapons were used other than the "personal" ones of fists and feet.

4. It is not the purpose of this writing to explore issues of weapon retention or to discuss retention training and policy considerations, but rather to advocate and illustrate the reality that a deadly force confrontation does not mean that everybody engaged in it starts out with a weapon. Even unarmed adversaries can justifiably be shot if they reasonably present an imminent risk of death or serious injury.

Although the obvious truth is that officers who are killed with their own weapon have it taken from them, obstructing access to the weapon while it is in the holster will also work to the detriment of officer safety and survival. It is doubtful that this same approach will reduce the incidence of law enforcement officers being killed with their own weapon. The annual statistics support this.

Law enforcement officers must be constantly aware of the fact that there is *always* a firearm present in every confrontation or interaction in which they engage—theirs. An unarmed man can immediately become an armed and dangerous adversary by taking the officer's weapon. This appears on its face to be one of those easy truisms too obvious to bear citing. The reality is that it is not. Law enforcement officers routinely treat unarmed people with less caution than those reasonably believed to be armed, even when the person is engaged in physical resistance, assault, or other aggressive activity. The recognition that a weapon is at hand must be a factor in the perception of risk and influence the resultant choice of responses. There are a variety of implements of less than deadly force available (chemical agents, impact weapons, electronic control devices) and techniques (swarming, for example) in which law enforcement officers are trained.[5]

However, a physical confrontation with an unarmed person always has the potential to become a deadly force confrontation even though the unarmed person never possesses a weapon. This possibility can never be ignored. An officer can lose the fight and thereby lose possession of his or her weapon. An officer may reasonably fear that the unarmed adversary is physically superior to him or her and if allowed to grapple or assault the officer, will win the fight and take the officer's weapon. In the course of a physical struggle with an unarmed adversary, the adversary does not have to be stronger, more skilled, or

---

5. Swarming has been used to subdue an individual in lieu of utilizing injurious force, even though such greater force may well be justified. The intent is to physically overwhelm the individual by sheer weight and force of numbers, force him to the ground, and restrict resistance by weight and physical control of limbs until additional assistance can arrive and/ or the individual can be restrained. The technique has been used against drunks, substance abusers, or otherwise distraught or disturbed individuals as an alternative to the use of justified, but more injurious means such as impact weapons, chemical agents, physical blows, or ultimately deadly force. Swarming is not appropriate where there exists reasonable belief that the individual is armed and a threat to the safety of the responding officers. It has been blamed for dubiously situational deaths such as "positional asphyxia" and thus widely discouraged, although one would think that if that were so then gang tackling in sports such as football would have a more noticeable death rate ascribed to it. It has been largely supplanted by the prevalence and effectiveness of electronic control devices.

more violent than the officer. The adversary merely has to be lucky enough to somehow get possession of the weapon. No officer is expected to take a beating, perhaps be hospitalized, and all in the mere hope that in the process the attacker does not take away his gun and kill him with it.

Using means other than deadly force, such as chemical agents or impact weapons, can be a consideration if such means are at hand. But if the situation is one in which the use of deadly force is reasonable and justified, the employment of such lesser means may unreasonably increase the risk to the officer(s) involved. Impact weapons are primarily intended to keep an assaultive adversary off an officer, to keep a person at arm's length until the person either surrenders or can be subdued. As well impact weapons can be used to compel compliance, for example to compel a person to move a leg or display a hand. Impact weapons can also be used as implements of deadly force. Any blow struck to a person's head meets the definition of deadly force[6] and therefore must also meet the same standards of reasonable necessity to be justified as any other use of deadly force.

Chemical agents are more problematic. The effectiveness of chemical agents has been vastly overrated. When used against individuals under the influence of alcohol, narcotics, or mental disturbance, chemical agents can exacerbate the situation by increasing the person's levels of rage and aggression more often than they will subdue the person. Individuals under such influences or even just adrenaline are often not dissuaded by chemical agents. They will exhibit the physical effects of exposure, but they continue to function in spite of them. Second, Murphy's Law dictates that chemical agents will invariably affect the law enforcement officers involved in the incident to a greater extent than the adversaries being confronted. The officers will not have the benefit of the ameliorating effects of alcohol, drugs, mental disturbance, or adrenaline. Third, people routinely continue to function in training programs and familiarization sessions when exposed to chemical agents as part of the curriculum, albeit with teary eyes and runny noses. It is unrealistic to expect an aggressive, physical assault perhaps augmented by adrenaline, substance abuse, mental aberration, or some combination thereof, to be dissuaded by the discomforting physical effects of a chemical agent.[7]

---

6. That force which when used can reasonably result in death or serious physical injury.

7. Clearly, chemical agents have a legitimate use in law enforcement. That subject is not for this writing. Rather, a rule of thumb that chemical agents are inappropriate in deadly force confrontations and why is the point because all too often they are suggested as realistic alternatives to deadly force and thus form the basis for allegations of excessive or unjustified force. Chemical agents are irritants, **not** incapacitants.

Every officer must be aware of this potential risk, but clearly every unarmed adversary cannot be shot. Law enforcement officers must be trained to recognize the potential risks and to understand their own capabilities. They must be trained to assess risk, and recognize the level of risk they are able to resolve. Law enforcement is not a risk-free profession, and it can never be so. But the risks can be managed through training, experience, and recognition of the level of risk being incurred. Each officer has the individual discretion to recognize when the risk exceeds his or her ability to manage it, and at that point the reasonable fear of death or serious injury that can justify the use of deadly force can become valid.

When a law enforcement officer does use deadly force against an unarmed person, it invariably results in public outcry and legal suits alleging excessive, unnecessary, and/or unjustified force. Police training is lamented as lacking and the unarmed adversary is portrayed as having posed no risk or threat that justified "gunning him down." While objective and informed analysis of the facts and circumstances may refute the allegations, the officer will be criticized for not attempting lesser means.

# Weapon Utilization

Another factor that comes into play in the tactical assessment of a deadly force confrontation and that is often misunderstood is the design of the weapons system in use and the use of those designed features. This consideration commonly arises in regard to the issue of placing a finger on the trigger of the weapon.

When a law enforcement officer anticipates the imminent onset of a possible deadly force confrontation, several precautionary responses can occur. Some of them are involuntary. For example, as a precursor to the potential advent of fight or flight (see Chapter 7), the body will begin to prepare itself—pulse will rise, mental attention will focus, hormones will begin to be dumped into the system with resultant "butterflies" in the stomach, and jumpy nerves and "nervous energy" will be felt. Some lack of fine dexterity will be experienced.

Equally involuntary will be physical preparations taken as a result of ingrained training and conditioned responses. The officer will unsnap the holster. The officer may grip the weapon in its holster, or draw the weapon and hold it unobtrusively at one side. These are all perfectly reasonable and sound precautionary actions. It is widely instructed in law enforcement training that if an officer thinks his firearm may be needed, the firearm should be in his hand. It is far easier to put the weapon away once it is recognized that it is not needed than it is to need it urgently and have to produce it.

And many officers will place their finger on the trigger of their weapon in response to a specific risk vector. This is a frequent and virtually unavoidable response, done below conscious levels. The law enforcement officer who steps into a darkened alley and believes that an armed and dangerous person is somewhere in that alley will have a finger on the trigger, and the particular weapon system should allow a margin of safety for that. The purpose for that margin of safety is to allow rational handling of the weapon while preventing an unintentional discharge.

Conventional handgun designs provide for that margin of safety by one of two means—length and weight of trigger pull, or the presence of a manual safety that requires a distinct and intentional effort to disengage. Length and weight of trigger pull is the typical design feature of double action (DA) revolvers and DA semiautomatic pistols. Typically the trigger requires a pressure of 12 pounds to move, and its movement is an arc of 0.5 inch or more. Length and weight thus require specific intent to pull the trigger through and fire the first shot. An officer can place a finger on the trigger and the margin of safety provided by length and weight of trigger pull will greatly mitigate the likelihood of an unintentional discharge of the weapon. The DA trigger design thereby permits the law enforcement agency to allow the officer by policy and training to do something the officer will almost certainly do in that dark alley regardless of policy or training.

Single action (SA) weapons are defined by short, light trigger pulls. The trigger requires pressure of 5–7 pounds or less and trigger travel on the order of 0.12 inch or so to fire the weapon. SA trigger weights and lengths of pull cannot be felt when fine muscle control and dexterity deteriorate under the influence of fight-or-flight stress. Most SA weapons are equipped with a manual safety that must be disengaged as a separate and distinct move prior to pulling the trigger and firing the weapon. This mechanical requirement for a separate and distinct act also mandates specific intent to pull the trigger and fire the first shot. The manual safety creates a safety margin in the conventional SA pistol that also allows an officer to have a finger safely on or near the trigger in anticipatory preparation.

A weapon that lacks length and weight of trigger pull, or lacks the separate and distinct manual safety, is not appropriate for law enforcement use. The most readily understood example is a cocked revolver (DA or SA design is immaterial for this discussion). When a revolver is cocked, the trigger pull is reduced in length and weight to less than 0.10 inch and less than four pounds. There is no manual safety on a revolver so *any* contact with the trigger that applies less than four pounds pressure will move the trigger the 0.10 inches necessary to fire the weapon. It is also true that the weapon is perfectly safe as long as there is no finger on the trigger. It cannot fire without pressure on the trigger. However, in this example there is absolutely no margin of safety, no mechanical allowance for error, and it would be imperative to prohibit placing the finger on the trigger until the moment that firing a shot was specifically intended.

An objective evaluation of the weapon system in use by a law enforcement agency can offer insight into the probable events that transpire in a deadly force incident. Some weapons are entirely too easy to shoot, a factor solely dependent on the trigger pull properties and safety mechanisms. Such weapons are susceptible to unintentional discharge, and most particularly in high-stress, high-risk situations wherein the body is preparing for "fight or flight," or engaged in fight or flight, and the fine muscle control, dexterity, and tactile sense necessary to feel and control the short length, light-weight trigger is simply not there.

The remedy that is dictated for using such weapons is to train officers to keep their fingers off the trigger until they intend to shoot the weapon. And this can be successfully accomplished in the controlled and practiced environs of a firearms range. Notwithstanding the feasibility of training officers to comply with a doctrine of "finger off the trigger until deciding to shoot," the issue is really whether such a practice can be ingrained reliably and effectively in the average officer given the time and resource constraints that apply to firearms training. Each officer, from the poorest performers to the larger body of average performers to the few high achievers, must be instilled with the instinctive confidence that keeping his or her finger outside the trigger guard until the decision to shoot is made will not impede his or her chance of survival.[8] It is the experience of the authors that even the training provided by leading agencies with ample resources and the time to invest in regular training will not accomplish this level of instinctive confidence and reliance on a slower technique.

It fails the test of actual practice when that same officer steps into that darkened alley believing that an armed and dangerous person is in there. The officer's finger finds the trigger to eliminate that one additional movement in the event the officer has to use the weapon to protect his or her life, or the life of another. It is inevitable. It is also clearly the manner in which law enforcement officers use firearms in the tactical realities of engaging in potentially life-threatening encounters. Even experienced law enforcement firearms instructors who believe in and instruct the "finger off the trigger" doctrine, admit that in similar scenarios they too place their finger on the trigger.

---

8. Bassett, DA, "Comments on the Finger on the Trigger Issue," IWBA, *Wound Ballistics Review*, Vol. 3 (3), 1997, page 10.

There is a small but definite tactical advantage that arises from having one's finger on the trigger. The average mean time required for a shot with finger on the trigger was 0.365 seconds in a controlled laboratory experiment where the decision to shoot was certain. This means that, on average, once an officer has perceived a stimulus, decided to shoot, and initiated the necessary nerve impulses to activate the necessary muscle groups, 0.365 seconds later the muzzle blast sounds. The mean time lapse for finger off the trigger was 0.677 seconds.[9] The simple mechanical time required to fire one shot with the finger on the trigger is 0.312 seconds (mean average) faster than with the finger off the trigger. In the short duration environment of a deadly force confrontation, that time difference could be the difference. And under the actual stresses and complications of high-risk, high-stress encounter, the time differential will only increase.

The weapon system used should be chosen to safely allow inevitable human behavior, rather than deny it. All too often in the aftermath of a shooting tragedy in which somebody is unintentionally shot, or (less tragically but no less deplorable) a car, window, mirror, store front, or other inexplicable object is shot, there is no consideration of the weapon system involved. Some handgun designs are just too susceptible to being fired unintentionally, especially in a stress situation. The real fault in such cases does not lie with the officer, but with the choice of weapon system required for use. Sadly, weapon selection is more commonly a budgetary concern with little recognition of tactical or safety of usage issues. When the unintentional shooting tragedy occurs, as it has and inevitably will again, it is an obfuscation to claim that the officer did not keep his finger off the trigger as training doctrine provides and make no deeper analysis. If the weapon system chosen is inappropriate for use in high-stress situations by human officers in high-stress situations, then similar tragedies will follow. Some weapons are simply too easy to shoot.

Imagine again the above example of a cocked revolver and assume, for illustrative purposes only, that a cocked revolver is the issued weapon. It is reliable and very easy to shoot—perhaps too easy to shoot—but that concern is resolved by dictating that officers keep their fingers off the trigger until they intend to fire the weapon. The dictate is made a key element of the training curriculum and relentlessly repeated and practiced in training because the gun *cannot* fire unless a finger nudges the trigger. If officers do as they are trained to do, the gun will be handled safely. Put another way, the gun is 100% safe, *if* the officers using it are 100% correct with it 100% of the time in 100% of the

---

9. Tobin EJ, Fackler, ML, MD, "Officer Reaction—Response Times in Firing a Handgun" IWBA, *Wound Ballistics Review*, Vol. 3 (1), 1997, pages 6–9.

situations in which they handle it. That may be considered a reasonable expectation by some for the small number of expertly adept and devoted firearms enthusiasts in the department, although the authors would argue against that. But in actual fact, it bears repeating that 100% of *all* of the departments' officers must be 100% correct in handling that weapon 100% of the time — there is no margin of safety, no margin for error at all, no mechanical safeguard. The weapon is unforgiving of any inadvertent or momentary carelessness or mistake. That is why consideration of the design of an issued weapon, and its trigger system in particular, as envisioned for use over the complete panoply of skill levels is so important. Unfortunately, it is also the least recognized and least considered factor in the selection of police firearms.

The point is that selecting and issuing a weapon system based on ease of shooting without regard to how law enforcement officers use weapons in high-stress encounters is setting the officers up for failure. A policy stipulation that mandates "finger off the trigger until the decision to shoot has been made" is then necessary. And when inadvertent discharges begin to occur because the weapon system is inappropriate to the manner in which firearms are used in high-stress encounters, the officer bears the full brunt of blame for violating the policy when in fact the policy restriction denies the reality of human nature in dangerous circumstances. A policy stricture that mandates an unlikely, if not impossible, restraint contrary to the overriding and irresistible responses that come into play in dangerous situations is unfair and unfairly puts the onus on the officer if something goes wrong. The officer will be blamed for "not handling the gun as he was trained to handle it" when in fact the selection of the weapon system created the near certainty that these unintentional discharges will happen.

> *"In essence, 'finger off-the-trigger until deciding to shoot' policy denies the officer the authority to assume the highest state of defensive preparedness (weapon trained on the suspect with finger on the trigger) short of making the decision and commitment to shoot."*[10]

A serious consideration in selecting a service weapon for a police department is the fact that most police officers are not expert gun-handlers. And most police officers will not become expertly adept in handling their firearm. They do not have the interest or the ambition for it. They will be safe, proficient, and qualified. They will train to the degree mandated by their department but no more. The the time and resources necessary to ingrain an expert skill level

---

10. Bassett, DA, page 9.

throughout a department and keep it there are neither practical nor available. So a weapon intended for general issue use in a department must be selected with the clear understanding that the entire department, in all its various skill levels, must be safe and capable with it in the practical necessity of that aforementioned darkened alley and not just a sterile and controlled range environment.

There is a second physical factor that also should affect consideration of the trigger system used in a weapon. The human "startle" reflex is an involuntary response to a sudden, surprising perceptual shock or physical contact. Simply put, when startled the fingers tend to contract slightly. Absent length and weight of trigger pull, or the presence of an independent safety mechanism, the result is an unintentional discharge. The officer will be blamed for violating the policy against having a finger on the trigger, and sadly most will accept that as the cause, including the officer who fired the unintentional shot. The truth of the matter is that a more forgiving trigger system would allow a more realistic policy, and also eliminate 75–90% of the unintentional discharges overall.

> *"It is unrealistic to instruct the Agent/officer to keep his finger off the trigger until he is intending to shoot. In actuality, the Agent/officer facing an unidentified subject in a potentially dangerous situation will have his finger on the trigger no matter what policy or instruction have said to the contrary, and common sense and survival instincts dictate that he should."*[11]

# Bouncing Bullets

In 1969 the FBI Firearms Training Unit published a report of testing and research done regarding bullet ricochets off hard surfaces, and the important tactical considerations involved in the phenomenon.[12] The modern urban environment has a lot of hard surfaces—paved roads, walls and surfaces of concrete or brick, steel objects; the examples are myriad and bullets that strike them ricochet. Ricochets have always been understood to constitute a serious hazard but the ramifications of that hazard have been deemed "common-sense"— intuitive deduction rather than fact. The truth is completely different.

Conventional wisdom about bullet ricochets pictures them acting in the same manner as billiard balls. That concept assumes that a bullet striking a

---

11. "Weapons Workshop: 5/16-19/1988," U.S. Department of Justice, FBI Academy, Quantico, Virginia. Participants included weapons experts from a wide variety of federal, state, and local law enforcement agencies plus entities of the U.S. military.

12. *FBI Law Enforcement Bulletin,* "Bouncing Bullets," 38, 1969.

hard surface at an acute angle will ricochet off that surface at a departure angle similar to the angle of impact in the same way that billiard balls carom off each other in accordance with the Law of Reflection.[13] The angle of departure is determined by the angle of impact. Conventional wisdom conceptualizes a bullet striking a hard surface at an angle of 30° will ricochet off that surface at an angle of 30°. However, while that tacitly understood concept is valid for nondeforming billiard balls of equal mass and density impacting at low velocities, it is not true for bullets—projectiles that impact at velocities several magnitudes greater than a billiard shot and that deform in the process.

When a bullet strikes a hard surface, be it brick, concrete, or steel, it deforms and flattens to some degree, although the amount of deformation appears to be insignificant relative to the effect it has upon the resulting angle of ricochet. The bullet does not ricochet off the surface at an angle anywhere near the angle of impact. Instead, it will fly very closely along the surface it struck, essentially skimming the surface for a considerable distance well within the usual range parameters of shooting incidents. Two shooting incidents in 1969 precipitated the interest of the FBI Firearms Training Unit.

> "In a small Midwestern city, a uniformed police officer responded to a burglar alarm ringing at a corner liquor store. Two suspects emerged through the front door, and one suspect appeared to have a gun in his right hand. The officer assumed a prone position in the street and shouted, 'Police Officer! Halt!' The suspect immediately fired at the officer. A .38 caliber bullet hit the concrete pavement six (6) feet in front of the officer, ricocheted and entered the officer's skull two inches below the bill of his cap."
>
> "In a large Midwestern city, detectives located an armed and dangerous fugitive in a modern steel and concrete building. One officer dropped to his knee and brought his sidearm to bear on the subject and ordered him to 'freeze.' The officer shot the subject as the latter attempted to draw an automatic. The subject recoiled backward after being hit and involuntarily fired at the floor. The bullet struck the tile-covered floor several

---

13. The scientific term for the angle at which a projectile strikes another object is "angle of incidence" and the angle at which that projectile departs after impact with the object is the "angle of reflection." The Law of Reflection states that when an object bounces off a flat surface, the angle at which it hits the surface will be equal to the angle at which it bounces away. However, for clarity and ease of understanding, the authors use the term "angle of impact" for the incoming angle of incidence and "angle of departure" or "angle of ricochet" for the outbound angle of reflection.

*feet in front of the officer, ricocheted, struck the officer, and severed a femoral artery, a mortal wound."*[14]

An experiment was conducted in 1988 that strikingly quantified the FBI's "bouncing bullet" phenomenon.[15] The results are critical for any discussion of shooting incidents and appropriate tactics designed to improve an officer's chances to prevail and survive.

The experiment consisted of firing four different handgun projectiles so that they struck a concrete wall at a precise angle of impact. A paper target was positioned down range from the impact point on the wall. The angle of ricochet and the projectile's passage along the wall was thus captured and measured. The researchers fired a .38 caliber lead ball; a .38 caliber lead hollow point (HP); a .38 caliber semi-jacketed hollow point (JHP), and a 9mm full metal-jacketed bullet (FMJ).[16] Each was fired from four feet (muzzle to wall) at three specific angles of impact: 45°, 30°, and 20°. The paper target was 36" by 45" and placed 19 feet down range.

At a 45° angle of impact, the lead HP angle of ricochet was 0.8 degrees for one shot (all others were fliers); the JHP mean angle of ricochet was 2.3 degrees (a maximum of 3.1°—minimum of 0.4°). All of the 9mm FMJ ricochets were fliers.[17,18]

At an angle of impact of 30°, the lead HP mean angle of ricochet was 2.3° (a maximum of 3.1°—minimum of 0.7°—one flier); the JHP mean angle of ricochet was 1.7° (a maximum of 3.2°—minimum of 0.7°—no fliers) and the

---

14. *FBI Law Enforcement Bulletin*, pages 1–9.

15. Burke TW, Griffin R, Rowe WF, "Bullet Ricochet from Concrete Surfaces: Implication for Officer Survival," *Journal of Police Science and Administration*, Vol. 16, No. 4 (1988).

16. The results of the shots using the .38 caliber lead sphere are excluded from the text in the interest of brevity. For information, the mean angle of ricochet for the lead sphere was 2.2° at a 45° angle of impact; 2.4° at a 30° angle of impact and 0.7° at the 20° angle of impact.

17. In recording the results, some shots did not hit the target. These shots were designated "fliers" since their flight path after hitting the wall was random enough to miss the target. It is apparent that this unpredictable flight path is a function of the angle of impact. The greater the angle of impact, the more likely it is that the projectile will be a "flier" with an unpredictable direction. This does not mean that the angle of ricochet was greater and the bullet ricocheted at a more pronounced angle. It means that the bullet still skimmed the surface but yawed in its flight path enough up or down to miss the target. This is due to the increased deformation of the projectile with a steeper angle of impact. Deformation destroys aerodynamic shape. The more deformed and irregular the projectile, the more susceptible it is to extreme variations in trajectory.

18. Burke, Griffin, Rowe, page 266.

9mm FMJ mean angle of ricochet was 5.1° (a maximum of 6.2°—minimum of 3.6°—no fliers).[19]

At the 20° angle of impact, the lead HP mean angle of ricochet was 0.7° (a maximum of 1.2°—minimum of 0.5°—no fliers); the JHP mean angle of impact was 0.5° (a maximum of 0.7°—minimum of 0.3°—no fliers) and the 9mm FMJ mean angle of ricochet was 0.5° (a maximum of 0.8°—minimum of 0.3°—one flier).[20]

The ramifications of this information are obvious, and important. Tactically, the law enforcement officer should keep an arm's length from any hard vertical surface. The adversary does not have to fire directly at the officer to hit him—a bullet strike anywhere on the surface within 20 feet of the officer can hit him. The officer would not even have to be visible to the shooter to get hit—a ricochet off the surface will travel along that surface and stay within the width of a torso for a significant distance along the surface. That has serious implications.

Two examples will suffice to illustrate the hazard. If a bullet ricochets off of a wall with an angle of ricochet (angle of departure) of 5°, it will be approximately 18-inches off the wall at a point 20 feet down range. If the angle of ricochet is 1°, the bullet will be approximately 4-inches off the wall 20 feet down range.

On the other hand, the "bouncing bullet" phenomenon works just as well for law enforcement. A law enforcement officer involved in a shooting can use it to advantage by intentionally shooting against the wall, street, or other hard surface in front of the adversary. As demonstrated, the shallower the angle of impact the better. A relevant example that is seldom recognized is that of an adversary taking cover behind a car. "Bouncing bullets" enable the law enforcement officer to hit the adversary by intentionally firing into the pavement and ricocheting the bullets underneath the car. Another consideration for using "bouncing bullets" is because of the possibility of any one shot being a "flyer," it should be obvious that multiple shots may be necessary in order to score meaningful hits. That is certainly consistent with the widely extant training admonishment to keep shooting until the threat is understood to be over.

# Body Armor

The fact that soft body armor is now a ubiquitous accoutrement of law enforcement is a positive development of the past 20 years. Even more encour-

---

19. *Ibid.* page 266.
20. *Ibid.* page 266.

aging is that the routine use of soft body armor is increasingly common.[21] Countless law enforcement officers over the years owe their lives to soft body armor. There are some caveats that do apply to body armor relative to deadly force confrontations.

First, soft body armor is a defense against unexpected attack no differently than the primary weapon, the handgun. It will prevent the penetration of those calibers of ammunition most likely to be confronted in a sudden attack—but it is not protection against all calibers. As well, soft body armor will not protect against a stabbing weapon such as a knife, ice pick, screwdriver, etc.

Second, body armor does not provide complete coverage of vital areas. As a rule, it covers the upper chest, front and back, and depending on the design, the sides to a degree. Law enforcement officers are intimately aware of this—the public is not. The pertinence of body armor limitations to a discussion of the tactical realities of deadly force confrontations is that it is in fact a limited and imperfect protective device. The aftermath of many justified shooting incidents is the allegation that the officer was not at risk because he or she was wearing body armor.

In the year 2014 (the most recent at the time of this writing for which figures are available), 51 law enforcement officers were feloniously killed. Of those 51 officers, 39 (76.5%) were wearing body armor when they were killed and 46 of the 51 were killed with firearms.[22] During the sixteen-year period of 1999–2014, 833 officers were killed. 765 of them were killed with firearms and 513 of those officers were wearing body armor when they were killed (67.0%).[23] To further break down those 513 deaths, 381 of the officers were struck in the head or neck, 174 in the upper torso (that area typically covered by body armor), and 31 died from wounds below the waist.[24]

Neither the public nor any individual law enforcement officer should consider body armor anything more than a partial and imperfect protective shield.

---

21. This is a self evident and laudatory development. The first edition of this book used FBI UCR data for the year 2002 (the most current at that time). In 2002, 56 law enforcement officers were feloniously killed. Of the 56, 35 (62.5%) were wearing body armor when they were killed. During the ten-year period prior to that (1992–2001), 594 officers were killed with firearms and 307 of them were wearing body armor when they were killed (52%). Contrast this data from 2002 with the current data from 2014 that is cited in the main text.

See: FBI Uniform Crime Reports, Law Enforcement Officers Killed and Assaulted 2001.

22. FBI Uniform Crime Reports, Law Enforcement Officers Killed and Assaulted 2014, Table 40.

23. *Ibid.* Tables 40 and 41 plus a compendium of data from FBI Uniform Crime Reports, Law Enforcement Officers Killed and Assaulted for the years 1999–2014.

24. Compendium of data from FBI Uniform Crime Reports, Law Enforcement Officers Killed and Assaulted for the years 1999–2014.

In a deadly force confrontation; no law enforcement officer should assume more personal risk wearing body armor than he or she would without it.[25] The presence or lack of body armor is irrelevant to the reasonable perception of a risk of death or serious injury and the justified decision to use deadly force to eliminate that risk. It is a fallacy to believe otherwise.

# The Matter of Vehicles

Frequently, deadly force incidents happen in and around motor vehicles. Almost as frequently, the motor vehicle is the weapon that is used in such a manner as to threaten death or serious injury that in turn results in the law enforcement decision to use deadly force. The fact that a car can be a weapon is widely unrecognized in the conventional public view of law enforcement practices and the use of deadly force.

However, by law an officer may use deadly force when necessary to protect self or others from the reasonably perceived threat of imminent death or serious injury. The discretionary authority to use deadly force is based on the need to prevent an imminent risk of death or injury from proceeding, or to stop a risk of death or serious injury that is in progress. There is no qualifying caveat regarding the means by which that risk is imposed.

The law and the sound law enforcement policies that derive from the law are focused on preventing or stopping imminent death or injury. There is no categorization of means, nor is there any mandate that certain weapons or tactics are more dangerous or more susceptible to result in injury than others. The person killed with a firearm is as dead as the person stabbed to death, the one kicked to death, or the one struck and killed with a car. Deadly force would be reasonable and justified to prevent any of these examples. However, as discussed at length, the decision to use deadly force can be made preemptively of any actual attempt to inflict death or serious injury. The law enforcement officer cannot and is not required to wait until he or she is certain of what is

---

25. Interestingly, some training programs take into account the vulnerable areas inherent to body armor. The Maine Criminal Justice Academy teaches the isosceles stance in its firearms program and advocates against the Weaver stance because the Weaver stance positions the shooter at an angle relative to the target—weak side forward. The Weaver stance thus turns the armhole of the body armor to the target—an obvious vulnerability that diminishes the protection of the armor. This is one small example of a well thought out and justified training dictum that is based on experience and is relevant to the needs of the officers under instruction.

going to happen. The officer must reasonably believe that the risk of death or injury is real and imminent and that the urgency of the risk is such that the only chance to dispel it is the use of deadly force rather than a lesser means.

The person who sees a gun pointed at him or her by an adversary can be in reasonable fear of imminent death or injury. So can the person who sees that adversary close by with a knife in his hand. So can the person whose unarmed adversary threatens to "kick the crap" out of him. And so can the person who sees the adversary drive a car at him. The law enforcement officer is authorized to use the means at hand most likely to negate or end the risk—not the least injurious or a progressive checklist of ever increasing force levels.

Whether the driver of the car intends to strike the officer or not is as irrelevant as the intent of the person who turns toward an officer with a gun in hand. It is not possible to discern the intent, nor does the urgency of preventing injury or death allow the luxury of time to wait and see what happens. If the driver operates the car in such a manner as to pose a threat to the officer or others, the car is the weapon and the driver is the individual employing it.

An officer involved in a vehicular-related incident must of course recognize the vehicle approaching, calculate its possible course of travel, assess his own vulnerability, assess the likelihood the vehicle will not stop and will endanger him as it proceeds, decide on a course of action that will best protect him from harm, and implement that course of action in time to protect himself from serious injury or death, and still satisfy his responsibility to protect himself and others in his community. Any time an officer interacts with a person in a motor vehicle, that motor vehicle can pose a real risk of death or injury. It does not matter whether the motor vehicle is operated as an intentional weapon or as the implement of escape. Intent of the driver is irrelevant—prevention of death or injury is the legitimate and reasonable purpose for use of deadly force.

Many vehicle-related incidents begin or end with high-speed pursuits that impose a significant risk upon the community at large and unrelated, unsuspecting citizens at random. These vehicle pursuits often result in incidents in which deadly force is used and the outcry that results when the occupant gets shot is evidence of a major misconception as to the dangerousness of the situation. When someone drives at extreme speeds, runs stop lights and stop signs, drives in the oncoming lanes, veers across lanes, drives off the road or refuses to stop in response to emergency lights and sirens, that individual is imposing an extreme and imminent risk upon citizens at large, as well as the law enforcement officers trying to stop or subdue him. The vehicle operated that way is an instrument of possible death and destruction. It is only by chance that another vehicle is not struck, or a pedestrian hit, or a bystander run down.

The operation of a vehicle in such a manner is clear reason to believe that the driver is dangerous, willing to injure or kill, and recklessly disregarding his own safety or that of anyone in his vicinity (recognized by the Supreme Court—see Chapter 3). When law enforcement finally succeeds in closing with the vehicle and its occupants, the presumption that the driver is dangerous has been clearly established by the events of the pursuit. If that driver now operates the vehicle in a manner that poses a perceptible risk to the officer(s) or others, the urgent need to stop or divert the use of the vehicle is equally clear. It is no different than a situation in which officers confront a subject with gun in hand who has just shot someone. The urgent and imminent nature of the risk being confronted has been established by the actions of the individual, and the individual's use of the weapon at hand.

The second reality of deciding to use deadly force to stop a risk of death or serious injury posed by the operation of a car is that it is absolutely physically impossible to stop a car with a bullet within the time constraints embodied by the concept of an imminent risk of death or serious injury. For example, a bullet that penetrated the radiator will in fact stop a car. However, it may take a few hours for the coolant to leak out and the engine to overheat and seize up. Shooting a tire flat will not work either. Cars are driven at length on flat tires with nearly monotonous regularity in chase events.

There is no vital area or critical point within the car itself that a bullet can disrupt and stop the car with any immediacy. Nor will a bullet physically stop a car any more than it will knock down a human being. It simply cannot be done. A typical sedan may weigh 5,000 lbs. A typical .45 bullet (to pick the largest handgun projectile commonly used in law enforcement) weighs 0.033 pounds (or about half an ounce).[26] The idea that a bullet will stop a car is absurd on its face.

To protect self or others from the imminent risk of death or injury posed by the operation of a motor vehicle requires that the one operating the vehicle be compelled to stop operating it in the hazardous manner. There is no other way. Law enforcement officers are best trained to shoot at the driver of a car when that car is operated in a manner that poses a reasonable threat of death or serious injury to the officer or others.

Shooting at the occupant of a car raises additional issues. A car is by and large excellent protection against small arms projectiles. In order to hit the occupant of a car, a bullet must penetrate into the passenger compartment of the vehicle. This can be difficult to accomplish except for shooting through the

---

26. The common bullet weight characteristic of the .45 ACP cartridge is 230 grains. There are 7,000 grains to the pound.

side windows. Side windows and rear windows usually offer little obstruction to bullets. Normally a side or rear window will shatter and fall apart, leaving no obstruction at all. However, the rest of a car is different.

Front windshields are made of laminated safety glass designed not to shatter and fall apart. Most handgun bullets will not stay intact when they penetrate front windshields.[27] They separate, bullet jackets from bullet cores, and lose mass in the process of penetrating the windshield. The resultant projectile that comes through is a misshaped piece of lead lacking stability and form plus jagged shards of bullet jacket. Some lightweight bullets won't penetrate at all. Even high-velocity rifle bullets are disfigured and deflected to varying degrees penetrating laminated safety glass.[28]

Car doors offer good protection against most handgun projectiles as well. A car door contains within it reinforcing bars, window operating mechanisms, support struts, brackets, etc. The likelihood of a handgun penetrating through a car door and into the passenger compartment with sufficient retained velocity and physical integrity to inflict a significant wound on the occupant is not good. Larger, heavier caliber projectiles offer a better possibility of success.[29]

---

27. All of the generalizations of bullet performance are based on the tabulated results of four years of ammunition testing conducted under the author's direction at the Firearms Training Unit, FBI Academy, Quantico, VA. The FBI Ammunition Test protocol was designed by the author and implemented in December 1988. Annual reports were published on a calendar year basis of the results. To wit:

"Ammunition Tests Vol. 1 — 1989," U.S. Department of Justice, FBI Academy, Quantico, Virginia — 27 rounds tested (6- .45ACP; 6- 10mm; 3- .357 Magnum; 6- .38 Special; 1- .380ACP; 5- 9mm).

"Ammunition Tests Vol. 2 — 1990," U.S. Department of Justice, FBI Academy, Quantico, Virginia — 33 rounds tested (6- .45ACP; 6- 10mm; 4- .40S&W; 1- .357 Magnum; 4- .38 Special; 12- 9mm).

"Ammunition Tests Vol. 3 — 1991," U.S. Department of Justice, FBI Academy, Quantico, Virginia — 21 rounds tested (1- 10mm; 4- .40S&W; 2- .357 Magnum; 2- .38 Special; 6- 9mm; 3- .380ACP; three SMG tests — one each 10mm, .40S&W, 9mm).

"Ammunition Tests Vol. 4 — 1992," U.S. Department of Justice, FBI Academy, Quantico, Virginia — 26 rounds tested (3- .45ACP; 4- 10mm; 4- .40S&W; 1- .357 Magnum; 2- .38 Special; 12- 9mm).

See also:

Hollabaugh, TL, Patrick, UW, "FBI Testing of Hydrashok Ammunition," U.S. Department of Justice, FBI Academy, Quantico, Virginia, July 1991.

28. Hollabaugh, TL, Quinn, ME, "FBI Testing of .308 Caliber Ammunition through Glass Barriers," U.S. Department of Justice, FBI Academy, Quantico, Virginia, November 1996.

29. One of the best possible rounds available to law enforcement for penetrating a car door while retaining the capability of inflicting a serious wound is the 12-gauge rifled slug.

Tactically, a car is a good source of cover against small arms fire by virtue of its construction and its mobility. Training of law enforcement officers in and around vehicles should stress this fact (see Chapter 6). Although it can be an excellent protective bunker, it can also become an equally good coffin, restricting an individual's ability to see and react to events, to move, and to respond to unfolding threats. It fixes the individual's location, *if* the vehicle is immobilized. In the case of a criminal within the vehicle, that can be a good thing. In the event of a police officer under attack, it can be bad. Coffin or cover—a car is always a significant factor when it is an element of a deadly force confrontation.

# Danger Signals

There is no more critical moment in law enforcement than when an officer and an adversary come within close proximity, whether incident to arrest, in pursuit of an investigatory end, or at the onset of a confrontation.

As noted before, during the 16-year period of 1999–2014, there were 765 officers killed with firearms, and 597 (78.0%) of them were killed within distances of 20 feet or less. There were 65 additional officers killed by other means, including knives, personal weapons (fists, feet), blunt instruments, cars, etc.[30] Proximity increases risk exponentially, yet proximity is also obligatory to the basic law enforcement functions. Close proximity (within reach) is necessary to make an arrest, to ask a question, to collect information, or to sort out events. It cannot be avoided.

Law enforcement officers must be thoroughly trained to recognize and evaluate danger signals. One of the first to manifest itself in most nascent confrontations is non-compliance on the part of the person that the officer(s) is facing. Non-compliance is a significant danger signal, and it can take several forms singly or in combination. The most obvious is non-compliance with verbal orders or commands. That is an elementary form of non-compliance that can arise in any law enforcement managed confrontation. It must be assessed in the context of the circumstances. For example, non-compliance with the command "Drop the knife!" would be symptomatic of a graver concern than non-compliance with the command "Sit down!" The difference between the

---

In handguns, any caliber smaller than .40 S&W is certain to disappoint, if not dismay, when used against vehicles.

30. Compendium of FBI Uniform Crime Reports, Law Enforcement Officers Killed and Assaulted 1999–2014.

two examples may seem clear, but the latter (obstinately standing), seemingly innocuous, non-compliance could be a precursor to a sudden attack (easier standing than sitting).

Non-compliance can occur in response to non-verbal commands as well. A high-speed pursuit is an example of non-compliance with visual and auditory commands—the flashing emergency lights and wailing sirens. It is willful, determined, and evidence of willingness, if not intent, to pose a risk of death or injury to others. The presence of a uniformed officer can be a command, especially if the officer is making a hand gesture (raised to signal "stop," for example). There are cases in which an officer was clearly visible, weapon drawn and pointed at a person, but the verbal commands could not be heard. Nevertheless, the clear image of an officer with weapon drawn is an unmistakable embodiment of the command to "stop" or "don't make a sudden move!" Refusal to acknowledge or respond to such a visual presence is as compelling an example of non-compliance as an intentional refusal to follow a verbal order.

Non-compliance is a danger signal and potentially an urgent one. But as a signal it has to be recognized and assessed within the parameters of the incident, the officer's knowledge of the individuals involved, the offense under investigation, and preceding events that have transpired. The context of the circumstances is critical.

Another truism common in law enforcement training is that a person's hands are the source of danger and a clear indicator of imminent risk. Hands out of sight, moving out of sight, or being displayed as weapons (clenched fists, for example) can all be signals of immediate danger. Two or more signals present in combination is an indicator of extreme risk that should not be ignored. For example a person's hands are not visible and the person is not compliant with commands to do something related, such as to show his hands or to freeze.

A third danger signal is implicit to any sudden uncontrolled, undirected, unanticipated, or unbidden action or movement by the subject of the incident. This is another flag that signals sudden increased potential for resistance if not violence. Non-compliance, unseen hands, aggressive or surprise movements, and persistent defiance are all signs that indicate that impending attack is both likely and imminent.

The necessity to be aware of where a person's hands are, the risk potential posed by areas that cannot be seen or actions that are not directed, and the fact that no person is under control until physically restrained and searched are paramount factors that all law enforcement officers must keep in the forefront of their awareness. However, police officers are not responsible for the actions of people they confront, regardless of the person's intentions. They are only responsible for the reasonable nature of the actions they take in response to what that person chose to do.

A fourth danger signal is the presence of other people. This factor is largely an unrecognized risk in conventional training doctrine and in conventional analyses of deadly force incidents. However, a large percentage of the law enforcement officers killed in the line of duty are slain by people who are not the focus of the officer's initial investigation or approach. In the only study of its kind, about 28% of the convicted cop killers investigated were in the company of others at the time of the incident (14 of 51). Eleven of those killers were not the subjects of the officer's attention (79%). They were family, friends, spouses, or bystanders. Significantly, 22% of the law enforcement officers killed in this study were killed by someone who was not the officer's original focus of investigation.[31] The presence of others is an important element that must reasonably heighten an officer's awareness and perceptions of potential danger.

# The Escaping Criminal

In 1985, the United States Supreme Court established that deadly force may be used when necessary to prevent the escape of a dangerous suspect. The Court said, " ... *if the suspect threatens the officer with a weapon, or if there is probable cause to believe that he has committed a crime involving the infliction or threatened infliction of serious physical harm, deadly force may be used if necessary to prevent escape, and if, where feasible, some warning has been given.*"[32]

The fact that a decision to use deadly force to prevent the escape of a dangerous suspect is constitutional is not widely understood. First, it is *not* subject to the same prerequisites of reasonable necessity as with the well understood "defense of self and others" rationale. This misconception centers on the fallacy that an individual who is "merely" trying to escape poses no risk of death or serious injury to the officer or others and therefore, it is unnecessary to prevent escape by using deadly force. To the contrary, a dangerous individual poses a clear threat to pursuing officers and to any citizens that may be encountered later in time. The Court recognized that the desirability of preventing potential harm to others justified the use of deadly force to prevent escape of individuals who were "dangerous" and thus a continuing threat if left at large.

---

31. "Killed in the Line of Duty—A Study of Selected Felonious Killings of Law Enforcement Officers," U.S. Department of Justice, Uniform Crime Reports Section, FBI Academy, Quantico, Virginia, September 1992, page 37.

32. *Tennessee v. Garner*, 471 U.S. 1, 10 (1985).

The Supreme Court clearly affirmed the authority of a law enforcement officer to act in the interest of the safety of himself, others in his proximity, and the community at large—*not* the physical wellbeing of an escaping dangerous suspect. Where an individual represents a continuing danger to others, even others remote from the setting of the encounter, the authority exists to protect them. An individual who threatens the life or well being of an officer trying to arrest him is also a threat to the life or well being of anyone encountered as he escapes. He is a threat to other officers who may be in the vicinity but unaware of his movements. He is a threat to innocent bystanders or uninvolved citizens who chance to cross his path. Some can pose significant threats well into the indeterminate future to unanticipated victims. The obvious example is a serial killer who will continue to kill as long as he is on the loose. This is not to say that dangerous people can be gunned down on sight. The use of deadly force to prevent escape is restricted to those incidents in which a dangerous suspect is escaping and there is no alternative to prevent it. As the Court specified, deadly force can be used to prevent escape "if necessary" and where a verbal warning has been given, "if feasible."

There is a three-pronged test to assess the legal justification of a use of deadly force to prevent escape. First, the individual must be "dangerous," as defined by the Court. That is to say, the individual must have threatened the officer with a weapon, or there must exist probable cause to believe the individual has committed a crime involving the infliction or *threatened* infliction of serious physical harm [emphasis added]. Second, the use of deadly force must be necessary to prevent escape. This would imply a last resort categorization of the decision to use deadly force. And third, "where feasible," some warning is given.

What happens far more often is that a law enforcement officer shoots a person during a deadly force confrontation as the person is turning away from the officer or moving away from the officer in a continuation of the incident. It can appear that the person is attempting to escape. The allegations will inevitably follow that escape was the intent and therefore the person did not pose a threat justifying deadly force. However, objective analysis will usually reveal that the most reasonable interpretation of the person's movement, *from the perspective of the officer*, is to gain tactical advantage. And it is the objectively reasonable perspective of an officer on the scene that has to control the analysis. Legally under these circumstances, it does not matter whether the person was attempting escape or seeking tactical advantage. In the former case, the person clearly meets the definition of a dangerous individual by having engaged in a deadly force confrontation. In the latter case, it is a prolongation of the imminent risk of death or injury sufficient to justify defense of self and others.

An armed and dangerous person moving during a deadly force confrontation is not unique. Nor is the movement predictable by the officer any more than any other human action or event can be. The person's intent is equally opaque to the officer. If it is reasonably perceived as pursuing a tactical advantage within the dynamics of the incident, then the officer may reasonably continue shooting to prevent that. It is a relatively ordinary event that occurs in law enforcement shootings that frequently results in the person being shot in the back, or shot as he runs away.

When this occurs it is not a case of using deadly force to prevent escape, although that can be and is argued. It is a continuation of the use of deadly force in protection of self and others. A deadly force confrontation is a continuous, dynamic event that entails extreme personal danger, high stress, inherent limitations on time and ability to respond, limited means with which to achieve protection and safety from harm, and a limited ability to control events.

A confrontation has a beginning and an end, and in between it has a series of actions, reactions, clear threats, less clear ones, and unanticipated events. Chance plays an inevitable role in all human endeavors. Thus the movement of the person and/or the location of wounds bear little relevance to an objective determination of the reasonableness of the decision to use deadly force, which is the measure of its justification. These things can be evidence of nothing more than the logical consequences of the tactical movements made by the person during the incident.

If a person moving away from an officer during a deadly force incident reaches a position of advantage, or gets out of sight, he is sheltered from outside view, free to either return fire from a barricaded position, ambush pursuit, or continue an escape attempt. The tactical advantage shifts severely in favor of the adversary, to the detriment of involved officers and others.

Numerous possibilities become feasible, none of which are desirable to the law enforcement officer(s) involved in the incident:

a.  The person can shoot as he runs.[33]
b.  The person can shoot from behind cover at exposed officers.
c.  The person can proceed unseen to have opportunity to attack perimeter officers by surprise.
d.  The person can take a hostage, if one opportunistically appears.

---

33. Plaintiffs' attorneys will always belittle this possibility, but it is in fact a common occurrence. Fleeing felons are not at all reluctant to spray random shots behind them to facilitate escape. Such shots are every bit as lethal if they hit someone as a deliberately aimed shot. To wit, one example in a discussion of the perils of foot pursuits:

> "After responding to a domestic abuse call, the victim officer saw a man fitting the suspect's description run into a field. The officer exited his patrol vehicle and chased the man through some tall weeds. During the pursuit, the suspect turned and fired

e. The person can force entry into adjacent locations occupied by innocent and uninvolved parties.

f. The person can exit the scene and escape, perhaps to harm others some other time, in some other place.

Training provided to law enforcement officers should never encourage them to willingly let an armed and dangerous person move unseen towards unsuspecting officers or possible innocent citizens. To the contrary, a training goal should change to prevent that scenario from occurring.

# Verbal Warnings

It is not unusual for law enforcement training to include the admonition to issue a verbal warning when feasible, i.e., when taking the time to issue such a warning will not delay the use of deadly force to such an extent as to increase the risk of death or serious injury, or prevent stopping such risk in a timely manner. The first provision that must be understood is that, constitutionally speaking, the *only* situation in which a verbal warning is required *when feasible* (emphasis added) is prior to the use of deadly force to prevent escape of a dangerous person. There is no constitutional requirement to issue a warning prior to the use of deadly force in defense of self or others. Some state laws and many departmental policies differ on this issue and include a requirement for a warning "*if feasible*" for all uses of deadly force. However, a warning in a defense of self and others scenario constitutes nothing more than a verbal bluff. If the situation does not merit the use of deadly force, officers are no more justified warning of it than they would be actually using it.

If deadly force is appropriate, the issuance of a warning is discretionary on the part of the officer involved. The training should stress that if the situation is such that the decision to use deadly force has been made, then it may not be feasible to issue a warning. Once the decision has been made, then the issue is one of life and death, protection of self and others, not dissuading the adversary from engaging in further threatening action. The officer may or may not attempt a verbal warning prior to using deadly force, or even while engaged in using deadly force. But the absence of a warning is not a measure of the reasonableness of the use of deadly force or its justification, especially in incidents

---

*a .380-caliber semiautomatic handgun, striking the officer in the wrist, twice in his protective vest, and once just above the vest … The officer died later at a local hospital."* U.S. Dept. of Justice, *FBI Law Enforcement Bulletin*, May 2000, page 13.

where the onset of the threat is sudden and unquestionable. Even in the case of a fleeing dangerous individual, the absence of a warning does not necessarily diminish the justification of a use of deadly force to prevent escape. The issue to examine is whether it was feasible to attempt issuing a warning. Taking the time to issue a warning and then inevitably waiting (even for a brief fraction of time) for a discernible response can raise the risk of death, injury, or escape to an unreasonable level. The hard reality of action versus reaction is not forgiving of delay.

Officers are not required to engage in a verbal warning prior to using deadly force any more than they are required to attempt a progression of lesser forms of force. They must react to the situation as it transpires and personally assess the time available for any attempt at using lesser means, such as a verbal warning. Assessment of the feasibility of a verbal warning is necessarily a situational exercise governed by the same factors of action/reaction, imminence of danger, risk of injury, and objectively reasonable perceptions of the officer(s) involved.

The use of a verbal warning is desirable "when feasible" in the language of the law, but it must be repeated that this requirement is legally imperative *only* when deadly force is being used to prevent the escape of a dangerous individual. There is no suggestion of any necessity to issue a verbal warning in the constitutional standards for using deadly force in defense of self and others. However, some jurisdictions and institutions do impose such a requirement by state law, by policy, and/or by training doctrine, for a verbal warning before any use of deadly force—but always " ... *when feasible.*" The caveat " ... *when feasible* ..." is important to recognize and understand. It is nevertheless frequently misunderstood. It means that the decision whether to attempt a warning or not is within the discretionary authority of the officer(s) involved in the incident.

Verbal warnings are notoriously ineffective in resolving physical confrontations. The authors' personal experience, supported by that related by countless other agents and police officers, is that the universal reaction to any verbal warning seems to be a redoubled effort on the part of the criminal—a warning such as "Stop, Police" seems to be heard as "Run Faster!" A subtle yet important fact that is often ignored even though it stares us in the face is that "in the greater scheme of things, when a criminal sees a police officer there is a primal instinct that causes the criminal to run from him or her."[34] Fleeing criminals generally do not stop for verbal warnings, and especially not when escape remains a hope. Resisting criminals do not stop resisting. Assaults do not suddenly cease.

A verbal warning is not a prerequisite to the use of deadly force if deadly force is reasonably justified. In fact, the attempt to utilize a verbal warning is an at-

---

34. Blum, LN, PhD, page 24.

tempt to use a less than lethal means no different than an attempt to use chemical agents, impact weapons, physical restraints, or negotiation. If time permits, and the level of risk will not preclude the additional time necessary to employ them, they may be tried. The decision to use other means remains within the discretion of the officer on the scene. But the law does not require officers to select the least intrusive force option, only a reasonable one.

# The Failure to Use Deadly Force

In the previously cited 1992 FBI study of cop killers it was discovered that in those incidents in which the victim officer had a partner or a back-up officer arrive on the scene during the assault, 92% of the time neither the partner nor the back-up officer employed deadly force against the attacker.[35] Approximately 85% of all the law enforcement officers feloniously killed in the line of duty *never* discharged their firearm.[36] It is sadly still not unusual for law enforcement officers to delay the use of deadly force or even decide not to use it at all, especially in situations where the threat of death or serious injury is not directed at them but at another. Although self-defense is widely recognized and officers generally engage in acts of self-defense with alacrity in overtly justifiable circumstances, the recognition that deadly force may be used with equal promptness in defense of others seems to give pause. This can easily result in the victim being injured to a degree beyond that which might have been prevented, regardless of whether the victim was a citizen or another law enforcement officer. It is notably encouraging that this tendency for indecision and delay is much less evident now than it was in 1992 at the time of the study, but it does still occur.

The failure to shoot in defense of others is not uncommon and is symptomatic of several factors. First, when confronted with sudden and unanticipated violence, there commonly occurs an overwhelming sense of disbelief, a reluctance or inability to comprehend the event and its potential for harm, which can also slow the reactions and responses of the witnessing officer or individual. Second, there is a pronounced reluctance to shoot someone in defense of others. And third, there is a reluctance to use deadly force against someone who is clearly dangerous, but not acting overtly dangerous *yet*. The reluctance to act is a significant factor because when the individual finally does

---

35. "Killed in the Line of Duty—A Study of Selected Felonious Killings of Law Enforcement Officers," U.S. Department of Justice, Uniform Crime Reports Section, FBI Academy, Quantico, Virginia, September 1992, page 44.

36. *Ibid.* page 44.

something overt that threatens injury or death, the officer can only react after the fact. Playing "catch-up" to looming death or injury is not a reliable way to prevent those consequences from occurring. The result is that police use of deadly force is rare, and because of the conditioning imparted by training or an inherent reluctance to actually kill someone, it is generally constrained to situations "in defense of self," and then as a last resort.

### Case History #1 (Reluctance to Use Deadly Force)[37]

On January 21, 2004, a man was walking south on Route 5 outside of Waterboro, Maine. He held a handgun in one hand, pointed at the ground as he walked. A passing motorist reported him to the York County (Maine) Sheriff's Office (York County SO) describing him and his clothing.

Sergeant Roger Hicks went to the reported location to investigate. He saw the man (later identified as Thomas E. Harrington) walking in the southbound breakdown lane along Route 5. Harrington was carrying a pistol in his right hand. It appeared to Sgt. Hicks to be a Luger, a distinctive German-designed semi-automatic pistol common during World War II.

Sgt. Hicks stopped his cruiser about 60 feet in front of Harrington and activated his blue emergency lights. Harrington continued walking toward the parked cruiser. Sgt. Hicks got out of his cruiser and stood there. Harrington stopped about 30 feet away.

Sgt. Hicks told Harrington to put the gun on the ground. Harrington said, "No." Hicks repeated his command. Harrington again refused, staring straight at Hicks in a manner later described by Hicks as "challenging." Sgt. Hicks drew his service weapon and pointed it at Harrington. He ordered him to get on the ground and to put the gun down. Harrington continued to look straight at Sgt. Hicks and responded, "F**k you pig. Shoot me!" or words to that effect.

Harrington turned around and started walking north on Route 5, crossing the two-lane roadway into the northbound lane and into the adjacent breakdown lane. He ignored Hicks's commands to stop. Sgt. Hicks got into his cruiser and radioed that the man (Harrington) was armed with a firearm in his right hand and that he wanted Hicks to shoot him.

Sgt. Hicks then made a series of unsuccessful attempts to stop Harrington and get him to drop his firearm. He repeatedly drove his cruiser up behind Harrington, got out of the car and ordered him to stop and put down his gun. Harrington just as repeatedly ignored Sgt. Hicks as he continued to walk along the

---

37. Findings of the Attorney General, State of Maine, regarding the investigation of the use of deadly force by police against Thomas E. Harrington, January 21, 2004.

roadway. Occasionally, he would verbally refuse to comply. As Harrington would walk past Sgt. Hicks, Hicks would get into his cruiser and repeat his approach.

At some point during this sequence of events, Sgt. Harvey Barr, York County SO, drove up from the south. He saw Hicks in his cruiser following a man walking in the breakdown lane who was holding a firearm in his right hand. Barr was in the southbound lane paralleling Sergeant Hick's cruiser in the northbound lane.

Thereafter, the officers alternated driving up behind Harrington. As each officer took his turn pulling up behind Harrington with his driver's side door open, the officer would stop, get out of his cruiser, and call upon Harrington to stop and put down his firearm. Harrington simply ignored them and continued to walk north. As he would pass the officer who was talking to him, the second officer would leapfrog past them and repeat the maneuver. The officers employed this leapfrogging tactic a number of times. When it happened to be Sgt. Barr's turn at one point, he got out and reached back into the cruiser to move the gearshift lever into park. At that moment, Harrington suddenly veered toward Sgt. Barr, raising his right arm and pointing his weapon directly at Barr from a distance of about 15 feet.

Hicks was standing outside his own cruiser at that moment. Sgt. Hicks fired one shot at Harrington from a distance of about 36 feet. In response, Harrington lowered his right arm to his side, turned towards Hicks and yelled, "You f**king missed me. You're a lousy f**king shot."

Harrington resumed walking north along Route 5, his weapon in hand at his side. Sgt. Hicks radioed that he had fired one shot at the armed man because he had raised his firearm at Sgt. Barr.

Meanwhile, Deputy David Scullion, York County SO, had arrived from the south and got out of his cruiser. He heard Hicks' gunshot. Deputy Scullion drew his service weapon and got behind Hicks' cruiser using it as a shield. Scullion saw that Harrington was carrying a gun in his right hand. It appeared to him to be a German Luger.

Sergeants Barr and Hicks resumed their leapfrogging tactics with Scullion walking along behind Hicks' cruiser. This continued for another 3/10 mile along Route 5 to the bridge across the Little Ossipee River. Harrington maintained a steady pace, ignoring the commands of the three officers to stop and lay his firearm on the ground. Occasionally, he would pause briefly and yell back over his shoulder at the officers.

Before Sgt. Hicks shot at Harrington, Maine State Police Trooper Jack Dow had arrived on the scene. He positioned himself on Route 5 well north of Hicks and Barr's location, but south of the bridge across the Little Ossipee River. Trooper Dow got out of his cruiser armed with a rifle. He stopped the traffic arriving from the north on Route 5. He was watching Harrington as he walked north toward Dow's position. He also saw that Harrington was carrying a gun in his hand, and he saw the two York County SO cruisers following Harrington as the officers employed their leapfrogging tactics.

Each time that Harrington neared his position, Trooper Dow backed his cruiser up the road to maintain a safe distance. Trooper Dow had moved his cruiser for the second or third time and was out of his car directing traffic away when he turned in time to see Harrington move towards Sgt. Barr. He saw Harrington raise his gun and heard a gunshot (fired by Hicks) but did not know who had fired. Then he saw Harrington resume walking towards his (Dow's) position.

Trooper Dow could hear the deputies ordering Harrington to stop and put down his gun as the entourage approached his position. Dow backed his cruiser up a final time to a position immediately beyond the north end of the bridge. He parked diagonally across the southbound lane. Just before Harrington reached the bridge, Sergeant Jonathan Shapiro of the Maine State Police arrived from the south and drove up behind Hicks and Barr. By radio, he directed Trooper Dow not to let Harrington get beyond his position because of all the people in cars and houses located behind Dow.

Harrington began to walk across the bridge. Trooper Dow put down the rifle he was carrying and drew his handgun. He yelled at Harrington numerous times to stop and put the gun down, which Harrington ignored. Harrington finally responded, "I'm not going to stop."

Dow continued to command Harrington to stop and put the gun down. As Harrington walked past Dow's position at the right rear of his cruiser, Dow started towards him. Harrington suddenly stopped and turned towards Dow. He brought his right arm up and around as if preparing to shoot Dow from a distance of 6 to 8 feet. Trooper Dow fired two shots at Harrington. One shot struck Harrington in the abdomen and he fell to the ground.

Harrington survived his wound. His weapon was later discovered to be a $CO_2$ pellet gun replica of a German Luger. This fact was only apparent after the weapon was recovered and is of no relevance to the assessment of the threat posed by Harrington during the event.

———————

This case history is notable for the extraordinary lengths undertaken to avoid initiating a use of deadly force by five officers over a lengthy period of engagement with Harrington. During the entire engagement, *from start to finish*, Harrington posed a clear, objectively reasonable threat of imminent death or serious injury. Yet not one of the officers employed deadly force, except very briefly when Harrington appeared to be attempting to shoot one of them, apparently convincing them to fire a shot (Sgt. Hicks) or two (Trooper Dow much later).

It highlights several important points. First, of course, is the fact that a decision to use deadly force is discretionary in the judgment of the officers involved. That judgment may not necessarily be correct although it is certainly fortuitous in a case like this, where none of the officers gets hurt. Second, it illustrates the extreme, if not foolish, measures officers will take to avoid using deadly force while accepting a level of risk to their own safety that is totally unnecessary and unreasonable. In the case history above, if Harrington had in fact possessed a real firearm and the inclination to use it, he could have shot and killed any one of these officers at will. Their only recourse would have been to shoot to prevent themselves from being hurt. A third point of note is that this case may have been an attempted suicide by cop. That phenomenon is discussed in greater depth in Chapter 9. This incident is also illustrative of the indecision and uncertainty that can overwhelm officer judgment in a situation where the threat is not immediate and unmistakable. Clearly, if Harrington had fired a shot at any point in any direction, all of the officers would have returned fire without hesitation. The reader will observe degrees of these elements of hesitation and indecision throughout the case histories and examples cited in this book. Eliminating or minimizing the effects is one of the most important goals of training.

Often a law enforcement officer will confront an individual who is a clear threat, an objectively reasonable risk of injury or death to the officer or others. The individual may be armed or not. The individual may actually intend harm to others, or not. Usually the individual will be engaged in non-specific acts of aggression, i.e., acts that are not yet directed at someone else. These circumstances are most likely to lead to a hesitation or failure to use deadly force even though deadly force is justified.

Certainly the decision to use deadly force, or not to use it, is completely within the individual discretion of the officer, guided by the officer's experience, training, temperament, and perception of risk. But an overriding factor that is not well recognized is the will to act: the will to use deadly force to prevent a looming risk of death or injury from becoming an actuality.

Human will to act is a fundamental factor. Few officers hesitate appreciably if at all in response to a specific physical threat suddenly directed against their person—the raised gun, the lunge with a knife, the blow or strike with a club or rock, the fired shot. When the threat is directed against someone else, hesitation becomes more prevalent. When the threat is real but non-specific, hesitation is more the order of the day. The decision to use deadly force to preempt a dangerous threat *before* it becomes an actual attempt to inflict injury requires the officer to muster the will to act despite the immensely negative factors in variance against such a decision.

The countervailing factors are the inevitable wave of criticism, second guessing, administrative and criminal allegations and implied liabilities, and public outrage fanned by ignorance of the realities of risk, or worse, fomented by special interests with the intent to promote their agendas at the expense of law enforcement and community safety (see Chapter 12—Aftermath & Impact). Zealous interests are immune to facts and a reality that weigh against the results they seek, dealing in emotional appeals and demagoguery. Frequently, the person confronted by law enforcement is possessed of a will to act dangerously that is stronger and more distinct in purpose than the will of the officers to prevent that act from rising to fruition. The Harrington case history above is a good example. The case histories cited in Chapter 9 are also enlightening.

It is always easier to stall, to delay a decisive and justifiable use of deadly force, to rationalize and deny, in hopes that events will work out optimally. Officers are prone to hope for the best rather than face the consequences of shooting an unarmed person or a person who had not attempted an overtly threatening act. The officer constantly must judge the degree of threat posed by the person and in the process assumes an excessive exposure to the risk of injury or death to self. The officers in the Harrington case spent the entire incident exposed to any sudden attempt by Harrington to shoot. When Harrington did commit an overt act, an officer immediately decided to use deadly force, but stopped with equal alacrity when Harrington ceased the specific act and resumed his non-specific threatening acts. The danger never lessened—just the officers' responses that rose and fell with their individual perceptions of Harrington's attempts to actually inflict an injury.

It is extraordinary how often and routinely law enforcement officers accept a risk of preventable injury or death in their dealings with patently dangerous people. Some of the reasons for hesitation are preventable by better, more comprehensive training. A more educated, well-informed community could eliminate some of the impetus for hesitation. The community at large can encourage the will to act by its officers through realistic assessments of the dangers faced and support for reasonable and justified measures taken to protect themselves even at the cost of imposing injury on the criminally dangerous. Both of these measures are functions of training and communications with the community at large. And lastly, some of the causes for hesitation are the ineluctable characteristics of individual human nature that will pertain regardless of training or community support, and about which little can be done.

Hesitation is almost universally present to some degree in the reactions of law enforcement officers confronted with the sudden onset of rapidly evolving violent confrontations. Empirical data support this assertion. There were 833 law enforcement officers feloniously killed in the 16-year period of 1999–2014. There were 909,434 law enforcement officers assaulted in that same 16-year period—an average of 56,840 documented assaults per year on law enforcement officers. The rate of injury for that 16-year reporting period was 27.6%—251,004 officers injured, an average of 15,688 per year. Of the 16-year total, 176,439 of the assaults involved the use of a dangerous weapon (11,027 average per year). 732,995 of the total assaults involved the attacker using personal weapons. These are assaults that were documented and reported to the U.S. Department of Justice.[38] The actual numbers are undoubtedly higher because almost 50% of the law enforcement departments in the United States do not file reports with the U.S. Department of Justice.

Meanwhile, law enforcement officers killed an average of 401 felons per year in the line of duty for the 11-year period 2004–2014 (the most current period for which there is data). This does not address individuals who are shot and not killed by law enforcement officers. The disparity in the number of assaults on law enforcement officers (average 56,840 per year—15,688 injured—11,027 involving a deadly weapon) relative to the number of felons justifiably killed by law enforcement (401 per year on average) clearly illustrates the reluctance of officers to use deadly force.[39] "Officers are quick to put themselves in harm's way but are then reluctant to use significant force."[40]

---

38. Compendium of FBI Uniform Crime Reports, Law Enforcement Officers Killed and Assaulted 1999–2014.

39. The annual figures for justifiable homicides by law enforcement are:

2004 — 367
2005 — 347
2006 — 386
2007 — 395
2008 — 368
2009 — 414
2010 — 397
2011 — 404
2012 — 426
2013 — 461
2014 — 444

See FBI Uniform Crime Reports for the years 2004–2014, Expanded Homicide Data Table 14. Justifiable homicide is defined by UCR as the killing of a felon by a law enforcement officer in the line of duty.

FBI Uniform Crime Reports, Law Enforcement Officers Killed and Assaulted reveals the following more current statistics for the 16-year period of 1999–2014 as follows: 90,434 assaults over the 16-year period; 176,439 of the total with dangerous weapons and 732,995 with personal weapons. For the year 2014, 11,027 of the 48,315 reported assaults were with dangerous weapons and 38,611 with personal weapons. The conclusion is unchanged.

40. Petrowski, TD, JD, "Use-of-Force Policies and Training—A Reasoned Approach," *FBI Law Enforcement Bulletin*, U.S. Department of Justice, Washington, DC, October 2002, page 28.

This reluctance to use deadly force in defense of others when clearly justified incurs a severe risk on the part of officers and other parties involved, although it is often viewed in the aftermath as desirable, even admirable restraint. It is further indicative of the lengths to which police officers routinely go to avoid the use of deadly force, with minimal recognition or credence given to the consequent risk. They ignore or deny the increased hazard to themselves and others with little or no awareness of the portent for catastrophically enhanced danger that may be the consequence.

This naturally prevalent inclination to hesitate can be encouraged and made even more inevitable by extraneous considerations such as the implementation of a force continuum policy and practice. Force continuum policies and practices build in a propensity for hesitation (see Chapter 6 — Training vs. Qualification). They also improperly require that any analysis of the reasonable use of force must hinge on the actions of the officer when the onus for the situation and the events rests rightly and solely on the offender. "It is the subject that dictates what use of force, if any, is necessary and reasonable."[41]

### Case History #2 (Hesitation in Use of Deadly Force)[42]

In the evening hours of February 25, 2002, two deputies from the Lincoln County Sheriff's Department went to the residence of Michael Buchanan to check on him. A local resident had asked for them to do so. The resident reported that Buchanan lived alone, he was mentally ill, and he had started a fire near the residence earlier in the day. The local citizen was concerned for Buchanan's welfare, and also for the safety and welfare of his neighbors. Deputy Hatch was assigned the call, and he asked Deputy Emerson to accompany him on the recommendation of a third deputy who recalled from a previous contact that Buchanan had a "mental problem" and had been violent in the past.

They had to walk the length of Buchanan's driveway (about 0.75 mile) because it had not been plowed. Lights were on in the house when they arrived at the front door. One of the deputies knocked on the door and then Buchanan was seen at a second floor window, apparently trying to open it. He was observed to be shouting but the deputies could not understand him.

Buchanan went to a different window that he was able to open. The deputies could hear him now, shouting incoherently about "Nazis," "Jewish ovens" and nonsensical rambling about the state police in Massachusetts and New York and some woman he described as a "Hun." The deputies tried to communi-

---

41. *Ibid.* page 27.

42. Findings of the Attorney General, State of Maine, regarding the investigation of the use of deadly force by police against Michael Buchanan, March 19, 2002.

cate with him, telling him they just wanted to make sure he was all right. Buchanan began to yell at the deputies to get off of his property and that he was going to kill them. He threw a liquid at them from an unidentified container, then closed the window and moved inside the house.

The deputies heard a loud noise that they thought at first was a gunshot. Deputy Emerson looked through a glass pane in the door and saw Buchanan coming down the stairwell with one hand bloodied. Deputy Emerson now believed that the loud noise had been the sound of Buchanan putting his hand through glass. Buchanan was yelling unintelligible statements about "warrants" and the "Commonwealth of Massachusetts" and the "federal government" as he opened the door and immediately spit on Deputy Emerson's chest. He then retreated into his house and headed back up the stairs, leaving the door open.

Deputy Emerson followed Buchanan with the intention of taking him into protective custody. He began to ascend the stairs after Buchanan. He saw Buchanan reach a landing at the top of the stairwell, enter a doorway there and close the door behind him. Meanwhile, Deputy Hatch had entered the house and started up the stairs behind Deputy Emerson when Buchanan reappeared on the landing with a kitchen knife in his hand, clearly visible to both deputies. Buchanan began to swing the knife at Deputy Emerson who was now near the landing.

Deputy Emerson attempted to grab Buchanan's arm, but was off-balance and still on the stairs slightly below Buchanan. Buchanan pulled the deputy down to a point that Deputy Emerson's upper body was partially on the landing. Buchanan began stabbing Deputy Emerson in the upper torso/shoulder area while the deputy continued to struggle. Buchanan was stabbing so violently that the blade of the knife actually broke off inside Deputy Emerson. He continued stabbing with the handle of the knife, although neither deputy was aware that the knife had broken.

Deputy Emerson felt the wound in his shoulder, and was aware that Buchanan was still stabbing him. He pleaded for Deputy Hatch to help him, saying he was unable to disarm Buchanan. Deputy Hatch, having observed Buchanan pull Deputy Emerson down and engage in his violent and continuous stabbing of the deputy, drew his firearm and shot Buchanan four times, killing him.

Deputy Emerson survived his wound. It is less sure he would have survived if the knife blade had not broken off on the first thrust.

----------

If there is a flaw in the universe of law enforcement training in the use of deadly force, it is the generic failure to stress the fact that a law enforcement officer may use deadly force when necessary to protect *self or others* from the risk of imminent death or serious injury and that it is not necessary to wait until the subject commits an overt, specific act against another.

# Chapter 9

# Suicide by Cop and the Mentally Ill Subject

There is a phenomenon that has been variously classified as "police assisted suicide" or "victim precipitated suicide." It is more popularly recognized as "suicide by cop." The phrase refers to an individual who wishes to die and uses the police to achieve that goal. It is more widespread than recognized and must not be ignored. It is an event that causes repercussions far beyond those associated with the "traditional" deadly force confrontation.

These individuals intentionally engage in life-threatening and criminal behavior with a lethal weapon, or what *appears* to be a lethal weapon, to engage the attention of law enforcement officers and attain their purpose. When law enforcement officers confront them, the suicidal individuals purposely disobey commands in order to compel the officers to kill them. They intentionally will escalate the perceptions of dangerous intent by threatening officers or bystanders with their weapon or even initiating an apparent assault. The conventional assumption is that law enforcement officers are selected by such individuals who are intent on dying because the officers are commonly known to be armed and are believed to be well trained in the use of deadly force. The police officer can be trusted to effectively achieve the suicidal goal.

The complexities and repercussions of suicide by cop are amplified when the underlying suicidal intent is concealed. The concept of hidden suicide has been well established. Many deaths appear to result from natural or accidental causes that might be classified as forms of suicide.[1] Many single-occupant car crashes have long been suspected as suicidal events, especially those that occur under excellent driving conditions.[2] Some researchers have attributed certain airplane

---

1. Kennedy, DB, PhD, Homant, RJ, PhD, Hupp, RT, MS, "Suicide by Cop," *FBI Law Enforcement Bulletin*, U.S. Department of Justice, Washington, DC, August 1998.

2. Selzer, M, Payne, C, "Automobile Accident, Suicide and Unconscious Motivation," *American Journal of Psychiatry* 119, 1962, pages 237–40.

crashes, parachute fatalities, and workplace fatalities to suicidal motivations.[3, 4, 5] Hidden suicide severely exacerbates the problem for law enforcement in the aftermath of a suicide by cop.

The ambiguity that can arise in determining whether a particular death is suicidal creates repercussions in the aftermath of a deadly force confrontation. The repercussions arise from the refusal of friends, family, or activists to recognize or accept the suicidal intent of the victim, which results in particularly emotional and intense allegations of police excess. They tend to create pressures on law enforcement to provide training or to initiate policy modifications to ensure law enforcement officers can quickly and efficiently identify the suicidal, no matter how well hidden the underlying intent may be.

One study attempted just that. The researchers examined the reports of 240 shooting incidents to determine the likelihood of suicide. They subsequently categorized the cases into five groups, listed here with the percentage of cases assigned to each category:

a.  Probable Suicide—4%
b.  Possible Suicide—12%
c.  Indeterminate—67%
d.  Suicide Unlikely—9%
e.  No Suicide Motive—9%[6]

Notice the large number of cases that are indeterminate despite careful, after-the-fact analysis performed clinically and at relative leisure. These cases are indeterminate even though analyzed in a stress-free atmosphere with no time constraints and including information that was not available to the officers involved during the confrontation. However, the researchers did note that 16% of the "indeterminate" cases did contain some evidence of probable or possible suicidal motivation, but insufficient for them to make a determination. This inability to reach a conclusion after the encounter is over is a clear illustration of why attempts to diagnose suicide by cop during the confrontation is doomed to failure as a general strategy.

An undeterminable number of suicides are camouflaged or hidden by the individual. This is true regardless of the venue of the suicide—by cop, by self-administered injury, by car crash, by contrived accidental means. The suicidal individual intends to die, but is equally determined that the death not be rec-

---

3. Phillips, D, "Airplane Accident Fatalities Increase Just after Newspaper Stories about Murder and Suicide," *Science* #201, 1978, pages 748–50.

4. Lester, D, *Questions and Answers about Suicide*, Charles Press, Philadelphia, PA, 1989.

5. Kinney, J, *Preventing Violence at Work*, Prentice-Hall, Englewood Cliffs, NJ, 1995.

6. Kennedy, DB, PhD, *et al.*, pages 4–6.

ognized as suicide. The motivation can be any of several fears—losing insurance, shame, family scandal, or hurting the feelings of family and friends. These fears are potent motivators in their own right. Hidden suicides may never be quantifiable. Nevertheless, they exist and they occur with probably equal regularity as overt suicides.

One large attraction of suicide by cop is quite likely the perception that it is a good way to be successful both in dying and in masking the suicidal intent. Thus, large numbers of police shootings that are examined as to whether they were in fact suicide by cop can only be classified as "indeterminate." Suicide by cop "occurs more than most people realize."[7]

Some of the first hard data compiled in support of the categorization of some law enforcement shootings as suicide by cop was compiled in British Columbia, Canada. Ten percent of the fatal law enforcement shootings in British Columbia from 1980 to 1994 were clear suicides precipitated by the victim. The characteristics associated with victim-precipitated suicide appeared to be a significant factor in roughly half of the 58 shooting incidents analyzed.[8] A study of police shootings by the Los Angeles Sheriff's Office over the ten-year period of 1987–1997 (425 incidents) determined that 11% of all officer-involved shootings (fatal and non-fatal) were incontestably "suicide by cop." Thirteen percent of all officer-involved justifiable homicides (fatal shootings) were incontestable suicides.[9, 10]

The suicide victims in Los Angeles were 98% male (i.e., 45 out of 46 cases). One of three stressors was commonly present. These stressors singly or in combination seem to have some causative effect on the victims. Either they were involved in a traumatic (to them) domestic dispute, they were confronting a return to prison, or some form of substance abuse was present. The suicidal intent was defined by the presence of one of four factors: a note, a verbal expression of the desire to be shot, indicative behavior such as holding a gun to one's own head, or non-compliance with clear and direct commands (such as "drop the weapon") and acting in direct opposition to the commands.[11]

---

7. Blum, LN, PhD, *Force Under Pressure—How Cops Live and Why They Die*, New York, Lantern Books, Booklight Inc., 2000, pages 115–16.

8. Parent, R, "Aspect of Police Use of Deadly Force in British Columbia: The Phenomenon of Victim-Precipitated Homicide," Simon Fraser University, Vancouver, Canada, 1996.

9. Hutson, RH, MD, "Suicide by Cop," *Annals of Emergency Medicine*, 32(6), December 1998, pages 685–89.

10. Anglin, D, MD, MPH, Hutson, RH, MD, Yarborough, J, "Police Assisted Suicide—A U.S. Perspective," Los Angeles Sheriff's Department, Los Angeles, CA, March 2001, page 3.

11. *Ibid.* pages 2–3.

In all of the unquestionable cases, the suicide victim acted to intentionally escalate the situation in some manner. An additional 15 shootings were potential suicides, but the criteria cited above were not sufficiently documented to make the determination. Of note was the fact that in the last year of the study (1997) the incidence of suicide by cop jumped sharply. In 1997, *25% of all officer involved shootings, and 27% of all officer involved justifiable homicides were clear cases of suicide* [emphasis added].[12]

These data describe the relative incidence of planned suicide by cop. Planned suicide can be documented or strongly inferred by a careful and thorough investigation in the aftermath of the incident. Two case histories will suffice.

### Case History #1 (A Planned Suicide)[13]

On March 16, 2001, James Levier drove a van into the parking lot of a shopping mall in Scarborough, Maine. Levier was deaf and had long been an activist in issues regarding the hearing impaired. The exterior of the van was covered with writings that expressed his dissatisfaction with the manner in which the hearing impaired were treated by the State of Maine. Witnesses saw Levier take up a sentry position outside his van holding a 30/30 caliber hunting rifle. They called police.

Officers from Scarborough, Maine State Police, and other area departments responded to the shopping mall. They established a perimeter around Levier's location and evacuated shoppers and employees from the stores, businesses, and a nearby daycare center. The officers repeatedly tried to persuade Levier to relinquish his rifle. Despite his hearing impairment, Levier appeared to acknowledge that he knew what they wanted. However, on several occasions during the standoff, Levier shouted for the officers to shoot him. Attempts to use an interpreter qualified in sign language were unsuccessful and planning was initiated to allow the interpreter to safely get closer to Levier.

Approximately one hour into the standoff, Levier walked to within 60 feet of a group of officers. He assumed a shooter's stance, raised the rifle to his shoulder and aimed at the group of officers. One of the officers in the group then fired a shot at Levier. Believing that it was Levier who fired the shot, three other officers at other locations fired at Levier. He was hit five times and was killed. His rifle was determined to be loaded with a round in the chamber and the hammer cocked, but he never fired a shot.

---

12. *Ibid.* page 5.

13. Findings of the Attorney General, State of Maine, regarding the investigation of the use of deadly force by police against James Levier, April 3, 2001.

A lengthy letter was recovered from Levier's residence that explained his intention to force police to kill him in order to dramatize the plight of the hearing impaired in Maine.

---

### Case History #2 (An Inferred Suicide)[14]

John Dawson was wanted for an armed robbery that occurred February 10, 2002, in Gardiner, Maine. It was believed that he was armed with the gun used in the robbery. Members of his family had told investigators that he had said he would not be taken without a fight. Police had his picture.

On February 12, 2002, in the early morning hours a sergeant with the Portland (Maine) Police Department observed Dawson in Portland. Dawson entered a taxicab and sat in the front seat beside the cab driver. Police followed the taxi and decided to stop it.

Meanwhile, inside the taxi Dawson noticed a vehicle following the taxi. He asked the cab driver if it was a police cruiser. The driver confirmed it was, and Dawson locked the taxi door on the passenger side. The police stopped the taxi and positioned themselves around it. Officer Black stood at the driver's door, Sgt. Hutcheson approached the passenger side, and Officer Letarte stood at the right rear corner of the cab. Dawson attempted to conceal his face, but the officers identified him.

Sgt. Hutcheson on the passenger side tapped on the window and ordered Dawson out. Sgt. Hutcheson tried to open the door, but it was locked. He saw Dawson reach into his coat, then turn and point a gun directly at him, no more than 18 inches away. Sgt. Hutcheson reacted by firing two shots at Dawson while simultaneously stepping back away from the car. He tripped on the street curb and fell backwards. One of his shots hit Dawson.

Officer Letarte also had seen Dawson pull out his gun. He heard the shots and saw Sgt. Hutcheson fall over backwards. Believing that Sgt. Hutcheson had been shot, Officer Letarte fired two shots at Dawson through the rear window of the cab. Both rounds lodged in the back of the passenger-side front seat.

The cab driver tried to physically subdue and/or disarm Dawson. Sgt. Hutcheson regained his footing and saw the two struggling in the front seat. He ordered Dawson several times to drop the gun without result. Sgt Hutcheson then fired several shots at Dawson through the window of the passenger-

---

14. Findings of the Attorney General, State of Maine, regarding the investigation of the use of deadly force by police against John Dawson, March 6, 2002.

side rear door. Dawson was hit four times in the neck and shoulder area and killed.

Dawson's gun was a 9mm semiautomatic pistol. It was not loaded.

———————

There is a more problematical form of suicide by cop that occurs with equal frequency. This is the unplanned suicidal impulse. The individual has not planned suicide, nor considered it an end in and of itself. Events transpire in such a way that the suicidal act is an impulse that arises in the duress of the moment. Suicidal impulses are a significant potentiality in cases involving alcohol abuse due to the resultant alcohol-induced depression that can influence an individual's cognitive processes. Substance abuse appears to be the most potent and dangerous factor in situations that escalate to deadly force confrontations.[15]

Suicidal impulse is also a concern in those cases in which an individual inexperienced in the processes of the legal system is suddenly confronted with unanticipated arrest, the perception of scandal, and the apprehension of humiliation and ruin. The result can be an overwhelming sense of despair and hopelessness, a perception that life is no longer worth living. The emotion is temporary but it can be powerfully compelling under the circumstances. If the individual does not succumb to the impulse or is unsuccessful in getting killed, he almost invariably loses all interest in suicide at some point afterwards. Many will become plaintiffs and allege excessive or homicidal force on the part of the police for using deadly force in response to the very real perception of attack. It is conveniently overlooked that the plaintiff created the danger that justified the use of deadly force in the first place. If they do get themselves killed, then the family or the estate will step in as the plaintiffs and make the same allegations, pointing out that the victim had no weapon, or an unloaded weapon, or a fake weapon, or should have been diagnosed as mentally ill.

One particular offender type that is at a very high risk for impulsive suicide is a current or former law enforcement officer. When approached and/or arrested for criminal violations, these individuals can be susceptible to extreme emotion and despair, fear of scandal, shame and dread of what is to follow. Incarceration is not kind to law enforcement officers. Some will weather the first arrest and incarceration all right, but the experience will harden them

———————

15. Chapman, L, "Deadly Force," *Maine Law Officer's Bulletin*, Special Edition, No. 7, April 10, 2000, page 3.

against ever allowing it to happen again. Former officers who are repeat offenders exposed to a second arrest and the looming prospects of incarceration are apparently more susceptible to impulsive suicide by cop acts at the moment of arrest. The long-time criminal who has "sworn never to go back" is equally susceptible to a sudden impulse under that circumstance. In both cases, if they survive the impulse they seldom resort to suicide by their own hand at a later date.

Characteristically, former law enforcement officers engaged in criminal pursuits are high-risk subjects for arrest anyway. They are typically well trained in weapons, police tactics, and survival measures. They know what to expect, and they can anticipate and initiate counter measures. They do not expect to be caught. A former law enforcement officer, especially one engaged in substantial criminal activity, is a dangerous individual to arrest. They are dangerous not just to the arresting officers but also to themselves as well. When confronted with arrest and the perception of no escape, they are significant suicide risks. Significantly, they have been trained and versed in exactly what actions are most likely to get them shot. Any law enforcement officer facing arrest certainly understands precisely what he needs to do to avoid provoking a deadly force response by the arresting officers.[16]

### *Case History #3 (A Substance Induced Suicide)*[17]

On August 3, 1997, police officers from the Bangor (Maine) Police Department responded to a call about Gregory Baker firing a handgun outside his girlfriend's apartment. Police surrounded the building after learning that Baker was inside on the second floor. Baker had been bailed from jail the previous evening after being charged with assaulting motorists and damaging public property. He obtained a .22 caliber handgun from a friend and bought 500 rounds of ammunition. He had been drinking extensively before the confrontation with police.

Police negotiators talked with Baker before he hung up after 12 minutes and during which he threatened to kill himself. Baker told the negotiator he would shoot any cop that showed up at the apartment, and he knew the building was surrounded. By now he had fired at least 17 rounds inside his car and either inside or outside of the building.

Baker climbed out a back window of the apartment and descended the outside stairwell. Police ordered him to drop his weapon. Baker turned toward

---

16. See *Pasteur v. U.S.* in Chapter 15 for an example of this exact scenario.

17. Findings of the Attorney General, State of Maine, regarding the investigation of the use of deadly force by police against Gregory Baker, September 1997.

an officer, raised his weapon and aimed it at the officer. The officer fired, hitting Baker once in the chest and killing him.

Gregory Baker was a former U.S. Navy SEAL, well versed and trained in weapons, shooting, and tactics. His gun was empty when he came out of the apartment. Investigation revealed he had been drinking heavily and habitually. He expressed deep depression over his life and his future.

---

### Case History #4 (Sudden Impulse Suicide)[18]

On January 24, 2000, Sidney Dunton left his residence in a mobile home park in Veazie, Maine, to elude officers who were preparing to execute a search warrant of his home. Dunton had been suspected of stealing from his employer, the University of Maine, and in fact numerous computers and other items were found in his residence that were university property. He departed the trailer park in a vehicle in such a reckless manner that a local Veazie officer was prompted to give chase. He was unable to catch up with Dunton and terminated his pursuit. Lookouts were broadcast.

Soon thereafter in the Bangor vicinity, Penobscot County Deputy William Flagg in his patrol car observed Dunton's vehicle approaching from the opposite direction. The deputy activated his emergency lights and siren and slowed to a near stop in preparation for turning in pursuit of Dunton. Dunton deliberately turned into Deputy Flagg's lane and struck the deputy's cruiser head-on.

The impact activated both airbags in the cruiser, pinning Deputy Flagg into his seat. Stunned by the impact of the crash, Deputy Flagg thought the cruiser was on fire, but the door was jammed and he could not open it. He radioed for help and continued to try to get out of the car. He succeeded and got out of his cruiser about the same time that Dunton got out of his car through the passenger side door. Dunton had a gun in his hand and was screaming that he was going to kill Deputy Flagg. He advanced on Flagg, ignoring repeated commands to drop his weapon. Deputy Flagg fired one shot as Dunton advanced on him and then his weapon jammed. He tried to elude Dunton as he frantically tried to clear the malfunction of his weapon.

Deputy Flagg retreated to his cruiser, and tried to keep it between Dunton and him. Dunton continued to advance on the deputy, screaming death threats the whole time. He forced Flagg away from his cruiser and into the open road-

---

18. Findings of the Attorney General, State of Maine, regarding the investigation of the use of deadly force by police against Sidney Dunton, February 17, 2000.

way. Deputy Flagg finally cleared the malfunction in his weapon and shot Dunton six more times. Dunton continued to advance on Deputy Flagg, threatening to kill him. A Veazie police officer arrived on the scene in response to Deputy Flagg's radio call and subdued Dunton.

Dunton was armed with a non-firing replica of a handgun. He survived his seven gunshot wounds and filed suit against the police alleging excessive force and inadequate training, among other failings on their part.

---

Often the incident is far more complex and encompasses a wide variety of factors and influences. Some will appear obvious, some distorted. It has to be kept in mind that the human condition is not always easily understood or resolved. The suicidal intent may be planned for some time, reinforced by depression-induced substance abuse, and pursued with unflinching determination only to dissipate entirely in the event. The sudden disappearance of a once firmly held and practiced suicidal intent can lead to severe and ill-founded misconceptions about the inevitability of the act itself.

The law enforcement officer can only react to what the individual does. The officer has no means to determine how serious the intent is, nor can the officer rely on the hope that the individual will suddenly experience an epiphany that changes his outlook and intentions. An officer can only contain the event, attempt to dissuade, and concurrently ensure that the individual is not permitted to harm the officer or others. To the extent that the officers involved can contain and control the risk of death or injury incurred by them or imposed on others, they can afford the luxury of taking time to try to defuse and resolve the confrontation without injury to the subject.

Law enforcement officers are not responsible for what that individual does. They cannot be responsible for the actions of the individual. There is no duty incumbent to law enforcement to prevent an individual from doing something that is dangerous or risky to that individual's life. If the individual does something that raises a reasonable perception of a risk of imminent death or serious injury to officers or others, then the greater responsibility for law enforcement is to prevent that risk from becoming real.

### *Case History #5 (Planned/Impulsive & Substance Induced Suicide)*[19]

During the evening of May 5, 2003, Christopher R. Pullen telephoned his estranged girlfriend and tried to persuade her to come talk with him at his

---

19. Findings of the Attorney General, State of Maine, regarding the investigation of the use of deadly force by police against Christopher R. Pullen, May 6, 2003.

house. She recognized he had been drinking and refused. At 11 p.m., Pullen appeared outside the girlfriend's residence, drunk and armed with a shotgun. She refused to let him in and closed her door. He opened the door and entered her residence, ignoring her demands that he leave. He told her she could not call the police because he had cut the phone lines (verified by the investigation after the incident).

Pullen repeatedly blamed her for all his difficulties, claimed he had nothing to live for, threatened to shoot her and her mother, and physically assaulted her. He also threatened to kill himself. At one point he placed the butt of the shotgun on the floor, put his face over the muzzle and reached for the trigger. The girlfriend pulled the barrel away and he slapped her. During this time, another resident in the house slipped away and called police from a neighbor's home. Pullen heard sirens from the fire department responding to the fire he had previously set at his own house. Alerts were broadcast for police to look for Pullen.

Approximately 30 minutes later, three deputies from the sheriff's office saw Pullen's pickup parked alongside a road. They positioned themselves to the rear of the truck from where they saw Pullen behind the wheel. Pullen got out of the truck with a shotgun in his right hand. The situation devolved into a standoff that lasted for three hours. During the standoff, Pullen was variously armed with the shotgun, a rifle he also took out of the truck, and a knife. One of the deputies talked with Pullen for two hours trying to persuade him to give up his weapons and surrender. Two negotiators from the Maine State Police relieved the deputy. They continued to negotiate with Pullen over the final hour.

During the three hours of the standoff, Pullen walked constantly around his vehicle and in the roadway between his pickup and the police vehicles. He continued drinking beer. He continuously threatened to kill himself and police. Occasionally he would lean both firearms against the side of his truck, but he never moved away from them. As he was opening another can of beer, a State Police negotiator told him that the officers were concerned for their safety when he was holding his guns. Pullen replied, "They should be."

Pullen put the muzzle of one of his guns under his chin and flipped off the safety. The negotiators convinced him not to shoot himself and he stopped. Sometimes as he walked around he would wave the weapons in a random fashion; sometimes he deliberately pointed them at the officers in a provocative fashion. At one point he walked straight towards the officers, shotgun in hand, despite repeated commands to stop. When he was about ten feet from one officer he yelled that if the officer shot him, he would kill the officer. Then he returned to his pickup.

Late in the standoff, Pullen renounced his original promise not to hurt any of the officers unless they approached. He advised them "someone's going to get hurt tonight." He tried to persuade the officers to shoot him. He told them that he would not leave there alive and asked what it would take to make them shoot him. Several times he opened his shirt and invited the police to shoot him in the heart. He waved his knife around, claiming he would fight the police hand-to-hand.

Finally Pullen retrieved a soft cooler with a shoulder strap from his truck and packed it full of beer. He slung it over his shoulder and announced he was walking into the woods and nobody better follow him. He had his shotgun in one hand, the rifle in the other, and walked towards the negotiator. He threw his truck keys to the negotiator and told him he could have the truck. He walked across an adjoining field towards the nearby woods.

Two members of the State Police Tactical Team were in the field with a State Police dog. They were instructed not to let Pullen get into the woods. The dog handler tried twice to set the dog on Pullen. Both times the dog went to Pullen and returned to its handler without taking any action against Pullen. Pullen warned them not to try it again.

Seconds later, Pullen raised both of his weapons at the two officers. He began to advance on them, pointing the firearms directly at them. The officers issued orders to "stop," to "drop the weapons." Pullen did not comply or even respond. He kept advancing on the officers when one of them fired two shots from about 56 feet. Both struck Pullen and he fell. Emergency first aid was rendered and he was transported to a hospital where he died. Both of Pullen's firearms were fully loaded.

The ensuing investigation revealed that he had told family members a couple days before that his life was over. He was going to burn down his house and have it out with the cops. He told one "Don't blame yourself for what I'm about to do." This same person told investigators that Pullen had no intention of hurting anyone, he just wanted to get killed and he did not want to shoot himself. Interestingly, and indicative of the impulsive nature of many suicide-by-cop events, once Pullen finally attained his objective and got himself shot, he implored the paramedics on the scene to not let him die.

———————

It is not just males who attempt suicide by cop. The whole idea of planning to create a deadly engagement with a police officer with the intent of inducing the officer to shoot one to death may seem to have little correlation with popular notions of the characteristics of female suicides. The conventional wisdom about female suicides does not include overt acts of confrontation and aggression designed to provoke a lethal response from a police officer. However, suicidal intent and attempts are not gender specific. Female suicide by cop does occur—admittedly less often than male suicide by cop—and the fact of it must be recognized.

### Case History #6 (Planned Female Suicide)[20]

On March 24, 2009, Barbara Stewart placed a 911 call to the Biddeford Police Department and told the dispatcher: "I'm gonna kill myself or somebody else and I have a gun." When the police dispatcher tried to engage Stewart in further conversation, she terminated the call. About three minutes after the call, Sgt. Jeffrey Greene, Sgt. Philip Greenwood, and Officer Benjamin Sholl arrived in separate cruisers. They arrived within seconds of one another near Stewart's apartment building.

Barbara Stewart was standing on the sidewalk at the base of the stairway leading to the apartment building in which she resided. Sgt. Greene observed Stewart but believed her to be a pedestrian unrelated to the call for service. Sgt. Greene walked toward Stewart. Officer Sholl had parked his cruiser and was still inside the cruiser when Greene walked past him. Sgt. Greenwood was on foot a short distance behind Sgt. Greene.

Sgt. Greene approached Stewart and asked her if she was a resident of the apartment house. Stewart responded that she was. Officer Sholl was now out of his cruiser, and Sgt. Greenwood was behind Sgt. Greene on the sidewalk. Sgt. Greene continued to walk towards the woman and from about 20 feet away, asked her which apartment she lived in. Stewart turned slightly so as to directly face Sgt. Greene, reached into her clothing, and displayed what appeared to Greene and the other officers to be a semi-automatic pistol. Sgt. Greene, while retreating, broadcast on his portable radio that "she's pointing a gun at me."

All three officers saw Stewart raise the pistol with two hands and point it directly at Sgt. Greene. All three officers drew their service weapons and began issuing commands for Stewart to drop her gun. Simultaneously, Stewart started walking directly toward Sgt. Greene as Greene and the other two officers retreated and sought cover. Sgt. Greenwood retreated close to a building next door, while Officer Sholl was able to retreat back to his cruiser. Sgt. Greene remained focused on Stewart as she advanced on him with the gun pointed directly at him. He first retreated into the street, and then took a stationery position next to a utility pole. Using the pole as partial cover, Sgt. Greene, as well as Officer Sholl and Sgt. Greenwood, continued to issue re-

---

20. Findings of the Attorney General, State of Maine, regarding the investigation of the use of deadly force by police against Barbara Stewart, March 24, 2009.

peated commands for Stewart to drop her weapon. There were at least 15 such commands. Stewart continued walking toward Greene with the gun pointed at him. She responded "no" at least twice to the commands to drop the gun.

When Stewart was about 10 feet from him, Sgt. Greene recalls asking her if the pistol was real and Stewart responding, "It's ready." He also recalls being aware that Officer Sholl and Sgt. Greenwood were somewhere close behind him. As Stewart continued to advance on him, still holding her gun in both hands pointed at him, Sgt. Greene fired the first of three rounds at Stewart, hitting her in the left shoulder. Stewart crouched forward and down and her gun struck the sidewalk. Immediately, however, she recovered and stood upright with the gun in her hand and pointed at Sgt. Greene. As she did so, Sgt. Greene fired two more rounds in quick succession, the second of which was later determined to have struck Stewart in the upper chest. Investigation determined that Stewart had advanced to within 9–11 feet of Sgt. Greene when she was shot. From the time Sgt. Greene arrived at the location on Main Street to the time he discharged his weapon at Stewart, one minute and 22 seconds elapsed.

The investigation that followed determined that Stewart was armed with a silver and black .177 caliber pellet pistol. The pistol is similar in appearance and configuration to a semi-automatic pistol. The investigation also disclosed that Stewart had left a dated, handwritten suicide note in her apartment in which she directed the disposition of her belongings.

———————

A final category that is pertinent to any consideration of suicide by cop is the mentally disturbed, also referred to as "emotionally disturbed persons."[21] Interaction between police and mentally disturbed or unbalanced individuals is a frequent occurrence. As a category, mentally disturbed individuals can be prone to engage in acts of aggression that lead to a reasonable and fully justified use of deadly force by the law enforcement officers. The act may be a planned and determined act of suicide to be consummated by the police. It may be an impulsive suicidal attempt. Or it may be the product of the individual's own demons and psychoses.

———————

21. "Emotionally disturbed person" is a vague and poorly conceived term that lends itself to application without clear guidelines or intuitive understanding. Emotionally disturbed can describe a host of perturbations—some temporary, some not. For example: drunken rage, jealousy, extreme grief, paranoia, schizophrenia, and narcotic induced psychoses can all be causes of emotional disturbance. All can engender different law enforcement awareness and responses.

If alcohol or narcotics are present, the potentiality for a suicidal act is even more likely. Advocates for the mentally ill point to national studies showing that substance abuse increases the likelihood of violence among people suffering from mental illness by a factor of five (500%).[22] Regardless, there is always an outcry that the police need to be better trained and better prepared to deal with the mentally ill. However, police officers are not mental health professionals. They are not diagnosticians. And they are not expected to permit the imposition of death or serious injury upon their selves or upon others— regardless of the mental capacity of the individual who poses the danger.

There are large numbers of mentally ill or mentally unbalanced individuals present in society, and both law enforcement and the mental health community recognize that most of them are neither dangerous nor criminal. In cases in which the non-dangerous or non-criminal mentally ill individual creates an incident that evokes a law enforcement response, there are numerous guidelines and training protocols that will guide the response to resolve the incident without harm to the instigator.[23]

Interactions between law enforcement and mentally unbalanced individuals are a common occurrence.[24] The vast majority of such incidents are nuisance

---

22. Chapman, L, page 3.

23. *Criminal Justice/Mental Health Consensus Project*, Council of State Governments, June 2002. Project partners include: Association of State Correctional Administrators; Bazelon Center for Mental Health Law; Center for Behavioral Health, Justice & Public Policy; National Association of State Mental Health Program Directors; Police Executive Research Forum; and Pretrial Services Resource Center. The *Criminal Justice/Mental Health Consensus Project* was an unprecedented national, two-year effort to prepare specific recommendations that local, state, and federal policymakers, and criminal justice and mental health professionals can use to improve the criminal justice system's response to people with mental illness. It was not a national guideline that carried any sanction upon law enforcement. To the contrary, the Project was a central clearinghouse for varied approaches and programs across the country that localities, institutions, and authorities can reference for use in creating their own, autonomous programs commensurate with needs, resources, and finances. The Project advisory groups included over 100 state lawmakers, police chiefs, officers, sheriffs, district attorneys, public defenders, judges, court administrators, state corrections directors, community corrections officials, victim advocates, consumers, family members and other mental health advocates, county commissioners, state mental health directors, behavioral health care providers, substance abuse experts, and clinicians. Since the Project defined the problem, more comprehensive models have been developed such as the eponymous "Memphis Model" discussed below.

24. "People with mental illness are significantly overrepresented among the segment of the population in contact with the criminal justice system. Approximately 5 percent of the U.S. population has a serious mental illness. The U.S. Department of Justice reported in 1999, however, that about 16 percent of the population in prison or jail has a serious mental ill-

crimes at worst. However, an emphasis on the physical well-being of the individual is not promoted at the expense of the safety of the public and the officers—it is when the individual's actions are not criminal or dangerous that such a personalized emphasis is feasible and can be considered. This distinction is clearly, and repetitively, stressed in prominent guidelines and recommendations for dealing with the mentally ill.[25]

When the individual is engaged in serious criminal or dangerous activity, the safety of the public, bystanders, and the officers involved is paramount and the law enforcement response necessarily must focus on threat assessment and resolution.[26] This is widely recognized and accepted within both the law enforcement and the mental health communities.

Law enforcement training, policy, and practice recognize that mentally ill individuals can pose a threat to themselves and to those around them even as it also understands that the incidence of mentally ill persons who are dangerous is miniscule relative to the vast number of interactions between police and mentally ill people. However, law enforcement training admonishes caution in dealing with the mentally ill for several reasons. One is the desire to avoid precipitating an attack or a suicide attempt, although that decision is solely in the hands of the person who will make that decision regardless of what the officers do or fail to do and regardless of the mental capacity of the person being confronted. The greater caution is to protect against a sudden attack upon the officer or others.

---

ness. Of the 10 million people booked into U.S. jails in 1997, at least 700,000 had a serious mental illness; approximately three-quarters of those individuals had a co-occurring substance abuse disorder." *Ibid.* page 4.

25. "In no way does this report minimize the importance of officer and public safety— they are of paramount importance. In fact, the policies outlined in this report are intended to prevent critical incidents through effective, earlier interventions. It also acknowledges those cases in which arrest is very appropriate, as with serious crimes. In those cases, the offender should be in the criminal justice system." *Ibid.* page 35.

26. "There are three distinct scenarios most often encountered by persons with mental illness and their families. The first scenario is that of the mentally ill family member arrested or incarcerated on misdemeanor criminal charges having nothing to do with his or her family. The second scenario occurs when a mentally ill family member is arrested or incarcerated on felony criminal charges having nothing to do with his or her family. In both of these cases, the objective of the family is to get the mentally ill family member released from custody, acquitted at trial, and access to appropriate treatment. The third common scenario occurs when a family is forced to call the police to intervene because of threatening or destructive actions of a mentally ill family member."

The National Alliance on Mental Illness (NAMI), "A Guide to Mental Illness and the Criminal Justice System," page 2.

Police officers are not, and cannot be, trained mental health professionals. In fact, trained mental health professionals routinely take days and weeks under controlled clinical circumstances to arrive at diagnoses that are frequently contradictory. It is pure folly to expect a police officer to diagnose reliably and accurately in stressful, uncontrolled, and time critical circumstances that a trained mental health professional would avoid. It is well recognized that law enforcement officers cannot be expected to diagnose mental illness.[27]

Police are routinely the first responders to incidents involving mentally ill individuals and thus the first authority figures to come into contact with them. There are numerous guidelines, training protocols, and resources that are variously available to assist police officers in these situations. All of them are targeted towards recognizing, handling, and treating the mentally ill individual relative to a face-to-face confrontational incident. All of them recognize the first police responsibility is to to protect themselves (the law enforcement officers) and others. The responsibility and care to be exercised by police officers, and for which they are trained, are focused on these direct confrontations between law enforcement and the mentally ill individual. Anything else is too speculative and disconnected from observable causality to be considered.

The National Alliance on Mental Illness (NAMI) is the most widely accepted and recognized authority on the interactions between law enforcement and the mentally ill. NAMI establishes and maintains relevant guidelines and standards, and is the certifying authority accrediting Crisis Intervention Teams (CIT) when established by law enforcement agencies.[28] The CIT program is

---

27. "The officer responding to the scene is not expected to diagnose any specific mental illness but is expected to recognize symptoms that may indicate that mental illness is a factor in the incident. Many of these symptoms represent internal, emotional states that are not readily observable from outward appearances, though they may become noticeable in conversation with the individual. In addition to the symptoms outlined, some specific types of behavior may also be signs of mental illness. These behaviors can include severe changes in behavior, unusual or bizarre mannerisms, hostility or distrust, one-sided conversations, and confused or nonsensical verbal communication. Officers may also notice inappropriate behavior, such as wearing layers of clothing in the summer. It should be noted that these behaviors can also be associated with cultural and personality differences, other medical conditions, drug or alcohol abuse, or reactions to very stressful situations. *As such, the presence of these behaviors should not be treated as conclusive proof of mental illness." Ibid.* page 64.

28. See: "Crisis Intervention Team Core Elements", The University of Memphis, School of Urban Affairs and Public Policy, Department of Criminology and Criminal Justice CIT Center, September 2007:

"The CIT program is an innovative national model of police-based crisis intervention with community mental health care and advocacy partnerships. Police officers receive intensive training to effectively respond to citizens experiencing a behavioral crisis. Patrol of-focused on the actual and commonly occurring, direct interactions between law enforcement and those individuals who are mentally disturbed.[29] It recognizes

---

ficers already have training and a basic understanding of the proper safety skills. Officers are encouraged to maintain these skills throughout the course, while incorporating new de-escalation techniques to more effectively approach a crisis situation. It is important that the individuals from the mental health, law enforcement, and advocacy communities play a critical role in the training curriculum in order to bring experience, ideas, information, and assistance to the CIT Officers in training."

29. The NAMI model CIT policy and procedures:

**I. Recognition of Mental Illness**

Signs or symptom which may indicate the presence of Mental Illnesses:
· Loss of memory/disorientation
· Delusions—These are false beliefs that are not based in reality. The individual will often focus on persecution or grandeur (he/she is God)
· Depression
· Hallucinations—hear voices, or see, smell, taste, or feel things
· Manic behavior—accelerated thinking and speaking or hyperactivity with no or little need for sleep—may also be delusional
· Anxiety—feelings are intense, state of panic or fright
· Incoherence—difficulty expressing themselves, disconnected ideas and/or thoughts
· Response—may process information more slowly

When an officer recognizes that they are potentially dealing with a mental consumer, they should consider applying some of the following de-escalation techniques. If the person is actively violent the officer may request assistance from a CIT Officer.

The officer should:
· Assess safety issues
· Introduce yourself and attempt to obtain the person's name.
· Remain calm and avoid overreacting
· Be helpful
· Present a genuine willingness to understand and help
· Speak slowly, low tone—using short sentences—repeating
· Move slowly
· Remove distractions or disruptive people from the area
· Demonstrate "active listening skills"—i.e., summary of verbal communications.

The officer should NOT:
· Engage in behaviors that can be interpreted as aggressive.
· Allow others to interact simultaneously while you are attempting to talk to the person and to stabilize the situation.
· Corner, or be cornered: (Give the person expanded space and ensure that you, the officer, has expanded space and a safe exit, if it should become necessary).
· Raise your voice, use a sharp edge in your speaking, or use threats to gain compliance.

that law enforcement has a clear and overriding responsibility to protect the safety of officers and others. It offers guidelines and training to facilitate police in accomplishing that responsibility while concurrently supporting the interests of the mentally ill individual to the extent it can be done without unreasonably sacrificing public safety.[30]

There occurs a common allegation in the aftermath of a police shooting involving a mentally ill individual that there is a fundamental rule for police interaction with the mentally ill mandating that police do nothing that will unnecessarily "excite or enrage" the individual into any adverse reaction. This is an invention. First, and broadly speaking, it creates the false implication that there exists a national authority that promulgates fundamental rules controlling police activities with the mentally ill *and* that binding authority to enforce those rules and sanction violations of those rules resides somewhere— presumably with the implied national authority. The proponents of the claim ignore the fact that there is more than one interest group organization studying, assessing, and devising guidelines and model policies for police practices regarding the mentally ill (as well as regarding all the other issues involving law enforcement in general). There is no authority or method by which one of them can be recognized as a controlling authority and the others are not. Law enforcement is authorized, defined, limited, and controlled by law, not by the concerns and recommendations of interest groups, no matter how well meaning, well researched, and well designed or efficacious those recommendations may be. They are helpful, often useful, but not binding.

The available references and authorities on police interactions with mentally ill persons provide guidelines for officer behavior *when in contact* with a men-

---

- Attempt to gain compliance based on the assumption that the person is as reasonable about things as you are.
- Argue

30. For example, see Hillsborough County Sheriff's Office Standard Operating Procedure Number GEN 522-01, Crisis Intervention Team; CIT:

"**B. First Responding Deputy:**

1. Responding deputy should perform the following:

**a.** Secure the scene, especially with regard to the deputy and subject's safety.

**b.** Determine if the circumstances require the continued response of the CIT deputy and inform the Communications Center of the status.

**c.** Gather all available information in preparation of briefing the CIT member upon their arrival. Information sources should include but are not limited to the following:

(1.) Observations of the person's actions, demeanor, etc.

(2.) Interview of family/friends on scene

(3.) Interview with the person (try to get information of diagnosis, medications, last time medication(s) were taken, look for medical alert bracelet, etc.)"

tally ill individual. These are not "rules" in the legally binding sense and they are not directed at officer behavior distant from a suspected mentally ill individual.[31]

_____

31. For example, see Seminole County Sheriff's Office, Florida, General Order G-52, "Mental Health and Substance Abuse," March 20, 2006 (one of several established CIT programs that NAMI offers as a model policy, generically called the Memphis Model) that provides:
"The following guidelines describe how to interact with a person suffering from mental illness and who may be a crime victim, witness, or suspect. These guidelines should be followed in all contacts, whether on the street or during more formal interviews and interrogations. To protect their safety and the safety of others Deputies should:
1. Remember that mentally ill persons in crisis situations are generally afraid,
2. Continually assess the situation for danger,
3. Maintain adequate space between the person,
4. Remain calm and avoid overreacting,
5. Be helpful and professional, offer assistance to make the person feel safer/calmer, etc.
6. Provide or obtain on-scene medical aid when treatment of an injury is needed,
7. Follow procedures indicated on any medical alert bracelet or necklace,
8. Indicate a willingness to understand and help,
9. Give firm, clear direction; speak simply and briefly. Only one Deputy should talk to the subject,
10. Move slowly,
11. Remove distractions, upsetting influences, and disruptive people from the scene,
12. Understand that a rational discussion may not take place, respond to delusions and hallucinations by talking about the person's feelings rather than what he/she is saying,
13. Recognize that the person may be overwhelmed by sensations, thoughts, frightening beliefs, sounds (voices), or the environment,
14. Be friendly, patient, accepting and encouraging, but remain firm and professional,
15. Be aware that the uniform, gun, handcuffs, etc., may frighten the person. Attempt to reassure them that no harm is intended,
16. Recognize and acknowledge that a person's delusional or hallucinatory experience is real to them,
17. Announce actions before initiating them,
18. Gather information from family or bystanders, and,
19. If the person is experiencing a psychiatric crisis, attempt to have a local mental health professional respond to the scene.
J. Each incident is different, and Deputies should be aware that their actions may have an adverse effect on the situation. Deputies should generally avoid:
1. Moving suddenly, giving rapid orders, or shouting,
2. Join into the behavior related to the person's mental illness; forcing discussion; challenging delusional or hallucinatory statements; agreeing or disagreeing with delusions or hallucinations,
3. Direct, continuous eye contact (staring at the subject),
4. Touching the person (unless essential for safety). While touching can be helpful to some people who are upset, for the disturbed mentally ill person it may

Law enforcement officers routinely respond to, and resolve, countless calls involving emotionally disturbed individuals.[32] A police officer can only be held to account for reasonably foreseeable events.

Secondly, there do exist national organizations that embody expertise in the sundry subject areas and issues regarding the mentally ill and interactions between the mentally ill and law enforcement. These organizations, such as the National Alliance on Mental Illness (NAMI), the International Association of Chiefs of Police (IACP) and the Council of State Governments Criminal Justice/Mental Health Consensus Project publish guidelines, recommendations, training content and, in the case of NAMI, administer CIT training and accreditation. As discussed above, none of the assorted guidelines and recommended practices rise to the level of national "rules," nor do they have standing or authority to sanction those who do not adopt and/or follow every guideline put forth. To the contrary, these organizations recognize the reality that communities have different needs and resources and the fact that individual police officers must and do have broad discretionary police powers and functions subject to the exercise of officer judgment in the circumstances at hand.

Finally, the references, guidelines, and expert authorities dealing with interactions between law enforcement and the mentally ill all focus on actual direct confrontations between police and an individual experiencing a mental crisis. There are often allegations made in the aftermath of a police use of deadly force against a violent mentally ill person that something done remote from the scene incited the violence, such as the sounds of sirens, the sight of armed officers

---

cause more fear and lead to violence,
   5. Crowding the person or moving into their comfort zone,
   6. Expressing anger, impatience, or irritation,
   7. Assuming that a person who does not respond cannot hear,
   8. Using inflammatory language, such as "mental" or "mental subject,"
   9. Deceiving the person (dishonesty increases fear and suspicion),
   10. Give multiple choices (multiple choices increase the person's confusion),
   11. Whisper, laugh, or joke about the situation (may increase the person's suspicions and the potential for violence), and,
   12. Misleading the person to believe that the Deputy thinks or feels the same way."

32. For example, in the claims and allegations following a 2012 shooting case in New York City involving an "emotionally disturbed person" the plaintiff noted that the NYPD "handles over 100,000 EDP calls per year." The plaintiff then attempted to illustrate a "long series of wrongful death incidents" in support of his claims, listing a total of seven incidents (out of context and with no attempt to assess justification) dating from 1984. Using the plaintiff's arithmetic, since 1984 the NYPD handled **3.1 million** EDP calls of which seven resulted in deaths (five by shooting). Even assuming that none of the seven were justified uses of force under the law and within NYPD policy (patently untrue), the nominal EDP death rate at the hands of NYPD is thus 2 millionths of one per cent over the 31 years in question.

approaching, or even the mere presence of uniformed officers in the person's line of sight. Allegations such as this are speculative fancy unrecognized by any of the recognized authorities on interactions with the mentally disturbed.

There exists a general reluctance in society to accept the premise that individuals can and do provoke law enforcement personnel by escalating the risk of imminent death or injury to self or others in order to be killed.[33] However, the phenomenon occurs far more often than realized. There have been a total of 115 police shootings in the State of Maine from 1990 through 2014.[34] At least eighteen of those 115 police shootings were cases of suicide by cop. Thus at least 15.7% of all police involved shootings in the State of Maine for the period 1990–2014 were suicide by cop. The examples of suicide by cop cited in this chapter all occurred within the state of Maine and were intentionally selected for that reason. This is a comprehensive database inclusive of all law enforcement jurisdictions and venues throughout the state.[35]

The compelling point to be made is that *even* in Maine, a relatively minor microcosm in the law enforcement universe that has few of the population pressures, racial dichotomies, societal stresses, and violent crime rates more endemic to denser urban and metropolitan areas elsewhere, this phenomenon occurs with regularity. Suicide by cop is a recurring phenomenon everywhere. The scope of the phenomenon is significant, but as yet not well defined or recognized. It is real and probably even more prevalent elsewhere. It is an ineluctable causative factor in law enforcement deadly force incidents that cannot be ignored. When it does occur, it gives rise to uninformed, emotional criticism of the officers involved and the department's training and policies, as if a suicidal individual bent on being killed poses a different and somehow more acceptable threat than an armed robber resisting arrest.

The Office of Investigations of the Maine State Attorney General's Office recognizes that suicide by cop is a recurrent phenomenon and it includes that awareness in its investigative process. The Office of Investigations has developed a series of indicators that can help diagnose a case of suicide by cop. Some of the indicators are unambiguous and unmistakable; some must be weighed

---

33. MacPherson, S, PhD, "Understanding the Law Enforcement Issues in Suicide by Cop," International Wound Ballistics Association (IWBA), *Wound Ballistics Review*, Vol. 4 (1), 1999, page 18.

34. Per Brian MacMaster, Director of Investigations, Office of the Attorney General, State of Maine, Augusta, ME, September 17, 2014.

35. Maine is unique in that every police use of deadly force within the state is investigated by the Maine State Attorney General's Office for compliance with Maine state law. This is a statutory requirement.

in concert with others. The indicators in whole or in part can assist in making a final informed judgment in police shootings where the suicide by cop motivation may be uncertain on its face.

<u>Indicators of Suicide by Cop:</u>

- The subject is barricaded and refuses to negotiate.
- The subject has just killed someone, particularly a close relative, his mother, wife, or child.
- The subject says that he has a life-threatening illness.
- The subject sets a deadline to be killed.
- The subject's demands of police do not include negotiations for escape or freedom.
- The subject has undergone one or more traumatic life changes (death of a loved one, divorce, financial devastation, etc.)
- Prior to the encounter, the subject has given away all of his money or possessions.
- The subject has a record of assaults.
- The subject says he will only surrender to the person in charge.
- The subject indicates that he has thought about planning his death.
- The subject has expressed an interest in wanting to die in a "macho" way.
- The subject has expressed interest in "going out in a big way."
- The subject expresses feelings of hopelessness or helplessness.
- The subject dictates his will to negotiators.
- The subject demands to be killed.
- The subject counting down or up.
    —This involves a counting cadence, often illustrated by a rocking motion that helps the suicidal subject take himself to "the point of release and fall."[36]

There is an equal reluctance to accept that some means other than deadly force could not have been found to deal with a mentally ill person. It is as if there exists a belief that only a person with clear intent and motivation can pose a threat that justifies deadly force. If the person lacks mental competency, then any use of deadly force is somehow suspect as excessive or ultimately unnecessary. Experience refutes this. There were thirteen law enforcement officers feloniously killed "handling person with mental illness" in the 15-year

---

36. Brian MacMaster, Director of Investigations, Office of the Attorney General, State of Maine, Augusta, ME, Maine Medico-Legal Society, 11/20/08.

period from 1999–2013.[37] There were 49,851 assaults on law enforcement officers reported in 2013 and 1,319 of those assaults were committed by "persons with mental illness."[38]

The local communities in which the incidents occur have a tendency to characterize the law enforcement behavior as aggressive and punitive. They deny the culpability of the true perpetrator—the suicidal or mentally disturbed individual who acts in a dangerous or threatening manner. This is even more acute in cases of hidden suicide and cases involving the mentally ill or the "emotionally disturbed"—the same individuals who comprise the "mentally ill" category utilized in classifying law enforcement assailants.

There is a measurable division in public attitudes toward these incidents. One segment that usually supports law enforcement generally sees no need to change police policies or practices, although they may not be sure why. The other segment considers law enforcement in general as an occupying force, community jackboots interested primarily in trampling civil liberties and acting aggressively to oppress people in need of help. They tend to view use-of-force interactions with the suicidal and the mentally ill as a validation of the need for law enforcement to respond differently. They reject the notion that deadly force could ever be justified against the suicidal or the mentally ill. And in incidents in which these critics must concede that the use of deadly force was justified, they blame law enforcement for creating the circumstances in which deadly force became necessary. Many of this ilk believe that law enforcement personnel are poorly trained and do not understand the psychological needs of the victim. In this view, law enforcement "should" have the skills of a mental health professional in order to prevent the death or injury of such persons. "These profound differences are driven by diverse and subjective societal beliefs, and are not objective observations and analysis."[39]

The unpredictable and impulsive mindset of an armed individual precludes any certainty that he will not initiate violence. A lack of mental competence does not mitigate the threat, nor is the law enforcement officer required to make those distinctions, nor essay a series of less than lethal options.

> " ... [t]here is no precedent ... which says that the Constitution requires law enforcement officers to use all feasible alternatives to avoid a situa-

---

37. Compendium of FBI Uniform Crime Reports, Law Enforcement Officers Killed and Assaulted 1999–2013.

38. FBI Uniform Crime Reports, Law Enforcement Officers Killed and Assaulted 2013, Table 68. "Handling person with mental illness "is a specific category utilized by Uniform Crime Reports.

39. MacPherson, S, PhD, page 20.

*tion where deadly force can justifiably be used. There are, however, cases which support the assertion that, where deadly force is otherwise justified under the Constitution, there is no constitutional duty to use non-deadly alternatives first."*[40]

When the issues move into the courts in the aftermath of a deadly force confrontation, advocates in litigation rely on perfect hindsight to interpret law enforcement actions as aggressive and insensitive to the state of mind of the subject. The clarity of hindsight is always remarkable.

The result is that they expect the police to possess a supernatural intuitive sense that will enable them to divine whether a person is ultimately going to be harmless or not. However, the law enforcement officer on the scene interacting with the mentally ill or the suicidal person has to make that determination with reliability and in mere seconds, at most. And the officer must always hold prevention of harm to himself and others first in priority. Injury to the subject of the encounter must always be subordinate to the necessity to prevent any chance of injury to others. If the officer retreats or refuses to intervene, where does that leave the public? It has to be so. All the vagaries of deadly force confrontations apply — action versus reaction, wound ballistic realities, sensory alterations, limited time and means, and the inescapable and undiminished responsibility to protect others at the expense of the one threatening violence.

Whenever a suicide by cop occurs or whenever law enforcement is compelled to use deadly force against one who is later determined to be mentally ill, the pressures on law enforcement increase to modify departmental use-of-force policies and training in dealing with emotionally disturbed persons who display life-threatening and criminal behavior with lethal weapons or their facsimiles. The impracticality of implementing this sort of modified use-of-force policy is well understood within law enforcement, but seriously misunderstood by much of the public and even some mental health professionals.[41]

Moreover, the common law enforcement experience is an encounter with an individual who is distressed or agitated and who does not initiate a subsequent assault on the officer. This is the norm, and it is a frequent occurrence. Distress and agitation are characteristics of the vast majority of people with whom a law enforcement officer must interact. So it is not atypical that officers do not expect or anticipate sudden assaults by a disturbed person even in cases where some external signs of their distress are obvious. The normal experience is that no attack occurs.

---

40. *Plakas v. Drinski*, 19 F.3d 1143 (7th Cir. 1994), page 1148.
41. *Ibid.* page 20.

As a result, this misunderstanding causes some segments of society to hold law enforcement accountable for any failure to compile a diagnostic psychological profile of the threatening person under volatile, unpredictable, high-stress, high-risk situations. Some even suggest that law enforcement "may be able to develop strategies for early recognition" in the handling of suicidal or mentally ill persons.[42] This implies training law enforcement officers to diagnose and manage severe mental pathology in an individual in the setting of an impending gunfight or knife attack. In effect, they are asking the law enforcement officer in the field to assess the threat based on a subjective belief regarding the mental status of the individual confronted and not what the officer sees as the threat posed to society at that moment.

> *"Putting responsibility on the officer to do a psychological analysis and to base his decisions on this psychological analysis requires him to modify departmental use of force policy (presumably thoughtfully chosen and precisely delineated) on the spur of the moment."*[43]

This is preposterous. It is also unreasonable and illogical and would serve only to place the officer and others in jeopardy. " ... [T]rained mental health professionals themselves often find difficulty in making an accurate diagnosis even under optimal conditions" (i.e., clinical surroundings) with no time pressures.[44] In fact, mental health professionals preparing to interact with a potentially violent or assaultive personality in controlled clinical conditions take precautionary measures to protect themselves against unpredictable attack. They are no more capable of being able to foresee and forestall sudden violence than any police officer could be—and they recognize that reality in their practices. Guidelines for handling emotionally disturbed/mentally ill people regularly include the caution "Do not turn your back on them!"

The mental health profession recognizes that an attack is always a clear and present risk, yet some of them would argue that a law enforcement officer facing a mentally disturbed person with a knife in an uncontrolled, free-form encounter with innocent lives at risk can afford to take greater liberties than they would recommend in a clinical setting with no weapons present. Many others recognize the reality:

> *"Just because someone has mental illness doesn't mean the cops should respond differently. That person is a danger. The key is to prevent that in-*

---

42. Hutson, RH, MD, pages 685–89.
43. MacPherson, S, PhD, page 21.
44. *Ibid.* page 21.

*dividual from reaching the point where the person is a danger to himself or others."*[45]

As further evidence of the irrationality of expecting a law enforcement officer to make a near instantaneous and accurate diagnosis while in the midst of an unfolding life-or-death scenario is the fact that well-credentialed mental health professionals appear on both sides in court cases wherein mental status is an issue, earnestly advocating totally different opinions. How many would want the life of their loved ones to depend upon this level of analytical precision?[46] In the end, any analysis and assessment of the use of deadly force by a law enforcement officer must look at what the subject of the deadly force did and was that reasonably perceived to pose an imminent risk of death or serious injury to the others present. Law enforcement agencies must have clearly delineated, unambiguous, use-of-force policies that allow their officers to respond to the observed or perceived threat and that do not attempt or require the utilization of on-the-spot psychoanalysis.

### Case History #7 (Events Are Driven by the Suicidal Individual)[47]

On February 16, 2008, at about 1:00 a.m., the Somerset County (Maine) Sheriff's Office received a 911 call from a cellular telephone. The caller identified himself as Dan McDowell,[48] said he had "just murdered someone," and "I have another person that I'm holding hostage right now." He told the dispatcher that the two persons were hitchhikers he had picked up on Route 150 between Athens and Harmony, and that he was presently on the South Road in Harmony. He told the dispatcher that the person he had killed was in the bed of his pickup truck, and responded in graphic terms when asked if he was sure the person was dead. McDowell described his pickup truck and his approximate location on the South Road, and told the dispatcher to have responding officers operating the blue lights on their cruisers "or I will shoot my hostage."

Asked by the dispatcher the reason he had killed someone and intended to kill another person, McDowell responded, "I plan to die tonight and I'm hop-

---

45. Katie Fullam, Deputy Commissioner, Maine Department of Mental Health and Mental Retardation, quoted in the Lewiston, ME, *Sun Journal*, April 9, 2000.

46. *Ibid.* page 21.

47. Findings of the Attorney General, State of Maine, regarding the investigation of the use of deadly force by police against Daniel L. McDowell, February 16, 2008.

48. The caller calmly provided his name and, in response to further questions from the dispatcher, his date of birth and address.

ing the officers will help me tonight." He also told the dispatcher, "When you send the cops, tell them that I'm armed and that I was trained by the military."

When asked by the dispatcher what he had for weapons, McDowell replied, "I'll let them [the responding officers] find out." At a point where the conversation became choppy because of a poor cellular connection, McDowell accused the dispatcher of trying to distract him and threatened to hang up. After additional brief conversation, the dispatcher asked McDowell to hold on so she could update the responding officers. McDowell responded by stating, "you got ten seconds starting now … nine, eight, seven …" at which time he disconnected the call.

The information from the 911 conversation was dispatched to Somerset County deputy sheriffs Michael Ross and Ritchie Putnam, as well as Maine State Police trooper Bernard Brunette. Each officer was in uniform and operating marked police cruisers. All three officers knew that McDowell had mental health issues and a military background. They knew from dispatch that McDowell wanted to commit "suicide by cop." He claimed to have murdered one person and was holding another hostage. They needed to respond quickly or he was going to shoot the hostage.

The three officers met and discussed a strategy to approach McDowell's location to gather further information for a planned call-out of the State Police Tactical Team.[49] They spoke with a motorist passing by their location, a local resident who told the officers of having just seen a man standing next to a pickup truck a few miles down the road. The officers started down the South Road in their respective cruisers with Trooper Brunette in the lead.

As the officers crested a knoll in the road and started down a grade, they observed the headlights come on in a stationary vehicle facing them. The officers stopped about 165 feet from the vehicle. Trooper Brunette used his spotlight to better illuminate the scene around the stationary vehicle to their front. He observed a man, later determined to be McDowell, standing next to the open driver's door of the vehicle. Trooper Brunette observed McDowell holding a rifle or shotgun at port arms, i.e., diagonally across his chest with the barrel of the weapon pointed upward. Trooper Brunette immediately alerted the other officers to the presence of the weapon. He then shouted to McDowell "Sir, put the gun down." Trooper Brunette and Deputy Ross saw McDowell raise the weapon to his shoulder and point it in their direction before

---

49. The commander of the State Police Tactical Team had already been consulted and requested that the responding officers assess the situation to determine if the team was actually needed.

momentarily disappearing from the officers' view. For protection, Trooper Brunette attempted to back up his cruiser, which was in the travel lane slightly toward the middle of the road. He was unable to do so because of the extremely icy roadway. Deputy Ross backed up his cruiser and positioned it at an angle on the left side of Trooper Brunette's cruiser. Deputy Putnam backed up his cruiser and positioned it on the right side of the roadway several feet behind Trooper Brunette's cruiser. All three officers then observed McDowell leave the vicinity of his vehicle and start walking toward them with his weapon held at port arms. The officers then observed McDowell level his weapon and point it at them as he continued to advance on them. Trooper Brunette shouted commands to McDowell to drop the weapon. McDowell ignored him and continued to walk toward the officers with his weapon aimed in their direction. All three officers simultaneously shot at McDowell until he fell to the ground.[50]

Trooper Brunette fired six rounds with his .45 handgun. Deputy Ross fired six rounds with his Colt M16 rifle. Deputy Putnam fired seven rounds with his Bushmaster AR15 rifle.

It was later determined that McDowell had walked about 27 feet from his parked vehicle toward the officers before being shot and killed. He was about 140 feet from the officers when he was shot. The chief medical examiner advised that McDowell's death was caused by a single gunshot wound to the chest. It was the only wound he suffered. It was determined that McDowell was armed with a 12-gauge shotgun with a slug round in the chamber and four birdshot rounds in the magazine. He had two additional rounds in his pocket. The safety mechanism on the shotgun was off. The investigation also disclosed that one of the rounds fired by the police struck and penetrated the barrel of McDowell's shotgun. There was no body in the bed of McDowell's pickup truck nor was a hostage found.

Lab analysis determined McDowell's blood-alcohol concentration to have been 0.203% at the time of his death. A lengthy suicide note and a handwritten "last will and testament" were found in McDowell's pickup truck. Three other notes, including one apologizing to "law enforcement authorities," were found in McDowell's residence.

---

50. The audio from the camera on Tr. Brunette's cruiser indicates that Tr. Brunette first shouted to McDowell "Sir, put the gun down" at 1:30:51 a.m. More than a minute later, when McDowell advanced toward the officers with his weapon raised and pointed in their direction, Tr. Brunette shouted (at 1:32:14), "Put the gun down. Do it now or I'm going to shoot!" Tr. Brunette repeated "Put it down or I'm going to shoot!" at 1:32:17. The officers first discharged their weapons at 1:32:20.

The public must accept that when they call the police, they will get a police response, not a psychiatric/sociological intervention. Law enforcement cannot refuse to act when there is a possibility that members of the public are at risk, nor can law enforcement stand idly by waiting for real harm to actually occur before they intervene. The law enforcement response must always focus on protection—protection of the officers on the scene, protection of the citizens present, and protection of the community at large. That, in a phrase, is the reason for being of law enforcement. No matter how hard officers strive to resolve things without injury to the antagonist in the encounter, if those goals are achieved without injury to the person posing the threat it is a credit to law enforcement training and discipline. But it is also ultimately fortuitous for it remains secondary to the critical need to protect all others first, and that depends exclusively on what the protagonist does—and what that protagonist allows the officer(s) to do.[51]

> *"Other than random attacks, all such cases begin with the decision of a police officer to do something, to help, to arrest, to inquire. If the officer had decided to do nothing, then no force would have been used. In this sense, the police officer always causes the trouble. But it is trouble which the police officer is sworn to cause, which society pays him to cause and which, if kept within constitutional limits, society praises the officer for causing."*[52]

---

51. The propensity of law enforcement officers to hesitate, their reluctance to use deadly force when it is clearly reasonable, is demonstrated repeatedly in the case histories related in this chapter. In addition, examples of many of the other realities discussed elsewhere in this book are also ever present, for example, the deterioration of marksmanship skills attributable to the stress, uncertainty, and dynamic nature of deadly force confrontation, and the realities of wound ballistics.

52. *Ibid. Plakas v. Drinski*, page 1150.

# Chapter 10

# Non-Deadly Force

*"Our Fourth Amendment jurisprudence has long recognized that the right to make an arrest or investigatory stop necessarily carries with it the right to use some degree of physical coercion or threat thereof to effect it."*
—*Graham v. Connor*, 490 U.S. 386, 396 (1989)

In a book that focuses on the use of deadly force by law enforcement officers, there are several reasons to include a discussion of non-deadly force. First, of the literally thousands of Fourth Amendment *seizures* made by officers every day, the overwhelming majority are effected through the use of non-deadly force. Second, the two subject areas are inextricably intertwined, not only by virtue of being governed by precisely the same constitutional rules, but because cases that initially involve the use of non-deadly force can quickly rise to the level of deadly force. The third reason is that despite being governed by the same constitutional principles, the distinct justifications for using deadly force and non-deadly force demand different treatment in practical application. Deadly force is justified in a very narrow set of circumstances, but when those circumstances arise *there is no gradation of deadly force* options. Conversely, when deadly force is not justified, there is an unlimited range of circumstances and non-deadly force options available to officers in making Fourth Amendment seizures. In making those choices, the Constitution requires only that they be reasonable. (Chapter 6 includes further discussion on distinctions between the applications of deadly force and non-deadly force.)

## The Constitutional Rules

In Chapter 3, we defined deadly force as that type or level of force that *creates* a significant risk of death. Conversely, non-deadly force is any type or level of force that *does not create* a significant risk of death. It should be observed that some types of non-deadly force may rise to the level of deadly force if the manner in which they are used creates a significant risk of death—e.g., whereas blows delivered to the limbs or torso with fists or impact weapons are viewed as non-deadly force, the same blows delivered to the head are viewed as deadly force.[1] Deadly force is constitutionally reasonable to defend against immediate threats of serious physical injury or when necessary to prevent the escape of a dangerous person. This chapter discusses the legal principles and the practicalities that determine the reasonable levels of force available to law enforcement officers when deadly force is not a constitutional option.

All Fourth Amendment *seizures* are *forcible*, meaning that they are not consensual. When law enforcement officers are justified in making a *seizure*, they are legally empowered to use whatever force is reasonably necessary to achieve their purpose. That decision is dependent initially on the type of seizure being conducted. The Supreme Court recognizes three distinct categories of seizures: arrests, investigative detentions, and *de minimus* seizures. Because the distinctive nature of each category of seizure can affect the reasonableness of different force options to achieve them, they will be addressed in turn. But first, one caveat is in order: Although the primary focus of this chapter is the authority of law enforcement officers to use non-deadly force to gain and maintain control of persons (regardless of the category of Fourth Amendment seizure at issue), this in no way affects their authority to use deadly force in defense of themselves or others when faced with immediate threats of serious physical injury, or to protect the community from fleeing, dangerous criminal suspects.

The use of force is justified in order to make an arrest—in fact, it is implicit to the concept of arrest (see below). The axiom that is the basis for law enforcement policy and training is that force may be used as reasonably necessary to achieve a legitimate law enforcement purpose. Examples of legitimate law enforcement purposes are: to compel compliance, to overcome resistance, to prevent escape, to subdue a resistant person for purposes of arrest or to preempt a risk of injury to the officers, to others, or to the individual being subdued, or to achieve any other legitimate law enforcement purpose that mere presence and verbal commands fail to accomplish. All of these are law enforcement functions that may require the use of force.

In all cases, examination of the reasonableness of the force actually used must consider the actions of the person being confronted, the circumstances of the confrontation, and the nature of the crime being investigated. Since the purpose (simplistically) is to compel the person to submit to the authority of the law enforcement officer, the person's determination (or lack thereof) to

---

1. See, *Davenport v. Causey*, 521 F.3d 544, 551 (6th Cir. 2008); and *Sallenger v. Oakes*, 473 F.3d 731, 740 (7th Cir. 2007).

resist that authority will dictate the force used, as will the reasonable expectation of danger inherent to the activity at issue. The physical circumstances in which the confrontation occurs will also affect the degree of force that may be reasonable.

If the force being used is not effective, officers may use higher levels of force or different means of force or combinations thereof. They may continue to apply force, and to attempt different means and levels of force, until the need for such force no longer exists because the person has either chosen to comply or has been restrained to the point that physical resistance no longer poses a risk of harm to the officers or others.

This leads to an interesting side issue that arises in use-of-force legal actions and analyses — the question of exactly what degree or means of force is necessary as the starting point, or entry-level force, when an officer decides to use force. Reliance upon use-of-force continua is particularly susceptible to allegations of policy violations and unreasonable "entry-level" force applications. This is another example of the inappropriate and misleading connotations that adhere to use-of-force continua, and why they have no place in use-of-force policies. (See Chapter 6.)

The simple truth is that there is no legal specification, policy, process, or procedure for choosing a specific level of force to apply — no starting point, *except* the objectively reasonable standard of the Fourth Amendment. Law enforcement officers are typically trained in a range of force levels, techniques, and implements of applying force to ensure that they have a variety of options available for their use. Therefore, when any particular use of force is ineffective, they may use other force options available to them, up and down any scale of severity.

The correct entry-level force is that level of force that the officer thinks will efficiently serve the purpose in a timely manner. If that level of force does not work, they may use more force. The officer may continue to use force, and to increase the level of force as necessary, until successful in accomplishing the purpose, whether it is to effect an arrest, to prevent a risk of injury to selves or others, to prevent a person from endangering himself or others, to compel compliance, or any other legitimate law enforcement purpose. The adverse is equally true — as the purpose is achieved, the force should diminish or end.

In law enforcement, the types of "force" available have been traditionally categorized as "deadly force" or "non-deadly force." We have defined "deadly force" as that force that creates a significant risk of death. The traditional law enforcement deadly force option is the use of a firearm. Other examples are readily evoked and easily understood — hitting someone in the head with a hard object, causing a speeding car to go out of control, striking someone with a vehicle, choking someone into unconsciousness, causing a fall from an unusual height onto a hard surface. These examples are not meant to be comprehensive by any means, serving merely to illustrate that a reasonable risk of causing death is the defining factor, not the implement or means of force used—and the probable consequence of death is not difficult to visualize.

"Non-deadly" force is simply that force that does *not* create a significant risk of death. Within the law enforcement world, non-deadly force is manifested in the use of all other types and forms of force—uniform presence, physical holds and grappling, use of the baton, blows struck with hands/feet/knees, physical restraint devices like handcuffs, and chemical agents are examples that again are meant to be illustrative and not a comprehensive list. The non-deadly force represented by these historically conventional forms and means have been in use forever, and, although death has occasionally resulted from their use, it is very rare, and certainly not probable. Non-deadly force, by definition, simply does not create a significant risk of death. When the improbable occurs, it does not convert the non-deadly force option into deadly force—the definition is not determined by the outcome, but by the means.

Modern law enforcement has seen the development and growth of innovative, technologically based means of exerting force. This development has spawned entirely new forms of non-deadly force that are significantly different from the traditional forms. These new forms attempt to replicate the efficacy of deadly force for incapacitation without the consequent prospects of serious injury or death. A supplementary motivation is the desire to be able to establish and maintain control of a person from a distance beyond arm's reach for the increased safety of the officer. Weapons devised for this purpose include electronic control devices, beanbag rounds, rubber bullets, immobilizing chemical foams, netting devices, and microwave transmitters—to cite some representative examples. As with other non-deadly force options, death is not a significant risk that adheres to the use of any of these newer, technologically based forms.

Nonetheless, along with these technological developments, there has emerged the appellation of *"less lethal"* force to describe them.[2] The origin and precise purpose of this label are obscure. It may reflect the aspiration, cited above, to equip officers with the means of effectively countering imminent threats of serious injury to themselves or others, while minimizing the risks of death or serious injury to their assailants. This book has frequently noted and described the heavy toll on law enforcement officers and their agencies even when deadly force is reasonably applied under the Constitution. It is understandable that the

---

2. To be clear, the law *only* recognizes "deadly force" and "non-deadly force"—it makes no other distinction.

law enforcement community would be receptive to claims that some new technological development will permit the safe achievement of law enforcement objectives and protect the officers and the community, while eliminating the negative impact consequent in an officer's use of deadly force. On the other hand, the unnecessary dangers to which law enforcement officers are exposed when required to try a non-deadly force option when deadly force is justified, have been amply described throughout this book. (See, for example, Chapters 5 and 7.)

The potential for failure of some of the most highly touted non-deadly force devices available to law enforcement is illustrated in many of the cases discussed later in this chapter. When a non-deadly force option fails to produce the anticipated result, the typical response of the officer to that failure is to persist in its application rather than to switch to deadly force. In the face of an imminent threat to an officer's life, encouraging or requiring an officer to try a lesser level of force before using constitutionally justified deadly force is requiring that officer to do precisely what the courts have said officers are not required by the Constitution to do—gamble with their lives.[3]

A final point regarding the use of the "less lethal" label to describe a subcategory of non-deadly force relates to the potential legal consequences that could follow from the ambiguity that the term creates. Read literally, "less lethal" means a lesser degree of lethal (deadly) force; it does not suggest a different or higher degree of non-deadly force. The resulting ambiguity invites plaintiffs to contend that the higher legal standards justifying the use of deadly force should apply. In making that argument, it is simple enough to point out that the law enforcement community itself recognizes these options as a lower form of "lethal" force. If such arguments should prevail, an important range of non-deadly force options could be denied to law enforcement officers in the very circumstances where they would be most effective. For these reasons, the authors decline to perpetuate the use of the expression "less lethal" force, choosing instead to use the traditional terms, deadly force and non-deadly force, as accepted by the courts and defined above.

# Arrests

"Arrest" is the most significant of the three categories of Fourth Amendment seizures recognized by the Supreme Court. An arrest is custodial. It in-

---

3. See, e.g., *Elliot v. Leavitt*, 99 F.3d 640, 641 (4th Cir. 1996).

volves taking an individual into custody; placing him in handcuffs; searching him and the area within his immediate control for evidence of any crime, weapons, or means of escape; and transporting him to a law enforcement facility where he can be fingerprinted, photographed, booked, and locked in a cell pending appearance before a magistrate.

An arrest is a highly intrusive seizure. For that reason, it must be supported by an arrest warrant or by the same level of information required by the Fourth Amendment to obtain an arrest warrant—i.e., probable cause. It is axiomatic that law enforcement officers may use the level of force reasonably necessary to make an arrest and maintain custody and control of the person. The Fourth Amendment standard of "reasonableness" requires officers to tailor their use of force to the circumstances confronting them. Officers are generally guided in their decisions by the demeanor of the arrestees, e.g., are they compliant, passively resistant, or actively resistant? Each may suggest a different application of force. For example, a compliant person who submits to an officer's commands will generally require no further force than the application of handcuffs for security. On the other hand, a passively non-compliant person will require some higher level of force to encourage compliance and, obviously, an actively non-compliant person may require yet a higher level of force to protect the officers and overcome resistance. When the purpose of using force is to overcome resistance, once it has achieved that purpose it is unreasonable to continue its application. The following cases illustrate a variety of non-deadly force applications and the manner in which the courts viewed them.

# Physical Force

*Drummond v. City of Anaheim*[4] is not a "pure" arrest case since Drummond was not a criminal suspect but a mentally disturbed person who was seized by the police for the purpose of transporting him to a medical facility. A neighbor called the police for fear that Drummond was going to hurt himself by darting into traffic. When three officers arrived, they found Drummond in a nearby parking lot, apparently hallucinating and in an agitated state, so they called for an ambulance. Before the ambulance arrived, the officers decided to take Drummond into custody for his own safety. In the inevitable lawsuit, plaintiff alleged that when the officers decided to take Drummond into custody "for his safety," they knocked him to the ground and cuffed his arms behind

---

4. 343 F.3d 1052 (9th Cir. 2003).

his back; as he lay on his stomach, one of the officers put his knees into his back and placed the weight of his body on him; a second officer put his knees and the weight of his body on Drummond's upper back, with one knee resting on his neck. Despite Drummond's complaints that he couldn't breath, the officers continued to place their weight on his back and neck while a third officer placed a "hobble" restraining device on his ankles. The officers were allegedly laughing during the course of these events. By the time the ambulance arrived, almost 30 minutes later, Drummond was unconscious. Although he was revived seven minutes later, he sustained brain damage and lapsed into a permanent vegetative state.

This description of events is the plaintiff's version of what happened, and the version that the federal district court was required to adopt in ruling on the defendants' motion for summary judgment. The court granted summary judgment, finding that there were no constitutional violations and that even if there were, the law was not sufficiently clearly established to place reasonable officers on notice that their conduct was unconstitutional. The federal appellate court reversed the district court's judgment. Relying on the same set of facts, the appellate court stated:

> "Here, some force was surely justified in restraining Drummond so that he could not injure either himself or the arresting officers. However, after he was handcuffed and lying on the ground, the force that the officers then applied was clearly constitutionally excessive when compared with the minimal amount that was warranted."[5]

The court then addressed the allegation that while Drummond was restrained on the ground, other officers "stood around and laughed." The court found that while the subjective motivation of the officer was not relevant to the reasonableness issue, their "*apparent lack of concern does indicate that Drummond was not sufficiently dangerous to others to warrant the use of the severe force applied.*"[6]

An additional factor in the court's decision was a training bulletin issued by the police department a year before this incident. The bulletin warned officers that kneeling on a person's back or neck to restrain him could result in compression asphyxia and death.

The reader is reminded that the appellate court did not rule that the officers violated the Constitution; it ruled that *if* the officers did what the plaintiff alleges they did, they violated the Constitution. The case was remanded to

---

5. *Id.*, at 1956.
6. *Id.*

the district court for resolution of the factual disputes. Even when there is no final resolution of facts, cases of this type are illustrative of the kinds of behavior the courts are likely to view as unreasonable. It is a well-established principle that force justified to address a specific problem, e.g., overcoming resistance, is no longer justified once that problem has been resolved.[7] When there are disputes between the parties regarding material facts, those disputes must be resolved by a jury.

In *Bozung v. Officer Travis, et al.*,[8] a police officer stopped a vehicle because he believed that a rosary hanging from the rear-view mirror obstructed the driver's vision. Bozung was the owner of the vehicle, but a friend was driving because Bozung's license had been suspended. As they approached Bozung's apartment the officer stopped them. The driver jumped from the vehicle and ran away, leaving the vehicle in the middle of the street. The officer pursued the individual in his patrol car but was unable to apprehend him. When the officer returned to the location of the stop he saw Bozung slowly driving his vehicle into an apartment complex parking lot. According to the officer he ordered Bozung to stop the vehicle; but Bozung claimed the officer said nothing. Once the officer approached the vehicle, he saw Bozung and another person seated inside. He asked for the identity of the person who fled, but they denied knowing him. The officer perceived that Bozung was intoxicated because of his demeanor and the smell of alcohol, and he had urinated himself. His blood alcohol level was later measured at .18%. A record check disclosed an outstanding misdemeanor warrant for failure to appear in court.

The officer informed Bozung that he was under arrest and ordered him to get out of the vehicle. Bozung was 54 years old, had suffered from a fractured ankle and had a hip replacement due to a bone deficiency. He also had health issues resulting from a stroke he suffered at age 28. He claimed that he informed the officer of his physical issues but the officer ordered him to spread his legs and began kicking the inside of his legs. The officer then used a straight-arm bar takedown technique that brought Bozung to the pavement. At about this time a second officer arrived. Bozung claimed that this officer participated in "throwing" him to the ground, and then put his foot on Bozung's neck while the first officer had his knee in the center of his back. As a result of these actions, Bozung suffered from lacerations to his face, a broken thumb, and permanent spinal cord injury. Bozung filed suit in federal court against the officers

---

7. *See, e.g., Abraham v. Raso,* 183 F.3d 279, 294 (3rd Cir. 1999); *Waterman v. Batton,* 393 F.3d 471 (4th Cir. 2005); *Dickerson v. McClellan,* 101 F.3d 1151, 1162 (6th Cir. 1996); and *Ellis v. Wynalda,* 999 F. 2d 243, 247 (7th Cir. 1993).

8. 439 Fed. Appx. 513 (6th Cir. 2011).

and the township, alleging excessive force by the officers and failure to train by the township. The federal district court granted summary judgment for the officers, finding that their actions were reasonable under the circumstances and even if they had made a mistake, they were entitled to qualified immunity. When his motion to reconsider was denied, Bozung appealed.

Considering the facts in the light most favorable to Bozung, the federal appellate court stated, " ... *it is clear it was reasonable for [the officer] to employ the straight-arm bar takedown technique to neutralize Bozung and to handcuff Bozung.*" It is interesting to read the court's reasoning in some detail:

> " ... *it was not clear to [the officer] at the time of the incident whether Bozung posed an immediate threat to him. Although there is no evidence to suggest Bozung possessed a weapon or made verbal or physical threats to the officers, the record indicates the officers did not have an opportunity to search Bozung or his vehicle prior to employing the straight-arm bar takedown technique.*"

With respect to the claim that the officer used excessive force by putting a knee on Bozung's back, the court concluded:[9]

> "*'Taking the evidence in the light most favorable to [Bozung], the kneeing ... occurred not when [Bozung] was neutralized, but while the officers were handcuffing him.' Therefore, such action was objectively reasonable.*"

***Galvan v. City of San Antonio, et al.***[10] provides an example of officers using a range of non-deadly options to subdue an actively resisting subject. At around 3:00 a.m., two police officers responded to a 911 call about shots being fired in a "rough" neighborhood—the area where the Galvans lived. There were also 911 "hang-up calls" from the Galvan's residence. Upon arrival at the residence the officers heard screaming and yelling in the distance and discovered that Mr. Galvan was the source. The officers identified themselves and offered their assistance, but Galvan ran away. During the ensuing chase Galvan threw something. When the officers caught up, one of them attempted to communicate with Galvan but Galvan responded by charging at the officer. The officer tried to fend Galvan off with two shots of pepper spray, but to no avail. Galvan then grabbed the canister from the officer. In the struggle both fell to the ground. Both officers attempted various empty-hand techniques without

---

9. Citing *Harris v. City of Circleville*, 583 F.3d 367 (6th Cir. 2009).
10. U.S. App. LEXIS 11114 (5th Cir. 2010).

success. One of the officers then warned Galvan that he would use his TASER. Despite the TASER, Galvan continued to struggle until eventually the officers were able to handcuff his hands behind his back. It was determined that Galvan was on cocaine at the time. Galvan died shortly thereafter, apparently as a consequence of the struggle, and his widow filed a lawsuit against the officers and the City of San Antonio.

The federal district court granted summary judgment for the officers, and that judgment was affirmed by the federal appellate court with this explanation:

> " ... when confronted with a rapidly evolving, volatile situation, the officers reacted with measured and ascending responses—verbal warnings, pepper spray, hand-and-arm-manipulation techniques, and then the use of a TASER. They did not use force until Mr. Galvan attacked [the officer.] Under such circumstances, we find that the force used by the officers was reasonable."

It is important to note that the officers were in a life-and-death struggle with Mr. Galvan, and in such circumstances would have been justified in using deadly force. Their response is typical of the many brave law enforcement officers who willingly assume greater risks than required by law to subdue a dangerous assailant.

In **Pershell v. Cook, et al.,**[11] the plaintiff sued four officers alleging excessive force during the execution of an arrest warrant. Pershell had called 911 shortly before the incident to report an altercation with a neighbor who would not leave Pershell's home. Shortly after that call, Pershell called 911 again to report that he no longer needed police assistance. He was informed that an officer would still need to respond to take a report. Unbeknownst to Pershell, the four officers had an outstanding warrant for his arrest on a misdemeanor charge of recklessly discharging a firearm while under the influence of alcohol.

Shortly after Pershell allowed the officers into his home, one of them pointed a TASER at him and said several times "I've got a TASER"; a second officer told him that he was under arrest. Pershell responded with profanity and ordered the officers to get out of his house. At some point during this interaction one of the officers said "Go," and another officer used a "leg sweep" that caused Pershell to fall face-first on the floor. Pershell alleged that while he was on the floor and handcuffed he felt a "forceful impact" on his left foot or ankle and two further

---

11. U.S. App. LEXIS 14549 (6th Cir. 2011).

impacts on his lower back. As a consequence of these blows he lost conscious-ness and it was later determined that he suffered a fractured hip.

The federal district court denied the officers' motions for summary judgment due to disputed facts regarding the officers' actions and the federal appellate court affirmed that decision:

> *"Taking the facts in a light most favorable to Pershell, officers performed a leg sweep, causing Pershell to fall on his face, handcuffed him once he was on the ground, and then struck him three times, causing him to lose con-sciousness and sustain a broken hip. The blows to Pershell's body, if in-tentionally applied, were not objectively reasonable, and therefore constituted a violation of the Fourth Amendment.... It was also clearly established at the time of the incident that striking a handcuffed and immobilized ar-restee is unreasonable conduct.... Using a leg sweep to knock Pershell face-first onto the floor was also objectively unreasonable."*[12]

For two instances where summary judgment was denied to officers who used their vehicles as a means to effect a seizure, see *Walker v. Davis, et al.,* 649 F.3d 502 (6th Cir. 2011), and *Gaillard v. Commins, et al.,* 562 Fed. Appx. 870 (11th Cir. 2014).

# Pepper Spray

An interesting case addressing the use of pepper spray is *McCormick v. City of Fort Lauderdale.*[13] In fact, this case involves police use of a firearm, a stun gun, a baton, and physical force, as well as the pepper spray. Since we've al-ready discussed the officer's use of deadly force against McCormick in Chap-ter 3, we will limit this discussion to his allegation that a police officer sprayed him with pepper spray without first issuing a verbal warning. As discussed elsewhere in this book, the only constitutional mandate for issuing a verbal warning to a potentially dangerous person prior to using force is the Supreme Court's ruling in *Tennessee v. Garner*[14] which requires such a warning, *when feasible,* before using deadly force to prevent the escape of a dangerous per-son. To McCormick's assertion that he should have been warned before being sprayed, the federal appellate court responded:

---

12. See also, *Cornejo v. City of Los Angeles, et al.,* 2015 U.S. App. LEXIS (9th Cir. 2015) (Officers held liable for fatally beating a man following a high-speed chase.).

13. 333 F.3d 1234 (11th Cir. 2003)

14. 471 U.S. 1 (1985).

"We read no such requirement into the Constitution ... The constitutional requirement that the use of force be reasonable includes no requirement to warn a violent felon—in circumstances like these—that the use of pepper spray is forthcoming."[15]

Characterizing pepper spray as *"an especially noninvasive weapon,"* the court added:

*"Shock and surprise may be proper and useful tools in avoiding unnecessary injury to everyone involved when dealing with potentially violent suspects."*[16]

It must be noted that the court's decision does not rule out the possibility that some warning might be viewed as necessary before using pepper spray on non-violent persons. It should also be noted that the pepper spray was not effective in subduing McCormick; he was sprayed at least three times, shot once with a firearm and then shot once with a stun gun before being physically wrestled to the ground. This comports with the authors' observations and experience that many highly touted non-deadly force measures or devices are not consistently effective against individuals in real-life encounters. To further emphasize that point, we remind the reader that in *City and County of San Francisco v. Sheehan*, discussed at length in Chapter 3, pepper spray failed to stop a knife-wielding woman, requiring officers to use their firearms.

# Impact Weapon

An impact weapon, e.g., a baton, beanbags, etc., is intended to impart energy to the area struck and induce compliance by stunning or inflicting pain. In *Bell v. Irwin*,[17] police officers responded to a domestic violence call at the Bell residence. They knew that Bell had a history of domestic violence, unlawful use of weapons, obstruction of justice, and drunk driving. The officers were unable to get Bell to come out of his house but were able to see him through a window holding several knives and a meat cleaver. He threw several knives into the yard in the direction of police officers and said that he would kill any officer who entered the house and then kill himself. Negotiations were unavailing, and one officer was authorized to use beanbag rounds if that proved

---

15. *Id.*, at 1245.
16. *Id.* See also, *Lawyer v. City of Council Bluffs*, 361 F.3d 1099 (8th Cir. 2004).
17. 321 F.3d 637 (7th Cir. 2003).

necessary. Bell threatened to blow up his home using propane and kerosene in tanks immediately outside. Officers saw him lean toward a propane tank with what appeared to be a cigarette lighter. An officer fired four beanbag rounds from a shotgun that struck Bell in the arm, the torso, and the head. He was taken to the hospital unconscious. He recovered sufficiently to become a plaintiff, alleging that the officer's use of the beanbag rounds was excessive force and that he suffered from memory loss as a result. The federal district court concluded that the officer acted reasonably to end the confrontation and to avoid further injury to Bell or to others. The federal appellate court concurred, and wrote;

> "*Like the district judge, we think that [Bell] should have thanked rather than sued the officers. True, he suffered injury at their hands, but in his depressed and irrational state, aggravated by liquor, he might have done himself or others greater injury had they not intervened.*"[18]

The court did not consider whether deadly force would have been justified to prevent Bell from lighting the propane and kerosene, as he appeared prepared to do. It seems fairly clear that his actions posed an immediate danger of serious physical injury to others in the vicinity and that deadly force would have been a reasonable response. In any event, the court concluded:

> "*The risks of intervention, unfortunately realized when one round hit Douglas in the head, still seem less than the risks of doing nothing.*"[19]

# Police Dogs

Over the past several years, dogs have taken their place in the arsenal of force options used by law enforcement to locate and seize criminal suspects. It can hardly be surprising that litigation has arisen from this development. A case in point is *Miller v. Clark County*.[20] An officer attempted to stop a car late one night when he discovered that it bore a license plate registered to another vehicle. Knowing the switched plate was a traffic infraction and suspecting that the vehicle might be stolen, he turned on his emergency lights and siren to pull the driver over. The driver slowed the vehicle momentarily to allow a passenger to get out, and then sped away. The unoccupied vehicle, with a

---

18. *Id.,* at 640.
19. *Id.*
20. 340 F.3d 959 (9th Cir. 2003).

seven- or eight-inch knife on the seat, was located later in front of a house where Miller lived with his parents. The officers knew that Miller was wanted for the felony of attempting to flee from police by driving a car "with a wanton or willful disregard for the lives of others." They were told that Miller had been seen running away from the house a few minutes earlier. The officers, assisted by a police dog, began a search of the dark, wooded terrain for Miller. The officer with the dog yelled, "This is the sheriff's office. You have five seconds to make yourself known or a police dog will be sent to find you." When no response was forthcoming, the dog was unleashed. Approximately a minute later, the officer heard a scream. He immediately entered the woods and within about 45 seconds found Miller with the dog biting his arm. Miller was taken to the hospital and treated for serious injuries to the muscles of his upper arm. Miller filed a lawsuit against the officer and the county, alleging that the use of the police dog to "seize and hold" in these circumstances was excessive force in violation of the Fourth Amendment. The federal district court resolved the case in favor of the officer and the county, and Miller appealed that decision.

The federal appellate court first considered whether the use of the police dog to bite and hold Miller constituted *deadly force*. Defining *deadly force* as "*force reasonably likely to kill*," the court noted:

> "*We have held that an officer's ordering a dog to bite a suspect does not pose more than a remote possibility of death in most circumstances.*"[21]

The court then turned to the issue of whether the use of the non-deadly force was nevertheless excessive, following the guidelines provided by the Supreme Court in **Graham v. Connor**:

(1) The severity of the crime. "*Miller was wanted not only for a misdemeanor traffic infraction, but also for a prior felony ... a crime deemed serious by the state.*"[22]

(2) Whether the suspect posed an immediate threat to the safety of officers or others.

> "*From [the officer's] viewpoint, Miller posed an immediate threat to officers' safety ... Miller had defied orders to stop ... [he] was a felony suspect wanted for ... a crime that evinces a willingness to threaten others' safety in an attempt to escape responsibility for past crimes ... Miller had possessed a knife moments earlier, a fact that suggests Miller had a propensity to carry a weapon (and perhaps a weapon more lethal than the one*

---

21. *Id.*, at 963.
22. *Id.*, at 964.

*he had left behind).... [The officer] was entitled to assume that Miller posed an immediate threat to his and to the other deputy's safety.*"[23]

(3)  Whether the suspect actively was resisting or attempting to evade arrest.

*"Although Miller had paused while hiding in the woods at the time of his arrest, Miller was still evading arrest by flight.*"[24]

Relying on this analysis, the court concluded:

*" ... [the officer's] use of a police dog to bite and hold Miller until deputies arrived on the scene less than a minute later was a reasonable seizure that did not violate Miller's Fourth Amendment rights.*"[25]

This case again highlights the importance of defining *deadly force* with precision. It also illustrates a reasonable use of *non-deadly force* that if used differently could have been considered excessive, or even *deadly force.*

# Electronic Control Devices (ECDs)

The ECD, also referred to as a "stun gun," has emerged in recent years as one of the more significant non-deadly force devices used by law enforcement. Its widespread use by law enforcement officers has been accompanied by considerable media coverage and increasing litigation. Like other non-deadly force options, an ECD offers the prospect of pre-empting or overcoming resistance to arrest without increasing danger to the officers and without creating a significant risk of death or serious injury to the persons against whom it is used. It accomplishes this by delivering an electrical charge to the person, inflicting some degree of pain, and, ideally, causing incapacitation by the disruption of voluntary muscle control characteristic of electrical shock effects. Unfortunately, as with other non-deadly force options, an ECD may not always work as advertised. Sometimes they have no discernible effect. Other times they have been associated with unintended and unanticipated injury and, albeit rarely, death.

An example of an ECD being ineffective is found in ***Williams v. Holley, et al.*,**[26] wherein an officer attempted to arrest a man on 23 outstanding nonviolent misdemeanor warrants. The officer located Williams at his residence, knocked on the door, and when Williams responded, told him that he was

23.  *Id.,* at 965.
24.  *Id.,* at 965–966.
25.  *Id.,* at 968.
26.  2014 U.S. App. LEXIS 16288 (8th Cir. 2014).

going to be arrested. Williams complained about being arrested and proffered two envelopes to prove that "he had business with the federal court." The officer grabbed Williams's arm, but Williams dragged the officer inside the residence. When the officer attempted to handcuff Williams, he passively resisted. The officer pushed Williams five to six feet away, drew his ECD, and ordered Williams to the floor. Williams remained passively non-compliant. The officer attempted to call for backup but the channel was in use. The officer then fired his ECD in dart mode which hit, but did not affect Williams. As the officer approached Williams with the intent of using the ECD in drive stun mode,[27] Williams grabbed the ECD and used it on the officer. The two men struggled, with Williams repeatedly using the ECD against the officer's left shoulder. The officer eventually managed to draw his pistol and shoot Williams twice in the stomach. Williams was still aggressively advancing when the officer fired four more rounds into Williams's chest at less than three feet. Williams then stood up and stumbled outside, where he collapsed. He was taken to a hospital where he died. In a subsequent law suit, the federal district court denied the officer's motion for summary judgment in light of disputed material facts, and the federal appellate court affirmed that decision.[28]

An example of debilitating injury resulting from being subjected to an ECD is found in *Goodwin v. City of Painesville*.[29] Two officers responded to a loud party complaint at an apartment complex where the Nall family resided. During their first encounter with Mr. and Mrs. Nall, the officers noted that Mr. Nall was wearing only blue jeans and appeared agitated by the officers' presence. After receiving assurances that the noise would be reduced, the officers left the apartment but remained close by. After a short time, the noise resumed and people were observed leaving the apartment. As the officers approached the apartment a second time, a woman came and told them that Nall was "crazy," that he had ripped her necklace off, and he was threatening to kill everyone in the apartment and the police. The officers called for backup

---

27. In "drive stun" mode, the TASER is held against the target without firing the projectiles. It is a form of pain compliance. This is accomplished by placing the TASER against the person's body. "Drive stun" mode can be accomplished without a cartridge in place or after a cartridge is deployed. The more widely recognized "Probe mode" is the firing of two small dart-like electrodes from a cartridge that remain contacted to the main unit by conductive wire. The cartridge contains a pair of electrodes and propellant. The electrodes are pointed to penetrate clothing and barbed to prevent removal once in place in skin. Both electrodes must penetrate the skin for the ECD to deliver its charge.

28. See also, *Buchanan v. Gulfport Police Department, et al.*, 530 Fed. Appx. 307 (5th Cir. 2013).

29. 2015 U.S. App. LEXIS 4417 (6th Cir. 2015).

and returned to the apartment with the intention of arresting Nall for disorderly conduct.

During their efforts to arrest Nall, he refused to step outside the apartment and returned to the living room, where the officers followed. Shortly thereafter, one of the officers discharged an ECD into Nall's chest from a distance of about six feet, causing him to fall to the floor. Nall was tased a second time with the ECD in the stun mode. The data file from the ECD indicated that the first tasing lasted 21 seconds, and the second lasted 5 seconds. After the second tasing it was observed that Nall was "foaming" at the mouth, he had urinated himself, and his eyes were open but he appeared to be unconscious. He went into cardiac arrest at the scene and was rushed to the hospital, where he remained for two weeks. As a result of the cardiac arrest and lack of oxygen to his brain, Nall suffered from severe cognitive impairment that affected his "memory and executive functioning."

The officers were sued in federal district court for, among other things, using excessive force. The court rejected the officers' motion for summary judgment and the federal appellate court concurred, writing:

> " ... a jury could reasonably find that [the officer] violated Mr. Nall's Fourth Amendment right to be free from excessive force ... "

An example of an ECD causing or contributing to the death of an individual is illustrated in *Sheffey v. City of Covington, et al.*[30] A man named Hughes, 52 years old, stood 6'6" tall and weighed 410 pounds. He was observed carrying a handgun with extra magazines and walking down a residential street in the vicinity of two elementary schools. Officers arrived in the vicinity, saw Hughes, and attempted to stop him. Hughes appeared to be intoxicated or mentally disturbed as he ignored commands to go to the ground. As Hughes continued to walk, either to approach one of the officers or to leave the scene, an officer deployed his ECD in "probe mode," striking Hughes in the upper left shoulder/chest area. Hughes did not react except to say "ouch." Hughes reached into his pocket and threw a box of ammunition at one of the officers. Another officer fired his ECD in probe mode twice into Hughes's back with little effect. Additional efforts were made to subdue and control Hughes, during which time officers used their ECDs in stun mode eight times. During the entire incident, Hughes was tased a total of 12 times. Shortly after he was cuffed and secured, Hughes exhibited signs of medical distress and was transported to hospital, where he died. The autopsy disclosed that he had

---

30. 564 Fed. Appx. 783 (6th Cir. 2014).

experienced "a cardiac event, due to myocardial hypertrophy and coronary atherosclerosis.... The pattern of circumstances with contributing morbid obesity and hypertrophic heart disease, and the use of the electrical stun devices suggests that this death could be assigned to excited delirium syndrome."

A suit was filed in federal district against the officers and the city, and summary was granted to the defendants. On appeal, the federal appellate court upheld the summary judgment decision, explaining:

> "*The officers' actions could not be said to be unreasonable ... [Hughes] was <u>known to be armed</u> in a school zone with children present, that he <u>consistently acted as if he was reaching for his waistband</u>, that <u>he attempted to flee the area</u>, and he <u>violently physically resisted arrest.</u>"*

The foregoing is yet another example of officers assuming unnecessary risks in the face of a threat of serious injury or death. The facts of this case, and the court's language (highlighted above), would have clearly justified the use of deadly force.

TASER[31] is the preeminent example of the ECD weapon category. Its use has become so ubiquitous throughout law enforcement as well as in the popular mind that the term "TASER" is synonymous with the concept of an Electronic Control Device. Its success and popularity has created substantive issues that are exclusive to the use of a TASER. Although this discussion is focused on the TASER because of its widespread adoption, these same considerations apply equally as well to other similar weapons and concepts.

Because of the close range at which a TASER must be employed, its limited but very real failure rate and the lack of any safety margin, TASER (as are all other similar weapons to date) is best suited for situations involving passive resisters, physical resisters lacking deadly weapons, and control of unruly or out-

---

31. The TASER fires two pronged darts that are connected by trailing wires to the TASER mechanism for transmission of the electrical charge. The individual firing a TASER should be within 15 feet and preferably within 10 feet of the target subject. Both barbs must imbed in the individual's skin. If one misses, or hangs up in clothing, it won't work effectively, if at all. When the trigger is pulled, the TASER discharges its electrical charge continuously for five seconds—this is termed a "ride" in the law enforcement vernacular. Once the "ride" starts, it cannot be stopped. A subject who gets "tased" (to use another term of law enforcement jargon) is going to get the full five-second ride regardless of any intervening event or development. It is all or nothing unless one or both of the barbs is pulled out or dislodged, breaking the circuit. However, a TASER can be used repeatedly as a direct contact stun gun (with or without its dart cartridge). This is called "direct drive" mode and obviously requires that the officer using it must directly contact the subject with the hand-held TASER device itself.

of-control subjects. In such circumstances, a TASER is more immediately effective and less injurious than traditional non-deadly force such as impact weapons, hand fighting, wrestling, and chemical agents. A TASER is often effective in preventing an otherwise unarmed subject from escalating in aggression or by assault the risk potential of the situation to a point that deadly force becomes necessary. When effective, a TASER protects both the law enforcement officer as well as the adversary, who is effectively prevented from doing something (intentionally or not) that gets him shot. Another limitation is that the TASER has one dart cartridge—once fired, that particular TASER has no further utility other than to continue to give rides to whoever is on the other end. If a second subject needs to be "tased," it will require a second TASER and presumably a second officer.[32]

However, a TASER is not a substitute for deadly force if deadly force is justified in defense of self or others. Neither must the use of a TASER be attempted in advance of using deadly force—no differently than any other non-deadly force must be tried. That means that if an imminent risk of serious injury emerges, the use of a TASER is not fundamentally logical. If it fails, for any of the several reasons that it can fail, the timely opportunity to protect self and others may be lost. The gravity of the consequences—serious injury or death of the officer or others—makes it irrational to willingly accept any diminution of chance that the threat can be ended or averted.

In the event of a sudden imminent risk of serious injury, the officer wielding the TASER has to be within lethal reach and thereby gamble that he can react to the attack, fire the TASER, have both barbs imbed in the subject's skin, and activate the TASER, before getting stabbed or shot or clubbed or assaulted.[33]

---

32. In the continuing march of technology, TASER International has developed a TASER that holds three dart cartridges and can be fired at three different subjects. That raises a different concern, because the "ride" is preprogrammed to five seconds and cannot be aborted or abated. That means that if Subject A is tased, he gets a five-second ride. If Subject B is tased with the second dart, then he gets a five-second ride and Subject A gets *another* five seconds. Now if Subject C is tased, he gets his five-second ride, Subject B gets a second ride for a total of ten seconds, and the unfortunate Subject A gets his third ride for a total of fifteen seconds.

33. TASER International has developed a TASER cartridge designed to be fired in a shotgun. This extends the range of the TASER user significantly—TASER claims an effective range of 100 feet (minimum safe range of 15 feet). It has four (longer) barbs and a run-time (ride) of 20 seconds to give the distant officers time to get to the incapacitated subject before the ride ends. However, in some states, the deployment of the ECD probes by shotgun may be considered deadly force by statutes that include discharging a firearm in the direction of a person as "deadly force." For example, this was the case in Maine until the law enforcement

In the case of a violent attack at close quarters, a weapon such as a TASER can be more of an impediment to safety than a logical alternative to deadly force, because the officer wielding it is far more likely to try to use it than to drop it and go for his gun. For this reason, it is imperative that an officer wielding a TASER have armed backup on hand for protection in the event the situation deteriorates and deadly force becomes necessary.

Apart from the technical limitations above, there are practical considerations that also must influence policy and practice relative to the TASER. One is that electricity does not take sides. That means that any officer who makes contact with a person during that person's ride is also going to experience the magic of electricity. Another concern is that the sound of the TASER firing is similar to the sound of a gun firing. That can precipitate perceptions of danger that may be premature or mistaken. A third practical consideration is that in most cases, the person who is incapacitated during the five second ride immediately recovers and is functional the moment the ride ends.

While many people appear to find the experience so unsettling that when the ride ends, they have lost all will or intent to continue to resist. That is by their choice. It is not physiologically compelled. They are capable of immediate resumption of resistance although they may choose not to. This raises the same serious safety connotations as were discussed in Chapter 5 regarding the problematic issue of physical incapacitation. Regardless, when the ride ends the officers still need to control, handcuff, search, restrain, and arrest and the object of this attention can still be dangerous, violent, and possibly even more agitated than before. Provision needs to be made in policy and in training to account for these considerations—to insure that officers are aware in advance of the deployment of the TASER and are trained to take position to handcuff or otherwise make contact with the person after the ride has ended.

A more insidious issue regarding the TASER is the all too human tendency to consider it a "magic wand" that obviates traditional uses of force and training. The "magic wand" syndrome is manifested in two ways. The first is the inappropriate use of the TASER to avoid traditional police chores such as handcuffing, dealing with recalcitrant individuals, overcoming passive resistance, or simply "going hands on" with people. It is the product of superficial defensive thinking. Numerous examples abound in this day and age of omnipresent video. An officer "tases" a middle-aged woman who refused to get out of her car pursuant to a routine traffic stop. An officer "tases" a hostile driver

---

community lobbied the Legislature in 2009 to exempt from the definition of "deadly force" the shotgun discharge of munitions not reasonably likely to cause serious bodily injury or death if deployed in the manner by which officers had been trained.

and, *during* the five-second ride orders him to put his hands behind his back then continues to "tase" him again—and again—and again when he doesn't. An officer "tases" a ten-year-old child. An officer "tases" a man on a ledge ten feet off the ground—with predictable, fatal results. The TASER is treated as a shield between the officer and the person being confronted that allows the officer to merely shout orders enforced by the consequences of the TASER— "put your hands behind your back"… (implication—or get tased)—"get out of the car"… (implication—or get tased)—"turn around and put your hands on the car"… (implication—or get tased). These are quotes from actual incidents, all of which resulted in the individual getting "tased." The authors expect sooner or later to see an officer conduct an entire seizure at the point of a TASER—

> "Get out of the car" (or get tased)
> "Empty your pockets" (or get tased)
> "Get face-down on the ground" (or get tased)
> "Put your hands behind your back" (or get tased)
> "Here are my handcuffs—cuff yourself" (or get tased)
> "Get up and walk over to my car" (or get tased)

The absurdity is sadly not too far removed from the reality. The TASER is a magnificent and effective tool, but it is not a substitute for traditional police chores. This aspect of the "magic wand" syndrome gets officers sued, disciplined, perhaps fired, and possibly jailed. It is easy to argue excessive or unreasonable force following the inappropriate use of a TASER to avoid routine police work. The cases cited below illustrate the sensitivity of the courts in this regard, and the authors would suggest that is merited.[34]

The second, and more dangerous, problem associated with the "magic wand" syndrome is reliance upon the TASER in situations where deadly force is, or may be, warranted. This aspect can get you killed. It can be attributed to any of several causative factors, individually or in concert. One is simple naïveté— the uncritical belief that this is indeed a "magic wand" that is certain to work as needed in any and all circumstances. Another is hesitation, alluded to above and throughout this book. The startle effect is another—the officer wielding

---

34. And, consider too, that the use of non-deadly force, e.g., the ECD, to counter or repel an imminent threat of deadly force may be problematic when deadly force is ultimately used when evaluating in later investigations or litigation whether an officer's perception of the imminency of a deadly threat was objectively reasonable. In other words, a plaintiff may argue that the perception was objectively unreasonable in the absence of a more immediate use of deadly force to counter or repel the threat.

a TASER will probably use it reflexively rather than drop it and draw his weapon in the face of a sudden imminent (or actual) threat of serious injury. Aggravating these problems is the reality that TASER-induced incapacitation is fleeting, lasting only for the duration of the "ride" and then dissipating virtually immediately. In the meantime, the person cannot be handcuffed or physically restrained because the electrical charge will equally affect any officer making contact. The dangerous person remains free and unrestrained at the end of the ride. Recovery and response can occur before it can be prevented. (See Chapter 7. Action always beats reaction). The consequences are best illustrated anecdotally:

> "On April 25, 2009, Deputy Burt Lopez and Deputy Skip York, Okaloosa County Sheriff's Office, Florida, were shot and killed while attempting to arrest a domestic violence suspect. The deputies were following up on a domestic assault report they had taken hours earlier, and located the suspect at a gun club in Crestview. The suspect was in the parking lot standing next to his truck. Deputy Lopez and Deputy York approached the suspect, had a brief conversation with him, and then informed him he was going to be arrested. As the deputies moved to handcuff him, he became uncooperative and began to resist arrest. Deputy York fired his Taser (conducted energy device) and hit the suspect. The suspect dropped to the ground during the five-second jolt of electricity. When the Taser cycle ended, the suspect immediately drew a concealed handgun and opened fire. Deputy Lopez was able to radio for assistance while he and Deputy York engaged the suspect in a gun battle. During the exchange of gunfire, Deputy Lopez was mortally wounded. The suspect then climbed in his truck to escape. Deputy York pulled the passenger-side door open and jumped inside in an effort to pull the suspect from the vehicle, but was shot and mortally wounded. The suspect fled the scene and opened fire at deputies from the Walton County Sheriff's Department during a vehicle pursuit. The suspect's vehicle was rammed by deputies, causing it to flip over near the intersection of U.S. Highway 331 and U.S. 90 in DeFuniak Springs. The suspect exited the truck, and opened fire at the deputies, who returned fire, killing the suspect. Deputies York and Lopez were airlifted to Sacred Heart Hospital in Pensacola. They succumbed to their injuries later in the day.[35]

---

35. Officer Down. http://www.odmp.org/officer/19924-deputy-sheriff-burton-(burt)-lopez. Also, see "Sheriff: Man killed 2 deputies after being stunned" by Melissa Nelson, Associated Press Writer (04-26) 13:05 PDT Pensacola, Fla. (AP).

*'When that Taser released after five seconds, he came up shooting,' Interim Okaloosa County Sheriff Edward Spooner said. 'He went from just being disagreeable to using deadly force in a matter of seconds. It was a very aggressive move with a concealed weapon on his part.'*

*'I don't think they did anything wrong. There was nothing to indicate he would be escalating this to any great level of violence,' Spooner said. Both deputies were wearing bulletproof vests but were shot in areas not protected by the vests, he said.*

*'When he had his crash, the truck flipped upside down, nose first, and he came out of the backside of the truck firing immediately and using the truck for cover,' Spooner said. Investigators say Cartwright and deputies exchanged about 60 rounds in 30 to 40 seconds before he was shot and killed.'*[36]

The cases discussed below provide some illustrations of potential problems and legal issues that may arise.

In *Heston v. City of Salinas*,[37] the jury concluded that a man's death was caused in part by being subjected to 20–23 discharges from ECDs manufactured by TASER International. Police officers were called to the Heston residence by Heston's father, who reported that his son was using drugs. The officers investigated but left when they were unable to establish that Heston was doing anything illegal. Shortly thereafter, Heston's father again called and reported that his son had knocked him down and was breaking household items. When the officers arrived, they saw Heston throwing items out the front door and one officer saw Heston's father on the floor where apparently he had just been knocked down by his son. Over the next several minutes, five different officers fired their TASERs at Heston. He was "tased" at least six times before he finally went down. He was tased several additional times as he laid on the floor because he did not comply with officers' commands to remove his left hand from beneath his body for handcuffing. Heston lost consciousness at the scene and died the next day in the hospital. It was later determined that he had ingested 300 milligrams of methamphetamines before the incident.

A lawsuit was filed against the officers and the city alleging violations of the Fourth Amendment, and a products liability suit was filed against TASER International. The federal district court denied motions for summary judgment

---

36. *Id.* Nelson. This incident is yet another example of the tenacity and will to prevail that makes immediate incapacitation so problematical with the adversary who will not quit, discussed at length in Chapter 5.

37. No. C05-03658 (NDCA 2007).

for the officers and the city and the case was submitted to a jury. The jury returned verdicts in favor of the officers and the city, finding that the officers had not used excessive force, but found that TASER International had failed to adequately advise police of the risks involved in using its product. The jury found that Heston was 85% responsible for his own death through his use of methamphetamines and other behavior and that TASER International was only 15% liable.[38]

Although the jury exonerated the officers, their judgment against TASER International for not adequately informing the police of the potential risks involved with using its product should not be ignored. Now that those risks are known—not only through this case but through the bulletin subsequently issued by the manufacturer—law enforcement officers are presumed to be on notice of the potential risks.

There are relatively few cases where the use of ECDs has resulted in death and in most of those cases (as in *Heston*), there are contributing factors such as the presence of drugs or a susceptible medical condition. For that reason, the use of an ECD does not fall within the definition of *deadly force*. Heston, it will be recalled, was hit with six charges before he went down, and another 14–17 before he apparently lost consciousness. The allegation against the officers was not that they improperly used *deadly force*, but that they used *excessive force*—an allegation that was rejected by the jury.

Undoubtedly, the growing number of lawsuits surrounding the use of ECDs is due in large part to the increasing frequency of their use, the wide variety of people against whom they are used, and the often dramatic effects—frequently captured on video and aired on the evening news. The courts and the public are understandably affected by the images of police officers using ECDs against seemingly nonviolent suspects, even more so because the video is seldom more than a mere snippet of the totality of the event, either through selective editing or simply incomplete recording. This induces the obvious, but hasty—if not misinformed—belief that a less dramatic option would have sufficed. These concerns may well be misplaced and ill-informed, but judges also watch the evening news and members of the public sit on juries.

In assessing the reasonableness of an officer's decision to use an ECD to effect a seizure, the courts look at a number of factors, including the nature of the underlying offense, the actions of the suspect, and the number of times

---

38. Shortly after this incident, TASER International issued a bulletin advising users that the recommended frontal target area should be the lower torso rather than the center mass (chest), and emphasizing that back shots remained the ideal target area when practical. TASER Training Bulletin Synopsis: 15.0 (Released November 6, 2009).

that the device was deployed against the suspect. Some courts have also focused on whether the suspect was given some warning before the ECD was used, particularly when the person appeared to be a non-violent misdemeanant. In *Brown v. City of Golden Valley*,[39] following a traffic stop during which her husband was taken into custody, a woman was subjected to one charge from a TASER for refusing an officer's commands to put down her cell phone and get out of the car. The officers had observed two liquor glasses on the floorboard at the woman's feet and thought there was liquor in them. After the TASER was used against her, she was removed from the car, handcuffed, and taken to the police station, where she was charged with "obstruction" and an "open bottle" violation. In the ensuing lawsuit, a federal district court denied summary judgment for the officers, and the federal appellate court affirmed, finding that on the facts alleged by the plaintiff they had violated her Fourth Amendment rights by using a TASER against her when she was suspected only of a minor non-violent offense, and was not resisting or trying to evade arrest. The district court also concluded that there was a "clearly established" requirement to provide a verbal warning before using an ECD, although the court based its conclusion on the absence of any case law to the contrary rather than on any affirmative case law asserting that position. In any case, the appellate court disagreed:

> "The clearly established right is not that [Brown] was entitled to a warning, but rather that she was entitled to be free from excessive force...."

Although there is some limited support for the notion that a warning is a legal requirement before an ECD can be used against a non-violent misdemeanant,[40] that position has not gained sufficient approval among the courts to be described as "clearly established" law. It should be noted that some law enforcement agencies require such a warning as a matter of policy, and in this specific, strictly limited, particularly defined circumstance, it would also seem to be sensible and reasonable.

A minor offense does not necessarily preclude the use of an ECD if the suspect is hostile and uncooperative. In *Draper v. Reynolds*[41] Officer Reynolds stopped a tractor-trailer truck because its tag light was not properly illuminated. The driver, Draper, paced back and forth, yelled obscenities at Officer

---

39. 574 F.3d 491 (8th Cir. 2009).
40. See, e.g., *Casey v. City of Federal Heights*, 529 F.3d 1278 (10th Cir. 2007).
41. 369 F.3d 1270 (11th Cir. 2004).

Reynolds, and refused to comply with five commands to retrieve certain documents from the truck. When Officer Reynolds attempted to handcuff him, Draper physically resisted. The officer used a TASER once to subdue and handcuff him. Draper filed a lawsuit against Officer Reynolds alleging excessive force. The federal district court granted summary judgment for the officer which the appellate court affirmed and held:

> *"Although being struck by a taser gun is an unpleasant experience, the amount of force [Officer] Reynolds used—a single use of the taser gun causing a one-time shocking—was reasonably proportionate to the need for force and did not inflict any serious injury."*[42]

The court in **Draper** was clearly influenced in its opinion by the fact that there was only one officer on the scene. It is notable that other courts have also taken account of the number of officers present at the time an ECD was used against a non-violent misdemeanant. It is apparent that courts tend to view the use of an ECD as a significant use of force, and therefore not appropriate in the absence of some additional justifying factors. In one recent case a federal appellate court noted that in a department's use-of-force "continuum," the use of a TASER was ranked just below the use of deadly force[43]—another good reason to avoid creating artificial gradations of force that bear little relationship to reality and serve only to further confuse the issue. (See Chapter 6).

To emphasize a point made above, once officers make an arrest, they may continue to use reasonable force to maintain custody and control. Individuals under arrest and physically restrained can still pose threats to officers. We cited a case in Chapter 3 where officers were compelled to use deadly force against a man who was under arrest, handcuffed, and sitting in a police vehicle when he produced a gun and pointed it at the officers.[44] The threats posed by handcuffed arrestees need not be life-threatening to justify officers taking countermeasures. In *Prymer v. Ogden*[45] two officers were escorting a handcuffed person to a police car when they heard him making "gurgling" noises in his throat as if he were preparing to spit on them. To preempt this imminent assault, one of the officers struck the arrestee with a straight-arm technique intended to "redirect his head." In the subsequent lawsuit, the arrestee alleged that the officer used excessive force by striking him in the head. A federal appellate court disagreed and concluded:

42. *Id.* at 1277–78 (11th Cir. 2004). See also, *Zivojinovich v. Barner*, 525 F.3d 1059 (11th Cir. 2008).
43. *Parker v. Gerrish*, 547 F.3d 1 (1st Cir. 2008).
44. *Elliot v. Leavitt*, 99 F.3d 640 (4th Cir. 1996).
45. 29 F.3d 1208 (7th Cir. 1994).

*" ... it was reasonable for an officer not to want to be spat upon ... we cannot say that [the officer's] reaction to [the arrestee's] attempt to spit on him was objectively unreasonable in the context of this case."*[46]

# Investigative Detentions

"Investigative detention" has been described by the Supreme Court as an "intermediate response" that gives officers a lawful alternative between either allowing a crime to occur or a criminal to escape, or making an illegal arrest without probable cause. In its 1968 decision of *Terry v. Ohio*[47] the Court held that the Constitution grants law enforcement officers the authority to briefly detain a suspect, without probable cause, for the purpose of investigating suspicious circumstances. While such a "detention" is not an arrest, it is a Fourth Amendment *seizure* and force may be used as necessary to accomplish it. Given a "reasonable suspicion" that some kind (any kind) of unlawful activity has occurred, is occurring, or is about to occur, law enforcement officers can intervene—i.e., "stop the action" so to speak—and attempt to determine what is happening. The underlying rationale is that this inquiry should take a relatively short period of time to either elevate the reasonable suspicion to probable cause for an arrest, or dispel the suspicion and release the suspect(s). The idea is to minimize the degree of intrusion, while allowing the investigation of suspicious circumstances. Accordingly, and unlike an arrest, an investigative detention does not automatically allow officers to handcuff a detainee, or transport him to another location. Furthermore, rather than allowing a full search of the detainee for weapons, evidence, or means of escape, officers are limited to a "frisk" or pat-down for weapons—and then only when they reasonably suspect the detainee is armed <u>and</u> dangerous. Nevertheless, as with any other Fourth Amendment seizure, officers have the authority to use whatever force is reasonably necessary to establish and maintain the seizure, and to protect themselves.

As a general rule, the force that will be necessary is determined by the willingness of the detainee to submit to the officers' control. If physical force is necessary, then it is reasonable—that includes handcuffing. It is not uncommon for resistance by the detainee to rise to the level of an assault on an officer, and then the detention will evolve into an arrest. The important point to note is that the authority to detain a person under suspicious circumstances carries with it the authority to enforce and maintain control over that person until

---

46. *Id.*, at 1216.
47. *Terry v. Ohio*, 392 U.S. 1 (1968).

the issue that prompted the detention has been resolved. The entire range of non-deadly force options is available to the officers, with the simple caveat that the force used must be proportionate to the need in order for it to be reasonable under the Fourth Amendment.

During the course of an investigative detention, an officer may perceive the need to use some force to protect himself, totally apart from the need to enforce the detention. In *Rucker v. Hampton*[48] this need arose when an officer attempted to detain the driver of a car whom he had just observed leaving a liquor store and driving on the wrong side of the road. The driver (Rucker) pulled into a residential driveway and got out of the vehicle. The officer requested his license and registration, and asked him to be seated in the back seat of the police cruiser while he checked the documents. Rucker refused to comply and entered the house. The officer did not know whose house Rucker had entered but followed him inside and requested that he go back outside. Inside the house were Rucker's wife and three children, aged 13, 11, and 9. Rucker resisted the officer's efforts to get him to leave the house, and at one point yelled to his wife, "Go get it, go get it, go get it." When she walked to the hallway, the officer became concerned that she was going to retrieve a weapon, so he drew his sidearm and backed out of the house. It is disputed whether the officer aimed his weapon at anyone or just displayed it.

Rucker filed suit in federal court alleging that the officer used excessive force in drawing his weapon. The district court determined that there were material facts in dispute, and denied the officer's motion for summary judgment. The federal appellate court reversed that decision, and wrote:

> "*The district court's conclusion that there are material facts in dispute which preclude summary judgment is in error because Trooper Hampton's conduct and his display of a weapon, even according to plaintiff's version of the incident, was objectively reasonable.*"[49]

This decision can be contrasted with an earlier decision by the same appellate court, holding that members of a SWAT team executing a misdemeanor arrest warrant used excessive force when they trained weapons on a four-year-old child for two seconds and held an eight-year-old and a fourteen-year-old on the floor at gunpoint for ten minutes.[50] The court explained that decision as follows:

---

48. 49 Fed. Appx. 806, 2002 WL 31341532 (10th Cir. 2002).

49. *Id.* at 809.

50. *Holland v. Harrington*, 268 F.3d 1179 (10th Cir. 2001), *cert. denied*, 122 S.Ct. 1914 (2002).

*"The display of weapons, and the pointing of firearms directly at persons inescapably involves the immediate threat of deadly force. Such a show of force should be predicated on at least a perceived risk of injury or danger to the officers or others, based on what the officers know at that time.... Where a person has submitted to the officers' show of force without resistance, and where an officer has no reasonable cause to believe that person poses a danger to the officer or to others, it may be excessive and unreasonable to continue to aim a loaded firearm directly at that person, in contrast to simply holding the weapon in a fashion ready for immediate use. Pointing a firearm directly at a child calls for even greater sensitivity...."*[51]

# De Minimus Seizures

"*De minimus* seizures" were first described by the Supreme Court in the 1977 case of ***Pennsylvania v. Mimms***.[52] Two officers stopped Mimms for driving an automobile with an expired license. One of the officers ordered Mimms to get out of the car. When Mimms complied, the officer noticed a suspicious bulge under his jacket. Suspecting the bulge to be a weapon, the officer frisked Mimms and found a revolver. Mimms' conviction for carrying a concealed weapon was reversed by the state supreme court on the ground that while the initial stop was a lawful *seizure*, ordering him to get out of the car was a separate and unreasonable *seizure*. As a separate *seizure*, it would not have been justified by the same facts that led to vehicle stop, and there was neither probable cause nor reasonable suspicion to justify any other kind of *seizure*. The U.S. Supreme Court reversed the state supreme court's ruling. Agreeing that ordering Mimms out of the car was a separate *seizure*, the Court held that it was reasonable in light of the "*inordinate risk confronting an officer as he approaches a person seated in an automobile.*" Citing statistics showing the number of officers killed and injured each year while making "routine" traffic stops, the Court wrote:

*"Against this important interest (in officers' safety) we are asked to weigh the intrusion into the driver's personal liberty occasioned not by the initial stop of the vehicle, which was admittedly justified, but by the order to get out of the car ... What is at most **a mere inconvenience** cannot*

---

51. *Id.* at 810–811.
52. 434 U.S. 106 (1977).

*prevail when **balanced against** legitimate concerns for the **officer's safety***
[emphasis added].[53]

The *Mimms* decision acknowledges the reality that the duties of law enforcement officers often compel them to engage in high-risk activities where there is no specific factual information to warn them of a potential threat. The Supreme Court has acknowledged the "perspective of a reasonable officer," which is grounded in the collective knowledge and experience of the law enforcement community. Thus, absent specific facts regarding the potential dangers inherent in certain kinds of police activity, officers are entitled to draw on that collective knowledge and experience. In *Mimms*, the Court noted that each year approximately 5,000 officers are injured while engaged in making "routine" vehicle stops, and approximately 10 percent of the officers killed each year are engaged in the same duties.[54]

In 1997, in its decision of **Wilson v. Maryland**,[55] the Supreme Court extended its ruling in *Mimms* to include passengers in a lawfully stopped vehicle. The Court stressed:

> *"The same weighty interest in officer safety is present regardless of whether the occupant of the stopped car is a driver or a passenger ... The risk of harm to both the police and the occupant [of a stopped vehicle] is minimized 'if the officers routinely exercise **unquestioned command** of the situation'"* [emphasis added.][56]

The emphasized portion of this opinion highlights the point that officers engaged in a lawful traffic stop have the authority to command the occupants to get out of the vehicle. That authority is not hinged on probable cause or reasonable suspicion or any other level of factual information. It is sufficient that the vehicle and its occupants have been lawfully stopped to justify the additional *de minimus seizure* of ordering them to get out.

---

53. *Id.*, at 111. The Court later applied the *Mimms* rule to passengers as well as drivers, based on *"the same weighty interest in officer safety."* *Maryland v. Wilson*, 519 U.S. 408, 418 (1997).

54. The statistics reported to the FBI for the year 2014 (most recent data available) reflect that traffic-related incidents accounted for 4022 officers assaulted and 18% of the officers feloniously killed in that one-year period. For the ten-year period 2005–2014, assaults in traffic-related circumstances were 9.6% of the 563,030 assaults on officers and officers feloniously killed in the same circumstances remain at the 18% level. FBI Uniform Crime Reports, *Law Enforcement Officers Killed and Assaulted*, 2014.

55. 519 U.S. 408 (1997).

56. *Id.* at 413–414.

What officers have the authority to command, they have the power to enforce—i.e., officers may use whatever reasonable force is necessary to compel compliance with their lawful commands. In addition, it was acknowledged that while making these *de minimus* seizures, officers could pat down the driver and any passengers if they reasonably suspected that they may be armed <u>and</u> dangerous.[57] In 2007 in **Brendlin v. California**,[58] the Court confirmed that when an officer makes a traffic stop, he *"effectively seizes 'everyone in the vehicle,' the driver and all the passengers"* **for the duration of the stop**.[59] Thus, not only may officers order all of the occupants out of a vehicle, they can maintain control of them at the scene until the legitimate purposes of the stop have been achieved.[60] The question then becomes one of timing. How long may officers maintain a *de minimus* seizure?

The Supreme Court had the opportunity to address that question in its 2009 decision of **Arizona v. Johnson**.[61] Three police officers, members of a gang task force, were patrolling a neighborhood associated with the Crips gang. At approximately 9 p.m. they pulled over a car after a license plate check revealed that the vehicle's registration had been suspended for an insurance-related violation—a civil infraction. At the time of the stop there were three males in the vehicle: the driver, a front-seat passenger, and a rear-seat passenger, Lemon Johnson. Two male officers attended to the front-seat occupants while a female officer focused her attention on Johnson. She observed that he was wearing clothing and a blue bandana that she considered consistent with Crips membership. She also noticed a scanner in his jacket pocket that she viewed as unusual and potentially indicative of someone who was interested in evading the police. Through questioning, she learned his name and the fact that he had served time in prison for burglary. She also learned that he was from a town that she knew was home to a Crips gang. She asked him to get out of the car because she wanted to question him away from the other two individuals. When he did so she patted him down, suspecting that he might have a weapon. The pat-down disclosed a gun in his waistband. At this point, Johnson began to struggle and the officer placed him in handcuffs.

Johnson was charged and convicted in state court with illegal possession of a firearm. A state appellate court reversed his conviction on the grounds that

---

57. See *Knowles v. Iowa*, 525 U.S. 113 (1998).

58. 551 U.S. 249 (2007).

59. *Id.*, at 255.

60. It should also be noted that implicit in an officer's authority to order occupants from a vehicle is the authority to order occupants to remain in the vehicle or to return to the vehicle.

61. 555 U.S. 222 (2009).

at the time of the pat down for a weapon, the initial lawful seizure had "*evolved into a separate, consensual encounter, stemming from an unrelated investigation by [the officer] of Johnson's possible gang affiliation.*" The court's view that this encounter had become consensual and no longer a *seizure* was apparently based on the belief, expressed by the officer during the trial, that Johnson could have refused to get out of the car or to turn around for the frisk. On that assumption, the court asserted that since the officer had no reason to believe that Johnson was involved in criminal activity, she "*had no right to pat him down for weapons, even if she had reason to suspect he was armed and dangerous.*"[62] The Supreme Court took the case on appeal and reversed the state court's decision. Addressing the assertion that the initial lawful *seizure* had ended, the Supreme Court explained:

> "*A lawful roadside stop begins when a vehicle is pulled over for investigation of a traffic violation. The temporary seizure of driver and passengers ordinarily continues, and remains reasonable, for the duration of the stop. Normally the stop ends when the police have no further **need to control the scene** [emphasis added], and inform the driver and passengers they are free to leave. An officer's inquiries into matters unrelated to the justification for the traffic stop, this Court has made plain, do not convert the encounter into something other than a lawful seizure, so long as those inquiries do not measurably extend the duration of the stop.*"

Applying those principles to the facts of this case, the Court concluded:

> "*In sum … a traffic stop of a car communicates to a reasonable passenger that he or she is not free to terminate the encounter with the police and move about at will. Nothing occurred in this case that would have conveyed to Johnson that, prior to the frisk, the traffic stop had ended or that he was otherwise free to 'depart without police permission.' [The officer] surely was not constitutionally required to give Johnson an opportunity to depart the scene after he exited the vehicle without first ensuring that, in so doing, she was not permitting a dangerous person to get behind her.*"

These cases explain and illustrate one category of *de minimus* seizures.[63] Those that occur during the course of a lawful traffic stop when a police offi-

---

62. 170 P.3d 667, 673 (2007).

63. A second category of *de minimus seizure* is the vehicle checkpoint, where vehicles are systematically stopped for brief periods for a legitimate societal interest. See, *Michigan v. Sitz*, 496 U.S. 444 (1990) (The Supreme Court approved properly restricted sobriety checkpoints based on the need to remove impaired drivers from the highway.); *Indianapolis v. Edmond*,

cer orders the occupants of a vehicle to get out of the car. Like all other Fourth Amendment *seizures, de minimus* seizures can be enforced. The issue is not whether officers can use force to achieve them. It is whether officers' use of force is reasonable under the circumstances. It is imperative that officers clearly understand their lawful authority in order to confidently and competently gain and maintain control over individuals when necessary.

Officers also need to fully understand the capabilities and limitations of the equipment available to address the range of challenges they are likely to confront. This is a persistent problem for law enforcement officers. The cases discussed in this chapter have focused on a variety of non-deadly force options commonly used throughout the law enforcement community today. In this small sampling of cases it is remarkable to note the number of instances where a particular non-deadly force option, e.g., pepper spray or an ECD, simply does not perform as officers have been led to expect. Take, for example, the resisting suspect who used a walking stick as a weapon and was sprayed with pepper spray three times with no effect;[64] or the subject who was hit with six shots from a TASER before going down, and then hit another 14–17 times before officers perceived that he was no longer resisting;[65] or the violently resisting motorist who proceeded to physically assault two police officers after being hit with a TASER at least twice, until deadly force finally brought his attacks to an end.[66]

There are logical explanations for why these things occur, and they occur far more often than conventional wisdom or promotional hype would lead us to believe. When an officer's expectations for a particular application of force are not realized, as the cases discussed throughout this book illustrate, it creates surprise, confusion, frustration, and fear, commonly resulting in repeated applications of the same force in hopes that sooner or later it will have the desired effect. That natural tendency can lead to unintended and undesired consequences, including increased risks to the officers who may delay the use of deadly force in circumstances where it is fully justified. The point is that training and indoctrination with new techniques, tools, and technology should

---

531 U.S. 32 (2000) (The Supreme Court disapproved of vehicle checkpoints designed to uncover illegal drug activities.); and *Illinois v. Lidster*, 540 U.S. 419 (2004) (The Supreme Court approved "informational checkpoints" designed to elicit the assistance of motorists regarding a recent hit-and-run vehicular homicide that had occurred in the area.).

64. *McCormick v. City of Fort Lauderdale*, 333 F.3d 1234 (11th Cir. 2003) (Discussed in Chapter 3).

65. *Hester v. City of Salinas, supra*, footnote 19.

66. *Davenport v. Causey*, 521 F.3d 544 (6th Cir. 2008) (Discussed in Chapter 3).

realistically prepare officers for the complete range of possible reactions, not just the preferred ones. What happens in the controlled and calm atmosphere of a training class rarely reflects what *can and is likely* to occur in real-life confrontations. Most importantly, the collective knowledge and experience of the law enforcement community with non-deadly force options—partially illustrated in the cases discussed in this chapter—should dispel any notion that they are viable alternatives to the use of deadly force when officers are faced with immediate threats of serious physical injury to themselves or others.

# Chapter 11

# Risks and Responsibilities

Law enforcement is a dangerous profession. It is not, nor can it ever be, risk-free. The men and women who practice the profession must accept that fact. The law enforcement role and its accompanying responsibilities within a community cannot be achieved without confronting the risk of injury. It is an everyday reality of the profession.

Those risks are generally well recognized throughout the broad community of shared law enforcement experience. Training, equipment, and policy are the ordinary measures that are utilized to provide the means and the guidelines for dealing with those sundry risks. Training, equipment, experience, and practice are the resources upon which every law enforcement officer must rely in order to recognize risk, to assess its gravity and potential for harm, and to minimize their exposure while still meeting the responsibilities of the profession—sworn responsibilities as well as implicit responsibilities expected of them. Nevertheless, it remains a truism that bears repeating: it is not possible to eliminate risk from law enforcement—regardless of how well trained, fully equipped, widely experienced, or expertly practiced the officer may be.

The law enforcement role within society has been long defined, well recognized, and multifaceted. Law enforcement is expected to keep the peace; to detect and investigate violations of law; to identify, locate, and arrest violators of the law; and to collect and organize evidence to ascertain the facts in support of prosecution and assignation of accountability. In the performance of this role, law enforcement protects and preserves society. It protects its community, of which it is a vital, coherent, and irreplaceable element—and the people who populate that community. Failing or refusing to understand the purpose, function, and rational goals of law enforcement infuses many of the allegations of wrongdoing that generally appear in the aftermath of a deadly force incident.

Reaction, analysis, and judgment of a deadly force incident are not limited to the legal system, where clear and controlling legal standards must be applied. Independent of the legal standards are segments of the public that will attempt to exploit the incident to advance other, broader agendas to the detriment of law enforcement and its role within the community. The allegations that arise are frequently based on ignorance or misunderstanding or distortion of the goals and priorities inherent to the law enforcement role within society. Ignored or misstated are the clear legal standards that are the impetus of much of this book. The decision to use deadly force is judged subjectively and emotionally, relying on results-based condemnation to energize support for a broader agenda of special interests and financial gain.

The role and functions of law enforcement are widely understood and recognized in society. The realization that it may be necessary to employ deadly force in the pursuit of those functions is less well accepted in some segments of society. Thus when an officer shoots and kills a person in the midst of a deadly force confrontation, the outrage over the death or injury of that particular individual will be the singular basis *after-the-fact* for criticism of or opposition to the decision to use deadly force. The generic allegation will always include the claim that deadly force was unnecessary and therefore wrong—that the officer could have stopped, or arrested, or negotiated or somehow, in some other way, using some other resource, resolved the confrontation. This is illustrative of a general misconception (either wittingly or not) that the decision to use deadly force is a failure to properly use any number of law enforcement tools or tactics that can be used in order to fulfill one of the law enforcement roles or functions.

The litany of charges will include a variety of claims. The person killed could have been arrested another day. The person killed had no idea the officer was in fact a police officer. The officer should have retreated and come back with more help. The officer should have been trained and equipped to deal with the person killed without having to use deadly force. The officer should have shot to wound. The allegations are endless. They are characterized by the incorrect assumption that the reason that deadly force was used was to arrest, or to detain, or to control, or to subdue.

The allegations are designed to throw blame upon the officer to the exclusion of the actions of the person against whom deadly force was used. Ignored are the unique and limited circumstances within which deadly force is justified. The use of deadly force is categorized as an option equally as available and pertinent to every function of law enforcement no different from handcuffing and note taking. But the use of deadly force is not a general purpose tool. It is clearly limited in use to the necessity of preventing an imminent risk of death or serious injury. It is not a force option or a technique or a tactic that can be employed independently of that specific circumstance.

To use a shorthand statement that encompasses a diverse array of responsibilities and duties, the civic function of law enforcement within a community is to enforce the law. The use of deadly force is not appropriate to subdue and arrest a subject, or to control an accident scene or to investigate a report of a crime in progress. It is true that in any one of the many functions that are encompassed in the law enforcement role, the necessity to use deadly force can erupt at any moment *if* it is necessary to prevent death or serious injury, and at that moment the successful defense of self and others becomes the preeminent goal above all others. Everything else is subordinated to the immediate and more urgent need to prevent death or serious injury. Once that is accomplished, then the normal law enforcement considerations of arrest, investigation, and regulation can resume and are controlling again. The argument that underlies the allegation of wrongdoing is that deadly force is just another technique to execute an arrest or a stop or enforce a command and, therefore, it is no different in the circumstances in which it is used than any other level or means of force. The officer "should" have done something else, or nothing at all. But in balancing the option of "no action" with the "duty to perform," we must remember that law enforcement officers are trained and practiced to protect themselves and the public. They are expected to be proactive in pursuit of their duty.

The reality is that the law enforcement role leads officers into situations in which real threats of death or injury regularly arise. They must confront these threats, assess their imminence and likelihood, adapt and accept the risk, and react to negate it. The duty inherent to the law enforcement function is to take action. If the circumstances are such that a decision is made to use deadly force, it is done in order to protect self and others from the reasonably perceived and imminently occurring risk of death or serious injury, or to prevent the escape of a dangerous individual. It is not justifiable for any other reason.

The decision to use deadly force is not made to keep the peace; to detect and investigate violations of law; to identify, locate, and arrest violators of the law; or to collect and organize evidence to ascertain the facts in support of prosecution and assignation of accountability. In fact, the utilization of deadly force is of no legal or moral use to fulfilling any of the well understood law enforcement functions except protection from death or serious injury. It is a means of preempting an imminent risk of death or serious injury, or terminating an actual and ongoing risk, or to prevent the escape of a dangerous individual. There are no other justifications for the use of deadly force.

When a law enforcement officer is engaged in a deadly force confrontation, the goal is survival—survival of the officer(s) and members of the community—not the performance of law enforcement functions.[1] The issue in the aftermath

---

1. This is not to say that the law enforcement role does not include protection of people—it clearly does. But that protection is encompassed within the entirety of the law enforcement concept—legal authority, uniformed presence, powers of arrest, and legal

is not whether deadly force was a poor choice to arrest or detain the subject, although that is the gist of the typical allegation. The issue is whether the perception of danger was reasonable and was the decision to use deadly force reasonably necessary to prevent or end that danger. Actions and judgments before and after that critical decision point may or may not be relevant to the law enforcement function and may or may not be valid points of criticism or signs of deficiency. They do not have a relevant bearing on the assessment of the rationale for the decision to use deadly force. It is a question of judgment—not criminal intent— and the attempt to treat it otherwise is unfair and destructive. Unless there is evidence of a criminal intent, the law enforcement use of deadly force is properly adjudicated through the civil process, not criminal proceedings.

Frequently, careful hindsight review of a deadly force confrontation can reveal mistakes in judgment, poor planning, incorrect tactics, or individual officer inadequacies. Nevertheless, such prelusive mistakes and errors are not germane to an assessment of the critical decision point in the use of deadly force. Analysis of the justification of a law enforcement use of force is based on a standard of objective reasonableness applied to the situation at the moment it devolved to a decision to use deadly force. It should not involve any subjective information regarding the officer who used the force, such as training, age, experience, or fallibility of prior planning.[2]

Planning is a desirable prerequisite for any action contemplated within the law enforcement role in society. Law enforcement doctrine requires that investigations should be planned, arrests must be planned, and utilization of personnel and materiel resources needs to be planned. Uninformed (or disingenuous) public post-shooting incident criticism will allege a lack of planning,

---

consequences. No police officer goes about the day expecting to shoot somebody in order to protect somebody else—they expect the full panoply of law enforcement powers and functions to suffice. When it does *not* suffice, the use of deadly force may be necessary— but that is a function of the inherent right of self-defense and not peculiar to the law enforcement role. Every citizen has the right to use deadly force in defense of self and others if it is necessary to prevent a reasonably perceived imminent risk of death or serious injury. The difference is that law enforcement officers are required to go in harm's way—citizens are not. Law enforcement officers accordingly benefit from a more affirmative authority to use deadly force. They are habitually in circumstances in which the likelihood of an imminent risk of serious injury is characteristically present. To put it more colloquially, the citizen may use deadly force when danger comes to him—the police officer must go into danger's way, and danger's way is a treacherous and precarious place to be.

2. Petrowski, TD, JD, "Use-of-Force Policies and Training—A Reasoned Approach," *FBI Law Enforcement Bulletin*, U.S. Department of Justice, Washington, DC, October 2002, page 26.

or incompetent or ineffective planning as the underlying cause that put the officers in the position that created the need to use deadly force. The accusation excuses the attacker as not responsible and claims the poor planning or lack of a plan is responsible for creating the circumstance in which he had to react, or defend himself, or otherwise act as he did. But the execution of a poor plan, or the lack of any plan at all, does not exonerate the subject of an attack or assault, or an act consistent with initiating an attack. It also does not nullify the officer's right to protect himself. It is the action of the subject that creates a reasonable and imminent perception of incipient death or injury. The police officer reacts to what the subject does.

An easily overlooked fact of law enforcement work is that officers routinely experience numerous, unforeseen encounters with suspects that cannot be planned in advance. When these encounters result in a decision to use deadly force, the allegations of improper or deficient planning will run even more rampant. Yet even in an unplanned encounter, the officer will rely upon experience, training, perceptions of events, personal skills and intuitions, and make decisions and initiate actions based on those factors, weighing responses or avenues of reaction within whatever time is available under the constraints of the encounter. The body of training, experience, and ability that an officer acquires cannot be erased. These factors will always influence the officer and affect the assessment of the situation and available responses. The harsh reality is that there is often little time for reflection and consideration of alternatives where surprise and the limited time factor inherent to an unplanned encounter are paramount. But once again, this happens because of the actions and choices of the person being confronted.

The well-trained, experienced, and well-practiced officer will not react mindlessly and reflexively, but will try to recognize, adapt, and act to prevail within the parameters of training, experience, and personal abilities. Some unplanned encounters will offer more time for planning than others. For example, two officers respond to a call and meet outside the location. Before going in, they briefly confer to decide who will enter first, who will follow as back-up, or whether to enter, and generally how they will proceed. They quickly weigh alternatives and decide what to do next. Perhaps the training they have received is such that it fits a training scenario and little conversation is necessary at all. Perhaps this is the tenth or 20th time they have engaged in this particular set of circumstances. The point is that although necessarily brief in ideation and implementation, it is still planning, no matter how severely abbreviated by the urgency of the encounter.

Yet other encounters are so sudden and unforeseen that any planning or consideration of alternative actions, no matter how brief, are simply not possible and the officer's reactions will ideally consist of conditioned reflexes in-

stilled by accumulated training and experience. But again, the need to act is compelled by what the individual does. Regardless, the individual is responsible
for what he does—the officer can only react and respond.

The plan, or lack of a plan, neither exonerates resistance nor induces it, nor
contributes to the decision of the subject involved to act in a threatening manner. In the simplest of resolutions, all the subject has to do is choose to surrender. Submit and comply. That is the one choice that is guaranteed to resolve
any situation with no harm to anybody, and that is not a choice the officer can
make. Law enforcement officers can and will do all that is reasonably possible
under the circumstances to induce "submit and comply" but they have no control over what the subject actually will do; they can only try to meet their responsibilities in as effective and safe a manner as possible.

Ultimately, a law enforcement officer can only react to what the individual
does during the time of the interaction between the officer and the individual. If the individual does something that reasonably raises the risk of death
or serious injury, then the officer may reasonably perceive it to be real and decide to respond with deadly force. In that event, the fact that a bad plan or
tactical mistake may have put the two protagonists in contact does not bear
on the reasonableness of the officer's decision to use deadly force at the moment it became necessary. It does not extinguish the innate right to defend self
or others from an imminent risk of serious injury.

Law enforcement officers and the general public recognize and accept the notion of using deadly force after an assault has begun. The image of a police officer suddenly under attack and responding with deadly force to save his life is
probably the most widely held in the public consciousness, and the most uncontroversial. On the other hand, there is another justification for deadly force
that does not find such popular understanding and acceptance.

The concept of striking after a threat is perceived but *before* the onset of an
actual assault is "preemptive" and can often lead to misconceptions regarding
the necessity or rationale for deadly force. However, the fact is that any reasonable
use of deadly force is always a preemptive use of force regardless of whether an
actual assault has started.[3] Deadly force lawfully used is employed to *prevent* (i.e.,
preempt) future injury. When an assault is in progress, the use of deadly force
is justified to prevent its continuation. It logically follows that deadly force
cannot be justified as an act of retribution or punishment. Law enforcement

---

3. Petrowski, TD, JD, "Use-of-Force Policies and Training—A Reasoned Approach (Part
Two)," *FBI Law Enforcement Bulletin*, U.S. Department of Justice, Washington, DC, November 2002, pages 27–28.

inherently bears the responsibility to preempt (prevent) harm from happening in the first place—to stop it from continuing, second.

A law enforcement officer cannot use deadly force to impose punishment or exact retribution. And the purpose for using deadly force is not to kill, although that is a common consequence. Deadly force is necessary and used because it is the only form and level of force available that promises a reasonable expectation of timely incapacitation to effectively prevent or stop injury. (See Chapter 5 for more regarding incapacitation.) This should be obvious by the fact that whenever a law enforcement use of deadly force ends and the incident is over, the officers do not continue to apply deadly force in order to assure fatal results. The law, their training, policies, and practices all prohibit it. They do not finish off the wounded. To the contrary, law enforcement officers routinely, immediately, and assiduously engage in Herculean efforts to save the life of the very person they just shot.

Quite apart from allegations of negligent or inadequate qualification, planning, training, judgment, supervision, or any of the host of other supposedly critical factors, even an incompetent police officer still has the right and authority to defend himself and others. The right of self-defense does not depend upon any factor except the reasonable perception of imminent death or serious injury.

A review of training records may reveal that the officer involved was not qualified to carry or use the weapon that was used in the incident. There may be some merit to such an allegation in an incident where the officer negligently or carelessly inflicts an unjustified injury on an individual, but in an incident wherein the officer's perception of risk was reasonable, it has no applicability at all. The logic of the allegation would imply that just because the officer was not qualified, he had no recourse other than to submit to whatever attack was imminent without resisting. The consequences of that implication are unreasonable when in fact the officer has the authority and the right to protect himself and others by any reasonable means at hand.

The law requires that a decision to use deadly force in defense of self or others be based on a perception of objectively reasonable and imminent risk of serious injury. If the decision is justified, there is no prescription in the law, nor should there be in policy or in the pantheon of law enforcement training and practices, that mandates the form or particularity that deadly force must take. It does not matter if an officer uses a weapon with which he or she has not qualified, provided the use of deadly force is justified. It does not matter if the form of the deadly force used is unconventional—a baton instead of a gun, a car instead of a firearm—if the use of deadly force is justified. It may well result in an allegation of improper or excessive deadly force, but the reality is that only the decision to use deadly force must be justified. It may also be the basis for administrative action if the officer violated some ill-advised stricture of policy. But that does not impute illegality. If the decision is justified, the means is assumed to be potentially lethal and thus irrelevant in its form or nature. In actuality, any such violations of policy tend to be assessed relative to the results— a good shooting that violates a policy stricture will be deemed an approved situational exception. (See Chapter 14 for more on policy considerations.)

The same reasoning applies to the use of deadly force to prevent the escape of a dangerous individual. If the prerequisite conditions established by the Supreme Court are present, then the officer has the legal authority to use deadly force to prevent escape. The form that deadly force takes is not pertinent to the justification.

All too often a law enforcement officer will lose track of the fact that the form of deadly force is irrelevant if the decision to use deadly force is justified. For example, an officer will be sitting in a cruiser with the engine running when a person (on foot or in a vehicle) shoots at him. Instead of staying within the excellent protective confines of the car and accelerating the car into the person, the officer will either try to shoot back from inside, or worse, get out of the vehicle to shoot back.[4]

To cite another example known to one of the authors, an undercover officer was engaged in an investigation of illegal gun traffickers. During the critical meeting, the officer loaded an illegal submachine gun and fired a short test burst in his undercover role as a potential buyer. When the situation went bad and the principal in the gun-running drew a weapon to shoot at incoming law enforcement personnel, the undercover officer put down the fully loaded, functional submachine gun he had just test fired to physically grapple with the subject six feet away—and he got shot for his troubles.

In the final analysis, it does not matter what form of deadly force is used. If the decision to use deadly force is justified, any form is acceptable. The legitimate and incontrovertible purpose is to dispel or terminate the risk of death or serious injury. It may offend the sensibilities of some segments of the community, especially among the plaintiffs' bar, to run a person down with a car, or gun him down with a heavy caliber machine gun, or strike him with a rock, club, or blunt object, but if the means used were the best and timeliest avail-

---

4. Although "knock-down power" is popularly used to describe the desirability of various handgun cartridges for self-defense, it is invalid, being scientifically impossible. However, the authors cannot resist pointing out that a moving car is a weapon that does in fact possess an abundance of scientifically authentic and reliably dependable "knock-down power." Where a bullet weighing 3% of one pound or less cannot knock a man down, a 4000-lb automobile assuredly can.

able for the justified purpose of defense of self or others (or to prevent the escape of a dangerous person), it is reasonable on its face. The ends do indeed justify the means in assessing the appropriate and justified use of deadly force.

A law enforcement officer has a singular responsibility to ensure that a decision to use deadly force is well justified and reasonable, and that the circumstances, perceptions, and events can be articulated in a manner that will explain the decision and its rationale. It is insufficient to merely say, "I was in fear for my life." That is not a magic phrase behind which an officer can hide and avoid further examination or accountability. There is no legal requirement in the federal standards that an officer subjectively fear death or injury.[5] The question is whether the officer was reasonable in believing that the facts and circumstances justified the use of deadly force. Personal fear of death or injury may well be an understandable consequence of those facts, but the underlying facts and the reasonable perceptions that are apparent to an objective observer devoid of personal fear are the decisive factors.

It is becoming apparent in the inevitable legal actions that ensue after law enforcement use of deadly force events that the courts are apprehensive of the uncorroborated "feared for my life" justification thrown up as a self-evident shield. There is a concern that unscrupulous or criminal acts could be hidden behind the bare assertion that "I feared for my life." Law enforcement must recognize this concern in the courts and within the community and understand it is a valid and profound point. The officer who believes that the statement "I was in fear for my life" is enough on its face is mistaken; it is not and cannot be. The fear may well have been real, but expressing it does not ab-

---

5. That is not necessarily true in self-defense laws at the state level. To cite but one example, under Maine law two requirements must be met for a law enforcement officer to be justified in using deadly force for purposes of self-protection or the protection of third persons. First, the officer *must actually and reasonably believe* that unlawful deadly force is imminently threatened against the officer or a third person. Second, the officer *must actually and reasonably believe* that the officer's use of deadly force is necessary to meet or counter that imminent threat of unlawful deadly force. The required *actual belief* is a subjective standard, unlike the objective federal standard.

Under certain limited circumstances, a Maine law enforcement officer is justified in using deadly force to make an arrest or prevent an escape. The officer *must actually and reasonably believe* that the person has committed a crime involving the use or threatened use of deadly force, or otherwise indicates that the person is likely to seriously endanger human life or to inflict serious bodily injury unless apprehended without delay.

It is beyond the scope and intent of this work to explain and discuss all the various statutory requirements for justified self-defense of the remaining 49 states. Maine is cited here solely to illustrate that differences can exist.

solve the officer from explaining it. The explanation is critical. Officers must be able to articulate a rational basis that led to the decision to use deadly force. Certainly, a well-founded fear of imminent death or serious injury stemming from the actions of the adversary is a substantiating factor, but it cannot be the only factor offered. The reasons for it must be explained in terms of facts, observations, knowledge, and circumstances—the elements of an objectively reasonable perception.

That "*an imminent risk of serious injury*" was reasonable should be the logical conclusion of those reviewing and analyzing the incident, not the proffered rationale "*I feared for my life*" by the officer who made the decision to use deadly force. A law enforcement officer is trained and sworn to be accountable. If the officer cannot articulate the underlying reasons that led to a fear of death or injury, there may be no sufficient underlying reasons to support the decision to use deadly force. An objective analysis will often reveal factors in support of the decision to use deadly force that were not apparent to the officer, or that the officer may have interpreted incorrectly. That does not invalidate the reasonable nature of the officer's actions.

However, the officer who makes the decision to use deadly force cannot merely rely upon the analysis and assessment of others following the event. The officer involved *must* be able to articulate what created the perception of imminent risk that led to the decision to use deadly force. It may be incomplete; it may be mistaken relative to a review based on hindsight; it may differ from the perceptions and recollections of others present; it may not square with some forensic evidence. But, it must be articulated, and it must be reasonable under the circumstances through the eyes of the officer himself.

The nature of the law enforcement profession requires officers to interact with dangerous people in dangerous situations. Some of the officers are targeted and killed simply because they are in the wrong place at the wrong time.[6] In all cases, police officers are killed and assaulted because the attacker made that choice, not because the officer precipitated the attack.

Risk is omnipresent in the law enforcement function. But not all risk is equal. This too is the responsibility of the individual officers involved. The de-

---

6. "Killed in the Line of Duty—A Study of Selected Felonious Killings of Law Enforcement Officers" Uniform Crime Reports Section, FBI, U.S. Department of Justice, September 1992. One of the findings was that 10–12% of the law enforcement officers killed every year are simply in the wrong place at the wrong time and nothing could prevent their murders, as opposed to the remainder who, variously, make tactical mistakes, fail to recognize symptomatic warning signs, or could have survived for other reasons discernible after the fact.

gree of risk to be accepted will vary with the individual involved and the situation in which it is occurring.

In general terms, an officer confronting an armed and dangerous person one-on-one can accept less risk and act more quickly and with less reservation than the same officer confronting an armed and dangerous person holding a hostage in front of him. In the first instance, any sudden act or change of demeanor may be reasonably interpreted as an escalation of risk compelling the use of deadly force to counter. In the second instance, the decision to use deadly force to protect one's self must be held in some abeyance to the greater need to protect the hostage, and therefore the officer may have to accept a somewhat increased degree of risk to himself. Risk is ever-present—but never equally intrinsic. Evaluation and judgment are necessarily situational.

To return to the example of a person wielding a knife, the level of risk incurred by the officer becomes a calculus of time, distance, and circumstances such as intervening obstacles. If the knife-wielding person is 50 feet away, there is relatively little risk of injury and more time. If the knife wielder is within 20–30 feet, the officer is at considerable risk of getting stabbed or slashed if there is a sudden attack. If an intervening obstacle obstructs or prevents the knife wielder from reaching the officer without hindrance, the risk is mitigated to the degree the hindrance precludes access to the officer.

If the knife wielder is holding a hostage, the officer may have to subsume risk to himself within the more urgent concern for prevention of harm to the hostage. Now the officer may need to willingly enter within the implicit danger radius to better protect the hostage, recognizing that at any moment the suspect may abandon the hostage and assault the officer with considerably better chances of success due to the proximity. In the latter example, closing the distance may be necessary to ensure that shooting the subject can be done with minimal risk to the hostage: for example, by putting the officer in position to ensure a hit in the central nervous system to prevent a desperate stab or slash of the hostage.

Looked at another way, law enforcement is a constant balancing of the functional demand for efficiency against the inherent need for personal safety. Most of the activities that a law enforcement officer initiates or in which the officer engages do not result in any overt risk of harm to the officer. That general and pervasive lack of overt risk generates two concerns. The law enforcement officer must always guard against complacency, the seductively appealing but extremely dangerous assumption that the current encounter will be just as harmless as all the previous, similar encounters in the officer's experience. At best, complacency inhibits the timely recognition and effective reaction to a sudden threat of injury or death. It fosters hesitation, denial, and delay. It can easily prevent a timely response with injury or death the result.

The second concern is the necessity for the individual law enforcement officer to constantly assess and balance perception of risk against the need to fulfill the responsibilities of the profession. For example, it is well recognized throughout law enforcement that car stops are dangerous.

In the 16-year period of 1999–2014, 146 officers were feloniously killed in circumstances involving cars and car stops (17.5% of the 833 officers feloniously killed in that time span).[7] There were 909,434 assaults of law enforcement officers in the same 16-year span, and consistently approximately 10% of the assaults occurred in circumstances involving cars and car stops. In 2014 (the most recent year for which data are available), there were 48,315 assaults reported—4,022 of them in situations involving motor vehicles (8.3%).[8]

The injury rate is relatively constant as well, fluctuating between a low of 26% per year to a singular high rate of 29.2% in 2013 (14,557 officers). The injury rate for 2014 (the most recent data available) was 28.3% (13,673).[9] Averaging the injury rate over the sixteen-year period of 1999–2014, 27.2% of the officers who were assaulted were also injured (over 247,366 officers injured).[10]

Nevertheless, it is not reasonable or even possible for a law enforcement officer to issue a speeding ticket from behind the cover of his or her cruiser. Sooner or later the officer must approach the vehicle. Officers must rely on training, experience, judgment, and personal confidence in their individual capabilities to assess, evaluate, and function while staying alert to maximize the recognition of any sudden changes or danger signals and the implications they represent.

Hypothetical examples can be imagined ad infinitum. A gun in the hand of the hypothetical adversary in any situation changes all the factoring of relative risks and reasonable inculcation of options in the calculus of risk assessment. A gun in the possession of a subject *is* an imminent risk of serious injury. The radius of risk expands significantly with a firearm. The person does not have to be skilled—a random "lucky" shot is all that is necessary to add to the officers killed statistics for the year. It takes less effort and far less time to pull a trigger than to stab or slash with a knife—a factor important to those assessing whether to use deadly force to protect the hostage. A spasmodic reflex action in response to a central nervous system wound may be sufficient to

---

7. Source: A compendium of the FBI Crime Reports "Law Enforcement Officers Killed & Assaulted" for the years 1999–2014.

8. FBI Uniform Crime Reports, "Law Enforcement Officers Killed and Assaulted 2014," Table 67.

9. *Ibid.*, Table 76.

10. Source: A compendium of the FBI Uniform Crime Reports "Law Enforcement Officers Killed & Assaulted" for the years 1999–2014.

cause a gun to fire—unlikely to be enough to cause a knife to injure. Range and cover considerations are even more critical in incidents involving firearms than knives, clubs, or other personal proximity weapons.[11]

Some officers will have greater confidence in their personal capabilities or their proficiency with particular weapons that may induce them to accept higher levels of risk than an officer with less ability or confidence. They may be correct in their personal, individualized recognition of the situation—and their individual actions must be assessed relative to these personalized perceptions. What is real for one officer is not necessarily real for another, yet each individual's perceptions are still real and valid for him.

This helps explain why it is not unusual in incidents involving several law enforcement officers confronting a potentially dangerous that one officer may be compelled to use deadly force while another never feels at risk. Equally as often, the critical incident is an event that is sudden and unexpected. The precipitous onset can result in a delayed realization of danger on the part of the witnessing officer—the stunned disbelief as illustrated by the expression common in the aftermath, "I could not believe this was happening." The delay prevents that officer from reacting as quickly and then the event is ended and the need to react has passed. And there is always the simple possibility that one officer simply did not see the action or event that precipitated the decision to use deadly force by the other.

A law enforcement officer must articulate the justification for his or her own individual decisions and acts. If a second officer on the scene perceived a different threat level, or no threat level, it is not proof of unreasonableness on the part of the other. Each is assessing the events from a different perspective of acuity, confidence, understanding, and simple observation. The officer who does not react may have simply not seen what the first officer saw—or may have interpreted it incorrectly. Each must be examined independently to understand and assess the actions of the individual officers involved.

Risk and responsibility are two edges of the same sword. The risk is always there, but not inevitably the same for all. The responsibility of the law enforcement officer is to understand that risk is unavoidable and seek to recognize and manage it, not preclude facing it. The authority to decide to use deadly force is within the personal discretion of every individual law enforcement officer. The courts and society have historically given law enforcement the ben-

---

11. Categorized as "personal proximity" weapons because they require that the wielder and the target be in close proximity to each other, and such weapons can only be wielded by the individual personally.

efit of the doubt when deadly force is used for all the many reasons explained in this book. Despite the advantage of the favorable presumption of necessity, law enforcement officers bear an undiluted responsibility to recognize that they cannot eliminate risk, and that when deadly force is used the individual officer must be able to articulate the facts and circumstances that led to the decision to use it. Anything less is unacceptable.

And finally, it is necessary for the bureaucratic entity that is the law enforcement department itself to accept responsibility for the risks that its officers incur, and to avoid increasing those risks by unnecessary restrictions or contradictory policy provisions and interpretations. A good example of such contradictory and risk-enhancing effects of a poor policy provision and its reverberating effects through training and into police practice is the following training scenario utilized by a state police organization:[12]

# State Police Training Scenario

**Relevant Factor:** Another safe alternative is available.

**Scenario:** Troopers possess a warrant to arrest a suspect for armed robbery of a bank the previous day. During the robbery, the suspect shot and wounded a bank guard. A team of several troopers sets up a perimeter around the house where the suspect is believed to be staying. The arrest plan calls for a trooper to announce their presence and purpose on a bullhorn and to demand the suspect's surrender.

Before the announcement can be made, the troopers see a man matching the suspect's description walking from the front door of the house toward a mailbox near the street. From a distance of about 25 yards, the troopers see what appears to be a handgun tucked into the waistband of the suspect's trousers.

A trooper announces on the bullhorn, "State Police! We have a warrant for your arrest! Put your hands up!" The subject turns quickly and runs back toward the front door of the house. One of the troopers fires two shots, striking the subject in the back.

**Discussion:** *This use of deadly force violates state police policy.* [Emphasis added by authors.]

**Necessity:** The troopers have probable cause to believe the suspect has committed a violent crime and is presently armed with a firearm. In addition, he

---

12. Unidentified only to avoid unfairly embarrassing the agency—there are far too many other departments and organizations who have similarly ignorant policy and training practices to single out this particular department alone.

is noncompliant. These factors satisfy the imminent danger element of this policy. However, based on these specific facts, there appears to be a safe alternative to the immediate use of deadly force.

The troopers are in positions of cover, not just concealment, thereby lessening the immediacy of the risks to themselves. Given these facts, if the suspect gets back into the house, the risks to the troopers appear to be no greater than if their original arrest plan, i.e., containment and negotiation, had been implemented.

[This scenario suggests that a safe alternative to the use of deadly force exists, not that the suspect poses no danger to the troopers. Different facts, e.g., lack of cover for the troopers or the presence of innocent third parties who would be endangered by the suspect, could give a different result.]

Despite the provisions of the state police policy, the use of deadly force contemplated in this situation is clearly legal (constitutional). A visibly armed, violent offender who has already demonstrated his willingness to shoot people is noncompliant, willfully changing direction and running to a position of tactical advantage despite the presence of armed troopers ordering him to stop. If there are other people inside the house, it would be a justified defense of self and others situation—if nobody is in the house, it would be arguably defense of troopers, but clearly conforms to the standard for use of deadly force to prevent the escape of a dangerous person. Importantly, a decision to use deadly force is discretionary—deadly force *may* be used—that does not mean it *must* be used. This interpretation of policy (deadly force *cannot* be used) removes that discretion from the troopers actually engaged and at risk.

Organizations certainly have the authority to establish policy as they see fit, but to the extent they try to remove the officer's judgment from the equation, they also remove the officer's experience, training, and observations. They attempt to create rote solutions to what are not rote problems. Thus, for example, a department adopts a policy that deadly force will not be used against people in vehicles, usually with the too-clever-by-half nuanced caveat "unless the vehicle is being used as a weapon against them." This despite the clear and regularly reaffirmed Supreme Court standard that when people create a grave public safety risk by the operation of a motor vehicle, the use of deadly force to stop them is justified. The motivation would seem to be to establish a policy to minimize public outrage rather than to maximize public and officer safety. Foreseeably, that same motivation could result in a policy restriction that no officer may draw his weapon unless confronting someone who has a weapon in hand and threatens the officer with it. That would be a foolish provision, but it is the sort of politically correct, public relations based policy provision that seems more and more popular with administrators these days, despite the clear and time tested legal standards to the contrary. Policy can always be more restrictive than legal standards, even when it creates a safe haven or unreasonable advantage for violent and/or dangerous people.

The policy in the training scenario above does exactly that. It creates a foolish safe haven in the interests of the "original" plan and passively allows the offender to use it. Basically, the policy and the instructional goal is to let him go and hope nothing worse happens rather than recognize the justified initiative in a changed circumstance to stop him before anything worse can happen, for example:

1. that the suspect will ultimately surrender without resistance—because ... he must?
2. that the suspect will not use his hidden, barricaded interior position to shoot at troopers or others outside;
3. that if the suspect shoots (aimed or randomly) he will not hit anyone (*anyone*) outside, either by intent or by chance—trooper or citizen;
4. that the suspect does not have more and perhaps more effective weapons inside;
5. that the suspect intends to eventually comply and surrender;
6. that there is nobody else inside who is at risk of being used as hostage, victimized in a murder/suicide, injured/killed as a collateral aspect of a forced entry, or injured/killed in any shootout that occurs;
7. that there is nobody inside who will contribute to the suspect's resistance and also shoot at troopers or others outside;
8. that in the event troopers must make entry the suspect will passively surrender and so will any confederate(s) inside;
9. that contrarily—if the suspect resists, no trooper will get hurt—even by a lucky shot;
10. that given time and opportunity to prepare, fortify, or booby-trap to retard or defeat an entry the suspect chooses not to do so.

The courts have made it clear that the consequences (risk) of stopping a grave risk to public safety are to be borne by those causing the risk—not those tasked with stopping it (police) or those (the public) that police are sworn to safeguard and protect. The law favors the endangered over the dangerous.

# Chapter 12

# Aftermath & Impact

*"To me, it doesn't matter how hardened a cop is, watching someone die violently is not a normal everyday human life experience. Furthermore, I think as police officers we operate with a set of simple rules and equations. If someone is speeding and they are going this fast over the limit, the fine amount is this. If someone satisfies element A and element B we have crime X. This is one of the only times in law enforcement where we have no time to consult a book of statutes or to run our decision by a supervisor, we have no hard and fast equation, we just react and although we may be psychologically prepared to do what is necessary I think we are rarely prepared for the aftermath or results of our actions."*[1]

There is no way to practice for a deadly force confrontation, no way to rehearse it. When that moment arrives, it will shock and surprise—it will involve obstacles, movements, and consequences that are unique to the specific circumstances and not replicable beforehand. Previous chapters have discussed and explained realties that are present, that unavoidably apply to deadly force incidents—wound ballistics, physiological responses, action/reaction cycles, tactical considerations, training content and issues, and the effects of life-or-death stress, to name but a few. What needs to be understood is that it all comes together instantly, an inundation of the senses and the mind.

Your "five-million-year-old" sub-conscious brain takes over when somebody is trying to kill you—in "fight or flight." Adrenaline and hydrocortisone flood your system. The blood is gone from your hands and fingers and they go numb. Your ears shut off and tunnel vision closes down your field of view. You are flooded with critical choices and looming consequences demanding that you make the right decisions, right now! The suddenly high stress slows your reaction times, and seriously impairs your ability to process and comprehend

---

1. James Gioia, Detective, Maine State Attorney General's Office. Gioia was a detective with Gardiner (Maine) Police Department when he confronted and shot a man threatening his wife and others with a rifle in 2007.

disparate information and events and formulate the necessary and proper responses.[2] You perform differently under stress and it all happens instantly.

Even in those situations where the officer has no doubt that a person presents an imminent threat of grave harm, uncertainty can still arise in the officer's mind as to whether shooting is justified. Fear of civil suits, criminal investigations, lurid headlines, and outraged segments of the community can implant doubt and hesitation even in situations where the threat is unmistakable. The limited wounding effectiveness of handguns, the lack of immediate response to wounds, and the problematical nature of rapid incapacitation mean that the officer cannot know if his shots are even striking the suspect. That creates additional uncertainty and stress.

In other situations the officer may be uncertain as to who or what or where is the threat and uncertain as to the nature of involvement of the person with whom he is interacting. The officer may have no reasonable suspicion of criminal activity or involvement at all. A law enforcement officer can end up shooting someone who appears innocent of wrongdoing, devoid of suspicion of involvement in a crime, or involved in an offense so innocuous and minor in nature that the sudden use of deadly force is assumed to be unjustified. Frequently, in such events the public will weigh the use of force against its opinion of the substance of the underlying offense, rather than the nature of the individual's actions and the reasonable threat of harm those actions signify. That public perception leads to accusations of police thuggery, excessive force, and racial profiling based upon the emotional, yet misinformed and inaccurate public claims of the decedent's family and friends that the officer stopped my son/brother/husband/friend who was doing nothing wrong, dangerous, or illegal. Public perception will focus on the minor infraction or misdemeanor and disregard an objective appraisal of what happened and the circumstances within which it happened. Or, in a different but frequent example, an officer stops someone who actually is a violent offender but the officer is unaware of that. The officer's interest in the individual may be innocuous. It may be related to some other event or minor offense.

But, even though the officer may not know the offender's recent past, the offender most certainly does. The offender knows what the officer does not—his criminal activity. The offender assumes that the officer's attention must be because of that criminal activity and that paranoid suspicion results in sud-

---

2. During World War II, U.S. bomber crews over Europe suffered a 71% casualty rate, killed in action and missing in action, second in magnitude only to German U-boat crews. One bomber pilot, in a talk about "what it was like" commented, "When you walked across the tarmac [to your plane] your IQ dropped by 50%."

den and unexpected (by the officer) resistance—flight, assault, even murder. The offender always knows—and what the offender knows establishes a mindset that can result in an unanticipated attack. And the officer, facing unexpected attack and suddenly at risk of serious injury, uses deadly force in self-defense because he has no other means at hand to stop the threat.

# A Presumption of Resistance

There is always uncertainty about what a person will do when confronted by police and the prospect of arrest and its immediately perceived consequences:

- loss of freedom
- end of his life as he knows
- destruction of his future and aspirations

Admittedly, most people will submit and comply ... but some don't. Most do nothing that would pose a threat of harm to the officer or others. It is easy for the officer to assume "this particular subject will not hurt me" ... depending on the specific circumstances that may in themselves be routine and nonthreatening ... but then some do.

To illustrate, assume 1,000 arrests with no use of preemptive force. Of those 1,000 people, if only 2% do not submit that means that 980 do no harm— but 20 of them do. Statistics tell us that one of the 20 will kill an officer and roughly ten others will attempt to seriously injure officers, and the officers are in the extremely vulnerable position of reacting after the fact of the attempted harm. By not acting with the precautionary mindset that all 1,000 persons were dangerous, law enforcement only insures that readily avoidable injuries will actually occur. The cost is unacceptably high and it can be prevented by the simple expedient of *presuming* that all 1,000 pose a risk of dangerous resistance and acting in such a way as to prevent *any* of them from reacting dangerously, either intentionally or impulsively. This best protects the two percent from causing harm—but the 980 people who did not resist are angry and offended because the officers "*should*" have known they weren't dangerous.

"People" are a random factor. Most people respond rationally when confronted with an overwhelmingly superior force and numbers—but some don't. Those few that don't are the reason that law enforcement treats all of them as dangerous until submission, compliance, and restraint are sufficient to insure otherwise.

The issue is not whether the vast majority of compliant people merit being treated with suspicion, but the severe and irremediable consequences of failing to restrain and control those few who will pose a risk of harm. The grave consequences of failing to presume resistance and acting to preempt the opportunity for it outweigh the seemingly disproportional anticipation of resistance from those who don't actually pose a threat. Unfortunately, there is no way to foretell who those 2% dangerous individuals are, so the latter is the cost of safeguarding against the former.

# An Intellectual Exercise: Clausewitz
## *On War* [& Law Enforcement]

The stress and uncertainty inherent to deadly force encounters in the law enforcement arena are a microcosm of the stresses and uncertainties inherent to war. Carl von Clausewitz[3] is the time-honored theorist of the nature and principles of war. His genius is also applicable to an understanding of the nature and principles of the much smaller scale phenomena of deadly force encounters in the world of law enforcement. We need only substitute law enforcement concepts and terms for the vastly larger scale military ones.

Clausewitz tells us that no plan survives contact with the [*subject*]. "Everything in [*law enforcement*] is very simple, but the simplest thing is difficult. The difficulties accumulate and end by producing a kind of friction that is inconceivable unless one has experienced [*actual arrest operations* … ] Countless minor incidents—the kind you can never really foresee—combine to lower the general level of performance, so that one always falls far short of the intended goal … Friction is the only concept that more or less corresponds to the factors that distinguish real [*arrest operations*] from [*arrest operations*] on paper."[4]

A good arrest plan—or a bad arrest plan—can only be assessed after the fact. Did the plan provide a framework to coordinate action and means to adapt to, and resolve, unknown events and developments? More simply—did the plan work? Did the officers know the mission and their roles, the resources on hand, the locations of the participants, and the known factors regarding the subject and the environs? Was there allowance for flexibility and initiative to react to unforeseen events in pursuit of the defined end goal?

---

3. Carl von Clausewitz (June 1, 1780–November 16, 1831) a Prussian general and military theorist whose most notable work *Vom Kriege* (*On War*) is widely respected to this day as a foundational treatise on the principles and nature of war.

4. Clausewitz, *On War* I: 7, page 119.

A good arrest plan is not a script—it is not a mandate. A good arrest plan is a prediction of what is expected to happen—and as uncertain as any other predictive tool in any other field of endeavor. Nevertheless, critics after the fact will always focus on those things that happened that were not foreseen in the "Plan"—and those things that "should" have been planned for but weren't—and things that were done in response to changing circumstances but weren't specified in sufficient detail in the "Plan." "Critical analysis is the application of theoretical truths to actual events."[5]

"They aim at fixed values; but in [*law enforcement*] everything is uncertain, and calculations have to be made with variable quantities. They direct the inquiry exclusively toward physical quantities, whereas all [*police*] action is intertwined with psychological forces and effects. They consider only the unilateral action, whereas [*law enforcement*] consists of a continuous interaction of opposites."[6]

Critics assume a level of rationality in human responses similar to that espoused by game theory. In game theory if all the players make rational choices of strategy, they all do as well as possible given the total rewards available in the game, but if one player acts irrationally in terms of the game he is sure to do worse. Therefore, when the subject appears to be acting irrationally, the assumption arises that it is a bluff and more pressure/forbearance can force rationality upon him. This is also taken as evidence of inadequate planning—a failure to assume rational responses and to compel rationality.

But Clausewitz tells us " … The conduct of [*law enforcement*] branches out in almost all directions and has no definite limits; while any system, any model, has the finite nature of a synthesis. An irreconcilable conflict exists between this type of theory and actual practice."[7]

## The Armed & Dangerous Caution Statement

When a person is categorized as "dangerous," it does not mean that law enforcement thinks he will absolutely act dangerously. It means that he has done so before, or has the means to do so now, and others just like him have done dangerous things in similar circumstances. It is a warning flag that law enforcement officers cannot bet their lives that this person won't act dangerously. It is an impetus to law enforcement officers to deter—or at least minimize—

---

5. Clausewitz, *On War* III: 5, page 156.
6. Clausewitz, *On War* II: 2, page 136.
7. Clausewitz, *On War* II: 2, page 134.

any dangerous acts by overwhelming any shred of opportunity for the impulse to arise. If the individual does not resist, does not react dangerously, and does not imperil the personal safety of the officers, then that is the optimal result— as it predominantly occurs in actuality. But " … the essential difference is that … in [*law enforcement*], the will is directed at an animate object that reacts."[8]

Equally important, the officers synchronously maximize their ability to respond effectively in the interest of their personal safety when an individual does not submit. The individual subject, his family and his friends may well aver after the fact that "he wouldn't have hurt anyone," but the officers cannot know that nor can they bet their lives on it being true. Otherwise, they are merely betting that when somebody someday proves the assumption untrue— they won't be the one hurt or killed.

> " … *The facts of [law enforcement] are often in total opposition to the facts of [civilian routine].*
>
> … The efficient [*police officer*] does not seek to use just enough means, but an excess of means. A [*police*] force that is just strong enough to take a position will suffer heavy casualties in doing so; a [*police*] force vastly superior to the [*subject's*] will do the job without serious loss …"[9]

## Post-Shooting Circumstances

There are two misconceptions that can arise in law enforcement thought, training, practices and policy. One is the notion that if a law enforcement officer acts with good faith within the law, complies with departmental policy and training doctrine, and makes a decision to use force that is objectively reasonable on its merits, no legal or community controversy or sanction will arise. This is implicitly assumed if not overtly promoted within law enforcement, all in good faith. The other is a pervasive administrative dread of getting sued, prosecuted, or both that gives rise to unreasonable restrictions on officer discretion and unwieldy micro-management by policy or training dictate. The truth is otherwise in both cases. The men and women of the law enforcement profession should be more fully informed, and better aware of the more likely reality of the aftermath of a decision to use deadly force.

---

8. Clausewitz, *On War* II: 3, page 149.

9. Mark S. Watson, "Chief of Staff: Pre-War Plans and Preparations (US Army in World War II)," Washington, DC: USGPO, 1950, page 12.

The first "good faith assumption" often results in alienation and bitterness in the minds of affected law enforcement officers as it is undermined by reality. The second, or "fear of suit phobia" is also unrealistic and it is damaging to officer safety. It affects the aftermath because it unduly restricts officer judgment and discretion to the detriment of the timely and efficient use of force to prevent serious injury. It is unfortunate but it is a fact that any use of force will bring a court action regardless of restrictive policies and practices.

No department or individual officer can avoid being sued. No policy or training regimen can be so deftly tailored to forestall civil suits. No artificial restriction on equipment, tactics, or intervention options will prevent allegations of legal liability. This is extremely important to understand in formulating training content and policy strictures. The popular and legal reactions that can erupt in the aftermath of a police shooting or other use of force are not symptoms of a need to reformulate policy and training or to add additional layers of restrictions and situation-specific force options. That is not to say that such lapses do not occur. Departments need to examine and assess every use of force by its members to validate training, policy and practice and to identify unforeseen issues and the justification of its officers' actions. But the focus of public emotion and outrage leading to legal action is not that. The reactions are indicia of ignorance, opportunistic demagoguery to promote special interests, or well-intentioned results-based dismay—either separately or in diverse combinations. On the other hand, such attempts to allay such responses and to prevent them from happening relative to future incidents, to guard against imagined or feared future legal actions, can have the very real consequence of increasing the risk of death or serious injury confronted by the officers in the performance of their duties. That also increases the risk of death or serious injury among the civilian population as well—a related consequence seldom considered.

Unfortunately, the heightened risks are tacitly acceptable (arguably not by intent) to community factions and departmental administrators who view the measures taken as necessary to prevent or limit controversy. This does require a faith that proscribing officer responses and options will somehow make future dangerous individuals less hazardous to confront. That alone is unrealistic on its face and reason enough to avoid subjective, reflexive changes. Actually, the unspoken hope is that it will prevent them from having to deal with controversial issues and emotional disputes. It is reflective, in effect, of an implicit preference (unintentional, and certainly unconscious) to mourn a dead hero rather than defend the decisions of a live officer whose actions are misconstrued or unpopular. The whole community rallies at the funeral of an officer tragically killed in the performance of duty. It is an uncontroversial and unifying event within the social context of any community. All segments of society unite to mourn the loss and commemorate the sacrifice.

On the other hand, consider the officer who shoots and kills a mentally disturbed person in a public setting when that person refuses to drop a small knife and runs at the officer. There is no dead hero here, but a surviving one. Typically this incident will create a firestorm of controversy.[10] Zealous interest groups will use the incident to promote an unfair and profoundly distorted view of law enforcement as a ruthless occupation force in the midst of an oppressed community. Activists for the mentally ill will agitate for restrictions on police action and increased resources to protect and assist the mentally disturbed. Friends and family of the victim will talk of the victim's life, portraying a lifelong love of children, animals, and the environment and possessing a non violent nature. The newspapers and the broadcast media will indiscriminately publicize all of the statements, opinions, issues, and claims of the family, friends, supporters, and interest groups. They will editorialize about the tragedy and the important questions they raise. They will demand answers. They will demand change. They will deplore the death of the unfortunate, mentally impaired victim.[11]

Too often, the public reaction to a police shooting will be driven by people with agendas rising from advocacy on behalf of subjective issues of mental capacity, race, cultural diversity, or social justice. The advocates demand that law enforcement customize its tactics, uses of force, and responses to service

---

10. The narrative that follows is admittedly a generalized composite of numerous law enforcement deadly force incidents over the years that the authors have reviewed, witnessed, studied, been retained in, or otherwise followed. It is intended to accomplish two ends. First, the generalized controversy depicted is evident, in part or in whole, in the aftermath of any use of deadly force by law enforcement. The irrational and destructive effects need to be recognized and understood. The hysterical rush to judgment and the determined distortion of information and events to pursue unrelated agendas or interests can drive a wedge of alienation between the community and its integral police department. That is deplorable and ultimately a dangerous consequence. General awareness coupled with education and a healthy skepticism of the excesses can counter the dangers. Second, individual police officers need to realize that the process will not afford them reassurance or vindication, whether the process is rational or not. The individual officer must seek the personal reassurance and vindication via other avenues and avoid the disillusion and bitterness that can result when the public process is ultimately resolved. The resolution will probably not provide comfort or vindication, and that is not going to change. The officer reading this hopefully will recognize that and accept it. It goes with the territory.

11. An economic factor that is frequently overlooked is that the media is in the business of selling its product with the intent of gaining readers and viewers, and controversy sells. This does not appear to be a motivating factor so much as it mitigates against actively trying to mediate or allay community reactions.

calls relative to those same subjective factors of mental capacity, race, and cultural and societal conventions instead of objectively reacting to the potential consequences of what the individual is doing. The result is not consistent with the facts of what actually happened.

> *"There are things that members of the community don't understand very well. They often don't understand the law, they don't understand police training, they don't understand the speed at which shootings unfold, and they don't understand the human factors involved. When a community calls for justice and seeks satisfaction, these are elements they need to understand."*[12]

On August 9, 2014, Michael Brown stole some items from a convenience store in Ferguson, MO, strong-arming the store clerk who attempted to intervene. The theft and a physical description of Brown were broadcast. Soon after, Ferguson police officer Darren Wilson saw Brown and an associate walking down the middle of the street. He stopped them and an altercation ensued. Brown assaulted Wilson, attempted to take Wilson's gun from him, and ultimately was shot several times and killed by Wilson. Wilson was white, Brown was black, and Brown's associate fabricated a story about Brown getting shot in the back as he raised his hands saying, "Don't shoot." This fabricated story was adopted at face value by those critics of law enforcement who insist that disparities in arrest and treatment of black subjects (12% of the population) relative to white ones are racially motivated, ignoring the widely documented fact that blacks commit disproportionately more crimes of violence (91%) than do whites.

The "hands up, don't shoot" mythology continues to characterize the shooting incident in Ferguson to this day, despite the fact that the evidence, witnesses, and forensic analysis all substantiated Officer Wilson's narrative and proved that the popular myth was and is in fact untrue in every particular.[13] Nevertheless, the lie lives on and law enforcement is unfairly branded as institutionally racist with the consequent demands that interactions with blacks be somehow different.

---

12. Lewinski, W, PhD, Force Science Institute, Mankato, MN, *Force Science News* #276.

13. As discussed in Chapter 1, on November 24, 2014, the St. Louis (Missouri) County grand jury declined to indict Officer Wilson after conducting an exhaustive and comprehensive examination of witnesses, evidence, and forensics. The grand jury's action was validated by a subsequent, independent, and even more exhaustive investigation by the U.S. Department of Justice that fully exonerated Officer Wilson.

See: For a thorough discussion and analysis of this incident see Chapter 1 and the "Department of Justice Report Regarding the Criminal Investigation into the Shooting Death of Michael Brown by Ferguson, Missouri Police Officer Darren Wilson, March 4, 2015."

Special interest advocacy groups that promote the interests of self-identified classifications of self-selected victims of alleged law enforcement bigotry and persecution routinely utilize sensationalized versions of incidents of police uses of force to promote their agendas regardless of the detrimental effects these efforts have on law enforcement, community safety, and the relations between police and those elements of the community most at risk from criminal violence. They demand that law enforcement modify its policies, tactics, and practices based on the categorization of the self-identified "victim." Their non-negotiable demand is that the police must somehow customize responses based on the social identity of the individual to whom they are responding as a favored racial minority, mentally ill, or otherwise specifically identified culturally or socially disadvantaged group. And the spokesman for the department will decline to comment about an ongoing investigation while privately the administrators and the management rue the day their officer shot that person. What they really regret is having to deal with the controversy that is imposed upon them.

The mentally ill are a class of individuals with which law enforcement must regularly and repetitively interact. They are more commonly referred to as "emotionally disturbed persons" (EDP) to create a more broadly inclusive category that also conveniently avoids the implied need for a qualified diagnosis of mental illness.[14] Critics of law enforcement uses of force and overzealous advocates for the mentally ill sensationalize incidents in which police have had to use force against an EDP to illustrate the "need" for customized police responses, ignoring the inconvenient truth that a law enforcement officer can only react to what a subject does, independently of the root causes that may underlie the subject's actions. If law enforcement officers are required to make special accommodations when confronting violent, life-threatening EDPs, officer safety and public safety will be compromised because officers will be forced

---

14. "Emotionally disturbed person" is uselessly ambiguous, but conveniently inclusive for the activist (see Chapter 9). Virtually everybody that a law enforcement officer confronts can be said to be "emotionally disturbed." The cause for that disturbance can vary widely. It may be simply irritation over the inconvenience of a summons and fine; it may be induced by the influence of drugs or alcohol; it may be a symptom of mental illness; it may be symptomatic of some other event or concern unknown to the officer. The point is that the officer cannot be expected to make a diagnosis of root causes before reacting to resolve reasonably recognized consequences of observed behavior within the known circumstances. The law enforcement officer can only react to what the individual does, or seems about to do, subject to the officer's knowledge, experience, training, and observations. And the law enforcement officer is *always* reacting to what the individual does, so he is always behind the action/reaction cycle. (See Chapter 7—Physiological Factors.)

to ascertain the causes of dangerous behavior instead of dealing with its effects. That will result in hesitation and delay during emergency situations and such hesitation and delay will then result in increased exposure to harm for the officer(s) and the public.

That said, EDPs are confronted by police officers regularly, by the thousands every year. Very few—a fraction of one percent of them—are subjected to deadly force. Most are not, because police officers are in fact well trained and well practiced in their jobs. They are capable and adept at resolving confrontations without resorting to deadly force. They do it literally every day, all the time—you don't read about that. Occasionally, the individual that is confronted *does something* that exceeds the officer's ability to protect the safety and physical well being of self and others, and the urgency of *that sudden threat of injury or death* may necessitate the use of deadly force to quickly and effectively stop that threat from maturing into actual physical harm, or from continuing to cause physical harm. That is the only reason an officer can use deadly force. Again—that is the *only* reason.

The problems confronting the mentally ill are societal—not police related. Society basically ignores them until and unless they provoke a police response. Society affords them wide discretion in life choices, accepting treatment, beneficial confinement—they are assumed to be harmless and allowed to be self-responsible until and unless they provoke a police response. Society has pretty much washed its hands of them, and left the problematic ones to the police—who are forced to become involved when they do something that threatens societal norms and community safety. That is not the solution—and police cannot act as mental health EMT first responders. They comprise a law enforcement function, not a mental health diagnostic and therapeutic resource.

If you call the police, you will get a police response … not a therapy session. Police must always be concerned with preventing harm to themselves and others. If the individual poses a threat of harm to the officer or others, deadly force may be the only way to stop that threat of harm from becoming an actual attempt at harm, or to keep an actual attempt from continuing. Critics ignore the fact that deadly force is only used in the circumstance of preventing imminent serious injury. The justified use of deadly force has nothing to do with mental state—it has everything to do with an urgent need to prevent harm *right now* and deadly force is the only measure available that holds the promise of doing that quickly enough to prevent harm. Most people (mentally ill or not) do not pose a threat of imminent physical harm … but those few who do cannot be ignored. An officer cannot wait until he or she is certain what will happen—the officer has to deal in reasonable likelihoods. If he waits for certainty, he insures others will be harmed who could have been protected.

Critics proceed from an assumption that because someone is an EDP, that person somehow poses less of a threat, or officers should take on more risk or allow others to take on that risk—but injured or dead police officers and civilians are just as injured or dead if harmed by a mentally impaired individual as by a mentally whole one. The purpose is prevention of harm to self and others—if the individual does something that makes harm likely, the officer must act—mental state is irrelevant. You want therapy to talk someone down regardless of risk to others—call a psychiatrist (but I bet you he won't come until the subject is under control and safe to approach). You want to prevent others from being hurt (first) and subdue the subject (second)—call a cop. They have a higher duty than merely making sure the subject doesn't get hurt.

Secondly, critics will point to the accumulated number of police shootings over some period of years that have been found justified, complaining that there are few if any that result in criminal charges or sanctions against the police. That would mean something if there was a statistical bell curve and if shootings were expected to fall on the curve like grades in a school. But shooting incidents don't—each shooting is a unique event that stands or falls on its own merits independently of all other shootings. Analysis cannot look at the total and make an assessment of the validity of the review process. Analysis must look at each single decision to use deadly force as if it were the only one ever—and judge that individual decision on its merits subject to the clear legal standards for the use of deadly force. If that shooting is then determined to be reasonable and justified, then it is so classified. The analyst can then consider the next incident in the accumulation and review it same way, without regard to other shootings before or since. If it is deemed justified, it goes in that category with the others—and so on. Then when each one has been examined and evaluated separately, independently, and on its own specific merits, if all of them have ended up in the reasonable and justified category that fact does not mean the review process is faulty—rather it indicates that the various departments and officers are well trained and acting responsibly, applying good judgment filtered by experience, training, and policy in stressful, dangerous, high-intensity situations. That is a testament to the professionalism and capabilities of the officers. It is not an indictment of the review process. The review process actually worked. In order to indict the review process, a credible critic must identify incidents in which the law was misapplied or the facts were misconstrued or the officer(s) lied or ignored evidence or otherwise did not do their job or acted without integrity.

When the investigations are done, the criminal charges or the civil suits, or both, will be filed with the energetic support and enthusiasm of all of the above.

The family of the deceased will claim that the loved one was murdered or a victim who was deprived of constitutionally guaranteed rights. They are now known as "plaintiffs." Sometimes the interest groups will precipitate the legal action. At the least, they will provide support in terms of time, money, and resources. They will produce a version events that will be characterized by microscopic and infallible hindsight, distorted facts, imputed meanings and intentions, and a series of misconceptions and fallacies that defy the realities discussed at length in this work. They will argue ideology and hindsight rather than legal principle and objective analysis.

Anomalies of time, evidence, or events will be considered proof of conspiracy. Conflicting witness statements will be contrasted, and the most favorable to the plaintiff's version of events will be asserted regardless of credibility or witness self-interest or the naturally occurring variations in perception and recall that afflict all eyewitness accounts. Investigative procedures and policies will be held up to scorn as further evidence of a conspiracy to cover up officer misconduct or defame the victim. A good example is the widely prevalent policy regarding the timing of the official interview of the officer who was involved in the deadly force confrontation.

The prevailing practice in law enforcement is to delay the official interview of the officer for some specified period of time after the event. This is strongly encouraged to provide a reflective interval for the officer to allow the distorting effects of fight or flight to dissipate, and for the trained and professional mind to reassert itself and recall events and sequences more accurately. It provides the officer time to gather emotions and replenish recollections. Plaintiffs and friends of the victim will claim it is evidence of a cover-up conspiracy, a ploy to prepare and coordinate stories, and an example of favoritism not afforded other "murder" suspects. They dispense with any differences between a suspect in a homicide and a police officer acting in the performance of his duty.

However, the differences are definitive. A law enforcement officer involved in a shooting is not suspected of a crime because he shot someone nor is there any reason to doubt that the officer will be available for interview and investigation. The officer is not going to become a fugitive or hide from the authorities. The department isn't going to secrete the officer or spirit him away to a foreign country with an alias and fake ID. The officer responded to a specific criminal act or potentially criminal situation; the officer did not foment one. The presumption is that the officer did not commit a crime. That is not favoritism—it is professionalism. Additionally, a reasonable delay in conducting the official interview is proven to enhance the investigation, not obstruct or subvert it.[15]

Nevertheless, the media will accept the conspiratorial version of events and uncritically publicize it. In the interest of fairness, the media will seek comment from the police department. The departmental spokesman will continue to decline to comment about an investigation while the administrators and management seriously rue the day they ever had to get involved with this mess.

The motivations that spur legal action are unlimited and diverse. Attorneys acting for the plaintiffs take many of these cases on a contingency basis. They do not get paid unless there is a judgment or settlement, in which case they keep a large percentage of the proceeds that result. The plaintiffs themselves commonly do not have to pay a thing—they can sue for free. Certainly, the calculation that there is money to be made somewhere has some influence on the process. The facts and the established law are either unknown, denied, or ignored. The attorneys may believe that if they can cause enough discomfort and controversy in the process that they can force a settlement offer just to end it all. Unfortunately, this tactic is often successful.

At this point, other factors may come into play. The insurance company that indemnifies the community, department, or individual officer may decide that its financial exposure is too large in the event the suit is lost and it will order a settlement of the case, preferring to spend a certain but lesser proffered dollar amount to end it rather than risk the considerably larger sum that would come due if plaintiffs win in court. This is strictly a cost/benefits analysis conducted by the insurance company or the municipality that ignores the right or wrong of the officer's actions as well as issues of principle and precedent. The analysis neither considers nor cares about right or wrong, merely minimizing cost. Frequently, a decision to settle will be made based on the same misrepresentative account using microscopic hindsight, distorted facts, imputed meanings and intentions, misconceptions, biases, and fallacies that have been publicized all along, juxtaposed against the refusal to comment by the authorities.

Once the insurance company or the municipality becomes sufficiently anxious about losing, the urgency of a settlement takes on a life of its own. Plain-

---

15. Artwohl, Alexis, PhD, "Perceptual and Memory Distortion during Officer-Involved Shootings," *FBI Law Enforcement Bulletin*, U.S. Department of Justice, Washington, DC, October 2002, pages 19–22. Research indicates that "traumatic situations" inevitably result in some degree of memory impairment. The research suggests that officers may make more thorough and accurate statements if the interview is delayed at least 24 hours, and they get some sleep in the interim. Sleep helps integrate memories and facilitate both learning and memory integration. This does not preclude an initial immediate "walk-through" briefing to assist the investigators by outlining what happened, when, and where.

tiffs' attorneys rely on this and go public with the version of events most help-ful to maintain the controversy and the emotional investment in the allegations against the department and the officer's heinous disregard for the civil rights and lives of disadvantaged members of the community. The officer will be accused of falsehood, unjustifiable violence, vendetta motivations, criminal intent, and/or sheer negligent incompetence. Spokesmen for the department continue to decline comment about an ongoing matter.

If no settlement is negotiated, the process enters the courts. Ultimately, this is the best thing to happen on behalf of the officer(s) involved. This is why the "fear of suits phobia" can be so harmful. "Fear of suits phobia" impedes effective training, policies, and guidelines by mandating unrealistic proscriptions, expectations, and layers of decision-making solely to prevent legal action—not to enhance the safety of officers and members of the public. When the inevitable legal action occurs anyway, the officer's case is weakened by the myriad of requirements and controls and mandates that "fear of suits phobia" threw up as a preventive measure. In truth, as stressed elsewhere in this book, since legal action *cannot* be prevented, it is imperative to provide realistic training and support that enhances the officer's ability to assess risk, weigh responses, and act decisively to best protect self or others from serious injury. That won't prevent legal action either—but it does provide the single best defense necessary to win the suit.

Suits alleging violations of constitutional rights can be brought in both state and federal courts. As a matter of practice, the suit almost always will be filed in federal court because it is only in federal court that plaintiffs can move beyond the officer(s) involved and implicate the deeper pockets of the department or the municipality (not that these financial considerations have any influence on the course of the legal process, but it is hard to imagine the coterie of attorneys, family members, and supporters being content with the assets of the average patrol officer or detective).

The federal court system is the law enforcement officer's best friend. This is not a matter of bias or favoritism. It is purely a matter of established legal principles and objective reasoning. Once the case enters the federal court system, some things change for the benefit of the officer(s) who are the focus of the whole maelstrom of allegations, invective, and one-sided portrayal of events. First, the facts and issues that are valid and material will be recognized and the inquiry will be limited to them. The clear, established standards discussed in Chapter 3 will be applied—an objectively reasonable officer looking from the eyes of the actual officer in the event. The law is very much on the side of the reasonable law enforcement officer, and it is uniformly and consistently applied in the federal court. Even the occasional aberrant adverse result can be successfully appealed.

To the extent that the U.S. district courts apply established law and precedent in deadly force cases with consistency and with objective analysis, the appellate level does so to an even greater degree and with greater certitude. The most desired result is that the police officer and the department or municipality ("defendants") will be awarded summary judgment or qualified immunity, affirmed on appeal if it is appealed, and the issue is finished. That occurs far more often than not, which is a confrimation that the federal court system is the law enforcement officer's best friend once legal actions are initiated.

Summary judgment is the required remedy when the material facts of the case are not at issue, although it does have to be requested—it is not automatic. Then the judge can apply the law to the facts and issue a summary ruling. A dispute over material facts is the basic purpose for a trial. If there is no dispute, then there is no need for a trial to determine material facts and the judge can simply apply the law and issue a judgment. A disagreement over the relevance of a fact, its substance, or its meaning, is not a dispute that necessarily requires a trial. Neither does the inevitable litany of allegations that unsupported claims or irrelevant facts or fallacious assertions are matters of dispute. If the fact is not material to the issues, it is not relevant to the issue of summary judgment regardless of any dispute about it.

An unfortunate byproduct of the process is that by the time a legal action over the use of deadly force arrives at this point in the federal system, the accused officer(s) is often embittered, apprehensive of possible consequences, and alienated from the community and the legal system. That is certainly an understandable human response, and it may be an unavoidable response. It does not have to be as pervasive or destructive in its effects as it all too frequently is. The law enforcement officer who is the focus of the public and legal controversy looks to his or her department and community for support and vindication. The use of deadly force was in service to the community, fulfilling the responsibilities and duties of the department in the face of imminent injury or death. The eagerness with which the contrary version of events is publicized and accepted can be dismaying. It can be damaging, too, in the long term. It is viewed as a betrayal of trust.

There is a relationship between the fundamental will to act in defense of self and others on the part of law enforcement officers and the fundamental will of the community at large to recognize and accept such acts as preferable to tolerating injured or killed officers and citizens. The relationship is a dynamic one, driven by the community at large to which law enforcement responds in turn. Law enforcement is an integral but subordinate part of the community. As fundamental community will rises or falls, individual police officer decisions to act decisively in the face of clear, and especially non-specific, threats is affected in direct relation. Accordingly, law enforcement has a serious responsibility to generate and sustain community understanding and support—to foster fundamental community will to recognize and accept the necessity for the lawful use of deadly force. This has to be a continuous process of education and honest appraisal because it has to inculcate knowledge, understanding, and facility with the use of deadly force in situations that are not Hollywood stereotypes (armed bank robbers shooting it out as they leave a trail of innocent bodies in their wake). Violent criminals engaging in armed resistance are seldom the focus of sympathetic community outrage. It is the less obvious danger represented by all the other people that police must confront and resolve that needs continuous explanation and education throughout the community. Law enforcement must be prepared to offer thorough, objective, timely, and informational responses in the aftermath of any use of force by an officer.

Realistically, the community at large does not pay much attention to its law enforcement department in the absence of a use-of-force incident. Police "violence" always raises interest levels and is the incentive for controversy. Law enforcement operates in the background, relative to the community at large. The status quo is taken for granted. It is incumbent upon law enforcement to exercise the initiative during the "status quo interregnum" to keep its practices, realities, and policies before the public eye. This interaction will provide a continuing educational enhancement for the general public that can create a basis for informed review, comment, analysis, and support when the status quo is inevitably altered by a sudden deadly force incident.

Every shooting incident will result in an investigation, and many will generate controversy. It is true that the department involved has limited discretion to discuss the incident; it is equally true that there is much about which the department can comment freely and at length. The facts and circumstances of the incident are the subject of investigation and that limits the scope of official comment. But the department can and should explain what the underlying principles and standards are that will guide the investigation (see Chapter 3), and what the general factors and realities are that appertain (much of this book is a source for just that). It should seek to educate and elucidate on the range of topics inherent to any analysis of a deadly force incident. Law enforcement may not be able to describe details of the incident in question, but it can certainly discuss the nature of deadly force incidents and the factors of risk assessment and defense of self and others.

The leadership and management of the department and/or municipality must face the controversy. Although it is proper that they do not comment on the specific facts of an investigation or court case, they can take the opportunity to educate the public in the realities of law enforcement deadly force. They can talk about the issues and factors that the investigation must examine without talking about the details of the case at hand. They can explain factors such as wound ballistics, action/reaction, physiological factors, tactical considerations, and the duties of law enforcement officers to the community. Some segments of the public will always refute or deny an objective discussion of these matters but the large majority of the community will be educated and able to evaluate based on science, physical necessity, and the greater good. None of this requires that the incident under investigation be used as an example. The information is pertinent to all deadly force incidents and investigations. It will counter a lot of misplaced concern and misconceived notions of what happens.

There should not be any changes of policy, procedures, or training doctrines proffered or agreed to until the results of the investigation can be assessed and a dispassionate determination made about whether there is in fact a need for change. Too often, change is seen as a cheap way to avert or abate the controversy regardless of merit. It never works that way. The cost may be deferred until the next deadly force confrontation, and even paid in an otherwise avoidable police death or injury, but it will come due.

One of the most common allegations that will arise in the aftermath of any law enforcement use of deadly force appears in one of two variants.[16] The first variant is that the actions of the officer and the training practices and policies of the department violated the law, and thus comprised a "license to kill" or a "renegade act" imposed upon the community with reckless disregard. However, the truth behind law enforcement training practices and policies is that they are supposed to be defined and constrained by the law. The law has clearly delineated the circumstances within which deadly force may be used, and clearly defined the factors necessary to justify a decision to use deadly force.

Law enforcement recognizes its obligation to establish policies and implement training practices that fall within the scope defined by the law, although it is undeniably true that an individual officer can violate the law—and some do. Those individuals are no less subject to criminal charges and proceedings than any other criminal. They must bear the consequences that their criminal acts incur. However, the decision to use deadly force to prevent an imminent risk of serious injury is not symptomatic of a criminal act. When criminal indictments and charges are instituted against a law enforcement officer for using deadly force, the impetus is predominantly political. The shooting incident

---

16. Both variants feed on the ever-expanding event-specific policies and training prescriptions that "fear of suits phobia" insists upon.

was controversial in the public eye, inflamed by segments of the community, and the filing of criminal charges is a political response to allay the emotional outrage of the affected activists. It is politically driven act, not a public interest one—a refutation of the existence of a civil system of law designed and intended to deal with precisely such issues in which harm was done but without criminal elements. This is patently unfair—but it happens.

In the civil arena, the attempt to use the actions of the individual as characteristic of the policies and practices of the organization is seldom more than a reach for "deeper pockets" that ignores the underlying, and inescapable, truth—police tactics, training, and policies are designed and intended to comport with the law. Although there are departments and jurisdictions in which training is deficient, or departmental policies are politically motivated to nullify criticism or pre-empt some ill-conceived and generalized potential liability, these deficiencies are unlikely to form the basis for successful lawsuits because they are not usually the cause of a constitutional violation. There cannot be a successful action without a violation of a constitutional right (see Chapter 3).

When the law changes, or is interpreted in a manner different than before, the tactics, training, and policies will be modified accordingly. It may not happen uniformly. It may not happen universally or in unison. It often will vary in some specific detail depending upon the federal circuit in which a department is located.[17] But there is a relatively constant coordination and related cross-checking of content that occurs within the universe of law enforcement training in general that over time generates a uniformity of legality throughout. Law enforcement tactics, training, and policies are legal, and great effort is made to keep them consistent with current law. An allegation of illegality is insufficient to justify conciliatory changes or amendments to

---

17. A good example of this is the differentiation of types of search warrants. As a rule, search warrants are meant to be served in daylight hours following a procedure commonly known as "Knock and Announce" that requires officers to make their identity and purpose known and then to wait a reasonable period of time before forcing entry. There are different interpretations of the scope of daylight hours, when and how announcements are made, and the duration of a reasonable period of time. There are also nighttime warrants, "No-Knock" warrants (an authorization to force entry without any prior announcement—a surprise entry) and other forms and conditions of warrant service that are subject to differing specifics among federal circuits. Law enforcement is bound by the rulings of the federal circuit in which it is located. There is no universally binding standard unless the U.S. Supreme Court has established one by a ruling on a circuit case. Of course, Supreme Court rulings are binding on all circuits equally.

policies and doctrines merely to allay criticism or forestall legal action. Neither will happen.

The second variant is the allegation that although the actions of the officer may be "technically" legal, they nevertheless violated "nationally recognized police standards and practices." This allegation is a common one in the aftermath of law enforcement-related deadly force incidents. However, there is no body of nationally recognized police standards and practices other than the body of legal principles and standards established over the years (see Chapter 3). They cannot be produced or reviewed. There is no national authority, no mandate, no central oversight body to define, implement, maintain, and monitor nationally recognized police standards and practices. Usually, the "nationally recognized police standards and practices" envisioned in the allegation are the concepts promoted by an expert witness retained on behalf of the plaintiff who recognizes that the law does not support the allegations being made so some means of judging the officer's actions other than the law must be advanced in order to make those actions appear wrong.

This also requires unrealistic, if not false, assumptions to be accepted as truisms. It must be "true" that the officer in question knew what the adversary intended to do, or knew that his or her (the officer's) actions would *inevitably* result in the opponent attacking or assaulting or acting in an irrational, perhaps threatening, but totally out of character manner. In other words, the officer is at fault for inducing the plaintiff to make a threatening gesture or otherwise act in a way that made it necessary for the office to use deadly force. This conveniently ignores the reality that no law enforcement officer can know what someone will do, and in fact, *most of the time* similar people in similar situations do nothing to threaten the officer. It also exonerates the subject from any responsibility for his own acts. There is no predetermined inevitability to individual reactions, nor is there a talent for prescience created in law enforcement training or practice. These are distractions intended to obscure the fact that the law and the reality of the event do not support the allegations. The officer can only react to what the subject of the event does—or reasonably appears to do within the context of the circumstances.

A second fallacy with this variant of the allegation is that it implies that there exists a standard for judging the legality of law enforcement actions other than the clear standards imposed by the law. The intent is to imply that the expert's guidelines or nationally recognized police standards and practices are legally binding mandates. That raises a host of questions that illustrate the absurdity of the original allegation.

If the "guidelines" or "nationally recognized police standards and practices" are binding, would that be by law or by policy? What legal authority encoded the policy? Where in the law are the terms of the policy constituted? Does a violation of policy represent a violation of a constitutional right? Does a violation of policy represent proof of a legal liability more than a violation of law? Then why use policies in addition to laws to prescribe and limit behavior? Aren't guidelines really aids to assist judgment in situations where it is impossible to foresee every eventuality, and thus not legally binding? Where in the espoused guidelines or nationally recognized police standards and practices is there recognition of a need to assess the risk of injury to others and protect them from it? Do police bear a greater responsibility to protect members of the community from perceived risks, or to act in a way to best ensure the well being of the source of the perceived risk and let the members of the community get by as best they can in the process? And exactly where in the law is that specified?

Ultimately, the argument in this variant is that police are responsible for thoughts, actions, and events over which they really have no control. It requires them to retreat, to abandon their duty to protect themselves and the public. This would ultimately create a vicious circle in which the police can never act responsibly and without liability because inevitably some unforeseeable harm can result—and by the reasoning of this allegation, they must be accountable for not foreseeing the unforeseeable harm. In reality, that is why an objective standard is necessary to judge police actions—not a situational one based on somebody's subjectively preferred outcomes. That objective standard is the law.

It should be apparent that it is impossible to avoid or prevent lawsuits in the aftermath of any use of force by a law enforcement officer. Policies should be formulated that allow an officer to respond based on informed threat assessment. Equipment and tactics must be selected in order to enhance the officer's ability to react to and stop an imminent risk of serious injury to self or others. Training content must be designed to give officers what they need to effectively and efficiently recognize and assess dangerous threats and to formulate the implementation of effective responses. Legal actions cannot be avoided; so the best that a department can do is provide the best training and support to meet the real needs of the officers at work and the members of the community they serve. Doing that provides the single best promise of winning the inevitable lawsuits.

Meanwhile, the individual officer's reaction to involvement in a deadly force incident is as varied as it is unpredictable. It is in many ways insidious, manifesting itself in unforeseen ways, at unpredictable times and with unexpected consequences in the officer's daily life and routine. It can be pernicious in its results. The after-the-fact of a shooting reaction is in many ways a continuance of the intense "fight-or-flight" syndrome, except it becomes a much bigger ordeal that plays out for hours, if not days. As previously noted, by statute all uses of deadly force by law enforcement in the State of Maine are investigated by the state attorney general's office. Maine's AG investigators have an extensive and widely varied exposure to law enforcement officers in the aftermaths of shootings that gives them a valuable and perceptive view of the post-shooting responses:

> "First I think that the fight or flight response that is so well documented is a microcosm of a much bigger chemistry reaction that plays out for hours if not days. Again, I'm not basing any of this on scientific studies or any knowledge in the field of psychology, just what I have seen. After the shots are fired I have seen anger, depression, fear, bewilderment, nervousness and really bad acting. That last one I think comes into play sometimes because as cops I think we have set a subconscious idea or standard for ourselves that goes something like this: '... if this happens to me, I should act a certain way because that's how people are supposed to act when something terrible like this happens' but in reality it comes out weird because it is competing with what we are truly feeling.
>
> Examples of the above in action: Shooting scene where three officers are interviewed who were all witness to the assailant being shot dead. Officer witness one is new on the job, is articulate in his responses to my questions and a good witness. He is visibly shaken but for some reason, probably because he has been taught that cops are tough, he is doing everything in his power to answer with no emotion. His chin quivers when he starts to talk about the moments before the shot is fired and he leans forward covering his chin with his hand as he answers. His answers sound almost robotic and rehearsed as he fights off his own emotions and puts on the tough exterior. He gets through the interview and the second the recorder is turned off he breathes a sigh of relief and with emotion in his voice tells me that it was the toughest thing he has ever had to go through in his life.
>
> Second officer witness has been on for a few years, has seen combat overseas and also answers my questions with very articulate responses, another great witness. This man is seemingly unaffected by what he has seen, it is as if it was any other incident that he has responded to and as if he is simply relaying pertinent information to another officer in the field. This officer was more nervous about talking with an investigator about what had happened than about what he had experienced and even relayed that to me later noting that the interview wasn't as painful as he imagined it would have been.

*Officer witness number three has been on the job for over a decade and like any cop that has worked the road for that long has seen much of what there is to see in this job. He is clearly in a state of shock as he answers my questions, so much so that it almost appears as if he is still trying to figure out if this is really happening. He is clearly still processing what he has seen and even comments that what he saw was a lot to process. After the interview as I walk him out he tells me with tears welling up that it was a really difficult experience to be involved in.*

*In a different shooting investigation I watched the shooter from a distance interacting with his attorney and clearly shaken and upset, still dealing with the remnants of the adrenaline surge that he had just experienced. I watched his demeanor and affect change completely when a fellow officer arrived on scene in street clothes just to support him. The shooter looked vulnerable and was holding back tears. I watched his demeanor change again significantly, almost as if he was reliving the experience, clearly upset, clearly not faking it and clearly taking steps to suppress his feelings through deep breathing as we approached him to discuss plans for the interview and walkthrough.*

*In another incident, the officer was almost killed and undoubtedly saved two lives in the process of returning fire on the assailant. This officer is a perfect example of someone whose training and muscle memory kicked in and worked great under really bad circumstances. After the incident I watched him shaken, exhausted and looking as if he had no direction whatsoever, lost inside his own police department, not physically but mentally. The investigator that interviewed him felt bad leaving him afterwards because he was so affected by what had happened. This officer struggled for a long time after the incident still riding the rollercoaster. He confided in me at a later date that he could barely breathe when he strapped his bulletproof vest on for the first time going back to work after the incident. His physiological response was long and drawn out, he over thought every possible 'what if' and was extremely uncomfortable being referred to as a hero for saving those two people. He will continue to ride that roller coaster for a long time I'm sure."*[18]

Individual officers in the aftermath of a deadly force confrontation are understandably anxious for reassurance that they did the right thing. They will

---

18. James Gioia, Detective, Maine State Attorney General's Office, email exchange with the author, Aug. 18, 2014.

not get that from the process. They will look for vindication through the course of the process, but it will not happen. The process is not concerned with vindicating the officer or commending him for a dangerous and difficult job rightly done. The all-too-human need for vindication will cause much of the bitterness and dismay that arises as frustration and disappointment increase while the process plays out. It is not going to happen and officers should not naively expect it. The process will be resolved through financial considerations, cost/benefit analysis, or relatively esoteric legal determinations that do not speak to right or wrong but merely affirm that the plaintiff's rights were not violated or that no case can be made supporting a constitutional wrong. Few if any participants in the process will tell the officer "You did the right thing—there was no other way."

The officer must seek understanding and vindication from among family, friends, and professional associates. That is the only viable avenue, and the most meaningful source. The officer who experiences this process as it plays out in the aftermath of a deadly force confrontation will be less traumatized and embittered with an honest and objective understanding that there are competing interests involved. These interests will use the officer's intense life-or-death decision making event to pursue issues and priorities that have no bearing on the officer's vindication or exoneration.

The law enforcement officer is as inseparable an element of the community as is the doctor, teacher, waiter, store clerk, or mechanic. The officer lives in the community, sends children to its schools, attends events, pays taxes, shops and browses, and engages others in daily interactions. Law enforcement officers have normal human hopes and aspirations. They share civic pride and a desire for community success and prosperity. They are parents, sons and daughters, husbands and wives. They are people with health issues, bills, family problems, and all the other common problems and daily stresses, routines, and triumphs. But unlike any other member of the community they are charged with the protection and preservation of that society and community for the benefit of all—themselves included. The risks of their profession are recognized, but little understood.

The law enforcement officer must understand that the relentless actions of the few that are bitterly and rightly perceived as condemnatory or defamatory are not the judgment of the community. Society extends the privilege of the benefit of the doubt—the law enforcement community must nurture that privilege with frank and objective information that will augment and improve wider and continued societal understanding of the risks, factors, and issues of deadly force confrontations.

After all, there is a covenant between the men and women who are the law enforcement officers out and about within their respective communities, and all the people who are in sum the composition of the communities (including fellow law enforcement officers).

> *"If you need me, I will be there for you. I will risk injury or death to get to you, because that is my promise."*[19]

---

19. The quotation is called the law enforcement promise. It is credited to James D. Harris, Los Angeles County Sheriff's Department, and cited by Lawrence M. Blum, PhD, in his book, *Force Under Pressure—How Cops Live and Why They Die*, New York, Lantern Books, Booklight Inc., 2000, Acknowledgments, page vii.

# Chapter 13

# The Plaintiffs' Dilemma

In legal actions, as in all disputes, there are always two sides to the story. As we have made clear throughout this book, the legal standards that govern the use of force (deadly and non-deadly) by law enforcement have been well and long established by the U.S. Supreme Court. Further, the standards have been consistently clarified and reaffirmed by the Court. They are durable and increasingly less susceptible to exceptions and nuanced differences of interpretation. Clarification and reaffirmation has constituted an informed recognition of the inescapable realities of deadly force confrontations that have also been explained at length in this book.

The application of these standards to an examination of the justification of use of force by law enforcement are grounded in these realities — action/reaction cycles, wound ballistics, physiological effects, tactical considerations, and the way such realities influence risk assessment and the consignment of consequences. The net effect is that the law and its application are weighted to the benefit of the police (who must assume the danger of great harm if not death) on behalf of the public (whose safety individually and in general is threatened by the risk of harm) at the expense of the one who creates that jeopardy.

This does not in any way imply that individual law enforcement officers do not use unreasonable force, or cannot be held accountable when they do. That does happen, but the occurrence is much less common than implied by the media or alleged by the plaintiffs' bar.[1]

The most prevalent instances of excessive force involve excessive *non-deadly* force. It will occur in several characteristic circumstances. One is the loss of professionalism for any of a number of innately human reasons, such as anger,

---

1. As discussed in Chapter 12 — Aftermath & Impact, the media thrives on conflict. In the absence of an objective account supported by evidence and knowledge of the issues, it will publish what it can get and that is the unfiltered allegations and suppositions of those with an agenda — personal or otherwise. The system does not favor the frank and unrestrained revelation of details, facts, realities, and legal and training standards and their applications to preserve the integrity of the legal processes.

humiliation, or demeaning treatment that incites the officer to react with an extra punch, a punitive kick, or a retributive blow to get even — so-called "street justice" in an overly generalized sense. Second, there can arise an institutional pattern of unreasonable force. This occurs when the "way we do it on the street"[2] creates a general form and degree of force that is expected and utilized indiscriminately. Non-deadly force is specifically limited to that degree of force reasonably necessary to achieve a legitimate law enforcement purpose. It must be necessary to the purpose and yet proportional to the circumstances. For example, the initial "entry level" force (see Chapter 10 — Non-Deadly Force) used to subdue and control a drunk and disorderly college student at a stadium tailgate party should be different than the initial force used to subdue and control a drunk and disorderly professional logger in a remote biker bar with a history of assaultive behavior. And yet, an institutional pattern of handling both the exact same way can arise because "that's the way we do it on the street," and that results in unreasonable force being used in the lesser encounters.[3] Any policy, practice or custom that promotes indiscriminate decision-making will inevitably lead to systemic excesses of force. It nullifies the critical element of officer judgment filtered through officer training, experience, capabilities and observations.

A third circumstance that can contribute to events of unreasonable non-deadly force is the adoption of new and highly promoted technological tools. The early history of the Taser is an excellent example. It becomes viewed as a "magic shield" that can resolve all compliance and control issues indiscriminately without the officer having to exercise any judgment or discretionary decision making. That in turn results in such patently unreasonable uses that have occurred such as "tasing" an uncooperative lady to make her get out of her car, or "tasing" an uncooperative person over and over until he or she presents a hand to be cuffed. (See Chapter 10 — Non-Deadly Force)

The relative rarity of incidents in which law enforcement officers use deadly force unreasonably is stark in comparison. It is attributable to several factors. Law enforcement officers are no more disposed to killing someone than is the

---

2. Tactics and practices that are preferred and expected of officers, and passed on and sustained by widely continued use and reinforcement by peer approval. Dissimilar practices (usually new, or training academy based) are dismissively considered "school tactics — not the way we do it on the street."

3. In one city whose practices the author was asked to review, a significant number of patrol officers routinely resolved every confrontation with the same first response at the first sign of uncooperative or noncompliant behavior — essentially, knock them down and kick them in the head — regardless of the circumstance. This tactic was used indiscriminately on college students, panhandlers, drunks, and aggravated citizens.

average citizen. A law enforcement officer may lose his temper and lash out, but not with deadly force. A loss of professionalism as mentioned above constitutes an emotional reaction to exert control and dominance, to "show him who's boss," to ignore training and discipline and exact retribution—not to kill him. The permanent and irremediable consequences of using deadly force and the cultural conventions against killing militate against the unreasonable use of deadly force. They also contribute to the much evident propensity of law enforcement officers to hesitate, to delay using deadly force far beyond the point in a confrontation where they could justifiably do so, at the cost of increased risk to themselves and others. All of which is not to say that the unreasonable use of deadly force does not happen at all. It does—but it is extremely rare. As well, the occasional "in-custody" deaths that create headlines and public outrage are characteristically unintentional deaths attributed to stress, physical and health impairments, chronic drug use, and/or the effects of the use of non-deadly force. These deaths are rare and do not occur from a use of deadly force.

Because the law and its application are well established, plaintiffs have a high bar to overcome to establish that a particular use of force was unreasonable. The first legal hurdle will be a motion for summary judgment and/or qualified immunity by the defendant police officer. By direction of the Supreme Court, the ruling court will apply the law to the material facts of the case only, ignoring as irrelevant nonmaterial facts and suppositional claims. Material facts are those that pertain to the perception of risk within the totality of circumstances in which the decision to use deadly force was made. The established legal principles that affirm and allow for the realities of deadly force incidents severely limit the scope of inquiry allowed. (See Chapter 3)

Plaintiffs will go to great lengths in an effort to establish facts as material that upon inspection are not. They will argue peripheral facts about an officer's tactical decisions or qualifications, the subject's state of mind or lack of intent or lack of capacity, the failure to utilize lesser means of force, the lack of availability of lesser means, the timing of the decision to use deadly force rather than wait longer, the lack of injury to anybody else, the perceptions of other officers, victims, and even distant witnesses who do not use deadly force or do not feel threatened, mythological doctrines attributed to law enforcement such as "shoot to kill," violations of policy, violations of training guidelines, disparities in witness statements, disparities in police statements, inconsistencies between officer narratives and forensic evidence, and disparities between statements and video evidence. The list of material irrelevancies is endless. The goal is to create a factual dispute to stave off summary judgment.

It is increasingly apparent that plaintiffs' attorneys in general are slowly understanding and accepting the established, and well defined, nature of deadly force law as it has been constituted and affirmed beginning with *Garner*.[4] It is not uncommon now for plaintiffs to ultimately agree (albeit grudgingly) that the decision to shoot may have been justified at the moment it was made, but the officer was wrong (for a litany of reasons—see the examples in the paragraph above) in what was done or decided or perceived during the preceding events and therefore it is the officer who precipitated the confluence of events that created the moment when deadly force was justifiably used. And that, of course, constructs the argument that the law enforcement officer was responsible, negligent, or otherwise at fault. The focus is upon the officer. The choices and actions of the person with whom the officer was interacting are ignored, except to the degree that they are alleged to have been induced by the officer.

Invariably, the plaintiff will begin with the deadly force event and work backwards—the very definition of 20/20 hindsight expressly prohibited by the Supreme Court. A confrontation occurs and at some point the subject creates a threat of imminent risk of serious injury. That subject is killed or wounded because a police officer decides to use deadly force to stop that threat. The death or injury of the subject is the basis of the claim. Plaintiffs work backwards from that event, focusing on every detail that could have been different and thus would have avoided that critical moment when deadly force was regrettably justified. What the officer did, as opposed to what could have been done, is second-guessed. Alternatives will be identified and the argument will be that these alternatives were obligations that the officer failed to recognize or perform. Thus, as goes the claim, the officer was negligent or incompetent and induced the moment in which deadly force was used—justifiably, but only because the failings of the officer engendered the critical moment when it became necessary.

This, of course, imputes a duty to the officer to know what is going to happen, to read minds and clairvoyantly ascertain actions and events. It ascribes to the officer a superhuman ability to function in a moment of sudden, extraordinarily traumatic, life-threatening stress with the cool, calm, and unerring judgment, perception, and responses of a pre-programmed machine. When the fully human officer does not rise to that standard of ability, it is the fault of the officer. It ignores the nature of the event and the intrinsic limitations of the human responses to stress. And it gives overriding weight, in hindsight, to factors that the officer could not know, did not know, or had no way of assessing in the time available to make immediately urgent decisions about how

---

4. *Tennessee v. Garner*, 471 U.S. 1 (1985).

to best protect his safety and that of others. This reasoning leads to irrational contradictions when carried out to its logical consequences. For example, the allegation is common that an officer who made a mistake, or who was not qualified with the weapon he used, or violated a policy provision was therefore not justified in using deadly force in the circumstances. But that presumes the ultimate conclusion that the officer forfeits the right to defend his life—a conclusion that is ridiculous on its face. The logical supposition is that officers have a greater duty to protect the safety and well-being of the person creating the threat than they do to protect themselves and others against the dire consequences of that threat.[5] This supposition mandates that the well-being of the person posing the threat of harm is privileged over the well-being of the law enforcement officers confronting the threat, or the public put at risk by the threat.

On August 28, 2010, in Hoonah, Alaska, two police officers (Matthew Tokuoka and Tony Wallace) were shot and killed by John Marvin. Marvin was long recognized in the community as "crazy"—he was a loner, often belligerent, erratic in behavior, who made people uncomfortable. He was well known to the police, who had often responded to citizen complaints about him trespassing or hanging around inside a store alienating customers. One year prior to the shooting, a woman found Marvin standing in her living room and registered a complaint. The two officers (Tokuoka and Wallace) went to Marvin's home to serve a misdemeanor trespass summons. Marvin refused to open his door and appeared to barricade himself inside. The two officers withdrew and called their chief for advice and assistance. As they waited, Marvin slipped out the back of his house, sneaked around behind the officers, and launched an assault on them. He was unarmed—it was a strictly physical surprise assault from behind. The two officers wrestled on the ground with him and ultimately subdued him physically and with the use of a Taser. The resultant charges were dropped following Marvin's agreement to undergo therapy.

One year later, Tokuoka and his family stopped at the Hoonah public dump—a trash receptacle in a parking lot beside the town's liquor store. The dumpster is over 100 yards away and across the street from Marvin's house.

---

5. See Chapter 15—Case Histories: *Joanne Woodward, Administratrix of the Estate of Robert Woodward, et al. v. Town of Brattleboro, Marshall Holbrook and Terrance Parker*, USDC, District of Vermont, Civil No: 1:02CV35, in which plaintiff's expert asserted the officers should never have entered the building in the first place, noting that if somebody had gotten hurt because they didn't enter, it would have been tragic but they would have the satisfaction of knowing that they had done the right thing. The details are presented in the case history.

Tokuoka's wife Haley saw Marvin in a lighted downstairs window banging a box on the floor. Soon thereafter, the lights went out and she could no longer see Marvin. Shortly after, Wallace pulled in behind the Tokuokas in his patrol vehicle and briefly flashed his lights. He may have chirped his siren—accounts differ. His mother was with him as part of an approved ride-along during her visit. Haley told Wallace what she had seen and he turned, briefly shined his light at Marvin's downstairs window (about 2 seconds), then, seeing nothing, turned his back and leaned on the Tokuoka car, playing with the children inside while Matthew and Haley were chatting with his (Wallace's) mother in the cruiser.

At this point, Marvin, from inside a darkened room upstairs in his house, shot Wallace twice in the back with a scoped hunting rifle using a prepared shooting position. Wallace went down and Tokuoka went to his aid, yelling at Haley to get out of there. Haley started to drive away with her children and Matthew stopped her long enough to drag Wallace out of the way of the car. Haley left the scene and Matthew Tokuoka was dragging Wallace to cover while using Wallace's chest mic to call for help when Marvin shot Tokuoka twice in the chest. Both officers died from their wounds. Marvin was convicted and sentenced to consecutive life terms in prison.

Haley Tokuoka ultimately filed suit against the town of Hoonah, despite having received substantial benefits from Alaska Workman's Compensation and the federal death benefits awarded for on-duty law enforcement deaths. She alleged that Hoonah police officer Wallace negligently caused Hoonah police officer Tokuoka's death because of a lack of training in dealing with the mentally ill, and his (Wallace's) negligence and his deficiency in following established police practices and procedures.[6] The "expert" retained on her behalf adamantly maintained that Marvin's murderous behavior was provoked by Wallace from 100 yards away, and that proper, reasonable police practices required Hoonah police officers to avoid letting Marvin see them even in the routine exercise of their duties independently of any activity by Marvin! He said that should a traffic stop be necessary in the vicinity of Marvin's house, the officers should wait until they were out of sight before initiating any lights or sirens to effect the stop, and if they had to respond to a complaint at the liquor store, for example, they should use their vehicles for cover to enter and exit the store. He said that properly trained officers would insure that they did not do anything within rifle range to unnecessarily attract Marvin's attention.

---

6. *Tokuoka v. City of Hoonah*, Superior Court State of Alaska, First Judicial District at Juneau, Case No: 1JU-12-776 CI, Plaintiffs' Complaint, 8/17/2012. The case went to jury trial in April 2015. On April 13, 2015, the jury returned a verdict for the City of Hoonah.

According to this expert, Marvin was so manifestly dangerous that the Hoonah police officers dared not attract his attention, based on his prior behavior and interactions with police, even though there was absolutely nothing in Marvin's history other than verbal belligerence, erratic behavior, and one incident of physical assault. Nothing about Marvin or his past history would have enabled even a forensic psychiatrist to foresee that he would shoot down two police officers from a hidden location 100 yards away while they were engaged in innocent activities irrelevant to Marvin in a public facility remote from his location. But this is typical of the illogical lengths to which plaintiffs' experts will go. Proper policing in Hoonah, according to him, required that officers avoid being seen by Marvin, as though some bubble of isolation at least a "rifle shot" in diameter surrounded him. I suppose that also meant they should monitor his movements in order to direct officers where they could and could not safely go as Marvin moved about the town. The absurdity is beyond parody, but it is not unique to this particular case.

The supposition that the welfare of the person causing the problem supersedes that of the police or the public is even more pronounced when the situation involves a person who is mentally ill or "emotionally disturbed." But law enforcement officers cannot be required to make special accommodations when confronting violent, life-threatening, mentally ill persons to ascertain the causes of dangerous behavior instead of dealing with its effects. Law enforcement officers cannot be held accountable for failing to exercise prescience in manifestly dangerous situations in which people are acting non-compliantly and in a manner consistent with causing serious harm. The imposition of unrealistic expectations will result in hesitation and delay during emergency situations, and result in more officers, and more innocent bystanders, being unreasonably injured and killed. The legal standards established by the Supreme Court recognize and account for this reality, and the lower courts understand it in their application of those standards and strictures.

Ultimately, the basic legal issue is simple—was the officer's perception of imminent risk of serious injury reasonable within the totality of circumstances when the decision to use deadly force was made? Plaintiffs strive mightily to adduce contested facts, subjective suppositions, and alleged duties disparate to the focused and objective examination required to answer that basic question. It all culminates in the opinions of so-called experts relied upon by plaintiffs' attorneys to substantiate their allegations.

Plaintiffs' experts will try to conflate the right of self-defense with legal restrictions and other rights, implying if not stating outright that self-defense is contingent upon the legality of other actions and events, when it is not. A police officer retains the right to defend himself against a reasonably perceived threat of imminent serious injury regardless of preceding events. Probable cause to arrest is not a precondition to the justified use of deadly force. People who are not subject to warrants or even the focus of investigative attention have attacked officers. Officers who are in error (good faith) do not lose the right to defend themselves—the choices and actions of the one they confront will establish the need for self-defense, not the legal necessities for arrest or entry or investigation. Officers react to what others do, and if what others do creates a reasonable perception of imminent serious harm, then the officer may use deadly force to stop it—independent of probable cause for arrest, existence of a warrant, or proper application of departmental policy. It is a stand-alone, fact-specific, independent, case-by-case analysis.

The plaintiffs' "experts" of this world argue that the justification for using deadly force is necessarily contingent upon, and subordinate to, extraneous legal/policy restrictions—must have probable cause, must have a warrant, must have proof, must have all manner of predicate factors ignoring what the individual actually did, the circumstances in which it was done, and what the officer saw, knew, or reasonably should have known. If that set of factors at the moment the decision to use deadly force was made support or create a perception of imminent or actual serious harm, deadly force is justified. All else becomes irrelevant regarding the use of deadly force because to make those other factors controlling requires an officer to passively accept being hurt if he lacks or violates any of those predicate conditions. That is absurd. That is further reason why law enforcement gets the benefit of the doubt.

Following are the expert opinions from four use-of-force cases, written by four *different* experts. These four opinions are exemplars of the nature and content of the allegations plaintiffs will make in attempting to overcome the hurdles of the otherwise unambiguous and unequivocal legal principles regarding the law enforcement use of deadly force.

Each case history begins with a narrative of the facts and sequence of events in the incident. The narrative is followed by the redacted report prepared by the plaintiff's expert in that case.[7] To the extent possible, we have also retained the original format used in each of the plaintiff's expert reports below. Following each expert report is a commentary regarding that report based on a rebuttal to the expert's opinion that was done as part of the respective case

---

7. The only information redacted is each expert's identity, credentials, background, and previous case experience. The case-pertinent analysis and opinion of each expert is presented unexpurgated, and unedited, including the original writer's emphases (bold and italic fonts). The typos, misstatements, and assorted errors that are more or less evident in each report are as found in the originals.

proceedings. There is a common thread throughout these examples. The plaintiff will diligently attempt to transform irrelevant facts into material facts in the mind of the judge to ward off summary judgment. Unfortunately, that will work sometimes with judges unwilling to make the distinction, or ignorant of the realities that underlie those distinctions. Then the case goes to trial to determine what the facts are.

# Case History #1

## Lisa Michelle Mena, et al. v. United States
U.S. District Court, Western District of Texas, El Paso Division
Civil No: EP-10-CV-282KC

On August 8, 2007, Senior U.S. Border Patrol Agent (BPA) Brian E. Ault, El Paso Texas Border Patrol Station, was on duty and assigned line watch duties. He was outside his vehicle just north of the bridge that spans the American Canal when he heard popping sounds coming from the border fence that parallels the Rio Grande River south of his location. As he walked across the bridge over the canal he saw four persons passing through a newly cut hole in the fence—the source of the popping noises he had heard.

The fence is a barrier between the northern cement embankment (apron) of the Rio Grande River and the levee road. The levee road (U.S. territory) is a gravel roadway that roughly parallels the Rio Grande providing access along the international boundary with Mexico. The fence itself is approximately ten feet tall. Its upper portion is chain link and its bottom structure is a galvanized oval patterned material thicker and heavier than chain link.

BPA Ault watched the four persons cross the levee road and walk west along the fence that runs along the south side of the American Canal. They were approaching his position on the bridge over the canal.

BPA Ault identified himself and attempted to apprehend the three men and one woman. All four reversed course and ran in the direction of the hole in the border fence. BPA Ault pursued them. He apprehended the fleeing woman [Contreras] approximately ten feet north of the hole in the fence. He saw one male standing nearby just north and east of the hole and a second male just on the other side of the fence yelling at him and waving a set of bolt cutters, banging them against the fence as he yelled at Ault. The man also yelled at Contreras urging her to resist BPA Ault. BPA Ault recognized the man as a smuggler who had assaulted Border Patrol personnel in the past, including BPA Ault recently. BPA Ault had lost sight of the third male.

As BPA Ault secured the woman, the unknown male nearby on the north side of the fence went through the hole and down onto the river apron. BPA Ault saw the second male with the bolt cutters lean through the hole in the fence. He was standing on the south side with his head, upper torso, and arms north of the fence extended through the hole. BPA Ault saw him reach down and pick up a rock from the ground and believed he was about to get "rocked."[8] The man raised the rock as if to throw it at BPA Ault, who was about ten feet away with the woman on her knees and in custody. BPA Ault drew and fired four shots at the man who fell back out of the hole in the fence and was helped across the Rio Grande by an unknown person who abandoned him once they were on the Mexican side of the river.

Mexican police were notified and directed to the location of the subject, later identified as Jose Alejandro Ortiz-Castillo. Ortiz was found dead in the location he had been abandoned by his unknown companion. He sustained three gunshot wounds, one of which was determined to be fatal.

## Case History #1: Plaintiff's Expert #1[9]

Agent Ault has testified that prior to that night he had multiple contacts with Mr. Ortiz-Castillo with the last occurring on July 29, 2007, just ten days prior to the date of this shooting. During that altercation Agent Ault has testified that he had confronted Mr. Ortiz-Castillo and another unidentified Mexican male apparently smuggling an illegal alien Mexican female thru a hole that had been cut in the border fence. Agent Ault testified that he was able to grab the female subject under the arms while she was trying to get back to the south side of the fence and was ultimately successful is pulling her back through the hole in the fence where he arrested her.

Agent Ault described that at the time, Mr. Ortiz-Castillo stood on the south side of the fence gesturing to Agent Ault with a raised pare of bolt cutters, shouting threats and obscenities. Agent Ault described how Mr. Ortiz-Castillo would match his evasive movements in his attempt to avoid being hit through the open hole in the fence by the raised bolt cutters. Ultimately Agent Ault decided that the use of Intermediate force was necessary and he sprayed Mr. Ortiz-Castillo, with OC Spray. In doing so, Mr. Ortiz-Castillo, was forced to

---

8. A USBP colloquialism that describes the act of an illegal immigrant throwing rocks at agents. It happens commonly along the border—agents get "rocked" in their cars and on foot. The potential for serious injury is obvious.

9. Note: This report is presented verbatim—misspellings, grammar, and syntax are in the original.

cease his assault, and after dropping the bolt cutters fled the immediate area. Agent Ault states that at that point Mr. Ortiz-Castillo's associate picked up the discarded bolt cutters and began to threaten Agent Ault in a similar manner but from a greater distance away.

On the date of the shooting, Agent Ault testified that he had been somewhat north of the 2nd Street crossing responding to directions from the surveillance camera operators regarding sighting of possible illegal aliens, or "Bodies" in the area. Upon failing to find the suspects, he returned to the 2nd Street crossing adjacent to fence gate #21.

Agent Ault parked his vehicle out of sight on the north of the canal crossing and walked to approximately the center of the bridge. At that time Agent Ault reports hearing the distinct sound of bolt cutters being used on the expanded metal fence just to the southeast. He can see an individual at the south side of the fence line cutting the fence. Later he estimated that a 3' by 3' "L" shaped cut had been made in the fence while he was watching. It should be noted that such a cut would take on the order of 36 individual cuts of the heavy gauge expanded metal fence.

However, even during the time that the individual was cutting the fence in an obvious illegal entry and smuggling attempt, Agent Ault has testified that he didn't believe it was necessary to contact backup Agents or the surveillance camera operators who would clearly have cameras capable of covering the area of intrusion.

Agent Ault waited and watched while four individuals, three males and one female climbed thru the cut in the fence and grouped on the north side on the fence on the levee road. Again, Agent Ault didn't notify backup Agents or the surveillance camera operators of the ongoing criminal activity. Agent Ault waited until the four individuals began walking west along the north side fence line of the levee and drew nearer to his position of the bridge before calling out to them and identifying himself as a Border Patrol Agent. Again, Agent Ault didn't notify backup Agents or the surveillance camera operators of the ongoing criminal activity when he clearly had the time to do so.

By this time, Agent Ault knew that he would be dealing with four individuals who were quickly nearing an avenue of escape, being the bridge that he was on and yet he still failed to alert any backup or the surveillance camera operators.

By this time Agent Ault was ignoring the customary and typical police practices of calling for backup when confronted by multiple suspects, something that would not only serve to provide more security for him but also afford resources to better insure the safe and effective capture of not only the "Coyotes" but their clients as well.

As might be expected, when Agent Ault identified himself, all four ran back to the cut in the fence in order to escape. Agent Ault called for them to stop and not move but Mr. Ortiz-Castillo and his unknown associate both managed to escape through the cut in the fence. Mr. Ortiz-Castillo and his associate called to the male and female still on the north side of the fence, later identified as Jesus Francisco Melendez Rivero and Laura Contreras-Escarcega, telling them to run and climb through the cut in the fence. Ultimately Jesus Francisco Melendez Rivero did just that and escaped to the south side of the fence.

At this point Laura Contreras-Escarcega apparently elected to submit to the orders of Agent Ault and knelt down on the levee road. Agent Ault describes this point as a standoff and a period of verbal altercation. Again Agent Ault does not call for backup or to alert the surveillance camera operators of the situation, when clearly he has the time to do so.

Agent Ault then describes how he approaches Mr. Ortiz-Castillo near the fence and asks him if he remembers him, obviously referring the incident ten days prior when he has successfully used intermediate force against him by spraying him with OC spray. Agent Ault describes that apparently this got Mr. Ortiz-Castillo's attention as he got quiet and seemed more intense.

Agent Ault described that he then approached Ms. Contreras-Escarcega as she was kneeling on the roadway and inexplicably knelt down behind her to further affect her arrest. When Agent Ault knelt down behind Ms. Contreras-Escarcega, it actually placed him in a more awkward position then standing. Prisoners are commanded to kneel so as to place them in an awkward position meant to prevent them from moving about readily and keep them from running. When Agent Ault did this he effectively put these constraints on himself.

Agent Ault then describes that when he looks back at Mr. Ortiz-Castillo, he sees that he has placed his upper torso thru the cut in the fence and has the bolt cutters in his right hand and is waiving it in a threatening manner and cursing him. The presence of the raised bolt cutters apparently didn't cause Agent Ault to use Deadly force. When Agent Ault noticed Mr. Ortiz-Castillo reached across his body with his left hand, and grab something, he didn't know what it was until Mr. Ortiz-Castillo raised his left hand and Agent Ault could see a rock pinned in his hand by his thumb. It was at this moment that Agent Ault says that he reacted to what he thought was an imminent threat of death to him by drawing his weapon from his holster and firing four times at Mr. Ortiz-Castillo.

Mr. Ortiz-Castillo, was struck three times in the body when the four rounds were fired at him. The first two bullets impacted him in the right forearm and elbow and also through the left side of his body as depicted in the below set of 3-D scene captures.[10]

The above view [screen shot 1] shows the trajectories of the three rounds fired that struck the body of Mr. Ortiz-Castillo. The placement of the trajectory lines was done by using a combination of the autopsy measurements and the placement estimates provided by Agent Ault. As can be seen, two of the bullets enter Mr. Ortiz-Castillo, from the same direction.

The below screen capture [screen shot 2] shows a view looking from behind the position of Agent Ault.

After the first two shots hit Mr. Ortiz-Castillo, a third shot hit him as depicted in the below screen shots [screen shot 3]. Note at this point Mr. Ortiz-Castillo has turned clockwise to his right as if backing out of the cut in the fence when he is hit the third time.

The below screen shot [screen shot 4] shows the scale view from behind Agent Ault when the third bullet strikes Mr. Ortiz-Castillo.

With regard to the threat of imminent Serious Bodily Injury or Death, witnesses, Ms. Contreras-Escarcega and Jesus Francisco Melendez Rivero, both state that the person in the fence line having at first picked up a rock, didn't throw it but instead dropped it to the ground before the shooting. Therefore there would not have been the imminent death threat described by Agent Ault just before he fired on Mr. Ortiz-Castillo. And therefore the Use of Deadly Force by Agent Ault would not have been justified.

Taking into consideration the description of the events as told by Agent Ault, the following considerations should be made: First, at the time of the alleged threat of imminent serious bodily injury or death, Mr. Ortiz-Castillo, was impinged within the confines of the "L" shaped cut in the fencing. Such a condition would have seriously restricted his upper body movements, especially with regard to throwing a rock. This restriction would have obviously prevented Mr. Ortiz-Castillo from "winding up" for a throw and would have in effect caused him to have to push or shove the rock forward instead of throwing it forward from behind the back in a normal fashion.

---

10. **Note:** The report includes four screen captures from a 3D computer simulation that [Expert #1] created based on autopsy results and *estimated* positions and movements. [Expert #1] also made unsupported assumptions about such basic data as the sequence of gunshots and the timing and direction of movement of the individuals' torsos and arms, the subject at the moment a specific bullet strikes him, among other things. It should be obvious that such a simulation is sheer speculation intended to illustrate predetermined subjective opinions, at specific moments frozen in simulated time as though they were factual depictions of real events. The screen shots have been excised for brevity—the captions have been retained to illustrate the disingenuous claims based on them.

In addition, Agent Ault testified that it was only when he saw the upraised hand with the rock exposed, that he reacted, drawing his weapon and firing. Agent Ault admits that the rock was never thrown, and that he doesn't know where it went to. From a time analysis, it is evident that Mr. Ortiz-Castillo, was not intending to throw the rock when he raised his left hand. If he had, then the rock would have been thrown well before Agent Ault had a chance to draw his weapon, let alone fire four times. This is based on the fact that all human beings require a certain Detection, Perception and Reaction process before taking any physical action. Typically, once this reaction process starts it takes approximately 1.5 seconds for the average person to physically respond to an unexpected stimulus. Considering that Agent Ault would have been in a heightened state of awareness, it would not be inappropriate to reduce this time to 1 second. Then the drawing of the weapon has to take place and this takes an additional time period. To this I would assign a nominal time period of 1 second. Agent Ault then needs to point the weapon, aim and commence firing. For this it would not be unreasonable to assign another 1 second, for a total of approximately 3 seconds.

Considering the time that it will take Agent Ault to react and fire, it is very unlikely that Mr. Ortiz-Castillo would have failed to somehow throw the rock if that had been his intent when he allegedly raised his left hand. Yet Agent Ault admits that the rock was never thrown.

It should also be noted that ten days prior Agent Ault was faced with almost the same circumstances with Mr. Ortiz-Castillo, yet he chose to make use of intermediate force to quell the assault and not Deadly Force as in this case.

Based on the above, it is my opinion that Agent Ault was not faced with a substantial risk that Mr. Ortiz-Castillo would cause seriously bodily injury or death at the point that he took Deadly Force against him. Therefore Agent Ault was not justified is using Deadly Force against Mr. Ortiz-Castillo on the evening of August 08, 2007.

## Case History #1: Discussion of Expert #1 Opinion

[Expert #1] makes no mention of the standards for the use of deadly force by law enforcement established by the U.S. Supreme Court, or the equally clear standard provided by the Court for judging the use of deadly force. [Expert #1] merely notes that Agent Ault expressed a fear of imminent death and then proceeds to propose an assessment based on after-the-fact assumptions and speculation that he argues proves that there was no "*substantial risk*" posed by Mr. Ortiz-Castillo. That is a misleading redefinition of the actual standard of risk that is applied by the law, by policy, and in training and practice.

To the contrary, deadly force policies implemented by law enforcement institutions offer objective standards, in compliance with the dictates of the U.S. Supreme Court, for assessing any use of force. The policies also establish the bounds for training officers in the proper and justified circumstances in which deadly force may be used. Specifically, deadly force may be used to prevent the *imminent risk* (NOT *substantial risk*) of death or serious injury to self and others.

First, [Expert #1] asserts that Mr. Ortiz-Castillo was so inhibited by his position within the cutout section of fence that he could not have thrown the rock " ... *forward from behind the back in a normal fashion*." Overlooking [Expert #1]'s odd description of a normal throw coming from behind the back, he ignores the fact that Agent Ault was within 10–12 feet of Mr. Ortiz-Castillo. That is literally point-blank range for rock throwing—it would not require much of a throw, or much throwing talent, to hit Agent Ault in the head with a rock from 10–12 feet away. There is no way to know how much injury a rock to the head would cause, or whether additional rocks would follow, or whether Mr. Ortiz-Castillo would continue his attack in other forms—nor is there any reason that Agent Ault had to wait to find out before reacting to insure his safety.

[Expert #1] assumes that even if Mr. Ortiz-Castillo threw a rock it would not have caused any injury, that no more rocks would have been thrown nor any other form of attack initiated. There is no possible way that Agent Ault could know any of that even if it were so. He had been threatened with attack with a rock at very close range. He was in a location where such attacks were common and increasing. He was confronting an individual he believed to be engaged in human smuggling—precisely the type of activity and individual responsible for most of the assaults on U.S. Border Patrol agents. He had no reason—legally, under policy, or by virtue of his training or experience—to believe one rock was the totality of the attack, or to wait and see if any further attack was made.

Mr. Ortiz-Castillo made his hostile intent unmistakable. Agent Ault believed the imminent assault was real and employed deadly force to prevent it from continuing. That is not unreasonable. In fact, the ideal use of deadly force is preemptive in nature, utilized to prevent a reasonably perceived *imminent* risk of injury from becoming an unmistakable *actual* attempt to injure.

Second, [Expert #1] states, "*From a time analysis, it is evident that Mr. Ortiz-Castillo, was not intending to throw the rock when he raised his left hand. If he had, then the rock would have been thrown well before Agent **Ault** had a chance to draw his weapon, let alone fire four times.*"

[Expert #1] ignores the relevant issue. The question is not whether it can be imputed after the fact whether Mr. Ortiz-Castillo intended to injure Agent Ault because he did not actually throw the rock before Agent Ault shot him.

The question is whether Agent Ault's perception of an imminent risk of serious injury was reasonable under the circumstances. He was looking at an aggressive and hostile individual he recognized from previous encounters who was acting in a threatening and belligerent manner in circumstances consistent with past attacks against Border Patrol agents. That individual was acting in a manner consistent with initiating a rock attack at point-blank range. Agent Ault was not shielded against such an attack. He lacked cover. Under these circumstances, Agent Ault's perception of an imminent risk of serious injury was reasonable.

Law enforcement officers in general, and Agent Ault in particular, are authorized to use deadly force " ... when the officer has a reasonable belief that the subject of such force poses an imminent danger of death or serious physical injury to the officer or to another person."[11] Getting hit with a rock from 10–12 feet away poses a manifest risk of serious injury that entails an even more serious risk of being incapacitated or debilitated. This in turn creates a far more serious risk of injury or death, for example by being shot with one's own gun.

[Expert #1] believes that because the rock was not actually thrown by Mr. Ortiz-Castillo before Agent Ault shot him, there could not have been a real threat to Agent Ault. This supposition ignores the very real risk of injury under *these particular* conditions and is disingenuous at best. Clearly, Agent Ault's perception of imminent risk was reasonable under the circumstances.

When Mr. Ortiz-Castillo made his threats and raised the rock in a manner consistent with throwing it, Agent Ault was under no obligation to wait and see what would happen. He could only act upon what he saw and knew, and what he believed might happen next. Waiting to see what an attacker does next is an unnecessary assumption of risk. His actions must not be judged after the fact with the clarity of 20/20 hindsight and the suppositional musings of [Expert #1] to fault him for facts and circumstances unknown and unknowable to him.

[Expert #1] cites two witness statements to substantiate his assertion that there was no "*imminent death threat*" (again misstating the standard) and thus Agent Ault's decision to use deadly force was unjustified. Much of their versions of the incident does not square with the forensic evidence and is inconsistent with prior statements they gave. [Expert #1] only mentions in passing their claims that the person with the rock dropped it before the shooting occurred. He passes on to an analysis that assumes the rock was not dropped.

---

11. U.S. Department of Justice Policy Statement: Use of Deadly Force (incorporated into INS Firearms Policy, USBP Deadly Force policy, & DHS Firearms Policy).

But if the rock was dropped, that could only have happened coterminous with Agent Ault bringing his firearm into use. He may or may not have seen it—but he was in the process of reacting to the immediacy of the imminent threat posed mere fractions of a second before. This is characteristic of deadly force confrontations and the inexact recall of precisely what transpired and when. The people involved are each acting independently and simultaneously. Action/reaction times are unavoidably in play. Incomplete recollection of what transpired is commonplace. Agent Ault was acting under the impetus of an incipient attack. Mr. Ortiz-Castillo may have dropped the rock and turned for cover as he saw Agent Ault drawing his weapon and firing it. As an aside, such movement on his part would also account for the different trajectory angles of his wounds. [Expert #1] uses computer simulations in his report based on assumptions and witness statements to illustrate bullet trajectories and torso positions that cannot possibly be accurate.

It is the decision to shoot that must be examined, not the location of the wound or the imagined intent of the adversary or the inability of the officer to choreograph with precision each move and nuance made by his adversary—factors over which Agent Ault had no control whatsoever. If his perception of imminent risk was reasonable, as it was, then his decision to use deadly force was justified. His inability to instantaneously recognize and react to Mr. Ortiz-Castillo's simultaneous reactions does not make that decision any less reasonable and justified. [Expert #1]'s observations here are not necessarily false—they just aren't relevant.

Also irrelevant is [Expert #1]'s observation, "*It should also be noted that ten days prior Agent Ault was faced with almost the same circumstances with Mr. Ortiz-Castillo, yet he chose to make use of intermediate force to quell the assault and not Deadly Force as in this case.*" The reasonableness of Agent Ault's decision to use deadly force must be judged within the context of the circumstances in which the decision was made. What he decided to do, or not do, in other circumstances at other times is immaterial to what he decided to do in the present circumstance except to the extent that it further substantiates his experience, knowledge, and perceptions regarding Mr. Ortiz-Castillo and the propensity for violence he represented in such confrontations.

[Expert #1] concludes, "*… it is my opinion that Agent Ault was not faced with a substantial risk that Mr. Ortiz-Castillo would cause seriously* [sic] *bodily injury or death at the point that he took Deadly Force against him. Therefore Agent Ault was not justified is* [sic] *using Deadly Force against Mr. Ortiz-Castillo on the evening of August 08, 2007.*" Again, [Expert #1] misstates the legal standard. Even a person who is clearly unarmed can pose a threat of imminent death or injury. That is why the totality of the circumstances at the moment the decision to shoot is made must be assessed, something [Expert #1] has not attempted.

Agent Ault was not hurt, nor was Mr. Ortiz-Castillo able to carry through an attempt to hurt Agent Ault, apparently detrimental factors in [Expert #1]'s analysis. But prevention of death or injury is the *only* reason for the use of deadly force in the first place. That is the sole legitimizing rationale for the justified use of deadly force. It is false, at best, to imply that an officer must be injured to some degree to justify a use of deadly force or to imply that lack of injury is symptomatic of a lack of justification. It is equally false to say that an officer may not justifiably use deadly force until an actual attempt to inflict injury has been made. Such a standard would mean that no law enforcement officer could prevent injury or death, but only react to real attempts. It should be obvious that such a standard implicitly assumes that the officer has the good fortune not to be injured or killed first.

[Expert #1] states, " ... *Agent Ault was not faced with a substantial risk that Mr. Ortiz-Castillo would cause seriously* [sic] *bodily injury or death....*" He is wrong. The *perception* of an imminent risk of death or serious injury must be reasonable. If it is, then the use of deadly force *to prevent that imminent risk* is justified. No officer is required to wait until he is certain that a "threat of deadly force" is real or "substantial." Any officer required to wait beyond a reasonable perception of an imminent risk is far more likely to get killed or injured than be able to prevent it.

[Expert #1] makes no mention at all of the U.S. Department of Justice Policy Statement Regarding Use of Deadly Force that states: "Law enforcement officers ... may use deadly force only when necessary, that is, _when the officer has a reasonable belief_ that the _subject of such force poses an imminent danger of death or serious physical injury_ to the officer or to another person."[12] (Emphasis added.)

[Expert #1] displays limited knowledge of deadly force confrontations and the factors that ineluctably come into play, such as action/reaction times, effects of stress, wound ballistics, the inability to foresee others' intents or actions, the consequences of delay and hesitation. All of these factors are recognized, understood, and are basic to the legal justification for deadly force and to the implementation of policies and training governing the use of deadly force.

[Expert #1] clearly disagrees with Agent Ault's decision to use deadly force, but on no basis other than his personal suppositions. His suppositions are irrelevant to any legal or expert assessment of the reasonableness of Agent Ault's perceptions and the justification of his decision to use deadly force.

---

12. U.S. Department of Justice Policy Statement: Use of Deadly Force. Adopted as the uniform federal deadly force policy in 1995; amended in 2004 (solely to further restrict the rules for use of deadly force to prevent escape) and incorporated into the INS Firearms Policy, USBP Deadly Force Policy, & DHS Firearms Policy.

# Case History #2
## Ofelia Rodriguez, et al. v. U.S., et al.
U.S. District Court, Southern District of California
Case No: 06-CV-2753-W (JMA)

On December 30, 2005, Senior U.S. Border Patrol Agent (BPA) Faustino Campos, Jr. was on duty in the Chula Vista Station's territory from 3:00 PM to 11:00 PM. He was dressed in the USBP rough duty uniform with prominent USBP patches, markings, and coloring and prominently displaying his USBP badge. He was specifically assigned to a stationary deterrent position in an area known to the Chula Vista personnel as Echo 2, indicating it is the second area located east of the San Ysidro Port of Entry. Echo 2 is approximately 300 yards east of the Port of Entry. BPA Campos was driving a USBP vehicle, a Ford Bronco bearing USBP official markings.

At or shortly after 7:00 PM, BPA Campos was notified by the USBP sensor dispatch center that a sensor had been activated at a location a couple of hundred yards east of his position in the Echo 4 area. At the time, BPA Campos was conversing with USBP Acting Field Operations Supervisor William Zucconi who was parked in his own USBP vehicle adjacent to BPA Campos' vehicle. BPA Zucconi told BPA Campos to go check Echo 4 for possible foot traffic while he covered Echo 2 for him.

There are two fences running along the international border in this area. The primary fence runs parallel to and in proximity to the international border between the United States and Mexico. It is offset north of the border to allow for inspection, maintenance, and repair as necessary without involving Mexican territory. A secondary fence is located north of the primary fence, running parallel to that primary fence. Between the two fences is an all-weather access road that enables USBP personnel to patrol along the border, between the two fences. The secondary fence has secure access gates located at intervals along its length. The land between the two fences is kept clear of cover and vegetation to facilitate surveillance and enforcement.

BPA Campos drove east on the all-weather access road between the primary and secondary border fences. He saw one individual north of the border at the secondary fence carrying a steel rebar ladder commonly used by smugglers. He saw this individual turning back towards the south as he drove into the area. BPA Campos reported his observations to the SBPA agent assigned surveillance of the area with an infrared telescope, and the scope operator verified seeing the same thing.

BPA Campos approached in his vehicle and the individual (subsequently identified as Guillermo Martinez-Rodriguez) started running south towards the border. He did not cross the border, but stopped on the edge of a roadway known variously as the "new road" or the "border road" that runs parallel to and south of the all-weather access road.

BPA Campos knew from extensive experience, both personal and institutional, that professional smugglers engaged in smuggling illegal aliens across the border routinely engage in behavior intended to delay or distract USBP agents from investigating or preventing the successful crossing of their human contraband. He believed that Martinez was a smuggler, as evidenced by his behavior and his possession of a ladder suitable for crossing over the fences. He assumed that Martinez had just guided a group of illegal aliens north of the secondary fence. At that time, BPA Campos did not consider Martinez a threat to his safety, nor did he consider him to be a likely illegal entrant.

BPA Campos drove to an adjacent access gate in the secondary fence, got out of his vehicle to open the gate, then drove north through the gate. His intention was to search north of the secondary fence for the group of illegal aliens that he believed Martinez had guided into the U.S. As he did so, he continued to monitor Martinez' location and movements. As he approached the gate in the secondary fence, BPA Campos observed Martinez move north from the edge of the "border road" to the secondary fence east of Campos' location. As he maneuvered through the gate, Campos saw Martinez running east towards the open gate.

BPA Campos believed this to be an attempt by Martinez to further delay his search for illegal aliens north of the fence, and/or an attempt to impede or jam the gate in an open/unlocked condition—both commonly experienced events in the frequent interactions between the USBP and the smugglers they confront.

BPA Campos put his vehicle in "park," got out, and ran towards Martinez to deter his advance and turn him away from the open gate and back to the south so that he (Campos) could then close the gate and continue his search for the illegal aliens he believed were somewhere close by, north of the secondary fence. BPA Campos saw Martinez turn away and run ahead of him, moving south in the direction of the primary fence. BPA Campos was not running at full speed, but the gap between them narrowed nevertheless.

Suddenly, Martinez stopped and turned to face BPA Campos. BPA Campos saw him squat down and grab a rock—BPA Campos perceived him to be gathering additional rocks. BPA Campos recognized that Martinez' actions represented an immediate danger of being "rocked" as he (Campos) got closer. "Rocking" by illegal immigrant smugglers is a common event along this area of the border. Martinez then stood up, cocked his arm, and threw a rock at BPA Campos that flew past his head.

BPA Campos had not been able to stop his forward momentum due to the suddenness of Martinez' actions. He drew his gun as he saw Martinez stand and cock his arm in a motion consistent with preparing to throw. BPA Campos saw Martinez execute the throw and fired one shot at him as the rock passed beside his (Campos) head.

BPA Campos saw Martinez grab his left arm as he turned and ran south, away from Campos. Martinez ran down the slope to the primary fence and ran some distance along it (BPA Campos estimated 200 yards) to an area known to have holes in the fence. BPA Campos lost sight of Martinez and assumed he had successfully crossed back into Mexico.

BPA Campos immediately radioed BPA Zucconi to come to his (Campos) location, at which time BPA Campos informed him about the incident and his belief that Martinez was injured. Information was received later that night that Martinez was in the Cruz Roja Hospital in Tijuana with a gunshot wound. The autopsy reported a single gunshot wound that entered Martinez' posterior right shoulder.

## Case History #2: Plaintiff's Expert #2[13]

I, [Expert #2], make the following report pursuant to Federal Rule of Civil Procedure 26. A true and correct copy of my CV is attached hereto. In formulating my opinions, I reviewed the entirety of the Border Patrol's CIIT report and the report prepared and statements taken by the San Diego Police Department. These voluminous documents total approximately 1200 pages.

After reviewing these documents, I have arrived at the following conclusions.

Central to the entire issue in that a law enforcement agent may use deadly force to meet deadly force. If the rock (and it could be a phantom rock) has already been thrown then the danger is past. Secondly, under normal conditions, a rock would not qualify as a lethal weapon. Mr. Martinez-Rodriguez was shot in thc back and it appears that he was probably fleeing when he was shot. Campos uses the phrase he "engaged" the deceased. This is a euphemism. He shot him dead. Mr. Martinez-Rodriguez did not have a weapon at the time he was shot. Campos suffered no injury. No one witnessed the rock throwing or the shooting. Martinez-Rodriguez was alone. Campos' claim that he shot him in the chest is contradicted by the physical evidence.

This was an unjustified use of deadly force. What Campos feared or thought was irrelevant. The threat of deadly force must be real. Here, even if Martinez-

---

13. Note: This report is presented verbatim—misspellings, grammar, and syntax are in the original.

Rodriguez did throw a rock at Campos, and even if his act in throwing that rock qualified as a use of deadly force (neither of which are apparent), the danger is passed after the rock has been thrown. Once the rock was thrown, Campos was no longer justified in shooting Martinez-Rodriguez. Accordingly, even under Campos' version of events, the shooting was not justified.

## Case History #2: Discussion of Expert #2's Opinion

First, [Expert #2] asserts that if a rock had been thrown at Agent Campos then the danger was past, presuming that no more rocks would be thrown nor any other form of attack initiated. There is no possible way that Agent Campos could know that even if it were so. He had been attacked with a rock. He was in a location where such attacks were common and increasing. He was confronting an individual he believed to be engaged in human smuggling— precisely the type of activity and individual responsible for most of the assaults on U.S. Border Patrol agents. He had no reason—legally, under policy, by virtue of his training or experience—to believe one rock was the totality of the attack, or to wait and see if any further attack was made.

Rodriguez made his hostile intent unmistakable—throwing a rock at Agent Campos' head at close range. Agent Campos believed the assault was real and employed deadly force to prevent it from continuing. That is not unreasonable.

Second, [Expert #2] contends, "under normal conditions, a rock would not qualify as a lethal weapon." There is no requirement under law, policy, or training that limits the use of deadly force to attacks with items deemed lethal weapons by [Expert #2]. To the contrary, law enforcement officers in general, and Agent Campos in particular, are authorized to use deadly force " … when the officer has a reasonable belief that the subject of such force poses an imminent danger of death or serious physical injury to the officer or to another person." It is reasonable to think that getting hit in the head with a rock poses a risk of serious injury that entails a consequent risk of being incapacitated, which leads to an even more serious risk of injury or death, for example by being shot with one's own gun.

There is no indication what the "normal conditions" are that [Expert #2] has in mind for throwing a rock at a uniformed law enforcement officer, but to ignore the very real risk of injury under *these particular* conditions is disingenuous, at best. Every year law enforcement officers are killed with "Blunt Instruments," "Personal Weapons," "Vehicles," "Cutting Weapons," and "Other" means. It is noteworthy that most of these categories of weapons used to actually kill police officers would not meet [Expert #2]'s definition of a "lethal weapon" under "normal conditions." The only relevant issue is whether Agent

Campos was reasonable in his perception that Rodriguez' actions posed an imminent risk of death or serious injury, not whether the weapon used by Rodriguez would "qualify" as a "lethal weapon."

Third, [Expert #2] points out that Rodriguez was shot in the back and "it appears that he was probably fleeing when he was shot"—a gratuitous supposition that has no basis in fact or bearing on the justification for Agent Campos' decision to shoot. Agent Campos' reaction and decision to use deadly force occurred simultaneously with Rodriguez' attack. Agent Campos was chasing Rodriguez when Rodriguez suddenly stopped running and initiated his attack. Agent Campos drew and fired his weapon as he saw Rodriguez raise his arm in a throwing motion. He was desperately trying to stop the first rock from being thrown (unsuccessfully) as his momentum carried him well inside point-blank rock range as well as prevent the continuation of the attack.

He acted upon what he saw and knew, and what he believed might happen next. Waiting to see what an attacker does next is unreasonable and an unnecessary assumption of risk. His actions cannot be judged with the clarity of 20/20 hindsight to fault him for facts and circumstances unknown and unknowable to him.

The bullet that struck Rodriguez hit him in the posterior right shoulder—not "in the back." The wound was not inflicted as Rodriguez ran away because the entry wound is located on the "posterior region of right shoulder ... projectile pathway from back to front, right to left and slightly downward." Rodriguez was hit as he completed his throwing motion, a follow-through that would expose the "posterior region of right shoulder" to Agent Campos at the moment the bullet happened to hit him. The wound track "from back to front, right to left and slightly downward" is consistent with the natural turning of the torso characteristic of a hard throw and follow-though. Further, due to the terrain and their positions, Rodriguez was slightly below Agent Campos—consistent with the wound track traveling slightly downward.

Agent Campos decided to shoot as he saw Rodriguez stand up and raise his arm to throw the rock—not after he completed the throw. The point is that when Agent Campos decided to shoot, Rodriguez was facing him as he said—but moving. When he actually shot and the bullet struck Rodriguez, the throw had been made and Rodriguez was in a different posture.

This is consistent with deadly force confrontations and the inexact recall of precisely what transpired and when. The people involved are each acting independently and simultaneously. Agent Campos was acting under the stress of an actual attack, perhaps more aware of the rock passing his head than of Rodriguez' precise movements, his vision masked by recoil and muzzle blast. These are physiological factors that commonly arise in high-stress incidents, and none are relevant to the reasonableness of his perception of risk at the moment he fired. *It is the decision to shoot that must be examined, not the location of the wound or the imagined intent of the adversary or the inability of the officer to choreograph with precision each move and nuance made by his adversary*—factors over which Agent Campos had no control whatsoever. If his perception of imminent risk was reasonable, as it was, then his decision to use deadly force was justified.

Fourth, [Expert #2] points out that Rodriguez was shot dead, that he did not have a weapon, that Agent Campos was not hurt, that nobody witnessed the incident, and that Rodriguez was alone. That is all true, yet none of those statements of fact pertain to the circumstances at the moment that Agent Campos decided to shoot. Rodriguez' death was clearly a result of Agent Campos' decision to shoot, but that is not a factor for assessing the reasonableness of that decision.

[Expert #2] states that Rodriguez "did not have a weapon" when actually he did, but he had used it and Agent Campos feared he would pick up and use another. Agent Campos saw him squat down and grab a rock and believed him to be gathering additional rocks. Even a person who is unarmed can pose a threat of imminent death or injury. That is why the totality of the circumstances at the moment the decision to shoot is made must be assessed.

Agent Campos was not hurt; a detrimental factor in [Expert #2]'s opinion. It is false to imply that an officer must be injured to justify the use of deadly force or to imply that lack of injury is symptomatic of a lack of justification. [Expert #2] points out that nobody witnessed the incident. That observation has no bearing on the assessment of the reasonable nature of Agent Campos' decision. In all shooting incidents, an assessment has to be made based on the evidence and accounts that are available. A lack of witnesses is not an indication of a lack of justification, any more than the fact that Rodriguez was alone. [Expert #2]'s implication to the contrary is merely another non sequitur.

[Expert #2] states, "The threat of deadly force must be real." He is wrong. The *perception* of an imminent risk of death or serious injury must be reasonable. If it is, then the use of deadly force *to prevent that imminent risk* is justified. No officer is required to wait until he is certain that a "threat of deadly force" is "real."

[Expert #2] states, " ... even if Martinez-Rodriguez did throw a rock at Campos, and even if his act in throwing that rock qualified as a use of deadly force ... the danger is passed after the rock has been thrown." He is wrong. [Expert #2] displays no knowledge of deadly force confrontations and the factors that ineluctably come into play, such as action/reaction times, effects of stress, wound ballistics, the inability to foresee others' intents or actions, the consequences of delay and hesitation. All of these factors are recognized, understood, and are basic to the legal justification for deadly force and to the implementation of policies and training governing the use of deadly force.

# Case History #3

## Labadie v. United States, et al.

U.S. District Court, Western District of Washington at Seattle
Civil No C09-1276-MJP

On September 9, 2006, Michel Labadie sought to enter the United States from Canada via the Pacific Highway Crossing at the Blaine, Washington, Port of Entry (POE). Entry into the United States is monitored and enforced by the U.S. Customs and Border Protection Service (CBP), an agency of the U.S. Department of Homeland Security (DHS). All people seeking to enter the United States are required to submit to a screening process intended to evaluate their legal status, suitability for entry of non-U.S. citizens, and the presence of contraband. The screening process is well established and routine in its administration.

Ports of Entry have a Primary Inspection station where individuals and vehicles entering the United States are subject to initial screening. The Ports of Entry also have a Secondary Inspection station where a more thorough inspection of a vehicle and/or an individual may be conducted if deemed necessary by CBP officers, or when directed by random computer referral, a process designated COMPEX in the CBP system. Notably, all individuals and their vehicles are subject to COMPEX referral. COMPEX is universally applied and any Secondary referrals that are directed are randomly chosen.

When individuals are directed to the Secondary inspection area, their inspection has not been completed until they have been cleared through both Primary and Secondary Inspection stations. Referral to a Secondary Inspection is a continuation of the mandatory screening process necessary for entry into the United States.

Individuals directed to Secondary Inspection by a COMPEX referral must undergo a more comprehensive inspection that includes a Customs Examination, an Immigration Examination, and any Agricultural Examination required to determine the admissibility of the person and accompanying merchandise into the United States. Secondary inspection includes the requirement that the individual's vehicle be searched.

All individuals referred to secondary inspection are queried through the Treasury Enforcement Communication System ("TECS"). TECS is principally owned and managed by CBP and is its principal law enforcement and anti-terrorism data base system. TECS is a law enforcement information collection, analysis, and sharing network that securely links telecommunications devices and personal computers to a centralized communications and database system. The TECS databases contain temporary and permanent enforcement, inspection, and intelligence records relevant to the anti-terrorism and law enforcement mission of CBP and the numerous other federal agencies that it supports. TECS also allows direct access to other major law enforcement data systems, including the Department of Justice's National Crime Information Center (NCIC), the National Law Enforcement Telecommunications Systems (NLETS), and the Canadian Police Information Centre (CPIC).

Labadie was in his vehicle undergoing screening at the Primary Inspection station when he was randomly selected by COMPEX for Secondary screening. The CBP officer directed him to proceed to the Secondary Inspection Station. Labadie did so, driving at an excessively high rate of speed. Two CBP officers (K.E. Ramsey and Isidoro Longoria) separately and individually ordered him to slow down because of the hazard he presented to pedestrians in the vicinity.

CBP Officer David Decker conducted Labadie's Secondary Screening. Labadie was agitated and impatient, questioning why he (Labadie) was being inspected. CBP Officer Decker asked Labadie to complete a Baggage Declaration (Labadie did so) and he answered Decker's routine questions relative to his (Labadie's) Customs Examination and Agricultural Examination. He provided identification to CBP Decker who then stepped away to query TECS regarding Labadie. The result of the TECS query is quoted in part:

> *Subject is 3rd degree black belt. Subject has numerous confrontations with enforcement officers in U.S. and Canada.*
>
> *Use extreme caution when encountering subject. Subject was encountered at the Pacific Highway POE and became very aggressive and assaulted officers during secondary inspection. Subject was taken down and put in restraints, Refer to incident report #20053004001991. May impersonate RCMP Officer.*
>
> *Both NCIC and CPIC checks revealed subject has extensive criminal history. Labadie has also been under arrest for agravated [sic] assault by a prisoner, impersonating a police officer, and interference with arresting officer in Salt Lake City, Utah. CPIC shows subject is under surveillance and was a former RCMP member misrepresenting himself as a current member.*

There was also a detailed entry describing the physical altercation at the Pacific Highway POE that occurred in July 2005.[14] The results of the TECS query raised doubts in CBP Decker's mind as to whether Labadie was admissible into the United States. Decker had not completed his Unified Primary Training and believed he did not have the expertise necessary to make that determination. He requested assistance from CBP Officer Edward Escobar who was the most senior officer on duty.

CBP Escobar had prior experience with Labadie from the incident in July 2005. He agreed to take over the Immigration Examination while CBP Officer Decker completed the Customs and Agricultural Examinations, i.e., the search of Labadie's vehicle. That search was negative.

Meanwhile, CBP Officer Escobar reviewed the results of the TECS inquiry and subsequently advised Labadie that he (Escobar) did not believe that Labadie was admissible. He attempted to explain that supervisory review would be necessary for a final determination,[15] but Labadie became belligerent and defiant, questioning Escobar's authority to send him back to Canada. CBP Officer Escobar directed Labadie to return to sit on a nearby bench while his (Escobar's) supervisor was briefed, but Labadie refused. Labadie threatened Escobar to " … put you on your ass again like the last time."

CBP Officer Escobar continued to command Labadie to go sit down, to unclench his fists, and to calm down. Labadie defied the commands and continued to yell belligerently at Escobar while exhibiting signs of impending physical aggression—clenched fists, combative stance, angry demeanor. CBP Officer Escobar attempted to take Labadie by the arm to escort him to the bench to sit, or out of the lobby if necessary. Labadie resisted and a struggle ensued. CBP Escobar, assisted by other CBP officers who had responded and stood near Labadie during the confrontation, took Labadie to the floor where he was restrained until they could get handcuffs on him, at which point he was helped to his feet and escorted to a holding cell pending interview and investigation by DHS Investigations.

CBP Officer Escobar was bitten on a finger severely enough to draw blood, and chipped a bone in his elbow against the floor in the process of taking Labadie to the floor.

---

14. During this incident, Labadie was belligerent, aggressive, and non-compliant with CBP orders. He physically resisted being escorted away by CBP agents and pushed CBP Agent Edward Escobar to the floor in the process. He was arrested but prosecution was declined. He was returned to Canada upon release.

15. It must be noted that final determination of admissibility requires supervisory review and confirmation. CBP Agent Escobar's assessment was not sufficient to deny admission to the U.S. without supervisory concurrence.

During his interview by DHS Investigative Agents Jeffrey Starrett and Charles Lehmann, Labadie complained of injuries to his forehead and to his shoulder and the agents immediately called paramedics in to examine and assess his physical condition. Whatcom County Medic-One paramedics examined Labadie and determined that he did not require hospitalization.

The agents completed their investigation and presented the facts of the case to the U.S. Attorney's Office. Arrest and prosecution was authorized for assaulting a federal officer. The agents returned to the holding cell to make the arrest and found Labadie being tended to by CBP officers. They found Labadie apparently choking and called an ambulance. He was transported to St. Joseph's Hospital, Bellingham, WA, where he was examined in the emergency room and immediately discharged. The agents placed him under arrest and placed him in the custody of the U.S. Marshals.

## Case History #3: Plaintiff's Expert #3[16]

My use of certain terms (i.e.— "*negligent*", "*reasonable suspicion*", "*probable cause*", "*objectively reasonable*", "*deliberately indifferent*", "*ratified*", "*unconstitutional*", etc.) merely reflects my training and experience, in applying reasonable standards of care to police officers' conduct, and does not presume or imply a statement of any legal opinion.

Similarly, my use of certain terms (i.e.— "*cyanosis*", "*petechiae*", "*apnic*", "*excited delirium*", "*carotid*", "*hyoid*", "*asphyxia*", "*mucosal*", etc.) merely reflects my training and experience in reviewing triage and/or autopsy reports and does not presume or imply a statement of any medical opinion.

Based upon my training, experience and a careful evaluation of the totality of circumstances in this matter, it is my considered professional opinion that the following facts appear to be undisputed in the record:

The DVD recordings are without sound but provide the best evidence of what physically occurred:

   a)  July 9, 2005 incident:
       12:21:10—Plaintiff was standing at the counter talking with some-
               one (off camera) and gesturing with his hands,
       12:22:02—Three CSP officers, including defendant officer sur-
               round plaintiff while he continues to communicate
               with the person behind the counter,

---

16. Note: This report is presented verbatim—misspellings, grammar, and syntax are in the original.

> 12:22:20 — The three CSP officers grab plaintiff and, in the process of taking plaintiff to the floor, defendant officer falls,
>
> 12:22:34 — A total of four officers swarm plaintiff and a fifth can been see to kick toward him but he is off camera,
>
> 12:23:33 — Plaintiff is raised to his feet and escorted off camera,

  b)  September 9, 2006 incident:

> 11:15:06 — Plaintiff, who had been waiting seated on a bench, is apparently beckoned to the counter and walks over to talk with someone,
>
> 11:15:27 — Two CBP officers, including defendant officer, confront plaintiff, immediately grab him and are soon joined by three other officers, all of whom participate in taking plaintiff to the floor on his back,
>
> 11:16:15 — Defendant officer separates from his fellow officers and stands to watch, while plaintiff's head can be seen to be facedown on the floor
>
> 11:16:55 — Plaintiff is raised to his feet and escorted off camera;

Both the July 9, 2005 and the September 9, 2006 incidents that are remarkably similar:

1) Plaintiff cannot be seen to make any threatening gestures or to take an aggressive posture;
2) Plaintiff is suddenly overwhelmed with the superior physical force of multiple officers.

Based upon my training, experience and a careful evaluation of the totality of circumstances in this matter, it is my considered professional opinion that plaintiff was a victim of unnecessary, unreasonable and therefore excessive force that appears to have been objectively unreasonable under the totality of circumstances. In reaching that conclusion I was especially mindful of the following information from the record:

  a.  All of the information previously described herein;

  b.  Neither plaintiff's conduct nor the circumstances of this encounter, as clearly portrayed on the video thereof, gave any indication whatsoever that he posed a risk of harm to defendant and/or his fellow officers and any contention to the contrary 'would be mere speculation:

      1)  His only alleged misconduct was defendant officer's contention that *"he was not a bona fide visitor for pleasure",*

    2) He did not pose an immediate threat to the safety of the officers:

        a)   He did not take an aggressive posture,

        b)   He was neither armed nor appeared to be armed with any weapon,

        c)   The number of officers were literally overwhelming,

    3) He was not actively resisting arrest,

    4) He was not attempting to flee;

        c.   Accordingly, defendant and his fellow officers did not have to make a decision under circumstances that were tense, uncertain, and rapidly evolving;

        d.   Nevertheless, defendant and his fellow officers seized plaintiff and forcibly took him down to the floor:

    1) Physical force was used against plaintiff immediately upon confronting him,

    2) There is no indication that he was told he was under arrest or given an opportunity to compliantly submit,

        e.   Ms. Gonzalez' analysis of the video is consistent with my review;

        f.   Plaintiff was needlessly injured from the physical force directed against him by defendant and his fellow officers;

        g.   In consequence of all of the foregoing reasons and as previously stated herein, plaintiff was the victim of unnecessary, unreasonable and therefore excessive force by defendant and his fellow officers.

Based upon my training, experience and a careful evaluation of the totality of circumstances in this matter, it is my considered professional opinion that defendant officer's response to plaintiff was more probably than not an example of what is known in the police vernacular as "*contempt of cop*". In reaching that conclusion, I was specifically mindful of the following information from the record:

    a.   All of the information previously described herein;

    b.   The elements of a "*contempt of cop*" scenario are well known and include:

        1) A citizen displays conduct that is perceived to be an "*attitude*" or a "*disrespectful*" challenge to an officer's authority,

        2) In direct consequence thereof, the officer responds to that perceived challenge by escalating the confrontation to conclusively demonstrate "*who's in-charge*",

    3) When the citizen does not submit to such intimidating be-
havior:
a) The officer further escalates the confrontation into physical force
that is unnecessary, excessive and essentially amounts to summary punishment,
b) The officer, who of course has overwhelming and immediately
available assistance, always *"wins"* that personality conflict,
c. Defendant officer and plaintiff had a similar and prior confrontation, in which the CBP investigation did not uphold defendant officer's allegation and plaintiff was released:
    1) Thereafter, defendant officer allegedly threatened plaintiff, *"If
I ever see you again, I will make you regret it!"*
    2) Between the July 9, 2005 and September 9, 2006 incidents,
plaintiff had made 23 uneventful border crossings, but primarily at Sumas rather than Blaine,
    3) On September 9, 2006, however, plaintiff encountered de-
fendant officer again and was refused entry, which he protested
by asking, *"Why, under what authority?"*
    4) The video clearly establishes that the September 9, 2006 event
was essentially a repetition of the July 9, 2005 event;
d. Both events are typical *"contempt of cop"* scenarios of the type that
I have reviewed numerous times over the past 25 years or more;
e. Unfortunately, this type of misconduct, while not prevalent, does
occur and is seen with sufficient frequency to be described in police literature as *"contempt of cop".*

## Case History #3: Discussion of Expert #3's Opinion

[Expert #3] does not utilize a standard by which he derives his opinion.
Rather, he opines " … that plaintiff was a victim of unnecessary, unreasonable and therefore excessive force that appears to have been objectively unreasonable under the totality of the circumstances." He bases his conclusion on several
factors that he lists in subparagraphs—discussed individually below:

Labadie did not pose a risk of harm, asserting that any contention to the contrary is *speculation.* This implies that law enforcement officers may use force
only when a subject poses a risk of harm. That is not true. The constitutional
standard that governs the use of non-deadly force by a law enforcement officer recognizes that the use of force is inherent to law enforcement and limits
the force used to that reasonably necessary to attain a legitimate law enforcement end. There is no caveat that a person must pose a risk of harm. [Expert

#3] is confusing the broad standard for using non-deadly force with the limited standard for using deadly force. Deadly force may only be used to prevent an imminent risk of serious injury. This incident is not a deadly force situation, nor did it even approximate one. This factor is irrelevant, even nonsensical.

Other factors cited by [Expert #3] in support of his conclusion are that plaintiff's only misconduct was "officer's contention he was not a bon-fide visitor for pleasure," that he "did not take an aggressive posture," "he was neither armed nor appeared to be armed with any weapon," "he was not actively resisting arrest," and "he was not attempting to flee." None of these alleged elements are relevant to the issue as to whether defendant officer's use of force was reasonably necessary to attain a legitimate law enforcement end.

[Expert #3] dismisses the responsibility and authority of duly vested officers of the U.S. Customs and Border Protection. He makes no offering that they lacked jurisdiction or that the defendant officer lacked the authority to make a determination regarding plaintiff's suitability for entry into the United States. Obviously he did have that authority by law, and final determination would be subject to supervisory review. [Expert #3] ignores the established procedures that the officers were attempting to follow, and thus implies that plaintiff was subjected to a manufactured charge or some other invention—which is not true.

The assortment of "risk" factors cited by [Expert #3] are a continuation of his conflation of deadly force guidelines with the broader standard for use of non-deadly force, combined with the implication that any use of force must entail some or all of his "factors." The use of non-deadly force must be assessed relative to the question of whether it was reasonably necessary under the circumstances to attain a legitimate law enforcement goal. [Expert #3] simply lists an assortment of circumstances that may or may not be present in any police incident and declares them necessary for all police incidents. The use of force must be evaluated under the totality of circumstances present when the force is used, and the presence of any of the factors listed by [Expert #3] would be part of that evaluation. But the absence of some or all of the factors he lists is not indicative of an unreasonable use of force. The presence or absence of some or all of his factors is merely one aspect of the totality of circumstances under which the actual use of force must be assessed.

[Expert #3] asserts that the "number of officers were [sic] literally overwhelming," to imply that any level of force other than their presence is thus unreasonable. But overwhelming presence is one of the tenets of police training. Overwhelming numbers will minimize the possibility of the person doing something rash, risky, or even dangerous—but it does not guarantee that the person won't do something rash, risky, or dangerous. It also better assures that in the event the person does not submit to the officers' presence, the overwhelming numbers can subdue and restrain the person more quickly, efficiently, and safely in the interests of all the parties involved. The presence of overwhelming numbers is a good thing, but it is no guarantee that more and greater force will not be needed. This is basic to police training and arrest policy and practice, and is institutionalized throughout law enforcement. [Expert #3] ignores that.

[Expert #3] asserts "Accordingly, defendant and his fellow officers did not have to make a decision under circumstances that were tense, uncertain, and rapidly evolving...." He is misusing widely cited language from *Graham*[17] from the Court's explanation of why any use of force must be assessed from the perspective of a reasonable officer at the moment the decision to use deadly force is made, and why 20/20 hindsight is expressly irrelevant. The language is *not* a definition of the circumstances necessary for a use of force, as attempted by [Expert #3].

[Expert #3] asserts that plaintiff was not given any opportunity to submit. This is not true. The interaction between plaintiff and the officers was extended in time, starting with his first appearance at the border. His intemperate attitude was evident early on and did not abate. The officers made continuous requests to him to calm down, to sit down, to step away from the counter inside the secondary inspection facility. He chose not to. When they acted to escort him away from the counter to a nearby bench to await supervisory review of his determination, they did so legitimately. He could have cooperated and complied. He did not. Plaintiff had ample opportunity to submit. His consistent refusal to submit, and his increasing level of anger and hostility to the officers were his choices—not theirs.

[Expert #3]'s contention that plaintiff was convicted and punished for "contempt of cop" is completely without merit. He alleges an ill-defined sociological construct that may be of limited academic interest for debating purposes, but that has no bearing in an assessment of a law enforcement use of force. It has no relevance to an assessment of the reasonable nature of a use of force by a law enforcement officer. The standard to be used is the objectively reasonable standard of the Fourth Amendment. As the Court has instructed, and law enforcement has embodied in its training curricula, use-of-force policies, and practices, objective reasonableness ignores subjective intent, preceding mistakes of judgment, and 20/20 hindsight in making its evaluation. The objec-

---

17. *Graham v. Connor*, 490 U.S. (1989).

tive determination is focused on the totality of circumstances at the moment the decision is made to use force.

[Expert #3] may well be an expert in "contempt of cop," as he declares himself to be, however it is irrelevant to the issue at hand. The only relevant issue is whether the defendant officer was reasonable in his perception that plaintiff's actions posed an imminent risk of increased resistance and aggression, not whether plaintiff was armed, attempting to flee, posing a risk of imminent harm, or committing "contempt of cop."

Officer Escobar had him by the arm to lead him to a nearby bench to await final determination of his status. Plaintiff had been hostile, belligerent, and non-cooperative. The so-called "escort position" enables an officer to immediately sense and detect incipient resistance—tightening of muscles, resistance to "steering," positioning of arms and legs, etc. These are indications of imminent physical resistance. No officer is required to wait until imminent physical resistance becomes actual physical assault. The officer can take action to pre-empt reasonably perceived imminent resistance before it erupts into something worse, more injurious, and more risky to the safety of all involved. That is a reasonable use of force, as was done here. The force used was proportional to the risk detected, reasonable to the goal to be attained—restraint of plaintiff to prevent a belligerent confrontation from suddenly becoming more violent. To the contrary, Officer Escobar was under no mandate to wait and see what plaintiff would do next. He could only act upon what he saw and knew, what he sensed from his grip on plaintiff's arm, and what he believed might happen next.

Law enforcement functions restrict the physical freedom of the affected individuals in a variety of ways. For example, being arrested, or resisting police directions (passively or actively), or attempting to escape, or intruding upon and obstructing police actions, or concealing/destroying evidence, or endangering themselves or others, or simply posing an obstruction by their presence at a police scene—all require some level of force to achieve the legitimate law enforcement purpose at hand. Further, every one of these examples can necessitate an escalation of force to the extent that initial efforts prove unsuccessful.

Since the purpose of using force is to compel a person to submit to the authority of the officer, the person's determination (or lack thereof) to resist that authority will dictate the force used, as will the reasonable expectation of danger inherent to the criminal activity (actual or suspected) at issue. The physical circumstances in which the confrontation occurs will also affect the degree of force that may be reasonable. If the force being used is not effective, officers may and should use higher levels of force or different means of force or combinations thereof. They are trained that they may continue to apply force, and to attempt different means and levels of force, until the need for such force no longer exists because the person has either chosen to comply or has been restrained to the point that physical resistance no longer poses a risk of harm to the officers or others. They are not expected to match force levels, or to use barely adequate force. They are allowed to use that force reasonably necessary.

# Case History #4

## Estate of Shane Tasi, et al. v. Municipality of Anchorage, et al.

USDC, District of Alaska
Case No: 3:13-cv-00234-SLG

On 6/9/2012, Anchorage Police Department (APD) received calls about a shirtless Samoan male in black shorts creating a disturbance by attacking a neighbor's dog while yelling at the dog's owner at 635 North Bunn Street. Seven APD officers responded to the area looking for the unnamed Samoan. A witness reported seeing him in the alley at 617 North Bunn.

Shortly thereafter, Willie Emry called APD dispatch to report a disturbance inside 707 North Bunn. He, Bronson Birdsell, and Jason Netter had been inside their apartment when they heard glass breaking outside at the apartment directly across from them. They saw the kitchen window smashed from the inside, pieces protruding out and broken glass strewn on the grass. They heard a woman screaming inside that apartment, "Get off of me" and "Someone help me!"

The three men attempted to intervene on behalf of the woman they heard screaming. They ran to the entryway of the apartment building but it was locked. The apartment in which the disturbance was happening was at ground level beside the entryway. They banged on a window of that apartment, yelling "stop." An upstairs resident opened the door for them and they entered the building. The resident told them that the occupants of the apartment had been fighting for a while and that there were children inside. The apartment door was ajar and Birdsell briefly saw a shirtless man inside with a stick who noticed him and slammed the door closed. He (Birdsell) saw blood on a wall inside and on the man's forehead. The three men went back outside to bang on the apartment window again.

They saw an APD patrol car on North Bunn Street at the western end of the building and flagged it down. Officer Trull saw them, stopped, reversed, and pulled over, parking on the street outside the building. As he was doing so, the three men turned back towards the entry and saw APD Officer Boaz Gionson in the alley at the opposite (eastern) end of the building. A sidewalk runs the length of the building from Bunn Street at the western end to the north/south alleyway at the eastern end. A low chainlink fence approximately 40 inches high runs parallel to the sidewalk. The sidewalk and the fence terminate at the parking areas located at each end of the building.

Officer Gionson was driving north in the alley when he saw the three men. He parked in the alley and got out of his cruiser, walking to where the chainlink fence and sidewalk ended. The three witnesses walked over to him (Gionson) and told him what they had heard and seen regarding the disturbance in the apartment and the man with the stick. As Officer Gionson listened to them, he drew his handgun and held it in a close guard position as a precautionary measure.[18, 19]

Gionson and the other APD officers were on the scene looking for a man because of the disturbances he had started—confrontations with a dog and then the occupants of a pickup truck. After talking with the three men had probable cause that the man in the apartment was armed with a stick and that something violent had occurred, possibly domestic violence.

Shortly after, an unknown Samoan male (later identified as Shane Tasi) came out of the apartment building walking directly at Gionson and the three men. Tasi was shirtless and wearing black shorts. He held a long stick in his right hand later determined to be 41.5″ in length. As he advanced on Gionson and the three men, he shifted the stick from his right to his left hand, struck the ground with it and as he got close to Officer Gionson, suddenly raised it while cocking his arm and hand back in a manner consistent with swinging it at Gionson. The three men talking to APD Officer Gionson dispersed as Tasi approached. Officer Gionson ordered Tasi to drop the stick "at least" two times

---

18. A "close guard position" means that the gun is held in the strong hand up against the front center chest, muzzle angled down and finger off the trigger. The gun hand is relaxed, and the offhand may overlay the gun hand. This allows the weapon to be held unobtrusively yet securely and yet have it immediately available in the event a sudden threat materializes. It is a precautionary, preparatory position that precludes the chance of a highly undesirable "fast-draw" circumstance should a serious danger suddenly materialize. Thus it serves the same purpose as any of several other ready gun positions, all of which are utilized for the same reason.

19. Police officers are trained that it is appropriate to draw their weapon if they have reason to think a situation may become violent. This is because the need to bring the weapon into play to protect their lives, or the lives of others, can erupt so suddenly and proximately that the time necessary to grip, draw, and effectively utilize their weapon could easily be the critical difference between success and failure. Officers are allowed to have a weapon in hand if in their judgment they think they might need it, and encouraged to holster as quickly as they determine it won't be needed.

as Tasi continued to advance. Tasi ignored him, continuing his advance without pause. When he got within striking distance and suddenly raised his stick as if to attack with it, Gionson shot him three times. He observed Tasi go down and ceased fire.

## Case History #4: Plaintiff's Expert #4's Opinion[20]

Mr. Weidner [plaintiff's attorney in this case] has asked me to render opinions in a number of potential areas: the use of force, particularly deadly force, by police officers; policy, training, and oversight pertinent to the use of force, particularly deadly force by police officers; incident management, particularly in high-risk police encounters; police practices regarding the investigation of the use of force, particularly deadly force, by police officers; police practices regarding the internal review and adjudication of the use of force, particularly deadly force, by police officers; and field tactics for managing high-risk encounters.

General Background

On June 9,2012 Mr. Shane Tasi, a 26-year-old Samoan male residing at 707N Bunn Street, Apartment C, was fatally shot by Anchorage Police Officer Boaz Gionson. The shooting occurred in the aftermath of a reported disturbance involving Mr. Tasi near his residence and, a short time later, another disturbance reported inside his N Bunn Street address. As Officer Gionson spoke to three male witnesses in an adjacent parking lot, Mr.Tasi exited the front door of the fourplex with a stick in hand and walked toward the officer and the witnesses. The stick turned out to be a yellow, 41", ¾" in diameter, light broom handle, from which the head had been removed. Officer Gionson, believing that Mr. Tasi intended to assault him with the broom stick, shot him three times in the chest, resulting in Mr. Tasi's death. At the time there was a 3' high, sturdy chain-link fence separating the officer and Mr. Tasi, who was moving down the sidewalk and not in a direct line toward the officer. A security video of the premises captured the officer's arrival, Mr. Tasi's exit, and the fatal encounter.

---

20. Note: This report is presented verbatim — misspellings, grammatical errors, typos, and other mistakes are in the original, indicative of the level of care exercised by the writer. This report is presented in its considerable length because it is an extraordinary example of the nature and forms of outlandish plaintiffs' allegations discussed in this chapter above. The footnotes and commentary included in [the Expert's] opinion #4 are also part of the original.

### The Initial Incident

The initial broadcast by APD dispatch at 21:25:08 was of a Samoan male creating a disturbance on "Bunn north of Thompson". The male was described as shirtless and wearing black shorts. He was reported screaming at passing cars in front of someone's house. An additional broadcast at 21:25:58 reported that the male was "yelling a people, attacking the neighbor's dog, and yelling at its owner". Responding police units, however, were unable to locate the male Samoan. Because the call was in his assigned area, Officer Boaz Gionson responded to the area.

APD dispatch received another call at 21:37:13 that reported a disturbance at 707N Bunn. As he drove through the alley east of the address, Officer Gionson was flagged down by three male witnesses, who told him that there was a fight in the lower left apartment. One witness said there was "blood everywhere"[in the apartment]. Officer Gionson was flagged down at 21:37:32 and another officer reported "shots fired" at 21:38:10. Hence, 48 seconds elapsed between the flag-down and the shooting, while 13 minutes and 2 seconds elapsed between the initial report and the shooting.

### Pre-encounter Information Known to the Officers

Responding officers knew the following[21]:

- A Samoan male was reported yelling and screaming at passing cars, attacking a neighbor's dog, and yelling at the owner. The male was shirtless.
- There was a "fight" in the lower left apartment at 707N Bunn.
- A witness had reported "blood everywhere" in the apartment.
- Witnesses had told Officer Trull, also at the location, that "it was an emergency". Officer Trull said that he radioed the location and asked for more officers.
- Dispatch advised officers that there were "children in the house".

Additionally, Officer Gionson knew the following based upon his observations and a pre-shooting conversation with the three male witnesses who had flagged him down:

---

21. [**Expert #4**]'s **footnote:** I requested a copy of the dispatch tape to make a definitive determination of the source, the timing, and the content of information that was broadcast or reported by officers at the scene. It is my experience that the incident history often does not correspond exactly with the incident dispatch tape, because the incident history involves manual updating by dispatchers and/or call-takers and usually, therefore, some entries are not real-time. Although I was provided a copy of the Incident History, I have not as yet been provided a copy of the dispatch tape, which is the best means of establishing an incident timeline.

- Witnesses told him, "He's inside there with a stick, he's bloody".
- The three male witnesses who flagged him down "were frantic" as they ran toward him.
- A female on the upper west side balcony at 707N Bunn told him that there were children in the apartment where the disturbance was reported.
- The male Samoan was "yielding (sic) a yellow broken off broom stick that appeared to be pointy side up".
- Officer Gionson, contrary to the witnesses' report, didn't recall seeing any blood as Mr. Tasi "walked towards me".
- He uses the words "walk" or "walking" 13 different times in his original interview to describe Mr. Tasi's movement between the entrance and the location where he was shot. He does qualify the term several times by describing Mr. Tasi's walk or walking as "aggressive" or "aggressively". When asked by Detective Huelskoetter what he meant by "aggressively, he said, "Like he was—he covered the distance between the front door, the front main door of the apartment building, and almost made it to me in a matter of a second, two seconds tops."

If Mr. Tasi had covered that distance—around 30'feet—in 2 seconds, as Officer Gionson claims, he would have been nearly sprinting at 10.2 mph, which is a 6-minute-milepace.

<u>Officer Gionson's Decision to Go to "Guard"</u>

Based upon what he knew from dispatch and the three witnesses, Officer Gionson states, "I went to guard just for safety purposes, you know." Mr. Tasi had not yet appeared. The "guard position", according to APD training documents, consists of the following:

Properly present[ing] the pistol from the holster, maintaining a proper stance and grip, trigger finger straight along the frame, isometric tension in the hands and arms. THIS IS A FIGH'I'ING POSITION!! (<u>capital letters and exclamation points in the original slide</u>). Do not relax into a two handed (sic) dangle. The muzzle is depressed (low enough to see the suspects (sic) hands.

The policy further states: "At Guard, before anything else, you must assess the current tactical situation...."

I assume that the above training slide refers to the "high guard" position. There are three positions of guard apparently used by APD: close, low, and high. Although he initially put his sidearm at "close guard"(against his chest, pointing to the ground), it's unclear from the video if he progressed through the "low and high guard" positions before shooting. It appears to me that he assumed a center-mass firing stance, arms extended at shoulder level, instantly as Mr. Tasi came out the door. Consequently, by "going to guard" quickly, Officer

Gionson reduced the time that would be required to react to and defend against an imminent deadly attack.[22]

Assuming a full shooting stance reduced that time even further. The video shows that Officer Gionson was beyond Mr. Tasi's reach, even with the stick, at the moment he shot. It also shows that Mr. Tasi never moved the stick to a typical striking position, or as Officer Trull claims had the stick "in his hands like a sword with the broken end pointed up."

From guard, Officer Gionson doesn't " … remember making the conscious decision of bringing my gun up, putting sights on target, it just happened, and I fired the first round." From the guard position, little upward movement is required to aim center mass and fire. He actually assumed a shooting stance at 13:30:40 in the video, just as Mr. Tasi was stepping onto the sidewalk from the grass and 4seconds before shooting.

<u>Officer Gionson's Account Compared to the Security Video of the Incident</u>

The security video provides the most definitive, reliable record of the encounter and fatal shooting of Mr. Tasi. Though compression[23] and the two-dimensional nature of the video make the more distant images less clear-cut, it is possible to make out the sequence of movements in the 6–7-second encounter that preceded the shooting. I have broken events down in a second-by-second comparison of Officer Gionson's account and what is seen in the video.

[Editor's note: at this point in the opinion, there is a tabular, second by second account of what the writer sees in the various security camera surveillance videos of the incident. He purports to describe, by the second, what Tasi is doing, what Officer Gionson is doing, and what the three witnesses are doing all concurrently with each other. In the interest of brevity, that table is not reproduced here.]

<u>Major Discrepancies between Officer Gionson's Account and the Security Video</u>

Note: The following excerpts numbered 1–11 are from Detective Huelskoetter's interview of Officer Gionson on June 12, 2012. Page numbers are

---

22. [**Expert #4**]'s **footnote:** He also reduced his cognitive load and, thus, freed up time to process perceptual inputs, weigh options, and assess other information. Hence, he should have been able to monitor the tactical situation and adjust his tactics accordingly, as his training requires in the guard position. I refer to this as "fast-cycle" thinking, deliberative process, or "OODA-looping". For instance, a trained, reasonable officer would have used the fence to his/her tactical advantage.

23. [**Expert #4**]'s **footnote:** It is difficult to estimate distances, particularly in the background of the video, though the relative positioning of persons and objects can be determined in some instance by locating fixed referents, like fence posts, building features, or surface markings, and then measuring the distance between two known points.

shown in parentheses. The 12th excerpt is from Sergeant Booker's Administrative Investigation interview of Officer Gionson on July 30, 2012.

1. "It was—it was a yellow, what appeared to be a broken broom handle. Q Where was it broken at, I mean, are we talking like half of a broom handle? A Talking—it—it was probably about three to four feet in length."

**The stick is 41 ½ ", ¾ ", 260 gm. It is unclear from the photos that were provided to me if it's broken with a "splintered" or sharp end, or if it was simply removed from the broom head, in which case both ends would normally be blunt unless they were subsequently altered. (In Officer Gionson's recent deposition, it was established that the stick was neither splintered nor sharpened.)**

2. "Now you mentioned when you first arrived you're standing on the north side of the fence. A Uh-huh (affirmative). Q At what point was it that you actually stepped into the courtyard? A I stepped into the courtyard between the two fences and into the pathway of where he was walking as he walked out of the—as he walked out of the—the apartment building. Q Distance wise? A Twenty to 25 feet."

<u>The video shows the officer on the north side of the fence the entire time leading up to the shooting.</u> **Hence, the fence remained between Mr. Tasi and the officer at all times. Additionally, the two were separated to the extent that Mr. Tasi could not have struck him with the stick because the officer was beyond his reach (I estimate Mr. Tasi's reach as 7' or so). He simply had no opportunity to assault the officer or the witnesses, even if that were his intent. He would have had to either scale the fence or go around the east end of it.**

<u>The video clearly refutes his claim that he " ... stepped into the courtyard between the two fences and into the pathway of where he was walking as he walked out of the ... apartment building...."</u>

3. "Okay. And how fast do you think he covered that distance? A Extremely fast. He got within six to eight feet of me. I would say he could reach out and touch me with that stick and hit me if he wanted to before I fired the first shot. over 'cause I had stepped into the—stepped into the gate way, or into the courtyard, so I covered a few feet myself."

*The officer remained north of the fence beyond Mr. Tasi's reach or range. The fence was a significant barrier if Mr. Tasi's intent was to attack the officer with the stick. He would have had to scale it or walk around it toward the officer, both taking time and signaling his intent to attack the officer. Because the officer was in a "fighting stance" and already aimed "center mass," he had sufficient time to respond if Mr. Tasi used either tactic to surmount the barrier and actually attack him. The officer did not step forward, as he claims, into the center of the sidewalk opening (he refers to it as the "gateway" and "into the courtyard" until 4 seconds after the shooting (he actually takes several steps to the east, then several to the south, as Mr. Tasi falls and rolls onto the grass). The video clearly refutes his claim.*

4. "Which shortened the distance between me and him also."(This refers to the above statement in which Officer Gionson claims he stepped forward, thereby closing the distance between him and Mr. Tasi.)

*The officer never moved closer prior to shooting, though he did take several steps to the east, which would have increased the separation between him and Mr. Tasi. Hence, the separation between him and Mr. Tasi never closed because he stepped forward, as claimed in his statement.* <u>*The video clearly refutes his claim.*</u>

5. "But he covered over half of it within a second, second and a half, two seconds. And he was close enough to me before I made that decision, I mean, he could hit me with the stick before I made that decision to actually fire the shot when he—when I got—when I got the impression he was not going to stop, he was not going to comply with anything I had to say, and he was fixated on doing whatever the heck he wanted to do, and I was not going to control him. could have jabbed me with it 'cause it was splintered on one end and that's the end that would have—"

*It took Mr. Tasi 6–7 seconds to walk—he does not appear to be walking particularly fast or ever running—to the point where he was shot. The officer had time to issue a* <u>*warning. but did not*</u>*. Mr. Tasi never placed the stick in a typical attack position. At the time he was shot the stick was close to his left side, parallel to the ground, about waist level. The officer describes Mr. Tasi's pace as either a "walk" or as "walking" in his interview with Detective Huelskoeter. He does describe the walk as "aggressive," but explains that by referring to his estimate about how much time it took Mr. Tasi to cover a distance of about 30'. His estimate—"within a second, second and a half, two seconds—is wrong by a factor of at least 3.* <u>*The video clearly refutes Officer Gionson's estimate of the time that elapsed from the time that he first saw Mr. Tasi to the time when he fired his first shot.*</u>

6. "Did—did you by any chance activate your recorder at any point? A No I did not."

<u>*The video clearly shows that he had ample time to do so before Mr. Tasi came out*</u>*. His failure to do so deprived himself, the department, and any prospective reviewers of critical evidence.*

7. "I don't recall seeing any blood as he walked towards me, but then again, I wasn't really worried about blood on him."

*This was discrepant information, was different from what he had previously been told, and indicated that witness accounts might be inaccurate. A reasonable officer would have factored it into his situation awareness and subsequent decision-making.*

8. "Yeah, basically where I was standing with the fence line that I was talking about. I was on the northeast basically side of the fence. I'm not going to give up ground when there's three people standing behind me. It's not my nature, it's not what I'm trained to do, that's not what I do. So the only other way for him to do—the only other thing for him to do is come toward—besides coming towards me was turn around and go the other way, and he didn't."

*The three witnesses were not behind him at any point, as the officer walked west and they moved away from the shooting scene almost immediately in response to Mr. Tasi's appearance. They all remained south of the officer and moved farther east and south just prior to the shooting. Their locations were an important part of the situational awareness that he was trained to develop and continuously update. However, he failed to monitor and factor their movements into his decision-making.*

9. "I gave him ample opportunity, I mean, he was close enough to hit me with the stick, the broom handle—the broken broom handle, before I fired the first shot. I mean, he was—he was close enough, I mean, when he fell he almost—I—I took a step back because he almost fell into me.

*The video clearly shows that Mr. Tasi would have had to scale or go around the fence in order to attack the officer. It was sufficiently high and sturdy enough to require some effort to scale and time to bypass. The officer had his weapon trained center mass on Mr. Tasi and could have reacted in a fraction of a second upon seeing him attempt to scale or bypass the fence in order to attack him. Mr. Tasi never did anything to indicate that that was his intent and he never raised the stick in a typical attack position. <u>The video clear/v refutes his claim that Mr.Tasi had an actual opportunity to attack him because o(the intervening fence and the distance between them.</u>*

*<u>The video also clearly refutes his claim that Mr. Tasi "… almost fell into me."</u> They were separated by the fence throughout the encounter and Mr. Tasi fell a significant distance from the officer and then rolled even farther away. The video does show him stepping to the east several steps as Mr. Tasi falls to the ground.*

10. "Oh, um, and you know the reason for stepping into the fence [opening]was because there was three civilians behind me…."

*He was always north of the three civilians, who moved quickly farther east and south as Mr. Tasi walked toward their location. They were always beyond Mr. Tasi's range if he intended to attack them with the stick. The officer also never stepped into the "fence" opening until 4 seconds after the shooting. The video clearly refutes both claims.*

11. "Like he was—he covered the distance between the front door, the front main door of the apartment building, and almost made it to me in a matter of a second, two seconds tops."

*Mr. Tasi was shot considerably short of Officer Gionson's position on the other side of the fence. To attack the officer, Mr. Tasi would have had to either vault or go around the fence. Both would have required additional time and movement. Mr. Tasi made no overt act to do either.*

<u>*The videotape clearly refutes his estimate of the time it took Mr. Tasi to "almost" reach his position—that is, "in a matter of a second, two seconds tops."*</u> *It actually took Mr. Tasi 6–7 seconds to reach the location where he was shot— considerably short of Officer Gionson—with the stick parallel to the ground, by his side, about waist high. His estimate of the elapsed time is wrong by at least a factor of 3.*[24]

12. "And it [the stick] landed right next to my feet and then he hits the ground shortly after that."

*As Mr. Tasi collapses to his right (toward the grass) and forward (toward the north post of the short fence running between the sidewalk and the fourplex), the stick can be seen in the video dropping from his left hand and landing next to the north post of the short fence (it is half off and on the sidewalk nearest the grass, or the south side of the sidewalk in the contemporaneous scene photos).*

*There is a series of photos—that show several officers working on Mr. Tasi immediately after the shooting. These may be the photos that Officer Lofton reports taking as he walked up to several officers trying to control and assist Mr. Tasi, who was bleeding and moving around on the ground. All but one of the photos—show the stick lying near the north post of the short fence running north to south from the corner of the fourplex. The stick is half on and half off the sidewalk, lying in an east to west direction (running parallel to the sidewalk's south edge and the chain-link fence separating the two fourplexes), nearest the grass side of the sidewalk.*

*The stick's location is also shown as "P1 Stick/Broom Handle (CM)" with a set of coordinates (12'N, and 0.5 E) with the origin the NE corner of 707 N Bunn. The north post of the fence running from the origin, or the NE corner of the fourplex, is shown as 7.4N, 0.3W. That is a difference of 4.6 feet, which I assume is the opening between the two fences, including the width of the sidewalk. At the time the stick lands near the north post of the short fence, Officer Gionson is standing just northeast of the east fencepost of the longer chain-link fence running between the two fourplexes.* <u>*The video clearly refutes his claim that the stick "... landed right next to [his] feet...."*</u>

---

24. **[Expert #4]'s footnote:** According to Runner's World magazine, " ... here is a general guideline on treadmill speeds: for most people 2 to 4 mph will be a walking speed; 4 to 5 mph will be a very fast walk or jog; and anything over 5 mph will be jogging or running. If Mr. Tasi covered approximately 28' in 7 seconds, he would have been walking at 2.73 mph, according to my calculation. (Runner's World, June 7, 2013)

This could simply be another discrepancy—among the many others—between the officer's account and what is seen on the video.[25] That, however, is only half of the story.

There is another set of photos, much more extensive and numbered as Bates 197-410. These are photos of the crime scene, including the interior and exterior of 707N Bunn. In the latter subgroup, there are several photos—numbered Bates 392 and Bates 409—showing the stick lying on the ground next to a yellow evidence placard with the number 1 on it (Bates 461). The stick is now 4.0 feet or so north of where it landed after being dropped by Mr. Tasi in the video and the location shown in Officer Lofton's series of contemporaneous scene photos. Plainly it was repositioned and then photographed in its new location—consistent with the officer's claim of the stick landing "right next to my feet"—and included as authentic evidence in the investigative file. It is a serious misrepresentation of a crucial fact.

The stick is actually shown in numerous photos.... There are also photos showing the location of the three shell casing from the rounds fired by Officer Gionson. All are well north of the center fence line, two (#3, #4) are west of a line extended between the east ends of the two fourplexes, and the third (#2) is east of the extended line and north of the fence line in the east end of the large oil stain.[26] The total length of the center chain-link fence is shown as 70.5' in Bates 463. The distance to the SE corner of the step leading to the common entry door is shown as 34.6'. Hence, Mr. Tasi was approximately 35' from the east end of the sidewalk when he emerged from the building.

There is one remaining photo that I find interesting, but I'm unable to find any documentation that explains what it shows or measures. It shows a measuring tape running north to south, perpendicular to the center chain-link fence, from just beyond evidence placard #2 to the stick's location by the east fence post of the center chain-link fence. The casing from which the tape extracts is positioned at the north-west "corner" of the oil stain.

There are two accounts of Mr. Tasi's fatal shooting: the officer's version and the one shown on the security video. They differ dramatically on key points,

---

25. [**Expert #4**]'s **footnote:** Whether stress or some other factor explains such major discrepancies is an open question and goes to his state of mind, which is outside the scope of this analysis.

26. [**Expert #4**]'s **footnote:** The location of ejected shell casing is commonly used to estimate a shooter's location, but that is not within the scope of my expertise. However, all suggest that he was both north of the fence line and west of the extended east-to-west, corner-to-corner building line at the time he fired.

which I've explained in the foregoing twelve-point comparative analysis. The two versions can't co-exist, so one must be credited as the trusted, verifiable account. That, without question, is the security video.

*Thus, not only is Officer Gionson's account refuted by the video and Officer Lofton's set of photos, but it appears that a critical piece of evidence was improperly handled — at the very least.*[27]

In contrast to my analysis and conclusions, APD's Administrative Investigation, conducted almost six months after the shooting (I understand that a recent policy change requires concurrent investigations, which is considered best practice in the industry), came to a radically different conclusion: "The video provided an exceptional view of the incident and supported the witness and officer's statements." (Sgt. J Bucher, IA January 8, 2013)[28]

<u>Officer Gionson's Deposition Testimony — October 2, 2014</u>

Officer Gionson was deposed almost 2 ½ years after the shooting. During the deposition, Officer Gioinson stated that he had reviewed the video prior to his testimony. He had also reviewed the video during the administrative interview with Sergeant Booker. Following are key excerpts from his deposition and my analysis:

1. " … that would mean that he was farther away from you than where he started to fall when you decided to shoot him; right? A Yes."

*This was his response to one in a series of questions that attempted to pin down the distance between Mr. Tasi and Officer Gionson at the time of the shooting. It is difficult to estimate actual distances from the video because of the compression factor.*[29] *However, several points are relevant to estimating the distance:*

- There was a lag between Officer Gionson's decision to shoot, executing that decision, and the bullet(s) striking Mr. Tasi;

---

27. [**Expert #4**]'s **footnote:** I am not implying any wrongdoing, but the error is major, misleading, and raises a question about the quality and integrity of APD OIS investigative practices. It certainly warrants a departmental inquiry to determine the source of the error and to take any needed corrective action.

28. [**Expert #4**]'s **footnote:** I am truly at a loss to explain the diametrically opposite conclusions that Sergeant Bucher and I reached after reviewing the same evidence, though several possible explanations, such as lax oversight and shoddy investigative practices, come readily to mind.

29. [**Expert #4**]'s **footnote:** Though I've asked several times to see a copy of the OIS scene diagram showing the relative positions of the officer and Mr. Tasi at the time of the shooting, none has been provided as yet.

- Mr. Tasi was moving at the time, though he appears to pause briefly when shot (his right heel comes off the pavement);
- Mr. Tasi did not fall immediately, but kept moving forward due to his momentum;
- *Mr. Tasi, who was 6', did not "crumple," but, rather, fell forward, fully extended, for the most part.*
- Officer Gionson was angled off to Mr. Tasi's left, north of the chain-link fence.

2. "In the video it shows Mr. Tasi raising a stick in a fighting position getting ready to swing just before he fell as I was shooting him."

*Officer Gionson does not use the term "fighting position" or any similar term, to describe Mr. Tasi's manipulation of the stick during his initial interview with Detective Huelskoeter. He was not aware of the security video at that time.*

3. "It's consistent with getting in a fighting position with a blunt object. Q Okay. Is it also consistent with raising your hands in the air with a broomstick in your hand? A No. It's a fighting position. He's assuming a fighting position."

*Again, Officer Gionson never characterizes Mr. Tasi's movement as assuming "a fighting position with a blunt object" in his original statement. In the video it is clear that Mr. Tasi proceeds east on the sidewalk in a straight line, that Officer Gionson is always at an angle behind the fence to Mr. Tasi's left, that Mr. Tasi never steps in Officer Gionson's direction as if to mount an attack, that Mr. Tasi's feet remain slightly separated, even with one another, and oriented in a north-to-south direction, and, finally, that Mr. Tasi remains on the right half (south half) just before being shot.*

4. "Well, do you admit or deny that when you said: He was close enough to hit me with the stick is when I decided he's not going to stop, that that wasn't accurate? A From my perception it was, at the time—at the time of the incident. Q But in truth and reality, in terms of how close he was, it's not accurate, is it? A It is accurate. Q So you're.... .A Because I'm—from my perception, it's from my perception.

*The video shows that Officer Gionson, who was on the north side of the center chain-link fence, was beyond Mr. Tasi's reach, even with the stick. Further, Mr. Tasi's orientation and direction of travel, as described in my response to point #3 above, were not consistent with mounting an attack on the officer.*

5. Q But, sir, you say right here: When he first stepped out, I stepped around the fence from where I was positioned into the courtyard between myself—I put myself between myself and the three civilians that had flagged me down. I basically I blocked the entrance to the alleyway and they were behind the gate behind me. Q That's not what we saw on the tape, is it? A Saw me moving in that direction. Q But you.... .A And it's based on my perception at the time. Q Okay. But you didn't actually step into the courtyard, did you? A No, I did not step into the courtyard. Q So when you made this statement that wasn't true, was it? A Based on my perception it was. Q Well, you're saying based on your perception and your claim, but the actual truth is you made a statement that was false, isn't it? A I made a statement based on my perception at the time and I was closing distance between him and myself. Q Okay. But the statement was false, wasn't it? A Not at the time. Q Well, it's not correct to say that you stepped into the courtyard before you shot him, is it? A I would say—no, it wouldn't. I would say that the video shows a true and actual depiction of what happened. But based on my perception at the time of this interview.... .Q Okay. A.... that's what happened

*We know from the video that both claims are false.*[30] *It's not what happened and, therefore, can't provide reasonable grounds for his decision to shoot. His assertion that his subjective beliefs are sufficient—based upon false perceptions that don't square with the objective reality shown in the video—is untenable.*

6. "A So from my perception of when the incident occurred that's what I did. Q But this statement that you just saw, that you gave to the officer, wasn't true, was it? A It wasn't accurate, but it was my perception at the time. Q But it wasn't true, was it? A It was true from my perception. Q But factually it was not.... .A After reviewing the video, I saw that I hadn't stepped into the courtyard ."

*Officer Gionson's repeated claim that, "It was true from my perception," has an Alice-in-Wonderland quality to it. That may have been, and still may be, his subjective belief at the time of the shooting, but it is not the objective real-*

---

30. [**Expert #4**]'s footnote: I am not suggesting that the officer is being untruthful; rather, I'm alluding to the fact that high stress can dramatically distort perception and recall.

*ity that existed when he shot and killed Mr. Tasi. He plainly was not where he claimed to be. Consequently, his inaccurate perceptions—contrary to the objective facts—cannot be relied upon as reasonable justification for the use of deadly force.*

Security Video Review: Sequence of Mr. Tasi's Movements with the Stick

To constitute an imminent deadly threat Mr. Tasi had to have the intent, the means, and the opportunity. His intent was unclear—though individual observers might infer very different intent from the same set of behaviors—but he did have the means to attack another person.

The stick, though apparently quite light and relatively small in diameter, could be used to inflict serious injuries. However, Mr. Tasi clearly lacked the opportunity because both the witnesses and Officer Gionson were beyond Mr. Tasi's range, even with the stick and his arm fully extended. **Of critical importance is the fact that an apparently sturdy, waist-high, chain-link fence separated Mr. Tasi and the officer**. I have done a second-by-second analysis of Mr. Tasi's movements with the stick:

13:30:38 Mr. Tasi exits the building with the stick in his right hand; the stick is pointed toward the ground at an angle.

13:30:40 Mr. Tasi, the stick still in his right hand, taps the ground with it.

13:30:42 Mr. Tasi moves the stick across the front of his body and switches it to his left hand. The stick is pointed to the ground at an angle and he taps the sidewalk with it.

13:30:43 Mr. Tasi moves the stick directly up with his left hand back behind his neck parallel to the ground and grabs the free end with his right hand. The stick is parallel to the ground at the back of his head. He then takes his right hand off and moves the stick straight down with his left hand, which travels close to his left side. The stick is waist high, parallel to the ground, and close to his body at this point.

13:30:44 Mr. Tasi's left arm and hand, which is holding the stick waist high, parallel to the ground, are close to his left side. He appears to react to being shot at this point.

13:30:45 Mr. Tasi collapses and drops the stick, which appears to land and come to a rest by the north post of the short fence running from the NE corner of 707 N Bunn to the SE corner of the sidewalk.

At no point on the video does Mr. Tasi position the stick in what is typically viewed as a striking position or make any motion signifying an imminent attack. He never extends his arms fully as if to prepare to strike somebody with the stick or raises it above his head. He never changes direction towards the officer. His arms and hands remain close to his body throughout the sequence.

### APD Policy, the Tactical Importance of the Fence, and the Meaning of Imminent

Sergeant Shaun Henry, APD's lead firearms trainer and force expert, asserts in his deposition that Mr. Tasi represented an imminent threat from the very moment he exited the building, despite the fact that he was walking fairly normal and carrying the stick toward the ground as he walked toward the sidewalk opening that leads to the east parking lot. During his deposition, the following exchange took place:

> MR. WEIDNER: Q "[When] Mr. Tasi first came out of the apartment with a broomstick, there was a sufficient threat of imminent deadly— imminent death or bodily injury that the officer could have shot? That's what you're telling me? SERGEANT HENRY: A Yes. It's consistent with policy and training, yes.

At the time he exited, Mr. Tasi was approximately 30' from the end of the fence that runs east and west between the two directly opposite fourplexes, it took him 6–7 seconds to reach the point where he was shot, and he carried the stick pointed to the ground for most of that time and distance. In his deposition Sergeant Henry was not asked, "How far away would Mr. Tasi have to be to no longer constitute an imminent threat?" That is a legitimate question and of great import for APD's training on the use of deadly force. Based upon the above testimony, it would have to be somewhere beyond 30'. And that's without factoring in the intervening fence, the effective range of the stick, and the fact that the officer was already in a full shooting stance.

If the sergeant's opinion is, in fact, an accurate recitation of APD policy, the officer would have been justified in shooting Mr. Tasi the second he exited the building—**even though, at that point, he was absolutely incapable of striking anybody, had not committed any serious crime, and had made no threats or threatening movements with the stick. No reasonable officer would believe that shooting Mr. Tasi in those circumstances was justifiable.**

Sergeant Henry further stated that the fence separating Mr. Tasi and Officer Gionson at the time of the shooting was "very small," "pretty low," "pretty wimpy," and that "[he] might be able to just step over it. (He had never seen the fence.) And certainly, just about anybody could jump over it as part of a moving instant act." Based upon his characterizations, I concluded that he regarded the intervening, waist-high, obviously sturdy chain-link fence as inconsequential in the fatal shooting of Mr. Tasi. He represented his opinion as

APD-approved training policy and procedure. He offered no written training material to substantiate that representation.[31]

Sergeant Henry did concede that sufficient time existed for the officer to warn Mr. Tasi that the he would shoot if Mr. Tasi didn't not comply with the officer's commands. Officer Gionson issued no such warning, nor did he turn on his digital recorder, though he had ample time to do both. A reasonable officer would know that such a warning was required, if feasible, before using deadly force. Further, a reasonable officer would have issued one in this situation.

Sergeant Henry acknowledges that, in effect, issuing a warning was feasible in the Tasi shooting and that there was no tactical reason for not doing so.

Witness Accounts (summary statements from APD Report #12-26605)

Note: I was not provided copies of the witnesses'APD taped statements.

Interview of Corie HUNTLEY (no indication that it was taped)

She heard "really loud smacks on the wall"(quotation marks in the report) and then heard a window break. She went onto her balcony and saw 3 males (neighbors) running toward the main entrance to her building. They said they needed to get into the building because there was a problem downstairs. She went down, let them in and returned to her balcony. She saw an officer with his gun out standing in the driveway. "Seconds later" she saw the man who got shot come out of the downstairs apartment carrying a "3–4 foot long stick," almost like a broomstick. The man walked towards the officer yelling, "What? What? What?" She heard the officer yell, "Put the stick down! Put the stick down!" The officer then shot the male. She said she heard 3 shots and went back inside.

Zachary STEWARD Interview (taped)

STEWARD was outside playing basketball when an officer (bald) asked him if he had seen a male causing a disturbance. He told the officer that he hadn't, but that he had heard a disturbance from the bottom apartment on the east end of 707 N Bunn. Later he saw an officer near the east end of the building next to the opening on the fence that blocked off the yard. He said that he heard the officer yell at a Samoan male that had a "bat" in his hand.

---

31. [**Expert #4**]'s footnote: The Las Vegas Metropolitan Police Department, in its policy on the use of force (6/002.00 USE OF FORCE, p.5) specifically mentions "physical barriers" as a factor in assessing the question of "opportunity". The section reads: "Opportunity exists when a person is in a position to effectively resist an officer's control or use force or violence upon the officer or another. Examples which (sic) may affect opportunity include: relative distance to the officer or others, and physical barriers between the subject and the officer."

The officer told the man to drop the bat three times, but the male kept coming toward him. The male was swinging the bat around while the officer was telling him to drop it. The male kept saying, "What you gonna do? What you gonna do?" He kept walking toward the officer and threatening him He said the male then grabbed the bat with two hands in a "baseball batter's style grip" and started to swing at the officer. That's when the officer shot. He said that the officer never retreated, but moved back some, staying near the opening of the fence. Earlier he had heard a loud disturbance in the same residence, including loud yelling and glass breaking. STEWARD told the officer that "the cop was totally in the clear in everything he did." At the end of the interview, CHILDERS transported him to APD HQ.

Bronson BIRDSELL Interview (Recorded)

BIRDSELL said he heard a "violent sounding disturbance) in the lower left hand apartment. He heard glass breaking and it sounded like someone "was getting killed inside." When officers arrived, a male carrying a stick 4' long and about an inch and a half in diameter "came out of the apartment. The male raised the stick like he was going to hit either BIRDSELL or the officer. "The suspect charged the officer, not at a sprint, but at a fast pace." The officer ordered the male to drop the weapon at least twice, but the male did not comply. The officer then shot the male.

(This interview was conducted by Officer Sutcliffe at the scene.)

Bronson BIRDSELL Interview (Recorded)

He heard the disturbance while watching a movie with his friends — glass breaking from the apartment behind his. They went outside and ran to the apartment. He could hear a female yelling, "Get off me." He banged on the apartment window to distract the persons involved in the disturbance. A lady let them in through the unit's secure front door and they went to the door of the apartment. The door was open about a foot, but the male inside closed it quickly. They went back outside and flagged down on officer driving on N Bunn Street. BIRDSELL then headed toward an officer in the alley. There is a fence that separates the two buildings and a small fence that separates the parking area. The male then exited the building with a stick in his left hand. BIRDSELL backed up and stood near a small SUV, as he thought the male was coming for him. He heard the officer tell the male to drop the stick at least twice. The male was within 3–5' of the officer when shots were fired. He felt that the male would have killed him if the officer wasn't there. The stick was 3'to 4' long.(This interview was conducted by Detective Huelskoetter at APD Headquarters.)

### Jason NETTER Interview (DVD Recorded)

NETTER told him that he was watching a movie with his friends Ray and Willie when they heard a loud bang and a window shatter. NEITER heard a woman screaming, "Get off me." He looked out the kitchen window and saw broken glass from the building next door. They ran to the building, tried the door and knocked on the window. NETTER said that a Samoan male came out of the apartment and was swinging a stick as he walked toward the officers. The officer told the male to drop the stick 3 times, but the male kept swinging the stick and coming towards the officer. The officer then fired at the male. He described the stick as "long, 5 feet." He said he didn't know how big around the stick was, but it was smaller than a baseball bat. NETTER placed the officer and TASI close enough that the officer could have been hit by the stick.

### Zachary STEWARD Interview (DVD Recorded)

He was playing basketball and heard glass crash and people screaming. He moved closer to check things out and saw an officer drive by. He told the officer about the disturbance. The male Samoan then came outside with a stick in his hand and approached the officer. The officer told the male to put the stick down and back away. The male then put two hands on the stick "like to swing it." The stick was 3–4' long and looked like a bat. STEWARD said that the male was "swinging the stick around in an aggressive manner." The officer fired three shots.

### Officer James TRULL Interview (Recorded)

He responded to the disturbance call, talked to a young man playing basketball, who told him that he had seen the male Samoan and pointed out 707 N Bunn, saying that he heard glass breaking there. TRULL was also flagged down by three males who directed him to the N Bunn address. They told him that it was an emergency, so TRULL requested additional officers. He exited his car and started walking down the sidewalk eastbound. He could see GIONSON on the northeast comer of the building. He then saw the male Samoan exit the apartment unit and walk toward GIONSON with something "like a broom or mop handle" that was about 4' long. The male had the handle in a two-handed grip, "like a sword." The male walked "aggressively" toward the officer, yelling something that TRULL couldn't make out. He saw GIONSON "at guard (pistol drawn)" commanding the male to "drop it." The male continued walking toward the officer, who then fired. TRULL estimated that the distance between the officer and the male at the time the officer shot was about 8–10'. He says that GIONSON was "just off the parking area at the end of the fence separating the buildings."

### William EMRY Interview (Recorded)

EMRY was home with BIRDSELL and NETTER when they heard the window break. He also heard the "muffled" sounds of a woman, "Get off me." All three ran to the apartment where the disturbance was occurring. BIRDSELL hit the window in an attempt to stop the disturbance. A woman let them into the building and he saw a Samoan male through the open door. The male shut the door. They then went outside to locate some police officers. They saw one car on N Bunn and another car in the alley. EMRY was near the officer in the alley when the male with the stick exited the apartment. He said the male was holding the stick "like you hold a rifle." He moved south in the alley, as he heard the officer tell the male to "Put it down, put it down, drop your weapon." He estimates that the male was about 6' to 8' from the officer when the shooting took place. He said the male was close enough to "puncture my skin." As the male walked toward the officer, he was saying something that EMRY couldn't understand. He said the male wasn't "charging," but " … like an angry person walking really hard." He added, "Walking like he wanted to hurt a person really bad."

### Corie HUNTLEY Interview (Recorded)

HUNTLEY lives upstairs at 707 N Bunn and heard banging and yelling coming from the apartment downstairs, and the heard glass breaking. She went out on her balcony to see what was going on. She saw nothing but kept hearing the disturbance. She then saw three men running from the alley and let them into the building. The police then began to arrive. She saw the male who lives downstairs come outside with a stick. The male walked toward the three men and the officer to whom they were talking in the alley. The officer told the male to drop the stick a couple of times, but the male kept saying, "What, what, what?" The officer then drew his weapon and shot the male. She said the male was pretty close to the officer, maybe 3' to 4' when he was shot. The male, to her, seemed more focused on the three men than the officer. She said the male was holding the stick up as he walked. She thought it might be a broom stick. She said that the officer's commands were clear and thought he was going to use a Tazer (sic) on the male.

### Annie LEVI Interview (Recorded)

LEVI works at New Concept 3, an assisted-living home at 798 N Bunn Street, was outside in the parking area and saw the shooting. She said that she saw "Shane" walk outside of the house, holding a stick. She also saw an officer at the corner and assumed he told "Shane" to drop the stick, but he didn't. A short time later she heard 3 shots. She knows TASI from the Holiday Gas Station where she also works. She was outside with Laura MARTIN when the shooting happened. She said that she was aware of the window being broken out, but didn't hear other signs of a disturbance. That was 2 to 3 minutes before the shooting. She described "Shane" as "swinging the stick around as he walked towards the officer who shot him."

There is general agreement among the witnesses, with some minor variations, about the following facts:

- Mr. Tasi had a yellow stick approximately 3' to 4' in length.
- Mr. Tasi manipulated the stick as he walked.
- Mr. Tasi was walking, not running.
- Officer Gionson commanded Mr. Tasi to drop the stick 2–3 times.
- Mr. Tasi did not comply with the commands to drop the stick.
- Mr. Tasi said something to the effect of "what, what, what," or "whata you gonna do," whata you gonna do."
- Mr. Tasi continued to walk at the same pace until he was shot.
- Officer Gionson fired a total of three shots.
- Officer Gionson never warned Mr. Tasi that he would shoot if he failed to comply with his commands and move near enough to use the stick as a weapon.

Several of the witnesses describe Mr. Tasi holding the stick with two hands, as if holding a baseball bat or sword. This is refuted by the video. The only time Mr. Tasi had the stick in both hands was when he held it behind his head. He had his hands on opposite ends of the stick at that time.

Three witnesses qualify their description of the manner in which Mr. Tasi walked toward the officer and the three males witnesses:

- BIRDSELL says that Mr. Tasi " … charged the officer, not at a sprint, but at a fast pace."
- Officer TRULL stated, "The male walked "aggressively" toward the officer."
- EMRY said, " … the male wasn't "charging," but " … like an angry person walking really hard."

Lastly, the witness accounts vary significantly in terms of the estimated distance between the officer and Mr. Tasi when the shooting occurred:

- BIRDSELL estimates the distance as 3' to 5'.
- NETTER says that Mr. Tasi was close enough to hit the officer, but does not put it in terms feet and inches.
- Officer TRULL estimates the distance as 8' to 10'.
- EMRY estimates the distance as 6' to 8'.
- HUNTLEY estimates the distance as "maybe 3' to 4'."
- NETTER states that the officer and Mr. Tasi were close enough " … that the officer could have been hit by the stick."

The summaries of the remaining witnesses include no estimate of the distance between the officer and Mr. Tasi. However, Mr. Weidner's investigator re-interviewed most of the witnesses, had several draw scene sketches, and reconstructed the incident based on the interviews and the sketches. The investigator measured the distance between the officer and Mr. Tasi in his reconstruction as 13'. This is shown in a photo dated June 20, 2012 taken at 18:49:03, which places Officer Gionson at the west edge of the large oil stain. I believe that this location is off by several feet, as the officer moved directly west and out of sight between the two buildings in the video that opens with Officer Gionson meeting with the three witnesses in the parking lot.[32] This movement placed the fence directly between Officer Gionson and Mr. Tasi. The angle between them is hard to estimate, given the compression in the video, but it appears to be somewhere between 40 and 60 degrees, using Mr. Tasi as the origin.

The investigator had four witnesses—HUNTLEY, BIRDSELL, EMRY, and LEVI—complete scene sketches on which they located Officer Gionson and Mr. Tasi at the time of the shooting. All put Mr. Tasi in approximately the same location. HUNTLEY and BIRDSELL placed Officer Gionson west of the east fence post and north of the chain-link fence. This is consistent with the video. EMRY places Officer Gionson in the sidewalk opening between the two fence posts. The video shows the officer in that position, but only after the shooting has occurred. LEVI places Officer Gionson at the east fence post. The video shows that he didn't move close to the fence post until after the shooting.[33]

---

32. [**Expert #4**]'s footnote: It is not clear how far the officer actually moved west into the alley between the fourplexes, but I estimate that it was several feet. Based upon that estimate, the distance between Mr. Tasi and the officer would have been approximately 11'. It doesn't appear that he moved either south or north, but the video compression makes it difficult to gauge distances accurately unless there is a definite referent. Mr. Tasi is 6'0" and fell forward after being shot, so his height is a significant factor in making any estimates from the video. The blood spatters on the sidewalk were 9.3 N and 4.3 W, but there seems to be no way to determine when in the sequence of him getting shot and falling they were deposited. Obviously, it was sometimes between the time Mr. Tasi was shot and he hit the ground.

33. [**Expert #4**]'s footnote: I assume that similar sketches were made during both the APD criminal and administrative investigations, but none have been provided to me. I have asked also for the OIS scene diagram(s), but none have been provided.

Moreover, I assume that the rough sketch provided to Mr. Weidner is not the same as the final, comprehensive scene diagram (or diagrams), which is a standard document in any OIS criminal or administrative investigation

<u>Professional Opinions</u>[34]

A reasonable, trained, prudent police officer would not have believed that Mr. Tasi was an immediate threat justifying the use of deadly force at the moment he was shot for a number of reasons:

1. There was a barrier between the officer and Mr. Tasi—a sturdy, 3' high chain-link fence—that impeded his path to the officer. Contrary to Sergeant Henry's opinion, Mr. Tasi could not have simply "stepped over" the fence. Officers are trained that such barriers are important tactical considerations in any encounter involving a potential threat. Although the fence did not constitute cover or concealment, as those terms are defined in police training, those issues are not relevant in this case because Mr. Tasi was not armed with a firearm, nor was there a need for concealment. Mr. Tasi also was walking directly east and did not move northeast toward the officer at any time. A reasonable officer would have factored the fence into his/her tactical decision-making even in a compressed time scale.

2. To strike the officer with the stick, Mr. Tasi would have had to vault the fence or go around the east end of it. He made no overt movement to do either. A trained, competent, reasonable officer would have continued to use the fence to his tactical advantage. Another possibility would have been for the officer to position himself at the fence close to Mr. Tasi's location—that is, within striking distance. Thus, if Mr. Tasi did intend to attack the officer with the stick, he would have had the opportunity to do so. However, officers are trained to avoid tactics that are foolhardy, provocative, or exceptionally high risk.

3. Opportunity is a critical element in any assault. Though Mr. Tasi had the means, and, possibly the intent, he did not have the opportunity, as Officer Gionson and the three witnesses were beyond Mr. Tasi's range at the time he was shot.

4. Though Mr. Tasi manipulated the stick as he walked, he never moved it to a typical striking position (high over his head, arm in an L configuration, stick cocked back) or jabbing position. At the time he was shot he was moving the stick down to his left side, parallel to the ground, about waist high. He did not extend his arm in the officer's direction as he did.

---

34. **[Expert #4]'s footnote:** I have requested other documents that I assume exist, such as taped statements of witnesses, taped statements of any involved officers, a copy of the dispatch tape, any depositions taken in the case, and a scene diagram, but I have not received them. Hence, for the record once again, I reserve the right to amend this Preliminary Report and, in particular, my opinions and any assumptions or conclusions underpinning them, if additional material is provided that warrants reconsideration.

5. APD policy, along with best practice in the field, stresses the need (the training slide actually uses the term "must assess") for officers to develop and maintain a high level of situation awareness (SA), which is defined as:

> *"The perception of the elements in the environment that matter, an understanding of their significance and the projection of scenarios in which their likely impacts are assessed and managed. Simply put, it is knowing what is going on around you."*

6. Officer Gionson failed to maintain a current, accurate level of situation awareness by failing to factor the chain-link fence into his tactical decision-making and by failing to monitor the location of the three witnesses, who, at the time of the shooting, had moved well out of Mr. Tasi's range. Hence, there was no imminent threat to any of them when he shot Mr. Tasi. As a result of his diminished level of SA, his account of the shooting deviates sharply from what is seen on the video. Fixating on Mr. Tasi early in the encounter probably contributed to his low level of SA.

7. Officer Gionson had sufficient time to issue a warning to Mr. Tasi that he would use deadly force if Mr. Tasi continued to advance with the stick and ignore his commands to drop it. He had already assumed a "guard" position before Mr. Tasi appeared, and then quickly went into a full shooting stance when he did appear. He had the fence between him and Mr. Tasi, who was over 30' away initially. It took Mr. Tasi 6–7 seconds to walk to the point where the officer shot him. Consequently, there were no tactical reasons to not issue a warning, nor was issuing a warning "infeasible." Sergeant Henry agreed that there was time to issue a warning. Had Officer Gionson done so, Mr. Tasi might have realized the seriousness of the situation[35] and then complied with the officer's commands which is exactly the rationale for issuing a warning. A trained, competent, reasonable officer would have issued a warning.

8. Sergeant Henry's understanding of the term "imminent threat" is far off the mark. Hence, APD should be concerned because he apparently is the department's lead trainer on use-of-force issues. His characterization of Mr. Tasi

---

35. [**Expert #4**]'s **footnote:** There remains a legitimate question of whether Officer Gionson was clearly identifiable as a police officer for several reasons: first, he did not have a hat on; two, his arms were extended fully from his shoulders in a full shooting stance upon Mr. Tasi's exit, probably concealing his badge; three, he would have been partially obscured by the fence (at least to his waist); and, four, his shoulder patches, because of his east-west orientation, probably weren't visible from Mr. Tasi's perspective. That is why officers are trained to identify themselves verbally in such situations. A trained, competent, reasonable officer would include "Police" in his/her standard command to an advancing subject with a stick in hand.

as an "imminent threat" at the very moment he exited the building—and therefore "shootable"—simply fails the test of objective reasonableness. No reasonable officer would agree with the interpretation of "imminent threat" that he articulates in his deposition.

## Case History #4: Discussion of Expert #4's Opinion

[Expert #4] ignores the standards for the use of deadly force by law enforcement established by the U.S. Supreme Court, as well as the equally clear standard provided by the Court for judging the use of deadly force.[36] The only passing reference is [Expert #4]'s assertion that APD Sergeant Henry's understanding of the term "imminent threat" is far off the mark.[37]

But the issue is whether Officer Gionson's perception of imminent threat was objectively reasonable under the circumstances. If it was, his decision to use deadly force was justified. Therefore it is necessary to assess his (Gionson's) perception of the imminent threat posed by Mr. Tasi.

[Expert #4] goes to great lengths to identify discrepancies between Officer Gionson's personal recall of the event, and the surveillance video of the event, apparently to show that Officer Gionson is being untruthful. Regarding Officer Gionson's recollections that Tasi was close enough to hit him (Gionson) with the stick and that he (Gionson) stepped around the short fence there to interpose himself between Tasi and the three civilians, [Expert #4] writes, "We know from the video that both claims are false." He adds a footnote saying, "I am not suggesting that the officer is being untruthful; rather, I'm alluding to the fact that high stress can dramatically distort perception and recall."[38]

---

36. *Tennessee v. Garner*, 471 U.S. 1 (1985), and *Graham v. Connor*, 490 U.S. (1989). These decisions are the legal basis for law enforcement deadly force policy and training throughout the United States, all of which must conform to the standards and limitations specified by the Court. One result is that deadly force policies, training, and practice are uniform throughout law enforcement in the United States—federal, state, and local. More recent decisions have reinforced the standards established in *Garner* and *Graham*, and have been incorporated into law enforcement use-of-force training.

37. See Expert #4 Report: "Sergeant Henry's understanding of the term 'imminent threat' is far off the mark. Hence, APD should be concerned because he apparently is the department's lead trainer on use-of-force issues." Yet, Sergeant Henry did not shoot anybody, nor was he even present when Officer Gionson shot Mr. Tasi. Sgt. Henry's understanding of "imminent threat" is irrelevant to an objective assessment of Officer Gionson's perception of risk and decision to shoot.

38. See [Expert #4] report above.

It is unreasonable and unrealistic to expect that the personal recollection of a participant in a high-stress incident must coincide with video of the event or forensic evidence examined in the aftermath. All police officers involved in deadly force confrontations experience the scientifically well-documented physiological, psychological, and perceptual stimuli that suddenly and inexorably arise. These stimuli affect the individual's ability to distinguish and recall the event comprehensively and with precision. Officers involved in shooting incidents seldom recall exact positions, distances, or times. They are focused on protecting themselves and others, singularly focused on the threat confronting them, and commonly unaware of incidental circumstances, subtleties of movement, observational details, or peripheral events. Officers commonly cannot recall how many shots they fired, exactly where they were in feet and inches relative to their opponent, how much time elapsed (except that they always seem to *overestimate* it), or any of the myriad other subtle and minute details that will be fleshed out by forensic analysis and/or video tape. [Expert #4] gives nodding recognition to this reality,[39] but ignores that reality throughout his report as he goes to great lengths to emphasize details of Officer Gionson's narrative that differ with [Expert #4]'s analysis of the surveillance videos of the incident.

There is no requirement in law or policy requiring that an officer's account of an incident cannot vary from any video or forensic evidence examined after the fact in order for the officer's decision to use deadly force to be justified. To the contrary, this is using 20/20 hindsight solely for the purpose of second guessing the officer, if not discrediting him outright, and does not comport with the objective reasonableness standard mandated for assessing any police use of force. If the officer is unable to accurately recall and describe every detail, it does not discredit the decision to use deadly force. It is an *objective* standard independent of subjective motivation or incomplete memory. The officer's decision is made based upon what his adversary does, and what that reasonably portends under the circumstances, as viewed by an objectively reasonable observer.

[Expert #4] does not do this. He dismisses any threat posed by Tasi in several ways. He notes there was a barrier between Tasi and Office Gionson that "impeded his path to the officer." He disputes Sgt. Henry's opinion about the height of the fence, an irrelevancy, and notes that Mr. Tasi "also was walking directly east and did not move northeast toward the officer at any time." [[Expert #4]'s Professional Opinion #1]

He returns to the fence in his second opinion, noting that Mr. Tasi made no "overt movement" to vault the fence or go around the east end of it, asserting

---

39. See [Expert #4]'s footnote 19, *supra.*

that was the only way for him to strike the officer with the stick. Or, [Expert #4] notes, were "the officer to position himself at the fence close to Mr. Tasi's location—that is within striking distance. Thus if Mr. Tasi did intend to attack the officer with the stick, he would have had the opportunity to do so. *However, officers are trained to avoid tactics that are foolhardy, provocative, or exceptionally high risk.*" (Emphasis added.) [[Expert #4]'s Professional Opinion #2]

Even if Officer Gionson made a tactical error, it would not invalidate his right to protect himself. Second, the presence of the fence ([Expert #4] Professional Opinion #1) does not invalidate Officer Gionson's decision to shoot. He does not have to assume an inability by Tasi to overcome the low fence. It runs parallel to the sidewalk that Tasi was walking on. The fence ends at the end of the sidewalk at an opening somewhat wider than the sidewalk. Officer Gionson was standing at the end of the fence to Tasi's left front as he (Tasi) approached, close enough to step into the opening directly. He did not approach Tasi at all—Tasi approached him, walking the length of the sidewalk as he manipulated the stick despite Officer Gionson's repeated orders to drop it. Gionson merely stood his ground until Tasi made an "overt movement" with the stick. But that is not the single issue of decision that [Expert #4] makes it out to be. The totality of the circumstances, including what was known of Tasi's prior behavior, the information relayed to Officer Gionson by witnesses, and Tasi's behavior and manner as he walked at Officer Gionson, created a clear and unmistakable impression of belligerence and intended violence. Officer Gionson was under no constraint requiring him to wait for an "overt movement" with the stick. The circumstances supported the belief that if Gionson waited any longer, Tasi would advance the additional one or two steps necessary to actually reach Gionson with the stick and simultaneously hit him with it. It is reasonable and justified to use deadly force to prevent an *imminent* threat of serious injury from becoming an *actual* attempt or infliction of injury. Police officers do not need to wait until they have been hit or are certain an attack is intended if the circumstances support the perception an attack is impending.

The foregoing refutes [Expert #4]'s third and fourth Professional Opinions, in which he writes:

> "Opportunity is a critical element in any assault. Though Mr. Tasi had the means, and, possibly the intent, he did not have the opportunity, as Officer Gionson and the three witnesses were beyond Mr. Tasi's range at the time he was shot." [[Expert #4]'s Professional Opinion #3]
>
> "Though Mr. Tasi manipulated the stick as he walked, he never moved it to atypical striking position (high over his head, arm in an

L configuration, stick cocked back) or jabbing position. At the time he was shot he was moving the stick down to his left side, parallel to the ground, about waist high. He did not extend his arm in the officer's direction as he did." [[Expert #4]'s Professional Opinion #4]

Opinion #4 makes the ridiculous assertion that specific manipulations or positions of the stick described by [Expert #4] are definitive to any determination of imminent threat posed by Tasi's holding and manipulating the stick. This ignores two realities.

One, as mentioned above, is that Tasi was moving forward. He was within one (two at most) steps of being within arm's reach of Officer Gionson. Had Officer Gionson not fired when he did, and had Tasi not fallen when he did, he would have easily been on top of Officer Gionson in mere fractions of a second. He was not static, standing still and waving the stick aimlessly from a safe distance. He was striding towards Officer Gionson without pause, with determination and purpose, and visibly accelerating his pace as he approached. He recognized and interacted with Officer Gionson, demanding in a confrontational manner "What are you gonna do? What are you gonna do?" in response to Officer Gionson's repetitive orders to drop the stick. Tasi was rapidly approaching the open end of the adjacent fence. Within one or two steps he would have reached the end point of the fence with unobstructed access to Officer Gionson.

Second, the presence of the weapon in Tasi's hands coupled with his manner and his inexorable approach manifested a clear and imminent threat regardless of exactly where or how he held his stick. A sudden attack with the stick could come from any aspect of his stance/grip/arm location. In tenths of a second he could suddenly slash or stab with the stick, or initiate another form of attack. The realities of action/reaction dictate that at such close range, Officer Gionson physically could not react fast enough to protect himself from getting hit. And as previously noted, police officers are not required to let themselves get struck or injured before deciding to use the force necessary to stop it.

[Expert #4] makes assumptions unsupportable by any evidence that Mr. Tasi had neither the intent to attack the officer nor the opportunity anyhow because of the way he held his stick and the short fence between them. But Officer Gionson couldn't know that even if it were so. He was facing an individual (Tasi) acting in a manner consistent with the intent of assault, and that perception in turn was consistent with the circumstances that focused Gionson on Tasi in the first place. Tasi ignored orders to drop his weapon. He did not vary or pause his approach. He did nothing to mitigate the situation; indeed his only responses to Officer Gionson were confrontational. Tasi created a clear impression of imminent threat, and it was reasonable for Officer Gionson to believe him. He had no reason—legally, under policy, or by virtue of his training or experience—to second-guess Tasi's intent or to wait to see if an attack actually occurred at such close quarters that he could not stop or avert.

Officer Gionson believed the imminent assault was real and employed deadly force to prevent it from continuing. That is not unreasonable. The best use of deadly force is preemptive in nature, utilized to prevent a reasonably perceived *imminent* risk of injury from becoming an unmistakable *actual* attempt to injure.

[Expert #4] states in his Professional Opinion #5 that Anchorage Police Department trains its officers to develop and maintain a high level of situational awareness. That is a self-evident truth documented in APD training materials. It is incongruous to present it as a "Professional Opinion" except to pad [Expert #4]'s facade of expertise. It has no bearing on the reasonableness of Officer Gionson's perception of an imminent threat posed by Mr. Tasi. It is an example of how a plaintiff will attempt to make an irrelevant fact into a material one in the mind of the judge to ward off summary judgment. Unfortunately, that does work sometimes.

[Expert #4] states in his Professional Opinion #6 that "Officer Gionson failed to maintain a current, accurate level of situation awareness by failing to factor the chain-link fence into his tactical decision making and by failing to monitor the location of the three witnesses, who, at the time of the shooting, had moved well out of Mr. Tasi's range. *Hence, there was no imminent threat to any of them when he shot Mr. Tasi.*" (Emphasis added.)

Again [Expert #4] disregards the relevant issue. The question is not whether it can be imputed after the fact whether Officer Gionson could have done something else, or whether he *should* have calibrated the level of threat to the witnesses, or whether it can be shown after the fact that the only imminent threat was to himself. The question is whether Officer Gionson's perception of an imminent threat of serious injury to himself or to others was reasonable under the circumstances at the moment he made the decision to shoot, not whether it can be proven with the luxury of calm and reflective hind-sight that perhaps the threat was not as urgent in some regards as he thought it was at the time.[40]

---

40. "The 'reasonableness' of a particular use of force must be judged from the perspective of a reasonable officer on the scene, rather than with the 20/20 vision of hindsight. The Fourth Amendment is not violated by an arrest based on probable cause, even though the wrong person is arrested, nor by the mistaken execution of a valid search warrant on the wrong premises. With respect to a claim of excessive force, the same standard of reasonableness at the moment applies: 'Not every push or shove, even if it may later seem unnecessary in the peace of a judge's chambers.' The calculus of reasonableness must embody allowance

Officer Gionson was confronting an aggressive and manifestly hostile individual reported by witnesses to have been involved in circumstances consistent with domestic violence. That individual had earlier been reported acting aggressively and erratically. Officer Gionson was not shielded against an attack by Tasi. He lacked cover. Tasi was within a step of reaching Gionson. At that moment and under these circumstances, Officer Gionson's perception of an imminent threat of serious injury was well grounded and reasonable. A reasonable officer could not fail to perceive a risk of injury in those circumstances. Despite [Expert #4]'s assertion to the contrary, it is clear that Officer Gionson's situational awareness was excellent. He knew where the threat was; he recognized how close he could permit Tasi to approach; and he understood that if he stood aside or did not stop Tasi, then Tasi could chase down and assault the three witnesses unimpeded regardless of where they were at that particular moment. That assumes that Tasi would have chosen to by-pass Officer Gionson to pursue the three witnesses, an assumption not supported by his actions. Officer Gionson recognized that the three witnesses were potential victims, and that he had a duty to protect them as well as himself. The critical question as to whether he would need to act to protect himself and the others depended entirely upon what Tasi chose to do. That is a well-trained, well-experienced officer employing appropriate, effective situational awareness and exercising his judgment commensurate with his training and knowledge within the circumstances of the event.

Law enforcement officers are authorized to use deadly force " … when the officer has a reasonable belief that the subject of such force poses an imminent danger of death or serious physical injury to the officer or to another person."[41] [Expert #4] derides the danger, but getting violently hit (perhaps in the head, or stabbed in the eye) with a hardwood stick is a manifest risk of serious injury that also entails a risk of being incapacitated or debilitated. Physical helplessness due to injury can lead to a far more serious consequence, for example, being shot with one's own gun. There is nothing in law, policy, or training that would even hint that Office Gionson must take such risks on the mere hope that the worst does not happen.

[Expert #4] opines in his Professional Opinion #7: "Officer Gionson had sufficient time to issue a warning to Mr. Tasi that he would use deadly force if

---

for the fact that police officers are often forced to make split-second judgments—in circumstances that are tense, uncertain, and rapidly evolving—about the amount of force that is necessary in a particular situation." *Graham v. Connor*, 490 U.S. 388 (1989).

41. U.S. Department of Justice Policy Statement: Use of Deadly Force—uniform with the language of APD Deadly Force Policy.

Mr. Tasi continued to advance with the stick and ignore his commands to drop it.... Had Officer Gionson done so, Mr. Tasi might have realized the seriousness of the situation and then complied with the officer's commands, which is exactly the rationale for issuing a warning. A trained, competent, reasonable officer would have issued a warning."

First, there is no requirement in law, policy, or training for an officer to issue a verbal warning before using deadly force in the defense of self and others circumstance. There is a caveat requiring the issuance of a verbal warning *when feasible* before using deadly force in the prevention of escape circumstance. The shooting of Mr. Tasi was unequivocally a defense of self and others circumstance. That said, Officer Gionson repeatedly ordered Tasi to drop the stick, pointing his handgun at him as he did so. Officer Gionson was in uniform. He verbally and visually presented an unmistakable warning to Tasi that if he continued his approach, weapon in hand, he was risking getting shot. Tasi's defiance of Officer Gionson is confirmation that he was well aware of Officer Gionson's armed police presence. Tasi did not drop his stick, did not alter or slow his approach, and repeatedly defied Officer Gionson, "What are you gonna do? What are you gonna do?"

[Expert #4] speculates in Professional Opinion #7, "Had Officer Gionson done so, Mr. Tasi might have realized the seriousness of the situation and then complied with the officer's commands, which is exactly the rationale for issuing a warning."

It is wishful thinking that Tasi would have stopped if Officer Gionson could have just composed the exact combination of words, warning, and inflection to persuade him. No "trained, competent, reasonable" (Expert #4's descriptors) police officer is required, or can be expected, to trust his physical safety to speculative desperation. More to the point, if Tasi had stopped, dropped his stick, or stepped to the side in response to Officer Gionson, he would not have been shot. If he had done anything to mitigate the appearance of defiance and aggression that he projected, he would not have been shot. But he did not. Tasi persisted in his actions despite the unmistakable presence of an armed police officer telling him not to.

In a footnote to his Professional Opinion #7 [Expert #4] questions whether Officer Gionson was clearly identifiable as a police officer, suggesting that because of that uncertainty that may or may not have existed, Officer Gionson bore the onus of insuring that he verbally identified himself as "Police!"[42] This requires that Officer Gionson had reason to suspect that his armed, uniformed

---

42. See [Expert #4]'s footnote 29, *supra.*

presence was somehow unclear, and that he was obligated to take time to remedy that. It requires that the justified use of deadly force in defense of one's self and others requires an affirmative action to eliminate any possible doubt regarding the identity of the assailant's target. That is simply not true. Justified self-defense depends upon the actions of the assailant and how the intended target or victim perceives those actions, within the circumstances in which they take place. Law enforcement officers (uniformed and plainclothes alike) do not lose their right to defend themselves because their assailant may not have a clear understanding of their police status. That right of self-defense is not contingent upon the acuity of the assailant, or his inability or refusal to recognize he is facing a police officer. The justified use of deadly force in self-defense is dependent upon the reasonable perception of imminent serious injury, for police and civilians alike.

[Expert #4]'s final Professional Opinion #8 is devoted to quarreling with APD Sergeant Henry's understanding of the term "imminent threat." But Sgt. Henry did not shoot anybody. Sgt. Henry was not present at the scene when Officer Gionson shot Tasi. Sgt. Henry did not coach Officer Gionson; he did not order him to shoot Tasi or influence Gionson's decision. Sgt. Henry had nothing to do with the use of force by Officer Gionson. [Expert #4]'s dispute with Sgt. Henry about the meaning of "imminent threat" may be debatable on its merits. It is irrelevant to a determination of whether Officer Gionson's decision to use deadly force was objectively reasonable within the totality of the circumstances in which he (Gionson) made that decision.

The fact that Officer Gionson was not hurt, nor was Mr. Tasi able to carry through an attempt to hurt Officer Gionson, are apparently detrimental factors in [Expert #4]'s view. Yet prevention of death or injury is the *only* justification for the use of deadly force in the first place. That is the sole legitimizing rationale for the justified use of deadly force. It is false, at best, to imply that an officer must be injured to justify a use of deadly force or to imply that lack of injury is an indication of a lack of justification. It is equally false to say that an officer may not justifiably use deadly force until an actual attempt to inflict injury has been made. Such a standard would mean that no law enforcement officer could prevent injury or death, but only react to real attempts after they occurred, assuming that the officer has the good fortune not to be injured or killed first.

[Expert #4] ignores the overt threat manifest by Tasi's actions. He implies that absent any overt threats, movement within reach or swings of the stick at Officer Gionson, there was no imminent threat. He is wrong. The *perception* of an imminent risk of death or serious injury must be reasonable. If it is, then the use of deadly force *to prevent that imminent risk* is justified.

# Chapter 14

# Deadly Force Policies

*" ... It would be unreasonable to require that police officers take unnecessary risks in the performance of their duties."*
— *Terry v. Ohio*, 392 U.S. 1, 23 (1968)

As noted in the discussion on constitutional rules, violations of departmental policy are seldom relevant to the question of whether an officer violated someone's constitutional rights. The issue is whether the officer violated the Constitution. That is not to suggest that policy can never have legal significance. It can be relevant in two instances: First, the policy itself can be the basis for a department's legal liability if it can be established that the policy *caused* a constitutional violation; and second, it is conceivable that a policy could be viewed by a court as *creating a legal duty* owed a person, although this has not emerged as a serious factor.

## Policy as a Basis for Departmental Liability

As discussed in Chapter 6, departmental liability can result if it can be shown that a constitutional violation committed by an employee of that department was *caused by a policy, practice, or custom* of the department. This is often confused with the doctrine of "vicarious liability," which refers to the legal principle that the employer is liable for any unlawful acts committed by an employee acting within the scope of employment. The Supreme Court has held that *vicarious liability* cannot be a basis for departmental liability when the allegation is that an employee of the department violated the Constitution. Put simply, the department is liable only if it *caused* a violation of the Constitution through its policies, practices, or customs. For example, if a department's policy permits the use of deadly force to prevent the escape of *any* fleeing suspect regardless of the nature or severity of his crime, that policy can potentially cause an officer to use deadly force to prevent the escape of a non-dangerous, unarmed fleeing suspect in violation of the Fourth Amendment. In such a case the officer could be held liable for violating the suspect's Fourth Amendment right to be free from an unreasonable "seizure," while the department could be held liable for implementing a policy that caused that violation.

# Policy That Creates Legal Duties

Throughout this book, we have repeatedly stated that policy violations are not synonymous with constitutional violations. But, there is one aspect of that issue that deserves some attention. In the case *Scott v. Henrich*,[1] a federal appellate court suggested *the possibility* that policies could be relevant to a constitutional violation if "*one of their purposes is to protect the individual against whom force is used.*" The court offered no illumination as to a policy that would do so, or why it would rise to constitutional significance. In the case before it, the court ruled that the policies or guidelines at issue " ... *were meant to safeguard the police and other innocent persons, not the suspect ...*"[2]

The court's statement undoubtedly reflects the purpose of most departmental deadly force policies, i.e., to safeguard the officers and other innocent persons. On the other hand, it could be argued that those policies that are deliberately framed to be more restrictive than the constitutional standards have the practical effect of shifting the burden of risk from the suspect to the officer and other innocent persons, and to the community. In this sense, they conceivably could be construed as creating legal duties owed to the suspect, above and beyond those found in the Constitution.

This prospect is sufficiently troublesome to prompt some departments to include a caveat in their policy statements to the effect that no such result is intended. One prominent example is the policy adopted by the U.S. Department of Justice in 1995, which contains the following statement:

> "*Nothing in this policy and the attached commentary is intended to create or does create an enforceable legal right or private right of action.*"

Whether such language will have the desired effect remains to be seen. The fact that it was included in the policy statement is a strong indicator that its authors recognized the potential for such a construction.

---

1. 978 F.2d 481 (9th Cir. 1992).

2. *Ibid.* at 484. This case was reconsidered by the appellate court at 39 F.3d 912 (1994), but nothing in the subsequent opinion altered this portion of the first. To date only the 9th Circuit Court of Appeals has suggested the possibility of a departmental policy creating a right for a criminal suspect.

# Upsetting the Balance of Interests

An unnecessarily restrictive policy has the practical effect of upsetting the delicate balance the Constitution strikes between the *dangerous* and the *endangered*. While no *legal* consequences associated with a gratuitously restrictive policy have yet emerged, the *practical* effect is to thwart the purposes of the law of the land and undermine the safety of the community and its law enforcement officers.

It is common for law enforcement agencies to adopt more restrictive deadly force policies than required by law and the Constitution. Until recent years there were understandable reasons to do so, the most significant being that there was scant case law to provide guidance. That began to change in 1985 when the U.S. Supreme Court decided *Tennessee v. Garner*[3] and established specific standards for the use of deadly force by law enforcement officers in immediate defense of themselves and others as well as to prevent the escape of "dangerous" fleeing suspects.[4] In 1989 the Court decided *Graham v. Connor*[5] and provided clear guidance regarding the use of any level of force by law enforcement officers to effect a Fourth Amendment *seizure*. In combination, these two landmark decisions, coupled with a multitude of lower federal court decisions applying them, provide clear guidance to law enforcement agencies for the development of departmental policies that preserve the ability of law enforcement officers to protect themselves and the community while respecting the constitutional rights of criminal suspects.

Ironically, a survey of modern use-of-force policies, including a number of "model" policies making the rounds, would lead one to believe that these positive developments in the law never occurred. As a consequence, use-of-force policies too frequently look much like they did 50 years ago. Rather than providing clear and concise guidance to inform an officer's decision-making in circumstances that are frequently "tense, uncertain, and rapidly evolving," they too often obscure core policy principles with irrelevant and extraneous matters, and subject officers and society to greater risks than those required by law.

Such an unfortunate result may not be intended, and yet it happens. Consider the following scenario that happens every day in America: an individual commits an armed robbery during which he brandishes a knife, demands money, and flees the scene. The police are called and given a detailed account

---

3. 471 U.S. 1 (1985).
4. See Chapter 3 for full discussion.
5. 490 U.S. 386 (1989).

of the crime and a description of the perpetrator. Shortly thereafter, police officers encounter an individual in the vicinity who matches the description of the suspect. When they seek to stop him, he refuses to comply and runs away. His description, the time, and his location give the officers reason to believe this is the person who committed the crime. The officers are unable to overtake him, and because their department's policy prohibits the use of deadly force absent an imminent threat—despite the **Garner** decision—he is allowed to escape.

So here is the situation. The officers had probable cause to believe that the suspect had committed a crime *"involving the infliction or threatened infliction of serious physical injury."* The Supreme Court has held that it is reasonable under the Constitution to use deadly force if necessary to prevent the escape of such a person. And yet this suspect will remain free in the community for the time being and law enforcement resources will be consumed in an effort to find him. When they do, perhaps he will surrender quietly or perhaps he will violently resist. While he is at large, perhaps he will not commit another crime or threaten to inflict serious injury. The point is that the Supreme Court's decision to place the burden of risk on the dangerous suspect rather than on the community has been overridden by a departmental policy.

It is acknowledged that pressures to create restrictive policies are often generated by individuals or groups who are ill intentioned and whose views are unaffected by either the facts or the law. Such individuals may be seen clamoring for the termination and prosecution of an officer following a shooting incident before the facts have even been established or when it is clear to any thoughtful person that no constitutional violation occurred. It may seem futile to argue against such views, but there is a larger audience beyond the activists. They are interested and will listen. Most people are willing to be informed.

With that notion in mind, it would seem to be wiser to develop policies that maintain the appropriate balance of risks reflected by the law, and then to aggressively inform and educate the community that those laws are for their protection, rather than to bend to the pressures of the ill-informed or the ill-intentioned.

As we have discussed previously, the law does not develop or exist in a vacuum. Rather, it reflects certain identifiable interests and realities. The use of deadly force by law enforcement is a perfect example of this point. Legislatures and courts can readily grasp the importance of a rule that permits the use of deadly force to defend against immediate dangers of death or serious physical injury. However, they are ill equipped to anticipate the infinite range of circumstances in which such dangers may arise or to provide useful criteria for officers to use in assessing the existence or imminence of such threats. These matters evolve through the institutionalized experience of law enforcement, filtered and refined through court decisions that reflect case-by-case review of the manner in which individual officers have *already* made judgments within specific factual contexts.

In the absence of guidance from the law, the law enforcement community necessarily relies upon its collective experience and wisdom to resolve the questions. And this is generally translated into policy and training. Even though departmental policy is not generally relevant to the legal question of whether officers responded appropriately in a given circumstance, the courts often rely upon the experience of law enforcement, often reflected in policies, as a means of acquiring the "*perspective of a reasonable officer on the scene.*"

A good illustration of how this process has worked in recent years is the acceptance by the courts of law enforcement's experience with knife-wielding suspects. Contrary to the common perception that a person armed with a knife poses no immediate threat to an armed officer who is out of reach, law enforcement experience suggested that this perception was wrong and that a person armed with a knife could cover a distance of several yards and stab or slash an officer before the officer could effectively respond and end the threat. Experience and experimentation led to the formulation of a "21-foot rule" to assist officers in assessing the imminence of the threat.[6] Consequently, when that issue has arisen in the courts, the practical experience of law enforcement has informed the courts in their decisions.[7] Had law enforcement agencies ignored their experience and waited upon the courts to fill the void, not only would more officers have fallen victim to assailants armed with knives, the current case law would undoubtedly reflect the misperceptions fostered by ignorance rather than the realities born of experience.

The important point is that the graver the issues, the more aggressive law enforcement policy makers should be in asserting the legitimate interests of law enforcement officers and the communities they serve. Policy and training are the obvious vehicles by which to accomplish this goal. Otherwise, the

---

6. See Chapter 8—Tactical Factors & Misconceptions for the history and provenance of the "21-foot rule." The continued evolution of experience and experiment within law enforcement has demonstrated that the danger radius is realistically 30–35 feet rather than the old 21-foot rule of thumb.

7. See, for example, *Sigman v. Town of Chapel Hill*, 161 F.3d 782 (4th Cir. 1998), where the court referred to the "21-foot rule" used by many law enforcement agencies to define the imminence of the threat posed by a knife-wielding suspect. See also, *Reynolds v. City of San Diego*, 84 F.3d 851 (9th Cir. 1996).

courts have little alternative but to presume that the myths and misperceptions are valid.

The law makes a distinction between the "*dangerous*" and the "*endangered*." Law enforcement deadly force policies should do the same. With that idea as a philosophical backdrop, here are some principles to consider in writing a deadly force policy.

**_Legality_**. The policy must be consistent with the law. For reasons noted above, a policy must not authorize unconstitutional behavior. To ensure that the policy is consistent with the law, it is first necessary to determine what the law is. That means careful research into both the statutes of the relevant jurisdiction, as well as the case law. The underlying legal imperative is that the federal constitutional standards are applicable to *all* law enforcement officers at *all* levels. State laws and departmental policies can be stricter than the federal constitutional standards; they cannot be less so.

**_Brevity_**. Unlike other law enforcement policies that can usually be reviewed in the manual before a decision is made, a deadly force policy addresses circumstances that do not permit prior reflection and review. Therefore, the fundamental principles of the policy must be capable of easy understanding and rapid application. In a word, the policy must become second nature to those who apply it. It isn't practicable to consult the manual in the midst of "circumstances that are tense, uncertain, and rapidly evolving...." That means that the policy itself should be reduced to a few clearly stated principles that can be elaborated upon and explained in a separate commentary or in training materials. It is noteworthy that the general constitutional principles describing the justification for the use of force—deadly or otherwise—can be articulated in a few sentences. There is a strong argument to be made in support of a deadly force policy that contains only two statements:

1. *Immediate defense of life.* A statement concerning the authority of officers to defend themselves or others from immediate threats of serious physical injury; and,
2. *To prevent escape.* A statement describing the general circumstances that justify the use of deadly force to prevent escape.

An example of the first clause could read as follows:

> **_Immediate defense of life._** *Officers may use deadly force when necessary, that is, when there is a reasonable belief that a person poses an immediate threat of serious physical injury to themselves or others.*

This statement is modeled on the policy adopted by the U.S. Department of Justice (DOJ) in 1995 and essentially mirrors the constitutional principles laid out in Supreme Court decisions. The policy bases the authority to use deadly force on *necessity*, but makes it clear that a reasonable belief in the immediacy of a threat creates that necessity. It is simple and it is straightforward. It tracks constitutional law, and it avoids any implication that an officer must consider lesser alternatives in the face of an immediate threat to himself or others. Moreover, it consists of 30 words, as contrasted with the 3,000 words comprising a recent "model" policy reviewed by the authors.

A simple *prevention of escape* clause would track the Supreme Court's decision in *Tennessee v. Garner* in language such as this:

> *Prevention of escape. Officers may use deadly force when necessary to prevent the escape of a fleeing suspect whenever they have reason to believe the suspect has committed a crime involving the infliction or threatened infliction of serious physical injury. When feasible, a verbal warning should be given before deadly force is used.*

As noted elsewhere in this book, despite the Supreme Court's decisions on this issue, many departments have opted to adopt a stricter policy or a blanket prohibition. Others attempt to write *prevention of escape* policies that fall between the opposite poles of full constitutional authority and blanket prohibition. This approach is illustrated by the 1995 DOJ policy described in Chapter 4 which sought to write a stricter policy by including an *imminent danger* component to the *prevention of escape* clause. The result was a meaningless statement that simply replicated the *immediate threat* clause and created so much confusion it was removed a few years later.

Some state and local departments have benefited from statutes that enumerate offenses that are deemed "dangerous." These specific offenses can be listed in the policy text, or, preferably, incorporated in training materials. Care should be taken to ensure that any "dangerous" crimes thus enumerated fit within the Supreme Court's definition in *Garner*—i.e., crimes "*involving infliction or threatened infliction of serious physical injury.*" The important point is that officers deserve clear guidance.

*Clarity.* At least one aspect of this principle is closely related to *brevity*. The key elements of a deadly force policy can be camouflaged by a mass of extraneous and irrelevant information, comments, and contingencies. Some departments attempt to address the entire range of circumstances under which officers may use their firearms, including firearms training, warning shots, shooting at vehicles, and shooting injured animals. A *deadly force policy* should not be confused with an overall *firearms policy* or *shooting policy*. To the extent that these topics need to be addressed, it is best that they be addressed in separate documents, manuals, or training materials.

One of the most obvious examples of unnecessary clutter in many deadly force policies is the separate treatment generally given to vehicles. Some policies forbid shooting *to disable a moving vehicle*. Such prohibitions are generally based on two factors. First, bullets are singularly ineffective at stopping vehicles; and second, in all cases deadly force should be directed at the threatening person rather than at the instrumentality. These are matters best covered in training. It is no more logical to have a specific policy statement regarding threats posed by vehicles than it is to have specific policy statements for each of the other countless instrumentalities that may be used to pose threats.

Some vehicle policies forbid shooting *at the driver or other occupants* of a vehicle even when it is being used as a weapon, *unless the threat is posed by some means other than the vehicle*. The rationale behind this rule is not obvious. What is obvious is the image of the driver chasing officers around the streets with impunity—as long as the vehicle is the only means used to pose a threat. The rule is consistent with a Keystone Kops script (a *fictional* comedic situation—to stress the point even further—where no actual person is harmed). As a real policy provision dealing with critical events that threaten serious injury or death, it is a travesty.

It is suggested that an officer can jump out of the path of an oncoming vehicle and thereby evade the danger, but that is not remarkably different from suggesting that officers who are being shot at can evade the danger by ducking behind cover or running away. The Constitution makes no distinction among instrumentalities that are being used to pose imminent threats of serious injury to officers or others, and an attempt to constrain by policy an officer's ability to defend himself or others from those threats is not only gratuitous, it contradicts *the inherent right of self-defense* discussed in Chapter 3. Specifically, the Supreme Court decisions in *Scott v. Harris*[8] and *Plumhoff v. Ricard*,[9] where the Court noted the dangers posed by individuals driving vehicles recklessly and upheld the use of deadly force to stop them.

It should be self-evident that a general policy statement permitting the use of deadly force to counter immediate threats of serious injury would subsume the entire universe of circumstances giving rise to such threats, regardless of the weapon or instrumentality used. It is incongruous to tell law enforcement officers that they can use deadly force to defend themselves and others from imminent threats of serious injury, and then create subcategories of imminent threats that do not qualify for that response. It is understood that killing or

---

8. 550 U.S. 372 (2008).
9. 572 U.S. _____ (2014).

injuring the driver of a moving vehicle creates separate concerns for the safety of pedestrians or others in the vicinity but training is the proper venue for these concerns in the same way that officers are trained to be aware of innocent bystanders when considering whether to fire at a dangerous suspect.

The authors believe that a deadly force policy need only address two issues: immediate threats to life, and prevention of escape. Issues relating to the use of non-deadly force should be addresssed separately, both in policy and training. No policy formulation should attempt to resolve all issues or answer all potential questions. To the contrary, the policy should provide the general principles to guide the mental processes by which issues and questions can be resolved. Once the policy is written, law enforcement officers must be trained to understand its terms, its scope, and its proper applications. Equally as important, they need to know that their leaders have the same comprehension. Commentaries or training materials that explain the terms of the policy and illustrate its proper application can provide deeper understanding and confidence as well as assurance that everyone at every level is "on the same page."

Most importantly, given the deference of the courts to the legitimate safety concerns of law enforcement officers and the compelling interests of society in protecting those who are charged with enforcing its laws, departmental policies should be constantly and carefully evaluated to ensure that those interests are safeguarded.

In closing this chapter, the authors feel compelled to address a recent development that could have a serious impact on the ability of law enforcement officers to lawfully defend themselves and others from imminent threats of death or serious physical injury. In January 2016, the Police Executive Research Forum (PERF) produced and disseminated a document discussing and proposing model policies relating to use of force and training by American law enforcement agencies. It is not within the scope and purpose of this book to provide a detailed analysis of the PERF work, but there are proposals therein that would significantly undermine the "*inherent right*" of law enforcement officers to defend themselves and others from imminent threats of death or serious injury. The most significant and troubling proposal is that agencies should " ... *go beyond the legal standard of 'objective reasonableness'* ... " established by the U.S. Supreme Court in 1989, and adopt a higher standard "*test of proportionality.*"

It is difficult to exaggerate the gravity of this proposal. Instead of assessing an event from " ... the perspective of a reasonable officer at the scene ... " and asking whether the officer's actions were "objectively reasonable" based on the facts and circumstances confronting him at the moment, the officer would be required to consider and assess, "How would the general public view the action? Would they think it was proportional to the entire situation and the severity of the threat posed ... "

As discussed in Chapter 3, "*objective reasonableness*" takes into account that "*officers must often make split-second judgments—in circumstances that are tense, uncertain, and rapidly evolving—about the amount of force that is necessary in a particular situation.*" By contrast, the PERF proposal describes "*a process which includes (1) Collecting information, (2) Assessing the situation, threats, and risks, (3) Considering police powers and agency policy, (4) Identifying options and determining the best course of action, and (5) Acting, reviewing, and reassessing the situation.*"

This 'process' provides "*a framework for going beyond the minimum legal standard of objective reasonableness.*" It certainly achieves that goal, and furthers the states purpose of imposing higher standards than those based on the Constitution. It also will inject highly subjective elements into the standards by which uses of force are judged to be justified or not.

One final proposal that deserves comment is the prohibition against shooting at or from a moving vehicle "*unless someone in the vehicle is using or threatening deadly force by means other than the vehicle itself.*" This policy has been incorporated by many law enforcement agencies for decades but it is difficult to discover its origin or its purpose. One hopes it is not based on the notion that vehicles cannot be used to pose imminent threats of death or injury and obviously shooting a car is unlikely to prevent it from striking someone. But this policy prohibits shooting the operator of a vehicle even if the driver actually is using it as a weapon. As noted in Chapter 3, the U.S. Supreme Court recently upheld the shooting of two men who were in a vehicle that endangered motorists on the highway, and when pursuing officers trapped them in a parking lot they continued using the vehicle in a manner that endangered the officers. This policy provision would have precluded the officers using deadly force to protect themselves since the driver was only threatening them with the vehicle! (See, **Plumhoff v. Rickard (2014)**, **Scott v. Harris (2008)**, and **Mullenix v. Luna (2015)**.

Earlier in this chapter it was noted that many law enforcement agencies have adopted policies that are more restrictive than is required by the constitutional standard of "*objective reasonableness.*" However, the PERF proposal and the progressive reform initiatives that give impetus to such efforts are extremely unusual because they propose a policy that openly rejects a clear Federal constitutional standard that directly affects the safety of law enforcement officers and the public. This is as unnecessary as it is unreasonable. The self evident truth is that law enforcement officers do not forfeit their inherent right of self-defense by putting on a badge.

# Chapter 15

# Case Histories

The 15 case histories presented here are offered in illustration of the various factors that arise in deadly force confrontations, the interplay and dynamics of such incidents, and the panoply of issues that can arise in the inevitable legal action that follows. Each of the following cases was decided in favor of the law enforcement agencies and officers involved—most through summary judgment. They illustrate the factors, issues, and misconceptions that have been discussed in this work. More importantly, each case cited involves a variety of the factors and issues presented, substantiating the complexities confronting both the law enforcement officer faced with having to decide if deadly force is reasonable and the post-incident expert analyzing the officer's actions.

For the convenience of the reader, a brief factual synopsis of each of the case histories is provided below in the same order as the unexpurgated version of each case appears following the summaries. This summary section will enable the reader to preview the subject matter of each case, recognizing that some cases may be more germane to the reader's interests than others. That said, the authors encourage reading all ten cases in their entirety—there is much to be gained from the collective experiences of these agents, officers, and departments whose uses of deadly force are comprehensively described and analyzed in the selected case histories that follow.

## Summaries

### *Patricia Pace, et al. v. Nicholas Capobianco, et al.*[1]

This case involved a lengthy car chase that terminated in a cul-de-sac. Police shot the driver when it appeared he was assaulting them with his car. The allegations in this case were centered on the use of deadly force against the

---

1. *Patricia Pace, et al., v. Nicholas Capobianco, et al.*, U.S. District Court, Southern District of Georgia, Case Number: CV100-032.

driver. The plaintiffs alleged that the driver was surrounded, had surrendered, and had no place to drive away, and that the officers used excessive force (too many shots) and were not in any danger anyway. They relied on the testimony of an eyewitness who was over 200 feet away from the scene. Secondly, it was alleged that the officers put themselves at risk by their reckless actions and the driver did nothing to endanger them. The case illustrates the use of a car as a weapon and the importance of prior behavior as an indicator of a propensity for violence. No other weapon was involved other than the car. Summary judgment was awarded on behalf of the defendants, affirmed on appeal by the U.S. Court of Appeals for the 11th Circuit.[2]

## A. Marie Pasteur v. United States of America, et al.[3]

Pasteur was a former sheriff's deputy who, upon his release from jail, attempted to engineer a cocaine deal. When the arrest was attempted, a vehicle stop was necessary that had not been anticipated or planned. Pasteur was surrounded in his car and made a sudden move that resulted in him being shot and killed. Plaintiffs in this case alleged inadequate supervision, improper planning, inadequate training between federal and local officers, confusing commands, and lack of control at the point of arrest. They alleged that Pasteur was not resisting and posed no threat to anyone at the scene because he was not armed (found to be true after the fact), and was merely trying to follow conflicting commands. Plaintiffs also made an issue of the fact that the agent who shot Pasteur used a weapon he was not qualified to carry in the field. This case is a probable suicide by cop. Summary judgment was awarded on behalf of the defendants.

## Estate of Errol Shaw v. David Krupinski[4]

Shaw, who was deaf, had been drunkenly assaulting a family member with a knife when police were called. Subsequently he picked up a rake in front of four police officers and used it to assault one officer. A different officer shot and killed him. The plaintiffs allege Shaw was not a threat to four armed police officers, and could not have understood them anyway. The fact that three of the

---

2. *Pace v. Capobianco*, 283 F.3d 1275, 1281 (11th Cir. 2002).

3. *A. Marie Pasteur v. United States of America, et al.*, U.S. District Court, Middle District of Florida, Orlando Division, Case No: 6:00-CV-591-ORL-22.

4. *Estate of Errol Shaw v. David Krupinski*, U.S. District Court, Eastern District of Michigan, Southern Division, Civil Action No: 00-73898.

four officers did not shoot at all was alleged as proof that Shaw did not pose a reasonable threat. The allegations included excessive force, unreasonable force, lack of training in dealing with handicapped persons, failure to use less-than-lethal means, and failure to plan or communicate. This case is interesting because of the use of a very unconventional proximity weapon and the handicap of the attacker. Deadly force was used solely in defense of another. Summary judgment was awarded on behalf of the defendant.

## Al Seymour and Peggy Sue Seymour v. City of Houston & J. G. Lopez[5]

Police routinely responded to back up a fire department dispatch of EMT personnel to an apartment complex housing mental patients. The patient in question attacked the EMTs with a knife in an uncontrollable rage, then turned on the police who retreated, pursued by the woman, until they could not retreat further and shot her. The allegations included excessive force, inadequate policies and training for dealing with the mentally disturbed, failure to use less-than-lethal means, failure to wait for a supervisor to intervene, and failure to retreat. Two of the three officers did not shoot, which gave rise to allegations that there was no threat meriting deadly force. The case illustrates the pervasive tendency for law enforcement officers to hesitate well beyond the point that the use of deadly force is clearly justified. Tragedy was averted only by chance — as the discussion of wound ballistics makes clear. The issue of non-lethal weapons was raised as a necessary policy mandate prior to confronting any psychiatric patient. Summary judgment was awarded on behalf of the defendants.

## Juan-Jose Guerra Morales v. U.S.[6]

The case involved an undercover drug buy. Instead of completing the buy, the drug traffickers planned a rip-off of the undercover agent. When they attempted their planned rip-off, the undercover agent reacted by shooting both drug dealers, killing one and paralyzing the other. The one killed had an unloaded gun. The other was unarmed and running away when he was shot in the back. The plaintiffs alleged that the surviving dealer did not know they were dealing with law enforcement or they would have surrendered, that the survivor was un-

---

5. *Al Seymour & Peggy Sue Seymour v. City of Houston & J. G. Lopez*, U.S. District Court, Southern District of Texas, Houston Division, Cause No. H-99-2198.

6. *Juan-Jose Guerra Morales v. U.S.*, U.S. District Court, Eastern District of Michigan, Southern Division, Civil Action No: 01-74269.

armed and no threat, and that the arrest team nearby with body armor and heavy weapons could have handled it if the undercover agents had just ducked out of the way and left it to them. The allegations include excessive force, unreasonable force, and unnecessary force and inadequate training.

Of interest is the prioritization of threats by the agent, the uncertain results of shooting the first subject and the shooting of the second subject running away (unarmed, but unknown at the time). Note that the total idiocy of the criminals' plan in formulation and execution was of no relevance. They engineered a drug rip-off attempt with one empty gun. In the words of an officer investigating the incident, these guys were criminally stupid. Summary judgment was awarded on all the allegations except the claim of excessive force in shooting the fleeing Morales in the back. That issue was tried before the judge, who rendered an unequivocal opinion and verdict for the defendants.

## *Estate of Robert Woodward v. Town of Brattleboro, et al.*[7]

Woodward intruded as parishioners were gathering to commence Sunday services. He took over the podium within the church, ranting about government conspiracies against him and his issues. He used a pocketknife to threaten suicide in response to attempts to get people to leave the church.

Three police officers arrived and attempted to discretely remove people still within the church while at the same time trying to talk to Woodward and defuse the situation. One officer moved to interpose himself between Woodward and parishioners who were sitting close by. Woodward suddenly ran at the officer and was shot and killed.

This case is an excellent example of the irrational expectations that can arise when police use deadly force against someone who is mentally ill. A segment of the community adopted Woodward as a *cause célèbre*, forming a group called "Friends of Woody" with a website and its own alternate report drafted in response to the official investigation. The group contended that the police should have recognized Woodward's mental illness and treated him differently, that the police should not have entered the church and exacerbated his paranoia, that the knife was not really a weapon, that the police should have done something different, that police were inadequately trained and unprepared, and that Woody was just seeking sanctuary and posed no threat to anyone and the police gunned him down.

---

7. *Estate of Robert Woodward v. Town of Brattleboro and Marshall Holbrook and Terrance Parker*, U.S. District Court, District of Vermont, Civil Case No: 1:02-cv-35.

The case is also a good example of the suicide by cop phenomenon and the manner in which a probable suicidal act can serve to inflame uninformed opinions, as well as a study in wound ballistics and the physiological effects that will come into play in a deadly force incident.

## Patricia Nelms, etc. v. U.S. Department of the Interior, et al.[8]

Nelms was a carjacker under the influence of PCP who had hijacked a taxicab earlier that morning. He was parked in an isolated, rural location early in the morning where a U.S. Park Ranger noticed him. The ranger was unaware of the circumstances and approached him because he simply thought it odd that a taxicab would be parked in this remote park area. What ensued was an extended and relentless attack by Nelms upon the park ranger that continued unabated over a distance of about 400 feet.

During the inexorable attack, the ranger attempted to use several different types of lesser force as he retreated in the face of Nelms' persistent attack—none of them worked. Ultimately, the ranger was pursued to a point he could retreat no further and Nelms was upon him with the ranger's baton, at which point he finally shot Nelms—and then had to keep shooting him because that did not stop the attack.

This case is unremarkable legally. It was resolved with the award of summary judgment to the defendants. There were no unusual allegations or interesting court rulings. It is included here because it is an unusually extended example of the impulse to hesitate, to desperately seek to avoid having to shoot somebody, which is an all too common reaction among law enforcement officers in the face of imminent serious injury. It also illustrates the problems with using non-lethal lesser force options in deadly force situations, including verbal warnings. And it is another example of the problematic issue of wounding effectiveness—incapacitation takes time.

## David Lopez, et al. v. LVMPD[9]

Lopez was arrested for committing a particularly heinous murder, shooting his victim three times at point blank range as the victim cried and begged for

---

8. *Patricia Nelms, etc. v. U.S. Department of the Interior, et al.*, U.S. District Court, District of Maryland, Southern Division, Civil Action No. AW-04-1126.

9. *David Lopez, et al. v. LVMPD*, U.S. District Court, District of Nevada, Case No. 2:06-cv-00951-BES-GWF.

his life. The victim was a young "groupie" enamored with Lopez' self-professed gangster lifestyle. Lopez wanted his car. Lopez was arrested without incident, searched twice, handcuffed with his hands behind his back and placed in a police car with the seatbelt fastened under his arms and around his torso. He managed to undo the seatbelt, get his hands in front but still with the cuffs on, and get out of the car.

A foot chase ensued with a large number of police officers in pursuit. The pursuing police officers gradually dropped out of the chase until two detectives remained as the closest pursuers. Each of them realized that Lopez was faster, unobstructed, and on the verge of getting away even though he was handcuffed. Each of them individually and repeatedly warned Lopez to stop or he would shoot. Each detective did shoot. The first detective fired one shot that grazed Lopez, the second fired one shot that killed him.

This incident is a rarity—a use of deadly force solely to prevent escape. There was no reasonable imminent risk of serious injury. Lopez had been searched twice, he was handcuffed, and he was steadily outrunning the pursuing officers. He was also an unquestionably dangerous individual.

## *Ralph J. Penley, Jr., et al. v. Donald F. Eslinger, et al.*[10]

Christopher Penley was a 14-year-old youth who used a pellet gun to commit suicide by cop. He terrorized his school, classmates, and school employees. He confronted several different sheriff's deputies over the course of the incident, variously threatening them with his gun, threatening to shoot himself, and talking about dying. He ended up cornered inside a school restroom where he continued to refuse to negotiate or put down his gun. He continued to aim his gun at the officers in his proximity who had some cover—one pair including the negotiator was using a ballistic shield. Finally, he was shot and killed by an officer with a scoped rifle who acted on his own volition to shoot him and end the stand-off.

The plaintiffs claimed that there was no danger to anybody—Penley was isolated and cornered with no avenue of escape and the police officers were all protected. They claimed that his youth required specialized handling skills and procedures, echoing the allegations that are common in the aftermath of incidents involving mentally disturbed subjects. They also claimed that Lt. Weippert—the officer who shot Penley—had neither the authority nor the necessity

---

10. *Ralph J. Penley, Jr., et al. v. Donald F. Eslinger, et al.*, U.S. District Court, Middle District of Florida, Orlando Division, Case No. 6:08-cv-00310-GAP-KRS.

to shoot. There were allegations of police cover-up of the facts and also that the officers should have known he did not have a real gun. In the end, the plaintiffs' allegations were not material to the issues.

The case was resolved with a grant of summary judgment based on the application of established law to undisputed facts. The U.S. Court of Appeals for the 11th Circuit affirmed the judgment.[11]

## *Whisman v. Regualos, et al.*[12]

Whisman ran through the security gate of an Air Force base in Detroit and led the base security officers and police on a high-speed chase around the base. Numerous attempts were made to stop him with traffic control points, pursuit, PIT maneuvers, mobile blockades, shooting at his car and ultimately, shooting at him. The case presents several interesting aspects—the legal determination of what constitutes a "seizure" (the numerous missed shots and shots not then intended to "seize" the individual were dismissed because they did not constitute seizures). The national security aspect of justified deadly force also is explained, although it did not factor into the resolution of the case.

## *Estate of John Garczynski v. Sheriff Ric Bradshaw (PBSO) et al.*[13]

Garczynski was suspected of being suicidal, known to be armed, and mobile in a car at an unknown location. When he is finally located inside his parked car, police make an approach and he turns his gun in their direction. They respond by shooting him. This is a good example of the suicidal individual scenario, and the uncertainties and dangers that are present in dealing with such an individual. The inevitable allegations of improper response to an emotionally disturbed person, inadequate training for interacting with emotionally disturbed persons, and the unjustified nature of shooting someone to stop them from committing suicide are dealt with. The case was resolved by summary judgment, and affirmed with a strongly supportive opinion in the Eleventh Circuit.

---

11. *Penley v. Eslinger*, 605 F.3d 843 (11th Cir. 2010).

12. *Whisman v. Regualos, et al.*, USDC, Eastern District of Michigan, Case No: 2:08-cv-12133.

13. *Estate of John Garczynski v. Sheriff Ric L. Bradshaw, et al.*, 573 F.3d 1158 (11th Cir. 2009).

## Kristi Cookson v. City of Lewiston, et al.[14]

Cookson was operating her vehicle "under the influence" and refused to pull over when a police officer attempted to stop her. A high-speed chase ensued, ending when she lost control and left the roadway. Her vehicle was temporarily stuck in the parking lot area that she skidded into, and the officers trying to arrest her were on foot beside her vehicle. As her relentless attempts to drive away continued, the officers tried several methods of stopping her— shooting her tires, shooting her, and finally stopping her with a Taser. This is a good example that despite a minor predicate offense (DUI), lack of any conventional weapon (gun, knife, etc.), and with an apparent intent only to escape, the perception of imminent harm is the only relevant factor to assess a use of deadly force. If that perception is reasonable, the use of force is justified. This case also illustrates the problematic nature of handgun wounds—they frequently have no apparent effect—and again, the problematic nature of stopping a motor vehicle against the will of its driver.

## Labensky, et al. v. Cornwell[15]

This is another vehicular pursuit that ends with the vehicle stuck, apparently immobilized, and yet the driver's determination to drive it out and away despite the close presence of police officers on foot creates a reasonable perception of imminent harm that justified the decision to shoot him. Interestingly, Officer Cornwell was to the side of the car and not directly at risk. There is no weapon in play other than Labensky's car. The district court's opinion explaining the award of summary judgment specifically applies the three factors suggested in *Graham* for determining whether lethal force is justified. This opinion is particularly good because it lays out why those three factors are not exclusive of other factors, and are also not mandatory in their entirety.

## Michael Tranter v. Officer Greg Orick, et al.[16]

Antonio Foreman attempted to shoot another man while being watched by Officer Orick. Orick was unseen; standing behind some shrubs about 50 yards

---

14. *Kristi Cookson v. City of Lewiston, et al.*, USDC, District of Maine, Case No: 2:11-cv-00460-DBH.

15. *Labensky, et al. v. Cornwell*, USDC, Southern District of Ohio, Western Division, Case No: 08-CV-42.

16. *Michael Tranter v. Officer Greg Orick, et al.*, USDC, Southern District of Ohio, Western Division, Case No: 09-CV-125.

away, his presence unknown to Foreman and the other man. Foreman fired two shots at his intended target. When he raised his gun for a third shot, Orick shot and killed him from his concealed position. The plaintiff alleged an unreasonable search and seizure by Orick, specifically citing the lack of any warning but the court granted him qualified immunity. This is an excellent example that a justified use of deadly force is made necessary by the imminence of the threat, and does not require unsuccessful attempts to use lesser means first. The court's opinion also provides a very good explanation of the principles of qualified immunity and its application.

### *Jonathan E. Mitchell v. Officer Robert Miller, et al.*[17]

Mitchell led Portland, Maine, officers on a high-speed chase ending up in a dead end. The officers on foot were subsequently endangered by Mitchell's operation of the car, executing a three-point U-turn and driving away. Officer Miller shot Mitchell in the process. The subsequent suit included allegations that the officers were never at risk, were standing beside the car, not in front of it, and shot Mitchell after he had driven past them at which point there was no risk at all. The district court dealt with these allegations and the distinctions raised in awarding qualified immunity to the officers. This case illuminates qualified immunity and the reasoning that underlies its application.

## Case Histories

### *Patricia Pace, et al. v. Nicholas Capobianco, et al.*

In February 1998, at approximately 7:45 p.m., Deputy Phillip Barnett, Richmond County Sheriff's Department (RCSD), stopped a Ford Tempo for driving without headlights on. He approached the vehicle on foot and asked the driver for his license and proof of insurance. There were three men in the vehicle—the driver and two passengers.

The driver produced proof of insurance, but stated he did not have his license with him. Deputy Barnett advised the driver of the reason for the stop, and the driver claimed to have been unaware of the fact his headlights were not on. The driver identified himself as Michael A. Davis and provided a date of birth and social security number that came back listed to a female, not a male.

---

17. *Jonathan E. Mitchell v. Officer Robert Miller, et al.*, USDC, District of Maine, Case No: 2:13-cv-00132-NT.

Deputy Barnett returned to the Davis vehicle and asked Davis to get out of the car and Davis did. They walked back to Barnett's cruiser where Deputy Barnett asked Davis to repeat his Social Security number. Davis provided the same number as before, and Deputy Barnett radioed it in for verification, both as a Social Security number and as a driver's license number. In both cases, the number was reported as registered to a female. Deputy Barnett instructed Davis to place his hands on the car in order to pat him down for weapons.

Davis complied, asking repeatedly if he was under arrest, to which Deputy Barnett replied in the negative. He told Davis he wanted to be sure Davis had no weapons on him and then he wanted to talk about the disparity regarding the Social Security number. Deputy Barnett did not find a weapon on Davis.

Davis began trying to walk away. When Deputy Barnett tried to physically constrain Davis from leaving, Davis began to resist, swinging his elbows to fight off Deputy Barnett. Deputy Barnett tried to pin Davis against the cruiser and handcuff him, but Davis threw him off balance and broke free, fleeing the scene on foot. Deputy Barnett pursued him on foot.

Davis ran around a nearby house, ran back to his vehicle (the Ford Tempo) and got in. He began to drive away and Deputy Barnett tried to stop him by pointing his handgun in the car at Davis while at the same time spraying Davis with a chemical agent through the open window. Davis drove away and Deputy Barnett returned to his vehicle and pursued. At some point in this sequence of events, both passengers had got out of the Davis vehicle and walked away. As Barnett pursued Davis, he issued a Signal-32, a preset emergency code established by the RCSD to signal that an officer needs help. By RCSD directive, all deputies receiving a Signal-32 are to cease any activities in which they are engaged and respond to the location of the officer needing help.

Deputy Barnett pursued Davis at high speeds through the adjacent residential area, back onto the main highway southbound to another subdivision, through that subdivision onto a secondary road, back into the subdivision to Jonathan Circle and then to Jonathan Court, a dead end cul-de-sac. Units responding to the Signal-32 joined in the pursuit of the Ford Tempo. Several of the responding deputies had to take sudden evasive action to avoid colliding with the Davis vehicle when Davis veered into their paths.

One deputy saw the Davis vehicle ahead of him approaching at a high rate of speed. The deputy stopped his vehicle with all of its emergency lights illuminated to establish a partial roadblock, leaving Davis an avenue of escape to one side should he not stop. The deputy had to move his vehicle to evade Davis who accelerated at him, showing no indication of slowing or trying to stop or attempting to bypass the roadblock.

Davis drove through a number of stop signs without slowing. He drove into oncoming traffic; he drove across a residential front lawn and he steered aggressively at responding RCSD units, forcing the drivers to take evasive actions to avoid collision with him. Speeds exceeded 55 to 60 miles per hour through residential areas. During the entire pursuit, Davis was driving in the dark with no lights on.

Ultimately, Davis turned into Jonathan Court, and came to a stop. Deputy Clark pulled alongside the right side of the Davis vehicle, Deputy Capobianco angled his cruiser across the left rear of Clark's unit, and to the rear of Davis' car. The other pursuing deputies also pulled into Jonathan Court, to the left and right of Deputy Capobianco, completely blocking off the street behind them and any egress from the cul-de-sac.

Deputy Clark got out of his vehicle and moved in front of the Davis vehicle with his weapon drawn, issuing loud verbal commands for Davis to get out of the car. Davis put his car in reverse and abruptly backed up at Deputy Capobianco. Deputy Capobianco had begun to get out of his car when he saw the Davis vehicle backing up. Davis first hit Deputy Clark's car in its left rear quarter, glanced off it, and continued in the direction of Deputy Capobianco, who was opening his car door.

Deputy Clark had crossed in front of the Davis vehicle to its driver's side. As it backed up past him, he thought it was going to strike Deputy Capobianco. He heard the sound of the Davis vehicle hitting his (Deputy Clark's) cruiser, and he fired at Davis through the windshield of the Ford Tempo.

Deputy Capobianco was out of his vehicle when he heard Clark's shots. He saw Deputy Clark to the left front of the Davis vehicle in close proximity to the car as he (Capobianco) moved to his left out of the rearward path of the Davis vehicle and to clear Deputy Clark's line of fire. Suddenly, Davis changed direction and began to accelerate forward in the direction of Deputy Clark. At this point, Deputy Capobianco fired several shots at Davis, first from the rear and then from the left rear side as he continued to move to the left of the Davis vehicle. He fired his last two shots at Davis through the left rear door and window and saw Davis slump over as the vehicle continued forward.

Simultaneously, Deputy Clark had seen the Davis car change direction and start to accelerate towards him. He continued to move to his right (towards the left side of Davis' car) to evade the car and fired several more shots at close range at Davis in the process. He ceased firing as the car drove past him. Deputy Clark fired seven shots in total; Deputy Capobianco fired a total of five.

The Davis vehicle continued straight ahead, drove over the curb, hit a telephone junction box, went through a chain-link fence, and came to rest in the backyard of 1604 Jonathan Court. Davis was dead.

## Discussion

Alfaigo Terell Davis began this incident by escalating a relatively minor traffic stop into aggressive physical resistance and flight, followed by a high-speed, recklessly dangerous vehicle escape attempt that endangered extensive swaths of the community at large. He attempted to ram three different deputies in the course of the pursuit. He continuously and resolutely refused to comply with abundant continuing police commands: verbal, visual (emergency lights), and aural (sirens)—all of which represented clear orders to stop. He sped through stop signs, heedless of the risks to others. He sped into oncoming traffic and across a residential front lawn.

From the inception of the pursuit to its end in the cul-de-sac of Jonathan Court, Davis' actions were a real and unabated threat to the lives and physical safety of the officers involved and the citizens of the community at large. He was reckless and determined to escape at all costs to any other. The reality of Davis' actions that comprised the events of this incident made it abundantly clear to the officers that they were pursuing a dangerous individual who had no regard at all for their safety or the safety of others.

Although he was successfully cornered on Jonathan Court and at a full stop, Davis chose to change gears and back into the cruisers behind him. That endangered Deputy Capobianco, who was in the direct path of Davis' car. Deputy Clark saw the sudden risk to Deputy Capobianco and shot at Davis to attempt to stop him from hitting Deputy Capobianco. Davis crashed into both cruisers behind him, then changed direction again and drove forward despite Deputy Clark's presence in front of the car.

Deputy Capobianco, now on foot outside of his cruiser, saw Deputy Clark in front of the Ford Tempo as it changed directions and began to accelerate, and he fired at Davis to try to stop him from hitting Deputy Clark. Neither deputy fired until he had perceived an imminent threat to the safety of the other, and neither deputy continued firing once it was apparent that the precipitating threat had passed.

Deputy Clark ceased fire as the vehicle passed him, moving away from where he and Deputy Capobianco stood. Deputy Capobianco ceased fire as the Ford Tempo moved away from him, and he saw Deputy Clark safely to the side of it. Neither fired as the car proceeded away from them into the empty yard to its front. Both immediately called for emergency medical treatment for Davis.

The entire shooting incident lasted approximately six seconds from the moment Deputy Capobianco pulled in behind Deputy Clark's cruiser and the Davis car. It was recorded by a camera in one of the other patrol cars on the scene. The FBI Laboratory established a timeline from the video. At time zero,

Deputy Clark's car has stopped and Clark is exiting the driver's side. Deputy Capobianco's car is to the left rear of Clark's and coming to a stop. Only 0.23 seconds later, the right rear light on the Ford Tempo appears as the vehicle is backing left to right in the direction of Capobianco. Since the lights were off in the Ford Tempo, this has to be the back up lights that automatically come on when a vehicle is in reverse gear. At the 1.20 seconds mark (elapsed time — 0.97 seconds after the Ford Tempo first appeared), the driver's side door of Deputy Capobianco's car begins to open. Davis' car has continued left to right, obstructing the view of the rear end of Deputy Clark's car.

At 0.40 seconds later (1.6 seconds elapsed time), the view of the rear of Deputy Clark's vehicle is blocked by the Ford Tempo and by the open driver's side door of Deputy Capobianco's car. At 2.6 seconds elapsed time, the Ford Tempo is stopped — backup lights off. By this point, it has hit the left rear of Deputy Clark's cruiser and continued in the direction of Deputy Capobianco's open door. It is assumed that Deputy Clark has fired his initial shots by this point. Only 0.16 seconds later, Deputy Capobianco exits his car. From the moment his door began to open until he leaves the vehicle, 1.56 seconds have elapsed, during which time the Ford Tempo continued to back up in his direction as he undertook to exit his vehicle.

Only 0.9 seconds later, the Ford Tempo begins forward movement, right to left. Deputy Capobianco is in view to the left rear side of the Ford Tempo, moving to his left. He exits the field of view to the left at 4.46 seconds, elapsed time (1.7 seconds after exiting his vehicle). About 1.5 seconds later, the Ford Tempo has exited the field of view.

The timeline analysis of the incident clearly shows that the two deputies (Clark and Capobianco) had mere fractions of a second, individually, in which to assess and react to a dynamic and changing situation. The incident took place at night and the interior of the Ford Tempo was dark. Each deputy perceived an imminent risk to the other occurring in close physical proximity and within a very limited time frame for assessment and reaction. Having properly recognized the Ford Tempo as the weapon, they reacted in the only way in which they could reasonably hope to protect themselves and others — by shooting at the driver.

The physical realities of cars and terminal ballistics prohibit any possibility of successfully affecting a vehicle's movement with a bullet. To have any reasonable chance of being effective when used, deadly force can only be directed against the individual posing the threat and not against the weapon being used. In cases involving the use of a car, the driver is the agent employing the weapon (the car) and is the proper focus for the use of deadly force to stop or dissipate the threat posed by the driver's use of the vehicle.

The gunshot wounds inflicted on Davis are illustrative. He suffered one penetrating head wound. None of the other wounds inflicted on him could have resulted in immediate involuntary physical incapacitation. Had that one shot not hit him in the head, he could have readily continued his attempt to flee, as he clearly was attempting to do. Given the conditions of darkness, stress, physical exertion, and movement inherent to this incident, the exact locations of Davis' wounds were largely a matter of chance. The deputies fired at him but given the poor lighting and the stress and movements, they could not and did not pick specific points of his anatomy at which to aim.

At the end of the incident when Deputy Clark and Deputy Capobianco were in close proximity to Davis in his car, his noncompliance with their verbal commands and total disregard of their presence substantiated their apprehension of injury and led them to believe he intended to hit them with his car, or did not care if he did so. That perception of imminent risk of serious injury in these circumstances was objectively reasonable. Despite being boxed in, despite the commands and presence of the officers, despite having backed into a clearly marked and identifiable sheriff's vehicle, despite being shot at and wounded, and despite a deputy in front of his vehicle, Davis changed gears from reverse to forward and was driving ahead at the moment he was struck in the head by one of the last shots fired.

At any time during this incident, if Davis had stopped fleeing and complied with the police commands being directed at him, he would not have been shot. However, police officers are not responsible for the actions of the persons they confront, regardless of what the person's intentions may or may not have been. They are responsible for the reasonable nature of the actions they take in response to what the person chooses to do. Davis' actions are the sole cause of the consequences. The fatal results were not the intent. Cessation of Davis' actions threatening their safety and the immediate dissipation of that threat was the intent.

A motion for summary judgment was denied by the district court. There was one witness (Hedge) who was located inside his house across the cul-de-sac from the incident. It was night. The scene was some 200 feet away and lit only by the headlamps and emergency lights of the police vehicles. Nevertheless Mr. Hedge's eyewitness account was that he saw the Davis vehicle stop, saw that it did not strike or threaten any officers, and saw Davis raise his hands and surrender. None of the numerous other eyewitnesses, civilian and law enforcement, supported the Hedge version, nor did the forensic evidence.

The district court judge identified the disputed facts between the Hedge account and the rest of the evidence as material to the issues at hand. Noting that he was required to assume that version of the facts most supportive of plaintiffs' position, he gave credence to the Hedge eyewitness account despite the other eyewitnesses, the investigation, and the videotape, and thus determined it to be a factual dispute needing resolution by jury. Therefore, because material facts were in dispute, he denied summary judgment. That decision was appealed.

The U.S. Court of Appeals for the Eleventh Circuit reversed and directed summary judgment.[18] In the language of the appellate court issued on behalf of the defendants, in part:

> *Plaintiff points to evidence attempting to establish two additional facts as material.... Plaintiff claims that evidence supports the fact that Davis had his hands raised when he stopped the car in the cul-de-sac. Plaintiff claims that evidence supports the fact that Davis posed no threat of serious physical harm to the officers when he was shot. The evidence pointed to for support of both of Plaintiff's alleged additional facts is an affidavit by Willie Hedge ("Hedge"), a witness to the events that occurred in the cul-de-sac.*
>
> *According to that affidavit, Hedge, from the front porch of his house on the cul-de-sac, "observed motion in the red car which I believe was [Davis] raising his hands towards the roof of his car in an attempt to surrender." The district court concluded that this statement was sufficient to create an issue of fact about whether Davis's hands were in the air. We disagree.*
>
> ...
>
> *According to the Hedge affidavit: "At no time did [Hedge] observe that the driver of the red car tried to run the deputies over. At no time did [Hedge] observe the driver of the red car aim his vehicle at the deputies. At no time did the red car appear to be a threat to any officer on the scene." The district court concluded that these statements created an issue of fact about whether Davis posed an immediate threat of serious physical harm to the officers in the cul-de-sac when he was shot.*
>
> *We have accepted the first two above-quoted sentences as factual statements, although they are hotly contested. But, we cannot accept that Hedge's opinion that "[a]t no time did the red car [Davis] appear to be a threat to any officer on the scene" is outcome determinative for summary judgment. Passing over the usual lurking problems of conclusory opinions in affidavits, the chief reason is that Hedge—unlike the deputies—did not know about the details of the spirited car chase lead-*

18. *Pace v. Capobianco*, 283 F.3d 1275, 1281 (11th Cir. 2002).

*ing up to the cars coming to the cul-de-sac.... Hedge's observation about the apparent threat is a conclusion that is inadequately supported. Hedge's opinion does not take into account legally material events that occurred at a time and place that Hedge could not observe: Davis's acts before and during the car chase. Hedge's view of events at the cul-de-sac was not in context; it is incomplete. So, even at the summary judgment stage, we need not accept Hedge's threat assessment as true and correct. His conclusory opinion is inadequate to create an issue of fact about the objective danger—in the light of all the circumstances—posed by Davis at the time of the shooting, much less about the objective danger that a reasonable officer in Deputy Clark's or Deputy Capobianco's position—considering all the circumstances—would have perceived at the time of the shooting.*[19]

*...*

*Briefly stated, the question then is whether, given the circumstances, Davis would have appeared to reasonable police officers to have been gravely dangerous.*

*The answer is "Yes."*

*First, we conclude that—given Davis's aggressive use of his automobile during the chase—probable cause existed to believe Davis had committed a felony involving the threatened infliction of serious physical harm: aggravated assault per Georgia Code § 16-5-2 1.*[20]

*Second, Davis, once he began the chase, never left his automobile or even turned the engine off. By the time of the shooting, Davis had used the automobile in a manner to give reasonable policemen probable cause to believe that it had become a deadly weapon with which Davis was armed.*[21]

*Given the facts in the light most favorable to Plaintiff, reasonable police officers could have believed that the chase was not over when the police fired on Davis. Even when we accept the Hedge affidavit as true that Davis's car, in the cul-de-sac, did not try to run over the deputies and that Davis, in the cul-de-sac, did not aim the car at the deputies, Davis's*

---

19. *Ibid.* 1279.

20. A person commits the offense of aggravated assault when he or she assaults ... [w]ith a deadly weapon or with any object, device, or instrument which, when used offensively against a person, is likely to or actually does result in serious bodily injury." Ga. Code Ann. § 16-5-(a)(2) (2001). Section 16-5-20 of the Georgia Code defines an assault as "an act which places another in reasonable apprehension of immediately receiving a violent injury." Ga. Code Ann. § 16-5-20(a)(2) (2001).

21. *Pace, et al.*, 283 F.3d at 1280.

*car was stopped for, at most, a very few seconds when shots were fired: no cooling time had passed for the officers in hot pursuit. Davis, while fleeing, had left the streets and driven through a residential yard before; so, that he had pushed the nose of his car to within 3 or 4 feet of a curb in the front of a home (as Hedge says) could mean little to the officers about whether the chase was finally over. And the police—before shooting— did yell to Davis to "get out of the car," which he never did.[22]*

*Given the facts and circumstances of this case, we cannot conclude that the Fourth Amendment ruled out the use of deadly force.[23]*

## A. Marie Pasteur v. United States of America, et al.

In November 1998, Robert Pasteur, then an inmate in the Orange County Jail, approached a fellow inmate to arrange the acquisition of a large amount of cocaine to sell upon his release from jail. Pasteur was a former deputy sheriff who had been convicted on charges of theft, burning to defraud an insurer, fraud and false Statements to obtain credit—offenses committed while he was employed as an Orange County sheriff's deputy. The inmate passed the information about Pasteur's request on to the police. Investigation revealed Pasteur's past history as a police officer, his experience investigating drug cases, his propensity for violence, and the obvious—he was actively attempting to traffic in cocaine. The U.S. Drug Enforcement Administration (DEA) was advised and requested to take over the investigation.

DEA planned to implement a "reverse sting operation" by working through the inmate to respond to Pasteur's initiatives, culminating with making available two kilograms of cocaine to be offered by an informant. When Pasteur paid for the narcotics and took possession of them, he would be arrested.

The investigation continued through December 1998 and into January 1999 as Pasteur and the informant settled on details of the transaction. Pasteur engaged in a variety of counter-law enforcement measures to negate risks of surveillance or recording, consistent with his law enforcement experience. Eventually, the deal was set for January 14, 1999. The informant told Pasteur to meet him in the parking lot of the Magic Mall Shopping Center to complete the sale and transfer of the cocaine.

DEA prepared an operations plan planning for the arrest of Pasteur upon conclusion of the drug deal. According to the plan, the cocaine would be lo-

---

22. *Ibid.* 1281.
23. *Ibid.* 1281.

cated in the trunk of a pre-positioned vehicle in the Magic Mall parking lot. Actual cocaine would be used to protect the informant in the event that Pasteur wanted to test the drug or otherwise verify its authenticity. The pre-positioned vehicle was disabled to prevent Pasteur or anybody else from driving it away. The informant was instructed to park his vehicle on the opposite side of the lot where he would meet with Pasteur and then walk with him to the vehicle containing the cocaine. Pasteur would be allowed to satisfy himself as to the authenticity of the cocaine and allowed to take possession of it. Pasteur would be arrested as he proceeded on foot back to his own vehicle.

The DEA primary arrest team was organized in two vehicles. DEA Special Agents Mark German and Jerald Lucas were in one vehicle, and DEA Special Agents Tim Jones and Jim Schrant in the second. Orlando Police Department (OPD) marked units controlled the perimeter of the arrest scene. In the event that Pasteur did enter his vehicle, OPD marked units were assigned to block it in and prevent it from moving. Several concerns were made clear. The informant was directed not to ride with anybody. Further, if Pasteur exhibited any qualms or uncertainties about the deal, its location, or its structuring, then the informant was to call it off. DEA made it clear that Pasteur was not to be allowed to leave the area with the cocaine. The operations plan specifically stated that Pasteur must not be allowed to enter a vehicle once he had custody of the drugs.

All participants in the operation were told that Pasteur was a former police officer with a reputation for violence and well versed in police drug operations. The covering units were warned to expect counter-surveillance measures by Pasteur. A tracking device was surreptitiously placed in Pasteur's vehicle to enable DEA to track his location from a greater distance as a precaution against any counter-surveillance measures he might employ. Participants were told that it was probable that Pasteur would resist arrest and he should be considered armed.

The investigation revealed that Pasteur had threatened the life of another deputy involved in his previous criminal case, and that he had threatened that if he ever went down he would kill everybody around him and himself. Pasteur was a very large and powerful man (over 300 pounds) who worked out regularly. He used his size and strength to intimidate people. He drank often and became more aggressive and belligerent when drunk. It was alleged that he used steroids to increase his muscle mass, but no evidence of that was ever produced. Pasteur was well versed in handling firearms, was trained in martial arts, and had engaged in teaching his fellow inmates in jail about police undercover activities, surveillance techniques, and how to identify undercover officers.

On the day of the planned arrest, Pasteur arrived at the mall shortly before the informant. He parked and entered a pizza shop located in the southeast corner of the plaza. Soon thereafter, Pasteur got back into his vehicle and drove around the parking lot and onto adjacent Colonial Drive. Meanwhile, the informant arrived at the mall and Pasteur met him in the southeast corner of the lot. Another individual (later identified as Angelo Krauss) left the pizza shop and joined them.

After a brief conversation, the three men walked to the vehicle containing the cocaine parked in the west end of the parking lot. A minute or two later, and before the cocaine was presented, Pasteur left and returned to his vehicle, which he entered and drove around the lots and roadways in the vicinity of the Magic Mall. Krauss took possession of the cocaine from the informant, and the signal for the arrests was given. Krauss was arrested on foot as he was crossing the parking lot.

Meanwhile, Pasteur was driving eastbound onto West Colonial Drive from the Western Way Plaza. He was across the street from the location where DEA Agents German and Lucas were waiting with DEA Agents Jones and Schrant, accompanied by an OPD car occupied by uniformed officers Chris Hall and Julie Mercks. They conferred and decided to use their three vehicles to stop Pasteur's car and place him under arrest.

The three law enforcement vehicles crossed Colonial Drive and blocked Pasteur's vehicle. Officers Hall and Mercks positioned their vehicle at the rear of Pasteur's car. DEA Agents German and Lucas positioned their vehicle across the front of Pasteur's car. DEA Agents Jones and Schrant stopped their vehicle roughly parallel to the car of DEA Agents German and Lucas, and on the side away from Pasteur's car. Officers Paul Bruining and Chris Myers arrived on the scene in a second OPD vehicle and positioned their vehicle in the traffic lanes alongside Pasteur's location. Pasteur was blocked in and sat in his vehicle with the engine running.

Agent Lucas got out of his vehicle and positioned himself at the left front of Pasteur's car. He was armed with a 9mm Colt submachine gun (SMG) that he kept aimed at Pasteur as he ordered him to get his hands up. Agent Lucas was not qualified with the SMG and not authorized to carry one. The SMG was issued to Agent German, who told Lucas to carry it because German was driving. Agent Lucas and Pasteur maintained direct eye contact throughout the ensuing incident. Pasteur's hands were visible to Agent Lucas, partially up above the steering wheel.

Officers Hall and Mercks got out of their vehicle and approached Pasteur's car from the rear. Officer Mercks was located on the passenger side of Pasteur's car, and Officer Hall was on the driver's side. Officer Hall saw the driver side door partially open and quickly approached. He opened the door the whole way, grabbed Pasteur by the left arm and ordered him to get out of the vehicle. Pasteur, without looking at him, replied that he had his seatbelt on at which point Officer Hall yelled "seatbelt on" one time. Officer Hall's stated intention was to take control of both of Pasteur's arms and then reach across him to unsnap the seatbelt. Pasteur never looked in his direction at any time—his attention was on Agent Lucas to his front. At this point, Pasteur suddenly reached down with his right hand in the direction of his seat or right side/hip area. Officer Hall saw this motion and leaned in closer to see what Pasteur was reaching for.

DEA Agent Lucas was watching through the front windshield. He could not see below the dashboard. When Pasteur suddenly reached down with his right hand, he fired one shot through the windshield that struck Pasteur in the chest. Pasteur made no further movements. He was extricated from the car and emergency aid was rendered. Pasteur died in the hospital emergency room. There was no gun on his person or in his car.

In an interview conducted by DEA following the shooting, Krauss advised he was Pasteur's oldest and closest friend. He said that on numerous occasions Pasteur told him he "would never go back to jail." Krauss understood that to mean that Pasteur would not submit to another arrest or possible time in jail.

### Discussion

The DEA Operations Plan was adequate, although limited in the scope of possible scenarios it covered. It only recognized two contingencies:

1. Pasteur displayed the money for the drugs, walked to the car, took possession of the drugs and was arrested while on foot; and
2. Pasteur insisted on seeing the drugs first, walked to the car, took possession of the drugs and was arrested while on foot.

All arrest situations are dynamic, fluid, and unpredictable as they evolve from start to finish. They all entail unanticipated, if not random, developments that must be recognized, adapted to, and resolved. No operations plan can ever comprehensively predict, foresee, or account for the actual development of events that occurs during the planned arrest. The problem is that the object of the plan is always an independent actor (or actors) who does not have access to the script. The subject of the arrest plan will react unpredictably, invariably in self interest, frequently in manners influenced by unforeseen factors such as fear, anger, pain, substance abuse, or, commonly, the sheer determination not to be caught, and almost always without reflection, acting on impulse. This in turn results in activities and events that the arrest planners did not or could not foresee.

Unsurprisingly, the sequence of events comprising the actual arrest of Pasteur occurred differently than planned. Pasteur did not take possession of the drugs himself, but employed a surrogate in the person of Krauss, presumably to interpose a buffer between himself and possession of the drugs in the event the drug deal was a setup.

Pasteur was present but at a distance in his car, driving about the vicinity presumably with the intent of rejoining Krauss and the cocaine after the deal was safely done. When the signal to execute the arrest was given, only one person (Krauss) fit the scenarios outlined in the operations plan. The primary subject of the investigation was at large in his car—something the arrest planners did not foresee. No arrest plan can be fully comprehensive, and this one was no exception. A plan is not a script—more accurately it is an informed estimation as to what is going to happen.

The arresting agents and officers needed to recognize the altered circumstances and react to resolve the situation within the guidelines of the operations plan. A good plan will offer pertinent guidance, defined goals, allocation of resources, and a structure within which the participating agents/officers can better employ their initiative and training as necessary to effect the desired results. This plan had made it clear that once the drugs were transferred to the target(s) of the investigation, the target(s) must not be allowed to leave with the drugs. That was a clear guideline. Second, the plan had provided that in the event the target(s) entered a vehicle, marked OPD units would block the vehicle and prevent it from moving.

When the order to execute the arrests was given, Pasteur just happened to be located in front of the agents assigned as the primary arrest team, and they acted to arrest him. Others acted to arrest Krauss, another eventuality not anticipated in the operations plan. When they moved to make the arrest, Officers Hall and Mercks positioned their vehicle at the rear of Pasteur's car while Agents German and Lucas blocked his forward progress. Each relied on the training and experience of the other to execute a basic car stop.

Arrest training subject matter includes a large body of universal tactics and principles that are common across the law enforcement community regardless of agency. The agency and the geographical location do not matter—much of the practical training is consistent, and especially so in the area of arrest tactics. Every law enforcement officer understands such basic tactics as triangulation to inhibit escape, rear approach for greater safety, non-compliance as a significant danger signal, see and control a subject's hands, the danger of areas that cannot be seen and actions that are not directed, and the reality that no subject is safely controlled until that subject is physically restrained and searched, etc. One lesson universal to law enforcement training is that any uncontrolled, undirected, unanticipated, or noncompliant action or movement by the subject of an arrest is an imperative precursor of imminent resistance if not violence.

Training for arrests in and around cars entails tactics that are relatively uniform across the law enforcement community. These tactics include the obvious practice that when a car stop is made, the officers in the rear will approach to make the arrest (i.e., physically restrain and control the subject) because that is the least risky avenue to do so, while those in front will maintain cover and communicate orders to the subject for the safety of all concerned, because that is the best vantage point for that responsibility. Training includes the necessity for the officers approaching from the rear to do so at the direction and under the guidance of the officers in the front. These are basic tactical considerations common to law enforcement car stop training.

Officer Hall approached Pasteur from the rear, opened the door, and grabbed his left arm. He should have waited to be directed to approach by Agent Lucas, but he did not. The dynamics of a situation and the aggressive nature of the officer involved can lead to an inadvisable haste in approaching the subject of the arrest. In this case, Officer Hall incurred excessive risk to his personal safety by rushing in on his own initiative. He should have held his position and approached when directed to do so by Agent Lucas and/or Agent German at the front.

At the same time, Agent Lucas was covering Pasteur and ordering him to raise his hands. Pasteur's hands were at least partially up. He was aware of Officer Hall's presence close beside Pasteur, but was so focused on Pasteur that he was not fully aware of what Officer Hall was doing. This is characteristic sensory alteration commonly present when people engage in high-risk, high-stress, life-threatening situations.

Distortions of sight, sound, feeling (sense of pain, for example), and time flow can occur singly or in combinations. The field of view narrows such that the focus is fairly limited to the perceived threat or agent of risk, and peripheral vision seems to dissipate. This tunnel vision was apparent in Agent Lucas' account of his focus on Pasteur. Also, Pasteur was probably "tunneled" on Agent Lucas and the weapon he held. Officer Mercks experienced tunnel vision on the periphery of the event, as she commented that she was "tunneling" in describing what she saw.

Auditory alterations also can be prevalent. Participants may or may not hear sounds, noises, or voices as the event unfolds. Many officers in shooting incidents have no recollection of the sound of their own gun, or never hear a partner's gun discharge, or the gun being fired at them. Time perception can become distorted, and the individual perceives the unfolding events in extreme slow motion or unnaturally speeded up. Sensory distortions are common among all participants in high-risk or deadly force confrontations, both on the part of the officers involved as well as the subjects themselves.

When he grabbed Pasteur by the left arm, Officer Hall did not expect or intend for him to lower his hands or make any movements. Officer Hall was in a particularly vulnerable position with his weapon holstered, his gun hand engaged in holding Pasteur by the arm, and he increased his vulnerability when he leaned further into the car to see what Pasteur was reaching for. If it had been a weapon of any sort, Officer Hall would have had little or no opportunity to defend himself.

From Agent Lucas' perspective, he was in front of and in direct eye contact with Pasteur. He was holding him at gunpoint and repeatedly issuing one simple and clear command, "Raise your hands." Pasteur was boxed in with no avenue of escape. He could either comply or resist. Agent Lucas could not see inside Pasteur's car below the level of the dash, but he could see both of Pasteur's hands, and he was aware of Officer Hall's close proximity to Pasteur. He also was aware of his own exposed position in front of Pasteur. And he believed Pasteur to be dangerous.

This reasonable belief arose from several sources of information. First, the situation was a drug bust, and the common experience universally held and substantiated throughout law enforcement is that drug arrests are inherently dangerous. Drug arrests typically involve people who are armed, who are willing to engage in violence, and who frequently do so. Drug transactions are even more dangerous because the participants regularly rob and assault their associates and counterparts. It is highly unusual for a drug trafficking deal to occur without weapons being present because drug traffickers fear getting robbed, held up, or assaulted in the course of their business more than they fear getting arrested.

Second, Pasteur was a former law enforcement officer. Former law enforcement officers engaged in criminal pursuits are high-risk subjects for arrest. They are often well trained in weapons, police tactics, and survival measures. They know what to expect, and they can anticipate and take counter measures. Former law enforcement officers, especially those engaged in substantial criminal activity, are dangerous individuals to arrest. They are dangerous not just to the arresting officers but also to themselves as well. When confronted with arrest and the perception of no escape, they can be significant suicide risks.

Third, the specific information available about Pasteur substantiated the belief he was dangerous. His background included a history of physical intimidation and coercion, a propensity to use physical force, training with firearms and in martial arts, acts of violence, threatening the life of another deputy involved in his previous criminal activities, and a willingness to engage in active criminal pursuits in violation of his public trust as a law enforcement officer. The precautionary advisory that he was considered to be armed and dangerous was a reasonable one.

Pasteur, for reasons known only to him, chose to reach down and out of sight with his right hand. Given Pasteur's extensive law enforcement training and experience, there can be no question he knew that in that situation the only safe response would be to stay still and do exactly as he was told. He probably engaged in countless training scenarios in which that particular lesson was driven home over and over. Nevertheless, in purposeful noncompliance of those orders Pasteur made a deliberate move fully consistent with reaching for a weapon in exactly the location that a weapon would be located—and Agent Lucas, in defense of himself and Officer Hall, shot him.

Agent Lucas had direct eye contact with Pasteur. He saw cognition in Pasteur's eyes, an awareness of his situation and certain arrest. Agent Lucas was facing a man he believed to be dangerous and who did not comply with the simple and clear command to get his hands up. He saw Pasteur suddenly reach down to where a weapon would be located. If Agent Lucas had waited to see what happened and Pasteur came up with a weapon, he could not have reacted quickly enough to protect Officer Hall or himself. If he had ducked or sought cover, he would have abandoned Officer Hall to Pasteur's intentions. In the space of less than half a second, Agent Lucas had to assess, decide, and respond to protect himself and Officer Hall.

One explanation for Pasteur's action is the phenomenon known as "suicide by cop." Pasteur is a very likely candidate in that he was a male, former police officer facing re-incarceration, and one who had expressed the resolute intent never to return to jail. He was in severe financial straits. He was separated from his wife and had no employment prospects. The drug transaction was his salvation, his ticket to financial health, and the remedy for his personal life disasters. All of a sudden this entire future disappeared, snatched away before his eyes. Pasteur certainly understood what he needed to do to avoid provoking a violent response by the arresting officers. The possibility that he reacted to his situation with the intention of provoking a shooting cannot be dismissed as unlikely.

The only other explanations for his voluntary and dangerous act of non-compliance are panic or confusion. Panic is unlikely given Pasteur's extensive training in law enforcement and his martial arts exposure, his belligerent personality, and his track record. He had been arrested before. For the same reasons, confusion is equally improbable. It would have compelled him to do nothing until the confusion could be sorted out, for he would have known that was the only safe approach.

The one certainty is that Pasteur chose to act as he did in direct non-compliance with the clear commands being directed at him. Pasteur never took his eyes off of Agent Lucas and did the one thing that he knew would probably result in him getting shot. Agent Lucas then had to decide in a fraction of a second if Pasteur's action posed a reasonable threat to him or to Officer Hall. Given his knowledge of Pasteur, his perception that Pasteur was an imminent threat of serious injury was objectively reasonable under the circumstances. Then he had to take action with the only reasonably effective means available to him and try to do so in sufficient time to neutralize or dissipate the threat to his safety and the safety of Officer Hall. Their close proximity to Pasteur and total lack of cover not only increased the relative level of risk incurred by them but also severely limited the practical likelihood that any attack could be successfully averted.

In November 2001, a motion for summary judgment was filed. The plaintiffs opposed the motion alleging that inadequate training, inadequate cross-training between DEA and OPD, conflicting orders and communications, the impromptu nature of the stop and arrest, inadequate planning, and the unqualified use of the weapon by Agent Lucas all violated Pasteur's assorted rights. They alleged material factual disputes over whether Pasteur was reaching for a weapon or his seat belt, whether he was in compliance with Officer Hall's directions or not, the content of the pre-arrest briefings, and the sufficiency of evidence that he was dangerous. The following is excerpted from plaintiffs' response:

> *Discrepancies surrounding the events of Pasteur's death create a contentious factual dispute regarding the reasonableness of Lucas' actions and propriety of his use of deadly force. It is disputed whether Pasteur ever posed a "threat" to anyone. Lucas claims he repeatedly instructed Pasteur to raise his hands but Pasteur refused and never raised his right hand.*
>
> *Several other law enforcement officers who were [there] present eyewitness accounts [that] sharply dispute Lucas' claim. Officer Hall saw both of Pasteur's hands raised.*
>
> *Hall points out that Pasteur's hands were raised even before Hall first approached Pasteur's vehicle. Hall never would have approached the vehicle if Pasteur's hands [had] not been raised. Moreover, Bruining, Schrant and Jones, who were further away from Pasteur than Lucas, saw Pasteur's hands were raised.*
>
> *Lucas further claims Pasteur's right shoulder dip[ped] downward, as if he were reaching for something. Lucas says this was a sudden movement and he was in fear for his life.*
>
> *Hall again sharply disagrees. Pasteur's movement was not fast or sudden. In fact, Pasteur's hand dropped in a normal fashion. This disputed fact is material. A reasonable officer would recognize lowering a hand in response to a command for a seat-belted occupant to get out of the car is in response to that command. Agent O'Rourke testified that he would instruct a seatbelted occupant to undo the seatbelt himself. Therefore Lucas should have anticipated this movement as well since O'Rourke was the Special Agent in charge at the time.*
>
> *Lucas claims because he took position in front of Pasteur's vehicle he was in control. Again, Hall differs on this point as well. Hall testified he had control of Pasteur when he grabbed Pasteur's arm. A reasonable of-*

ficer would conclude the person closest to Pasteur who has actual physical control of his arm is the one Pasteur will react to.

Lucas suggests he shot Pasteur because he was not doing what he was told. Hall refutes any claim Pasteur was resisting. In point of fact, Hall confirms Pasteur was not resisting at all. Pasteur had surrendered. Pasteur had not threatened Hall or anyone else. Hall, who saw Pasteur's right arm move towards the seatbelt area, was stunned when Pasteur was shot. Hall did not anticipate Lucas firing his weapon. Neither did Pasteur.

Lucas claims he never heard Hall yell at the top of his lungs "seatbelt on"! Lucas makes this claim despite being only a mere three to five feet away from Hall at the time it was yelled. This signal is given to alert everyone for the need of the occupant to remove the seatbelt. Lucas denies hearing when he was just a mere three to five feet away from Hall at the time it was yelled.

Moreover, three other officers heard Hall yell seatbelt on! And they were further away than Lucas! These disputes call into serious question Lucas' account as to why that fatal shot was fired. A jury is the appropriate body to determine the credibility of Lucas' claim that he did not hear Hall warn of Pasteur's seatbelt.

Pasteur made no aggressive movement toward the officers, he did not verbally threaten the officers, there was no evidence suggesting that Pasteur was armed at the time, and they did not observe anything, such as a bulge in his clothing, to indicate he had a weapon. Given these facts, as well as the disputed facts above, Lucas is not entitled to qualified immunity as a matter of law; it is a jury question as to whether Pasteur posed a threat of death or serious bodily harm to the officers.

It is also important that Lucas was not qualified to use this submachine. Lucas' attempt to suggest this as unimportant defies logic. Lucas, who claims to have loaded the SMG, loaded the weapon beyond its capacity. The SMG had 33 bullets. The manufacture only permits 32. A person qualified on an SMG would know the gun was loaded beyond its capacity making it prone to an accidental discharge if stress is put on the trigger after the safety is removed.

When the SMG was cleared at the scene, two bullets ejected. This is not supposed to occur. Lucas also used mixed ammunition. This is not recommended by the DEA. OPD's Homicide Detective Barbara Bergin, testified she in all of her other investigations, she has never seen mixed ammunition used in law enforcement. [As an aside, the authors are greatly bemused at this claim!]

Lucas also has a history of having his gun accidentally discharge. (See accidental discharge document from Production Request.) A fact omit-

*ted by Lucas. This illustrates another example of Lucas' unawareness of a bullet in the chamber!*

*In addition, O'Rourke admitted discussions occurred at DEA's Heathrow location about this shooting being an accidental. Both the DEA and OPD participated in these types of discussion.*

*The United States' own expert reluctantly admitted an SMG like the unauthorized one Lucas was using could unintentionally discharge if there is a round in the chamber (as in this case) and the safety is taken off and they put their finger on the trigger in stress—it's a fairly short trigger throw. Ironically, this expert thinks Lucas was aware there was a round in the chamber because he claims Lucas watched German load the SMG. Lucas claims he was aware there was a round in the chamber because Lucas loaded it himself. German, on the other hand, said that he was the one who loaded the SMG. The only conversation German remembers having with Lucas about the gun was for Lucas to check and see if there is a round in the chamber.*

*The SMG, a weapon Lucas was not qualified to use, which was loaded beyond its capacity with mixed, unauthorized, ammunition would not be in the hands of a reasonable officer for fear of accidentally shooting someone. It is more than a curiosity why Lucas' non-qualified use of the SMG weapon that took a man's life was never made known to OPD.*

*Lucas' decision to use an SMG even though he was not qualified was a choice he deliberately made. It was reckless and inexcusable and is supportive of the notion that Pasteur very well may have been killed as a result of an accidental discharge.*

*Moreover, if Lucas' story about the conversation he says took place behind the Lincoln-Mercury dealership, wherein Hall was to perform the back block and be hands-on is true, then Lucas failed to secure any understanding from Hall that DEA procedures were to be followed.*

*If Lucas is to be believed, the following must be true: Pasteur never had his right hand up, Pasteur never surrendered, Pasteur dropped his shoulder suddenly, Lucas never heard seatbelt, Lucas did not hear others yelling conflicting commands, Hall knew Lucas was in charge and was to give commands, and Hall knew he was to perform the back-block and be hands-on.*

*All of these disputed facts go towards the reasonableness of Lucas' actions. Due to their materiality and whose version will be deemed credible this case presents a jury question. Accordingly, summary judgment should be denied.*

...

*In this case, Pasteur had not harmed anyone. Pasteur had not threat-
ened anyone. His car was in park. He was not resisting. His hands were
up by his ears. He had surrendered. Hall, standing at Pasteur's driver's
side door, had physical control of Pasteur. Pasteur, in an attempt to comply with Hall's commands, lowered his right hand and was fatally shot.
Hall testified he was stunned when Pasteur was shot. Hall was not anticipating Pasteur being shot.*

*Law enforcement officers should be trained for this type of dynamic sit-
uation. Lucas did not react reasonably. A reasonable officer would not
have shot Pasteur. A reasonable officer would not have used his partners
SMG which he was not qualified to use. A reasonable officer would have
been aware of his surroundings, including the location of other officers and
the series of conflicting commands they are yelling. A reasonable officer
would have recognized ordering a seatbelted occupant out of a car would
have necessitated the lowering of an arm to unfasten the belt in order to
comply with this command.* [Emphases in original.][24]

Notice the attempt to impute surrender by Pasteur, to advocate the perceptions of officers who did not shoot as somehow invalidating the perception of the one who did. There is much made of extraneous facts that have no
relevance to Lucas' perception of imminent risk—the weapon, the loading,
the ammunition, and the assertion that Officer Hall, having grasped Pasteur's
left arm, thus had control of Pasteur. Some facts are even misstated. The court
dispensed with the assorted allegations and supposed disputes of material facts,
viewing the circumstances objectively from Agent Lucas' perspective and found
that his perception of imminent risk was reasonable and his use of deadly force
was justified. Summary judgment was awarded. Agent Lucas was administratively censored for accepting the SMG for use, and Agent German was censored for giving it to him, but that had no effect on the legal resolution. He was
justified in shooting Pasteur, and he used the weapon he had at hand.

## *Estate of Errol Shaw v. David Krupinski*

In August 2000, Officers Brandon Seed and David Krupinski, Detroit
(Michigan) Police Department (DPD), were dispatched to a residence for a
report of family trouble—man with a weapon—that had been called in by

---

24. *Pasteur v. United States*; USDC Middle District of Florida, Orlando Division; Case
No: 6:00-CV-591-ORL-22KRS; Plaintiffs Response to Defendant, Jerald Lucas' Motion for
Summary Judgment, 12/01.

a neighbor. Two other DPD Officers (Brandon Hunt and Bradley Clark) responded as well. At the address, they queried a young girl sitting on a parked car. She did not answer, but pointed across the street to the Shaw residence.

The four police officers walked to the residence. They saw a man (later identified as Errol F. Shaw) standing at the front end of a Cadillac parked in the driveway. At the rear of the Cadillac was a young man later identified as Shaw's son. The four officers walked up the driveway. Officer Hunt was left of the Cadillac on the driver's side and the other three officers on the passenger side. Officer Hunt spoke to the son, who identified the man at the front of the Cadillac as his father and told Officer Hunt that his father had been chasing him with a knife. Shaw Sr. turned and ran through a gate into the backyard but still in sight of the police officers. Officer Clark asked people on the front porch what was going on, and one of them told him "he's high on crack and chasing his son with a knife." Shaw Sr. had been drinking heavily as well.

Meanwhile, Officer Hunt on the left side of the Cadillac and Officer Krupinski on the right side had moved up the driveway in front of the car from where they could see Shaw Sr. in back of the house as he bent over picking up something. Officers Clark and Seed were behind Officer Krupinski and to his side. Shaw came back through the gate from the rear of the house holding a steel pronged garden rake in both hands, the rake laid back across his right shoulder. He held it near the end of the shaft like a baseball bat. He walked directly towards the officers at a fast pace with the rake cocked back across his right shoulder.

The officers variously ordered him to halt, to stop, and to put down the rake. Shaw continued in their direction. The officers backed up as they continued to order him to stop and to drop the rake. Officer Hunt held his left hand up in a "halt" gesture. He backed into the Cadillac and moved to his left a step or two away from the car. Officer Krupinski also backed up to the car. Officers Hunt, Krupinski, and Clark each drew his weapon as Shaw continued to approach. Officer Seed, standing behind Officer Krupinski, had his hand on his weapon.

Despite the orders, the hand gestures, the drawn weapons, and the unmistakable presence of four uniformed police officers, Shaw continued to approach, picking up his pace. He altered his direction so that he was moving directly at Office Hunt, who was alone on the driver's side of the car. As he neared Officer Hunt, he raised the rake off his shoulder, holding it in two hands above his head. All four officers continued to order him to stop and to drop the rake. As Shaw started to swing the rake at Officer Hunt, Officer Krupinski shot him two times. Shaw died from the gunshot wounds. The investigation that followed determined that Errol Shaw Sr. was deaf.

## Discussion

The officers involved in this incident knew that they were likely to confront a person armed with a weapon. That was the basis of the call made requesting police intervention. They had no further information before arriving on the scene.

On arrival, the officers learned more. A bystander pointed them to the Shaw residence. Shaw's son told them that his father had been chasing him with a knife. Shaw ran away as the officers walked up the driveway. A witness on the porch told them "he's high on crack and chasing his son with a knife." The circumstances put the officers on guard and focused them on Shaw. Because they did not lose sight of Shaw, they did not pursue him. Shaw had not done anything up to this point to threaten or endanger the officers or others in the officers' presence.

Before the officers could attempt any further investigation or inquiry, Shaw returned with a steel pronged garden rake held in both hands, walking at a fast pace directly towards the officers. He refused to stop or to drop the rake. Although he was deaf, a fact not known to the officers and one they had neither opportunity nor time to discover, Shaw was not blind. The presence of four uniformed officers arrayed in front of him, focused on him, gesturing at him and obviously speaking forcefully, holding guns in their hands, presented a clear and unambiguous visual command to stop. Shaw did not stop, and in fact quickened his pace in the direction of the one police officer standing alone to one side of the Cadillac. It appears that Shaw chose to attack the single officer on the driver's side of the Cadillac, ignoring the three officers on the other side of the car.

Shaw's noncompliance and his continued, even hastened, approach was a clear and present danger, a threat to the physical safety of the officers. An array of four police officers, three with guns drawn, confronted Shaw, gesturing for him to halt even as they tried to back up and stay out of reach of his weapon. Although he was deaf, he could see them speaking and gesturing. He may not have heard what they said, but he could not have failed to recognize that they were saying something and saying it with force and urgency. If anything, the command to stop was even more clear and compelling visually. Shaw did not stop, did not comply, and suddenly began to swing his rake like a baseball bat at Officer Hunt.

Officer Krupinski reacted to Shaw's sudden attack by shooting him twice in defense of Officer Hunt. Officers Hunt and Clark stated later that they did not shoot only because Officer Krupinski reacted more quickly and Shaw went down. However, the fact that they did not shoot was later alleged to be proof that no threat existed, overlooking the specific reason the officers admitted for not shooting—they were too slow.

Officer Krupinski was not required to wait until Officer Hunt was actually struck by the rake. He was not required to wait to see if Officer Hunt was seriously hurt. All four officers recognized that a steel headed garden rake wielded in a two-handed swing like a bat could inflict serious if not fatal injuries and that the individual wielding it was doing so deliberately. The threat posed by Shaw at the onset of this incident that brought police there had disappeared. The officers were seeking clarification. They approached with weapons holstered. As Shaw first evaded them, and then confronted them menacingly with a weapon in hand and readied for use, they tried to gain compliance by gesture, command, and presence. But Shaw refused to submit and escalated the incident, continuing to defy the officers and then press home his threatening approach.

As he drew nearer to Officer Hunt the imminent threat of serious injury changed suddenly, in a split second, to a genuine risk of serious injury, if not death. An individual who may pose no objectively reasonable threat of death or serious bodily harm can, by a sudden and non-compliant choice, act in such a manner as to abruptly transform himself into the instrument of a real and ongoing risk of death or injury. In that fraction of a second, officers must recognize the sudden looming danger, react to it, and resolve it in a manner best able to protect themselves or others.

The inability to predict or control what an individual chooses to do creates the uncertainty and risk in police work. The officer can only react to the circumstances he or she faces, the decisions made by the person being confronted, and the actions that person chooses to pursue. Officer Krupinski and his fellow officers gave Shaw an extended opportunity to comply with their commands, to submit and defuse the situation. The plaintiffs alleged that it was unreasonable to expect a deaf man to understand their verbal commands. But the officers' presence, their actions, and their obvious focus on him comprised a visually imperative image that unmistakably mandated he stop. Shaw did not need to hear them to recognize and understand what they wanted him to do. For reasons of his own, he chose not to comply with that imperative. His actions created an objectively reasonable belief that he intended to assault Officer Hunt with the rake. Officer Krupinski's perception that Shaw was a direct risk of serious injury to Officer Hunt was reasonable, and his decision to use deadly force was justified. The court dispensed with Shaw's deafness as irrelevant to the issues because the officers could not have known. The civil suit ended with the award of summary judgment.

## Al Seymour and Peggy Sue Seymour v. City of Houston & J. G. Lopez

In January 1999, Sheryl Sue Seymour made two calls three minutes apart to the Houston 911 Emergency Response system in the very early morning hours. Seymour was abusive, incoherent, and threatening. She demanded an ambulance to take her to Rosewood Psychiatric Hospital. The Houston Fire Department (HFD) dispatched an ambulance with two Emergency Medical Technicians (EMT) to her address.

In accordance with HFD policy, the Houston Police Department (HPD) was advised of the dispatch. HPD then dispatched two officers, J. G. Lopez and W. L. Meeler, to Seymour's address. They arrived shortly after the EMTs. A third HPD officer, Earl Dean Morrison, heard the dispatch and went to the Seymour address on his own initiative.

As the officers entered the stairwell of the apartment building leading up to the second floor where Seymour's apartment was located, they heard unintelligible yelling and screaming. The hallways run north and south. The officers emerged on the second floor at the south end of the hallway. Seymour's apartment was over 100 feet away at the north end, second from the north end stairwell.

The three officers saw the two EMTs standing at Seymour's door. Seymour was yelling unintelligibly through the closed door and the EMTs were trying to talk to her. The HPD officers walked up the hallway within 15 feet of the doorway when Seymour suddenly burst through the doorway and attacked one of the EMTs with a large butcher knife. She turned her back to the officers as the EMT retreated northwards up the hallway to the stairwell. Seymour went after him, stabbing and slashing with the knife as he retreated from her.

The second EMT saw the three HPD officers behind him in the hallway as they were telling him to get away from her. He moved and got behind the three officers. The first EMT successfully avoided injury as he ran down the north end stairwell and as Seymour's attention was diverted to the police officers. She turned and began to advance on the officers, all the while stabbing and slashing with the knife in her right hand and yelling that she was going to kill them. She was alternating between walking and running towards the officers. At four locations along the hallway, she stabbed and slashed the wall as she advanced towards the officers who backed away from her.

The three officers were in a triangular formation in the hallway. Officers Lopez and Morrison were side by side in front, with Officer Meeler behind them. Officer Lopez was on the right, looking northward up the hallway, Officer Morrison on his left. Both had drawn their side arms when they witnessed Seymour's initial attack on the EMT. Officer Meeler never did draw his weapon throughout the incident.

At the urgings of Officer Lopez, the three officers retreated southwards down the hallway in the face of Seymour's unremitting attack. They backed up, facing Seymour the whole time, and all the while alternately ordering her to drop the knife, to stop, and also attempting to reason with her. Regardless, she continued to advance on them with no perceptible diminution of her rage or her determination to attack them with her knife. At one point during Seymour's extended attack down the hallway, Officer Morrison called HPD Dispatch to send a sergeant with a TASER.

The officers arrived at the stairwell landing at the south end of the hallway. The landing angles to the southwest, providing entryway to the adjacent apartment building as well as the stairs between the buildings. The EMT entered the stairwell and left the building. The three officers were crowded together in the angle of the landing. Officer Lopez' back was against the stairwell railing. Seymour was now within 10 feet of them with the knife raised over her head in her right hand in position to stab downwards. She started to run at them, yelling that she was going to kill them.

Officer Lopez fired one shot at her that struck her in the right shoulder, right of the anterior midline. It penetrated into her chest cavity, through the upper lobe of her right lung and severed her spinal cord at thoracic vertebra #5. She immediately collapsed. Officer Morrison kicked the knife out of her hand and radioed "Female down" to HPD Dispatch.

The location of the entry wound in Seymour's shoulder was consistent with her motion at the time Officer Lopez fired at her. She was moving towards him and Officer Morrison and was stabbing down violently with the knife in her right hand. The motion caused her torso to turn towards the left as her right hand and arm swung down and across her body. Thus the bullet penetrated the anterior right side of her shoulder and chest.

A timeline established from HPD communications logs reveals that 5 minutes 6 seconds after the dispatch of Officers Lopez and Meeler, Officer Morrison called for a sergeant—less than 3 minutes after his own arrival on the scene. One minute later he radioed "Female down." The entire incident, from initial attack to "Female down" transpired in less than 2 minutes.

The two EMTs rendered immediate emergency treatment, assisted by the HPD officers. A second ambulance was called for with paramedics who promptly arrived and transported her to a hospital, where she entered emergency surgery and was declared dead soon thereafter.

### Discussion

When the HPD Officers arrived, they did not know they were going to have to deal with a violent individual. They did not know where the responding EMTs were located. They had been dispatched on a routine basis (no lights, no siren) to provide precautionary backup to an ambulance crew "dealing with a

female psychiatric patient." The HPD officers had no basis to suspect potential violence, and they had no reason to react differently.

A number of the allegations in the resultant legal action claimed that HFD
should have delayed responding to Seymour until she had been restrained by
HPD and that HPD should have had a policy of responding to psychiatric patients with a sergeant carrying non-lethal weapons or that they should contain a situation until the non-lethal means could arrive on scene.

HFD Emergency Services had a history with Seymour. This was not the first
time she had called 911 for an ambulance. Seymour was habitually abusive, incoherent, and threatening over the phone, stressing the urgency of her needs
and using her anger to give weight to her demands. She had previously been
physically difficult with the responding personnel. Emergency Services personnel dealt with such individuals routinely. At the time, they had no basis to believe this event would be any different this time than their previous experiences
with Seymour.

Further, in addition to their institutional history with Seymour, Emergency
Services has a primary duty of rendering first response care and support to
those needing it in as prompt and efficient a manner as possible. To do otherwise absent a clear indication of danger is to risk injury or loss of life for failure to respond—dereliction of duty on the part of the Houston Fire
Department—refuting the later allegations by plaintiffs that they should have
waited for HPD. Plaintiffs also claimed that the lack of a policy *requiring* contact to be initiated by the police in advance of EMT personnel was negligent in
this case.

Psychiatric patients being abusive and threatening while interacting with
caregivers are common. HFD relied on the experience and judgment of its personnel involved at the time to enable the quickest and most effective response.
A policy that requires emergency personnel to delay responding in deference
to the police is irresponsible when there is no evidence of a material risk to
the lives of the HFD crews. There was no reason to believe that Seymour would
be a danger to the EMTs this time. She had not been dangerous before—just
abusive. HFD relayed the dispatch to HPD as a routine precautionary notifi-
cation that is required by policy.

In turn, HPD had no information beyond the situational advisory that HFD
was responding to a female psychiatric patient. The purpose of the relay from
HFD was to notify HPD that it was responding to a difficult and possibly abusive individual. The situation might need support from HPD and officers were
dispatched as a precaution. To mandate a delay in the services provided to psychiatric, disabled, and disturbed people for reasons of abusive language is unreasonable. It would deny them the prompt and efficient service that all other

citizens rely upon for emergency aid and rescue. The HFD did not have probable cause to believe that the situation with Sheryl Seymour would develop into one beyond their training and abilities to handle, or that it would threaten their safety.

The plaintiffs alleged negligence because the officers did not back off and call in support. HPD policy required calling in a supervisor with a TASER to confront disturbed individuals who might be physically violent. But the HPD officers had no reason to anticipate a violent confrontation. Lacking any basis to back off and call a supervisor, they did not. There was no fact or suspicion available to them that could have triggered the policy to the contrary, until the situation exploded before them and they were immersed in a deadly confrontation without warning or time to act otherwise.

The first indicator the officers had that it was a violent confrontation was when they saw Sheryl Seymour burst from her apartment 15 feet in front of them and attack an EMT with a large butcher knife. The three officers would have been fully justified in shooting Seymour at this moment to protect the EMT. The justified use of deadly force does not require that someone actually be killed or injured before deadly force can be used to protect them. It is justified to prevent *the imminent risk* of serious injury, not just to prevent the fact of it. But they *hesitated.*

The failure to shoot in defense of others is not uncommon and is symptomatic of several factors. First, when confronted with sudden, unanticipated violence there commonly occurs a sense of stunned disbelief, a reluctance or inability to comprehend the event and its potential for harm. That factor unavoidably slows the reactions and responses of the witnessing officer or individual. Secondly, there is also a pronounced reluctance to shoot someone "in defense of others." Police use of deadly force is rare, and by training is typically constrained to situations "in defense of self." The reluctance to use deadly force "in defense of others" when clearly justified can facilitate the unnecessary imposition of severe risks upon officers and other parties involved, although it is often viewed in the aftermath as desirable restraint, especially if fortuitously nobody was hurt.

The officers did not use deadly force. They verbally attracted Seymour's attention away from the EMT and towards themselves. From this point on, they were in an unmistakable "defense of selves" situation. Seymour turned on them and advanced, stabbing, slashing, and threatening to kill them the whole while. The officers retreated over 90 feet down the hallway, desperately trying to stop her attack with verbal commands and suasion as well as a display of weapons and their presence. It did not work, and at the distance of 10 feet she suddenly pressed her attack, knife above her head and stabbing down. That is when Officer Lopez fired the one shot that severed her spinal cord and terminated the attack.

These officers waited too long to shoot, and they let her get too close to them in pressing her attack. In actual fact, their delay in using deadly force put them at certain risk of death or serious injury. An attacker with a knife can initiate an assault and stab an individual with a holstered weapon from over 30 feet away before the individual can draw and fire a shot (action versus reaction). The attacker can successfully persevere against an officer despite being fatally wounded in the process because incapacitation due to hemorrhage requires time to occur. The only way to achieve incapacitation quickly enough in close quarters is to hit the central nervous system of the attacker— as happened here.

Seymour started her final attack from 10 feet. She had the knife overhead and was stabbing down with it. Had the bullet not severed her spine, there was no physiological damage done to her that could have stopped that attack. One of the three officers would have been stabbed. The autopsy notes point out that the damage to the spinal cord caused her to collapse—*nothing else did*. That damage occurred by mere chance. Given her level of rage and emotional disturbance and the extremely close quarters of the attack (inside of 10 feet), the bullet wound she suffered could not have slowed her down at all otherwise.

The three HPD officers waited much longer than they needed to before one of them acted to protect the three of them, and that shot was taken in desperation. This may be looked upon as a commendable effort on their part to avoid hurting Seymour and to dissipate the incident without violence, but it exposed them to an unabated, unambiguous, and unreasonable risk in the process. They avoided injury only by mere chance. They gambled with their lives and won through no skill or expertise of their own—merely the fortuitous happenstance of the bullet striking her in just the right way to sever her spine. Had it not done so, Seymour would not have dropped.

In the civil suit that followed, the plaintiffs' postulations as to what the participants should have known or should have done consisted of working back from the actual shooting and assuming that everything was an ineluctable progression from one post-determined action or fact to another. However, post-event suppositional reasoning is not supported by the facts and events as they transpired.

The supposition was made that she would not have been killed if the officers had left the floor, or otherwise stayed out of her reach until a sergeant with a TASER could arrive. This supposition has to assume that no innocent resident or bystander emerged into her path, and that she would not evade the three officers when out of their sight and disappear to endanger unknown others in unknown other locations. It also has to assume that she would not harm herself. More to the point, this supposition assumes that the opportunity to use the TASER would present itself and be effective before she succeeded in stabbing someone somewhere. It also requires an implicit faith in the infallible effectiveness of the TASER itself.

In order to be effective, the individual firing a TASER should be within 15 feet and preferably within 10 feet of the target subject. Both barbs must imbed in the individual's skin. If one misses, or hangs up in clothing, it won't work effectively, if at all. In this case, the individual wielding the TASER would have to be within Seymour's lethal reach. That implies that the officer approach within 10 feet and gamble that he can react to the attack, fire the TASER, have both barbs imbed in the subject's skin, and discharge the TASER, before getting stabbed. In the case of a violent attack at close quarters, a less-lethal weapon such as a TASER is more of an impediment to safety than a reasonable alternative to deadly force.

TASER is the preeminent example of the "less-lethal" weapon category. "Less-lethal" weapons are increasingly alleged to be the "reasonable" and "necessary" first option to be used instead of deadly force in violent confrontations because of the ability to incapacitate without causing serious injury.[25] Failure to use a TASER to resolve a violent confrontation is claimed to be evidence of excessive and unreasonable force as well as deficient policies, supervision, and training.

However, because of the close range at which the TASER must be employed, the small but very real failure rate, and the lack of any safety margin, the TASER (and all other less-lethal weapons to date) is better suited for situations involving passive resisters, physical resisters lacking deadly weapons, and control of unruly or out-of-control subjects. In such instances, a TASER is more effective and less injurious, than traditional non-deadly force such as impact weapons, hand fighting, wrestling, and chemical agents. A TASER is an excellent means of preventing an otherwise unarmed subject from escalating the risk potential of the situation to a point that deadly force becomes necessary. However, a TASER is not reasonable when the use of deadly force in defense of self or others is necessary and justified at the outset. The attempt to employ non-deadly alternatives delays the use of deadly force, raising the risk of death or serious

---

25. The insistence upon the priority of using so-called "less-lethal" weapons is particularly characteristic of plaintiff allegations on behalf of "non-conventional" dangerous subjects, such as the mentally ill or minors. Seymour is a case in point.

injury. It is frequently overlooked, but the justified use of deadly force is a life-saving option, employed in the face of imminent loss of life.[26]

It is a truism that if Sheryl Seymour had dropped her knife at some point in her advance down the hallway, she would be alive. She did not. To suppose any or all of the above is to suppose facts and events not in evidence in the incident and to ignore the severely limited time frame in which this incident occurred. It encompassed less than two minutes from start to finish, which made the decision to use deadly force all the more necessary given the real and severe limitations of action vs. reaction and wounding factors.

A final supposition that is common in the allegations that arise in cases like this is there should have been a policy in place that was detailed and restrictive enough to have prevented this specific shooting. The allegation that there should be a policy requiring a series of prerequisite actions and precautionary preparations prior to confronting psychiatric patients was one of the principal bases for legal action. On its face, this is an attractive notion that appeals to the uninformed in the aftermath of an incident involving a mentally ill person. It seems to be an easy solution. But a policy proscription that supplants the collective judgment, training, and experience of professional responders before the fact is a device that will only obstruct and delay the emergency response system.

A supposedly comprehensive and proscriptive policy controlling risk will inevitably run up against the random, unanticipated, and unwarranted violent act unforeseen by the policy, or not covered by its terms, in which case the resultant criticism for violating policy would discourage future responses except as specifically authorized. The problem with such a policy is that it cannot anticipate and delineate the random and aberrant act. There will always be something that, with clear and reflective hindsight, the police and fire department *should* or *could* have known. The outcome then inevitably becomes the blanket application of the policy and all emergency responses are delayed until a police supervisor with non-lethal means at hand can make first contact, thereby eliminating the application of any judgment, experience, or training to the

---

26. The same allegations are made regarding other so-called "less-lethal" forms of force, such as shotgun beanbag rounds. The "less-lethal" appellation is popular, especially among those interests making allegations of unjustified deadly force. It has acquired an unfortunate cachet in the conventional wisdom as a sophisticated distinction between deadly force on the one hand and the conventional non-deadly force options such as batons, chemical agents, strikes with hand/foot/knee, grappling, pressure points, control holds, and pain induced compliance on the other. That is problematic, as explained in Chapter 9. It is all non-deadly force. Non-deadly force ("less-lethal" if we must be all inclusive) is not necessary or reasonable to resolve an imminent risk of serious injury. It is also neither necessary nor reasonable in advance of the use of deadly force.

contrary, and ignoring the very real limitations inherent to any non-lethal alternative. The emergency response system is diminished by delay for some of those needing it the most, at increased cost to life or trauma. And there can be no culpability because it is a matter of policy mandated to ensure everybody's safety. Such a solution defies reality, pre-empts experience and training, and although well intentioned, is far more harmful in its effect.

But police and emergency response personnel are trained to assess risk relative to their respective missions. The assessment of risk is a responsibility that has to be trusted to their collective judgment, training, and experience.

In the final analysis, within moments of their arrival on the scene, the three HPD officers faced Seymour's surprise attack on the EMT and were inextricably engaged. From that point they were joined in an intense, close range, and rapidly unfolding threat to their lives. They had neither the time nor the opportunity to do any more than what they did. They gambled by letting Seymour continue her attack unabated until the very last second and then one officer was able to stave it off only by the merest chance of the single bullet fired severing her spine.

## Juan-Jose Guerra Morales v. U.S.

In December 1997, the U.S. Drug Enforcement Administration (DEA) initiated an investigation of a group of reputed narcotics traffickers in Detroit, Michigan. Special Agent (SA) Dawn Ohanian was acting in an undercover capacity with her partner Task Force Officer (TFO) Bodek as drug dealers from Cleveland. Morales and his associates claimed to have two kilos of cocaine to sell. SA Ohanian had previously displayed $48,000 in cash to Raul Guerrero, the point of contact for the group. Unknown to the agents, Morales, Guerrero, and Walt Morris (a third associate) had no intention of consummating the drug deal. They planned to steal the cash at gunpoint.

The plan was that Morales and Morris would engage the robbery after Guerrero showed them where Ohanian was located in the motel where the buy was supposed to happen. They would do the robbery after Guerrero had left, or they would make it look like they were robbing Ohanian and Guerrero together to cover his involvement. Their goal was to conduct the "rip off" and make it seem as if Guerrero was not involved so that the supposed drug dealers from Cleveland could not track them down and take retribution. Regardless, they intended to do the robbery whether or not Guerrero was covered. Morris had a gun he would bring, although he had no ammunition for it. Guerrero told him that this was "just a little lady" (referring to Ohanian) and he didn't see any need for ammunition—it would be an easy thing to do.

SA Ohanian was in room 204 at the motel. The room was equipped for audio and video surveillance monitored by four agents in room 206 immediately next door. The motel wing where the room was located is situated with the long axis running south to north (front to back). Room 204 was on the second level facing west into the parking lot between the two wings of the motel. There were two stairwells to the second floor—one at the far north end of the building, and one in the middle of the building. Both stairwells had entries on each side of the building. In addition to the four agents inside room 206, additional agents and officers formed a perimeter around the motel.

SA Ohanian met Guerrero in the parking lot near the front (south end of the motel wing). She asked Guerrero where the owner of the cocaine was and noticed two men walking across the north end of the parking lot. She asked Guerrero if the two men were his people, which he confirmed. She told Guerrero to have them come meet with her.

The two men were Morales and Morris. They came to the parking lot and she asked the trio if they were ready to sell the cocaine and added that she wanted to see it. Morales told her that he would not show her the kilos until he saw the money. SA Ohanian protested that she had already shown the money but Morales insisted that he needed to see the money before the cocaine would be delivered. Although their original plans to rob Ohanian in a way that concealed Guerrero's involvement had now been made irrelevant, that did not stop them. The men just wanted to ensure the money was on hand.

SA Ohanian told Morales to come with her to the room and the money would be brought there for inspection. Morales followed her to room 204 and they entered. Morales sat in a chair beside the door to the room. SA Ohanian sat in a chair across the room from him. TFO Bodek telephoned and she told him to bring the money to the room. At some point in this sequence of events, the outside surveillance teams lost sight of Morris. He used the middle stairwell to go up to the second floor where room 204 was located. Morris and Morales were the ones designated to conduct the robbery.

TFO Bodek walked to the north end of the motel wing and used the stairwell to go up to the second level. He began to walk south along the balcony that runs the length of the building. He was proceeding from the northern end of the building (room 230) towards room 204 at the far southern end. The stairwell located at the midpoint is between rooms 214 and 216. Room 230 is the northern most; room 202 is the southern most. Room 204 abuts room 202. The balcony is five feet wide and the top of the railing is 12'8" above the ground.

TFO Bodek saw Morris with his hands in the pockets of his sweatshirt standing near room 204. TFO Bodek asked Morris why he had his hands in his pockets and Morris replied, "It's cold." The two walked together to room 204 and TFO Bodek knocked on the door. Morris stood facing the parking lot, his back towards Bodek. The hidden camera located inside room 204 videotaped the ensuing incident.

At the knock, SA Ohanian rose from her seat, walked to the door, and opened it. TFO Bodek started to enter the room. Morris turned around from the railing behind him with the gun in his right hand. TFO Bodek grabbed Morris' gun hand with his left hand and a struggle ensued which carried the two men back onto the balcony to the right side of the doorway.

SA Ohanian's first reaction was an involuntary half step backwards behind the door. Then she drew her handgun and stepped forward through the doorway trailing closely behind the two struggling men. She shot Morris three times at very close range (within 18 inches by forensic examination). She did not see any effect, but now felt physical contact from her rear and turned to confront Morales. Morris continued to struggle with TFO Bodek after SA Ohanian turned away from them until he succumbed to his wounds. He was struck by all three shots and died on the scene.

As SA Ohanian stepped through the door, Morales rose from his seat beside the door and followed her. He raised both hands towards her shoulders from the rear in a motion consistent with grabbing her, contacting her at about the same instant she shot Morris. The contact appears to cause SA Ohanian to stagger forward slightly. At the sound of the shots, Morales broke contact with SA Ohanian and turned to his left, disappearing from view behind the doorframe as he ran towards the south end of the balcony.

SA Ohanian turned to her left in the direction he had gone. By her account, she saw Morales briefly facing her as she turned her weapon towards him and moved in his direction (and out of camera view). He was running towards the end of the wing. At the end of the wing, the balcony turns left into a sheltered walkway to the other side of the building. The distance from the edge of the doorframe to the corner of the building is 20 feet 6 inches. SA Ohanian fired two shots at Morales, one of which struck him in the back of the neck. He fell at the corner of the building and is now a quadriplegic.

At this point, the arrest/surveillance team located in room 206 appeared in the camera's view through the doorway after SA Ohanian moved out of view to the left.

## Discussion

The illegal drug trade is characterized by the prevalence of firearms and the propensity for violence. Participants in the illegal drug trade are known to be dangerous. People engaged in illegal drug trafficking must constantly recognize and provide for the ever-present risk that they are exposed to armed assaults and robberies conducted by their competitors, their cohorts, or others engaged in the trade. People who engage in illegal drug trafficking are correctly presumed to be armed and to have a propensity for violence. They must guard against the risk of detection and arrest by lawful authorities as well as the risk of assault and robbery by those with whom they are dealing. It is an illegal activity in which participants operate in a manner best understood as "survival of the fittest" or "law of the jungle."

A narcotics deal involves a buyer and a seller. Each possesses an asset the other wants—one has a large sum of money, the other a large quantity of illicit and valuable narcotics. Each must guard against the other taking that asset by force and violence (known as "rip-offs" in the vernacular). When a rip-off occurs, the victims of the rip-off are commonly hurt and/or killed to shield the perpetrators of the assault from retributive actions by cohorts of their victims.

The agents involved in this undercover narcotics operation were fully aware of the risk of a rip-off and took care to provide security measures against that possibility. A cover and arrest team of four agents was positioned in the room abutting room 204. The room occupied by SA Ohanian was equipped with covert surveillance cameras that recorded what occurred within the room. The arrest team next door had monitors enabling them to see and hear what the camera recorded as it occurred. Additional agents and TFOs were positioned around the motel forming an outer perimeter.

The plaintiffs alleged that the presence of the cover team armed with submachine guns and wearing body armor made it unreasonable for SA Ohanian to act in her own defense. They claimed that Morales was unarmed and posing no threat to anybody when he was shot as he was merely trying to flee. They argued that if Ohanian did think Morales was a threat, she should have ducked back into her room and let the cover team deal with him. They argued that even if Morales was armed and reached cover around the corner of the building, the cover team was safe from return fire because of their body armor. All of these allegations were dispensed with by the judge.

An undercover agent does not function risk free. The need to successfully pursue an undercover operation to its desired conclusion requires undercover personnel to assess personal risks and to accept and manage those risks. Cover teams are a last resort intervention to save the undercover personnel from imminent death or injury. However, they cannot intervene to resolve lesser risks without exposing and nullifying the entire undercover operation. Thus, undercover agents are armed and trained to defend themselves as the first resort in an assault or attack. The cover team can only react to what it sees and hears, which means that any action it can take will always lag events. The undercover agent has the initiative in self-defense, which will either resolve the incident or buy sufficient time for the cover team to effectively respond and resolve the incident. This is a given in any undercover operation.

The primary responsibilities of the perimeter agents and officers were to monitor the movements of involved parties to and from the vicinity of the motel, control avenues of escape, provide surveillance as needed and possible, and contain all involved people to the location when the arrest occurred. Because they were in uniform or wearing identifiable law enforcement apparel and using clearly identifiable official cars, it was incumbent upon all the perimeter personnel to select locations close enough to control the perimeter but distant enough not to be spotted by the subjects of the operation.

A perimeter team is not the primary responder when or if something goes wrong. That is the function of the cover and arrest team. In the event the operation goes awry, the perimeter team is expected to seal the perimeter and contain the principals within that perimeter. Secondarily, the team must respond to the event, but in doing so it can incur the risk of a sudden and dangerous confrontation. For example, the perimeter agents in this incident heard the shots fired by SA Ohanian. They did not know who fired the shots or why. As some of them responded on foot, they could have run unaware into an armed and dangerous person or an ambush situation for which they were unprepared in those circumstances. These dangers are a matter of experience and precedent, and law enforcement personnel must recognize the potential for injury or death to others coincident to the scene of a violent confrontation.

Plaintiffs claimed that this incident was not one shooting, but actually two separate and distinct events—first the shooting of Morris that they reluctantly agreed might be reasonable (see below), and the later shooting of Morales that was not. Lastly, they claimed that shooting Morales in the back as he fled was excessive force.

When TFO Bodek saw Morris to his right with a gun in his hand, he grabbed Morris' gun hand with his left hand, precluding him from drawing his own weapon (Bodek is left-handed). The struggle quickly carried them back outside onto the balcony beyond the doorway.

SA Ohanian immediately recognized the most immediate threat was Morris. She glanced at Morales as she drew her handgun, moved through the doorway and fired three shots into Morris. She did not see any reaction from Morris and did not know if she hit him. This is not unusual. The most common physical reaction to being hit by a handgun bullet is no reaction. The thought occurred to her that she could have just shot her partner.

In actuality, all three shots struck Morris but none of the wounds struck any part of his central nervous system, so none of them would have forced immediate incapacitation upon him by the physiological damage they caused. Morris continued to resist and struggle until the accumulating blood loss stopped him. Of note is that the three bullet wounds had widely divergent entry points. One entered his left shoulder, one his lower left abdomen, and one entered his lower right back. Plaintiffs took this as evidence of unreasonable force—shooting Morris in the back—distinguishing that from the location of his other two wounds. Plaintiffs agreed that one or two of the shots fired at Morris could be justified, but the one in the back was not. Actually, the divergent entry points were a result of the violent physical struggle between Morris and Bodek, twisting and turning as they fought over Morris' gun. SA Ohanian was stationary when she fired, she did not run around Morris shooting him from the various angles. This is a good example of why the location of a bullet wound is irrelevant. The issue is the justification for the decision to shoot, not where the shots happen to strike.

Morris did not surrender when he was shot. He is heard to say "OK, OK" on the tape but that is indicative of nothing substantive. He could have been attempting a ruse or simply making an involuntary expression induced by surprise. There is no way to know what he meant, but he did not release the gun or cease to struggle with TFO Bodek, who wrestled him to the deck. Finally, the effects of his wounds caught up with him and the struggle ended. This is another lesson in the realities of wound ballistics.

Simultaneously with SA Ohanian's movement through the doorway, Morales followed her. He did not turn left or right as would be expected if he were merely trying to flee as alleged. He followed directly behind her and raised both hands in a manner consistent with grabbing her from behind. In the video, she can be seen to step or stagger slightly forward from the contact. At the same instant SA Ohanian fired her three shots Morales immediately broke contact and turned to his left and ran along the balcony towards the walkway at the end of the wing.

Morales' actions are consistent with executing the rip-off. As Morris struggled with Bodek, Morales went after Ohanian with both hands when the sudden shots occurred. Apparently none of these would-be rip-off artists anticipated that their intended victims might be armed and resist. Until the moment that SA Ohanian shot Morris, nothing had occurred to change their assault and robbery plans. The plaintiffs claimed that the empty gun was evidence that Morales and Morris were no threat, but the agents had no way to know that. Moreover, Morales and Morris wanted their intended victims to believe the gun was loaded and that they would shoot them with it. Their plan relied exclusively on the believable nature of the threat they intended to represent. They succeeded in that endeavor.

SA Ohanian felt the contact from the rear by Morales. She now had a second imminent threat to confront. It was certainly reasonable for her to believe that both of the men were armed. Drug rip-offs are armed confrontations. She had already seen one gun in the hand of an assailant. She had to assume the second assailant was armed, too, and now she was caught between the two of them.

SA Ohanian had shot Morris with no noticeable effect and suddenly she had a second assailant on her. She turned and saw him running to a position of tactical advantage. By her own account, she expected to be shot in the back at any second as she turned from Morris. The distance from the doorframe to the corner of the building where the walkway across the end of building begins is 20 feet 6 inches. Morales was over half way there by the time it took SA Ohanian to turn, follow, and shoot.

The walkway would provide an excellent position of cover. It runs across the southern end of the building, connecting the balcony on the west side to the balcony on the east side. It has a wall running the width of the building and is covered by the roof, forming an alcove or hidden access way from one side to the other. If Morales had turned the corner, he would have been sheltered from outside view, free to either return fire from a barricaded position, ambush pursuit, or continue an escape attempt. In the space of less than a second, SA Ohanian had to resolve the following issues:

Was Morales armed? The reasonable assumption under the circumstances was "yes." Guns are easily hidden on the person, as Morris had amply demonstrated mere moments before.

Can he shoot as he runs? The answer is "yes." Nothing precludes an individual from shooting as he runs.

Was she at risk? She was unprotected, standing in the open in close proximity to Morales (within 10 feet). If he suddenly fired a shot in her direction, she could easily be hit. She could not react fast enough to get out of the way or take cover from a sudden shot. In the process of trying to move to cover, she would abandon her unprotected partner to any shots fired by Morales.

What happens if Morales gets around the corner? He would be protected behind cover while she was in the open and exposed. He would be free to shoot at her with relative impunity. He would have gained tactical advantage if she had hesitated. And tactical advantage increases the threat of serious harm to the officers. It is not unreasonable to refuse to concede tactical advantage in an active engagement.

Was Morales a threat to others? Given the totality of the circumstances and his actions, the answer is "yes." He was reasonably believed to be armed and escaping a violent confrontation. There were perimeter agents unaware of his location or actions that could be victims of ambush or sudden assault. There were innocent citizens residing in the motel who could step unaware into harm's way and be injured or be taken hostage.

SA Ohanian did not wait to see what Morales would do next. She recognized the danger and she fired two shots at him. One of the shots struck him in the back of the neck and he fell immediately. She did not shoot again.

While SA Ohanian moved after Morales, the cover team emerged from room 206 and took control of Morris. They responded as quickly as they could possibly have managed. Morris was not within view of their surveillance equipment as he stood outside room 204. He became visible as TFO Bodek stepped into the doorway and then turned to grapple with him. In the time it took them to recognize the onset of the attack and move to the front door of room 206, SA Ohanian had already acted in defense of herself and TFO Bodek as she was trained and expected to do. The surprise rip-off put the cover team in the unavoidable position of lagging behind events. The reality of action versus reaction is always present.

A basis for many of the primary allegations in the resulting legal action was that two separate and distinct shooting incidents occurred that had to be assessed and justified independently. This view alleged that Morales' actions were clearly no threat, merely fleeing, and the use of deadly force against him was reckless and unjustified because he was unarmed. Much was made of the fact that Ohanian acted against Morris and turned her back on Morales, arguing this proved she did not reasonably perceive or fear any threat from Morales. The reality is that the incident was one continuous attack perpetrated by two assailants working together and not two or more separate and distinct events. It also was alleged that the agent was required to issue a verbal warning before using deadly force in the alleged "second" incident, and had she done so, Morales would have immediately surrendered. The fact that Morales was hit in the back was alleged as proof of the unreasonable and excessive use of force against him.

Morales abruptly changed direction at the sound of the gunshots, turning to his left and moving towards the corner of the building some 20 feet away. This was a change in tactics, not the end of one incident and start of another in sequence. The entire shooting incident from first shot to fifth shot occurred in the space of 2.4 seconds, as timed from the surveillance videotape. This is consistent with the statistical norm for law enforcement shooting experience — over 90% of all law enforcement shootings occur in 3 seconds or less.

A more detailed analysis of the time line of this particular incident is possible due to the videotape of the shooting that contains all five clear and specific gunshots as audible markers. For the sake of clarity, the first gunshot is assigned a starting time of 0.0. The second shot occurred 0.4 seconds later, and the third shot 0.5 seconds after that. These are the three shots that hit Morris. The next two shots were fired at Morales. Shot 4 occurs 1.1 seconds after shot 3, and shot 5 follows 0.4 seconds later.

As detailed in Chapter 6, an officer with a finger on the trigger will perceive a stimulus, decide to shoot, initiate the necessary nerve impulse, and an average 0.365 seconds later, the muzzle blast sounds. These times are simple, no-choice-required reaction times. This is the mechanical time necessary to fire a shot, once the judgment and decision have been made to shoot.

In looking at SA Ohanian's five shots, this mechanical time is obvious between shots 1 to 2 to 3, and shot 4 to 5. It is simply the mechanical time necessary for her brain to form the impulse to pull the trigger, send that impulse to the gun hand, have the gun hand pull the trigger, have the trigger move, the hammer fall, the primer detonate, the powder charge burn, and the projectile exit the muzzle (the point at which muzzle blast is audible). Having decided to shoot and fired shot 1, SA Ohanian needs 0.4–0.5 seconds for the sheer mechanical action of firing the subsequent shots.

Decision time, defined as that time necessary to perceive a signal, identify it, and make the decision to fire a shot, is another component of reaction time. A complex scenario predictably increases decision time and total reaction time. Two or more choices increase reaction time exponentially, and stress generally increases reaction time by a factor of 50% to 100%. The critical imperative of action/reaction times in the law enforcement setting is that the officer's time lapse (decision plus response time resulting in a shot fired) *begins* in response to an action initiated by the person confronted. A law enforcement officer cannot see the future or read minds. The officer can only react to what the assailant does.

Relating this data to SA Ohanian's sequence of shots, her mechanical time was 0.4–0.5 seconds. There was an interval of 1.1 seconds between shot 3 and shot 4. Subtracting the mechanical time necessary to fire shot 4, which leaves an interval of at most 0.7 seconds during which she turned, followed after Morales, and *decided* to fire shot 4. The obvious question is what, if anything, could have changed in that 0.7 seconds that would have precluded shooting at Morales or made feasible a verbal warning, and *would have been known* to SA Ohanian.

It is helpful to re-examine what she could have known, or reasonably believed, at this point in the incident. She and TFO Bodek were dealing with a group of drug traffickers that included Morales and Morris. She and TFO Bodek were the targets of a sudden attack initiated by Morales and Morris. Drug rip-offs are characterized by the prevalence of extreme violence, a fact known to the agents based on training, experience, and the institutional experience of the DEA amassed over years of intimate involvement with drug traffickers. For the same reasons, she believed that Morales and Morris were armed and would inflict death or injury upon her and TFO Bodek in the course of the rip-off. It was objectively reasonable for her to believe Morales and Morris were armed from the outset. When Morris actually drew and aimed a handgun at them, she was not surprised to learn that he had a weapon. She was amazed after it was over to learn that Morales did not have one.

The training provided to law enforcement officers in general stresses that they must recognize risks of imminent death or serious injury and react to protect themselves *and others.* One training goal is to enhance the ability to recognize and prioritize threats, and react against those threats quickly and efficiently *in order of risk* to self and others. For example, confronted with two targets at 10 yards, one with a knife and one with a gun, the agent should shoot at the one with the gun first, then deal with the knife wielder. At arm's reach, the problem becomes more complex since either can inflict injury—which requires first attention, and which can wait a second or fraction of a second.

Training deals with multiple threats. The agent may not be able to afford to wait and see if the first threat has been successfully resolved before addressing the next one. It is extremely unlikely that an agent could know whether or not any shots fired were successful in the time available in such a scenario. SA Ohanian's experience is a case in point.

In simple terms, officers are trained to shoot at least two shots at the first threat then immediately respond to the next threat—fire at that one—and then move to the next one or be prepared to re-address the first one. A threat may not be resolved, but at least it may be disrupted or deflected sufficiently to serve the ultimate goal: protection of self and others. Agents also are trained to keep shooting as long as the threat presents itself, and stop as soon as they see that the threat has ended.

SA Ohanian did as she had been trained to do, and as she was expected to perform. She recognized that two men working together had initiated an armed assault. She saw one with a gun in hand struggling with her partner. She knew the second one was to her rear as she reacted. She prioritized the threats— Morris with gun in hand versus Morales with no visible weapon yet. She dealt with the higher threat posed by Morris, shooting him three times. Without waiting to see if that threat had been resolved (and convinced in her own mind that it had not been), she turned to deal with the second threat—Morales who had reaffirmed his threat status by coming up behind her and making contact.

Then Morales turned and ran south along the balcony towards the building corner 20 feet away. Ohanian had not seen a weapon, but she believed he was armed and she understood that if he turned the corner he would be in a position of significant advantage from which he could shoot at her and TFO Bodek with relative impunity. He could turn and shoot while he ran down the balcony.

She saw Morales turned enough to be looking at her. He certainly would have been compelled to look and see what was happening behind him. He of course saw her directing her attention to him—probably his worst fear at the moment. They were not taking turns, each reacting to the other in linear fashion. Each was acting independently of the other and also simultaneously as their actions overlapped. This is why the location of the bullet wound in the back of his neck is not relevant.

SA Ohanian made the decision to shoot as she saw him looking at her. Meanwhile, Morales was making or continuing his turn away in furtherance of his movement to get to the corner as she went through the "decision time/reaction time" necessary for shot 4 to actually fire. The physical positioning and configuration of the two when the decision to shoot was made and implemented had changed completely by the moment that the bullet struck.

SA Ohanian remembered shooting Morales as he looked at her, a statement used to allege deception on her part. Yet, it is a fact that actual wound locations often do not square with memories of how the parties were positioned when the decision to shoot was made. This is a common occurrence in shooting incidents. It is fully explained by the forensic reality of human and mechanical reaction times and the dynamic of overlaid, independent actions/reactions occurring more or less simultaneously. The only issue is whether the decision to shoot was reasonable and justified at the moment it was made, not the ultimate location of the wound.

Some other issues merit discussion in this example. First is the issue raised concerning a verbal warning. Neither of the agents had time to contemplate a verbal warning, or attempt one, or await a response as they were suddenly and without warning confronted with the immediate prospect of being shot and a desperate physical struggle to divert the gun held in Morris' hand. A warning was not feasible, not legally required, and the agents cannot be faulted for not attempting one any more than they could be faulted for not attempting to talk Morris into giving up his gun.

Plaintiffs contended that SA Ohanian should have ducked back into room 204 and left Morales to the other agents in the area. However, to do so would have been to abandon TFO Bodek to the risk of Morales shooting as he ran, or shooting from behind the protection of the building corner. Law enforcement officers are not trained to take *no action* to protect themselves and others. They are expected to be proactive in the pursuit of their duty.

One of the more outrageous allegations made by plaintiffs was that SA Ohanian should have done exactly that—run for cover because her cover agents were all wearing body armor and thus were "safe." This allegation appears with regularity in lawsuits filed against law enforcement officers using deadly force— the presence of body armor diminishes the necessity to use deadly force because it renders the officer safe from return fire. Contrarily, if body armor is not present the allegation is made that the officer was at fault for not wearing it and thereby "caused" the risk by recklessly and unreasonably increasing his vulnerability. Neither is true—both are nonsense. Neither the public, nor any individual law enforcement officer, should consider body armor anything more than a partial and imperfect protective shield. In a deadly force confrontation, no law enforcement officer should assume more personal risk wearing body armor than he or she would without it.[27]

Once Morales turned the corner, he would have been out of sight of every agent at the motel. The walkway provides an excellent position of cover. It runs across the southern end of the building, connecting the balcony on the west side to the balcony on the east side. It has a wall running the width of the building and is covered by the roof, forming an alcove or hidden access way from one side to the other. If Morales had turned the corner, he would have been sheltered from outside view, free to return fire from a barricaded position, ambush pursuit, or continue to escape by running north along the east side balcony. He had numerous options if he turned the corner:

1. Fire on SA Ohanian and TFO Bodek from behind cover.
2. Fire on the agents from room 206 as they emerged in view.
3. Proceed unseen across to the eastern side of the building and move unseen to either of the two stairwells in the building—one in the middle, one at the north end, and have opportunity to attack perimeter agents by surprise from the vantage of the walled balcony.
4. Take a hostage from among the numerous motel residents, or attack a resident, if one opportunistically appeared.
5. Force entry into a room occupied by another resident of the motel.

---

27. During the sixteen-year period of 1999–2014, 833 officers were killed. 797 of them were killed with firearms and 513 of those officers were wearing body armor when they were killed (64.4%). To further break down those deaths, 381 of the officers were struck in the head or neck, 174 in the upper torso (that area typically covered by body armor), and 31 died from wounds below the waist. Compiled from a compendium of FBI Uniform Crime Reports, Law Enforcement Officers Killed and Assaulted from 1999–2014.

6.  Exit via the stairwell in the middle, from which he could emerge on the eastern side or the western side, and have opportunity to attack perimeter agents by surprise.
7.  Exit via the stairwell at the north end, from which he could emerge on the eastern side or the western side, and have opportunity to attack perimeter agents by surprise.
8.  Shoot at any of the perimeter agents, all of whom were distracted and dealing with Raul Guerrero and Virginia Guerrero as they fled in their cars.
9.  Escape, probably unseen.

To the contrary, the responsibility is to prevent exactly such a scenario from occurring.

In the final analysis, arguing that a law enforcement officer has a legal duty to keep a particular person from engaging in a particular behavior is to argue that the officer is responsible for a person's acts. It defies logic and reality and is ludicrous on its face, impossible in fact. Law enforcement officers cannot divine intents, read minds, or eliminate chance influence. They can only react to what happens. They are not responsible for what another person does — only what they do in response. If that response is objectively reasonable, it is justified.

All of the plaintiffs' allegations were dispensed with and summary judgment awarded except for the allegation of excessive, unreasonable force based upon Ohanian shooting Morales in the back as he ran, which went to trial. The judge trying the case on that one issue found a verdict of judgment for the defendants.[28] The opinion detailed several "Conclusions of Law," including:

> *"In evaluating the reasonableness of the actions, the officer's training and experience may be taken into account."*[29]
>
> *"The fact that Morales was unarmed at the time of the incident is irrelevant in determining the objective reasonableness of Ohanian's discharge of her weapon."*[30]
>
> *"Ohanian was not required to wait to see if in fact Morales was reaching for a weapon when she saw his arm movements. 'Courts cannot ask*

---

28. *Juan-Jose Guerra Morales v. U.S.*, U.S. District Court, Eastern District of Michigan, Southern Division, Civil Action No: 01-74269, *Findings of Fact and Conclusions of Law*, U.S. District Judge Robert H. Cleland, May 30, 2003.
29. *Ibid.* page 4.
30. *Ibid.*

*an officer to hold fire in order to ascertain whether the suspect will, in fact, injure or murder the officer.'"[31]*

*"There is no proper inquiry into Morales' state of mind or intentions, for the officer is not required to speculate as to what is in the mind of an opponent."[32]*

*" ... claims of excessive force are fact-driven and require careful analysis and attention to details, particularly when events are tense, uncertain, and rapidly evolving."[33]*

*"It is unavailing to assert 'that a surrounded subject presents no danger to others.'"[34]*

*"A 'feasible' warning is not one that is simply possible.... In the cool aftermath, it is deceptively easy to say:*

*'What harm can come from giving a warning? In the split-second reality of a deadly police chase, that warning ... might permit the suspect to turn and fire a weapon or otherwise facilitate his escape, putting at risk innocent police and civilians who he encounters in the path of his flight.'"[35]*

The judge's concluding finding of fact stated, in part:

*"It was objectively reasonable in the totality of the circumstances for Ohanian to shoot Morales to resolve the threat of imminent danger which he presented."[36]*

## *Estate of Robert Woodward v. Brattleboro, et al.*

On a Sunday in December 2001, at approximately 10:00 a.m., a man later identified as Robert Woodward entered All Souls Church in Brattleboro, Vermont. The church was occupied by a large number of parishioners—men, women and children—variously estimated to number between 50 and 65 people congregating for their regularly scheduled church service. Woodward was a stranger entirely unknown to the church members and his entrance was a surprise.

Woodward ran to the pulpit at the front of the room and began addressing the congregation at large. He was emotionally agitated, distressed, and ranting loudly of conspiracies against him by the government: CIA plots against his life and CIA-engineered assassinations of celebrities such as Bob Marley and

---

31. *Ibid.* page 5.
32. *Ibid.*
33. *Ibid.* page 7.
34. *Ibid.*
35. *Ibid.* pages 7–9.
36. *Ibid.* page 28.

George Harrison. He passed out slips of paper on which he had written messages such as: "I have received threats of death, torture, harm to friends and family and arrest on trumped up charges from CIA." Another message read: "The unitarians (sic) should create and promote national networks of buyers, co-ops for energy efficient vehicles." The messages were written on blank checks for Woodward's bank account.

Some parishioners decided that they had to get people to leave the church and began quietly telling members of the congregation to leave. Others in the congregation had taken it upon themselves to quietly remove the dozen or so children from the room. One member called 911 to report the incident. Woodward noticed people leaving and pulled a folding knife from his pocket, opened the blade and held it to his right eye, telling people not to leave or else he would kill himself.

The first dispatch broadcast was that there was an unwanted individual at the church who would not leave. Officers Terrance Parker and William Davies, Brattleboro Police Department, responded in one car. Subsequently, the dispatcher advised responding officers that the subject was armed with a knife, was refusing to let people leave, and was threatening suicide. Officer Marshall Holbrook also responded to the church when he heard the dispatch that the subject was armed and arrived moments before Officers Parker and Davies.

Inside the church Woodward continued to brandish his knife and threaten suicide if people left or did not listen to him. Two members of the congregation happened to be mental health professionals, a psychiatrist and a psychiatric nurse. Both interceded with Woodward to attempt to de-escalate the situation. The psychiatrist urged the minister to get people to leave quietly and slowly while Woodward was self-absorbed in his ranting.

The nurse was concerned for the safety of several elderly parishioners seated in the front row in close proximity to Woodward. She moved forward and sat with them in the front row, telling Woodward that he was scaring people with his knife. Woodward put the knife back in his pocket and apologized for scaring people, but told her that he needed to take desperate action; "I feel justified because such drastic action has been taken against me."

The psychiatrist approached Woodward and offered to listen to him. He tried to call people at Woodward's request on a cell phone but did not reach anyone. Then a church member entered the room and told everybody to leave. Woodward got up from his chair beside the psychiatrist, pulled his knife out and threatened suicide again, holding the knife to his right eye while demanding that nobody leave. The psychiatrist backed slowly away, trying to keep the pulpit between him and Woodward. He later stated he was in fear of imminent assault at this point. The responding police officers arrived on the scene approximately at this point in the sequence of events.

Woodward moved away from the pulpit to an open area 15–20 feet away, near a Christmas tree in the corner of the room. There was a double door behind him that opened into an adjacent room. Additionally, a ramp providing access to the room ran along the same wall leading from near the Christmas tree to an exit from the meeting room at the rear. Woodward began pacing back and forth between the tree and the pulpit in an agitated manner with his knife held to his eye as he ranted about being killed and about killing himself.

People standing outside directed Officer Holbrook inside the church. Officers Parker and Davies followed him into the church building. They conferred inside the entryway/foyer out of Woodward's sight. They briefly surveyed the scene from behind cover and decided to remove the remaining members of the congregation before trying to establish a dialog with Woodward.

The three officers entered the meeting room. The chairs for the congregation were set up in two banks of rows separated by a center aisle with the pulpit positioned in line with the central aisle. The officers entered from the left rear corner of the room (facing the pulpit at the front and diagonally across from the Christmas tree). Officer Holbrook stayed to the left side of the room, moving forward along the rows of chairs to the front of the room left of the pulpit. Officer Parker moved through the left side bank of chairs to the center aisle, and moved forward in the center aisle. Officer Davies followed Officer Parker, but stayed towards the rear of the center aisle to encourage and direct people leaving. All three officers were signaling people to leave with hand gestures and quietly telling them to leave, as the officers moved forward.

Woodward saw the police officers enter the room and his level of agitation increased substantially. He was yelling at them not to come in or he would kill himself. He gripped his knife in one hand with the point in or at his eye and his other hand cupping the knife hand in a manner consistent with making a two-handed stabbing thrust.[37] He continued pacing about the area to the right of the pulpit in the vicinity of the Christmas tree.

Officer Parker tried to talk with Woodward as he moved forward, telling him to drop the knife and that nobody would hurt him, that he didn't need to hurt himself. Woodward did not respond. He continued his frenetic movements and his monologue about suicide. Officer Parker saw several parishioners seated in the right front row within eight to ten feet of Woodward. He

---

37. In fact, the autopsy revealed several cuts in the vicinity of Woodward's right eye (one deep one) that could only have been caused by a knife.

began to move forward slowly to interpose himself between them and Woodward. Officer Holbrook was to the left of the pulpit, keeping the pulpit between himself and Woodward. Both officers had drawn their handguns as they approached, holding them down out of sight. Officer Davies did not draw his weapon because he was to the rear, behind Officer Parker who obstructed his line of fire to Woodward.

As Officer Parker neared the front of the aisle, Woodward made eye contact with him. He stood still for a moment, appeared to take a deep breath, then suddenly dropped his knife hand from his eye and ran at Officer Parker. Officer Parker reacted initially by yelling at Woodward to stop and to drop the knife as he raised his gun. Woodward did not stop nor did he drop the knife. Officer Parke shot him once. The bullet struck Woodward in the right arm and he briefly paused then resumed his attack. Officer Parker fired three more shots and Officer Holbrook fired three shots. Woodward fell to the floor in front of the pulpit, approximately six feet in front of Officer Parker. The officers had to physically wrest the knife from Woodward's hand as they handcuffed him.

Officer Holbrook immediately called for emergency medical services. Two members of the congregation with medical training rendered first aid until the EMTs arrived. Woodard was transported to a nearby hospital where he later died of his wounds. Several of the EMTs heard Woodward apologize for his actions, saying he forced the officers to shoot him and he did not intend to hurt them.

### Discussion

The three officers arriving at the church knew:

1. An unknown man had intruded on the church service and would not leave;
2. The intruder was armed with a knife;
3. The intruder would not let members of the congregation leave; and
4. The intruder was threatening suicide.

When the officers arrived on the scene, they had no knowledge where the intruder was located. Members of the congregation standing outside the church directed them inside where other members advised them where the intruder was located. This situation developed in such a manner that the officers could not stay outside the church and await developments. They knew that innocent people were inside the church in close proximity to a man armed with a knife and threatening suicide, and preventing those people from leaving. The police function does not encompass leaving members of the public at risk while waiting to see what a potentially violent individual may choose to do or not do.

The fact that the intruder had not attacked anyone yet was no guarantee that he would not.

The responsibility of a law enforcement officer is first and foremost to protect the public. That is a proactive, dynamic responsibility, not a passive function based on a hope that things will work out for the best. The officers had to enter the church to identify and assess the public threat posed by the intruder and to plan and initiate action reasonably intended to best safeguard the members of the public then at risk. Nevertheless, the plaintiffs' expert hired to opine on the police decisions stated unequivocally that the police were irresponsible and wrong to enter the church. In so doing they inflamed the situation and thus negligently created the conditions that compelled them to kill Woodward.

Inside the church the officers saw Woodward and the parishioners seated within Woodward's reach. They observed that Woodward was acting irrationally, was armed, and heard his threats of suicide. Woodward was obviously mentally unbalanced, and the officers knew that they should try to avoid aggravating him while attempting to protect those parishioners within his reach. As police always must do in violent incidents involving the mentally ill, the officers had to balance the danger to Woodward that an attack would create against the unacceptable cost of failing to safeguard parishioners in danger. Plaintiffs in the ensuing legal action clearly argued that Woodward's safety was more important than the safety of any of the innocent people in his presence. That allegation is common, either overtly or implicitly, in legal actions contesting the use of deadly force against somebody who is mentally ill.

There are large numbers of mentally ill or mentally unbalanced individuals present in society, and both law enforcement and the mental health community recognize that most of them are neither dangerous nor criminal. In cases in which the non-dangerous or non-criminal mentally ill individual creates an incident that evokes a law enforcement response, there are numerous guidelines and training protocols that can serve to guide the response to better resolve the incident without harm to the instigator.[38]

---

38. "Criminal Justice/Mental Health Consensus Project," Council of State Governments, June 2002. Project partners include: Association of State Correctional Administrators; Bazelon Center for Mental Health Law; Center for Behavioral Health, Justice & Public Policy; National Association of State Mental Health Program Directors; Police Executive Research Forum; and Pretrial Services Resource Center. The Criminal Justice/Mental Health Consensus Project is an unprecedented national, two-year effort to prepare specific recommendations that local, state, and federal policymakers, and criminal justice and mental health professionals can use to improve the criminal justice system's response to people with mental illness. It is not a national guideline that carries any sanction upon law en-

Interactions between law enforcement and mentally unbalanced individuals are a common occurrence.[39] People do not call a psychiatrist when a mentally disturbed individual causes a problem—they call the police. The vast majority of such incidents are nuisance crimes. However, an emphasis on the physical wellbeing of the problem individual cannot be promoted at the expense of the safety of the public and the officers—it is when the individual's actions are not criminal or dangerous that such a personalized emphasis is feasible and can be considered. This distinction is clearly drawn in the various guidelines and recommendations for dealing with the mentally ill.[40]

When the individual is engaged in serious criminal or dangerous activity, the safety of the public, bystanders, and the officers involved is paramount and the law enforcement response must focus on threat assessment and resolution. This is also recognized and accepted by both law enforcement and the mental health community. The plaintiffs' criticisms of the officers' actions in this incident start with the uncritical assumption that Woodward was neither criminal nor dangerous to anyone.

It is a tenet of both law enforcement training and mental health training that suicidal individuals are a threat to themselves and to those around them. Law enforcement training admonishes caution in approaching suicidal threats for several reasons. One is the need to avoid precipitating the suicide attempt, although that decision is solely in the hands of the person who will make that

---

forcement. To the contrary, the project is a central clearinghouse for varied approaches and programs across the country that localities, institutions, and authorities can reference for use in creating their own, autonomous programs commensurate with needs, resources, and finances. The project advisory groups included more than 100 state lawmakers, police chiefs, officers, sheriffs, district attorneys, public defenders, judges, court administrators, state corrections directors, community corrections officials, victim advocates, consumers, family members and other mental health advocates, county commissioners, state mental health directors, behavioral health care providers, substance abuse experts, and clinicians.

39. "People with mental illness are significantly overrepresented among the segment of the population in contact with the criminal justice system. Approximately 5 percent of the U.S. population has a serious mental illness. The U.S. Department of Justice reported in 1999, however, that about 16 percent of the population in prison or jail has a serious mental illness. Of the 10 million people booked into U.S. jails in 1997, at least 700,000 had a serious mental illness and approximately three-quarters of those individuals had a co-occurring substance abuse disorder." *Ibid.* page 4.

40. "*In no way does this report minimize the importance of officer and public safety—they are of paramount importance. In fact, the policies outlined in this report are intended to prevent critical incidents through effective, earlier interventions. It also acknowledges those cases in which arrest is very appropriate, as with serious crimes. In those cases, the offender should be in the criminal justice system.*" *Ibid.* page 35.

decision regardless of what the officers do or fail to do. The greater caution is to protect against a sudden attack upon the officer or others due to a change of focus from hurting self to hurting others or a desire to have company in death, or to compel the officer to become the instrument of suicide.

Another allegation common in plaintiff claims was present in this case—the officers did not diagnose Woodward as an "emotionally disturbed person" (EDP). The allegation was that an EDP requires special handling and tactics different from that appropriate to a non-EDP who creates a similar risk to the safety of innocent bystanders. In other words, the plaintiffs alleged, a reasonable police response must be dictated by the mental health of the individual posing the risk of injury and not by the risk of injury alone. In the view of the plaintiffs, a sane man with a knife is different than an EDP with a knife and the two must be handled differently. However, the term "emotionally disturbed person" is a generalization that cannot be functionally defined. Arguably, "emotionally disturbed" describes just about every person a law enforcement officer confronts, from the domestic abuser to the substance abuser to the family of an arrested violator to the violent criminal bent on escape at any cost. Even a disgruntled citizen receiving a traffic citation can be "emotionally disturbed." The term cannot be delimited.

One expert retained by the Friends of Woody maintained that the police were to blame for entering the building in uniform and "confronting" Woodward. The expert was unequivocal that the officers should have stayed outside until mental health professionals were brought into play (overlooking the fact that two mental health professionals were already in play inside, both of whom believed that Woodward was dangerous). The expert claimed that in the event Woodard hurt one of the parishioners, the officers would at least have the satisfaction of knowing that they had done the right thing. The police are supposed to have been willing to see one of the parishioners hurt or killed rather than risk provoking Woodward. Utter nonsense.

Police officers are not and cannot be trained mental health professionals. Trained mental health professionals will take days and weeks under controlled clinical circumstances to arrive at diagnoses that are frequently contradictory. Police have seconds—minutes at best—to assess and resolve dangerous situations. Law enforcement officers cannot be expected to diagnose mental illness.[41]

---

41. "The officer responding to the scene is not expected to diagnose any specific mental illness, but is expected to recognize symptoms that may indicate that mental illness is a factor in the incident. Many of these symptoms represent internal, emotional states that are not readily observable from outward appearances, though they may become noticeable in conversation with the individual. In addition to the symptoms outlined, some specific types of behavior may also be signs of mental illness. These behaviors can include severe

The officers recognized from their own experience and training that mental illness was a factor in Woodward's behavior. Woodward posed a clear threat to the safety of those within his proximity. The officers' first priority was to remove those people at risk while attempting to interpose themselves between potential victims and Woodward and simultaneously engaging Woodward in a dialog to either maintain the status quo or defuse it. The officers did nothing to goad Woodward. Once the bystanders were safe, they would have allowed the dialog with Woodward to last as long as necessary to resolve the incident without any use of force. Time and circumstances as dictated solely by Woodward did not permit this incident to evolve that way.

The most common law enforcement experience is that such interactions are resolved without the use of deadly force. The officers involved in this incident each had considerable prior experience dealing with mentally unbalanced individuals, some of them violent.[42] The approach they used with Woodward was successful in their collective past experience, and was consistent with their training. It did not work with Woodward, but there was nothing that would have led them to believe otherwise. The officers' actions were dictated by their responsibility to protect the members of the community.

Law enforcement officers are trained to keep an obstacle between themselves and a person armed with a knife or other personal or proximity weapons.[43] Officer Holbrook did exactly that, keeping the pulpit between himself and Woodward as he moved. However, the only obstacles between Officer Parker and Woodward were the folding chairs *and the elderly parishioners sitting in them*. Officer Parker could have chosen to use those people as protection for himself, staying behind them so they would bear the brunt of any attack. To his credit, he did not do so but instead chose to move forward and incur greater personal risk in order to better protect them.

He did so with his weapon in hand because of Woodward's proximity. A determined adversary who launches a sudden attack without warning from 20 to 25 feet away can be on top of an officer before that officer can draw and fire

---

changes in behavior, unusual or bizarre mannerisms, hostility or distrust, one-sided conversations, and confused or nonsensical verbal communication. Officers may also notice unusual behavior, such as wearing layers of clothing in the summer. It should be noted that these behaviors can also be associated with cultural and personality differences, other medical conditions, drug or alcohol abuse, or reactions to very stressful situations. *As such, the presence of these behaviors should not be treated as conclusive proof of mental illness."* Ibid. page 64.

42. There is a large mental health institution located in Brattleboro.

43. Weapons that require closeness for use, i.e., knives, clubs, sticks, fists, feet, etc.

a shot.[44] The additional realities of wound ballistics are such that even if the officer succeeds in shooting an attacker, it is unlikely that the attack will be stopped before it reaches the officer, as discussed in Chapter 4. An attacker armed with a knife can still stab an officer despite receiving a mortal wound in the process of the attack. The "Friends of Woody" denied that the knife was in any way dangerous to the "heavily armed" police officers, and to bolster their claim, asserted that Woodward did not even point the knife at the officers. It is incomprehensible as to how a knife can only be dangerous when pointed at another as neither slashing nor stabbing necessitate "aiming" the knife prior to the attack.

The "Friends of Woody" asserted with conviction that Woodward never meant to harm anyone, including himself. Yet prior to his appearance at the church that day, Woodward had never been in Brattleboro and was a complete stranger to the community. Not one of the "Friends of Woody" had ever met him. And they denied the reality of the attack Woodward did make, ignoring the abundant forensic evidence to the contrary. All of the witnesses (even the "Friends of Woody") placed Woodward near the Christmas tree before he was shot and he fell at Officer Parker's feet some 20 or more feet away from the tree. The "Friends of Woody" admit they cannot explain that, yet insist that Woodward never charged the officer. A few even suggested that somebody unknown and unseen dragged Woodward's body to the pulpit in front of Officer Parker where he ended up and where the EMTs treated him. One member of "Friends of Woody" even agreed under oath that she would lie if it would help Robert Woodward.

These are all examples of the emotional and ill informed posturing that can arise in denial of the realities of deadly force confrontations. People engaging law enforcement in dangerous acts have full, but unpredictable, freedom of will to do as they choose, no matter how foolish or irrational it may appear to the sensibilities of the community. It also illustrates the illogical lengths and disregard for physical realities that some segments of a community will insist upon in pursuit of their opposition to any police use of force or to any police action that offends their sense of what *should have* happened. Chapter 11 discusses this consequence of deadly force incidents at greater length.

Officer Parker had moved within 20–25 feet of Woodward, who was armed with a knife and threatening suicide, and acting in an irrational if not mentally unbalanced manner. Woodward was not responsive to Officer Parker. He was not compliant. Woodward stopped his pacing and took a deep breath as he

---

44. This is the "30-foot rule" as discussed in Chapter 8.

made eye contact with Officer Parker and appeared to gather himself.[45] Then he suddenly ran at Officer Parker. The distance between them was approximately 25 feet. Woodward could have covered that distance in about a second. As noted in Chapter 6, in a clinical setting it can take a second for an officer to recognize a shooting situation and react to it by shooting. Woodward's attack in these close circumstances eliminated all reasonable options available to Officer Parker except for shooting.

Officer Parker could have retreated and abandoned the very people he was trying to protect. He could have grappled with Woodward and gambled his safety on the mere chance that somehow Woodward did not or could not stab him. This would also risk that Woodward might gain control of Officer Parker's pistol and then be an irrational, suicidal individual armed with a gun instead of a knife.

Officer Parker responded to Woodward by shooting him once. The effect of the wound did not stop the attack or deter Woodward's decision to attack. This is not unusual, as detailed in Chapter 5. Woodward continued his attack and Officer Parker shot him three more times, stopping when he saw Woodward go down. After the first shot from Officer Parker, Officer Holbrook also shot Woodward to stop his attack from reaching Officer Parker.

It is notable that all four shots fired by Officer Parker struck Woodward in the hand and arm holding the knife. This is more common than conventional wisdom recognizes. When the fight-or-flight phenomenon occurs, the impetus and the focus are the threat to life and limb. Thus tunnel vision centers on the threat, and often that restricted field of vision is further limited to the actual weapon that will cause injury. In this case, Officer Parker was "tunneled" on the knife in Woodward's right hand. Correlate this with police firearms training practices, which condition the shooter to raise the firearm into the line of sight as the eyes are on the target, thus interposing the sights within the line of sight in one coordinated action for rapid, efficient, and accurate shooting. If the eyes are focused on the *weapon*, then it should be no surprise that is where the shots strike even though the officer will be unaware of it. Officer Parker had no recollection of aiming at Woodward's knife hand—but that is where all of his shots struck. From his position to the side, Officer Holbrook saw *Woodward* as the threat attacking Officer Parker, and all of his shots hit Woodward in the torso. This is validation of the issues raised in Chapter 7 and the realities of wound ballistics as discussed in Chapter 5. Despite multiple severe wounds to his right arm and hand that destroyed the bone and mus-

---

45. See the indicators of "suicide by cop" listed in Chapter 9.

culature of his hand and wrist, Woodward never dropped the knife. It had to be pried from his grasp.

Some other issues merit discussion. The lack of a verbal warning was alleged to be another sign of unreasonable, unjustified deadly force. But as noted repeatedly, officers are not required to use a verbal warning prior to using deadly force any more than they are required to attempt a progression of lesser uses of force. They must react to the situation as it transpires and personally (and immediately) assess the time available for any attempt at using lesser means, such as a verbal warning. Verbal warnings are notoriously ineffective in resolving physical confrontations. Taking the time to issue a warning and then waiting for a discernible response actually represents an attempt to utilize non-lethal force in its own right that may elevate the likelihood of death or serious injury to an unreasonable level by delaying the use of justifiable deadly force.

In this incident, Officer Parker did not issue a verbal warning prior to shooting, but he did urgently shout at Woodward to stop and to drop the knife even as he raised his pistol to a firing position. That visual imperative coupled with the loud frantic commands represented an unmistakable warning of an immediately imminent use of deadly force. Woodward ignored it and pressed on with his attack.

A final consideration is illustrated in the Woodward shooting—the phenomenon popularly referred to as "suicide by cop," more accurately called "victim precipitated suicide" or "police assisted suicide" discussed at length in Chapter 9. A large number of cases are indeterminate despite careful, after-the-fact analysis performed at relative leisure, and both the "Friends of Woody" and the plaintiffs in this case insist Woodward never intended to kill himself.

Woodward had two avenues of escape immediately available to him that he ignored. A double door entryway right beside the Christmas tree display led into an adjacent room out of sight of the officers. Woodward did not know where the doorway led, but he made no attempt to use it. Also immediately at hand was a ramp that ran along the right side wall of the meeting room from Woodward's location to an exit door at the rear of the room. There were no police or other obstructions to prevent him using either means of egress to avoid and/or evade the officers. The direct indications that Woodward was committing suicide were his frequent threats to do exactly that, his distinct pause to gather himself as though confirming a decision made, his then sudden attack with a knife against armed officers, and his final apology and comment that he intended to force them to shoot. It is not unreasonable to take him at his word.

The Court granted summary judgment to the defendants (Officers Parker and Holbrook plus the Town of Brattleboro) in a written decision that confirmed the long-established legal standards applicable to law enforcement use-of-force actions.[46] The opinion affirmed the analysis of the incident as detailed above, but in an abbreviated fashion that is a testament to the clarity and lack of ambiguity inherent to the state of the law in this field. It was upheld by the 2nd Circuit Court of Appeals.

> *The plaintiffs have attempted to create a material factual dispute on the specific issue of whether, immediately prior to the shooting, Woodward pointed the knife at Parker and lunged at him ... This apparent discrepancy, involving nuanced interpretations of the admittedly emotionally disturbed man's rapid and unpredictable actions and motivations, does not preclude the entry of summary judgment in this case.*
>
> *In this context, 'we are not concerned with the correctness of the defendants' conduct, but rather the "objective reasonableness" of their chosen course of action given the circumstances confronting them at the scene.'* Lennon v. Miller, 66 F.3d 416, 421 (2d Cir. 1995). *Thus, the plaintiffs' disputed facts, which speculate on Woodward's subjective motivations and question whether the police officers could have handled an EDP like Mr. Woodward differently,* **are not material***; the issue is whether the defendants, given what they knew at the time of the incident, objectively acted reasonably, not whether, as a matter of factual hindsight, they could have made a better decision or ultimately made the correct decision.* [Emphasis added.][47]

The decision first addresses the alleged violation of Woodward's constitutional rights:

> *The facts, as related by the dispatcher or known by the officers, were that Woodward (1) was armed with a knife, (2) had refused to put down the weapon, (3) had threatened members of the congregation, (4) was acting irrationally, (5) was in close proximity to several individuals, and (6) was continuing to move back and forth. Under these circumstances, it was rea-*

---

46. *Joanne Woodward, Administratrix of the Estate of Robert Woodward, et al. v. Town of Brattleboro, Marshall Holbrook and Terrance Parker*, U.S. District Court, District of Vermont, Civil No: 1:02CV35, *Ruling on Defendants' Motions for Summary Judgment*, U.S. District Judge J. Garvan Murtha, July 1, 2004.

47. *Ibid.* page 23. Judge Murtha cites two pertinent cases: *Wood v. City of Lakeland*, 203 F.3d 1288, 1292 (11th Cir. 2000) (Despite plaintiff's assertion that the decedent posed no immediate threat and only intended to injure himself with a knife, the shooting officer was entitled to qualified immunity unless a fact finder could find that "no reasonable person in the defendant's position could have thought the facts" indicated the decedent posed a threat.); *Reynolds v. County of San Diego*, 84 F.3d 1162, 1170 (9th Cir. 1996) (In a case where police fatally shot a knife-wielding man, "[t]he fact that an expert disagrees with an officer's actions does not render the officer's actions unreasonable.") *Ibid.* at page 24. Strongly reasserted by the U.S. Supreme Court in *San Francisco v. Sheehan* (see Chapter 2).

*sonable for the officers to approach Woodward, to confine him, and to disarm him. Given the split-second judgment which the defendants had to make, the Court is unable to find the officers' conduct objectively unreasonable and therefore violated Mr. Woodward's constitutional rights.*[48]

Regarding allegations of a violation of constitutional rights under the Fourth Amendment, the Court explained that it:[49]

> *... must afford the defendants qualified immunity if the constitutional right was not clearly established at the time of the violation. This inquiry focuses on whether it would be clear to a reasonable officer that his conduct was unlawful in the situation he confronted. The concern of the immunity inquiry is to acknowledge that reasonable mistakes can be made as to the legal constraints on particular police conduct. It is sometimes difficult for an officer to determine how the relevant legal doctrine, here excessive force,*[50] *will apply to the factual situation the officer confronts. An officer might correctly perceive all of the relevant facts but have a mistaken understanding as to whether a particular amount of force is legal in those circumstances. If the officer's mistake as to what the law requires is reasonable, however, the officer is entitled to the immunity defense.*[51, 52, 53]

---

48. *Ibid.* pages 24–25.

49. *Ibid.* pages 25–26.

50. The Court references *Cowan v. Breen,* 352 F.3d 756, 761 (2d Cir. 2003), that dealt with allegations of excessive force.

51. The Court references *Saucier v. Katz,* 533 U.S. 194 (2001), wherein the U.S. Supreme Court instructed that resolution of an excessive force claim requires a two-part analysis: (1) would a constitutional right have been violated on the facts alleged and (2) assuming a violation is established, was the right clearly established at the time of the violation, i.e., would a reasonable officer know that his conduct was unlawful in the situation he confronted.

52. Judge Murtha also applies a Second Circuit case (*O'Bert v. Vargo,* 331 F.3d at 36), that addressed the nature of a court's review involving not merely excessive, but deadly force, to wit:

> A government official sued in his individual capacity is entitled to qualified immunity (1) if the conduct attributed to him is not prohibited by federal law; or (2) where that conduct is so prohibited, if the plaintiff's right not to be subjected to such conduct by the defendant was not clearly established at the time of the conduct; or (3) if the defendant's action was objectively legally reasonable in light of the legal rules that were clearly established at the time it was taken. In a case involving the use of deadly force, only the objective reasonableness branch of this test presents any possibility for a qualified immunity defense. Accordingly, if the Court determines that Officers Holbrook and Parker's actions, viewed objectively and in a light most favorable to the plaintiff, were reasonable, then they are entitled to qualified immunity.

53. See: *Malley v. Briggs,* 475 U.S. 335, 341 (1986), "all but the plainly incompetent or those who knowingly violate the law" are protected by qualified immunity.

And finally:

> "*Here, the Court is unable to conclude that the officers' use of deadly force was objectively unreasonable. Given the undisputed fact that Mr. Woodward was armed and uncooperative, it was objectively reasonable for officers to believe that either their lives or the lives of others in the area were in danger. The individual defendants' Motion for Summary Judgment on plaintiffs' federal claims is GRANTED.*"[54]

One additional point must be noted. Nowhere in the Court's opinion is the issue of suicide addressed except to the extent that it is reaffirmed that the subjective intents or motivations on the part of the plaintiff (actual or alleged after the fact) are not material. The critical issue is the reasonable perceptions and beliefs that arise in the minds of the officers confronting the individual. This highlights the danger of the suicidal-motivated individuals. The atmosphere of danger that can be created by their actions can create a clear perception of imminent injury or death to the officer and others. The reasonable nature of that perception is the basis for justifying a use of force, not the allegation that inevitably arises in the aftermath that the individual was only a risk to himself.

## Patricia Nelms, etc. v. U.S. Department of the Interior, et al.

In January 2003, just prior to 8:00 a.m., U.S. Park Ranger Derek W. Anderson, U.S. National Park Service, was on routine patrol when he pulled into the Edwards Ferry landing along the C&O Canal. Ranger Anderson was in uniform and driving a marked Park Service Jeep Cherokee. He noticed a taxicab parked at the far end of the landing facing the water. The driver's side door was open and an unidentified black male (later identified as Paul Nelms) was standing beside the door, facing the water. Ranger Anderson drove the length of the landing and parked directly behind the cab.

Nelms turned and looked at him as Ranger Anderson got out of his vehicle and asked Nelms how he was doing; was everything OK? Nelms' response was incoherent. Ranger Anderson asked Nelms for identification. Nelms felt through his pockets, and then said that his ID was in the cab. Ranger Anderson was

---

54. *Joanne Woodward, Administratrix of the Estate of Robert Woodward, et al. v. Town of Brattleboro, Marshall Holbrook and Terrance Parker*, U.S. District Court, District of Vermont, Civil No: 1:02CV35, *Ruling on Defendants' Motions for Summary Judgment*, U.S. District Judge J. Garvan Murtha, July 1, 2004, at page 27.

standing at the front fender of his Jeep and told Nelms he was going to "call this in." When he turned towards the door of his Jeep, Nelms advanced aggressively while verbally attacking the ranger.

Ranger Anderson turned to confront the suddenly hostile Nelms, drawing his chemical agent dispenser from his belt and pointing it at him. He ordered Nelms to stop, put up his hands, and get back. Nelms did stop, asking Ranger Anderson why he was doing this to him. Nelms repeated that his ID was in the cab and he returned to the cab despite Ranger Anderson's orders to stop. Ranger Anderson followed him back to the cab and was located beside its half open door as Nelms reached into the interior of the vehicle, leaning across the driver's seat to reach the passenger side. Ranger Anderson had been continuously ordering Nelms, "Stop—don't move," but Nelms ignored him. Suddenly Nelms kicked or pushed the driver's side door, striking Ranger Anderson at which point Anderson sprayed Nelms with his chemical agent (oleo capsicum).

Nelms immediately assaulted Ranger Anderson, punching and striking him twice on the left side of the head. Ranger Anderson grappled with Nelms. Nelms kicked Ranger Anderson in the legs. Ranger Anderson finally pushed Nelms away and retreated backwards past his Jeep to gain separation. He holstered his chemical agent dispenser and drew his collapsible baton (ASP), extending it in the process. Ranger Anderson continued to order Nelms to stop and to get on the ground. Nelms continued to advance upon Ranger Anderson.

Ranger Anderson attempted to call for backup on his portable radio. Nelms heard him and told him "you're a long way from anybody; there is nobody coming." He advanced, and Ranger Anderson struck him on his left bicep with the ASP as Ranger Anderson continued to retreat to keep his distance from Nelms. Nelms continued to advance on him. Ranger Anderson struck Nelms again with the ASP as the Ranger continued to retreat. Nelms continued his advance. Nelms was telling him that he (Ranger Anderson) "can't do anything to me."

As he continued to retreat, Ranger Anderson attempted another radio call for help. At this point, Nelms told him "Do you know where you are? You're at Harper's Ferry. You need to relax—this is where you are going to die."

Nelms continued to advance on Ranger Anderson. Ranger Anderson pushed him back with one hand and Nelms told him to put away the baton. Ranger Anderson struck Nelms again with the ASP, and this time Nelms grabbed him and they both fell to the ground fighting for control of the baton. Ranger Anderson had to relinquish his control of the baton in order to push Nelms away and thus disengage and get to his feet. Nelms also got up and raised the ASP in a striking motion. Ranger Anderson drew his firearm and aimed it at Nelms, ordering him to stop and to drop the baton.

Ranger Anderson continued to back away from Nelms, holding him at gunpoint and "screaming" orders for him (Nelms) to stop. Nelms ignored Ranger Anderson's orders and continued to advance on him, this time with the baton. Ranger Anderson shot Nelms at a range of about 10 feet but Nelms continued to come at him. Ranger Anderson continued to back away and continued to shoot as Nelms pursued him until he saw Nelms go down on the ground. Nelms was hit a total of seven times before he stopped attacking Ranger Anderson and went down. He was declared dead at the scene—almost 400 feet away from the taxicab's door.

## Discussion

Ranger Anderson observed an individual at an unusual hour, in an out of the way location, in unusual circumstances. The man, apparently the driver of a taxicab parked at the water's edge, was standing alone at a remote landing isolated by surrounding woods. In fact, the man was Paul Nelms, who had committed an assault and carjacking that morning that had resulted in his possession of the cab. Nelms was also under the influence of PCP, as determined at his subsequent autopsy. Ranger Anderson knew none of these facts.

Nelms' responses to Ranger Anderson's routine approach and initial inquiry were not reassuring. He mumbled and could not be understood, and he failed to produce any identification. He aggressively followed Ranger Anderson back to his Jeep, engaging in an argumentative and hostile verbal attack that Ranger Anderson countered with the display of his chemical agent dispenser and verbal commands. When Nelms stopped and returned to the cab, Ranger Anderson followed, ordering him not to enter the cab. Nelms had no discernible weapon on him, but he was also unidentified and hostile and his presence and purpose there were unexplained. The interior of the cab could contain a weapon, evidence, or some other pertinent item. Nelms ignored Ranger Anderson's commands and Ranger Anderson sprayed him with his chemical agent to compel compliance. Nelms' immediate reaction was a sudden physical attack on Ranger Anderson, striking him in the head and kicking him in the legs.

The disruptive effects of surprise caused by the sudden or unanticipated actions of the person being confronted can also affect officer responses. "The impact upon an officer of unexpected, rapidly changing, or chaotic circumstances will often be a disruption, disturbance, or lag in time in decisionmaking and tactical responses until he or she accurately identifies what has to be done. This disruption occurs because the brain experiences a temporary perceptual shock when something serious happens that it wasn't ready for."[55]

The unusual feature of this incident is the hesitation by Ranger Anderson to use deadly force when it was clearly reasonable. He could have decided to use deadly force as soon as he was attacked. At that initial stage of the confrontation, Ranger Anderson was suddenly the target of a violent physical attack that put him at risk of being beaten, of losing control of his firearm, of being seriously injured or even killed at the hands of his assailant. Yet Ranger Anderson chose to attempt various lesser means of force such as grappling, chemical agent use, and baton strikes, all coupled with retreat and continuous verbal commands to buy time while desperately trying to end the inexorable and relentless attack. The distance from the front door of the taxi where the attack began to the location of Nelms' body on the ground was almost 400 feet.

Nelms had been unyielding in his non-compliance. He had been relentless and undeterred in his attack on Ranger Anderson. He even told Ranger Anderson what his intentions were. He ignored all of Ranger Anderson's attempts to use lesser force—he was unaffected by pepper spray and impassive to baton strikes. His intentions to harm Ranger Anderson were unmistakable by virtue of his actions and his words, and he pressed his attack against the retreating ranger for almost 400 feet. In the end, Ranger Anderson shot him only when he could not retreat any further and Nelms was upon him with the baton—and that was only after first warning him to stop.

Although the inevitable legal action was filed in the aftermath of this shooting, there was nothing remarkable in its process and the case was resolved with the award of summary judgment to the defendant. The remarkable aspect of this case that makes it worth reviewing is the incredible length to which Ranger Anderson went to delay, deny, or avoid the use of deadly force. Hesitation is one of the most significant weaknesses that will act to diminish the ability of a police officer to protect himself or others. This is an unusually extended example of that unfortunately all too common human characteristic.

## David Lopez, et al. v. LVMPD

In May 13, 2006, Swauve Davon Lopez was located and arrested without incident for the murder of Kyle Staheli three days before. The investigation

---

55. Blum, LN, Ph.D, *Force Under Pressure—How Cops Live and Why They Die*, New York, Lantern Books, Booklight Inc., 2000. Page 39.

was conducted by Homicide Detective Kenneth Hardy and Major Crimes Unit Detective Shane Womack, Las Vegas Metropolitan Police Department (LVMPD), working with numerous other members of the LVMPD.

In the course of the investigation, friends and associates of Lopez[56] told LVMPD investigators that:

1. Lopez had lured Staheli into the adjacent hills, riding in Staheli's car on the pretext of doing a drug deal with unnamed others.
2. Lopez killed Staheli for his car; Staheli begged for his life as Lopez shot him three times at point blank range.
3. Lopez and an associate, James Carter, returned to the murder scene the next day and burned Staheli's body in an attempt to destroy it and conceal the murder.
4. Lopez was driving Staheli's car after the murder and crashed it, fleeing the scene when police responded.
5. Lopez was always armed with a .45 caliber pistol that he carried inside his pants.
6. Lopez threatened people with his pistol on several occasions.
7. Lopez claimed to be an Asian "hit man" and to have a "crew" that was getting more guns and getting big.
8. Lopez repeatedly said that he would not go back to jail; that he would shoot any police officer who confronted him; and that he would kill anybody who talked to the police.
9. Lopez was engaged in an argument with Michael Starr, and was looking for him in order to kill him. Starr was in hiding.
10. Lopez intended to kill the Forrest brothers.
11. Lopez would find out they were talking to the police and would kill them.

Lopez' friends and associates abandoned their residences in fear of him and met with LVMPD officers at a local Walmart parking lot. The information they provided about Lopez killing Staheli was the basis for the homicide investigation that followed. The detectives discovered Staheli's burned body and three .45 caliber cartridge casings on a hillside overlooking Las Vegas. Gasoline was poured over his face and upper body and then ignited. Investigating officers located Staheli's car where Lopez abandoned it after crashing it. There was an empty gasoline can in it. The detectives interviewed Holloway at the crash scene who at first claimed he had been carjacked, but then later admitted that

---

56. Specifically, Shandel Flowers, Michael Starr, Derrick Holloway, Kelvin Coleman, Franklin Demichael, and Jack Strosnider.

Lopez was driving the car and fled after the crash, telling him to make up a story about a carjacking.

Eventually, LVMPD detectives located Lopez at 5250 East Stewart, apartment 1003, home of Neva Buford and her son Devin. Lopez and James Carter were arrested without incident as they slept in Devin Buford's bedroom. Lopez was handcuffed and searched. A .45 pistol was found inside his pants and removed. He was escorted out of the Buford apartment and handed over to Detective James Mitchell, LVMPD.

Detective Mitchell placed his own handcuffs on Lopez and walked him to his (Mitchell's) car where he patted down Lopez for weapons and contraband, and placed him in the right front seat of the car. Lopez was handcuffed with his hands behind his back. Detective Mitchell laced the seat belt under Lopez' right arm and across his chest, snapping the buckle of the belt together. He closed the door and walked to the rear of his car where he engaged another officer in conversation.

Soon thereafter, the detectives saw Lopez open the door of the car and stand up. His hands were still in cuffs, but were now located in front of his body. Despite orders from a number of nearby LVMPD officers and detectives to stop, Lopez turned and ran, proceeding east to the north/south access road and then heading north along that roadway. An undetermined number of LVMPD officers pursued Lopez, running after him as he fled, ordering him to stop. Lopez did not stop.

Detectives Hardy, Womack, and Trevor Alsup were leading the pack of officers chasing Lopez. Sergeant Rocky Alby was driving his marked LVMPD car south as Lopez ran north and he turned his vehicle into Lopez' path to stop him. Lopez dodged the car and continued to run. Sergeant Alby did succeed in picking off Detective Alsup who was knocked out of the chase. Detectives Hardy and Womack continued pursuit, although each was unaware of the other. By this point, the pack of pursuing officers was spread out behind the two detectives and falling off.

Detective Hardy was ordering Lopez to stop. He realized that Lopez was gaining ground and he could not catch him. He knew there was no police officer or police presence ahead of Lopez. He yelled "Stop or I'll shoot" at least twice. When Lopez did not stop, Detective Hardy fired one shot at him from about 45 feet away. Lopez did not react to the shot and appeared to run even faster. Detective Hardy could not shoot again because at this point Detective Womack crossed in front of him and obstructed his line of fire.

Detective Womack was running after Lopez, unaware of Detective Hardy's presence to his left. As he passed Sgt. Alby's car, he realized that Lopez was pulling away from him and that he was not going to catch him. He described Lopez as being in a "full sprint."

Detective Womack knew that there was nobody ahead of Lopez. Lopez ignored Womack's repeated orders to stop and warnings that he would shoot. Womack heard the shot fired by Detective Hardy and saw no reaction or response by Lopez other than continued flight. Detective Womack fired one shot from about 30 feet away and Lopez went down. Pursuing police officers quickly arrived and emergency medical services were immediately requested for Lopez. He was hit twice — a grazing wound to his side from Detective Hardy's shot, and a fatal wound from the shot fired by Detective Womack.

### Discussion

The use of deadly force is justified in two broad scenarios (see Chapter 3):

a.  Defense of Self or Others to prevent an imminent risk of serious injury before it comes to fruition, or to end an actual risk of death or serious injury before it can go any further.
b.  Prevention of Escape of a "dangerous" person.

The self-defense option is by far the predominant scenario in which police officers use deadly force. The shooting of Swauve Lopez does not fall within the scope of deadly force used in defense of self and others. Factors, issues, and considerations necessary to justify a use of deadly force in defense of self or others do not apply to the Lopez shooting. The Lopez shooting is that rarity that clearly falls within the second scenario for the justified use of deadly force — prevention of escape — and must be analyzed as such.

Deadly force *may* be used when necessary to prevent the escape of a "dangerous person" as defined by the U.S. Supreme Court in ***Tennessee v. Garner***.[57] This use of deadly force to prevent escape of a dangerous person has been specifically addressed by the Court and incorporated within general law enforcement policies, training, and practices. LVMPD policy 6/002.00 Use of Force — Deadly Force Parameters for Use states:

"Department members are authorized to use deadly force in accordance with NRS 171.1455 to:

1.  Protect themselves or others from what is reasonably believed to be an IMMEDIATE THREAT OF DEATH OR SERIOUS BODILY HARM;
2.  Prevent the escape of a fleeing felon who the member has probable cause to believe will pose A SIGNIFICANT THREAT TO HUMAN

---

57. The Court defined a "dangerous person" as one who has "committed a crime involving the infliction or threatened infliction of serious physical harm." 471 U.S. 1 (1985).

LIFE if escape should occur; and that the justification for the action must be CLEAR and IMMEDIATE.

3.  Kill an animal…." [Emphasis in original.]

*Prevention of escape* has no pre-requisite perception of imminent risk of death or injury, as there is when deadly force is used in *defense of self and others*. There is a requirement to issue a verbal warning where feasible, which is logical where there is no imminent threat to others, thereby affording the fleeing person a reasonable opportunity to surrender and avoid getting shot.[58]

Clearly, Lopez fits the Court's definition of a "dangerous" person. The officers had evidence that Lopez had "inflicted" physical harm by murdering Kyle Staheli. They had evidence that he "threatened to inflict" physical harm from the testimony of the various witness accounts regarding Lopez' violent nature, his threats to kill anybody talking to the cops, and his expressed intent to kill Starr and the Forrest brothers. They had probable cause to believe Lopez would make good his threats to shoot it out with police. Detectives Hardy and Womack were the primary investigators in the homicide case against Lopez. They were fully versed in the results of the investigation and the evidence in support of Lopez' arrest for murder. They were equally informed of the threats made by Lopez against witnesses and police.

The detectives knew that Lopez represented a "significant threat to human life" if successful in escaping (language of the LVMPD policy.) They recognized that Lopez' escape was imminent because he was out-running them and there was no officer or police presence ahead of him. Also, they did not know what lay ahead in terms of escape avenues, hiding places, or obstacles to pursuit.

Lopez made a determined and resolute attempt to escape from custody. He had been arrested, searched twice, handcuffed, and strapped into a police car parked among a dozen or more police officers. Despite the proximate presence of over a dozen police officers, Lopez ran. Despite being pursued by all of those police officers repeatedly commanding him to stop, he continued to run. Despite Sgt. Alby's attempt with his vehicle to obstruct his flight, Lopez continued to run. He continued to run after being warned repeatedly that his pursuers would shoot. He continued to run despite being shot at and receiving a grazing wound. He continued to run despite continued orders to stop and warnings of shooting from Detective Womack after Detective Hardy's shot. This merits par-

---

58. Of course, the issuance of a verbal warning may not be feasible or logical where the fleeing subject does pose an imminent threat to self or others, as can be the case. In that eventuality the use of deadly force is more accurately seen *in defense of self and others*, not to prevent escape. Such is not the case here.

ticular note—the fact that Lopez ignored the initial shot fired by Detective Hardy even though it had grazed his chest. Despite being wounded and facing unmistakable proof that the pursuing officer(s) would in fact shoot as they were warning him that they would, Lopez still chose to persist in attempting to escape.

In the words of the Supreme Court in the *Garner* decision " … deadly force may be used if necessary to prevent escape, and if, where feasible, some warning has been given." The use of deadly force to prevent Lopez' escape is a perfect example of exactly that scenario. On March 2, 2009, the judge issued an order granting summary judgment to the defendants, quoted at some length here because of the rarity of the circumstances of this case, and the judge's discussion of both the use of deadly force and the alleged liability of the municipality.

> " … When a constitutional violation occurs, 'law enforcement officers nonetheless are entitled to qualified immunity if they act reasonably under the circumstances.' See KRL v. Estate of Moore, 512 F.3d 1184, 1189 (9th Cir. 2008) (citing Wilson v. Layve, 526 U.S. 603, 614 (1999)). The United States Supreme Court outlined a two-step qualified immunity analysis in Saucier v. Katz, 533 U.S. 194 (2001), which requires district courts to first determine whether the officer's conduct violated a constitutional right. Saucier, 533 U.S. at 201. If no constitutional right was violated, the court need not inquire further. Id. If a constitutional violation has occurred, the court's second inquiry under Saucier is to ask whether the law was 'clearly established' at the time of defendant's alleged misconduct. Id. The Supreme Court recently modified the procedure outlined in Saucier and concluded that the sequence set forth therein should no longer be regarded as mandatory in all cases. Pearson v. Callahan, No 07-751, 2009 WL 128768, at \*9 (U.S. Jan. 21, 2009). Following Pearson, courts are now 'permitted to exercise their sound discretion in deciding which of the two prongs of the qualified immunity analysis should be addressed first in light of the circumstances in the particular case at hand.' Id. The Supreme Court noted, however, that the sequence set forth in Saucier often is the appropriate analytical sequence. Id. In this case, the Court concludes that the two-step analysis of Saucier, although no longer required, is the appropriate analysis.
>
> ### 1. Use of Deadly Force
>
> Under Saucier, the Court first analyzes whether Plaintiffs have shown a constitutional violation. Claims of excessive and deadly force are analyzed under the Fourth Amendment's reasonableness standard. Long v. City and County of Honolulu, 511 F.3d 901, 906 (9th Cir. 2007) (citing Graham v. Connor, 490 U.S. 386, 394–95 (1989); Tennessee v. Gar-

ner, *471 U.S. 1 (1985)). The use of deadly force to prevent the escape of a felony suspect is constitutionally reasonable 'if the officer has probable cause to believe that the suspect poses a significant threat of death or serious physical injury to the officer or others.'* See Scott v. Henrich, *39 F.3rd 912, 914 (9th Cir. 1994) (quoting* Garner, *471 U.S. at 3). Factors to consider include 'the severity of the crime at issue, whether the suspect poses an immediate threat to the safety of the officers or others, and whether he is actively resisting arrest or attempting to evade arrest by flight.'* Long, *511 F.3d at 906 (quoting* Graham, *490 U.S. at 396); see also* Garner, *471 U.S. at 11–12 (if there is probable cause to believe that the suspect has committed a 'crime involving the infliction or threatened infliction of serious physical harm, deadly force may be used if necessary to prevent escape, and if, where feasible, some warning has been given.').*
*In judging reasonableness, the Court also considers the risk of harm that Defendants' actions posed in light of the threat that they were attempting to eliminate.* Scott v. Harris, *550 U.S. 372 (2007). In weighing these risks, it is 'appropriate ... to take into account not only the number of the lives at risk, but also their relative culpability'* Id.

*Plaintiffs' Fourth Amendment claim does not survive summary judgment because Hardy and Womack were reasonable in using deadly force to prevent Lopez's escape. Although Plaintiffs disagree that the use of deadly force was reasonable under the circumstances of this case, the facts relevant to the inquiry are undisputed. Plaintiffs concede that Defendants had probable cause to believe Lopez had committed a heinous 'crime involving the infliction or threatened infliction of serious physical harm.'* Garner, *471 U.S. at 11. Plaintiffs also concede that Lopez was attempting to escape from police custody, that he failed to stop when ordered to do so, and that Defendants warned that [they] would shoot. Finally, Plaintiffs do not dispute Defendants' perception that Lopez was potentially armed or that he was capable of posing a serious threat of harm to others if he escaped. Plaintiffs submit the deposition testimony of Officer Cannon and liability expert Donald P. Van Blaricom to establish that Defendants' use of deadly force was unnecessary because one of the many police officers chasing Lopez should have been able to catch Lopez and run him to the ground without the use of deadly force. Plaintiffs claim that Womack, at least, was close enough when he shot at Lopez that he should have been able to catch him. However, whether somebody should have been able to outrun Lopez is immaterial. Moreover. Plaintiffs' evidence does not create a triable issue of material fact because it does not contradict Defendants' perception that Lopez posed an immediate danger to others or that Lopez was about to successfully evade arrest by flight.*

*The circumstances of this case are similar to the facts present in* Forrett v. Richardson, *112 F.3d 416, 419 (9th Cir. 1997), overruled on other grounds by* Chroma Lighting v. GTE Products Corp., *127 F.3d 1136 (9th Cir. 1997).* Forrett *involved a suspect who shot his victim at point-blank range, stole a number of guns, eluded the police in a residential area, and was in the process of scaling a backyard wall in order to escape when he was shot. The suspect had been told to stop and surrender, but refused.* Id. *at 418. The court reasoned that using deadly force was justified because the police reasonably feared the suspect 'would seize an opportunity to take an innocent bystander hostage.'* Id. *at 421. As the Ninth Circuit Court has emphasized. 'broad discretion ... must he afforded to police officers who face a tense situation' and courts should defer 'to the judgment of reasonable officers on the scene.'* Jeffers v. Gomez, *267 F. 3d 895, 909 (9th Cir. 2001).*

*In light of the foregoing analysis, the Court finds the use of deadly force by Hardy and Womack was reasonable and did not constitute an unconstitutional use of excessive force. Even assuming the existence of some triable issues as to the question of whether the use of deadly force was constitutional in this case, Defendants Hardy and Womack would be entitled to qualified immunity because the law was not sufficiently settled, at the time of the incident, that Defendants could not use deadly force in the circumstances they confronted. See, e.g.,* Brosseau v. Haugen, *543 U.S. 194, 200–01 (2004) (finding, where officer shot fleeing suspect who presented risk to others, Fourth Amendment law not 'clearly established'; noting 'this area is one in which the result depends very much on the facts of each case'). Moreover, Plaintiffs have completely failed to carry their burden of showing that, at the time Hardy and Womack allegedly violated decedent's Fourth Amendment rights, such rights were clearly established. See* Kennedy v. Ridgefield, *439 F.3d 1055, 1065 (9th Cir. 2006) (plaintiff has the burden of showing, at the time of the alleged violation, the constitutional right at issue was clearly established). Plaintiffs have proffered no meaningful argument and no case law to support their contention that 'there is no haziness' in this case because '[t]he constitutional limits on the use of excessive force had been clearly established for almost two decades at the time the Decedent was shot.' (Opp (#146), p. 10).*

*Accordingly, the Court finds that even it Lopez' Fourth Amendment rights were violated, Defendants Hardy and Womack are entitled to qual-*

*ified immunity. The Court therefore grants Defendants' Motion for Summary Judgment on Plaintiffs' First Cause of Action.*

### 2. Right of Familial Association

*Plaintiffs allege that by violating Lopez' Fourth Amendment rights, Defendants also violated Plaintiffs' Fourteenth Amendment rights by interfering with their familial relationship with Lopez. Defendants argue that because no constitutional violation occurred, they are entitled to summary judgment on this claim. The parents and children of a person killed by law enforcement officers may assert a substantive due process claim under the Fourteenth Amendment based on the deprivation of their liberty interest arising out of their relationship with the decedent. See* Moreland v. Las Vegas Metropolitan Police Dept, *159 F.3d 365, 371 (9th Cir. 1998). In the context of police pursuit of a fleeing suspect, a plaintiff must establish that the officer used excessive force with the intent to harm the suspect physically or to worsen his legal plight to establish § 1983 liability. See* Bingue v. Prunchak, *512 F.3d 1169, 1174 (9th Cir. 2008) (citing* County of Sacramento v. Lewis, *523 U.S. 833. 854 (1998)). If the officer's actions were objectively reasonable, 'it follows that his conduct d[oes] not offend the more stringent standard applicable to substantive due process claims.'* Moreland, *159 F.3d at 371, n. 4.*

*Because the Court has concluded that Defendants' conduct was reasonable and therefore did not result in a constitutional violation, Defendants are also entitled to summary judgment on Plaintiffs' familial relationship claim. See, e.g.,* Galipo v. City of Las Vegas, *2007 WL 1381774, at \*6 (D.Nev. 2007); see also* Gausvik v. Perez, *392 F.3d 1006, 1008 (9th Cir. 2004) (familial interference claim is moot where there was no violation of any underlying constitutional rights of plaintiff).*

### C. Municipal Liability under 42 U.S.C. § 1983

*In their Amended Complaint, Plaintiffs allege that they were deprived of their constitutional rights as a result of Defendant LVMPD's policy, practice and custom of 'tolerat[ing] and ratify[ing] the use of excessive, unreasonable and deadly force by its officers.' (Am. Comp. (#87) at ¶ 32). Plaintiffs also allege that LVMPD had a policy, practice and custom of 'negligently hir[ing], train[ing] and supervis[ing] its officers, agents, and employees.' Id. At ¶ 33.*

*To impose § 1983 liability on a municipality, a plaintiff must show: (1) that the plaintiff possessed a constitutional right of which he was deprived; (2) that the municipality had a policy; (3) that this policy 'amounts to deliberate indifference' to the plaintiffs constitutional right; and (4) that the policy is the 'moving force behind the constitutional violation.'* Plumeau v. School Dist. No. 40 County of Yamhill, *130 F.3d 432,438 (9th Cir. 1997) (quoting* Oviatt By and Through Waugh v. Pearce, *954 F.2d 1470, 1474 (9th Cir. 1992)); see also* Monell v. Dep't of Social Servs., *436 U.S. 658 (1978) ('a municipality cannot be held liable under § 1983 on a respondeat superior theory'). In the context of summary judgment, the plaintiff 'must offer enough evidence to create a genuine issue of material fact as to both the existence of a constitutional violation and municipal responsibility for that violation.'* Herrera v. Las Vegas Metropolitan Police Dep't, *298 F.Supp. 2d 1043, 1052 (D.Nev. 2004) (citing* Monell, *436 U.S. at 690–91).*

*Assuming arguendo that a constitutional violation occurred as a result of the use of deadly force, in order to defeat a motion for summary judgment and establish municipal liability, Plaintiffs 'must provide evidence from which a reasonable jury could find that there was an inadequate training program, and that the Defendant was deliberately indifferent to whether its officers received adequate training. There must also be actual causation between the inadequate training and the deprivation of the Plaintiff's rights.'* Id. *(citing* Merritt v. County of Los Angeles, *875 F.2d 765, 770 (9th Cir. 1989)). To this end, a plaintiff must proffer actual evidence of inadequate training; proof of a single incident of deviant official action is not enough.* Id.

*Defendant LVMPD argues that it is entitled to summary judgment because Plaintiffs have failed to offer any evidence to substantiate their allegation regarding the existence of a policy, practice or custom that could be causally related to the alleged constitutional deprivations. (Motion (#139), p. 22). In fact, LVMPD points out that Plaintiffs' expert and deposition testimony concedes that no evidence exists to suggest that Hardy and Womack were inadequately trained, supervised, hired, or retained (Reply (#148), pp. 13–14). The Court finds that Plaintiffs have failed to present evidence to establish a question of fact as to whether a policy, custom or practice was the cause of Lopez's death. Consequently, Defendant LVMPD is entitled to judgment as a matter of law on Plaintiffs' constitutional claims."*[59]

## *Ralph J. Penley, Jr., et al. v. Donald F. Eslinger, et al.*

In January 2006 around 9:30 a.m., 14-year-old Christopher Penley displayed a handgun in his waistband to other students in his class at Milwee Middle

---

59. *David Lopez, et al. v. LVMPD*, USDC District of Nevada, Case No: 2:06-cv-00951-BES-GWF, Order, 3/2/09, pp. 5–10.

School. Penley told them it was real and it was a "nine," implying a 9mm caliber weapon. One student notified a teacher who telephoned the administration office. The office initiated a "Code Red" lock-down of the school facilities and grounds.

Meanwhile Penley drew his weapon, turned off the lights in the classroom, and manipulated the weapon in a manner described by students as "he cocked" the gun. Students were fleeing from the classroom. Penley held one student (Matthew Cotey) at gunpoint, ordering him up against the chalkboard. Cotey pleaded with Penley, "Please don't shoot me." Cotey turned and grabbed at Penley's handgun and they struggled momentarily. Cotey was able to push Penley away and escape the classroom.

Eliseo Badillo, a security officer at Milwee School, responded. He saw students running from the classroom as he approached. Badillo looked into the room and saw Penley holding Cotey at gunpoint. Penley saw Badillo and turned his weapon on him. Badillo advised everybody to run as he closed the classroom door and notified Seminole County Sheriff's Office (SCSO) Deputy Matthew Parker, the assigned school resource officer.

Deputy Parker responded to Badillo's location outside the classroom in Building 11. Badillo told him that Penley was inside a closet in the classroom, but unknown to Badillo and Parker was that Penley had left the classroom through a side door into an adjacent work area occupied by a teacher's assistant who saw him holding the handgun as he went by. He entered a second classroom and traversed it, waving his weapon, leaving through a back door.

Deputy Parker was still outside the first classroom when he heard another teacher (Harold Hitt) say that he (the gunman) was running in the rear of Building 7. Deputy Parker saw the teacher running from the rear of Building 7, and he saw a white male with a black handgun (Penley) there as well. He yelled orders at Penley to drop the weapon, but Penley ignored him and ran to the rear of Building 7. Deputy Parker notified SCSO via radio that he was in foot pursuit of an armed subject on the school property. This call was made at 9:38 a.m. and other SCSO officers immediately began responding to the school.

Penley was outside between two portable classrooms. Hitt heard the "Code Red" and was moving students to safety and securing the portable classrooms when Penley appeared approximately 15 feet away holding his handgun to his side. Hitt said later that Penley was staring at him "coldly" and he pleaded with Penley, "Please don't shoot me. I didn't do anything to you." He ran and that was when Deputy Parker noticed him (Hitt) and subsequently, Penley.

Penley was still moving. Deputy Parker next saw him on the second floor of Building 7; then he saw him on the second floor of Building 10. SCSO Deputy Jake Bramer arrived in the vicinity of Building 10. He saw Penley and ordered him to stop and get down on the ground, but Penley ignored him. Subsequently, Deputy Parker saw Penley aim the gun at his own neck and making his way back towards Building 7. Deputy Bramer was joined by SCSO Deputy Charles Hilton, and they were moving towards the second floor of Building 7 when they were notified by radio that Penley was now on the first floor of the opposite side of the building.

SCSO Deputy Teresa Maiorano[60] arrived in the back of the school property. She saw Penley armed with a handgun on the second floor of Building 7, running south. After broadcasting that information, she lost sight of Penley. She approached the building on foot with her weapon drawn when she saw Penley walking toward her. He was approximately 30 feet away and held his handgun pointed up under his chin. Deputy Maiorano aimed her gun at Penley and repeatedly ordered him to put down his gun. In her account, Penley "looked at me, right dead in the eyes, and he said, 'I'm going to die one way or another.'" He briefly lowered his weapon and Deputy Maiorano thought he was going to point it at her but he did not. He again pointed it up under his chin and entered a nearby restroom located on the ground floor of Building 7 near the southeast corner.

Meanwhile, SCSO Deputy Christopher Maiorano arrived on the scene. He heard Deputy T. Maiorano yelling loud orders and ran to her location in time to see Penley enter the restroom. He placed himself in a position that enabled him to see Penley inside the restroom and close enough to attempt to engage him in conversation. SCSO Sergeant Vincent Kauffman joined him trying to communicate with Penley, to no avail. Penley continued to hold his gun pointed up under his chin.

The restroom had a wide, roll-up door that was rolled up so that the entry was wide open with no impediment to looking inside. The door opened to the outside courtyard and was the only entry into the restroom. Inside the restroom were stalls along one side (west wall) and sinks and a drinking fountain along the opposite wall. Throughout the incident, Penley was variously in and out of view of the surrounding officers as he moved about the restroom and in and out of the stalls.

When Deputy C. Maiorano asked Penley to drop his gun and to stop pointing it at his chin; Penley told him that he needed to drop his gun first. Deputy C. Maiorano was behind some cover. He holstered his own gun and displayed his empty hands to Penley, telling him, "I put my gun down, now it's your turn

---

60. Two deputies with the surname Maiorano were involved in this incident: Teresa Maiorano and Christopher Maiorano. For the sake of clarity, we will include their respective first name initial as necessary to specifically identify each one.

to put your gun down." Penley did not comply. Instead, he squared off and aimed his gun at Deputy C. Maiorano who said he was looking down the front of the barrel. He also described Penley's movements within the restroom as tactical, minimizing exposure and using cover. Deputy C. Maiorano drew his gun and took cover, advising the other officers on the scene of what had transpired.

Sergeant Kevin Brubaker, the SCSO hostage negotiator arrived on the scene. He took over negotiations with Penley. Penley did not respond to Brubaker as he continued to move in and out of the view of Deputy C. Maiorano several times, aiming his gun at him every time. Initially, Sgt. Brubaker was in an exposed position in front of the restroom doorway until SCSO Sergeant Dave Dalka joined him with a ballistic shield that provided them a degree of cover.

Penley continued pacing about the restroom, moving in and out of Brubaker's sight. Most of the time, Penley held his gun pointed up under his chin. He was not responsive to Sgt. Brubaker's attempts to engage him in conversation or to persuade him to give up his gun. On the other hand, when Penley moved out of sight, Sgt. Brubaker would ask him to come back into view and he (Penley) always did so.

SCSO Lieutenant Michael Weippert arrived on the scene. He joined Deputy Hilton first, but he could not see inside the restroom well enough from there. He noticed Deputy C. Maiorano suddenly duck and take cover and realized that vantage point offered a better sightline into the restroom. He moved to join Deputy C. Maiorano, from where he could see Penley as he moved about the restroom. Lt. Weippert was the SCSO SWAT sniper and was armed with a .223 caliber AR-15 with a 3x telescopic sight. He and Deputy C. Maiorano were positioned about 50 feet from the restroom doorway.

By now, Brubaker was behind the ballistic shield and continuing to talk to Penley. Lt. Weippert could not hear Penley respond to Brubaker, but he could see Penley moving inside the restroom, always with his gun in hand—sometimes pointed up under his chin, sometimes aimed at individual officers outside the restroom. Lt. Weippert said that Penley was moving tactically, in and out of view, sidestepping across the restroom, holding his gun in a two-handed grip and looking through the sights at Sgt. Brubaker and Deputy C. Maiorano as well as himself (Weippert). He appeared to be minimizing his own exposure, remaining in sight only 1–2 seconds as he moved from one place of cover to another. He would stay out of sight for 4–5 seconds, and then sidestep quickly across the room to another spot out of sight aiming his gun at them as he did so.

Lt. Weippert said that Penley stopped looking at Sgt. Brubaker and focused his attention on the other officers—Weippert and Deputy C. Maiorano—as though he knew they were the ones pointing guns at him. Lt. Weippert did not know if there was anybody else inside the restroom with Penley. He did know that there were classrooms behind him, directly across from the restroom.[61] Lt. Weippert said that Penley seemed to be reaching a decision point, to make police shoot or to hurt someone and he (Weippert) decided, "I wasn't going to let him shoot us first."

By his (Weippert) account, the fourth time that Penley appeared in view, aiming his gun at the officers in front of the restroom, Lt. Weippert fired one shot striking Penley in the head. Penley immediately dropped out of sight as Deputy C. Maiorano called him down. Penley was found laying on his side with a bullet wound to the left side of his head. He died from the effects of the wound. His weapon was recovered near him. It was a .24 caliber Daisy AirStrike Model 240 air gun pistol designed to replicate a Beretta Model 92 9mm pistol in appearance. Daisy manufactures this gun to be orange in color, but it had been painted black making its outward appearance identical to that of a Beretta M92 pistol.[62]

### Discussion

An analysis of a decision to use deadly force by a law enforcement officer must look at what the officer knew or reasonably believed at the moment the decision was made. The issue is whether the officer was reasonable in believing that there was an imminent danger of death or serious injury to self or others. If the perception of imminent danger was reasonable, then the decision to use deadly force is a reasonable response — not the only conceivable response, not a last resort, but reasonable because of its necessity given the imperative of "imminent danger" of serious injury. As noted throughout this book, the reasonable perception of risk is assessed independently of mental capacity, subjective intent, ability, armament, sex or, as here, age.

Christopher Penley was a disturbed, immature 14-year-old youth. His age and his mental state were the facts that underlay the plaintiffs' allegations of unreasonable force and negligent training and police actions that led to the killing of this "child." When police shoot a minor, the aftermath is virtually identical to that which follows the shooting of a mentally disturbed person. It does emphasize the reality that is stressed in the law, and through training, that the single underlying reason that justifies the use of deadly force is an imminent risk of serous injury. No officer is required to risk serious injury — or death —

---

61. SCSO Sergeant Tom Johnson and Corporal Dave Nagowski were on the second floor directly above the restroom and advised that the classrooms across from Penley — and thus in his line of fire — were full of kids, and that they (the two officers) could see people at the windows and in the doorways looking out.

62. The investigation found that Penley had painted his orange pistol black a couple of weeks prior to this incident.

be inflicted on himself, or upon others, merely because the individual posing the risk is young, or ill, or in some other seemingly innocent category that is regarded sympathetically by segments of society.

The issue to address is whether the perception of imminent danger at the moment that Lt. Weippert decided to shoot was reasonable. The officers were confronting an individual armed with a handgun who was acting in a threatening and non-compliant manner wholly consistent with the intent to shoot others and/or himself. Penley made no efforts to conceal or minimize his dangerousness. He aimed his gun at other students, teachers, sheriff's deputies, and himself. Their inference that he was willing to use it was unavoidable. All of them believed they were in danger of being shot and killed. Penley told Deputy T. Maiorano that he was "going to die one way or another." She believed him. His actions were also indicators of an intention to commit suicide by cop.[63]

Law enforcement officers are trained that suicidal individuals pose a threat to themselves and to those around them. Officers are cautioned about approaching suicidal threats for several reasons. One is the desire to avoid precipitating the suicide attempt, although that decision is solely in the hands of the person who will make that choice regardless. The efforts of the SCSO deputies to defuse and resolve the incident by attempting extensive verbal engagement and by avoiding any attempt at physical control is evidence of this. However, the greater caution is always to protect against a sudden attack upon the officer or others.

"Suicide by cop" has become a more widely recognized phenomenon. It is a significant factor in a significant percentage of police involved shootings, and one that creates by design an immediate threat to a police officer. The intention is to create such a clear and present danger that the officer is compelled to shoot, accomplishing the suicidal individual's goal of dying. People seeking to provoke police into killing them are aware that they must do something immediately and believably dangerous. That may be a ruse in some cases, but it also can and does mean inflicting actual injury or death in the process. Police officers are not expected to wait and see if the attempt to inflict injury is real or not. Training regarding the phenomenon instills the recognition that such an individual poses an imminent threat of serious injury and officers should be aware of that risk as they attempt to resolve the issue by lesser means—to the extent the individual gives them the time and opportunity to attempt lesser means.

---

63. See Chapter 9. One study cited therein diagnosed suicide by cop by the presence of one of four factors: a note; a verbal expression of the desire to be shot; indicative behavior such as holding a gun to one's own head; or non-compliance with clear and direct commands (such as "drop the weapon") and acting in direct opposition to the commands. There are other indicators.

In the incident involving Christopher Penley, there was little uncertainty as to Penley's intent. He made that clear—he intended to die. He repeatedly held the gun up under his chin—a suicidal gesture. He repeatedly aimed his gun at individual officers—an unmistakable threat of harm intended to provoke a police officer into shooting him. The officers had no reason to disbelieve him.

The one uncertainty they did face was whether Penley would follow through on his demonstrated, vocalized intent and actually act on it. Each individual officer who interacted with Penley was convinced that he posed an imminent risk. Nevertheless, the officers allowed the incident to continue to develop at considerable length (in time and distance), all the while attempting to dissuade Penley from any overtly dangerous act.

For that reason, Lt. Weippert correctly aimed his shot at Penley's head, the only option he had to force physical incapacitation upon Penley quickly enough to prevent him from pulling his trigger. Penley was moving as Lt. Weippert went through the process of making his shot. The fact that the bullet struck the left side of his head is indicative of that—in the time that Lt. Weippert aimed and fired and the bullet traveled to its target, Penley continued moving and turning independently of Lt. Weippert's perceptions and actions.

Lt. Weippert had been watching Penley move back and forth across the restroom, moving in a tactical manner, in and out of view. He watched Penley aim his handgun at the individual officers (including Weippert himself) in close proximity to him (Penley). He had observed and listened to the lengthy attempts by Sgt. Brubaker to communicate and negotiate with Penley to deescalate the situation, without response or results. Finally, Lt. Weippert decided that the imminent danger manifest in Penley's actions could not be allowed to continue.[64]

Lesser options had been attempted at length over the extended distance of the school facilities and lasting well over 30 minutes: continuous attempts at verbal commands, arguments and pleadings, and the uniform presence of nu-

---

64. The necessity for an officer to make immediate decisions in order to best protect his life or the life of another under urgent, dire, and extremely stressful conditions is accepted and well recognized throughout law enforcement practice, training, and policy. For example: "Determining whether deadly force is necessary may involve instantaneous decisions that encompass many factors, such as the likelihood that the subject will use deadly force on the officer or others if such force is not used by the officer; the officer's knowledge that the subject will likely acquiesce in arrest or recapture if the officer uses lesser force or no force at all; the capabilities of the subject; the subject's access to cover and weapons; the presence of other persons who may be at risk if force is or is not used; and the nature and the severity of the subject's criminal conduct or the danger posed."

U.S. Department of Justice Commentary Regarding the Use of Deadly Force in Non-Custodial Situations; Section III, Principles on Use of Deadly Force.

merous armed police officers—none of which dissuaded Penley. As the situation continued to develop, the likelihood that Penley would actually attempt to shoot one of the officers increased. He did nothing to mitigate that possibility. To the contrary, his actions were consistent with forcing a confrontation with police, aiming a weapon with the readiness and intent to use it. Lt. Weippert realized that if he waited until Penley actually fired a shot from the handgun he was aiming at the officers, he could not prevent that shot from hitting someone. And in his words, "I wasn't going to let him shoot us first."

On June 5, 2009, summary judgment was granted to the defendants. The judge addressed the issues in a written order:

" ...

### II.  Legal Standards
### Summary Judgment

*A party is entitled to summary judgment when the party can show that there is no genuine issue as to any material fact. Fed.R.Civ.P. 56(c). Which facts are material depends on the substantive law applicable to the case.* Anderson v. Liberty Lobby, Inc., 477 U.S. 242, 248 (1986). *The moving party bears the burden of showing that no genuine issue of material fact exists.* Clark v. Coats & Clark, Inc., 929 F.2d 604, 608 (11th Cir. 1991).

*When a party moving for summary judgment points out an absence of evidence on a dispositive issue for which the non-moving party bears the burden of proof at trial, the nonmoving party must 'go beyond the pleadings and by [his] own affidavits, or by the depositions, answers to interrogatories, and admissions on file, designate specific facts showing that there is a genuine issue for trial.'* Celotex Corp. v. Catrett, 477 U.S. 317, 324–25 (1986) *(internal quotations and citation omitted). Thereafter, summary judgment is mandated against the nonmoving party who fails to make a showing sufficient to establish a genuine issue of fact for trial.* Id. *at 322, 324–25. The party opposing a motion for summary judgment must rely on more than conclusory statements or allegations unsupported by facts.* Evers v. Gen. Motors Corp., 770 F.2d 984, 986 (11th Cir. 1985) *('conclusory allegations without specific supporting facts have no probative value'). The Court must consider all inferences drawn from the underlying facts in a light most favorable to the party opposing the motion, and resolve all reasonable doubts against the moving party.* Anderson, 477 U.S. at 255. *The Court is not, however, required to accept all of the non-movant's factual characterizations and legal arguments.* Beal v. Paramount Pictures Corp., 20 F.3d 454, 458–59 (11th Cir. 1994).

*Qualified Immunity*

*Qualified immunity protects government officials performing discretionary functions from individual liability as long as their conduct does not violate 'clearly established statutory or constitutional rights of which a reasonable person would have known.'* Harlow v. Fitzgerald, *457 U.S. 800, 818, 102 S.Ct. 2727, 2738, 73 L.Ed.2d 396 (1982). Qualified immunity is an immunity from suit rather than a mere defense to liability, and it is effectively lost if a case is erroneously permitted to go to trial.* Mitchell v. Forsyth, *472 U.S. 511, 526, 105 S.Ct. 2806, 2815, 86 L.Ed.2d 411 (1985). Qualified immunity decisions should be resolved at earliest possible stage in the litigation.* Hunter v. Bryant, *502 U.S. 224, 227, 112 S.Ct. 534, 116 L.Ed.2d 589 (1991) (per curiam). Unless the plaintiff's allegations state a claim of violation of a clearly established constitutional right, a defendant pleading qualified immunity is entitled to dismissal before the commencement of discovery.* Chesser v. Sparks, *248 F.3d 1117, 1121(11th Cir. 2001).*

*Even if the plaintiff's complaint adequately alleges the commission of acts that violated clearly established law, the defendant is entitled to summary judgment if discovery fails to uncover evidence sufficient to create a genuine issue as to whether the defendant in question in fact committed those acts. To receive qualified immunity, a government official first must prove that he was acting within his discretionary authority.* Gonzalez v. Reno, *325 F.2d 1228, 1234 (11th Cir. 2003). Once the defendants establish this, the burden shifts to the plaintiffs to show that qualified immunity is not appropriate.* Id. *The Supreme Court has established a two-part test to determine whether qualified immunity should apply. 'The threshold inquiry a court must undertake in a qualified immunity analysis is whether plaintiff's allegations, if true, establish a constitutional violation.'* Hope v. Pelzer, *536 U.S. 730, 736, 122 S.Ct. 2508, 2514, 153 L.Ed.2d 666 (2002). To resolve that inquiry, the Court must determine whether the facts alleged, taken in the light most favorable to the party asserting the injury, show the officer's conduct violated a constitutional right.* Gonzalez, *325 F.3d at 1234. If so, the Court must then determine whether the right was 'clearly established.'* Id.

### III. Analysis
### A. Section 1983 claim against Weippert

*There is no dispute as to whether Weippert was acting within his discretionary authority at the time he shot Penley. Thus the burden lies with the Plaintiffs to establish that Weippert is not entitled to qualified immu-*

*nity in regard to the Section 1983 claim. And to establish that, the Plaintiffs must show that Weippert's actions violated Penley's constitutional rights.*

*A police officer's apprehension of a suspect by the use of deadly force is a 'seizure' subject to the reasonableness requirement of the Fourth Amendment.* Tennessee v. Garner, *471 U.S. 1, 7, 105 S.Ct. 1694, 1698, 85 L.Ed.2d 1(1985). 'The "reasonableness" of a particular use of force must be judged from the perspective of a reasonable officer on the scene, rather than with the 20/20 vision of hindsight.'* Graham v. Connor, *490 U.S. 386, 396, 109 S.Ct. 1865, 1872, 105 L.Ed.2d 443 (1989). To determine the constitutionality of a seizure, the Court must balance the nature and quality of the intrusion on the individual's Fourth Amendment interests against the countervailing governmental interests at stake. Id. at 396, 109 S.Ct. at 1871. The intrusiveness of a seizure by means of deadly force is 'unmatched,'* Garner *at 9, 105 S.Ct. at 1700, justified only by the strongest governmental interests. However, where the officer has probable cause to believe that the suspect poses a threat of serious physical harm, either to the officer or others, it is not constitutionally unreasonable to employ deadly force to accomplish the seizure.* Garner *at 11, 105 S.Ct. at 1701.*

*The Plaintiffs argue that, at the moment Weippert decided to pull the trigger, a reasonable officer in his position would not have thought that Penley posed a threat of serious physical harm. They assert that Penley was essentially contained in the bathroom, because it had no exit aside from the one that was covered by the weapons of at least half a dozen police officers, and because he made no effort to exit the bathroom during the approximately 40 minutes he was in there before he was shot. They argue that Weippert and the other officers surrounding the bathroom had 'acceptable' cover, such as ballistic shields for Brubaker and others,[65] and the corner of a building for Weippert and Chris Maiorano. And they point out that Brubaker, who was closest to Penley during the standoff, testified that he did not feel threatened by Penley.*

*However, even when viewed in the light most favorable to the Plaintiffs, the evidence does not support these contentions, or the Plaintiffs' larger point. Although Penley was no longer running around the campus, he was not truly 'contained,' as he retained the ability to run out the open*

---

65. The plaintiffs also allege that, in addition to the wall that was partially shielding them, Weippert and Chris Maiorano had the benefit of ballistic shields. This issue is addressed below.

*door at any time with his gun, perhaps toward one of the still-occupied classrooms.*[66] *More importantly, he did not need to leave the bathroom to pose a serious threat to others.*

*Even though the officers deemed their cover 'acceptable,' that cover did not eliminate the threat to their safety posed by Penley's (apparently real) firearm. From within the restroom, Penley continued to threaten to shoot Chris Maiorano and Weippert, who only had the partial cover offered by a corner of a building.*[67] *And ballistic shields do not necessarily offer perfect cover, particular when the officers employing them are moving around and when two officers are seeking shelter behind one shield, as was the case with Brubaker and the officer who brought him the shield. Finally, a reasonable officer on the scene that day would have had to consider the possibility that one of the students in the buildings bordering the courtyard might choose the wrong moment to peer out a window.*

*As for Brubaker, he was not in the same position as Weippert. Because of their different viewpoints, Brubaker and Weippert saw Penley at different times. According to his testimony, Brubaker did not see Penley repeatedly aiming his handgun at Chris Maiorano, Weippert, or anyone else. As such, Brubaker's estimate of the danger posed by Penley would likely differ from that of an officer in Weippert's position, and Brubaker obviously did believe that Penley posed some danger, as demonstrated by his taking cover behind a ballistic shield while attempting to negotiate.*

*The evidence shows that, at the time he decided to take the shot, Weippert had probable cause to believe that Penley had, among other things, threatened the lives of two police officers—himself and Chris Maiorano. Indeed, according to the officer's uncontradicted testimony, Penley was aiming his gun at Weippert at the moment Weippert fired. As such, it was not constitutionally unreasonable for Weippert to employ deadly force against him. The implicit threats made by Penley that day against his classmates and the other officers on the scene bolster this conclusion, but are not necessary for it.*

---

66. The plaintiffs point out that one of the portables bordering the courtyard was evacuated. (Doc. 55 at 12). However, there is no evidence that all of the buildings around the courtyard were evacuated, much less all of the buildings in the school. In addition, the evacuation of the one portable occurred during the standoff with Penley, and there is no evidence that Weippert was aware of the evacuation at the time it occurred. A reasonable officer in Weippert's position would have thought at least some of the nearby buildings were still occupied.

67. As noted above, there is no evidence that any of the officers knew that Penley's gun was not capable of firing real bullets.

*Seeking to undermine Weippert's credibility, the Plaintiffs present the expert testimony of William Gaut ('Gaut'). Gaut, a police practices expert, reviewed a school videotape showing a portion of the courtyard during the events at issue in this suit. Toward the end of the standoff with Penley, two officers are seen crouching behind a ballistic shield and advancing from left to right across the courtyard, toward Penley's position in the bathroom. Gaut contends that one of these two officers is Weippert[68] and that the ballistic shield 'negated any danger' from Penley, and that therefore there was no justification for Weippert to employ deadly force. However, neither Gaut nor the Plaintiffs present any evidence from which a reasonable juror could identify either of the officers behind the shield as Weippert. (Gaut is an expert in police practices, not videotape identification or anything of similar relevance to this issue.) For their part, the Defendants have produced affidavits from two other officers — David Dowda and Jarrit Negri — attesting that they are the two individuals seen utilizing the ballistic shield and moving across the courtyard on the videotape. Based on this evidence, no reasonable jury could conclude that Weippert was one of the officers seen on the videotape advancing behind a ballistic shield.*

*The Plaintiffs also argue that Weippert's failure to warn Penley prior to employing deadly force against him fell short of the constitutional minimum. It is true that in Garner, the seminal case on the employment of deadly force, the Supreme Court imposed a requirement of a warning in some circumstances. More particularly in that case, in which the police shot an unarmed fleeing burglary suspect, the Court stated that 'if the suspect threatens the officer with a weapon or there is probable cause to believe that he has committed a crime involving the infliction or threatened infliction of serious physical harm, deadly force may be used if necessary to prevent escape and if, where feasible, some warning has been given.' Garner at 11–12, 105 S.Ct. at 1701. However, the instant case did not involve a fleeing suspect. Rather, it involved a suspect who was pointing a gun at an officer at the moment he was shot. As such, the Garner warning requirement did not apply. In addition, by training their weapons on Penley, the officers implicitly warned him that he might be shot if he threatened them or failed to obey their commands. And the evidence shows that Penley understood this warning: When Teresa Maiorano*

---

68. The plaintiffs contend that the other officer behind the shield is Chris Maiorano, but Gaut does not make this contention in his affidavit.

*pointed her weapon at him and ordered him to drop his gun, Penley re-*
*sponded to the effect that he was going to die one way or another.*

*Weippert did not violate Penley's constitutional rights when he employed*
*deadly force against him. Weippert is therefore entitled to qualified im-*
*munity on the Plaintiffs' Section 1983 claim. Because there was no un-*
*derlying constitutional violation, the Plaintiff's Section 1983 claim against*
*the Sheriff fails as a matter of law.* Rooney v. Watson, *101 F.3d 1378,*
*1381–82 (11th Cir. 1996)."* [References to case documents have been
deleted—footnotes are in the original.][69]

On May 3, 2010, the U.S. Court of Appeals for the 11th Circuit affirmed the
grant of summary judgment. In its opinion, the Court said, in part:

*" ... as set out in* Garner, *the use of deadly force is more likely reasonable*
*if: the suspect poses an immediate threat of serious physical harm to of-*
*ficers or others; the suspect committed a crime involving the infliction or*
*threatened infliction of serious harm, such that his being at large repre-*
*sents an inherent risk to the general public; and the officers either issued*
*a warning or could not feasibly have done so before using deadly force.*
*See 471 U.S. at 11–12, 105 S. Ct. at 1701. But, once again, none of these*
*conditions are prerequisites to the lawful application of deadly force by*
*an officer seizing a suspect.... As this Court has clarified, the second fac-*
*tor can be reduced to a single question: 'whether, given the circumstances,*
*[the suspect] would have appeared to reasonable police officers to have been*
*gravely dangerous.'* Pace v. Capobianco, *283 F.3d 1275, 1281 (11th Cir.*
*2002).*

*Mr. Penley demonstrated his dangerous proclivities by bringing to*
*school what reasonable officers would believe was a real gun. He refused*
*to drop the weapon when repeatedly commanded to do so. Most impor-*
*tantly, he pointed his weapon several times at Lieutenant Weippert and*
*Deputy Maiorano. We have held that a suspect posed a grave danger*
*under less perilous circumstances than those confronted by Lieutenant*
*Weippert.*

*The Penleys' reliance on Sergeant Brubaker's statement that he did*
*not feel threatened is misplaced.* **The relevant question is whether a rea-**
**sonable officer in Lieutenant Weippert's shoes would have believed that**
**Mr. Penley was gravely dangerous.** *... The bulk of the Penleys' appeal*
*amounts to a challenge to the district court's conclusion that no issues of*

---

69. *Ralph J. Penley, Jr. et al. v. Donald F. Eslinger, et al.*, USDC, Middle District of Florida,
Orlando Division, Case No. 6:08-cv-00310-GAP-KRS, Order, 6/5/09.

*fact preclude summary judgment. However, we find no error in the district court's decision that summary judgment was warranted.*

*The Penleys argue that Lieutenant Weippert knew that the buildings around him had been evacuated. But, the deposition of Sergeant Vincent Kauffman ... does not support this contention. Instead it indicates no more than that one of the nearby classrooms was evacuated. Furthermore, even absent the presence of students, Lieutenant Weippert would have been justified in using deadly force because he had 'probable cause to believe that his own life [was] in peril.'*

*The Penleys claim that a jury could find that 'the physical evidence is not consistent with Lt. Weippert's version [of the event].' ... for instance, that Mr. Penley was not pointing his weapon at Lieutenant Weippert when he was killed, but, instead, was walking away from the door with his back to the officer.*

*However, the record does not support [that] position ... The deposition and report of the Medical Examiner ... describe Mr. Penley's wound, but do not shed light on how the boy's head and arms were positioned at the time he was shot. In fact, the wound is not inconsistent with Lieutenant Weippert's testimony about the last moments of this tragic standoff. [Defendants] presented an expert report that explained that the wounds sustained were actually consistent with Mr. Penley's independent movements.*

*Furthermore, Deputy Maiorano's testimony corroborates Lieutenant Weippert's version of the story. Consequently, the evidence to which the Penleys cite does not create a fact issue sufficient to alter our evaluation of Mr. Penley's posture towards Lieutenant Weippert and Deputy Maiorano and, therefore, does not preclude summary judgment.*

*The Penleys also contend that because the officers had adequate cover and Mr. Penley was contained in the bathroom, any threat posed by Mr. Penley was 'eliminated or significantly reduced,' and, therefore, the use of deadly force was unreasonable and excessive.*

***However, the fact that Mr. Penley was surrounded would not have prevented him from firing a weapon at Lieutenant Weippert, Deputy Maiorano, other officers, or students behind windows in neighboring buildings....***

*The Penleys dedicate a significant portion of their briefs to the argument that Garner mandated Lieutenant Weippert to issue a warning before shooting Mr. Penley. Their argument fails for several reasons. First, as this Court has noted, 'Garner says something about deadly force but not everything.' Long, 508 F.3d at 580. The Supreme Court has also ob-*

served that '[w]hatever Garner *said about the factors that might have justified shooting the suspect in that case, such 'preconditions' have scant applicability to [a] case which has vastly different facts.'* Scott, 550 U.S. at 383, 127 S. Ct. at 1777.... *Unlike in* Garner, *Lieutenant Weippert had probable cause to believe the suspect posed a real threat to the lives of officers and others. Mr. Penley was armed and not fleeing; he repeatedly refused to drop his weapon; and, at the moment Mr. Penley was shot, evidence demonstrates that he was pointing his weapon at Lieutenant Weippert....*

**We have '"decline[d] ... to fashion an inflexible rule that, in order to avoid civil liability, an officer must always warn his suspect before firing—particularly where ... such a warning might easily have cost the officer his life."'** Carr, *338 F.3d at 1269 n.19 (quoting* McLenagan, *27 F.3d at 1007). In this case, Mr. Penley had his weapon trained on Lieutenant Weippert, who believed that the boy was going to fire. Particularly in light of various officers' repeated commands that Mr. Penley drop his weapon and the fact that the officers had their own guns pointed at Mr. Penley, Lieutenant Weippert's failure to explicitly warn Mr. Penley does not alter our conclusion that the use of lethal force was objectively reasonable....*

*At bottom, the Penleys have asked us to question with 20/20 hindsight vision the field decision of a twenty-year veteran of the police force.* **The relevant inquiry remains whether Lieutenant Weippert 'had probable cause to believe that [Mr. Penley] posed a threat of serious physical harm.'** *See* Robinson, *415 F.3d at 1256. In other words, would Mr. Penley 'have appeared to reasonable police officers to have been gravely dangerous'? See* Pace, *283 F.3d at 1281. Under the tragic circumstances of this case and in light of this Court's binding precedent, we must answer this question in the affirmative. We therefore hold that Lieutenant Weippert did not violate Mr. Penley's constitutional rights, thereby ending our qualified immunity analysis."* [Emphasis added.][70]

## *Whisman v. Regualos, et al.*[71]

Selfridge Air National Guard Base (ANGB) is an active military air base located within Detroit, Michigan. The military assets that are located on the base include numerous aircraft, fuel stores, an armed aircraft alert facility, and mu-

---

70. *Ralph J. Penley, Jr., et al. v. Donald F. Eslinger, et al.*, 605 F.3d 843 (11th Cir. 2010).

71. *Whisman v. Regualos, et al.*, USDC, Eastern District of Michigan, Case No: 2:08-cv-12133.

nitions. The base is populated with Air Force and Air National Guard personnel, their dependents and families, civilian employees, and other Department of Defense (DOD) personnel. The main gate is clearly marked and vehicle lanes are designed to control access. There are concrete barriers positioned to direct traffic flow into a one lane serpentine to impede uninterrupted traffic flow. The serpentine lane directs traffic to the main gate checkpoint manned by security personnel. Drivers are required to stop, show identification, and proceed when so directed by the security guards manning the gate. The main gate is located in the northeastern corner of the base.

On May 17, 2006, Tim Whisman breached the main gate of the ANGB at about 7:50 p.m. Whisman was blowing his horn as he approached the gate checkpoint in his red Geo Tracker. He proceeded through the gate security without stopping or slowing down, veering around vehicles ahead of him at the gate and accelerated south on Jefferson Road. The main gate guards broadcast the breach and ANGB security personnel responded.

Staff Sergeant Charlie Mitchell (a one-man unit) was ahead of Whisman on Jefferson. He joined with a two-man unit, Staff Sergeants Bradley Vermeesch and Patrick Probyn, to form a roadblock across Jefferson. They positioned their vehicles in such a manner as to block all three lanes of Jefferson Road, angled to direct Whisman off the road. Both units had their emergency lights on and were positioned head-on to the oncoming Geo. Whisman evaded the roadblock without slowing down. Sgt Mitchell fell in behind Whisman in pursuit, followed by Tech Sergeant David Christian (another one-man unit) and SSgts Vermeesch and Probyn in their vehicle. Speeds exceeded 70 mph.

Whisman continued south. Jefferson turned east, becoming Wilbur Wright Boulevard. He drove east on Wilbur Wright until it merged into George Avenue. He drove southeast on George at 90 mph until it turned south, becoming General Andrews Road. SSgt Mitchell observed him zigzagging "all over the road" and people pulling children back from the sidewalks.

Whisman continued on General Andrews Road through the base golf course. General Andrews Road turned west in the vicinity of the Golf Gate, becoming South Perimeter Road across the southern end of the base. SSgt Mitchell observed golfers running out of the way as Whisman drove through at 70 to 90 mph. The posted speed limit is 25 mph. Whisman drove west on South Perimeter across the length of the southern extremity of the ANGB, driving in the middle of the road. TSgt Christian tried several times to pass Whisman's car in order to box it in to slow Whisman down and bring him to a stop, but every time he attempted to pass, Whisman swerved back and forth across the road, forcing Christian to fall back in order to avoid being forced off the road at 90 mph. Whisman was actively countering the attempts to box in his car. TSgt

Christian switched positions with SSgt Mitchell behind Whisman. The pursuit sequence now consisted of TSgt Christian in his vehicle, followed by SSgt Mitchell in his, followed by two two-man units—TSgt. Jonathan Southern and SSgt William Heatley in one, followed by SSgts Vermeesch and Probyn in another. All of the pursuing vehicles were operating emergency lights and sirens.

At the southwestern corner of the ANGB, South Perimeter turns north, becoming West Perimeter Road. Whisman continued north on West Perimeter Road until it intersected Joy Road, about midway along the western boundary of the ANGB. Intercept Security Officer John Berry had set up a Traffic Control Point[72] (TCP) on the south side of this intersection to attempt to stop Whisman. Berry placed his vehicle in one lane as he stood in the other lane. Whisman drove right at Berry at high speed, forcing him to run for cover to avoid being hit. Another two-man unit, SSgt Keith Werhnyak and Airman Raymond King had established a second TCP on the northern side of the intersection.

Whisman turned east on Joy Road and drove towards the ANGB Tower. Joy Road also accesses the runways and flight line beyond the Control Tower. It is a gated access through the fence line that bounds the runways and the gate was closed. Whisman turned south off Joy Road into the tower parking lot using the eastern-most entry into the lot and stopped. TSgt Christian stopped behind him. SSgt Mitchell had turned into the lot using its middle entrance and was stopped ahead of Whisman, facing him about one car-length away. SSgts Vermeesch and Probyn stopped and set up a TCP on southbound West Perimeter Road above Joy Road. SSgts. Southern and Heatley moved their vehicle to set up a TCP inside the western-most entrance to the parking lot and they got out of their vehicle.

SSgt Mitchell began to get out of his vehicle when Whisman accelerated at him, striking his vehicle in the left front fender and an adjacent parked vehicle as he passed and forced SSgt Mitchell to jump back into his vehicle to avoid being hit. Whisman drove out of the parking lot and turned west on Joy Road driving past SSgts Southern and Heatley. SSgt Heatley fired four shots with his M4 carbine at Whisman's vehicle as it passed in an attempt to disable it.

Whisman turned south on West Perimeter Road, reversing his previous route and again evading the TCP set up there by Berry. He drove south on West Perimeter to the southwestern corner of the ANGB where West Perimeter turned

---

72. Traffic Control Point is the terminology used by the ANGB security personnel for a partial roadblock intended to induce an oncoming vehicle to slow down, stop, or leave the roadway. It entails blocking the lane of travel of the oncoming vehicle, but leaving other lanes open, to induce compliance without forcing a crash.

east and became South Perimeter Road, pursued (in order) by TSgt Christian, SSgt Mitchell, and then SSgts Southern and Heatley. TSgt Christian fired one shot from his handgun at Whisman as he pursued him south on West Perimeter. The pursuit continued onto South Perimeter Road, headed east.

Meanwhile, SSgt Werhnyak with Senior Airman King, SSgts Vermeesch and Probyn, and Berry all proceeded north on West Perimeter Road in their respective vehicles in an attempt to get ahead of the pursuit by driving around the northern end of the base to intercept Whisman on the other side.

TSgt Christian tried again to pass Whisman's car in order to box it in, but Whisman countered by swerving towards Christian despite a 5–7' drop along the roadway at that location. TSgt Christian was forced to steer to the left side to avoid contact. SSgt Mitchell saw the danger to TSgt Christian and aligned his vehicle behind Whisman's. He fired his handgun out his driver's side window at Whisman as they sped down Perimeter Road. The pursuit continued past Golf Gate where South Perimeter turns north, becoming General Andrews Road. Whisman continued along General Andrews at 70–80 mph to where it turns northwest and becomes George Avenue. Department of Defense (DOD) officers Canty and Careathers had set up a TCP there, but Whisman drove off the road and around it with people on foot scrambling out of his way. He proceeded up George Avenue, driving at DOD Officer Scott, who was on foot in the opposing lane. Scott had to run out of the way to avoid being hit. Both DOD units joined the pursuit.

Whisman drove the length of George Avenue, passing Wilbur Wright Boulevard, towards the intersection of George and Jefferson. SSgts. Southern and Heatley cut through the base commissary parking lot to try to get ahead of Whisman. SSgt Werhnyak with Airman King had succeeded in getting ahead of the pursuit. They were stopped and out of their vehicle in the intersection of George and Jefferson. Whisman drove at them at a high rate of speed, forcing Airman King to take evasive action. SSgt Werhnyak fired three shots at him with his handgun.

Whisman drove across Jefferson and turned south in front of the base fire department, leaving the roadway to drive across the grass to Supply Street. His vehicle was briefly airborne when he left the road, but he kept going, turning east and returning to Jefferson, turning north and driving back through the intersection with George Avenue. SSgt Werhnyak and Airman King were still on foot in the intersection. As Whisman evaded their TCP and Airman King dodged him again, SSgt Werhnyak fired three more shots with his handgun at the Geo's engine and front tires. Airman King fired one shot with his handgun at Whisman. Whisman drove off the road in front of Building 806 and then returned, now driving north on Jefferson. He evaded another TCP established by SSgts Southern and Heatley near the intersection with Johnson Street.

SSgt Mitchell was now directly behind Whisman as they proceeded north-bound on Jefferson. He fired two shots at Whisman with his handgun, shooting left-handed out of his driver's side window in the vicinity of Building 781. He saw Whisman arch his back and lean to his right. Whisman's vehicle began to drift to the right. TSgt Christian passed SSgt Mitchell and struck the left rear end of Whisman's Geo, causing it to spin out of control and leave the road to the right. The Geo came to a stop in a grassy area between Buildings 780 and 970, facing to the southwest.

Whisman was not responsive to orders from the officers approaching him on foot. He was pulled out of the Geo and handcuffed. He had a pulse and shallow breathing. Emergency medical assistance was requested and the ANGB Emergency Medical Services and Fire Department responded. Whisman had been hit by two gunshots and subsequently died from his wounds.

From the Main Gate located in the northeast corner of the ANGB, Whisman had driven along the entire length of the east side of the ANGB, through base facilities, residential areas, and the golf course and then across the length of the southern boundary of the base and halfway up the western side of the base, where he turned into the Control Tower and towards the flight line. He reversed course through the tower parking lot, and retraced his route—down the western side of the base, across the southern end, and up the eastern side through the golf course, residential areas, and base facilities. The pursuit attained speeds as high as 90 mph.

### Discussion

*"Law enforcement and correctional officers ... may use deadly force only when necessary, that is, when the officer has a reasonable belief that the subject of such force poses an imminent danger of death or serious physical injury to the officer or to another person."*[73]

---

73. U.S. Department of Justice Policy Statement: Use of Deadly Force. Air Force Instruction 31-207 (1 September 1999) "Arming and Use of Force by Air Force Personnel" is fully consistent with the DOJ policy, to wit:

"§ 1.4.1 You may use force, including deadly force, when you reasonably believe yourself or others to be in imminent danger of death or serious bodily harm."

The 1999 version of 31-207 was in force at the time of the Whisman shooting at Selfridge. Air Force Instruction 31-207 "Arming and Use of Force by Air Force Personnel" was revised as of 29 January 2009. This revision did not change the policy provisions, to wit: " ... Deadly force is authorized under the following circumstances ..."

"§ 1.5.1 Inherent Right of Self-Defense. Applies when an individual reasonably believes he/she is in imminent danger of death or serious bodily harm. Deadly force is authorized when individuals reasonably believe that a person poses an imminent threat of death or se-

As events unfolded, Whisman continuously and aggressively defied all of the police officers trying to stop him over the extended course of his vehicular flight. He recklessly and unremittingly evaded and eluded the officers pursuing him. He ignored an array of official vehicles with emergency lights and sirens activated. He ignored numerous uniformed personnel ordering him to stop, many of them in his path and gesturing for him to stop. He drove through or around numerous traffic control points that were set up serially in his path to stop him. He maintained speeds ranging from 70 to 90 mph through residential, pedestrian, recreational, and business areas of the base, scattering pedestrians and officers in his wake. He resisted and aggressively countered attempts to box him in with pursuing vehicles, endangering the officers attempting to do so by trying to force them off the road at high speed.

Whisman never slowed down or made any effort to moderate the grave risk to public safety that his high-speed flight created to both those pursuing him and innocent bystanders in his vicinity. The only time he paused in his flight was in the parking lot of the flight tower when he momentarily stopped in front of SSgt Mitchell, inducing Mitchell to exit his vehicle to approach. However, he then accelerated directly at Mitchell, who had to jump back into his vehicle to avoid being hit, and the pursuit resumed.

Whisman could have chosen to comply at any point during the extensive pursuit but did not. He continuously and determinedly refused to comply, using his car as an instrument of assault and escape. He created an unmistakable and unabated danger to everyone in his vicinity—police officers and citizens alike. Whisman did nothing to signify any intention to surrender or even diminish the danger his actions created. To the contrary, his sustained and reckless flight elevated the risk of death or serious injury to the officers in his proximity and to innocent bystanders who happened to be in his way.

In the civil suit that followed, the contentions were that Whisman had no intent to cause harm and therefore posed no danger. However, it was not his intentions that justified the use of deadly force. His intentions were not, and could not have been, known by any of the law enforcement and security personnel dealing with him. It was his actions that created an unmistakable and clearly present danger. The officers could only respond to what Whisman did. Their individual and collective responses necessarily derived from the recognition that

---

rious bodily harm to DoD forces. Unit self-defense includes the defense of other DoD forces in the vicinity.

§1.5.2 Defense of Others. When an officer/sentry reasonably believes others are in imminent danger of death or serious bodily harm. Deadly force is authorized in defense of non-DoD persons in the vicinity, when directly related to the assigned mission."

what he (Whisman) persisted in doing created grave, significant risks to their safety and security and to the safety and security of the ANGB and its populace.

They had a responsibility to protect their selves as well as the safety of the public at large. That responsibility ultimately superseded the natural desire and sincere efforts to resolve the danger posed by Whisman without injuring him (Whisman). Notably, they had attempted extensive efforts to do exactly that, setting up numerous TCPs, pursuing with an array of official vehicles all with lights and sirens activated, and with various uniformed personnel repeatedly on foot gesturing and ordering "stop." They also attempted several times to disable Whisman's car with gunfire, shooting at the car and not Whisman! None of it worked—there was no diminution of the danger posed by Whisman's behavior. As Whisman continued, the risks only intensified and the probability of seriously injurious consequences increased. Although they could have chosen to continue the pursuit indefinitely—trying again and again to induce him to stop while allowing the danger to continue unabated, that becomes increasingly unreasonable as the failures mount. It is not reasonable to allow an obvious danger to continue unabated upon the mere hope that nobody will get hurt before it comes to an eventual but uncertain end.

The officers involved recognized the imminent and continuing danger of death or serious injury Whisman had created. Throughout the pursuit, Whisman was aggressively noncompliant. He repeatedly used his car as a weapon. In addition to their physical safety, and the safety of every bystander who happened to be in Whisman's way, the officers also had the additional concern unique to national security interests—the security of base military assets. They had to protect against an attack upon DoD assets that could result in even more widespread death and destruction.[74] His behavior was not inconsistent

---

74. There are additional provisions for the authorized use of deadly force that are unique to the Department of Defense and its singular responsibility to protect the national security. Air Force Instruction 31-207 (1 September 1999) "Arming and Use of Force by Air Force Personnel" stated these additional authorized uses of deadly force:

§ 1.4.2 You may use force, including deadly force, to protect DoD assets designated as vital to the national security.

§ 1.4.3 You may use force, including deadly force, to protect DoD assets not involving the national security but inherently dangerous to others.

§ 1.4.4 You may use force, including deadly force, to prevent the commission of a serious offense involving violence and threatening death or serious bodily harm.

§ 1.4.5 You may use force; to include deadly force, when it reasonably appears necessary to detain, apprehend, or prevent the escape of a person suspected of committing an offense of the nature specified in paragraphs 1.4.1, 1.4.2, 1.4.3, and 1.4.4, and it reasonably appears that the suspect presents an immediate danger to you or to others.

with that of an aspiring car-bomber, and Selfridge ANGB is obviously in a target category that is subject to terrorist attack.

There is nothing in law enforcement training or practice that would suggest or require that any one of the officers who fired their weapons should have waited instead to see what Whisman would do next. Whisman chose to act as he did, endangering everybody in his vicinity in defiance of the verbal commands and manifest visual presences directed at him throughout his flight. He ignored uniformed, armed officers waving, gesturing, pointing guns at him, and shooting at him. He ignored increasing numbers of marked cruisers pursuing him with lights and sirens activated. He ignored a persistent series of roadblocks and traffic control points and several instances of shots being fired at his vehicle. He actively countered attempts by his pursuers to box him in. He endangered innocent bystanders who happened to be in his way as he sped through residential areas and the golf course. Efforts to dissuade or contain him had all failed. Whisman's behavior throughout the incident created a clear, reasonably perceived, and continuous risk of death or serious injury. He never did anything to abate that risk. Nevertheless, with the exception of the final three shots by SSgt Mitchell, none of the officers or airmen actually shot *at* Whisman. They all shot at his car. Notably, that had no effect on the speed, direction, or duration of the pursuit or Whisman's use of the car to imperil others.

SSgt Heatley had participated in the pursuit from its inception. He recognized that he had a safe field of fire as Whisman left the Control Tower parking lot and evaded the TCP that he and SSgt Southern had set up. He decided to shoot at Whisman's tires as he drove by.

TSgt Christian had also been involved in the pursuit from its inception, and had experienced Whisman's determined vehicular flight. He had been personally endangered by Whisman's attempts to force him off the road at high speed. He was directly behind Whisman in close pursuit when he fired one shot at the rear window in a self-described attempt to "distract" Whisman and induce him to slow down.

SSgt Mitchell saw Whisman try to force Christian off the road. SSgt Mitchell had been involved in the pursuit from its onset, and also a witness to Whis-

---

These authorized uses of deadly force are retained, and expanded upon, in the current version of 31-207 (29 January 2009). See:
   § 1.5.3 Assets Vital to National Security
   § 1.5.4 Inherently Dangerous Property
   § 1.5.5 National Critical Infrastructure
   § 1.5.6 Serious Offenses Against Persons

man's reckless endangerment of everybody in his path and in his vicinity. Whisman had driven directly at him in the Control Tower parking lot, and now he saw Whisman trying to force Christian off the road for a second time. He fired at Whisman and saw Whisman duck down as he disengaged from Christian's vehicle.

When the pursuit returned to the intersection of Jefferson and George, Whisman's operation of his car became more even dangerous due to the numbers of people and officers present and the closer confines of buildings and obstructions. Whisman drove off the road, ran through intersections, and drove through traffic control points forcing officers on foot to dodge him. SSgt Werhnyak actually thought Whisman had run down Airman King. He shot at Whisman's engine. Airman King had not been hit, but he had been forced to dodge Whisman's vehicle and he also fired at Whisman's car to try to disable it. When Whisman returned through the TCP that SSgt Werhnyak and Airman King had set up, SSgt Werhnyak fired at his car yet again to stop it.

It is notable that despite being shot at by five different officers at five distinct and widely separated moments during this extended pursuit, Whisman never slowed down or mitigated his behavior in any way consistent with abating the risk he was creating. He gave no indication of any intention to comply with the widely separated, numerous, continuous, and unmistakable command stimuli to stop. Ultimately, SSgt Mitchell shot twice more at Whisman as he pursued him north on Jefferson. Whisman was hit and visibly reacted to the wound(s). Concurrently, TSgt Christian succeeded in forcing the Whisman vehicle out of control and off the road. The car was still operable when the officers approached it, and it is certain that only the effects of his two gunshot wounds terminated Whisman's flight.

Much of what law enforcement does involves vehicles, and consequently it is common for vehicles to be operated in manner that threatens the safety of law enforcement and others. Shootings centered in and around the operation of a motor vehicle are frequently controversial because the operator of the vehicle is often "unarmed," often under the influence of drugs or alcohol, and often suspected of nothing more than non-violent offenses and mere misdemeanors. That controversy misunderstands that the dangerous operation of a vehicle creates an imminent risk of serious injury independently of the underlying offense, actual intent, or peripheral activities of the driver.

Law enforcement training and policies recognize that a vehicle can be operated in a manner to threaten imminent risk of death or serious injury, and that there is no reasonable way to disable a moving vehicle with a firearm. In the DOJ Commentary provided to facilitate understanding and implementation of the DOJ Uniform Policy on the Use of Deadly Force, the DOJ specifically states: " ... Shooting to disable a moving motor vehicle is forbidden ... An officer who has reason to believe that a driver or occupant poses an imminent danger of death or serious physical injury to the officer or others may fire at the driver or an occupant only when such shots are necessary to avoid death or serious physical injury to the officer or another, and only if the public safety benefits of using such force reasonably appear to outweigh any risks to the officer or the public, such as from a crash, ricocheting bullets, or return fire from the subject or another person."[75]

As an aside, this shooting incident involving Whisman is exactly the "public safety benefit" envisioned in the DOJ commentary, i.e., the other officers and bystanders were in the path of a vehicle being operated in an imminently dangerous and threatening manner and their close proximity made any attempts at avoidance or eluding the threat difficult, if not unreasonable.

Ultimately, events were driven by Whisman's choices and actions. Whisman chose to resist and to flee, driving recklessly and in total disregard for the safety of others. His actions created an imminent and continuous danger of death or serious injury to officers and bystanders. His decision to ignore all the sustained, preceding attempts to induce or compel him to stop, in disregard of the risks to others around him, made the decisions to use deadly force by the involved officers reasonable.

In the ensuing civil suit, the Plaintiff alleged *"that defendants Christian, Heatley, King, Mitchell, and Werhmnyak violated Mr. Whisman's Fourth Amendment right to be free from unreasonable force when being seized by law enforcement officers ..."*[76]

The Court offers an excellent discussion of the concept of a Fourth Amendment "seizure" that is concise, cogent, and specifically relevant to the facts in this case:

> " *... a court should first determine whether a Fourth Amendment seizure occurred.* Adams v. City of Auburn Hills, *336 F.3d 515, 519 (6th Cir. 2003). If no seizure occurred, no consideration of the reasonableness of an officer's conduct is necessary.* Id. *A Fourth Amendment seizure 'occurs only when government actors have, "by means of physical force or show of authority, ... in some way restrained the liberty of a citizen."'* Id., *quoting,* Terry v. Ohio, *392 U.S. 1, 19 n. 16 (1968). The Supreme Court has held that a show of authority by police is not a Fourth Amendment seizure if the suspect does not yield.* Id., *citing* California v. Hodari D., *499 U.S.*

---

75. U.S. Department of Justice Commentary Regarding the Use of Deadly Force in Non-Custodial Situations; Section IV, subsection: Motor Vehicles and their Occupants.

76. *Whisman v. Regualos, et al.*, U.S. District Court, Eastern District of Michigan, Case No: 2:08-cv-12133.

*621 (1991). In Cameron v. City of Pontiac, the Sixth Circuit held that 'deadly force alone does not constitute a seizure, absent an actual physical restraint or physical seizure.' Cameron v. City of Pontiac, 813 F.2d 782, 784 (6th Cir. 1987). 'Shooting at a fleeing person, but missing, is not a "seizure."' Adams, 336 F.3d at 519. Courts outside of the Sixth Circuit have also addressed this issue. Id., citing, Latta v. Keryte, 118 F.3d 693, 699–700 (l0th Cir. 1997) (a plaintiff was 'seized' only when he stopped at a roadblock and not when the defendant-officer shot the tires of plaintiff's car in an unsuccessful pursuit.)"*[77]

The Court noted that the numerous pursuing vehicles all with flashing lights and sirens activated, the multiple attempted roadblocks, and the various security personnel on foot that he endangered demonstrated *"beyond any reasonable dispute that Mr. Whisman was aware that he was being pursued and that he had chosen to flee from the security forces."*[78]

Of particular note in this case history is the disposition the Court makes of the shots fired at Whisman and/or his car that did not hit him, constituting missed shots. Whisman was never seized until the final moments when he was actually struck by shots fired at him for the purpose of stopping his continued flight.

*" ... when Sgt. Christian, Sgt.Heatley, Senior Airman King, Sgt. Mitchell (first shot only), and Sgt. Werhnyak discharged their weapons at Mr. Whisman and his vehicle, they were firing at a fleeing suspect that refused to stop. Third, these shots did not hit Mr. Whisman, nor did they cause him to cease his flight. Hence, Mr. Whisman was never seized by defendants Christian, Heatley, King, Mitchell (first shot only), and Werhnyak. As there was no seizure for Fourth Amendment purposes by these defendants, plaintiff has not alleged a constitutional violation to support a Bivens action and these defendants are entitled to summary judgment on this claim."*[79]

As in so many incidents involving the operation of a motor vehicle, the allegation is invariably made that the risks of bodily harm posed by the driver's operation of the vehicle do not justify the use of deadly force. The driver is variously "just" driving away, not "directly" threatening anybody, "induced" to act rashly by the aggressive pursuit with its high-stress lights and sirens, not armed, or engaged in nothing more than a misdemeanor traffic violation, or that other officers did not feel in danger. But ...

---

77. *Whisman v.Michigan Air National Guard, 127th Security Force et al.*, 2:08-cv-12133, No. 90 (E.D.Mich. Jul. 6, 2011).

78. *Ibid.*

79. *Ibid.*

"*In* Scott v. Harris, *the Supreme Court stated that 'in judging whether [a defendant's] actions were reasonable, we must consider the risk of bodily harm that [defendant's] actions posed to [the suspect] in light of the threat to the public that [the defendant] was trying to eliminate.' In measuring these risks, it is appropriate to 'take into account not only the number of lives at risk, but also their relative culpability.' In Scott, the Court considered the fact that it was the plaintiff 'who intentionally placed himself and the public in danger by unlawfully engaging in the reckless, high-speed flight that ultimately produced the choice between evils that [the defendant] confronted.' The Court also noted that '[m]ultiple police cars, with blue lights flashing and sirens blaring, had been chasing respondent for nearly 10 miles, but [the plaintiff] ignored their warning to stop.' Finally the court stated that 'by contrast, those who might have been harmed had [the defendant] not taken the action he did were entirely innocent.' For these reasons, the Court concluded that it was reasonable for the defendant in the case to take the action, executing a pit maneuver, he did. Similarly, in this incident, Mr. Whisman intentionally placed himself, the residents of Selfridge, and the officers engaged in his pursuit in danger by unlawfully engaging in a reckless high-speed chase. Multiple Security Squadron vehicles pursued Mr. Whisman with their lights flashing and sirens blaring for more than 12 miles, but Mr. Whisman ignored their warnings to stop. Mr. Whisman produced the choice of evils Sgt. Mitchell and his fellow officers faced. Those Mr. Whisman might have harmed by his actions, residents of Selfridge and the pursuing officers, were entirely innocent, while Mr. Whisman was responsible for causing the high speed chase.*

*Plaintiff relies heavily on Sgt. Christian's testimony that he was not in fear of his life at the particular moment when Sgt. Mitchell pulled out his gun. In the view of the undersigned, this does not mean that Mr. Whisman did not, throughout the 15 minute chase, prove that 'he would do almost anything to avoid capture' and that his actions posed a significant threat to the officers that had set up multiple roadblocks in his path of travel. Moreover, the use of deadly force may be justified where the officers reasonably believe that a suspect's actions pose a threat to the public and any pedestrians, which was certainly the case here.*[80]

*Deadly force is also justifiable if there is 'a significant threat of death or serious physical injury ... [to] others.' Washington v. Starke, 433 N.W.2d 834, 837 (Mich. Ct. App. 1988) As discussed earlier, Mr. Whis-*

---

80. *Ibid*, citations removed.

*man intentionally placed himself, the residents of Selfridge, and the officers engaged in his pursuit, in danger of death or serious physical injury by unlawfully engaging in a reckless high-speed chase. Mr. Whisman was pursued by multiple Security Squadron vehicles, with their lights flashing and sirens blaring, for more than 12 miles, but ignored their warnings to stop. Mr. Whisman drove at a high rate of speed through residential areas. Perhaps most significantly, Mr. Whisman intentionally or recklessly directed his vehicle at the officers attempting to stop his flight and caused a collision with a Sgt. Mitchell's vehicle. Defendants had cause to reasonably assume that Mr. Whisman, by his actions, would cause death or significant injury, if not stopped. For this reason, the use of deadly force was justified."*[81]

Summary judgment was granted on September 13, 2011, by the U.S. District Court affirming and adopting the report and recommendations of the magistrate judge hearing the case.

## *Estate of John Garczynski v. Sheriff Ric Bradshaw (PBSO) et al.*[82]

In March 2005, deputies of the Palm Beach Sheriff's Office (PBSO) responded to the residence of Leigh Garczynski in Boca Raton, Florida, in response to her report that her estranged husband John Garczynski was suicidal. She had received a suicide note and she was unable to locate him. Four PBSO deputies were initially present at Leigh Garczynski's home when John Garczynski called Leigh on his cell phone telling her he had a gun and was going to kill himself. He remained on the phone with her for the next two hours, monitored by a deputy as she persistently tried to discover his location so that the PBSO could find him and help him.

Descriptions of John Garczynski and his car (a Ford Explorer) were broadcast. The PBSO and Garczynski's mobile phone provider were able to triangulate his location on the beach within a radius of 8,000 yards. Deputies went to the area to search for him and the Boca Raton Police Department (BRPD) was advised.

About 11:00 p.m., the PBSO deputies met in the vicinity to get briefed on the situation. They were advised that Garczynski was suicidal, in possession of a handgun, and walking around talking on his cell phone. They had descriptions

---

81. *Ibid.*
82. *Estate of John Garczynski v. Sheriff Ric L. Bradshaw, et al.*, 573 F.3d 1158 (11th Cir. 2009).

of Garczynski and of his Ford Explorer, and they knew he was in their general area because of the triangulation done by the cell phone company.

After the briefing, Deputies Rod Withrow and Shawn Goddard were riding together when they saw a man matching Garczynski's description walking with a cell phone in his left hand and his right hand in his pocket. They reversed course and lost sight of the man, but did locate Garczynski's Ford Explorer parked in the lot outside an apartment building.

They could not see inside the car because the back and side windows were heavily tinted and the front windshield was fogged up and opaque. The deputies were unable to see whether Garczynski was in the car or not. The car was backed into a parking space on the east side of the lot. There was only one entrance/exit to the lot at its north end. Deputies took positions to cover the parking lot and Deputy Withrow put "stop sticks" across the entrance/exit. Boca Raton PD K-9 officer Robert Adams joined them. PBSO Lt. Jay Hart was the senior officer on the scene.

The weather conditions were cold, windy, dark, and rainy. Garczynski was still talking with Leigh Garczynski on his cell phone. At the suggestion of Deputy Wildove back at the house, Leigh suggested to Garczynski that he get into his car to warm himself up. Then PBSO Sgt. Robert Sandt radioed from the house that Garczynski would be walking back to his car but none of the officers saw him and none of them had any idea where he was until Deputy Dana MacLeod saw the dome light in Garczynski's car turn on. He reported that Garczynski was in the car. And then the Ford Explorer's engine started. That was the officers' first indication of Garczynski's presence and Lt. Hart immediately radioed "don't let him (Garczynski) leave the lot." The officers approached Garczynski's vehicle on foot.

Deputy MacLeod and Officer Adams were on the passenger side of Garczynski's car near its right front quarter. They could not see inside the car, but they could discern Garczynski in the glow of his cell phone as he held it in his left hand. Deputies Withrow and Goddard also approached the passenger side of Garczynski's car from the right rear, using an adjacent vehicle for cover. They could not see inside.

The officers verbally identified themselves and commanded Garczynski to show his hands and to place his hands on the steering wheel. Deputy Withrow decided to move up to the car and break out the front passenger side window so that Deputy MacLeod and Officer Adams (positioned at the right front quarter) could see inside. He did so, using his flashlight. Then he broke the right rear passenger side window so that he and Deputy Goddard could see inside.

Deputy MacLeod and Officer Adams saw Garczynski through the broken window sitting in the driver's seat holding a cell phone to his left ear with his left hand. He held a handgun in his right hand that he pointed at his right temple. The officers immediately began ordering him to drop the gun.

Garczynski was non-responsive to the officers' presence or their commands. When Deputy Withrow broke the right rear passenger window, Garczynski turned in his seat in the direction of Deputy Withrow, still holding the cell phone in his left hand and the gun in his right. The officers continued to order him to drop the gun. Garczynski turned the gun from his right temple in the direction of Deputy MacLeod and Officer Adams at the right front quarter. Garczynski continued his motion swinging the gun past them to his right and bringing it to bear on Deputy Withrow at the right rear window.

All four officers shot at Garczynski. Deputy Withrow tripped and fell as he tried to back away from Garczynski's gun and Deputy Goddard thought Withrow had been shot. The four deputies fired a total of 30 rounds. Garczynski was hit eleven times and died of his wounds.

### Discussion

Obviously, when law enforcement responds to a situation involving a suicidal subject the singular purpose is to prevent that individual from actually committing the act. But suicidal situations present law enforcement with a complex problem that extends to dimensions beyond the seemingly simple imperative of preventing the suicide. (See Chapter 9.)

The suicidal individual is self-evidently a clear threat to his self. But the suicidal individual is (perhaps less evidently to the observer) a significant danger to others as well.[83] When Garczynski was at large, location unknown, it created an even more dangerous and uncertain situation—that of an armed, ostensibly suicidal (and thus potentially violent) individual whose location was unknown and further complicated by the mobility of a car at his disposal.

Motor vehicles always present serious tactical problems because of the mobility inherent to vehicles, the potential of causing serious harm with the vehicle, and the bunker-like protection a vehicle can provide to hostile or resistant persons. A person in a car and loose on the streets has freedom of action, mobility, and the not insubstantial ballistic protection provided by the car itself. The car is essentially a mobile bunker in which the person has the initiative. The problem is compounded because the unconstrained operation of the car can impose an unreasonable risk on the public at large, for example by reckless

---

83. Interestingly, and by policy, Maine State Police dispatch reports of suicidal individuals as "man with a gun" calls, rather than "threatened suicide" calls to avoid inducing any assumptions among responding troopers that the subject of the call is not a potential danger to responding officers and others as well as to himself.

operation such as ramming; speeding; driving off roads, against traffic, and through pedestrian areas; ignoring traffic signals; etc. In the event of armed resistance, there is the substantial risk of indiscriminate shooting by the occupant(s) from within the car. The risks to police officers trying to deal with such a situation are significantly increased, for all these same reasons.

When the deputies located Garczynski's car they recognized that to be their best opportunity to locate him because they knew that he was returning to the car. They set up a discrete surveillance of the car not knowing if Garczynski was inside the car or somewhere close and returning to it. To reduce the chances for Garczynski to leave in the car, they set out stop strips across the exit of the parking lot. Anticipating an approach (suicidal individual armed with a gun) they called for ballistic shields to be brought to the scene (and one was in fact on its way when the incident climaxed). They called for a K-9 officer and Officer Adams, a BRPD K-9 officer, responded. They called for helicopter coverage, but the inclement weather prevented it. All of these measures were intended to contain Garczynski in or near his car and to enhance the safety of the officers, who would have to approach him for the purpose of subduing and disarming him.

As it happened, Garczynski entered his car unobserved. The officers' first indication of his presence was the illumination of the interior dome light after Garczynski had gotten into his car and started the engine. Suddenly events had transpired to force a decision between the only two options available to them— approach or passively await further events.

Waiting was unreasonable because it would only make the situation worse, portending ever more severe consequences. Even though there were stop sticks across the parking lot exit, a car can continue to travel for an extended distance as its tires flatten—and that assumes the driver actually crossed the stop sticks in the first place and did not drive around them. A car can continue to move, albeit with difficulty, even on flattened tires. Passivity assumed that Garczynski eventually would submit without harming himself or others (he had a gun)—unwarranted under the circumstances—or that when he drives away, he will do so in a controlled and safe manner that does not imperil anybody else, also unreasonable given the suicidal state of mind ascribed to him. Secondarily, driving a car on flattened tires is by design not a safe and controllable endeavor. Flattening the tires simply makes driving the vehicle difficult and conducive to loss of control so that if the driver does not quickly stop of his own volition, he will lose control sooner or later and still come to a stop. The four officers on foot in the vicinity of the car could have been at risk of injury. Others on the perimeter or responding to the scene would have been at risk. Tactically, no helicopter was available so the only remaining option if Garczynski did not submit would have been some form of vehicle pursuit with its attendant risks and uncertainties to officers and the public. And if Garczynski somehow succeeded in eluding the police, he would have been at large again—either in the car or fleeing on foot if he abandoned the car—and this time fully aware of the police presence.

As it happened, when Lieutenant Hart heard the car start he immediately ordered, "don't let him leave"—a reasonable and necessary decision under the circumstances. In response to Hart's order, the four officers on foot approached the car. Two of them (MacLeod and Adams) moved to the front right quarter of the Garczynski car, using an adjacent parked car for some cover. The other two (Withrow and Goddard) moved to the right rear quarter of the Garczynski car, also using the adjacent parked car for cover. Both pairs were positioned on the passenger side of Garczynski's vehicle and at either end of it, avoiding a crossfire situation. They had positions with some cover that were close enough to manifest their presence, keep them away from the front of the vehicle, and enable them to attempt verbal communications.

The officers had their weapons out, given that they were approaching an individual with a gun. Deputy Withrow shined his flashlight into the car and saw Garczynski in the driver's seat with a cell phone in his left hand. MacLeod and Adams identified themselves and ordered Garczynski to put down his cell phone and show his hands but Garczynski did not respond or comply. None of the officers could see Garczynski's right hand. Deputy Withrow moved along the side of Garczynski's vehicle to break the front passenger window in order to give MacLeod and Adams a clear view inside the car. It took him several tries with his flashlight to actually break the window. When it finally broke he stepped back to break the right rear passenger side window to give himself and Goddard a clear view inside. This was compelled by the physical realities of the situation—windows fogged, visibility into the car inhibited, no idea where the gun was, and Garczynski ignoring the officers.

When the front passenger window broke, they immediately saw the gun in Garczynski's right hand held to his head. He turned as he moved the gun away from his head and pointed it at Adams and MacLeod, who began shooting at him. He continued to swing the gun to his right in the direction of Deputy Withrow's location at the rear side window. Deputy Withrow saw the gun aimed at him and he began shooting at Garczynski as he stepped back in reaction to seeing the gun pointed at him. In the process Deputy Withrow tripped and fell. Deputy Goddard saw him go down and, believing Withrow had been shot, also fired at Garczynski.

Each one of the officers recognized the situation was inherently risky. They were confronting a self-declared, potential suicide who was known to possess a gun, and who had substantiated his intent during his lengthy conversation with his estranged wife. Potential suicides are dangerous to others as well as themselves, and most particularly to the law enforcement officers seeking to engage them. Additionally, the widely recognized phenomenon of suicide by cop is a significant factor that cannot be dismissed from consideration in any confrontation between police and a demonstrably suicidal individual. People planning suicide can, and have, acted to provoke police into killing them.[84]

Law enforcement training recognizes that the suicidal individual is in fact an imminent threat of death or serious injury. Training and experience thus mandate that officers must be aware of the risk as they attempt to resolve the issue by lesser means—to the extent the suicidal individual gives them the time and opportunity to attempt lesser means. The ignorant and the ill-informed look on this as a paradox—police prepared to kill someone in order to stop them from killing themselves. The truth is that police will desperately try to stop the suicidal individual from harming himself, but cannot in the process let down their guard and permit that individual to harm them or others.

The tactics used by the officers attest to their recognition of the risk represented by Garczynski—they separated to reduce vulnerability; they used available cover; they continuously attempted to gain compliance; they were attempting lesser means of force by way of their presence, commands, and numbers—all prudent and reasonable tactics to attempt to dissuade an imminent suicidal act coupled with the urgent exigency of preventing Garczynski from driving away.

There was no uncertainty about Garczynski's intent. He had made that clear. The officers had to believe him. Neither was there any uncertainty whether he was armed. The uncertainty they faced was whether Garczynski would follow through on his expressed intent and act on it. Each officer individually recognized that Garczynski was a credible, imminent risk and each officer was reasonable in that perception under the circumstances.

The presence and degree of various danger signals in conjunction with the situational context of an expressed suicidal intent coupled with the officers' proximity to Garczynski and their inabilities to get compliance led to the reasonable perception of an imminent risk of death or serious injury. When Garczynski suddenly acted by turning his gun on the officers, their respective perceptions of an imminent risk of death or serious injury became more than reasonable—it became unmistakable. And suddenly the unavoidable imperative of reaction times made waiting unreasonable.[85]

---

84. See Chapter 9.
85. See Chapter 7.

At the moment Garczynski turned his gun on them, each of the four officers had to recognize and immediately react to the following critical question:

Did Garczynski pose an "imminent threat of death or serious injury" to one or any of the officers?

Each of the four officers clearly decided that question affirmatively and each one of them decided to use deadly force at once rather than await confirmation of the threat by delaying until Garczynski actually shot at them.

Lesser options had been attempted with Garczynski: persuasion via his wife, continuous verbal commands, and the uniform presence of four armed police officers — all of which were unsuccessful. Garczynski's actions did nothing to signal a possibility he would submit and comply. When that is coupled with his suicidal intent and the gun in his hand, his final action in turning and pointing that gun at the officers was consistent with the actions of someone aiming a weapon with the intent to use it. Each one of the officers individually chose not to wait to see if Garczynski would in fact shoot at them.

The Garczynski estate sued and the district court granted summary judgment as to the Estate's § 1983 claims of excessive and deadly force on grounds that the officers were entitled to qualified immunity. The court first concluded that Sergeant Sandt and Deputy Wildove did not violate Garczynski's constitutional rights by failing to convey to the Boca house officers that Garczynski was calm and started his car at his wife's instruction. Additionally, the court determined that the style and timing of the dynamic approach by Deputies Withrow, MacLeod, and Goddard did not violate Garczynski's constitutional rights. Next, the district court concluded that the officers' use of deadly force was objectively reasonable under the circumstances because *"the officers faced an imminent threat of danger when Garczynski failed to drop the gun as he was commanded to do and pointed it at them."* Because Garczynski's constitutional rights were not violated, the district court held that the Estate's § 1983 claims of deliberate indifference against Sheriff Bradshaw, acting in his official capacity, necessarily failed.[86] The Estate appealed the grant of summary judgment and the U.S. Court of Appeals for the Eleventh Circuit affirmed summary judgment, noting, *"Any claim that a law enforcement officer used excessive force— whether deadly or not—during a seizure of a free citizen must be analyzed under the Fourth Amendment's 'reasonableness' standard."*[87]

---

86. *Estate of John Garczynski v. Sheriff Ric L. Bradshaw, et al.*, USDC Southern District of Florida, Case No. 06-80943-CIV-KAM.

87. *Estate of John Garczynski v. Sheriff Ric L. Bradshaw, et al.*, 573 F.3d 1158 (11th Cir. 2009).

*"The Estate's central argument is that the officers had no reasonable objective basis for their dynamic approach and use of deadly force. The Estate emphasizes that Garczynski had no criminal record, was not breaking any laws, had never been violent, and had been calmly discussing reconciliation with his estranged wife at the time the officers confronted him. The Estate suggests that the officers should have allowed that conversation to continue as long as possible to defuse Garczynski's suicidal emotions. Additionally, the police could have waited for the ballistic shield or relied on the stop sticks. Instead, the officers rushed in with their guns drawn, shouted commands, and bashed in windows. There was no probable cause for this dynamic approach, according to the Estate, and the use of force was therefore excessive."*[88]

The Court pointed out,

*"Our task is not to evaluate what the officers could or should have done in hindsight. The sole inquiry is whether the officer's actions, as taken, were objectively reasonable under all the circumstances. In this case, they were. The situation facing the officers the night of 9 March 2005 was urgent and inherently dangerous: a man armed with a gun had written his own obituary for that very day and no one knew where to find him."*[89]

The Eleventh Circuit assessed the tactics used by the officers, their decisions to use force, and the circumstances within which they were acting:

*"The officers were not required to wait and see if Garczynski remained stationary, or rely on the stop sticks and surrounding police officers to deter him should he suddenly become mobile. 'We think the police need not have taken that chance and hoped for the best.'*

*Furthermore, the escalation into deadly force was justified by Garczynski's refusal to comply with the officers' commands. After identifying themselves, the officers repeatedly ordered Garczynski to show his hands. They also repeatedly commanded him to drop the phone and then, after he raised a gun to his head, to drop his gun. Instead of obeying these commands, Garczynski swung the gun from his head in the direction of the officers, at which point they fired. The officers reasonably reacted to what they perceived as an immediate threat of serious harm to themselves. This is exactly the type of 'tense, uncertain, and rapidly evolving' crisis envisioned by the Supreme Court. Graham, 490 U.S. at 397, 109*

---

88. *Ibid.*
89. *Ibid.*

*S. Ct. at 1872. Judged from the perspective of a reasonable officer on the scene, the officers' use of deadly force was objectively reasonable under the circumstances.*[90]

...

*Even if we assumed that Garczynski did not point his gun in the officers' direction, the fact that Garczynski did not comply with the officers' repeated commands to drop his gun justified the use of deadly force under these particular circumstances. [Montoute v. Carr, 114 F.3d at 185] ... At least where orders to drop the weapon have gone unheeded, an officer is not required to wait until an armed and dangerous felon has drawn a bead on the officer or others before using deadly force.*

...

*The officers could reasonably believe that the weapon was loaded, as it actually was, given Garczynski's expressed intent to commit suicide.... Garczynski repeatedly disobeyed the officers' orders, first to show his hands and then to drop his gun. These factors, even assuming that Garczynski never pointed the gun at the officers, provided a sufficient basis for the officers reasonably to believe that Garczynski posed an immediate risk of serious harm to them."*[91]

## *Kristi Cookson v. City of Lewiston, et al.*[92]

On December 1, 2009, Officer Raymond Vega, Lewiston (Maine) Police Department (LPD), was patrolling in a marked LPD police cruiser. He noticed a pickup truck stopped ahead of him at an intersection. The truck remained stopped in place for an extended period of time despite the lack of any traffic on the crossing street. Officer Vega checked the registration and determined the truck was one he had stopped previously at which time he had arrested the driver Kristi Cookson for operating under the influence.

The truck suddenly moved, turning right with no signal. Officer Vega followed. The driver of the truck made another right hand turn without signaling, this time driving up over the adjacent curb in the process. Officer Vega decided to initiate a traffic stop and turned on the emergency lights of his cruiser. The driver of the pickup truck (later identified as Kristi Cookson) did not stop. Officer Vega honked his horn, shined his spotlight on Cookson, and activated

---

90. *Ibid.*

91. *Ibid.*

92. *Kristi Cookson v. City of Lewiston, et al.*, USDC, District of Maine, Case No: 2:11-cv-00460-DBH.

his siren. Cookson accelerated and Officer Vega pursued, reporting the pursuit to LPD dispatch.

Cookson drove at high speed through several residential and downtown streets, veered around a construction site and up on the sidewalk. She sped through five separate stop signs and one red light without slowing. She drove against traffic on a one-way street. She reached speeds up to 80 mph and was pulling away from Officer Vega when she failed to negotiate a right hand curve and skidded off the road into a small parking lot beside an apartment house there. Cookson crashed into a parked vehicle with sufficient force to push that vehicle over 15 feet sideways into the side of a second parked vehicle and in turn impel that second parked vehicle into a third one. Cookson's pickup truck came to rest with its front end lodged in the driver's side of the first parked vehicle.[93]

Officer Vega pulled alongside the Cookson vehicle and got out of his cruiser. As he did so, Cookson attempted to dislodge her vehicle and back away from the crash, shifting gears and revving her engine. Office Vega ran to the driver's side of the Cookson vehicle and ordered her to stop, pointing his handgun at her. He recognized Cookson from his previous arrest of her for operating under the influence. Cookson looked directly at him but ignored his commands and continued her efforts to dislodge the truck, gunning the engine, rocking the truck forwards and backwards by shifting repeatedly from forward to reverse, turning the steering wheel left and right as she did so. Officer Vega saw her tires spinning and digging into the grass. He banged on the closed drivers side window with his hand, ordering Cookson to stop. He noticed that another LPD officer, Keith Caouette, had arrived on the scene and was on foot at the rear of the Cookson pickup.

Officer Caouette had joined the pursuit earlier. He got out of his cruiser at the crash site and ran past the rear of the Cookson vehicle to join Officer Vega on the driver's side, drawing his weapon in the process. His intention was to eliminate any possibility of a crossfire situation. As he went around the rear of the pickup, it began moving in reverse. He heard Officer Vega yelling commands, and he heard gunshots that he believed were from Vega.

Cookson had dislodged her pickup from its entanglement with the wreckage of the car it had hit and she began backing away. Officer Vega fired two shots into the left front tire in an unsuccessful attempt to disable the vehicle.

---

93. Crash reconstruction revealed that Cookson's pickup skidded 140 feet off the road, across a lawn, and into the parking lot before impacting the first parked vehicle. It revealed that she was traveling at 81 mph at a point five seconds before impact. The brakes were engaged and the speed one second before impact was 30 mph.

Cookson cleared the parked vehicle and sped in reverse in the direction that Officer Vega had last seen Officer Caouette on foot. Vega moved to a position in front of the Cookson vehicle and fired one shot at her. He heard other gunshots, and he fired two more shots at Cookson without noticeable effect.

Meanwhile, Officer Caouette had moved to the left front quarter of Cookson's vehicle off Officer Vega's right side when he saw the truck suddenly lurch forward in their direction and he fired at the vehicle. He heard Officer Vega shooting as well. The two officers were between the truck and the apartment building and that restricted their movements. Cookson reversed direction again.

She accelerated in reverse across the adjacent yard and driveway then over a small shoulder bordering the driveway until she hit a stand of trees halting her backwards movement. Office Vega holstered his weapon and ran to the driver's side of the pickup. Officer Caouette initially ran towards his cruiser because he thought the pursuit was about to resume since she had broken free of the wreckage in the parking lot. When he saw that Cookson was stuck against the trees he ran to Officer Vega's side.

The driver's side window was shattered. Officer Vega ordered Cookson to get out of the pickup, but she ignored him, revving the engine and trying to drive away. The tires of the pickup were digging into the ground, throwing up dirt and grass. As she continued her efforts to drive away, Officer Vega attempted to open the driver's side door. It was locked so he reached through the shattered window and grabbed Cookson in an attempt to remove her from the vehicle and stop her attempts to drive away. She physically resisted him so Officer Caouette Tasered her and she was subdued. She was removed from the pickup truck, handcuffed, and arrested, during which time the officers discovered that she had a single gunshot wound to the neck. First aid was rendered and she was transported to a local hospital where she was treated and released.

### Discussion

As events unfolded, Cookson relentlessly defied the police officers trying to stop her over the course of her flight. She drove through multiple stop signs and a red traffic light and sped the wrong way down a one-way street. She was heedless to the endangerment of other motorists, pedestrians, and passersby.

Even after she lost control of her vehicle and crashed, she was undeterred in her determination to get away, gunning her engine and rocking her vehicle back and forth to break loose and escape, despite the presence of uniformed police officers at her window ordering her to stop. She never took her foot off the gas or made any attempt to stop. She never turned off her vehicle's engine—in fact it was still on and in gear after she had been removed from it. She was so desperate to get away that she spun her tires several inches deep into the ground where her truck was stuck.

Cookson's response to a uniformed law enforcement officer on foot giving her loud clear commands at gunpoint was to repeatedly shift gears, gun her engine, and yank her steering wheel back and forth in a continuous attempt to break free and escape, endangering the officers on foot and in close proximity with vehicle. Cookson did not stop or comply despite being shot at and wounded in the neck. At the end, she had shifted into drive, kept her foot on the gas, and was spinning her wheels against the trees to her rear even as Officer Vega was grappling with her through the window to make her stop.

Cookson could have chosen to comply at any point during the long lasting incident but did not. She could have simply pulled over at the start—but did not. She was unrelenting in trying to escape in her vehicle. She created a severe and unmistakable risk of imminent danger to everyone in her vicinity—police officers and citizens alike. Cookson did nothing consistent with any intention to surrender or quit or to mitigate the hazard to others that her actions created. To the contrary, she sustained and extended her actions, elevating the risk of death or serious injury to the officers chasing her and all others in her proximity. She ran stop signs and a red light, she drove over sidewalks and a lawn, she drove against the flow of a one-way street—and she did it at speeds in excess of 80 mph. It was only by the stroke of sheer good fortune that no one was injured by her reckless high-speed flight through the streets of Lewiston.[94]

At the crash site, when Officer Vega saw Cookson's vehicle begin to dislodge from the wreckage and move backwards, that is when he fired two shots into the front left tire of Cookson's vehicle in an attempt to disable it. Notably, police officers are trained that shooting at a vehicle's tires will not disable the vehicle. Shooting at a vehicle cannot stop the vehicle in sufficient time to prevent injury—actual or imminent. It is a physical impossibility with small arms projectiles. Nevertheless, Officer Vega made the attempt in an effort to end the threat posed by Cookson's operation of the vehicle without using force against Cookson herself. Predictably, it did not work. (See Chapter 8.)

---

94. The driver of the first parked car that Cookson hit at the apartment building had left her car only seconds before the crash. Had she been in or beside her car, she could not have avoided serious injury or death. This is but one instance illustrative of the severe danger of harm that Cookson's behavior imposed upon others during her heedlessly reckless attempts to flee Officer Vega.

Cookson broke free of the entanglement with the parked car she had hit and accelerated to the rear despite Officer Vega shooting out her front left tire. Office Vega recognized the danger that now threatened Officer Carouette, whose location he had last noticed was to behind her vehicle. He stepped in line with her as she backed away and now shot at her, the driver.

Although Officer Vega did not have to gamble on the situation becoming more dangerous by waiting to see if Cookson could succeed in driving in reverse, he *did exactly that* when he tried to disable the vehicle by shooting the front tire. When that did not work and Cookson's operation of the truck directly endangered Officer Carouette he also did not have to wait to see if she would actually hit Carouette.

Police officers involved in shooting incidents are typically unaware whether their shots have actually struck their target until the incident has ended. Thus police training in the use of deadly force teaches that an officer may shoot to prevent an imminent risk of serious injury, and an officer should continue to shoot until the officer perceives that the risk has ended. That reality is illustrated in this incident—Cookson was shot at 6 times and struck once in the neck and that did not stop or alter her behavior. Neither officer was even aware that she had been hit until they removed her from the truck and observed the wound to her neck.

As Cookson ignored him and drove her truck in reverse, Officer Vega shot at her three times. He believed that Cookson could and would hit Officer Carouette to her rear. As it happened, none of his shots struck her. In the meantime, Officer Caouette had moved alongside Officer Vega. The close quarters between the Cookson vehicle and the apartment house behind them restricted the officers' ability to move. He heard Vega's shots, and when he saw the pickup truck lurch in their direction as Cookson continued to try to break away, he fired three shots at her in his own attempt to stop her from endangering them with her truck. It did not work.

Of note is that, with the exception of the two shots Officer Vega intentionally fired into her front tire, both officers fired to stop the actions of the driver, the actual threat of harm by means of her operation of the vehicle, and not at the vehicle to disable it. That is consistent with training and with ballistic realities. A vehicle cannot be mechanically disabled with a bullet in a timely enough fashion to prevent imminent injury, as Officer Vega's initial attempt to disable Cookson's vehicle demonstrated.

As an aside, the use of a Taser by Officer Caouette is what finally incapacitated Cookson long enough for the officers to restrain her. The effects of the Taser temporarily incapacitated her so that the officers could remove her from her vehicle and handcuff her, ending her resistance and the incident. Although the Taser was effective, this point in the incident was the first and only moment in which it could have been utilized.

Officers are trained that the level of force reasonably necessary in any confrontation will rise and fall as the dynamics of the incident change and evolve over time and circumstance. Prior to this moment, the only option the officers had with which to stop her aggressive and dangerous operation of the truck was shooting at her. The urgency of protecting themselves dictated the necessity of using deadly force to stop her. However, once she was stuck against the trees with the officers beside her and her window broken out, an opportunity to use lesser force was created. Although there was a risk her tires could suddenly gain traction and she could accelerate away at any moment, the officers did not continue using deadly force. Officer Vega attempted to physically subdue her—and she aggressively resisted his efforts—while Officer Caouette recognized the opportunity (proximity and open window) to employ his Taser. That enabled the officers to end the incident without further injury to Cookson, or increased likelihood of injury to their selves.

> "*The use of deadly force is reasonable when a suspect 'poses a significant threat of death or serious physical injury' to the officers involved. Tennessee v. Garner, 471 U.S. 1, 3 (1985). Here, the plaintiff argues that the officers used deadly force three times: when Vega fired into the tire of her truck, when Vega and Caouette shot at her, and when Caouette shot her with his Taser.*
>
> *With respect to the shooting of the tire, case law establishes that, independent of the question of whether such activity constitutes the use of deadly force, no seizure has taken place when the shots are fired in an unsuccessful attempt to stop a vehicle, so no Fourth Amendment claim will lie.*[95]
>
> ...
>
> *Nor does the use of a Taser constitute the use of deadly force.... Thus, only the shot which hit the plaintiff need be considered under the standard applicable to the use of deadly force.*[96]
>
> *The use of the Taser does not present a close question, on the facts submitted. The plaintiff had refused to comply with the officers' orders to stop, crashed into a parked vehicle in an apartment complex's parking lot, backed out of the debris of that crash and lurched backward while Caouette was behind the vehicle, drove in reverse across the lawn and driveway of the apartment building and crashed into some trees at the*

---

95. *Kristi Cookson v. City of Lewiston, et al.*, U.S. District Court, District of Maine Case No: 2:11-cv-00460-DBH, page 15.

96. *Ibid.* page 17. Citations removed.

*top of an embankment, then continued to spin the tires and rev the engine until Vega reached in through the broken driver's side window, whereupon she physically resisted his efforts, pulling away from him and kicking at him. At the time the Taser was fired, the plaintiff posed a threat to the safety of the officers, and to the public, should she have succeeded in repulsing the officers and again been able to drive away. She was certainly attempting to evade arrest and to continue her flight from the officers.* All of the Cote factors [here the Court is referring to the factors cited in *Graham v. Connor* quoted in the cited case[97]] *are met in a manner that can only lead to the conclusion that the firing of the Taser was reasonable under the circumstances.*

*That leaves the firing of the officers' weapons. The first and third Cote factors remain the same: the crime at issue was or could have been a felony,*[98] *and the plaintiff was attempting to evade arrest and continue her flight. The deadly force standard applies here: did the plaintiff's actions at the time the shots were fired 'pose a significant threat of death or serious physical injury?' At the time the officers fired at Plaintiff, her vehicle was in motion and the officers believed they were in danger of being run over or pinned against one of the nearby structures by Plaintiff.*
*An officer who reasonably believed that a suspect might run over him or another officer with the suspect's vehicle is justified in using deadly force. While the reasonableness of the use of deadly force is a fact-specific inquiry, on the undisputed facts in the summary judgment record, and with consideration of paragraphs 2 and 3 of the plaintiff's statement of material facts, and given the Supreme Court's admonition to avoid second-guessing the split-second decisions of law enforcement officers, no rea-*

---

97. " ... three factors are relevant to determine the reasonableness of the force: (1) 'the severity of the crime at issue'; (2) 'whether the suspect poses an immediate threat to the safety of the officers or others'; and (3) 'whether he is actively resisting arrest or attempting to evade arrest by flight.' " *Ibid.* pages 13–14. Citations removed.

98. The Court's footnote [#3 in the text] reads "With respect to the seriousness of the offense, the First Circuit said ... that '[t]hough driving while intoxicated is a serious offense, it does not present a risk of danger to the arresting officer that is presented when an officer confronts a suspect engaged in an offense like robbery or assault.' The First Circuit found it significant for the purpose of evaluating the first *Cote* element that the suspect 'complied with [the officer's] requests and exited the vehicle voluntarily,' so that he no longer posed the threat of driving while intoxicated. The latter facts distinguish this case..., but even if [it were not so] were to require this court to construe the first element of the test in the plaintiff's favor, the second and third factors favor the defendants." *Ibid.* page 21. Citations removed.

*sonable jury could conclude that the officers' discharge of their weapons under the circumstances of this case was unreasonable."*[99]

Summary judgment was granted.

## *Labensky, et al. v. Cornwell*[100]

On May 5, 2008, a BP gas station in Dayton, Ohio, was robbed. A short time later at about 11:10 p.m., a Rite Aid drugstore was also robbed. Based on surveillance camera photos, descriptions, and victim interviews, the Montgomery County Sheriff's Office (MCSO) determined that the same individual committed both robberies. MCSO Deputy Joshua Walters responded to the Rite Aid robbery and a K-9 unit briefly tracked the suspect fleeing the Rite Aid robbery.

Shortly after midnight Deputy Walters saw a silver Pontiac Grand Am at a stop sign at an intersection in the same area to which the K-9 unit had tracked the robbery suspect. Deputy Walters used his spotlight to look at the driver of the Pontiac and identified him as the robbery suspect. The driver (later identified as Larry R. Labensky) ducked to avoid the spotlight and accelerated away. Deputy Walters advised MCSO dispatch as he initiated pursuit, using his emergency lights and siren.

Labensky did not stop. He continued south on Salem Avenue until he lost control of his vehicle and left the roadway at the intersection with Gotham Avenue. He came to a stop in the yard of the residence on Gotham Avenue. Deputy Walters approached on foot and ordered Labensky at gunpoint to show his hands. Labensky ducked inside the car, backed out of the yard, and accelerated away. Deputy Walters returned to his cruiser and resumed the pursuit. The pursuit went east on Gotham, north on Falmouth, east on Detroit, north on Madison, west on Michigan, then north on Monroe, where Labensky drove through the side and backyards of a residence on Monroe Avenue to get across to the parallel street, Otis Drive. He continued to flee on Otis. Deputy Walters lost sight of him by this point but other units spotted Labensky when he turned off Otis Drive onto Williamson Drive.

Labensky turned off Williamson Drive into the side yard of a residence. He hit the corner of the house as he passed into the backyard. He drove diagonally across the backyard then veered to his right and crashed through a 6-ft tall wooden privacy fence into the backyard of a residence on Saylor. Saylor parallels Williamson Drive and Labensky was duplicating his previous tactic of driving across lawns

---

99. *Ibid.* pages 22–23. Citations removed.

100. *Labensky, et al. v. Cornwell*, USDC, Southern District of Ohio, Western Division, Case No: 08-CV-42.

and yards to access the parallel street. After he drove through the fence he turned right and drove across the backyard of the residence, running over the back steps of the garage and assorted children's toys on the ground. He drove into a 6' tall wooden privacy fence and its parallel chain-link fence separating that residence from its neighbor. The only reason he did not successfully crash through the fences was that this residence had a garage situated immediately behind the fence at the spot that Labensky hit. Apparently, when he couldn't get through the fence, he floored his accelerator, attempting to force his way through the fence only to succeed in digging his front tires deep into the ground.

The pursuit and its series of events was broadcast by MCSO dispatch and monitored as well by Dayton Police Department (DPD) officers. DPD Officer Christopher Cornwell responded to the area of the pursuit to assist. He was driving south on Williamson with his emergency lights on when he saw Labensky's vehicle coming towards him, followed by several cruisers with their emergency lights and sirens activated. Labensky veered across Cornwell's path to his (Labensky's) right (east) into the yard of the residence on the south side of Williamson (see above). Officer Cornwell got out of his vehicle and ran up the driveway on foot. As he got to the rear corner of the residence, he saw the Labensky Pontiac driving across the backyard. He lost sight of it behind a large shed to his front left.

Officer Cornwell ran around the shed in the direction the Pontiac had gone. He heard crashing sounds as the car drove through the 6' tall wooden privacy fence between that residence on Williamson and the one behind it on Saylor. He saw the tail lights as Labensky turned right on the far side of the fence, driving across the backyard of the Saylor residence. Officer Cornwell ran after the Pontiac, thinking the car would continue to crash through fences and across yards until the driver got back to the street, and he wanted to be able to broadcast the direction the Pontiac went in order to facilitate the pursuit.

However, as Officer Cornwell ran over the debris of the fence left in the Pontiac's wake, he saw the car run up against the 6' tall wooden privacy fence on the other side of the backyard of the Saylor residence. The engine was racing at high revs, consistent with the accelerator being floored. Dirt and mud were being thrown all over by the tires of the Pontiac as they spun uncontrollably in place. Officer Cornwell drew his handgun and approached the car from the driver's side. He was aware of other officers (MCSO deputies and DPD officers) approaching on foot along the car's track to his (Cornwell's) right rear.

Officer Cornwell stood about 10 feet from the driver's side of the Pontiac with his flashlight in his left hand and his firearm in his right. The driver's side window was open. He illuminated the driver with the flashlight as he yelled orders to stop. And he warned that he would shoot.

The driver (Labensky) never acknowledged Officer Cornwell's presence. He never looked at Officer Cornwell, and he never eased off on the accelerator. Officer Cornwell said that the tires never stopped spinning, the engine never stopped racing at full speed. Despite his repeated orders, Officer Cornwell saw the driver move his right hand from the steering wheel to the gearshift lever. He thought that he saw the car move backwards. He knew other officers were behind the car and he began shooting at the driver, backing away from the car as he did so. He fired five shots.

After he fired, Officer Cornwell saw the car go forward, engine racing and tires spinning, dirt and debris still being thrown up by the tires. The tires began to burn and throw off pieces of tread from the friction with the ground. Labensky continued to move around inside the car for a few seconds before he reclined his head against the headrest. The engine continued to race and the tires continued to spin. Smoke from the burning tires enveloped the interior of the car and Officer Cornwell lost sight of Labensky. The car continued to run at high speed until officers turned off the ignition.

Labensky was hit by all five shots fired by Cornwell and died from his wounds.

## Discussion

As events unfolded, Labensky recklessly and continuously defied all of the police officers trying to stop him over the course of his vehicular flight. He aggressively and recklessly attempted to evade and elude the officers pursuing him prior to ending up in the backyard of 4237 Saylor. Labensky fled when Deputy Walters merely shined his spotlight on him. He drove through residential neighborhoods recklessly, losing control of his car and ending up in a residential front yard. Deputy Walters approached him on foot, gun in hand, ordering him to stop but Labensky ignored him and accelerated away in reverse. He willfully drove through residential yards in the dark attempting to escape the police, with reckless disregard for the safety of anybody who might be present in those yards. He sideswiped one house in the process. He crashed through fences totally unaware of who or what might be on the other side, and clearly unconcerned about the possibility of hitting someone with his car. The fences prevented any possibility that Labensky could see who or what might be on the other side. Labensky drove through them anyway. He knocked down a children's playhouse behind 4237 Saylor as he crashed through the fence. He ran over children's toys. He made a determined and aggressive, but unsuccessful, attempt to crash through the south side fence. He kept his accelerator floored in his desperate flight, and ultimately spun his tires into the ground and burned away the tread as he was unable to break through the fence and garage of the adjacent residence.

Once rammed up against the fence, Labensky never turned off his car's engine. He never took his foot off the gas. His reaction to a uniformed law enforcement officer on foot giving him loud clear commands at gunpoint was to engage reverse gear and attempt to back away, recklessly using his car as a weapon endangering the officers in close proximity to his rear. Labensky did not stop or comply despite being shot. He shifted into drive, kept his foot on the gas and again spun his wheels against the fence to his front even as he was dying from his wounds.

Labensky could have chosen to comply at any point during the extensive pursuit but did not. He continuously resisted, using his car as an instrument of assault and escape. His actions created an unmistakable imminent danger to everyone in the vicinity of his car—police officers and citizens alike. Labensky had done nothing to indicate any intention to surrender or quit his resistance. To the contrary, his sustained and reckless flight served to elevate the risk of death or serious injury to the officers in his proximity and to any innocent bystanders in the area.

Labensky had been aggressively noncompliant throughout the incident. He had made repeated use of his car as a weapon. Officer Cornwell had witnessed Labensky's reckless driving through yards and blind fences. And he saw Labensky reversing direction despite the close presence of officers behind him, despite Officer Cornwell's unmistakable presence ten feet way, and in defiance of Officer Cornwell's loud and clear commands. If Labensky suddenly gained traction and shot to the rear, the officers behind him could be run over. And if he did gain traction and shot to the rear, it would be impossible for Officer Cornwell to then stop him or the car at all.

Law enforcement officers do not have to gamble life or physical safety on sheer chance. Officer Cornwell did not have to gamble with the lives of the other officers by waiting to see if Labensky could succeed in driving in reverse—or waiting to see if he actually hit one of them. There are also the physical realities of wound ballistics that dictate that even if an officer succeeds in shooting an attacker, it is no guarantee that the attack will be stopped before it causes injury or death.[101] An attacker using a car can still change gears, accelerate, and steer, as Labensky notably did for several seconds despite having been shot five times.

There is nothing in law enforcement training or practice that would suggest or require that Officer Cornwell should have waited to see what Labensky would do next, or to assume that he could not "unstick" his car. Labensky chose to act as he did, endangering everybody in his vicinity in defiance of the verbal commands and manifest visual presences directed at him throughout

---

101. See Chapter 5.

his flight. He ignored uniformed, armed officers pointing guns at him (Walters and Cornwell). He ignored increasing numbers of marked cruisers pursuing him with lights and sirens activated. He willfully endangered all who might happen to be in his way as he veered across residential yards and crashed through blind fences. Officer Cornwell did not have the luxuries of time or containment affording him the option of safely waiting to see what happened next. Labensky's behavior throughout was heedless of harm to others. He never did anything to diminish that perception of risk.

Labensky continued to ignore him and put his car in reverse. Officer Cornwell recognized the ongoing danger and he shot him.[102] He believed that Labensky could and would endanger him and others with the car if he succeeded in getting it moving again. The only means he had at hand that could effectively stop or pre-empt the danger in time was his weapon. Notably Officer Cornwell fired to stop the actions of the driver, the source of the threat, and not at the car to disable it. A car cannot be mechanically disabled with a bullet in a timely or effective fashion.

Law enforcement training and policies recognize that a vehicle can be operated in a manner to threaten imminent risk of death or serious injury, and that there is no reasonable way to disable a moving vehicle with a firearm. For example, in the DOJ Commentary provided to facilitate understanding and implementation of the DOJ Uniform Policy on the Use of Deadly Force, the DOJ specifically states: " ... Shooting to disable a moving motor vehicle is forbidden ... An officer who has reason to believe that a driver or occupant poses an imminent danger of death or serious physical injury to the officer or others may fire at the driver or an occupant only when such shots are necessary to avoid death or serious physical injury to the officer or another, and only if the public safety benefits of using such force reasonably appear to outweigh any risks to the officer or the public, such as from a crash, ricocheting bullets, or return fire from the subject or another person."[103]

---

102. It is not exceptional for an officer armed with a semi-automatic weapon to be able to fire numerous shots in the space of a second or less. Concurrently, it is not exceptional for someone being shot—even multiple times—to take several seconds or even minutes to exhibit the effects of the wounds. Thus DPD officers are properly trained to keep shooting until they perceive that the threat has ended. They can and do end up shooting dangerous people multiple times because it takes time for wounds to take effect—seconds, sometimes minutes. During that interval between beginning to shoot and wounds taking effect, it is not exceptional for a trained officer to fire numerous shots. In this case, Officer Cornwell fired five shots in less than a second as he stepped back.

103. U.S. Department of Justice Commentary Regarding the Use of Deadly Force in Non-Custodial Situations; Section IV, subsection: Motor Vehicles and their Occupants.

As an aside, this shooting incident involving Labensky is exactly the "public safety benefit" envisioned in the DOJ commentary, i.e., the other officers were in the path of a vehicle being operated in an imminently dangerous and threatening manner and their close proximity made any attempts at avoidance or eluding the threat unreasonable. Law enforcement officers are trained that this is the type of circumstance in which employing deadly force against the driver is reasonable, as opposed to a passing vehicle, or a vehicle some distance away, or one on the other side of an obstacle.

Events were driven by Labensky's choices and actions. Labensky chose to resist and to flee. He chose to drive recklessly and with total disregard for the safety of others. His choices created an imminent and continuous danger of death or serious injury to officers and bystanders. He chose to ignore Officer Cornwell and to try to accelerate away yet again, in disregard of the risk to others around him, putting Officer Cornwell in the circumstance where he decided he could not wait any longer to see what happened. He decided he had to act to stop Labensky. Finally, Labensky never chose to submit, the one act that would have immediately ended this situation without incident and without injury.

The District Court cited *Graham v. Connor*:

> "*In determining whether a particular use of force was excessive, the Court must examine three factors: (1) the severity of the crime at issue; (2) whether the suspect posed an immediate threat to the safety of the police officers or others; and (3) whether the suspect actively resisted arrest or attempted to evade arrest by flight. Given this non-exhaustive list of factors, the ultimate question is 'whether the totality of the circumstances justifies a particular sort of seizure.'*"[104]

The Court noted (citations omitted):

> "*To use force, actual danger need not threaten the officer or other officers; an officer need only have a reasonable perception of danger.*
> [ ... ]
> *An officer need not see a weapon to presume that a suspect may be reaching for or attempting to use a weapon ... (Sixth Circuit); the Fifth Circuit considered the absence of a gun to be 'irrelevant,' because all that matters is whether an officer has a reasonable belief a dangerous weapon is in the possession of a suspect and that the suspect may use it.*"[105]

---

104. *Harold G. Labensky, Administrator of the Estate v. Cornwell*; USDC, Southern District of Ohio, Western Division at Dayton (Case No. 3:08-CV-429) *Entry and Order Granting Defendant Christopher Cornwell's Motion for Summary Judgment*, 9/1/10, page 7.

105. *Ibid*, pages 7–8.

The Court determined that Labensky's Fourth Amendment right was not violated, and granted Cornwell's motion for summary judgment.

> "*Turning toward the instant case, of the three explicit factors for determining whether lethal force is justified, the first and third factors are undisputed. Neither party disputes the fact that the officers were pursuing a suspected felon. Neither party disputes the fact that the decedent was actively attempting to evade arrest by flight, even up to the moment he was shot. The second* Graham *factor and the only disputed factor relevant here is whether the officer reasonably believed that the decedent posed an immediate threat to the safety of the officers or others. Defendant argues that because the car began moving backwards toward other officers who were approaching from behind, his use of force was justified. Plaintiff counters that decedent could not have shifted his vehicle into reverse and, as such, posed no immediate threat to the officers.*
>
> *Plaintiff has produced several experts, who concluded that was there no evidence suggesting that the vehicle had attempted to move backwards[106] and that putting the car in reverse was impossible if the engine was running. Because the Court must take all inferences in the light most favorable to the Plaintiff, for the purposes of summary judgment, the Court assumes decedent never put the vehicle in reverse.*
>
> *Assuming decedent did not put the car in reverse, the Court must nonetheless examine the reasonableness of the situation 'from the perspective of a reasonable officer on the scene, rather than with the 20/20 vision of hindsight.' Plaintiff erroneously relies on* Green *in his assertion that Defendant acted unreasonably in his application of force. While the facts may seem similar at first glance, the outcome rests on several factors for which the situations differ.*
>
> [ ... ]
>
> *Plaintiff has not produced any evidence which directly contradicts Cornwell's testimony that he 'saw his right hand move from the steering wheel down' and believed that 'the vehicle and driver posed an immediate threat.'... it is not enough in the Sixth Circuit for a party to cast circumstantial doubt on one set of facts. A party must present direct evidence such as witness testimony that creates two distinct sets of facts. Plaintiff's*

---

106. In a footnote on page 12, the Court notes " ... Plaintiff states that the evidence shows that 'decedent's vehicle was not moving backward at any point.'" The actual testimony is that "none of the photographs demonstrate any evidence that the car was in reverse."

*experts do not contradict the reasonableness of Defendant's interpreta-
tion of the potential danger.* [ … ]

    *Plaintiff's insistence on the importance of the stuck tires, and the im-
possibility of the decedent shifting the vehicle into reverse has little bearing on the primary inquiry: Was Defendant reasonable in believing that
decedent posed a serious threat? Assuming everything Plaintiff claims is
factually true, it is only through hindsight that Defendant's actions can
appear unreasonable.*

    *Given the totality of the circumstances, including the failure of dece-
dent to comply with the commands of police officers who reasonably suspected him to be a felon, the recklessness of decedent in his repeated attempts
to escape, and the officer's reasonable belief that decedent was imminently
putting other officers' lives in danger, Defendant did not violate decedent's
Fourth Amendment right through use of deadly force. Having led police on
a chase, having once resumed that chase after crashing, and having crashed
again, Plaintiff needed to keep his hands on the driver's wheel, or raise them
in the air. Instead, Plaintiff chose a different course of action, which was
reasonably perceived as a threat to others.*" [Citations omitted.][107]

## *Michael Tranter v. Officer Greg Orick, et al.*[108]

In the early morning hours of April 2, 2007, Dayton (Ohio) Police Department (DPD) Officer Greg Orick was dispatched to several disturbance calls
reporting people fighting and shots fired on Basswood Street. The dispatch
advised that two black males were involved—one with "puffy" braids wearing
a white t-shirt and another with braids wearing a white jersey with the number "32" on it.

Officer Orick parked his cruiser on the street adjacent to and paralleling
Basswood. He walked up a small alleyway to the front of a house on Basswood,
standing at the front corner where he was partially concealed by shrubbery
and the structure of the house. He had a clear field of view down Basswood and
the intersection of Basswood and Theodore.

The first activity he noticed was a black male wearing a white t-shirt who
was constantly peeking out from behind the drapes in the front window of a
ground floor apartment in the apartment building diagonally across Basswood
east of his location. Then he saw a second black male wearing a red t-shirt who

---

107. *Ibid*, pages 12–14

108. *Michael Tranter v. Officer Greg Orick, et al.*, USDC, Southern District of Ohio,
Western Division, Case No: 09-CV-125.

appeared to his right (Orick's) walking east on Basswood. This individual entered the apartment building and was let into apartment #1.

Then Officer Orick observed a third black male walking on Basswood west of its intersection with Theodore. This individual (Antonio R. Foreman) was wearing a white jersey with the number "32" on the front. He passed the intersection, still on Basswood, and stopped, standing still. As he did so, the black male in the white t-shirt who had been looking out of the apartment window (Nolan Hunter) walked out of the apartment building and stood on the front stoop. Foreman raised his arms in the air and Hunter said, "I'm gonna smoke your ass." Foreman said, "Do what you gotta do" at which point Hunter raised his right arm and fired a shot in the air.

Officer Orick saw and heard the exchange between the two men and the gunshot that Hunter fired into the air. Foreman walked down the middle of the street until he stood directly in front of the apartment building. Hunter left the front stoop and walked 25–30 feet towards Foreman, standing in the grass just off of the sidewalk. The unknown black male in the red t-shirt also came out and stood several feet to Hunter's left. A black female was yelling for them to get back inside.

Hunter and Foreman were yelling at each other and Officer Orick could not distinguish what they were saying. He was using his radio to broadcast the shot fired and to request backup when suddenly Hunter raised his right hand and fired a second shot, this time shooting at Foreman. Before Orick could react, Hunter raised his right hand again and fired another shot at Foreman. As Hunter raised his right hand a third time, pointing his gun at Foreman, Officer Orick dropped his microphone, drew his service weapon, and fired one shot at Hunter from his concealed position about 50 yards away. That shot hit Hunter in the neck and traversed into his chest.

Officer Orick saw Hunter stagger, spin away from Foreman, and fall to the ground. He notified dispatch that he had shot Hunter and backup was needed. Meanwhile, Hunter regained his feet and ran hunched over into the apartment building and into apartment #1. He died from his wound. His gun was recovered outside where he had dropped it in the grass.

## Discussion

The best use of justified deadly force is preemptive. That means that it is timely enough, and effective enough, to prevent an *imminent* risk of serious injury (about to happen) from becoming an *actual* attempt to cause serious injury (in fact happening). Often, the decision to use deadly force is not timely enough to be preemptive (for any number of reasons such as hesitation, the action/reaction cycle, sudden encounter with an ongoing attack, etc.). Then the justified use of deadly force can only be preventive in nature—intended to stop the ongoing attempt to cause injury, or the real infliction of injury, from continuing. In this case, however, the risk of serious injury was not imminent—it was overt and ongoing. Hunter was trying to shoot Foreman.

Officer Orick watched Hunter and Foreman yelling at each other. He saw Hunter fire one shot in the air, so he knew Hunter was armed with a gun. He saw Hunter suddenly fire two more shots aimed at Foreman before he could do anything to intervene. There was no uncertainty about Hunter's intentions or the gravity of the risk to Foreman. The risk of death or serious injury to Foreman was not imminent—it was occurring and obvious. When Hunter raised his gun hand one more time, Officer Orick immediately responded by drawing his own weapon and firing at Hunter to stop him.

There was no uncertainty in Officer Orick's mind as to Hunter's intent or the threat he posed. Hunter's actions were unmistakable. He had fired two shots directly at Foreman and was in the process of firing a third shot at him. Officer Orick reacted by drawing his weapon and firing one shot.

Officer Orick could have chosen to use a verbal warning first before using his firearm, but that would have been unreasonable under the circumstances. It was also unnecessary. He was 50 yards away from Hunter and if he had tried to yell a warning he would have gambled with Foreman's safety in the hope that Hunter would miss him with that impending third shot, as well as the hope that he would not shoot again after that. Hunter was actively engaged in shooting at Foreman again—the shot would have been fired by the time he could have heard any warning from Officer Orick. No law enforcement officer is trained or expected to passively allow the continuation of an unmistakable, ongoing attack while the officer yells verbal warnings in the hope of being both heard *and* obeyed.

A police officer cannot see the future or read minds. The officer can only react to what the suspect does, and what that action reasonably portends.[109] There

---

109. The necessity for an officer to make nearly instantaneous decisions in order to best protect his life or the life of others under urgent, dire, and extremely stressful conditions is accepted and well recognized throughout law enforcement practice, training, and policy. For example: "Determining whether deadly force is necessary may involve instantaneous decisions that encompass many factors, such as the likelihood that the subject will use deadly force on the officer or others if such force is not used by the officer; the officer's knowledge that the subject will likely acquiesce in arrest or recapture if the officer uses lesser force or no force at all; the capabilities of the subject; the subject's access to cover and weapons; the presence of other persons who may be at risk if force is or is not used; and the nature and the severity of the subject's criminal conduct or the danger posed."
U.S. Department of Justice Commentary Regarding the Use of Deadly Force in Non-Custodial Situations; Section III, Principles on Use of Deadly Force. DPD policy and training are consistent with the DOJ Commentary.

is no requirement in law, policy, or training to run through a laundry list of various force options. There is no requirement in the law, in policy, or in training that preordains a sequence of actions prior to the use of deadly force " ... in the defense of human life." Officer Orick did not have time to issue a verbal warning before shooting, nor was he required to do so. Police officers are trained to issue a verbal warning *only where feasible*, i.e., when taking the time to issue such a warning will not delay the use of deadly force to such an extent as to increase the risk of death or serious injury.[110] However, the fact that Office Orick did not attempt any sort of verbal warning or other notice of his presence did form the basis for the allegations of unjustified force in the ensuing civil action.

There are several concerns affecting the use of a verbal warning. The first is that deadly force is, or may be, justified in the first place, else there would be no cause to consider a warning. Otherwise, a warning is nothing more than a verbal bluff. Officers are trained that if the situation does not merit the use of deadly force, they are no more justified warning of it than they would be actually using it. In fact, issuing a verbal warning is nothing more than an attempt to utilize a lesser force option in a deadly force situation. As noted above, however, if Officer Orick had decided to delay the use of deadly force while he issued a verbal warning as Hunter was actively engaged in shooting at Foreman, he effectively would have only allowed Hunter the unimpeded opportunity to continue shooting at Foreman at least one more time.

If deadly force is appropriate, the issuance of a warning is necessarily left to the discretion of the officer involved—the intrinsic meaning of *"when feasible."* But the officer who is engaged in and reacting to the event is the only one who can make that determination. That officer may or may not attempt a verbal warning prior to using deadly force, or even while engaged in using deadly force. But the absence of a warning is not a measure of the reasonableness or the justification for the use of deadly force, especially in incidents such as this one, where the threat is immediate, in progress, and unmistakable in the perception of the officer involved.

Whereas verbal warnings have some limited foundation in the law, i.e., they are necessary *when feasible* solely within the narrow and specific circumstance of preventing the escape of a dangerous individual, such was clearly not the circumstance here. In this case, it is uncertain that Hunter would have even heard Officer Orick from 50 yards away over the heated yelling and gunshots between him and Foreman, much less understood who

---

110. Note that this is a common policy statement—not a stricture of law.

was yelling and what was being yelled, and then decided to obey it. Ultimately it was not necessary for Officer Orick to gamble Foreman's life on a verbal warning, and it was objectively reasonable for him not to make the attempt.

The plaintiff, Michael Tranter, claimed that Officer Orick violated Hunter's Fourth Amendment right to be free from unreasonable searches and seizures when Officer Orick shot and killed Hunter. Officer Orick responded that he was entitled to qualified immunity from this claim, moving for summary judgment. The Court granted the motion.[111]

The Supreme Court has set forth a two-step process for resolving qualified immunity claims. In this case, the court first addressed whether Tranter's allegations represented a violation of the Fourth Amendment with regard to Hunter's death, the first step in the process. Tranter alleged a Fourth Amendment violation in his complaint but the court determined that the Rule 56 evidence developed in discovery revealed otherwise, and Officer Orick presented Rule 56 evidence that his use of force was constitutionally permissible. The burden then shifted to Tranter to identify Rule 56 evidence showing that Officer Orick's actions were not constitutionally permissible. This he has not accomplished.[112]

> *"However, the mere existence of a scintilla of evidence in support of the nonmoving party is not sufficient to avoid summary judgment. 'There must be evidence on which the jury could reasonably find for the plaintiff.' The inquiry, then, is whether reasonable jurors could find by a preponderance of the evidence that the nonmoving party is entitled to a verdict.*

---

111. *Michael Tranter v. Officer Greg Orick, et al.*, U.S. District Court, Southern District of Ohio, Western Division,Case No: 09-CV-125, *Entry and Order Granting Orick's Motion for Summary Judgment and Terminating This Case*, 7/8/10.

112. The standard of review applicable to motions for summary judgment is established by Federal Rule of Civil Procedure 56 and associated case law. Rule 56 provides that summary judgment "shall be rendered forthwith if the pleadings, depositions, answers to interrogatories, and admissions on file, together with the affidavits, if any, show that there is no genuine issue as to any material fact and that the moving party is entitled to a judgment as a matter of law." Alternatively, summary judgment is denied if " ... there are any genuine factual issues that properly can be resolved only by a finder of fact because they may reasonably be resolved in favor of either party." Thus, summary judgment must be entered "against a party who fails to make a showing sufficient to establish the existence of an element essential to that party's case, and on which that party will bear the burden of proof at trial." See Federal Rules of Civil Procedure 56(c).

*Finally, in ruling on a motion for summary judgment, '[a] district court is not ... obligated to wade through and search the entire record for some specific facts that might support the nonmoving party's claim.'*[113]

*The use of deadly force, a form of excessive force, is constitutionally permissible only if, judged from the perspective of a reasonable officer on the scene, Officer Orick had to shoot Hunter because he thought Hunter posed a threat of serious physical harm to Foreman. In this case, a reasonable officer on the scene would have believed that Hunter posed a threat of serious physical harm to Foreman. Prior to arriving at the scene, Officer Orick had been told that he was approaching a disturbance with two black males fighting and shots fired. Upon arrival, Officer Orick observed and heard Hunter and Foreman arguing in the street. He also observed Hunter shoot a .25 caliber handgun once into the air and twice at Foreman. When Hunter appeared to be firing at Foreman for the third time, Officer Orick fatally shot Hunter.*[114]

[ ... ]

*Tranter first argues that Officer Orick should have warned Hunter before he shot at him. However, courts have held that a warning is not required in this situation. Tranter also argues that there is an issue of material fact because only one casing from Hunter's .25 caliber handgun was found. However, Detective Hall, who has performed many homicide investigations, testified that projectiles and casings are not always recovered. Thus, this argument is not enough to create an issue of material fact. Finally, Tranter argues that there are additional issues of material fact given that two supportable versions of the incident exist. However, Tranter has not presented Rule 56 evidence of another supportable version.*

[ ... ]

*In sum, there are no genuine issues of material fact and Officer Orick's actions were constitutionally permissible. Further, since Officer Orick's actions were constitutionally permissible, the Court need not address whether the constitutional right was "clearly established" at the time, the second step in the process. Officer Orick is, therefore, entitled to qualified immunity from Tranter's § 1983 claim. Officer Orick's Motion for Summary Judgment on Tranter's § 1983 claim is granted.*[115]

[ ... ]

---

113. *Tranter*, op.cit. page 14. Citations removed.
114. *Ibid.* page 20. Citations removed.
115. *Ibid.* pages 26–28. Citations removed.

*The use of deadly force, a form of excessive force, is only constitutionally permissible if the officer has probable cause to believe that the suspect poses a threat of serious physical harm to either the officer or to others. Further, a police officer need not always call out a warning before using deadly force. The time frame considered is important in excessive force cases. Other than where there is a random attack, the analysis of whether excess force was used begins with the decision of the police officer to do something, to help, to arrest, to inquire.*"[116]

On February 7, 2012, the U.S. Court of Appeals for the Sixth Circuit affirmed the decision: *"Finding no error, we affirm."*[117]

## *Jonathan E. Mitchell v. Officer Robert Miller, et al.*[118]

On April 10, 2011, Portland (Maine) Police Department (PPD) Officer Robert Miller heard a dispatch concerning a burglary in progress. Dispatch provided information that the complainant was a woman and the reported offender was Jonathan Mitchell, her former husband/domestic partner who was subject to a court order prohibiting any contact with her. Mitchell was described as a sexual predator. The complainant said he was unstable. Dispatch advised that Mitchell might be on drugs or might be intoxicated. He had broken into her apartment and refused to leave when she confronted him. He fled the apartment when she called 911, driving a black Volkswagen Jetta reported to be heading towards Washington Avenue.

Officer Miller drove along Washington Avenue looking for Mitchell. He saw a black Volkswagen Jetta passing him in the opposing traffic lane and reversed course to follow it.

Mitchell, in the Jetta, turned left off of Washington Avenue onto East Kidder Street. Officer Miller followed and closed within ten feet of the Jetta, both vehicles traveling at approximately 25 mph. He advised Dispatch of the Jetta's license plate number and that he was continuing to follow. Mitchell turned right onto Sherwood Street. Dispatch advised Officer Miller that Jonathan Mitchell was the suspected operator of the Jetta and that he was a habitual offender believed to be under the influence of alcohol or drugs.

---

116. *Ibid.* page 20. Citations removed.

117. *Michael Tranter v. Greg Orick*, U.S. Court of Appeals for the Sixth Circuit, File Name: 12a0144n.06, No. 10-3945, *Opinion*, 2/7/12.

118. *Jonathan E. Mitchell v. Officer Robert Miller, et al.*, USDC, District of Maine Case No: 2:13-cv-00132-NT.

Mitchell turned left onto Inverness Street and Officer Miller activated the emergency lights on his cruiser to initiate a vehicle stop. Mitchell did not stop and Officer Miller activated the cruiser's siren as well. Mitchell turned right onto Berkshire Street, right again onto Presumpscot Street followed by a left back onto Sherwood Street, at which point he suddenly accelerated to a speed in excess of 60 mph, pulling away from Officer Miller. Sherwood Street was lined with parked cars along both sides such that extensive sections of the street only had room for a single lane of travel.[119] Officer Miller pursued.

Mitchell ran the stop sign at the intersection with Veranda Street as he made a sharp left turn onto Veranda with Officer Miller in pursuit. Mitchell's speed increased in excess of 70 mph along the residential streets lined with parked cars. PPD Supervisory Sergeant Glen S. McGary directed all officers to terminate pursuit because of the high speeds involved in accordance with PPD policy. Concurrently, Officer Miller saw Mitchell turn onto Fairfield Street, known to him as a dead end street, and he followed Mitchell despite Sgt. McGary's order.

Officer Miller pulled in behind Mitchell's car at the end of the dead end street. The Jetta was stopped off of the pavement, pulled up on a small berm beside a guardrail marking the end of the street. Officer Miller parked about ten feet behind and to the driver's side of Mitchell's car, at an angle facing the door. He left his emergency lights and siren on. He exited his cruiser and approached on foot, ordering Mitchell to get out of the car. As he did so, Mitchell backed the car to his (Mitchell's) right rear alongside Officer Miller's cruiser as though maneuvering to reverse course and drive away. Officer Miller was on foot, gun in hand, and ordering Mitchell to get out of the car. He opened the driver's door of the Jetta, ordering Mitchell to turn off the engine and to get out of the car. The Jetta suddenly lurched forward as Officer Miller stood in the open doorway. Officer Miller reached inside the car to turn off the ignition, but Mitchell swatted his hand away.

Meanwhile, PPD Officer David Schertz had arrived on the scene. He parked to the left rear of Officer Miller's cruiser. He exited his cruiser and was on foot at Officer Miller's left rear, holding the door open as Officer Miller stood inside the open door issuing commands to Mitchell. The Jetta was momentarily still as Officer Miller continued to order Mitchell out. After Mitchell swatted

---

119. The entire event from the moment Mitchell initiated his high-speed flight through the final confrontation when the shooting occurred was captured in detail by the dash cam video from Officer Miller's cruiser. The dash camera from Officer Schertz's cruiser also captured the final confrontation but from a different angle. The video vividly supports the narrative.

his hand away from the ignition, he grabbed Mitchell by his clothing using his left hand.

Mitchell ignored the orders and he suddenly drove forward, compelling Officer Miller to move along with the car as well as Officer Schertz, who was then located ahead of the open door. Officer Miller continued to order Mitchell to turn off the car and get out as he held onto Mitchell's clothing with his left hand.

The Jetta rolled backwards briefly for approximately three to four feet and came to a stop as Officer Miller continued trying to hold onto Mitchell through the open doorway. He (Miller) repeatedly grabbed Mitchell's clothing but could not maintain his grip as Mitchell vigorously fought him off. As Officer Miller continued trying to grab and hold Mitchell, Mitchell accelerated forward, turning sharply left as he did so. The Jetta fishtailed and its tires spun against the pavement. Officer Miller was briefly pulled along by the impetus of the sudden acceleration before he could let go. He was aware that the car was headed in the direction that he had last known Officer Schertz to be located.

Officer Miller released Mitchell and fired two shots at Mitchell. At that moment, Officer Schertz was inside the open doorway to Miller's left trying to assist in extracting Mitchell when the car accelerated. He had to evade the vehicle for his own safety. Mitchell continued to accelerate and fled the scene. Neither officer was aware that he (Mitchell) had been struck by the shots. Mitchell was located and arrested without incident later that day at the residence of a female friend of his. He had two gunshot wounds.

### Discussion

As events unfolded, Mitchell's high-speed flight endangered other motorists, pedestrians, and passersby who might have happened into his path, as well as the safety of the pursuing officers. This reckless and determined endangerment to others posed by Mitchell's vehicular flight induced Sergeant McGary to order termination of the pursuit in accordance with PPD policy. But when Mitchell turned into a known dead end street, Officer Miller recognized that Mitchell would not be able to continue to flee and exercised his discretion to follow him (Mitchell) into the dead end despite the termination directive. This was the basis for one of the allegations by Mitchell in his civil suit, that Officer Miller disobeyed Sgt. McCrary's orders and violated PPD policy. But Officer Miller had recognized that Mitchell was boxed in and the pursuit could not continue. He exercised his initiative and judgment to take advantage of circumstances that suddenly arose to apprehend Miller without the continuation of the high-speed chase.

Even after Mitchell was constricted within the confines of a dead end street and at a standstill with two police cars in his rear with lights and sirens activated, he refused to submit. He adamantly refused to comply with repeated orders to stop the car and to get out. He never took his foot off the gas or made any other effort to stop. He never turned off his vehicle's engine. He fought off Officer Miller's attempts to turn off the ignition and his attempts to grab him (Mitchell) by his clothing to pull him out of the car.

Despite the uniformed law enforcement officer on foot beside him issuing loud and unambiguous commands at gunpoint, Mitchell repeatedly shifted gears, revved the engine of his car, and executed a multi-point U-turn, tires squealing and car fishtailing. In the process, Mitchell (whether by design or not) employed his vehicle as a weapon endangering the officers on foot in close proximity to him. And finally, Mitchell did not stop or comply despite being shot at and wounded. To the contrary, he accelerated away and made good his escape, only to be located and apprehended later that day.

Officer Miller had experienced Mitchell's dangerous operation of his vehicle from the outset. He witnessed Mitchell's disregard for the safety of others. And when he approached Mitchell on foot in order to attempt to compel compliance he was aware of Officer Schertz's presence to his left. As Mitchell continued to execute the reversal and drive away despite the two officers standing beside him, Officer Miller had mere fractions of a second to disengage. In the stress of the moment as he (Miller) was being pulled into and along with the car, focused upon Mitchell as he was, his understanding of exactly where Officer Schertz was then located was based upon his last recollection of Schertz standing beside him and at risk of being in the path of Mitchell's car. Simultaneously he decided to shoot at Mitchell in an attempt to protect himself and Officer Schertz.[120]

This, of course, gave rise to Mitchell's allegation of unjustified deadly force. Mitchell claimed that since the two officers were beside the car, not in front of

---

120. As the risk of serious injury to Officer Miller increased due to Mitchell's actions, Officer Miller's vision inexorably narrowed onto Mitchell—the source of the threat. This is the "tunnel vision" that is the most prevalent physiological response to sudden, direct recognition of a grave physical threat. The threatened individual's field of view narrows to the threat, excluding visual discernment outside that "tunneled" field of view. Officer Miller knew that Officer Schertz was on foot and close to his left—in the same direction that Mitchell was steering his car. The imperative of the threat precluded him from looking around to track Schertz' movements—time and circumstances did not allow that given the urgency of the sudden threat by Mitchell's actions. Miller was further compelled to focus on Mitchell by his (Miller's) efforts to grapple with him and to evade the erratic movements of the car. His tunnel vision prevented him from monitoring Schertz' movements in his peripheral vision because that peripheral vision was severely diminished. At the moment of risk when he decided to shoot, Officer Miller's impression that Schertz was closer and thus at risk was reasonable and logical.

it, and that because of the car's movement Mitchell was ahead of them when Miller shot (the entry wounds were located in his left rear shoulder and neck), there was no imminent danger to either officer.

There is no ignoring the realities of reaction times. It is unreasonable to expect a law enforcement officer to allow an attacker a fair chance to prevail either through greater skill, strength, or the vagaries of mere chance. The attacker need only be lucky to succeed. Law enforcement officers do not have to gamble life or physical safety on sheer chance. Officer Miller did not have to gamble on the outcome by waiting to see if Mitchell actually struck Officer Schertz with the car, or waiting to see if he himself was actually pulled under a wheel or otherwise injured. He perceived a sudden, imminent risk of serious injury from Mitchell's operation of the Jetta in defiance of police orders and presence and he reacted in that fraction of a second available to him to diminish or terminate that risk. His decision to do so under the urgent exigencies of the moment was reasonable. Mitchell's actions coupled with what Officer Miller knew about him had established that he was heedlessly dangerous to them.

An important aspect of the action/reaction cycle that cannot be overlooked is that all parties to the confrontation are acting/reacting/moving and making decisions simultaneously and independently of each other. The police officer has no ability to predict what the adversary is going to do. By that same token, the adversary is reacting to what the police officer does, moving and responding unpredictably even as the officer is reacting to the adversary. This dynamic reality is illustrated most frequently when the location of wounds inflicted on the adversary is assessed against the officer's account of events.

When the officer decides to shoot, at that moment of imminent risk he sees the adversary in a specific posture posing a specific threat. Having made the decision to shoot, his focus is on the threat and the act of shooting. The officer's peripheral awareness is limited to the perceived threat, intensified by the effects of physiological phenomena such as tunnel vision. Meanwhile, the adversary is continuing to move and respond, independently of and simultaneously with the officer. It takes an actual, finite amount of time for the officer to bring his weapon to bear, execute the shot or shots fired, and recognize/respond to ensuing results. During that same time frame, the adversary has also been moving—frequently unobserved by the officer in the momentary stress and urgency of trying to prevent death or serious injury. (See Chapter 7.)

The result is that the actual locations of bullet wounds are seldom consistent with an officer's recollection of positions and postures at the moment he decided to shoot. Commonly the adversary (acting/reacting simultaneously with yet independently of the officer) sees the officer's weapon coming to bear and/or being fired and turns away in an avoidance response as the officer begins firing. The officer's specific recollection is that the adversary was facing him when he began shooting, but the bullet wounds are determined after the fact to be located in the adversary's side or in his back. This appears to contradict the officer's narrative of events, and is frequently so alleged in legal proceedings against the officer, but that is as misleading as it is irrelevant. To the contrary, it is fully consistent with, and indicative of, the dynamics of deadly force incidents and the independent and unpredictable interplay of independent simultaneous movements.

The location of wounds is not a relevant factor in assessing the justification for the use of deadly force anymore than is the number of shots fired. The critical issue is whether *the perception of imminent risk that precipitated the decision to shoot* was reasonable at the moment the decision was made. If that perception of risk was reasonable in the circumstances, the decision to use deadly force was justified and clearly the resultant location of wounds is irrelevant.

Mitchell was in motion at the moment of risk that precipitated Officer Miller's decision to shoot. Miller raised his gun, aimed, and fired, tracking Mitchell with his gun as Mitchell simultaneously accelerated past him. In the fractional time between deciding to shoot and actually shooting, Mitchell's concurrent motion put him further to Miller's left and the shots hit him (Mitchell) from his left rear. This is the reality of the dynamics of shooting incidents. Officer Schertz substantiated the dynamic when, in response to a question, he agreed that he was not in the path of the vehicle when Miller fired *but* noted that he was in the vehicle's path before that.[121]

There is nothing in law enforcement training or practice that would suggest or require that Officer Miller should have waited to see if Mitchell's operation of the Jetta became a certain risk of injury to himself or Officer Schertz. His ac-

---

121. Schertz Deposition, Item (w) above, page 28. To wit:
*Q. When the shots were fired, you were not in the path of the vehicle, true?*
*A. Yes.*
*Q. So when the shots were fired, you weren't in danger of being run over by the car?*
*A. I was previous to that; but, yes, that's correct. I wasn't in the path of the vehicle at the time Officer Miller fired.*
*Q. Right. I really just want to focus on and I think this case is going to be focused on what the situation was at the very moment that deadly force was used. So at the moment that deadly force was used you were not in danger of being run over by the car, true?*
*A. Not immediately. I have no idea what the car was going to do. It obviously had changed directions three times in about—less than 10 seconds as you said.*

tions throughout the pursuit and the confrontation at the end of Fairfield Street had established his willingness to endanger others. He ignored uniformed, armed officers, one of whom was pointing a gun at him. He ignored marked cruisers pursuing him with lights and sirens activated. He endangered everyone who might happen to be in his way as he fled at high-speed from the pursuing officers. Officer Miller did not have the luxuries of time or containment affording him the option of waiting to see what happened next. Mitchell's behavior throughout the incident created a clear, reasonable, and continuous risk of death or serious injury. Importantly, he never did anything to diminish that risk.

The time factor is integral to this incident. From start to finish, the total confrontation lasted approximately 24 seconds.[122] More precisely, at the moment of acute risk when Mitchell's actions suddenly created Officer Miller's perception of an imminent threat to himself and Schertz, he (Miller) had fractions of a second to react to the implications of Mitchell's actions, assess the degree of danger created, and if necessary act to stop it to protect himself and Schertz. "Fractions of a second" is not a time frame conducive to reflective analysis and tranquil contemplation of factors and alternatives.

As Mitchell ignored him and continued to execute his U-turn and drive away, Officer Miller recognized the danger and shot at him two times. He believed that Mitchell could and would hit him (Miller) or Officer Schertz to his left. Of note is that Officer Miller intentionally fired to stop the actions of the driver, the actual threat of harm by means of his operation of the vehicle, and not at the vehicle to disable it. That is consistent with training and with ballistic realities.

Officers are trained that the level of force reasonably necessary in any confrontation will rise and fall as the dynamics of the incident change and evolve over time and circumstance. Initially, the officers had only their presence and non-deadly force options (grabbing and restraining) available to try to control and apprehend Mitchell. At the moment that Mitchell endangered them with his operation of his car, the urgency of protecting themselves from sudden imminent harm dictated the necessity of using deadly force to stop him. However, once Mitchell had driven past them—mere fractions of a second after being shot—he no longer posed an imminent risk and Officer Miller did not shoot at him again. At that point, he was "merely" escaping and not en-

---

122. The elapsed time is taken from the dash cam video of Officer Schertz' cruiser, starting with the opening of Officer Miller's car door and ending at Miller's second shot and the Mitchell car's departure from the camera's field of view (± 0.5 seconds). But the elapsed time when Mitchell suddenly accelerates forward as Officer Miller has hold of his shirt to the first shot is less than 1.5 seconds.

dangering others in the process. Officer Miller recognized that the threat of harm had passed and immediately ceased his use of deadly force.

These distinctions were not lost on the court in its analysis leading to a grant of qualified immunity for Officer Mitchell. The Court noted,

> "*The inquiry is conducted 'from the perspective of a reasonable officer on the scene, rather than with the 20/20 vision of hindsight.' It 'must account for the fact that police officers are often forced to make split-second judgments—in circumstances that are tense, uncertain, and rapidly evolving—about the amount of force that is necessary in a particular situation.'*"

> "*Courts applying the excessive force reasonableness test sometimes consider such factors as '(1) the severity of the crime at issue, (2) whether the suspect poses an immediate threat to the safety of the officers or others, and (3) whether [the suspect] is actively resisting arrest or attempting to evade arrest by flight.' However, the critical judgment must be made in light of the 'totality of the circumstances,' not through mechanical application of a multi-factor test. [I]n the end we must still slosh our way through the fact bound morass of 'reasonableness.'*"[123]

Courts "employ a two-prong analysis in determining whether a defendant is entitled to qualified immunity," asking "(l) whether the facts alleged or shown by the plaintiff make out a violation of a constitutional right; and (2) if so, whether the right was 'clearly established' at the time of the defendant's alleged violation." The second prong itself has two parts.

First, the court asks, "whether 'the contours of the right were sufficiently clear that a reasonable official would understand that what he is doing violates that right.'" This inquiry "focuses on the clarity of the law at the time of the alleged civil rights violation."

Second, the court asks, "whether in the specific context of the case, 'a reasonable defendant would have understood that his conduct violated the plaintiffs' constitutional rights.'" This inquiry "focuses more concretely on the facts of the particular case and whether a reasonable defendant would have understood that his conduct violated the plaintiffs' constitutional rights."

Where the facts warrant doing so, trial courts have discretion to skip the first prong of the qualified immunity analysis (whether the facts make out a constitutional violation) and instead move immediately to the second prong

---

123. *Jonathan E. Mitchell v. Officer Robert Miller, et al.*, USDC District of Maine, Case No: 2:13-cv-00132-NT, *Order On Defendant's Motion for Summary Judgment*, 9/26/14. Page 9. Citations removed.

(whether the right was clearly established). If the court reaches the second prong, the burden of demonstrating the law was clearly established at the time of the alleged constitutional violation is on the plaintiff."[124]

> "*Here, as [ … ] allows, the Court passes over the question of whether 'the facts make out a triable Fourth Amendment claim and looks first to whether Officer Miller violated a right that was "clearly established" as of April 10, 2011, the date the incident in question occurred.*
>
> *To answer that question, the Court is aided by* Brosseau v. Haugen, *a case in which the Supreme Court granted qualified immunity to a police officer who, like Officer Miller, shot and wounded a suspect fleeing arrest in a car. The incident at issue in* Brosseau *took place on February 21, 1999, so that decision acts as a guidepost as to what was and was not 'clearly established' in this area of Fourth Amendment jurisprudence as of that date. As the First Circuit instructed [ … ]:*
>
>> '*[T]o overcome summary judgment under the second prong of the qualified immunity analysis in a case where a police officer fired at a fleeing driver to protect those whom his flight might endanger, a plaintiff would have to show "at a minimum" that the officer's conduct is "materially different from the conduct in* Brosseau*" or that between February 21, 1999, and the date of the alleged constitutional violation "there emerged either controlling authority or a robust consensus of cases of persuasive authority that would alter our analysis of the qualified immunity question.*"'[125]
>
> [ … ]
>
> *In both the case before this Court and in* Brosseau: *(1) a police officer tried to wrest a fleeing criminal suspect from a car; (2) the suspect refused to exit the car even when threatened with a gun; (3) the suspect attempted to drive away with the officer immediately beside the car and at least one other person in the immediate vicinity; (4) the officer fired while still physically reeling from the suspect's sudden attempt to drive away; (5) the action unfolded so quickly that the officer had no time to react and could reasonably have believed at least one other person in the immediate vicinity was in great danger, even though the suspect ultimately managed to get away without hurting anyone. The Court sees no principled basis to distinguish the facts of this case from those faced by the Supreme Court in* Brosseau. *If anything, the facts here are more favorable to the*

---

124. *Ibid.* page 10, citations removed.
125. *Ibid.* page 11, citations removed.

*defendant officer. For instance, there was no indication in* Brosseau *that the fleeing suspect was intoxicated or possibly unstable, nor had the suspect in* Brosseau *already engaged police in a high-speed chase.*

*Because the Plaintiff cannot materially distinguish* Brosseau, *he must point to 'controlling authority' or 'a robust consensus of cases of persuasive authority' that developed between February 20, 1999, the date the* Brosseau *incident occurred, and the morning of April 10, 2011, which meaningfully alters the analysis. The Plaintiff falls far short of this mark. The majority of the Plaintiff's opposition is concerned with distinguishing the facts at bar from those in cases involving greater danger to police officers or others nearby where qualified immunity was granted. Those holdings represent instances where courts found the law was not clearly established; they provide little if any guidance as to where the law is clearly established.*

*In fact, the Plaintiff cites just a singe case (*Lytle v. Bexar County, 560 F.3d 404 (5th Cir. 2009)) *where a court denied qualified immunity.* Lytle *is a much different case than this one. The facts in* Lytle, *viewed in the light most favorable to the plaintiff, were that the officer fired into the car as many as ten seconds after any immediate danger to the officer had passed, when the car was three or four houses down the block. Additionally, the officer fired indiscriminately into the car and struck a 15-year-old passenger, not the driver responsible for the chase. The Court's analysis of Officer Mitchell's decision to fire into the Jetta would be a very different one if a similar amount of time had elapsed and an innocent third party had been trapped inside the car. But, even if* Lytle *were more helpful to the Plaintiff, a single out-of-circuit case decided on the basis of a highly fact-specific test does not add up to a robust consensus. Officer Mitchell is therefore entitled to qualified immunity.*"[126]

---

126. *Ibid.* pages 12–14, citations removed.

# Cases

# Index